Penguin Books
The Malayan Trilogy

Anthony Burgess was born in Manchester in 1917 and
is a graduate of the University there. After six years in
the Army he worked as an instructor for the Central
Advisory Council for Forces Education, as a lecturer
in Speech and Drama and as a grammar school master.
From 1954 till 1960 he was an education officer in the
Colonial Service, stationed in Malaya and Borneo.

He became a full-time writer in 1960, though he had
already by then published three novels and a history
of English literature. A late starter in the art of
fiction, he had previously spent much creative energy
on music, and has composed many full-scale works for
orchestra and other media. His third symphony was
performed in the USA in 1975.

Anthony Burgess believes that in the fusion of
musical and literary form lies a possible future for the
novel. His *Napoleon Symphony* attempts to impose
the shape of Beethoven's Eroica on the career of the
Corsican conqueror. His other books include the
Enderby Novels; *Tremor of Intent*, a biography of
Shakespeare intended to act as a foil to his Shakespeare
novel, *Nothing Like the Sun*; *Honey for the Bears*;
The Wanting Seed; *MF*; *Urgent Copy*; *Beard's
Roman Women*; *ABBA ABBA*; and *A Clockwork
Orange*, made into a film classic by Stanley Kubrick.

Mr Burgess lives with his second wife and his son in
France, Monaco and Italy, but mostly on the road in a
Bedford Dormobile.

Anthony Burgess

The Malayan Trilogy

Time for a Tiger
The Enemy in the Blanket
Beds in the East

Penguin Books

Penguin Books Ltd, Harmondsworth,
Middlesex, England
Penguin Books, 625 Madison Avenue,
New York, New York 10022, U.S.A.
Penguin Books Australia Ltd, Ringwood,
Victoria, Australia
Penguin Books Canada Ltd, 2801 John Street,
Markham, Ontario, Canada L3R 1B4
Penguin Books (N.Z.) Ltd, 182–190 Wairau Road,
Auckland 10, New Zealand.

The trilogy consists of three novels, *Time for a Tiger*,
The Enemy in the Blanket, and *Beds in the East*,
first published by William Heinemann in 1956, 1958
and 1959 respectively
Published in Penguin Books 1972
Reprinted 1973, 1978, 1979

Made and printed in Great Britain by
Hazell Watson & Viney Ltd
Aylesbury, Bucks
Set in Linotype Baskerville

Contents

Time for a Tiger

Dedication

كڤد صحابة۲ ساي
دتانه ملايو

The Malay state of Lanchap and its towns and inhabitants do not really exist.

I

'East? They wouldn't know the bloody East if they saw it. Not if you was to hand it to them on a plate would they know it was the East. That's where the East is, there.' He waved his hand wildly into the black night. 'Out there, west. You wasn't there, so you wouldn't know. Now I was. Palestine Police from the end of the war till we packed up. That was the East. You was in India, and that's not the East any more than this is. So you know nothing about it either. So you needn't be talking.'

Nabby Adams, supine on the bed, grunted. It was four o'clock in the morning and he did not want to be talking. He had had a confused coloured dream about Bombay, shot with sharp pangs of unpaid bills. Over it all had brooded thirst, thirst for a warmish bottle of Tiger beer. Or Anchor. Or Carlsberg. He said, 'Did you bring any beer back with you?'

Flaherty jerked like a puppet. 'What did I tell you? What am I always saying? May God strike me down dead this instant if I wasn't just thinking to myself as I came in that that's the first bloody question you'd ask. Beer, beer, beer. For God's sake, man, haven't you another blessed thought in your head at all but beer? And supposing I had put a few bottles for myself in the fridge, don't you think it would be the same as always? You lumbering downstairs with your great bloody big weight and that dog after you, clanking its bloody anti-rabies medal against the treads of the stairs, and you draining the lot of it before breakfast and leaving the bloody empties on the floor for any self-respecting decent man who keeps Christian hours to trip over. I did not bring any beer back, though those soldiers is generous to a fault and was for plying me with loads of the stuff and as much as you want, they said, any time you like and all at N.A.A.F.I. prices.'

Nabby Adams stirred on his bed and the dog beneath it stirred too, the medal on its collar clinking like money on the floor. Should he get up now and drink water? He shuddered at the thought of the clean, cold, neuter taste. But thirst seemed to grip his whole body like a fever. He levered himself up slowly, six feet eight inches of thirst, ghostlike behind the darned and frayed mosquito-net.

'I'm worried about you, Nabby,' said Police-Lieutenant Flaherty. 'Worried to death. I was saying tonight that you're not the person I made you into at the end of your last tour. By God, you're not. By Christ, you're back to the old days in Johore with the *towkays* round at the end of the month waving their bills round the office and me not able to go into a *kedai* at all for fear of the big bloody smarmy smiles on their yellow faces and they saying. "Where's the big *tuan*?" and "Has the big *tuan* got his pay yet, *tuan*?" and "The big *tuan* has a big *kira, tuan*, and when in the name of God is he going to pay?" Christ, man, I was ashamed of my white skin. You letting the side down like that. And I got you right. I got you clear. I got you on that bloody boat with money in your pocket. And now look at you.' Flaherty dithered in a palsy of indignation. 'I've covered up for you, by God I have. There was the other day with the C.P.O. round and you on the beer again in that filthy bloody *kedai* where I'd be ashamed to be seen, boozing away with that corporal of yours. Leading him astray, and he a bloody Muslim.'

'You leave him alone,' said Nabby Adams. He was on his feet, a little unsteady, a huge hand stained with tobacco-tar seeking support from the dressing-table. Gaunt, yellow-brown, towering, he moved another step. The black bitch came from under the bed and shook herself. Her medal clanked. Her tail stirred as she looked up, happy and worshipping, at the vast man in shrunken dirty pyjamas. 'You leave him alone. He's all right.'

'Christ, man, I wouldn't touch him with my walking-stick. They're talking, I tell you, about you letting the side down, slinking from *kedai* to *kedai* with your bloody corporal at your tail. Why don't you mix a bit more with your own race, man? Some damn good nights in the Club and they're the salt of the earth in the Sergeants' Mess, and that fellow Crabbe was playing the piano the other night, a real good singsong, and all you do is prowl around looking for credit in dirty little *kedais*.'

'I do mix with my own race.' Nabby Adams was moving slowly towards the door. The dog stood expectant by the stairhead, waiting to escort him to the refrigerator. Her tail beat dully on the door of the bedroom of Police-Lieutenant Keir. 'And you wouldn't speak like that if you wasn't tight.'

'Tight! Tight!' Flaherty danced on his bottom, gripping the chair-seat as if he thought it would take off. 'Listen who's talking about being tight. Oh, God, man, get wise to yourself. And make up your mind about what bloody race you belong to. One minute it's all about being a farmer's boy in Northamptonshire and the next you're on about the old days in Calcutta and what the British have done to Mother India and the snake-charmers and the bloody temple-bells. Ah, wake up, for God's sake. You're English right enough but you're forgetting how to speak the bloody language, what with traipsing about with Punjabis and Sikhs and God knows what. You talk Hindustani in your sleep, man. Sort it out, for God's sake. If you want to put a loincloth on, get cracking, but don't expect the privileges –' (the word came out in a wet blurr; the needle stuck for a couple of grooves) 'the privileges, the privileges ...'

Nabby Adams went slowly down the stairs. Clank, clank, clank came after him, and a dog's happy panting. He switched on the light in the big, bare, dirty room where he and his brother officers ate and lounged and yawned over the illustrated papers. He opened the refrigerator door. He saw only chill bottles of water. In the deep-freeze compartment was a rich bed of snow with incrustations of month-old ice on the metal walls. He took a bottle of water and gulped down mouthful after mouthful, but the thirst abated not at all, rather the lust for a real drink mounted to an obscene pitch. What day was it? Confused, he wondered whether this was late in the night or early in the morning. Outside the smeared uncurtained windows was solid black, heavy and humid, and there was not a sound, not even a distant cock-crow. It was near the end of the month, of that he was sure, a day or two off at the most. Must be, because of the petrol returns. But then, what difference did that make? Gloomily he watched bills parade and curtsy before his inward eye.

Lim Kean Swee	$395
Chee Sin Hye	$120
Tan Meng Kwang	$250

And these shadowy bills, further back, grown as familiar as a wart or a jagged tooth. And the accounts in the drinking-shops. And the club-bill, three months old. And the letter that blasted swine Hart had written to his boss. Hart, the treasurer, the Field Force major, hail-fellow-well-met with the Sultan's A.D.C., bowing with joined pudgy hands to H.H., well in, the man with the big future. 'I'll get him,' thought Nabby Adams. 'I'll get that bloody car of his. I'll have the Land Rover waiting next Friday because he's always at the Club on Fridays and when he drives out I'll give him a nice bloody little nick on his offside mudguard. He can't do that to me.' Proud, tall, unseeing, clutching the belly of the water-bottle, Nabby Adams stood, thinking up revenge, while the dog adored, panting.

'That was the East, man. Palestine. You wasn't there, so you wouldn't know. There was one place I used to go to and there was a bint there who did a bit of the old belly-dancing. You know, you've seen it on the pictures. If you haven't, you're bloody ignorant. You know.' Flaherty got up and gyrated clumsily, lifting arms to show sweat-

soaked armpits in his off-white shirt. He crooned a
sinuous dirge as accompaniment. Then he sat down and
watched Nabby Adams move to his bed and fall heavily
upon it. With a clank the dog disappeared under the bed.
'You know,' said Flaherty, 'you're not bloody interested.
You're not interested in anything, that's your bloody
trouble. I've travelled the world and I tell you about this
bint and what we did in the back room and you don't
take a blind bit of notice. Here.' Flaherty took a cigarette
from the tin on Nabby Adams's bedside table. 'Here.
Watch this. And I bet these aren't paid for either. Here.'
He lit the cigarette and puffed till the end glowed
brightly. Then he began to chew. Nabby Adams watched,
open-mouthed, as the cigarette disappeared behind the
working lips. It all went in, including the red glow, and
it did not come out again. 'Easy,' said Flaherty. 'If you're
fit, which you're bloody well not. Watch this.' He took a
tumbler from the table and began to eat that too.

'Oh, no,' groaned Nabby Adams, as he heard the brittle
crunching. Eyes shut, he saw, white against red:

| The Happy Coffee Shop | $67 |
| Chop Fatt | $35 |

'Easy.' Flaherty spat blood and glass on the floor. 'By
Christ, it was a good night tonight. You should have been
there, Nabby, drinking with decent people, salt of the
earth. Laugh? I never laughed so much. Here, listen.
There's a Malay sergeant-major there. They call him
Tong, see? That's Malay for a barrel, but you wouldn't
know that, being ignorant. I never seen such a beer-belly.
Well, he told a story . . .'

'Oh, go to bloody bed,' said Nabby Adams. Eyes closed,
he lay as in death, his huge calloused feet projecting
beyond the end of the bed, pushing out the mosquito-
net.

Flaherty was hurt, dignified in sorrow. 'All right,' he
said. 'Gratitude. After all I've done. Gratitude. But I'll
show you the act of a gentleman. We still make gentlemen

where I come from. Wait. Just wait. I'll make you feel bloody small.'

He lurched out to his own room. He lurched back in again. Nabby Adams heard an approaching clink. In wonder and hope he opened his eyes. Flaherty was carrying a carrier-bag covered with Chinese ideograms, and in the bag were three bottles.

'There,' said Flaherty. 'The things I do for you.'

'Oh, thank God, thank God,' prayed Nabby Adams. 'God bless you, Paddy.' He was out of bed, alive, quick in his movements, looking for the opener, must be here somewhere, left it in that drawer. Thank God, thank God. The metal top clinked on the floor, answered by the emerging clank of the dog. Nabby Adams raised to his lips the frothing bottle and drank life. Bliss. His body drank, fresh blood flowed through his arteries, the electric light seemed brighter, what were a few bills anyway?

Flaherty watched indulgently, as a mother watches. 'Don't say I don't do anything for you,' he repeated.

'Yes, yes,' gasped Nabby Adams, breathless after the first draught, his body hungering for the next. 'Yes, Paddy.' He raised the bottle and drank life to the lees. Now he could afford to sit down, smoke a cigarette, drink the next bottle at leisure. But wait. What time was it? Four forty-five, said the alarm-clock. That meant he would have to go back to bed and sleep for a little. For if he didn't what the hell was he going to do? Three bottles wouldn't last him till it was time to go to the Transport Office. But in any case if he drank another bottle now that would mean only one bottle to wake up with. And no bottle for breakfast. He groaned to himself: there was no end to his troubles.

'Those Japanese tattooists,' said Flaherty. 'Bloody clever. By God they are. I seen one fellow in Jerusalem, wait, I'm telling a lie, it was in Alex, when I went there for a bit of leave, one fellow with a complete foxhunt on his back. Bloody marvellous. Horses and hounds and huntsmen, and the bloody bugle blowing tally-ho and you could just see the tail of the fox, the bloody brush you know, disappearing up his. What's the bloody matter with you?' He writhed in petulance, his lined frowning face stern and beetled. 'In God's name what's the matter? I bring you home food and drink and expect a bit of gratitude and a bit of cheerful company and what do I get? The bloody miseries.' He loped round the room, hands clasped behind, head bent, shoulders hunched, in a mime of lively dejection. 'Here,' he said, straightening, 'this won't do. Do you know what the bloody time is? If you can sit up all night I can't. We do a bit of work in Operations. We help to kill the bloody bandits. Bang bang bang.' He sprayed the room with a sub-machine-gun of air. 'Takka takka takka takka takka.' Stiff-legged he moved over to Nabby Adams and laid a comforting hand on his shoulder. 'Never you mind, Nabby my boy, it'll all be the same in a hundred bloody years. As Shakespeare says. Listen.' Eagerly he sat down, leaning forward with crackling eagerness. 'Shakespeare. You've never read any, being bloody ignorant. Or Robbie Burns. Drunk as a fiddler's bitch.' He leaned back comfortably with closed eyes, singing with wide gestures:

'Oh, Mary, this London's a wonderful sight,
   With the people all working by day and by night.'

'You'll wake them up,' said Nabby Adams.

'And what if I do,' said Flaherty. 'What have they ever done for me? That bloody Jock Keir with the money rattling in his pocket. Tack wallah's joy-bells. Saving it up, bloody boat-happy, but he'll down another man's pint as soon as look and with never a word out of him. Have you seen his book at the Club, man? Virgin soil. Three bucks' worth of orange squash in six bloody months. Where is he till I get at him?' Flaherty sent the chair flying and tore raggedly out of the room. On the landing he forgot his mission and could be heard bumping and slithering down the stairs. Nabby Adams listened for the flush of the lavatory, but there was no sound more to be heard. No-thing except the dog truffling for fleas, the tick of the rusty alarm-clock. Nabby Adams went back to bed, the dog rattled her way under it, then he realised he hadn't put out the light. Never mind.

He dozed. Soon the *bilal* could be heard, calling over the dark. The *bilal*, old and crotchety, had climbed the worm-gnawed stairs to the minaret, had paused a while at the top, panting, and then intoned his first summons to prayer, the first *waktu* of the long indifferent day.

'*La ilaha illa'llah. La ilaha illa'llah.*'

There is no God but God, but what did anybody care? Below and about him was dark, and the dark shrouded the bungalow of the District Officer, the two gaudy cine-mas, the drinking-shops where the *towkays* snored on their pallets, the Istana – empty now, for the Sultan was in Bangkok with his latest Chinese dance-hostess, the Raja Perempuan at Singapore for the race-meetings – and the dirty, drying river.

'*La iliha illa'lah.*'

Like a lonely Rhine-daughter he sang the thin liquids, remembering again the trip to Mecca he had made, out of his own money too, savings helped by judicious bets on tipped horses and a very good piece of advice about rub-ber given by a Chinese business-man. Gambling indeed was forbidden, *haram*, but he had wanted to go to Mecca and become a *haji*. By Allah, he had become a *haji*, Tuan Haji Mohammed Nasir bin Abdul Talib, and, by Allah, all would be forgiven. Now, having seen the glory of the great mosque at Mecca, the *Masjid-ul-Haram*, he despised a little his superstitious fellow-countrymen who, osten-sibly Muslim, yet clung to their animistic beliefs and left bananas on graves to feed the spirits of the dead. He had it on good authority that Inche Idris bin Zainal, teacher in the school and a big man in the Nationalist Movement, had once ordered eggs and bacon in a restaurant in Tahi Panas. He knew that Inche Jamaluddin drank brandy and that Inche Abu Zakaria sneaked off to small villages during the fasting month so that he might eat and drink without interference from the prowling police.

'*La ilaha illa'lah.*'

God knoweth best. *Allahu alam.* The nether fires awaited such, a hot house in *naraka.* Not for them the Garden with the river flowing beneath. He looked down on the blackness, trying to pierce it with his thin voice, seeking to irradicate with the Word the opacity of Kuala Hantu. But the town slept on. The white men turned in their sleep uneasily, dreaming of pints of draught bitter in wintry English hotels. The *mems* slept in adjoining beds, their dreams oppressed by servants who remained impassive in the face of hard words and feigned not to understand kitchen-Malay made up of Midland vowels. Only in a planter's bungalow was there a dim show of light, but this was out of the town, some miles along the Timah road. The fair-haired young man in the Drainage and Irrigation Department was leaving, sibilating a sweet good-morning to the paunched planter who was his friend. He stole to his little car, turning to wave in the dark at the lighted porch.

'Good-bye, Geoffrey. Tomorrow night, then.'

'Tomorrow night, Julian. Be good?'

But soon the dawn came up, heaving over the eastern edge like a huge flower in a nature-film. The stage electrician, under notice, slammed his flat hands on the dimmers and there was a swift suffusion of light. The sky was vast over the mountains with their crowns of jungle, over the river and the *attap* huts. The Malayan dawn, unseen of all save the *bilal* and the Tamil gardeners, grew and grew and mounted with an obscene tropical swiftness, and morning announced itself as a state, not a process.

At seven o'clock Nabby Adams awoke and reached for the remaining bottle. The dog came from under the bed and stretched with a long groan. Nabby Adams put on yesterday's shirt and slacks and thrust his huge feet into old slippers. Then he went softly down the stairs, followed closely by the clank clank clank of the dog. The Chinese boy, their only servant, was laying the table – a grey-white cloth, plates, cups, two bottles of sauce. Nabby Adams approached him ingratiatingly. Though he had been in the Federation for six years he spoke neither Malay nor Chinese: his languages were Hindustani, Urdu, a little Punjabi, Northamptonshire English. He said:

'Tuan Flaherty he give you money yesterday?'

'*Tuan?*'

'*Wang, wang.* You got *wang* to buy *makan*? Fat *tuan*, he give *wang*?'

'*Tuan kasi lima linggit.*'

Lima ringgit. That was five dollars. 'You give *lima ringgit* to me.'

'*Tuan?*'

'You give *lima ringgit* to *saya. Saya* buy bloody *makan.*'

The squat, ugly, slant-eyed boy hesitated, then pulled from his pocket a five-dollar note.

'*Tuan beli sayur?* Vegitibubbles?'

'Yes, yes. Leave it to *saya.*'

Nabby Adams went through the dirty stucco portico of the little police mess, out into the tiny *kampong*. The police mess had formerly been a maternity home for the wives of the Sultans of the state. Faded and tatty, peeling, floorboards eaten and unpolished, its philoprogenitive glory was a memory only. Now the spider had many homes, the chichaks, scuttling up the walls, throve on the many insects, and tattered calendars showed long-dead months. The cook-boy was not very efficient. His sole qualification for looking after four police-lieutenants was the fact that he had himself been a police-constable, discharged because of bad feet. Now he fed his masters expensively on tinned soups, tinned sausages, tinned milk, tinned cheese, tinned steak-and-kidney pudding, tinned ham. Anything untinned was suspect to him, and bread was rarely served with a meal. The porch was littered with flattened cigarette-ends, and the bath had a coating of immemorial grime. When plaster fell from the ceiling it lay to be trampled by heavy jungle-boots. But nobody cared, for nobody wanted to think of the place as a home. Nabby Adams thirsted for Bombay, Flaherty yearned for Palestine, Keir would soon be back in Glasgow and Vorpal had a Chinese widow in Malacca.

Where, in the old days of many royal confinements, there had been a field and a lane, now straggled a village. Villages were appearing now in the oddest places: the Communist terrorists had forced the Government to move long-established *kampong* populations to new sites, places where there was no danger of ideological infection, of help given to the terrorists freely or under duress. This newish village, on the hem of the town's skirt, already looked age-old. As Nabby Adams moved like a broken Coriolanus through the heavy morning heat, he saw the signatures of the old Malaya – warm, slummy comfort as permanent as the surrounding mountain-jungle. Naked brown children were sluicing themselves at the pump, an old mottled Chinese *nonya* champed her gums at the open door, a young Malay father of magnificent physique nursed a new child. His wife, her sarong wound under her armpits, proffered to Nabby Adams a smile of black and gold. Neither he nor his dog responded. They both made straight for the *hedai* of Guan Moh Chan, where he owed a mere hundred dollars or so. Would this tribute of five soften the hard heart of the *towkay*? He could feel already the sweat of anxiety more than heat stirring beneath his shirt. He needed at least two large bottles.

The shutters were being taken down by the youngest son of the large family – huge planks that fitted into the shop-front like the pieces of a Chinese puzzle. The *towkay*, in working costume of vest and underpants, grinned, nodded, sucked a black cigar. His head was that of an old idol, shrunken, yellow, painted with a false benignity. Nabby Adams addressed his prayers to it.

'*Saya* bring *wang*. *Saya* bring more *wang* tomorrow.'

The *towkay*, happy, chirping laughter, produced a book

and pointed to a total with a bone of a finger. '*Salatus tujoh puloh linggit lima puloh sen.*'

'How much?' He read for himself: $170.50. Christ, as much as that. 'Here. Give us a couple of bottles, big ones. *Dua.* You'll get some more *wang* tomorrow.'

Clucking happily, the old man took the five-dollar note and handed Nabby Adams a single dusty small bottle of Tiger beer. 'You mean old bastard,' he said. 'Come on, be a sport.'

It was no good. Nabby Adams went back with the one bottle hidden in his vast hand. He felt, irrationally, cheated. Five dollars. One dollar seventy a big bottle. The bloody old thief. Man and dog entered the mess to find Keir and Vorpal already at breakfast. Keir, in jungle green, sneered up at Nabby Adams, and Nabby felt a sweat of hatred for the Glasgow whine and the smug meanness. Vorpal, eupeptically bubbling greetings, bathed a sausage in a swimming plate of sauce. The cook-boy stood by, anxious, and said:

'*Tuan beli* vegitibubbles?'

'Yes,' said Nabby Adams, 'he's sending them round.' He then prepared to mount the stairs with his bottle. Keir said:

'I hope you made enough row in the night. I couldn't get a wink of sleep with your banging around and your drunken singing.'

Nabby Adams felt his neck-muscles tighten. Something in the mere quality of the impure vowels smote at his nerves. He said nothing.

Vorpal had the trick of adding a Malay enclitic to his utterances. This also had power to irritate, especially in the mornings. It irritated Nabby Adams that this should irritate him, but somewhere at the back of his brain was the contempt of the man learned in languages for the silly show-off, jingling the small change of 'wallah' and *charpoy*. The irritation was exacerbated by Nabby Adams's realization that Vorpal was not a bad type.

'Let the boy have his fun-*lah*. If you took a wee drappie

yourself you'd sleep through it like I do.' He crammed a dripping forkful in his mouth, chewing with appetite. 'Old Nabby's quiet enough during the day-*lah*.'

'Paddy's ill, too,' said Keir. 'He can't get up this morning. You might have a bit of consideration for a sick man.'

Nabby Adams turned to reply and saw at that moment a sight that brought a fearful thirst to his throat. His beating blood had dulled his ears to the sound of the approaching car, the car that now slid into the porch and stopped. Next to the Malay police-driver was the Contingent Transport Officer, Hood, who now, tubby and important, slammed the car door and prepared to enter the mess. Nabby fled up the stairs, the dog panting and clanking after him.

With the dry razor on his chin, Nabby Adams listened to salutations below, condescending, servile. The bottle stood on the dressing-table and grinned mockingly at him.

'Adams!'

Adams. Usually it was Nabby. Things must be bad. Nabby Adams called down, 'Yes, sir, shan't be a minute, sir,' in the big confident voice, manly but not unrefined, he had learnt as a regimental sergeant-major. He tore into uniform shirt and slacks, cursing the dog as she lovingly got under his feet. He clumped down the stairs, composing his features to calm and welcome, putting on the mask of a man eager for the new day. The unopened bottle sneered at his descending back.

'There you are, Adams.' Hood was standing waiting, a high-polished cap shading his flabby clean face. 'We're going to Sawan Lenja.'

'Sir.' Keir and Vorpal were out on the porch, waiting for transport to the police station. 'Anything wrong there, sir?'

'Too many vehicles off the road. What's these stories I've been hearing about you?'

'Stories, sir?'

'Don't act daft. You know what I mean. You've been hitting it again. I thought that was all over. Anyway, I'm getting all sorts of tales up at Timah, and Timah's a bloody long way from here. What's going on?'

'Nothing, sir. I have given it up, sir. It's a mug's game. A man in my position can't afford it, sir.'

'I should bloody well think not. Anyway, they tell me they couldn't find you anywhere last week and then they picked you up half-slewed in a shop in Sungai Kajar. Where did that come from?'

'Enemies, sir. There's a lot of Chinese on to me, sir. They want me to fiddle the accident reports and I won't, sir.'

'I should bloody well think not.' His face creased suddenly in a tight pain. 'Christ, I'll have to use your lavatory.'

Nabby's face melted in sympathy. 'Dysentery, sir?'

'Christ. Where is it?'

When Hood was safely closeted, Nabby Adams wildly hovered between two immediate courses of action – the telephone or the bottle? The bottle would have to wait. He picked up the dusty receiver. Fook Onn was at the other end, and Fook Onn spoke English.

'Alladad Khan? Where the hell is he? Get him, get the lot of them. Get them lined up. Hood's on his way.' Normally the Transport Pool began its operations at nine o'clock or thereabouts; this was a convenient arrangement for everybody. Officially it began to function at eight. The Chinese at the other end of the line was maddeningly urbane and slow. 'Get a move on,' urged Nabby Adams. 'He's coming now, I tell you.' As he replaced the receiver there was a flushing sound from the water-closet. Nabby recomposed his features as Hood re-entered.

'Better, sir?'

'It's an awful bloody business. Never know when it's going to come.' Hood sat down gingerly.

'What you could do with is a nice strong cup of tea, sir. I'll tell the *kuki* to make you one.'

'Does it really do any good, Nabby?' (That was better.) 'I've tried every damn thing.'

'Perfect, sir. It always puts me right.'

Hood looked at his wrist-watch. 'We haven't got much time, you know. I want to go to your place before Sawan Lenja.'

'That's all right, sir. I think he's got the kettle boiling.' Nabby Adams moved to the stairs, the dog following him.

'I can see your cook out there,' said Hood. 'What are you going upstairs for?'

'Oh. I thought he'd gone up to make the beds, sir.' Nabby Adams went to the kitchen and said, 'Make some *teh* for the *tuan besar.*'

Hood said, 'Sit down Nabby. Why are you running through the petrol so bloody fast? You're fifty-four gallons over and the month isn't ended yet.'

'I've got the file upstairs, sir. I'll bring it down.'

'It doesn't matter. I'll see it later.'

'I'd rather you saw it now, sir.' Nabby Adams moved again to the stairs.

'You're bloody restless, aren't you? Have you got a woman upstairs or something?' At that moment a groan of penitence came from an upper room. It was Flaherty, ill. God's most deep decree bitter would have him taste.

'That's Flaherty, sir. He's got fever. I'll just go up and see if he wants anything.' Nabby Adams made decisively for the stairs. The dog was waiting for him, her paws on the second tread, pere regardant with a happy lolling tongue. Nabby Adams nearly tripped over her. 'God blast you,' he said.

'That's no way to speak to an animal,' said Hood. 'I've got a dog myself. Come on, old boy.' The dog ignored him, following her master with a hasty clank clank clank.

Up in his room Nabby jerked off the bottle-top with trembling hands. The life-giving beer gurgled down his throat. Too soon the stream dried up. He threw the empty bottle with disgust on the bed. Then he went down again, feeling a little better, but, into the vacuum made by the removal of his immediate need, there nudged a more extensive, blunter anxiety: the long day, no money, Robin

Hood tut-tutting like a bloody parson, the lies, the subterfuges, the *towkays* wanting their money up in Sawan Lenja.

'So you didn't bring that file down, Nabby?' said Hood.

'No, sir. I thought it was upstairs. It must be in the office, sir.'

The tea came, not very strong but very milky, with a flotsam of leaves on its pale surface. 'Aren't you having any?' said Hood.

'No, thank you, sir,' said Nabby Adams. 'I've had my breakfast.'

Hood was downing the tea too rapidly. Nabby Adams calculated that he would have to give Corporal Alladad Khan at least another fifteen minutes. 'Will you have another cup, sir?' he asked.

'I've not finished this one yet. No, I don't think I will have another. Your boy makes bloody awful tea. How much do you pay him?'

'Hundred a month, between the four of us, that is.'

'Too much. Now, when I was in Perak, I got everything done for eighty, including garden and car cleaning.'

'Did you really, sir? That's very cheap, sir.'

'Well, we can't spend all day talking about the cost of labour.' Hood put down his cup and rose slowly. 'Christ,' he said. 'The bloody guts-ache. That tea wasn't much of an idea, Adams.'

'Give it time, sir. It'll do you the world of good. Just rest for a few minutes.'

'Well.' Hood sat down again. 'I suppose we're not worried over a few minutes, are we, Nabby?'

Nabby Adams breathed thanks to an unknown god. 'No, sir. Plenty of time. It's only an hour's run.'

'Hour and a half. Christ.' Hood was off again to the toilet. Nabby Adams wiped sweat off his face with a grey handkerchief. He stole noiselessly to the telephone, whispered the number, whispered:

'Is he there yet? Well, get hold of him quick. Get the lot of them. For God's sake get a move on.'

Hood came out amid the sound of rushing water. 'On our way,' he said.

'Yes, sir,' said Nabby Adams. 'I'll just get my cap.' Slowly he mounted the stairs, passed Flaherty's door and heard him moaning softly. He was gall, he was heartburn. Nabby Adams looked in the mirror, arranging his cap. He saw a bilious-yellow face, enlivened with a razor-cut. The body of his death.

There was some difficulty in getting the dog out of the car. At last they were off, she gamely running after down the *kampong* street. They soon lost her.

'You ought to train that dog properly,' said Hood. 'Mine wouldn't do that. You've got to have obedience in animals.'

His heart beating faster, his throat drying. Nabby whispered to the driver, 'Not so bloody fast.'

'*Tuan?*'

'All right, all right.' One of these days he must really get down to the language. There never seemed to be time, somehow.

They passed the Tamil Vernacular School, the town *padang*, the Anglo-Chinese School, the Government Girls' English School, the Iblis Club, the toddy-shop, the Town Board Offices, the Mosque, a row of Asian clerk's bungalows, and then came the Police Station, and next to it Police Transport, and now Nabby Adams swallowed lump after lump of anxiety, because the place seemed deserted, unopened, desolate, abandoned ... They rounded the corner and entered the vehicle park, and there were, thank God, the whole bloody lot of them lined up, calm, been waiting for hours and, as they left the car Corporal Alladad Khan barked, 'Ten Shun!' and they came to attention and Nabby Adams, police-lieutenant in charge of transport for the Police Circle, was proud and happy.

Relief brought an aching desire to be sitting in a *kedai* with a large bottle of Tiger or Anchor or Carlsberg in front of him. That, of course, was impossible. While Robin Hood was using the *jamban* at the back of the yard, Nabby

Adams urgently begged a loan of ten dollars from Corporal Alladad Khan. He spoke clean grammatical Urdu.

'Your wife is away. When she returns you may tell her that you required a new pair of trousers to be made. And then when I pay you back you can buy the pair of trousers.'

'But I do not need a pair of trousers.' Alladad Khan's melting brown eyes were serious over the proud nose, the ample, neat moustache.

'I shall have repaid you by the time she returns, however. So perhaps there will be no need for any story.'

'Wait,' said Alladad Khan. He had a long colloquy in Punjabi with a Sikh constable. He returned with ten dollars. 'I have borrowed this from Hari Singh. I shall have to open my wife's saving-box to repay him, because he needs the money today. I shall give you this and then you can pay me at the end of the month.'

'Thank you, Alladad Khan.' Hood was returning, saying, 'I'll have to get some hard-boiled eggs on the way.'

It was a wearisome, dry morning. They sped along the Timah road, through terrorist country, past regular neat woods of rubber trees. They saw tin-dredgers at work; they saw lorries loaded with latex; they went through villages and one largish town called Sungai Kajar – a wide main street, several drinking-shops, a Cinemascope advertisement – and by the time they got to Sawan Lenja Nabby Adams was near death. But he had to stoop over vehicles, examine engines, castigate inefficient corporal-fitters. At length Robin Hood said it was time for tiffin and they sought the rest house.

Hood ordered a portion of fried fish, a steak with onions and chipped potatoes, a dish of chopped pineapple and tinned cream. Nabby Adams said he would have a small round of cheese sandwiches.

'You ought to eat a good tiffin,' said Hood, 'because you need it in this climate. Thank God, I think my dysentery's a bit better. Have a beer if you want it,' he added generously. 'I'll have a small Tiger with you.'

'No,' said Nabby Adams. 'It's no good starting again.

I've finished with it, once and for all. It's better to give it up completely.'

'I'm glad to hear that from your lips, Nabby. You know, all your confidential reports have said the same thing: "A good man, first-class, but hits the bottle".'

'Never again,' said Nabby Adams. 'It's a mug's game.'

They ate, Hood sipping his small Tiger genteelly, Nabby Adams gloomily toying with a sandwich of tinned white cheese. They were alone in the single room that served as a restaurant and lounge. There was little sound: only the sucking noises that made Hood's every course seem like soup, the slow champing of Nabby's dry mouth, the whirr of the fan, the hoicking of the Chinese boy in the kitchen.

Soon Hood belched repletion, picked his teeth and eyed the rattan couch. 'It's only ten-past one,' he said. 'I'll just have a few minutes. It's been a hard morning.'

'It has, sir.'

'You haven't had this dysentery like I have. It takes it out of you.'

'You've put it back in again, sir.'

'I'll just have a few minutes, Nabby.' He stretched his small tubby form on the couch, crossed hands on his full belly. Nabby Adams watched him with great intensity. The eyes were closed, the breathing seemed relaxed and regular. Nabby Adams tiptoed over to the serving-hatch, watching still, narrowly. Hood sighed, turned, said, 'Don't let me oversleep, Nabby.'

'Not likely, sir.' Nabby Adams beckoned the boy sibilantly, went through the motions of pouring, drinking, indicated a large one with huge hands a cubit apart. The boy said, loudly, cheerfully, 'Anchor beer.'

'Not so bloody loud, man.' Nabby Adams made a hair-tearing gesture with a pair of gorilla arms, his face a devil's mask. He took the proffered glass and bottle, poured, downed, poured, downed, poured. A sleepy sigh came from the couch. Nabby Adams downed the last of it and tiptoed back, sitting at the table, good as gold.

Hood opened his eyes and said, 'How's the time going?'

'Quite all right, sir. Plenty of time. You have a sleep, sir.'

Hood turned over with his fat bottom towards Nabby Adams. Thank God. Nabby Adams tiptoed over again to the serving-hatch, ordered another, downed it. He began to feel a great deal better. After yet another he felt better still. Poor old Robin Hood wasn't a bad type. Stupid, didn't know a gear-box from a spare tyre, but he meant well. The world generally looked better. The sun shone, the palms shook in the faint breeze, a really lovely Malay girl passed by the window. Proud of carriage, in tight *baju* and rich sarong, she balanced voluptuous haunches. Her blue-black hair had some sort of a flower in it; how delicate the warm brown of her flat flower-like face.

'What time is it, Nabby?'

Nabby Adams gulped down his beer nervously. 'This clock says quarter to, sir, but I think it's a bit fast.'

'We're not worrying about five minutes, are we, Nabby?'

'No, sir.' Thank God he didn't turn over. Another bottle would make six dollars eighty. That meant he could finish the day with a bottle of *samsu*. He didn't like the burnt taste of the rice-spirit, but he didn't worry about the awful tales of the high lead-content. Or he could send the *kuki* to the toddy-shop, after dark, of course, because it was illegal to consume toddy off the premises. Toddy was cheap enough. The smell of decay was ghastly, but you could always hold your nose. The taste wasn't so good either: burnt brown paper. Still, it was a drink. Good for you, too. If it wasn't for the smell and the taste it would be a damn good drink.

Nabby Adams drank another bottle. At the end of it he heard Hood stirring with deep sighs, yawns, a creaking of rattan. This was it then. Two o'clock. He moved from the serving-hatch to the dining-room-lounge. Hood was sitting on the edge of the couch, rubbing sleepy eyes, then scratching through scant greying hair.

'On the job again, Nabby.'

'Yes, sir.'

The Chinese boy came in jauntily with a bill for Nabby Adams. Nabby Adams gave him a look of such malevolence that the boy's mouth, open to announce the amount of the bill, clapped, like a rat-trap, shut.

'Here, boy, give me that bill,' said Hood. 'I'll pay, Nabby. Your cheese sandwiches won't break me.'

'No, sir.' Nabby Adams grabbed the bill in panic. 'On me, sir. I mean, let's pay for our own.'

'I'll pay, Nabby. You deserve something for reforming your bad habits. How much, boy?'

'On me, sir, please,' begged Nabby Adams.

'Well.' Hood yawned widely and long showing back fillings and a softly rising uvula. 'You must be rolling in it now, Nabby, giving it up like you said. You must be saving pots of money. All right, I'll pay next time.'

Ten dollars was far from enough. Nabby Adams told the boy, while Hood was stretching on the veranda, that he'd give him the rest next time. The boy protested. Nabby Adams asserted six feet eight inches of Caucasian manhood and said he could whistle for the five dollars forty. The boy went for the *towkay*. Nabby Adams hastened Hood to the waiting car.

The mean bastard. Nabby Adams felt ill-used. The afternoon stretched, an arid scrubland of carburettors and oil-gaskets. The night? Nabby Adams groaned in his very stomach. Was ever grief like mine?

2

Victor Crabbe slept through the *bilal's bang* (inept Persian word for the faint unheeded call), would sleep till the *bangbang* (apt Javanese word) of the brontoid dawn brought him tea and bananas. He slept on the second floor of the old Residency, which overlooked the river.

The river Lanchap gives the state its name. It has its source in deep jungle, where it is a watering-place for a hundred or so little negroid people who worship thunder and can count only up to two. They share it with tigers, hamadryads, bootlace-snakes, leeches, pelandoks and the rest of the bewildering fauna of up-stream Malaya. As the Sungai Lanchap winds on, it encounters outposts of a more complex culture: Malay villages where the Koran is known, where the prophets jostle with nymphs and tree-gods in a pantheon of unimaginable variety. Here a little work in the paddy-fields suffices to maintain a heliotropic, pullulating subsistence. There are fish in the river, guarded, however, by crocodile-gods of fearful malignity; coconuts drop or are hurled down by trained monkeys called *beroks*; the durian sheds its rich fetid smell in the season of durians. Erotic pantuns and Hindu myths soothe away the depression of an occasional *accidia*. As the Lanchap approaches the coast a more progressive civilization appears: the two modern towns of Timah and Tahi Panas, made fat on tin and rubber, supporting large populations of Chinese, Malays, Indians, Eurasians, Arabs, Scots, Christian Brothers, and pale English administrators. The towns echo with trishaw-bells, the horns of smooth, smug American cars, radios blaring sentimental pentatonic Chinese tunes, the morning hawking and spitting of the *towkays*, the call of the East. Where the Lan-chap meets the Sungai Hantu stands the royal town, dominated by an Istana designed by a Los Angeles archi-tect, blessed by a mosque as bulbous as a clutch of onions, cursed by a lowering sky and high humidity. This is Kuala Hantu.

Victor Crabbe slept soundly, drawn into that dark world where history melts into myth.

The history of the state differs little from that of its great neighbours, Johore and Pahang. A prince of Malacca settled on its river at the time of the Portuguese invasions. He had known the old days of quiet and leisure, the silken girls bringing sherbet, the long, subtle theological debates with visiting Islamic philosophers. The Portuguese, sweat-ing in trunk-hose, brought a niggling concern with com-merce and the salvation of pagan souls. Francis Xavier preached about the love of an alien God, tried to fracture the indivisible numen and establish a crude triune struc-ture, set up schools where dreary hymns were sung, and finally condoned the rack and the thumbscrew. Now the royal house of Malacca began to substantiate its old hypo-thetical claim to overlordship of the entire peninsula. Ben-dahara Yusuf set up a meagre palace on the swampy shore of the Lanchap and tried to divert the outrageous revenues collected by the chiefs into his own coffers. He bequeathed to his successors an arduous task, made no easier by the bullyings of the Achinese and the ubiquitous Bugis, ex-acerbated by the ruthless greed of the trumpeting Dutch. The rulers themselves lived unedifying lives. Yahya never moved out of an opium-trance; Ahmad died of a surfeit of Persian sweetmeats; Mohammed lashed at least one slave to death every day; Aziz had syphilis and died at the age of eighteen; Hussain had a hundred wives.

Victor Crabbe had been married twice. His second wife breathed and murmured now in deep sleep induced by barbiturates.

At the time of Stamford Raffles's first appointment, while, in the East India Company Offices in Penang, that great Englishman fretted over the decay of Malacca and learned his Malay verbs, then it was that Sultan Iblis – may God be mericful to him – crashed his mighty fist on the table, slaughtered a few Bugis, tortured a few chiefs, reformed the laws of inheritance, centralized the Customs and Excise, affirmed that women had souls, and limited wives to four in number. His name is remembered, his achievements commemorated in numerous institutions: the Iblis Club in the royal town, the Iblis Power Station at Timah, the Iblis Cinema in Tahi Panas, the Iblis Koran School at Bukit Tinggi, Iblis Mineral Waters (Swee Hong & Co., Singapore and Kuala Lumpur).

Victor Crabbe was a member of the Iblis Club but did not drink Iblis Mineral Waters.

After the death of Sultan Iblis there was trouble again. Five chiefs claimed the throne, only one of them – the Crown Prince Mansor – with any right. The bad days of anarchy returned, the kris whistled through the air and lopped innocent heads, there was pillaging and arson in up-river *kampongs*, the Bugis appeared again – a portent, like the anti-Christ Danes at the time of Bishop Wulfstan – and even the Siamese, who already held Patani, Kelantan and Trengganu, began to be interested. It was now that the British intervened. Mansor fled to Singapore, imploring help from the Governor. Yes, yes, he would most certainly accept a British Resident if he could be guaranteed a safe throne, a permanent bodyguard and a pension of $15,000 a month. And so the wars gradually died down like a wind, though not before some British blood had been spilled on that inhospitable soil. The state began to prosper. Rubber throve, and the Chinese dredged for tin with frantic industry. Sultan Mansor became Anglophile, wore tweeds even in his own palace, was graciously received by Queen Victoria, adopted as his state anthem a Mendelssohnian salon piece composed by the late Prince Consort, frequented the race-meetings in Singapore, and established that tradition of heavy gambling which has ever since been a feature of the royal house of Lanchap.

His successors have been men-of-the-world, cosmopolitan, fond of new cars, insensitive to many of the sanctions of Islam. Pork, indeed, has never appeared at state banquets, and polygamy and concubinage have been practised with traditional piety, but the Istana has a well-stocked cellar and every Sultan has to drink brandy on doctor's orders. The work of governing Lanchap has been carried on quietly and with moderate efficiency by the British Advisers – mostly colourless, uxorious men with a taste for fishing or collecting matchboxes or writing competent monographs on the more accessible Malay village customs.

Victor Crabbe was in the Education Service, a resident master at the Mansor School.

On his first visit to England, Sultan Mansor had been fascinated by the public school system. He had been shown round Eton, Harrow, Winchester, Rugby and Shrewsbury, and one of his dreams had been a public school in his own state, in his own royal town, reproducing many of the features of its English prototypes – cricket, a wall-game, and pancake-scramble on the eve of Puasa, housemasters, prefects, fags, and, of course, a curriculum which should open the doors of European culture to brown little boys in Eton collars and bum-freezers. The limitations he placed on the scheme killed its realization, however. He was a cosmopolitan when abroad, at ease in the hotels of the Western capitals, but in his own country he was parochial, his vision bounded by his own blood and his own river. He wanted a school for the Malay aristocracy of his own state, but, philoprogenitive and imaginative as he was, he could not but see that his own loins would never produce a sufficient first-form entry in his own lifetime.

Victor Crabbe, though thirty-five years of age, had no children.

Sultan Aladdin preferred Chinese and European mistresses to his own Malay wives, and had love-children of many colours. He found it easy to see that the future of

Malaya in general, and of Lanchap in particular, rested not with the Malays alone but with the harmonious working-together of all the component races. He had few illusions about his own people: amiable, well-favoured, courteous, they loved rest better than industry; through them the peninsula would never advance – rather their function was to remind the toiling Chinese, Indians and British of the ultimate vanity of labour. He saw in the mingling of many cultures the possibility of a unique and aesthetically valuable pattern, and before his early death he had laid out his plan for a Malayan public school in a letter which he sent to all the Sultans. Written in exquisite, courtly Malay, made flavoursome with neologisms drawn from Sanskrit and Arabic, this letter may be found in those anthologies of Malay prose – compiled by scholars like Ashenden, Pink and Inche Redzwan bin Latiff, B.A. – which oppress pupils up and down the Federation.

Actually, it was an Englishman who realized the visionary project, an able Inspector of Schools, F.M.S., called Pocock. He spoke with energy and zeal to the Resident-General, his enthusiasm infected a Residents' Conference, and soon the High Commissioner himself saw the value of an educational establishment which should be a microcosm of the teeming, various world which was Malaya and yet be a symbol too of the calm British governmental process.

And so the Mansor School came into being in Mansor's own royal town. To it came Chinese, Malays, Indians and Eurasians – all of 'good family' (a qualification which, though never defined, had been a *Leitmotif* in Pocock's original prospectus). Teachers came from England and India and the Straits Settlements. The School grew steadily, established traditions slowly. After some years it was decided that the climate was unsuitable for stiff collars and striped serge trousers, but an adequate school uniform was eventually found in white ducks, striped tie and Harrovian boater. The many buildings of the School represent a whole museum of colonial architecture, ranging from the original *attap* huts, through stucco palladian, to broiling Corbusier glass-houses on high stilts. All subjects have always been taught in English, and the occidental bias in the curriculum has made many of the alumni despite their own rich cultures, leading them, deracinated, to a yearning for the furthest west of all. Thus, the myths of cinema and syndicated cartoon have served to unite the diverse races far more than the clump of the cricket-ball and the clipped rebukes and laudations of their masters.

Victor Crabbe taught history.

Headmasters came and went, officers in the Education Service who did well or ill, but always moved on to retirement or to less arduous posts. Some ruled as they had been used to when they were form-masters in tough London or Liverpool secondary schools; they were baffled by tears in moustached sixth-formers, by walls of impassivity in the Lower School, by silent conspiracies which nullified the rules. One master was axed and another knifed during one harsh reign, that of the hated Gillespie. Him a local *pawang* was hired to kill by sympathetic magic, but Gillespie was too tough or insensitive to feel the lethal waves sent out from his pin-pricked image. Headmasters who cooed their love of the Asians found that love was infectious, and that Eros stalked the dormitories in two of his many divine forms. Moreover they were ostracized in the Club, shunned as betrayers of the British Way of Life. Only one headmaster was removed for pederasty and he with regret, for he was a superb cricketer. The problem of rule seemed insuperable. A sort of Malayan unity only appeared when the discipline was tyrannous; when a laxer humanity prevailed the Chinese warred with the Malays and both warred with the Indians and the Indians warred among themselves. Only one man had ever achieved the compromise of a firm liberalism. This had been Roberts, an Oriental scholar of deep human insight and warm charm. But under him the public school spirit began to evaporate.

Cricket ceased to be played because only a few boys seemed able to understand it; two years went by without a Sports Day, and the headmaster was once seen working in a sarong. Roberts was transferred to an obscure post in Kelantan. At times it was thought that an American might be appointed, who, because he would combine the familiar and the exotic and would carry on his breath the magic of the sound-track, might arouse in the boys a strong religious devotion. But an American might introduce rounders. Besides, such an appointment would be a complete betrayal of the ideals on which the Mansor School was based, surrender to a culture which, however inevitable its global spread, must for as long as possible meet a show of resistance. An Australian was once appointed on contract, but he swore too much. And so makeshift and second-best have continued. Victor Crabbe's headmaster was a little man called Boothby with a third-class Durham degree, a paunchy sportsman with a taste for whisky-water and fast cars, who subscribed to a popular book-club and had many long-playing records, who invited people to curry tiffin and said, 'Take a pew.'

Victor Crabbe was a housemaster.

The difficulties of organizing a house-system in a school of this kind had been partly solved through weak compromise. At first it had been proposed to call the houses after major prophets – Nabi Adams, Nabi Idris, Nabi Isa, Nabi Mohammed – but everyone except the Muslims protested. Then it seemed microcosmically fitting to allot boys to houses bearing the names of their home states. It happened, however, that an obscurantist Sultan and a Union of Chinese Secret Societies in one state forbade, independently of each other, any patronization of the new educational venture. Thus it fell out that a rich and important territory was represented in the Mansor School by a Eurasian, the son of a Bengali money-lender, a Tamil and a dull but happy Sikh. The pupils themselves, through their prefects, pressed the advantages of a racial division. The Chinese feared that the Malays would run amok in the dormitories and use knives; the Malays said they did not like the smell of the Indians; the various Indian races preferred to conduct vendettas only among themselves. Besides, there was the question of food. The Chinese cried out for pork which, to the Muslims, was *haram* and disgusting; the Hindus would not eat meat at all, despite the persuasions of the British matron; other Indians demanded burning curries and could not stomach the insipid *lauk* of the Malays. Finally the houses were given the names of Britons who had helped to build the new Malaya. Allocation to houses was arbitrary – the dormitories buzzed with different prayers in different tongues – and everybody had to eat cold rice with a warmish *lauk* of buffalo-meat or vegetables. Nobody was satisfied but nobody could think of anything better.

Thus it was that Victor Crabbe had the post of Master of Light House, named after Francis Light, founder of British Penang. The house was not very felicitously titled, said many: it was no academic pharos. Still, Birch House (a sop to the shade of the murdered Perak Resident) had no more than its normal share of flagellation, and Raffles House did not exceed the others in its interest in the Federation Lottery. Low House (named after the great Hugh) often came high in games and athletics; so, in fine, the names had no paranomastic propriety. All they showed was a lack of imagination on the part of those who had chosen them.

Victor Crabbe, as dawn approached, stirred uneasily, his eyes tightly closed, his brow creased. He fended something off with his arms.

A centre of culture, Kuala Hantu is also a centre of Communist activity. A man may walk in moderate safety through the town at night, but let him not venture too far out into the scrublands. A grenade was once hurled into a *kedai* where Home Guards sat drinking; pamphlets calling on Asians to exterminate the white capitalist parasites are found on café tables and in long-parked cars. A mile or so out, on the Timah and Tahi Panas roads, there are frequent 'incidents'. On rubber estates the terrorists appear capricously, at unpredictable intervals, to decapitate tappers or disembowel them – a ceremony followed by harangues about the Brotherhood of Man and the Federation of the World. At Grantham Estate, seven miles outside Kuala Hantu, there have been five new managers in two years. A planter carries a gun not in hope of prevailing against the terrorists, but because he prefers the clean end of a shot to the tearing-out of his intestines. Lanchap, like most other states, is at war. Even outside the smart store of Blackthorn Bros, in Tahi Panas, armour-plated cars may be seen, parked while the summer-frocked mems go shopping. Military convoys trundle down the roads, bombs rattle windows, aeroplanes zoom, questing, over the jungle hideouts. The car-driver, hoping yet once more to get away with it, to speed through the bad nine miles and heave, once more, a sigh of gratitude at the end, sees at last the tree-trunk laid across the road and soon the ambushing grinning yellow men emerging. Some think the war will never end. The troops move into the steaming leech-haunted nightmare and emerge now and again with sullen prisoners who have names like Lotus Blossom, Dawn Lily or Elegant Tiger. But there are no decisive engagements, no real victories. It goes on and on, the sniping, the gutting, the garrotting, the thin streams of jungle-green troops, the colossal waste, and the anarchic days of the Bugis and the Achinese seem not far away after all.

Victor Crabbe woke up sweating. He had been dreaming about his first wife whom, eight years previously, he had killed. At the inquest he had been exonerated from all blame and the coroner had condoned with him all too eloquently and publicly. The car had skidded on the January road, had become a mad thing, resisting all control, had crashed through the weak bridge-fence and fallen – his stomach fell now, as his sleeping body had fallen time and time again in the nightmare reliving of the nightmare – fallen, it seemed endlessly, till it shattered the ice and the icy water beneath, and sank with loud heavy bubbles. His lungs bursting, he had felt the still body in the passenger-seat, had torn desperately at the driver's door, and risen, suffocating, through what seemed fathom after fathom of icy bubbling lead. It was a long time ago. He had been exonerated from all blame but he knew he was guilty.

He was grateful now for the warmth of the Malayan morning, for the familiar sound of Ibrahim on swift bare feet bringing the rattling tray, set for one, to the veranda. Fenella, his living wife, would sleep on, long, killing the hot morning in sleep. She wanted to go home, but she would not go home without him. She wanted the two of them to be together. She believed her love was reciprocated. To some extent it was.

'Morden or Surbiton with palm trees. A ramshackle inland Bournemouth. Little suburban minds. Bridge and gossip. Tea and gossip. Tennis and gossip. Red Cross sewing parties and gossip. Look.' She would show, as they sat in the deserted Club, a copy of *Country Life*. 'We could save enough to buy that in three years. If we go steady. Ideal for a private school.'

Or again, flopped in one of the standard-pattern armchairs supplied by the Public Works Department, drinking in the wind of the ceiling-fan, she would gasp, 'It's so damned hot.' It had not been so damned hot in that English January. 'Doesn't it ever get any cooler?'

'I like the heat.'

'I thought I did. I used to in Italy. It must be the humidity.'

The humidity could be blamed for many things: the need for a siesta, corpulence, the use of the car for a hundred-yard journey, the mildew on the shoes, the sweat-rot in the armpits of dresses, the lost bridge-rubber or tennis-set, the dislike felt for the whole country.

'I quite like the country.'

'But what is there to like? Scabby children, spitting pot-bellied shopkeepers, terrorists, burglars, scorpions, those blasted flying-beetles. And the noise of the radios and the eternal shouting. Are they all deaf or something? Where is this glamorous East they talk about? It's just a horrible sweating travesty of Europe. And I haven't met a soul I can talk to. All those morons in the Malay Regiment and those louts of planters, and as for the wives ...'

'We're together. We can talk to each other.'

'Why should we have to come out here to do that? It was more comfortable in London.'

'The pay's better.'

'It goes nowhere. Have you seen this month's Cold Storage bill? And this dress from Blackthorn's – eighty dollars, and it's going already under the arms.'

'Yes. I see your point.'

Having eaten two bananas and drunk three cups of tea, Victor Crabbe stood naked in the second bathroom, shaving. Between the first and last razor-strokes the morning grew from bud to full flower. Between the louvres of frosted glass Crabbe could see the descending terraces of lawn and the thin, black Tamil gardeners watering away with quarrelling cries. This country was not rich in flowers, but the semi-public garden of the Residency had bougainvillea, hibiscus, frangipani, rain trees and a single banyan. Across the road that bounded the lowest terrace the Hantu met the Lanchap, a meagre confluence now, the water smelling foul with a salty decay, bicycle tyres high and dry and bits of stick and iron lying like bones on rare mud islands.

In a sense, infidelity to one's second wife was an act of homage to one's first. His dead wife was in all women. Pointless to moon about, as his father had done, hugging a memory putting flowers on the grave, decking them with the brine of self-pity. That was necrophily. He had learned a lot from his father. The body of his own wife had been burnt and dispersed in vapour, had become atoms suspended in air or liquid, breathed in or drained down. A memory had no significance. History was not memory but a living pattern. Dreams were not memory.

His hands, screwing the safety-razor apart, trembled, and a piece of steel fell into the wash-basin with a resonant clatter. Dreaming, one was not oneself. One was used by something, something stupidly malignant, a lolling idiot with a thousand volts at his command. 'But why do you still have this feeling of guilt? Why won't you swim any more or drive a car again?'

'Nerves,' he answered. 'Something resident in the nerves. I married again to quieten my nerves. I think it was a mistake now, but it was a natural one. Perhaps that's where the sense of guilt is really coming from. It's not been fair to her. The remembered dead wife and the palpable living wife must, to some extent, be identified. Or, at least, those well-worn tracks of the brain identify them. Then one is seeing her with the wrong eyes, judging, weighing, comparing. The dead woman was brought to life, and it was not fair, it was unnatural, to give life to the dead. The dead are fractured, atomized, dust in the sunlight, dregs in the beer. Yet the fact of love remains, and to love the dead is, in the nature of things, impossible. One must love the living, the living fractured and atomized into individual bodies and minds that can never be close, never important. For if one were to mean more than the others, then we should be back again, identifying and, with sudden shocks, contrasting, and bringing the dead back to life. The dead are dead.

'And so spread and atomize that love. But how about her, sleeping there in the big dark bedroom, what does she deserve? It was all a mistake, it should never have happened. She deserves whole wells of pity, tasting and looking like love.'

Victor Crabbe put on clean starched white slacks and a cool, fresh-smelling, white shirt, open at the neck. He did this quietly in their bedroom, having opened one of the shutters to let in some light. The precaution of quiet was unnecessary, a mere habit. She slept a drugged sleep. If anything could wake her, it would be the row of the dormitories, the clatter of the boys to the dining-room, the

43

exhortations of the prefects, the ringing of bicycle-bells and the crunching feet on the gravel of the drive below. She would not wake till midday. He picked up his dispatch-case, mildewed under the buckles, from the desk-chair in the lounge, and walked to the door which led from the flat to the world of boys. The swing-doors which opened on to his dining-room creaked, and Ibrahim said softly, '*Tuan.*'

'Ibrahim?' (People had said, 'I don't know why the hell you keep that boy on. You'll be getting yourself talked about. He was down outside the cinema the other night, wearing women's clothes. It's a good job you're married, you know. He was thrown out of the Officers' Mess for waggling his bottom and upsetting the men. He may be a good cook, and all that, but still ... You've got to be careful.')

Ibrahim squirmed and simpered. '*Minta belanja, tuan.*'

'But it's only three days to the end of the month. What do you do with the money?'

'*Tuan?*'

'How much do you want?'

'*Lima ringgit, tuan.*'

'Buy some hair-clips with it,' said Crabbe in English, handing over a five-dollar note. 'Mem says you're pinching hers.'

'*Tuan?*'

'Never mind.'

'*Terima kaseh, tuan,*' smirked Ibrahim, tucking the note in the waist of his sarong.

'*Sama sama.*' Victor Crabbe opened the flimsy door that separated him from the boys of Light House, and walked slowly – for fear of slipping on worn treads – down the wide seedy staircase that had once been so imposing. At the bottom the duty prefect waited, Narayanasamy, rich black face vivid above the white shirt and slacks. The entrance-hall was full of boys leaving for the Main School, a counterpoint of colour united by the pedal-note of the snowy uniform.

'Sir, we are trying to work because we are having to take the examination in a very brief time from now, but the younger boys are not realizing the importance of our labours and they are creating veritable pandemoniums while we are immersed in our studies. To us who are their lawful and appointed superiors they are giving overmuch insolence, nor are they sufficiently overawed by our frequent threatenings. I would be taking it, sir, as inestimable favour if you would deliver harsh words and verbal punishing to them all, sir, especially the Malay boys, who are severely lacking in due respectfulness and incorrigible to discipline also.'

'Very well,' said Victor Crabbe, 'tonight at dinner.' Once a week he dined with the boys. Pursued by respectful salutations he strode down the cracked stone steps, flight after flight, to reach the road leading to the Main School. He alone of the Europeans in Kuala Hantu did not possess a car. By the time he reached the War Memorial damp had soaked through the breasts of his shirt.

The citizens of Kuala Hantu watched him go by. Workless Malays in worn white trousers squatted on the low wall of the public fountain and discussed him.

'He walks to the School. He has no car. Yet he is rich.'

'He saves money to be richer still. He will go back to England with full pockets and do no more work.'

'That is wise enough. He is no banana-eating child.'

The two old *hajis* who sat near the door of the coffee-shop spoke together.

'The horn-bill pairs with his own kind, and so does the sparrow. The white men will say it is not seemly for him to walk to work like a labourer.'

'His heart is not swollen. Enter a goat's pen bleating, enter a buffalo's stall bellowing. He believes so. He would be like the ordinary people.'

'That I will believe when cats have horns.'

A wizened hanger-on, hoping to cadge some early-morning coffee, volunteered, 'Water in his grasp does not drip.'

45

The more charitable *haji* said. 'A black fowl flies by night, it is true. But do not measure another's coat on your own body.'

A Chinese shopkeeper's wife, surrounded by quarrelling children, said to her husband in plangent Hokkien:

> 'All time he walk.
> On his face sweat.
> Red-haired dogs rich,
> Pay what we ask.
> Yet day by day
> He go on foot
> Car he has not.'

Her white-powdered moon-face pondered the small mystery for a short time only. Then in a passion of plucked strings and little cracked bells she let fly at a weeping child, pushed by his fellows into a sugar-bin.

The Indian letter-writers, awaiting clients, fresh paper and carbons rolled into their machines, greeted Victor Crabbe with smiles and waved hands. With them once or twice, in the Coronation and the Jubilee and Fun Hwa's, he had drunk beer and discussed the decay of the times.

Victor Crabbe passed by the pathetic little Paradise Cabaret and swallowed a small lump of guilt that rose in his throat. Here, in search of a drink and an hour's solitude, he had met Rahimah, the sole dance-hostess, who poured beer, changed the records, and shuffled with the customers round the floor. Small, light brown, short-haired, wearing a European frock, she was amiable, complaisant, very feminine. She was a divorcee, thrown out by her husband on some thin pretext backed by the grim male force of Islamic law. She had one child, a small boy called Mat. Two unlaborious professions only were open to Malay divorcées, and in practice the higher embraced the lower. A dance-hostess earned little enough in such places as this, and the descent from polygamous wedlock to prostitution seemed a mere stumble. Victor Crabbe liked to believe that she had sold nothing to him, that the ten-dollar notes he hid in her warm uneager hand were gratuitous, a help – 'Buy something for Mat.' He felt, in her small room, that he was somehow piercing to the heart of the country, of the East itself. Also he was placating that unquiet ghost. But he must not grow too fond of Rahimah. Love must be fractured, pulverized, as that loved body had finally been. Fenella believed that he went off to the School debates, meetings of the Historical Society. He must drop the liaison soon. But there would have to be others.

An aged Sikh, high on his cart of dung, king of two placid oxen, was coiling hanks of grey hair into place, stuffing them beneath his rakish turban. His face, all beard, smiled at Victor Crabbe. Crabbe waved, wiped sweat off his forehead. Little boys, on their way to the Chinese School, looked up at him in that intense wonder which characterizes the faces of the Chinese young. Victor Crabbe turned the corner by the Police Barracks. If only the School buildings were not so dispersed, like Oxford Colleges. He must really carry a change of shirt in his dispatch-case. He observed small cats with twisted tails stalking hens from the dry monsoon-drains. His feet trod a litter of palm-tree pods, like segments of blackened bicycle tyre. He was nearing the Main School now.

Corporal Alladad Khan, unaware as yet of the urgent telephone summons that was animating the Transport Office, shaved at leisure, seeing Victor Crabbe walk, too briskly for the climate, to his work. He saw nothing un-natural in this walking. He, Alladad Khan, spent his life now among motor vehicles and sometimes yearned for the old village days in the Punjab. He liked to feel the solid ground under his feet, or, better still, the warm moving flanks of a horse between his knees. Motor vehicles plagued his dreams, spare parts and indents for spare parts pricked him like mosquitoes. That a man should prefer to have nothing to do with motor engines seemed reasonable and even laudable. But . . .

Corporal Alladad Khan swept his cut-throat razor across his throat and cut his throat slightly. He swore in English. All the English he knew was: names of cars and car-parts; army terms, including words of command; brands of beer and cigarettes; swear-words. He had been long in the Army of India – he had joined as a boy of thirteen, stating his age wrong. Now, at thirty, he saw another ten years before he could leave the Malayan Police with a pension and return to the Punjab. But ...

'Bloody liar!' he said to the razor. 'Fock off!' It was behaving badly this morning. He did not really like even the simplest machine. Even a razor had a nasty malicious little soul, squat, grinning at him from the blue shine of metal. 'Silly bastard!' He could swear aloud because his wife, who knew some English, was away in Kuala Lumpur, staying with an uncle and an aunt, making lavish and leisurely preparations to have a baby, their first. Alladad Khan did not want any children. He was not a very ortho-dox Muslim. He had ideas which shocked his wife. He had once said that the thought of eating a pork sausage did not horrify him. He liked beer, though he could not afford much of it. He could afford even less of it now that Adams Sahib insisted on taking him around. He had seen kissing in English and American films and had once suggested to his wife that they try this erotic novelty. She had been hor-rified, accusing him of perversion and the blackest sensual depravity. She had even threatened to report him to her brother.

He had found the Malay term '*Tida' apa*' useful when she spoke like that. '*Tida' apa*' meant so much more than 'It doesn't matter' or 'Who cares?'. There was something indefinable and satisfying about it, implying that the universe would carry on, the sun shine, the durians fall whatever she, or anybody else, said or did. Her brother. That was the whole trouble. Her brother, Abdul Khan, was an Officer Commanding a Police District, a big man, unmarried, who had been trained at an English Police College and thought a lot of himself. Her parents, their parents, were dead. It was up to the brother to arrange a marriage for her, and naturally she had to marry a Khan. No matter what he did, no matter what his position in life, so long as he was not a *servant* (which, naturally, a Khan could not be), she had to have a Khan. Well, she had a Khan, him, Alladad Khan. Shutting his razor with a clack he wished her well of him, Alladad Khan. Alladad Khan laughed grimly into his mirror before he washed the shaving-soap off his face and trimmed his moustache with nail-scissors. He had been a good husband, faithful, careful with money, loving, moderately passionate; what more could she want? Ha! It was not a question of what she wanted but of what he, Alladad Khan, wanted.

In the small living-room he buttoned his shirt, looking sardonically at their wedding photograph. When that photograph was taken he had known her precisely two hours and ten minutes. He had seen her picture before, and she had observed him through a hole in a curtain, but they had never spoken together, held hands or done that terrible erotic thing which was a commonplace of the English and American films. The long gruelling courtship was about to commence. There he was, with a background of photographer's potted palms, awkward in his best suit and a *songkok*, while she rested an arm confidently on his knee and showed her long strong nose and cannibal teeth to the Chinese photographer. Allah, she had known all about courtship.

But there was the memsahib, Mrs Crabbe, very much in his thoughts now. He had never met her, but he had seen her often, sweating in the heat as she walked to the Club or to the shops. He, Crabbe the teacher, might not wish to have a car, but it was not right that his wife should have to walk in the sun, her golden hair darkened at the forehead by sweat, her delicate white face dripping with sweat, the back of her frock stained and defiled by sweat. He had often to stifle the mad desire to run down to her as she walked by the Transport Office, offering her the Land Rover, or the A70, or the old Ford, or whatever vehicle sweltered in the yard, together with a police-driver who would, for once, behave properly and not hawk or belch or lower the driver's window yet further to spit out of it. But shyness held him back. He did not speak English; he did not know whether she spoke Malay. Besides, there was the question of propriety, of morality. Who was he to rush up on clumsy booted feet, stopping before her with a frightful heel-click and a stiff salute to say, 'Memsahib, I observe you walking in the heat. You will be struck by the sun. Allow me to provide you with transport to wherever you wish to go,' or words to that effect? It was impossible. But he must meet her, at least see her closely, to examine her blue eyes and appraise her slim form and hear her English voice. Blue-eyed women he believed there were in Kashmir, but here was the mythical Englishry of fair hair as well. He had to meet her. That was where Police-Lieutenant Adams would have to help him. That would be a small return for many small loans whose repayment he did not press. An Englishwoman who walked; that was a barrier down before he started, a barrier of slammed elegant blue or red or green doors, the calmness of one who waits, smugly, to be driven to where she will.

The entrance of a small, elderly Malay driver broke his dreams. Kassim, who had never mastered the philosophy of gears, who dragged mucus into his throat horribly, even on parade, who had undertaken the impossible task of keeping two wives on a driver's pay, Kassim spoke.

'The big man speaks by the telephone. There is the other big man from Timah here. He will inspect the transport now.'

'There is no God but Allah,' said Alladad Khan piously. He rushed out, followed by Kassim. He banged at doors, he cursed and entreated, he sent frantic messages. He dashed to the Transport Office. He smacked two Malay drivers on the cheek to recall them from lethargy, he checked tyres, he checked uniforms, he checked the alignment of the vehicles. Soon he had his men drawn up. Then he heard the approaching car, horrible as Juggernaut. He saw the car enter the park. He called, 'Ten Shun!'

There they were, thank God, the whole bloody lot of them lined up, been waiting for hours. As they came to attention Nabby Adams, police-lieutenant in charge of transport for the Police Circle, was proud and happy.

3

Victor Crabbe stood before his form and knew something was wrong. He scanned the faces, row after row, in a silence churned gently by the two ceiling-fans. The serious, mature faces looked back at him – yellow, gold, sallow-brown, coffee-brown, black. Malay and Indian eyes were wide and luminous. Chinese eyes sunken in a kind of quizzical astonishment. Crabbe saw the empty desk and said:

'Where's Hamidin?'

The boys stirred, some looking over their shoulders to where Chop Toong Cheong was rising. Assured that their form-captain would speak, they veered their heads delicately round towards Victor Crabbe, looking at him seriously, judicially.

'Toong Cheong?'

'Hamidin has been sent home, sir.'

'Home? But I saw him yesterday evening on the sports-field.'

'He was sent home last night, sir, on the midnight mail-train. He has been expelled, sir.'

Expelled! The very word is like a bell. Crabbe felt the old thrill of horror. That horror must also be in the boys' nerves, even though English words carried so few over-tones for them. England, mother, sister, honour, cad, decency, empire, expelled. The officer-voice of Henry Newbolt whispered in the fans.

'And why in the name of God has he been expelled?' Crabbe saw the squat brown face of Hamidin, the neat lithe body in soccer-rig. Expulsion had to be confirmed by the Mentri Besar of the boy's own state, but confirmation was always automatic.

Toong Cheong had been brought up a Methodist. His eyes narrowed in embarrassment behind serious thick spectacles. 'It is a delicate matter, sir. They say he was in house-boy's room with a woman. House-boy also was there with another woman. A prefect found them and reported to Headmaster, sir. Headmaster sent him home at once on midnight mail-train.'

'Well.' Crabbe did not know what to say. 'That's bad luck,' he offered, lamely.

'But, sir.' Toong Cheong spoke more rapidly now, and urgency and embarrassment reduced his speech to essential semantemes. 'We think he was framed, sir. Prefect no friend of his. He did nothing with woman in house-boy's room. Prefect deliberate lie to Headmaster.'

'Who was the prefect?'

'Pushpanathan, sir.'

'Ah.' Crabbe felt that he had to say something significant. He was not quite sure who Pushpanathan was. 'Ah,' he said again, drawing out the vocable in a falling tone, the tone of complete comprehension.

'We wish you to tell Headmaster, sir, Hamidin wrongly expelled. Injustice, sir. He is a member of our form. We must stick by him.'

Crabbe was touched. The form had welded itself into a single unity on this issue. Tamils, Bengalis, and one Sikh, the Malays, the one Eurasian, the Chinese had found a loyalty that transcended race. Then, hopelessly, Crabbe saw that this unity was only a common banding against British injustice.

'Well.' He began walking up and down, between the window and the open door. He knew he was about to embark on a speech whose indiscretions would sweep the School. 'Well.' The face of a moustached Malay in the front row glowed with attention. 'Please sit down, Toong Cheong.' The Chinese form-captain sat down. Crabbe turned to the blackboard, observing equations of yesterday in thick yellow chalk. Yellow chalk was a nuisance; it defiled hands and white trousers; one's handkerchief was sickly with it; it stained, like lipstick, the mouth of the tea-cup at break.

'Hamidin,' he said, 'should not have been in the house-boy's room. Those quarters are out-of-bounds. I cannot believe that the meeting of Hamidin and this woman was accidental. I cannot believe that Hamidin would merely want to discuss politics or the differential calculus with this woman. Who was she, anyway?' He stopped his promenade and craned his neck at Toong Cheong.

Toong Cheong stood up. 'She is a schoolgirl, sir. From Government English Girls' School.' He sat down again.

'Well.' Crabbe resumed his walk. 'Frankly, speaking as a private individual and not as a member of this staff, I would say that, whatever Hamidin was doing in that room with that girl . . .' He turned again towards Toong Cheong. 'What was it alleged that he was doing, by the way?'

This time there was a serpentine chorus. 'Kissing. Kissing, sir. They said he was kissing her, sir. Pushpanathan alleged they were kissing, sir. Kissing.'

'Oh, kissing.' Crabbe faced them squarely. Toong Cheong sat down, still hissing the word quietly. 'All of you here are of marriageable age. Some of you would have been married years ago, perhaps, if the Japanese occupation had not played havoc with your educational careers. I, personally, can see no great crime in a young man of nineteen consorting innocently with a girl. I can see no great crime, frankly, in a young man's kissing a girl. Though I had thought that kissing was not practised by Malays. Still, it seems to me one of the less harmful Western importations.'

He caught shy smiles, delicate as foam.

'I do not, speaking again as a private individual, think that such conduct merits expulsion. Even,' he added, 'if it could be proved that such conduct took place. Did Pushpanathan have any witnesses, other than himself? What did the house-boy say?'

'The house-boy was expelled, too,' said Toong Cheong, levering himself up to a half-standing position.

'Dismissed, you mean.'

'Dismissed, sir. He was told to go by Headmaster right away.' Toong Cheong sat down.

'So,' said Crabbe, 'it was Pushpanathan's word against Hamidin's. And the Headmaster sent Hamidin home immediately, and Hamidin's career is ruined. Is that the right story?'

More quiet hisses, hisses of affirmation.

'Has Hamidin's Housemaster been approached about this matter?'

A thin bright-eyed Tamil stood up to say, 'Mr Crichton said he would do nothing because Headmaster's decision is a right one and it is right that Hamidin should be expelled. That is why we ask you as form-master to tell the Headmaster that it is not right and that grave injustice have been done to the innocent.' He sat down with grace and dignity.

'Well.' Crabbe looked at them all. 'It seems possible, probable indeed, that a very hasty decision has been taken, and that an injustice may have been done. Of course, I don't know the whole story. But expulsion is certainly a terrible thing. It is your wish then that I convey to the Headmaster your dissatisfaction with his summary procedure, his harsh sentence, his decision made on what seems to you insufficient evidence?'

There were eager hisses, a controlled tiny surge, a wind-ripple, of excitement. The class tasted the word 'harsh'. It was the right word, the word they had been looking for. 'Harsh.' Its sound was harsh; it was a harsh word.

'I will see the Headmaster as soon as I can this morning, then,' said Victor Crabbe. 'And now we must learn a little more about the Industrial Revolution.'

They turned obediently to text-books and note-books, the word 'harsh' echoing still through the creaking of desk-lids, the borrowing of a fill of ink. Crabbe realized he had gone too far. Somebody would now tell Crichton or Wallis that Mr Crabbe had talked about the Head-master's 'harsh sentence', and Crichton or Wallis would pass this back to the Headmaster, and then there would be talk of loyalty and not letting the side down, and at Christmas an adverse report, perhaps, but certainly more material for Club calumny. 'He likes the Asians too much. He tells the Asians too much. Why, he complains about the Europeans on the staff to the Asian kids. What's he after, anyway?'

Tida' apa.

The fact was that Victor Crabbe, after a mere six months in the Federation, had reached that position common among veteran expatriates – he saw that a white skin was an abnormality, and that the white man's ways were fundamentally eccentric. In the early days of the war he had been in an Emergency Hospital, a temporary establishment which had taken over a wing of a huge County Mental Hospital. Most of the patients suffered from General Paralysis of the Insane, but the spirocaete, before breaking down the brain completely, seemed to enjoy engendering perverse and useless talents in otherwise moronic minds. Thus, one dribbling patient was able to state the precise day of the week for any given date in history; no ratiocinative process was involved: the coin went in and the answer came out. Another was able to add up correctly the most complicated lists of figures in less time than a comptometer. Yet another found a rare musical talent blossoming shortly before death; he made a swan-like end. The Europeans were rather like these lunatics. The syllogism had been the chancre, the distant fanfare of the disease, and out of it had come eventually the refrigerator and the hydrogen bomb, G.P.I. The Communists in the jungle subscribed, however remotely, to the Hellenic tradition: an abstract desideratum and a dialectical technique. Yet the process of which he, Victor Crabbe, was a part, was an ineluctable process. His being here, in the brown country, sweltering in an alien class-room, was pre-figured and ordained by history. For the end of the Western pattern was the conquest of time and space. But out of time and space came point-instants, and out of point-instants came a universe. So it was right that he stood here now, teaching the East about the Industrial Revolution. It was right that these boys too should bellow through loudspeakers, check bomb-loads, judge Shakespeare by the Aristotelian yardstick, hear five-part counterpoint and find it intelligible.

But it was also right that he himself should draw great breaths of refreshment from the East, even out of the winds of garlic and dried fish and turmeric. And it was right that, lying with Rahimah, he should feel like calling on the sun to drench his pallor in this natural gold, so that he might be accepted by the East. And, if not right, it was at least excusable if he felt more loyalty to these pupils than to the etiolated, ginger-haired slug who yawned in the Headmaster's office. His indiscretion was based on something better than mere irresponsibility.

'But surely, sir, it was not good if these machines made people have no work, and they were right, sir, if they wished to destroy them.' The Malay sat down, awaiting an answer. The West always had an answer.

'You must remember,' said Crabbe, 'that technological progress has always, in theory, at any rate, sought to serve the end of greater and greater human happiness.' The Malay boy nodded vigorously. 'Man was not born to work.' All the Malays nodded. 'He was born to be happy.' The solitary Sikh smiled through his sparse beard. 'Man needs leisure to cultivate his mind and his senses. A great Italian poet said, "Consider your origins: you were not formed to live like brutes but to follow virtue and know-ledge." But we cannot follow virtue and knowledge or the pleasures of the senses – which are just as important – if we have little leisure. And so the machines come along and they do more and more of our work for us and give us more leisure.'

The Malay boy seemed puzzled. 'But, sir, in the *kampongs* they have no machines but they have a lot of leisure. They sit in the sun and do no work and they are happy. I do not see how machines can give leisure.'

'But,' said Crabbe, 'surely we all want more out of life than a *kampong* existence can give us. You, Salim, like gramophone records of American singers. Darianathan here is a photographer and needs cameras. You cannot expect these to fall like coconuts from the trees. Again, you all wear shoes. These have to be made, and making them is work. We have to work to get the things we need. The more things we need the more advanced is our civilization; that is how the argument runs. If we can get machines to make these things for us, well, we get the best of both worlds. We get many pleasures to feed our souls and our bodies and we get plenty of leisure in which to enjoy them.'

'Sir,' said Ahmad, a Malay boy with a moustache and a pitted complexion, 'we only need to wear shoes because the British built roads which hurt our feet.'

'But roads were not built so that your feet might be hurt. They were built for transport, so that the things you need could be brought quickly from distant towns.'

'But, sir, they could be brought by the railway,' said a small Tamil with a radiant smile.

'Or by aeroplane,' said Latiff bin Haji Abbas.

'The aeroplane is more expensive than the railway.'

'That is not true. It costs thirty dollars less by aeroplane than by railway to come from Alor Star. I know, because I inquired about it.' This was a tall, thin Chinese boy named Fang Yong Sheak.

'All right, all right!' Crabbe scotched the argument at birth. 'Don't get off the point.' But, he realized, they had never been on the point. Again he felt hopeless. This was the East. Logic was a Western importation which, unlike films and refrigerators, had a small market.

The bell sounded. It was a hand-bell, rung by a boy in the next class-room. He rang it early when he was bored with the lesson or thought he was likely to be asked a question to which he did not know the answer. Very occasionally he rang the bell late. That was when he was dreaming about being a film-star, or the great Malay singer or the leader of U.M.N.O. He did not dare nowadays to extend the mid-morning break by more than ten minutes. Once he had extended it by as much as forty-five minutes. Nobody had minded except the Headmaster, who had given him detention. Just now he was roughly on time.

Crabbe had a free period, so he went straight to the Headmaster's office. He knocked on the swing-door and was told to enter. The Malay Chief Clerk was saying something about estimates. Files were spread on the desk. The swift blades of the ceiling-fan were reflected in the rare naked parts of the glass top, on which Boothby leaned his chubby elbows.

'Dese estimates den we must do six copies of.'

'Awwwww!' Boothby yawned with great vigour. He was fond of yawning. He would yawn at dinner parties, at staff-meetings, at debates, elocution competitions, sports days. He probably yawned when in bed with his wife. His yawning seemed almost a deliberate physical exercise, involving squaring of the shoulders, bracing of the hands on the chair-arms, throwing back the whole of the upper body. When Crabbe had first seen him yawn in the middle of a passionate speech about religious holidays made by 'Che Jamaluddin at a staff-meeting, he had thought that Boothby was going to sing. 'Awwwwww!' The boys had often said, 'But, sir, if we go to see him about this he will only yawn at us.' Now Boothby turned to Crabbe, yawned, and said, 'Take a pew.' The Malay Chief Clerk went back to the noise of gossip and typewriters.

'This pew seems to have hymn-books on it. May I move them?'

'Those are copies of the new Malayan History for Schools. Cooper at K.L. wrote it. Awwwwww! You'll be using it next year.'

'I don't know whether it's any good yet. Cooper's a woodwork specialist, isn't he?' Crabbe looked at the first chapter. 'This Malaya of ours is a very old country. It is a country with a very long history. History is a sort of story. The story of our country is a very interesting story.' Crabbe closed the book quickly.

'What can I do for you, Victor?' Boothby had thinning ginger hair and ginger eyebrows. He had a sulky frog's mouth, perhaps enlarged by much yawning, a potato nose, and pale eyes framed by large reading-glasses.

'It's about Hamidin. The boys in Form Five think he shouldn't have been expelled. They say that there was no real evidence and that the duty prefect had it in for the boy. They talked about injustice.'

'They did, did they? And what do they know about injustice?'

'They asked me to say something to you about this business. I've said something. Perhaps you have something to say to them.'

'Yes. You can tell them to mind their own bloody business. No,' Boothby added with haste, 'tell them that I am perfectly satisfied my decision was the right one.'

'It seems a very considerable punishment for a slight offence.'

'You call fornication a slight offence? On School premises, too?'

'Pushpanathan said he was kissing the girl. That may or may not be true. Anyway, you can't call kissing fornication. Otherwise I shall have to admit that I fornicated with your wife last Christmas. Under the mistletoe.'

Boothby killed a yawn at birth. 'Eh?'

'Expulsion's a terrible thing.'

'Look here,' said Boothby, 'I know the facts and you don't. Their clothes were disarranged. It's obvious what was going to happen. You haven't been here as long as I have. These Wogs are hot-blooded. There was a very bad case in Gill's time. Gill himself was nearly thrown out.'

'I didn't realize that Hamidin was a Wog. I thought he was a Malay.'

'Look here, Victor, I've been here since the end of the

war. I tried the bloody sympathy business when I started teaching at Swettenham College in Penang. It doesn't work. They let you down if they think you're soft. You've got to take quick action. Don't worry.' He yawned. 'They'll forget about it. Anyway, tell them that from me: I am perfectly satisfied my decision was the right one.' Boothby began to look for a file.

'You've only got Pushpanathan's word for it.'

'I trust Pushpenny. He's a good lad. He's better than most of them.'

'Well, you know how the form feels. You know how I feel. Presumably there's nothing more to be said. Except that I think you're being damned autocratic.'

Boothby was angry. The quick red of the ginger-haired suffused his untanned face. 'Wait till you've been in the country a few bloody years longer. You'll learn that you've got to be able to make decisions, and make them quickly. Who the hell do you think you are, anyway, telling me how to run this place? Come back in ten years' time and tell me I'm being damned autocratic.' Crabbe caught a hint of clumsy parody in Boothby's pronunciation of these last two words. Boothby had a Northumberland whine which he rarely took the trouble to mask. He threw Crabbe's words back at him with a jaw-dropping affectation of gentility. Crabbe prepared to leave. As he pushed open the swing-door Boothby called after him, 'Oh, by the way!'

'Yes?'

'Where's your report-book? It should have been handed in on the 26th.'

'What do you want it for?'

'It's laid down in those rules you got when you came. Twice a term you hand it in to me. I didn't mention it last time because you were new. I must know what the boys are learning and how they're getting on.'

'You get the examination results.'

'I must know what the syllabuses are. I must have some idea of whether the boys are learning anything or not. I want to see their marks for prep, and classwork.'

'Well, you know what I'm teaching. English History and Malayan History.'

'Yes, but I want to see how much they're taking in.'

'But, look here, I'm not a probationary teacher. Surely you can leave it to your staff to get on with the work they know best.'

'I can't trust the Wogs on the staff. I've got to know what they're doing.'

'Presumably we're all Wogs, then?'

'That's the rule. Report-books in twice a term. Bring yours in today.'

Swing-doors cannot be slammed; they can only swing. This one swung viciously. Crabbe went to the staff-room in a flaming temper. There he found Mr Raj and Mr Roper exchanging grievances. Mr Raj had been lured from Ceylon to train Malayan teachers. He was a man of rich culture of which he would give anybody the benefit in long, slow, rolling, montonous monologues. He had already spent two years in the Mansor School, teaching Geography to junior forms. His subjects were Education and Asian History. He complained endlessly in the staff-room about the wrongs that had been done to him. Mr Roper was a Eurasian, the son of an English planter and Tamil woman of low birth. He could never forgive the English for this act of miscegenation, even though it had produced in him a singular beauty. Tall, muscular, golden-skinned, he ranted bitterly about the injustice done to him pre-natally. Crabbe could hear him now.

'I applied for this increment, but they would not give it to me. And why? Because I am not a white man, an *orang puteh*. They say I am not well-qualified, but, believe me, they are not thinking of university degrees. I can see what is in their minds. He is not an *orang puteh*, they are thinking all the time. He is dirt, he must be kept down, the money is for the *orang puteh*.'

And yet he owned a rubber-plantation and the finest car in Kuala Hantu. And Crabbe, for one, envied that intense physical beauty, a beauty which was a mark of shame to its possessor. How complicated life was for the Eurasian.

Raj rumbled in reply. The sesquipedalian words flowed in an unintelligible sound-pattern. The calm orgy of bitterness would continue till the bell rang.

Crabbe sat at his table, which was piled with unmarked books, and rested his head in his sweating hands. He could hear Crichton's Australian voice from the far corner, talking about Shykespeare and Bycon. Crichton taught English. Crabbe thought, 'I should want to go home, like Fenella. I should be so tired of the shambles here, the obscurantism, the colour-prejudice, the laziness and ignorance, as to desire nothing better than a headship in a cold stone country school in England. But I love this country. I feel protective towards it. Sometimes, just before dawn breaks, I feel that I somehow enclose it, contain it. I feel that it needs me. This is absurd, because snakes and scorpions are ready to bite me, a drunken Tamil is prepared to knife me, the Chinese in the town would like to spit at me, some day a Malay boy will run amok and try to tear me apart. But it doesn't matter. I want to live here; I want to be wanted. Despite the sweat, the fever, the prickly heat, the mosquitoes, the terrorists, the fools at the bar of the Club, despite Fenella.'

Fenella. The long teaching morning limped towards its end, hot and airless. White shirts were sodden; sweat dripped on to the wet ink of exercise-books and blurred the words; even Tuan Haji Mohamed Noor, the Koran teacher, had to take off his turban the better to wipe his hair-roots. The fans whirred their fastest but they beat the air as impotently as the fists of a fretful child. The bell went early today.

Fenella Crabbe got out of bed as soon as she heard the first returning cyclists. The boys were coming back for lunch. Victor would be at least another fifteen minutes, unless someone gave him a lift. He insisted on walking usually. Penance. Fenella had not been sleeping all the time. She had on the bedside table a jug of tepid water which had, an hour ago, been ice. There was also a bottle of gin and a saucer containing sliced limes. She had a slight bout of fever, and gin helped a little. At the foot of the bed was a copy of *Persuasion*, a volume of John Betjeman's poems and a work of literary criticism by Professor Cleanth Brooks. In her slightly trembling hands she had just been holding the day's issue of the *Timah Gazette*, a badly-printed rag with scare headlines – 'Tapper's Eyes Gouged Out by C.T.s', '70-year-old Chinese Convicted Of Rape'; 'Singapore Riot Threat'. She had been interested to read that a Film Society had just been inaugurated in Timah, and that there would be a meeting once a fortnight. The first films scheduled were: *The Battleship Potemkin*; *The Cabinet of Dr Caligari*; *Sang d'un Poète*; *Metropolis*; *Les Visiteurs du Soir*. It was too ridiculous that they hadn't a car and that Victor seemed unwilling to be friendly with any European in the place, for all Europeans – except the Crabbes – had cars. She felt that in Timah there must be people of her own kind, people who would discuss books and ballet and music. If only they could join this Film Society. But what was the use if they hadn't a car? It was about time Victor got over this stupid nonsense of refusing to drive again. She herself could not drive, but why should she have to do what was her husband's job? She should be driven. Perhaps they could afford a driver – say, eighty dollars a month. But Victor was stubborn about buying a car. He was like a man who feared water and would not even sit on the beach. And in a sense that was true also. There was a Swimming Club in Timah. He refused to swim, and that meant that she could not go there. But, in any case, how could she without a car? Without a car life in Malaya was impossible. Life in Malaya was impossible anyway.

She wiped the sweat from her face with a towel. Perhaps if he could be persuaded to buy a car she might learn to drive. But who was there to teach her? And again she was much too nervous a type, much too highly strung. The roads were treacherous with erratic cyclists and trishaw men. As she made up her face, cursing the sweat that clogged the powder, she was sick for London, coolly making up for a dance in the evening, or for the ballet, or for a concert. Civilization is only possible in a temperate zone. She had written a poem about that.

> Where sweat starts, nothing starts. True, life runs
> Round in its way, in rings of dust like Saturn's,
> But creating is creating arid patterns
> Whose signatures prove, always, the arid sun's.

She heard the boys shrilly entering the dining-hall downstairs, not heeding the prefects' unsure barks. The noise made her head throb. Oh God, to have this added to the sheer, damned, uncultured emptiness. Noise from now on till the games period started. Hearty noise after till dinner-time. Noise before and after prep. Noise in the dormitories. Why didn't Victor control them better?

Victor's feet could be heard, entering the lounge, the feet of a tired man. Fenella, in a dressing-gown, went out to greet him. He kissed her on the cheek, and she felt the sweat of his upper lip. His face dripped with sweat. She said:

'Do change your shirt before lunch, darling. That one's soaked.'

'It's bloody warm walking home. It's not too bad in the mornings. Can I have a drink?' He flopped into an armchair.

Ibrahim had heard him come in and a sound of approaching rattling glasses and bottles came from the direction of the distant kitchen. Ibrahim entered, bearing a tray, simpering at his master, dressed in wide-sleeved, wide-trousered silk. He had dyed the front bang of his hair a vivid red.

'For God's sake don't try and look like Boothby,' said Crabbe.

'Tuan?'

'But there's no danger of that. Nobody could call Boothby a pretty boy.'

'Saya ta' erti, tuan.'

'I said that looks pretty. *Itu chantek, Ibrahim.*'

'*Terima kaseh, tuan.*' Ibrahim went out, smirking pleasure, waggling his bottom.

'You shouldn't encourage him,' said Fenella. 'I don't mind our being a little eccentric, but I don't like it reaching a point where people will laugh at us.'

'Are people laughing at us? Because we keep Ibrahim?' Crabbe drank off a tumbler of lemon squash with a double gin in it. 'Are we supposed to get some sour-faced ancient Chinese who swigs the brandy while we're out? I don't know the correct procedure. I'd better consult the D.O. about it.'

'Oh, don't be silly.' Fenella was still shaky. The long drugged sleep always left her exhausted and irritable. The fever would not go.

'I'm sorry, dear.' Hastily he remembered his responsibility to her, the pity she deserved. 'It's been a hell of a morning. Boothby got on my nerves rather.'

She did not ask what Boothby had done to get on his nerves. She walked to the veranda which swept, in a huge curve, round the entire flat. 'There doesn't seem to be any air,' she said. Crabbe looked at her as she leaned over the stone balustrade, trying to drink in air from the green lawns below. She was tall, elegant in the flowered thin dressing-gown, her yellowish hair hanging almost to her shouders. The hair was lank and stringy with the wet heat. He put down his refilled glass and walked over to her. He put an arm round her, feeling damp through the thin stuff of the dressing-gown.

'Aren't you feeling any better, dear?'

'I'll feel better in two and a half years' time. When we can get away. For good.'

'If you really want to go home, I can arrange your passage any time you like. You can wait for me there.

> '. . . I shall not fail
> To meet you back in Maida Vale.'

'Oh, don't be so damned heartless all the time.' She

turned on him, shaking. 'I really think you don't care a bit about what I feel.'

Another little tropical storm brewing. Another classical colonial row between tuan and mem. Crabbe said nothing.

'I want us to be together,' she said. 'I wouldn't dream of leaving you here on your own. I thought you felt that way about me.'

'All right, darling. But, in the meantime, we've got to live here. We've got to try and make some sort of life in this country. It's no good fighting against it all the time. You've got to accept that this isn't London, that the climate's tropical, that there aren't concerts and theatres and ballets. But there are other things. The people themselves the little drinking-shops, the incredible mixture of religions and cultures and languages. That's what we're here for – to absorb the country.' 'Or be absorbed by it,' he said to himself.

'But we're stuck here all the time. The noise is driving me mad. Boys yelling all over the place. And when the boys are on holiday the workmen come in, spitting and belching, scraping the walls, sawing wood. If only we could get into some decent company for a change, go to Timah a couple of times a week, meet people of our own type.'

'Timah's full of hearty planters and Malay Regiment officers.'

'All right.' She was calmer now, wiping her face with a small handkerchief, turning away from the vista of lawn and mountain and jungle and river. 'There must be some reasonable people there because they're starting a Film Society. It's in today's paper. They're showing good films, French films.'

'Very well, let's join it.'

'How do we get in?'

Here it was again, not at all conventional material for a row, most unusual, eccentric – that was her word – in a land where all the white men had cars, where a car was an essential limb, sense, faculty.

'We could use the bus. There's quite a good service.'

'And you expect me to sit there, stared at like something in a sideshow, and have garlic breathed on to me, and the sweat, and the dirt . . .'

'You didn't object to garlic in France. Or in Soho.'

'Oh, don't be a fool, Victor. You just can't do that sort of thing. I thought even you would have enough bloody sense to see that . . .'

'I can't understand your inconsistency. At home you were Bohemian, prided yourself on it, loved being different from everybody else. The buses and tubes were good enough for you then.'

'But it's different here.' She almost shouted at him, spacing the words out like the announcement of a radio programme. 'We were all Europeans in Europe.' She shook violently. We can't live like the Asians . . .'

'All right, all right.' He gripped her by the elbows, then tried to take her in his arms. 'We'll find some way.'

Ibrahim came in softly, looking with wide serious eyes, to announce that lunch was ready.

'*Makan sudah siap, tuan.*'

'*Baik-lah, Ibrahim.*'

They went silently into the hot dining-room, fanless, its windows overlooking a final spread of veranda which itself overlooked the boys' lavatories and showers. Ibrahim served chilled tomato juice, seriously, gracefully. Crabbe said:

'You want a car, is that it?'

'We've got to have a car.'

'You know I don't want to drive any more. I'm sorry about that, but there it is.'

'We could get a driver.'

'Can we afford it?' Eighty dollars a month at least, and at the moment he was giving about sixty to Rahimah.

'We can try.'

And of course repayment of a Government loan for a car would come to about a hundred and fifty a month. There was some money in the bank, however, the dwindling remnant of their small capital.

68

'All right. I'll think about it.'

'We could get a second-hand one. We've enough money for that.'

'Yes, just what I was thinking.'

Ibrahim had brought in tinned salmon and a salad. As she served him she said, 'It will make such a difference. It will almost reconcile me to being here.'

It would bring her the breath of a temperate climate. Him, too, for that matter. The very cold breath of a temperate climate. He began to eat his tinned salmon.

4

His ears still ringing with the protests of his shut-in dog, Nabby Adams entered the Club. He entered it rather shyly, six feet eight inches of diffidence, though he had as much right to be there as anyone else. More perhaps, for he owed the Club no money. That was more than could be said for those two bastards tee-heeing away over there by the bookshelves. But he felt uncomfortable in the Club; he would much rather have been entering a little *kedai* with Alladad Khan. Still it was precisely because this was the only place for miles around where he did not owe money that he was there tonight. Hart, that fat bastard over there, had written a letter about Nabby Adams's bill to the Officer Superintending Police Circle. The O.S.P.C. had been very nice about it. He had told Nabby Adams that he must pay the bill right away, and, to ensure that the bill was paid right away, the O.S.P.C. said he would arrange for a single deduction to be made from Nabby Adams's salary. The deduction had been made and there had been damn near nothing left of Nabby Adams's salary. Still, there was one bill paid, and a bloody big one.

Nabby Adams had told Alladad Khan to go and sit in the servants' yard at the back of the Club. Nabby Adams had promised to send out a large bottle of beer to him. Alladad Khan was to try to make that last as long as possible. Nabby Adams called the Club waiter. To Nabby Adams's trained eye it looked pretty much as if the Club waiter, Hong or Wong or whatever his name was, took opium. He had pin-point pupils. He would not look straight at Nabby Adams, as though he knew that he, Nabby Adams, knew.

'*Dua* Tiger. One for me and one for him out there.' If Alladad Khan wanted more beer desperately he was to whistle shrilly. Nabby Adams would be able to hear that from the bar.

The beer was too cold. Nabby Adams was used to the exiguous amenities of oil-lamp-lighted drinking-shops, and, had, during twenty-odd years in the East, developed a taste for warm beer. A liking for iced beer was effeminate, decadent and American. During his last leave Nabby Adams had met an American in his local pub. This American had had some sort of refrigerating apparatus in the boot of his car. The car had, otherwise, been a lovely job. This American had said, 'We sure would appreciate to have a man of your size in Texas.' He had insisted on thrusting gracious living on Nabby Adams – a bottle of beer so cold it had felt red-hot. Nabby Adams had been sick after that Arctic, astringent, tooth-probing draught.

He let his Tiger stand for a time on the bar counter to take the chill off. He smoked a ship's Woodbine from a tin donated by a grateful Chinese race-horse owner whose car he had repaired when it had broken down on the road. Nabby Adams's huge fingers were so impregnated with tobacco-tar that they looked as if they were painted with iodine or something. They made him feel a little sick whenever he held a sandwich. That was another reason for not eating much.

Nabby Adams did not propose to stay in the Club for the entire evening. Somebody might come in and stand by the bar and Nabby Adams might have to talk to him. Nabby Adams was not very happy about his English lately. He liked to speak a language well, and he was conscious that his English grammar was deteriorating, his vocabulary becoming so weak that he had to eke it out with Indian words, and his pronunciation hardly proper for patrician society. He was content to speak Urdu with Alladad Khan, sitting nice and cosy in one of them little *kedais*.

He heard Alladad Khan's shrill whistle. He sent him

out another bottle, a small one this time. That bugger was drinking faster than he himself, Nabby Adams, was. Getting uppish. Asking to be introduced to memsahibs. And him with a charming wife in silk trousers and sari having a baby in Cooler Lumpur. Nabby Adams always pronounced 'Kuala' as 'Cooler'. He could not take Malay seriously. It was not a real language, not like Urdu or Punjabi. And as for Chinese. Plink, plank, plonk. Anybody could speak that. It was a bloody hoax.

Nabby Adams was in the Club primarily to see if he could borrow fifty dollars from the old Chinese who ran the place, Ah Hun. It could be put down in his book or Nabby Adams could sign an I.O.U. Nabby Adams would always sign an I.O.U. It was only a bit of paper anyway. Besides, Ah Hun was the richest man in Cooler Hantu. He ran a sort of auxiliary Club for his friends at the back of the real Club. That was pure profit, for all the drink came out of the real Club. The gin and whisky were watered and always short-measured. That was why it was better to drink beer. They couldn't fiddle with that. Ah Hun was a turf commission agent, an opium peddlar, an abortionist, a car salesman, a barber, a pimp and a distiller of illicit *samsu*. He had three wives, too, although he said he was a Christian. That was why he was never in the Club doing his bloody job. He was hard to get hold of. When committee members were present – and there were two of them there – Ah Hun sometimes came in, busy and brow-lined with bills and accounts and God knows what. Nabby Adams decided to ask this opium-eating sod where his dad was. He didn't want to waste the evening in here.

'Ah Hun,' said Nabby Adams, '*Saya* want a word with Ah Hun.'

Wong or Hong or whatever his bloody name was gurgled something, his shifty eyes on the counter.

'Where is he?' asked Nabby Adams. 'I want to see him.'

The opium-eating sod sidled off, gurgling.

He hadn't understood. Nabby Adams shuddered to think what opium could do to a man if it became a habit.

An addict, that was the word. To become an addict was to invite early death.

Nabby Adams heard Alladad Khan's shrill whistle.

Let the bugger wait. Getting too big for his bloody boots. Memsahibs and going out with his superiors in rank. Nabby Adams drank placidly.

Nabby Adams thought for a while about something he rarely thought about nowadays, namely women, wives and whatnot. It did not pain him that desire had fled. It had not pained him for the last fifteen years. Now, at forty-five, he was safely past all danger. In calm waters. Besides, his vocation involved celibacy. But there had been a time, in the Army in India, there had been a time, working on the railways in India, when it had been very different. Every afternoon, after tiffin, when he climbed on the *charpoy* for a rest, that little amah had climbed after him. Every afternoon, when he woke for tea, she had brought the tea and it had been left to get too cold to drink. And that other time there had been the major's lady. And back in England, when he had been a sexton, that time with Mrs Amos on the gravestone. Nabby Adams shook his huge head. His real wife, his houri, his paramour was everywhere waiting, genie-like, in a bottle. The hymeneal gouging-off of the bottle-top, the kiss of the brown bitter yeasty flow, the euphoria far beyond the release of detumescence.

But there was this Chinese with three wives, and Alladad Khan with one wife but thirsting randily after a memsahib. And there was Crabbe with this same memsahib but carrying on with a Malay girl in the Paradise Cabaret down the road. He had seen him on his way there tonight. They had spoken together for a while, and Crabbe had said he was on his way to a meeting. Which was true enough, but that wasn't the meeting he had meant, the bloody liar. And he had said that he was looking for a second-hand car. Nabby Adams thought of money wasted on wives and cabaret-girls and second-hand cars.

With surprise and hope Nabby Adams saw Ah Hun

come in. shrunken and bespectacled, seriously conning an account-book. 'Here,' said Nabby Adams. But at the same time there were booted footsteps approaching the bar. Nabby Adams turned to see Gurney, the O.S.P.C., still in uniform, though it was nearly nine o'clock. Gurney, long and cadaverous and tired-looking. Of all the bloody luck.

Nabby Adams said, 'Good evening, sir,' in refined, confident R.S.M. tones.

'Hallo, Nabby. What are you going to have?'

'Thank you, sir. A small beer, sir.'

'And, Nabby, sorry to talk shop, but you mustn't go up to Melawas without an escort. That's the rule, you know. You'll get shot up. Another incident today.'

'To save petrol, sir. Them scout-cars use a lot of petrol, sir.' But the real reason couldn't be given. You can't keep stopping at little *kedais* with a bloody escort watching every mouthful you drink and blabbing about it when they get back.

'If you use police transport, Nabby, you've got to have an escort. Cheers.'

Hart and the other bloke, Rivers, came to the bar from their colloquy in the far corner.

'Hallo, Nigel.'

'How's it going, Doug?'

'Wotcher, Nigel.'

Nabby Adams felt uncomfortable. He wanted to be out of here. He couldn't stand Hart, and Rivers, the ex-army type planter up the Tahi Panas road, got on his bloody nerves. But he had accepted a Tiger, and the others had accepted drinks too, and Nabby Adams saw, in horror, the prospect of having to stand a round himself. And there was Ah Hun, grinning at everybody, having shown his bloody face, off again, and the opium-eater leering at everybody from the back of the bar.

'Trouble again at Kelapa Estate,' said Gurney.

'Oh God, Kelapa again?' Rivers clutched the right wing of his rank moustache as though it were a talisman.

'Withers shot his way out. They got that Tamil bloke

though. Cut his guts out and then sang "The Red Flag" in Chinese.' Gurney sipped his pink gin.

'That's an unlucky estate,' said Hart, nursing a fat bare knee. 'There was Roebuck and then Fotheringay and that young assistant, what's-his-name. They'll get Withers.'

'It's bound to be our turn again, any day now,' said Rivers nervously. A tic throbbed under his left eye. 'Roll on that bloody boat. Three weeks to go. No, two weeks and five days.'

'There's a big battle-cry going on up there,' said Gurney. ' "Death to Withers". What hurts the C.T.s is that they gave him a chance to pay protection money, but he wouldn't do it.'

'Couldn't do it, I should think,' said Hart. 'Debts all over the place.' Nabby Adams listened sympathetically.

Nabby Adams said, by way of making conversation, 'Withers and Rivers sound a bit alike. It might be "Death to Rivers".'

Rivers writhed and showed big teeth under the pelmet of the moustache. 'If you think that's funny, old man . . .'

'No,' said Nabby Adams. 'I mean, serious, the two names . . .'

'All right, all right,' said Gurney softly. 'Let's have another drink.'

'My turn,' said Hart. 'Here, boy.'

'Joking on one side,' said Nabby Adams, 'the two names . . .'

They heard a shrill whistle from the servants' yard. Rivers's hand went fast to his holster. They all listened. The whistle, shriller, was repeated.

'Who the hell's that?' said Gurney.

Rivers said, 'They're getting out of hand. Bloody Club servants. I'll tan his black hide. I'll put a bullet through him. I'll castrate him. I'll pull out his toenails with pincers. Insubordinate bastards. Hey!' he shouted. 'Stop that bloody row!'

A softer, more plaintive, whistle could now be heard.

'Do you hear?' raged Rivers. '*Diam*, you sod, bloody well *diam*!'

'You mustn't shout at these people,' said Gurney. 'They take it as a sign of weakness. Go round and tell him.'

'I'll go,' said Nabby Adams with energy. 'I'll tell him, sir.'

'Never mind,' said Hart. 'They're shutting him up.' Nabby Adams could hear importunate Hokkien and Alladad Khan pleading the rights of man in Punjabi.

'I'll be glad to get away,' brooded Rivers. 'Coolies all day long, cretins, bloody morons, and not even here in the Club can you be free of them. I'll be glad if I never see another black skin as long as I live. They give me the shudders. Discipline, that's what they need. When I was in the Army I could handle them all right. Ten days' pay stopped. Round the square with full pack at the double. Try it here on the estates and you get a knife in your back.' He scratched his shoulder-blades petulantly. Prickly heat.

'That was in Africa, wasn't it?' said Gurney. 'A bit different, you know.'

'They're all the same,' said Rivers. 'Niggers. Black bastards.'

Nabby Adams looked at the arrogant white nose, the scornful nostrils whence the moustache flowed, a cornucopia of hair. He longed to have just one little crack at it. But he kept his temper, drank the beer that Hart had bought for him, and wondered if he could slip round the back without Gurney getting suspicious. For the lavatory was at the other end of the Club. That bloody Ah Hun was walking round the yard: he could hear him scolding his wives; he could almost hear the crackle of bunches of ten-dollar notes in his pockets. And that damned fool Alladad Khan would start again in a minute. 'Wait,' thought Nabby Adams, 'I'll say good-night, walk out, and then slip round the back.'

Nabby Adams drained his glass and said with a froth-flecked mouth, 'Must be going now, sir.'

'I'll give you a lift, Nabby,' said Gurney.

Oh God, why did these things always happen? 'That's very kind, sir. I'm not going back to the mess. Thought I'd have a stroll round.'

'Oh well, one for the road then.'

'Push the boat out, Adams,' said Hart. '*Stengah* for me.'

Nabby Adams saw, in delirium, a vision of Bombay set in a sea of blood. He called the waiter with a single savage bark.

'You'll have to hurry up with that car,' said Gurney to Rivers. 'When do you go?'

'Two weeks five days.'

'How much are you asking for it?'

'Two thousand.'

'You won't get it.'

There was a discussion about the merits of Rivers's car. Nabby Adams indicated, in urgent pantomime, that Hong or Wong or whatever his bloody name was should take another bottle to Alladad Khan and tell him to keep his trap shut. The opium-eater opened the bottle with insolent loudness and clomped out with it, singing. Thank God, the others hadn't noticed.

'There's a chance for you, Nabby,' said Gurney. 'A '52 Abelard. One thousand eight hundred.'

'That's my lowest,' said Rivers. 'I'm losing money as it is.'

'You could take it up to Melawas without an escort,' said Gurney, a glint in his eye. 'Save petrol for the firm.'

'I'll think about it,' said Nabby Adams.

Strangely enough, Nabby Adams did think about it. His mind's dark waters were ringed with jumping plans. Soon Gurney went. Soon two officers of the Malay Regiment came in, morbidly eupeptic. One was Major Latiff bin Haji Mahmud, the other Captain Frank Harley. They spoke a facetious mixture of Malay and English which made Nabby Adams shudder.

'*Selemat* evening.'

'Good *malam*.'

'*Apa* news?'

'What *khabar*?'

Rivers called to the waiter, '*Siap meja.*'

'*Tuan?*'

'Get the billiard-table ready. *Kita main* snooker.'

There was a foursome. The billiard-table was screened off from the bar, but the click of the balls and the boyish jeers and shouts made Nabby Adams shake with nerves. And that bloody fool Rivers had left his gun on the bar. 'Serve him right if I pinch it and flog it to Ah Hun.' Nabby Adams took a sly glance at the debit total in Rivers's bar-book and found, to his grim satisfaction, that Rivers owed the Club $1,347.55. He turned over the pages of Hart's book with a great yellow hand. $942.70. So. There was he, Nabby Adams, owing a mere five hundred odd, and that bastard had reported him. One law for the rich. Right. He would buy that car of Rivers. Or rather Crabbe should buy it. Right.

Nabby Adams tiptoed out of the Club, making the boards creak. Nobody noticed him. Right. Among the potted plants and the hanging coconut-shells full of withering flowers he breathed in the blue Malayan night. The palms swayed in front of the Town Board offices. A swaying Tamil workman tottered from the toddy-shop. A loud radio sang in Hindustani from the Police Barracks. Nabby Adams picked his way through dustbins and bicycle-tyres to the servants' yard behind the Club and found Alladad Khan sitting with an empty glass at a huge dirty table. Doll-like children with straight fringes squabbled around him, and a shapeless young Chinese woman in pyjamas ironed shirts with some vigour.

Nabby Adams spoke in his clean, grammatical Urdu.

'Where is the Chinese man who is in charge of this Club? I wish to borrow money off him.'

'He has gone out, sahib.'

'Another thing. What advantage do you expect to gain from the loud noises you were continually making while I was in there drinking? Surely you realized that the other sahibs in there displayed a considerable measure of anger.

Moreover, the O.S.P.C. nearly came out to you. That would undoubtedly have spelt disaster for both of us, but more especially for you.'

'I was tortured with thirst, sahib.'

'Well, next time you're thirsty you can pay for your bloody own,' said Nabby Adams in violent English. 'Do you think I'm made of bloody beer?'

'Sahib?'

'Listen.' Nabby Adams returned to Urdu. 'We are going to injure a car. We then shall buy it. Then we shall sell it. We shall buy it cheap and sell it dear, as is the way of merchants.'

'I have no money to buy a car. Nor, I think, have you.'

'That is no matter. First we must get the car away from here. It is at the front of the Club. It is an Abelard. Then we shall do what things are meet to be done.'

Nabby Adams and Alladad Khan walked quietly through the dark to the parking area of the Club. The polished Abelard shone ghostly, a vision of the future, in the faint street-lamp. From within the Club came ball-clicks and happy cries. Alladad Khan evinced little enthusiasm for Nabby Adams's plan.

'It is a simple matter of making the engine seem hard to start and to knock violently also. Wait here.'

Nabby Adams entered the Club again. There were only a few colours left on the table.

'*Dalam* the hole.'

'Into the *lobang*.'

The neat Malay major, cat-graceful, sleek with toothed charm, sank the blue.

Nabby Adams said to Rivers, 'Can I just try it out?'

'Are you going to buy it?'

'I think I can raise the money.'

Rivers fumbled in his pocket, found the ignition-key and threw it over. It was fixed by a ring to a tiny model of a bulldog. Nabby Adams caught it in huge fielding paws.

'Look after it. Don't be too long.'

Outside the Club Nabby Adams said to Alladad Khan, 'First you shall drive to the Paradise Cabaret.'

'Why?'

'To sell the car to Mr Crabbe.'

'You promised you would introduce me to the mem-sahib.'

'One thing at a time. There is no call for impatience.'

'How can we sell the car when we have not yet bought it?'

'I will take charge of all that aspect of the matter.'

They drove slowly along Jalan Mansor. Music and light blared from coffee-shops. Trishaw-drivers swerved and sidled with their human burdens. Young Malay bloods cycled many abreast, heedless of Alladad Khan's warning honk.

'The horn is good,' he said.

Crisp, exquisite, the Chinese girls toddled in sororities, their cheongsams split to their thin thighs. A half-naked Tamil carried the corpse of a fish. Chettiars in *dhotis* waved money-loving arms, talking excitedly with frank smiles. Wrinkled Chinese patriarchs raked their throats for residuary phlegm. A Sikh fortune-teller jabbed re-peatedly at a client's palm. Sellers of *sateh* – pieces of tripe and liver on a skewer – breathed in the fumes of their fires. Soft-drink sellers brooded over blue and green and yellow bottles. In the barber-shops the many customers lay back like the sheeted dead. Over all presided the fetid, exciting reek of durian, for this was the season of durians. Nabby Adams had once been to a durian party. It was like, he thought, eating a sweet raspberry blancmange in the lavatory. Alladad Khan drove slowly.

'The brakes are good,' he said. Calmly he watched the uninjured child crawl back to play in the monsoon-drain. They passed the Queen's Cinema where a huge hoarding announced a Tamil film – squiggles and curlicues three feet high, a fat female face contorted with fear. They passed, with regret, the beer-garden of Kong Huat. Soon they came to the Paradise Cabaret – dim lights and a hoarse record, the manager in evening dress of shorts and singlet and cigar standing, dim-descried, at the curtained door.

'*Achcha*,' said Nabby Adams. 'We will go in here.'

'We have no money.'

'*Achcha*. Crabbe will pay.'

Crabbe will pay. Crabbe sat in the shadows at a little table with Rahimah. They were sharing a tepid bottle of Anchor beer. Rahimah's charming small face, lost in shadow, Rahimah's charming small body, lost tonight in loose silk pyjamas, Rahimah herself, still, restrained, not yet resigned. Crabbe spoke his slow Malay over a record which, to samba rhythm, recounted in a skirl of grace-notes the principles of religion – '*Rukun Islam*.'

> 'If you do not observe all these tenets,
>   And pray to Allah day and night as well,
> Then you may find it much too late for penance,
>   And a house will await you in Hell.'

The record changed. Crabbe went on, weakly, with his one tune.

'*Maalum-lah*, there are difficulties. People talk. Perhaps I am thrown out of my work.'

'We could go from here and live together. We could go to Penang. You could play the piano and I could be a dance-hostess there. We could earn perhaps three hundred dollars a month together.'

'But there is the matter of my wife.'

'You could enter Islam. Four wives are allowed. But two surely would be enough.'

'But that would not do. I dare not lose my present post. That would be the end of me.'

'You wish to be rid of me, like Rahman my husband.'

'But the difficulties are very great. And I cannot give you money any more. I am becoming a poor man.'

She said nothing. Crabbe gloomily drank beer. The record of 'Seven Lonely Nights' stuck and squawked psittacinely. 'Seven lo seven lo seven lo.' Rahimah went to change it. She came back and held his big white hand in her two small brown ones.

'The money does not matter. You will not leave me. If people talk that is their affair. *Tida' apa.*'

Crabbe heard heavy footsteps and, raising his head, saw with something like relief a huge man approaching him, followed by a moustached Indian in white shirt and black trousers. They came to the table.

'I hope I'm not interrupting you, Mr Crabbe.' It was a deep voice, apt for much morning coughing. The lines of the huge yellow-brown face came into the lamplight.

'Good evening, memsahib.' Alladad Khan bowed, proud of his English.

'Don't be a bloody fool,' said Nabby Adams savagely, 'Beg your pardon, Mr Crabbe. He's three parts pissed, that's his trouble. Can't see straight. Do you mind if I join you for a minute?' He sat down on a tiny chair, like father at a dolls' tea-party. Alladad Khan sat down too. He saw, with embarrassment, that Mr Crabbe had, hidden in the shadows, a woman not his wife. He felt bitter towards Crabbe, who could thus deceive, thus betray, when he had a golden-haired blue-eyed goddess awaiting him at home in trust and love.

'*Dua botol lagi, Rahimah,*' said Crabbe. Rahimah went obediently to fetch more beer.

'Not out of the fridge,' said Nabby Adams. 'Tell her that.'

'Everything's warm here,' said Crabbe.

'You remember you saying about wanting a car?' said Nabby Adams. 'I've got a car outside for you, dirt-cheap. An Abelard, '52 model. Only two thousand.'

'Miles?'

'Dollars.'

'Whose is it?'

'The planter with the tash, the one who's going home. Withers.'

'Rivers?'

'That's right. Withers is the one who's going to die.'

'What are you doing with it if it belongs to Rivers?'

'Well, you see.' Nabby Adams leaned closer, showing confidential huge horse-teeth, brown, black, broken. 'He wanted two-five, you see, and I wouldn't say as how it's not worth it. But you see, me and him' – he jerked a shoulder towards Alladad Khan, calm, moustache-smoothing – 'buggered the works up a bit and I told him this was wrong and that was wrong, so he said two thousand. Licensed and insured till the end of the year.'

'You buggered the works up? For me?'

'For both of us,' said Nabby Adams. 'I'll do a deal with you. Lend me that car, say, two days a month, and I'll look after it for you. Service it and see to the oil. Petrol I can't manage. Too risky. But everything else.'

Rahimah came back with the beer. Nabby Adams said, 'Good health, Mr Crabbe. Good health, Miss er.' Alladad Khan said, '*Shukria, sahib,*' and drank thirstily.

'What do you want it twice a month for?' asked Crabbe.

'So I can go up to Melawas without an escort. As it might be yourself, I like the odd bottle, but you can't stop off with them escorts gawping at you when you go into a *kedai*. Same as yourself, I don't like too many knowing my business.'

'Yes,' said Crabbe. 'Let's try the car out.'

'No hurry,' said Nabby Adams. 'When we've had another bottle.'

'*Shukria, sahib,*' said Alladad Khan.

Nabby Adams turned on him in passionate Urdu. 'Nobody, to my knowledge, suggested that you should sit here all night drinking at other people's expense. You have had more than enough for one evening. You are already intoxicated.' He turned to Crabbe. 'Getting above himself. And drinking's forbidden by his religion, too.'

They had another bottle. Nabby Adams looked round the little dance-hall empty save for their own party and a couple of fat Chinese business-men in crumpled white. 'A nice little place,' he said unconvincingly. 'I think I'll open an account here.'

When the three men were outside, having said good-night to Rahimah, the girl waving her wrist ruefully about, crushed in the bear-hug of Nabby Adams's handshake, Crabbe felt his betrayal of her was complete. There stood the car, gleaming as with blue butter under the fairy-lights in the little garden. A recrudescence of the past, the victory of Fenella over one already long-vanquished, a means of getting out of the Malaya he wanted to know. He climbed into the back of the car.

'You'd better try it yourself,' said Nabby Adams.

'No. I'll never drive again. I'll have to employ a driver.'

'There is your chance,' said Nabby Adams to Alladad Khan. 'You can drive for this gentleman and his wife when you are off-duty. Undoubtedly they will pay you.'

'Thank you. I am a Khan. I am no man's servant. But the memsahib I will gladly drive anywhere.'

'I've got a driver for you,' said Nabby Adams to Crabbe.

A bargain was eventually concluded in a little *kedai* on the Timah road. Here the beer was sun-warmed day-long, and the tepid froth soothed Nabby Adams' bad teeth. Alladad Khan was happy, his eyes shining in the dim light of the oil-lamps. Crabbe, resigned, promised to go to the Treasury the next day, draw out two thousand dollars in cash and hand this over to Nabby Adams in a little *kedai* near the Mansor School. Nabby Adams would see to everything.

Later in the evening, Nabby Adams and Alladad Khan brought a maimed and coughing car into the Club porch. Alladad Khan was singing softly Punjabi folk-songs about young love in the hay.

'Quiet now,' said Nabby Adams. 'I am going in to fetch this man Rivers. He will undoubtedly be astonished by the state of his engine, not realizing that all we have done is to adjust a few little wires and things of that sort.'

Rivers was now very drunk. He tottered about the Club shouting, 'Lash them, beat them, nail them to the door, pepper them with hot lead, ha, ha. Treat them as they deserve to be treated. Speak to them in the only language they understand. Go through them like a dose of salts, ha ha.' Raja Ahmad, the Sultan's A.D.C., was performing a Spanish *jota*. At the worn grand piano sat Hart, playing old songs in N.A.A.F.I. style. Raja Azman sat placidly with his latest wife, smiling at vacancy, drinking gin and tonic water. He was very old.

Nabby Adams said, 'I've brought it back, Mr Rivers.'

Rivers said, 'Major Rivers to you. I insist on my rights. I insist on my rank being respected. We shall have discipline if it's the last thing we do.' He writhed against the bar as if it were a scratching-post. 'One thousand eight hundred. Not a penny less.'

Nabby Adams said, 'Come out and see it.'

The warm night air made Rivers sway and clutch a porch-pillar for support. 'Take me home this instant,' he said. 'I insist on my rights. There's no discipline round here.'

'Get in,' said Nabby Adams, 'and just you listen to that bloody engine.'

Rivers fell in, sprawling on the cushions, shouting, 'Discipline, sir. There is no discipline in this battalion.' At the wheel Alladad Khan sang happily.

'For Christ's sake,' said Nabby Adams. 'Like a bloody loony-bin. Here, let me drive.' He snatched the wheel from Alladad Khan, pushing him rudely into the front passenger-seat. Alladad Khan sang of the fulfilment of love, of the spring moon riding like a huge pearl above the marriage-bed. They drove off down the Tahi Panas road.

'You saw what it was like starting,' said Nabby Adams. 'Now listen to that knock. Hear it? Tearing its guts out. One thousand five hundred, and that's a fair offer.'

The only response was a loud snore from the back. Rivers was out like a light. Nabby Adams pleaded, 'Wake up, listen to that bloody engine. *Please* listen to that bloody engine.' Rivers snored on.

About half a mile from Jagut Estate they ran out of

petrol. Nabby Adams quarrelled petulantly with Alladad Khan.

'It was your responsibility to check the petrol. That is why you carry two stripes. You obviously cannot be trusted to do your work efficiently.'

'This car is no responsibility of mine, sahib.'

'Yes it is. You're going to drive it, aren't you? It's no good. We'll have to leave it here by the roadside.'

'But the sahib is sleeping inside. The terrorists will get him.'

'That's his bloody funeral.'

'Sahib?'

'All right. We'll push it.'

And so they pushed it, their snoring freight oblivious, stretched on the back cushions in deep rest. Nabby Adams grumbled and cursed and reviled Alladad Khan. Alladad Khan sang in rapture an old ploughing song. Under the glowing moon they laboured up the road. The demons of the half-tamed jungle watched them impassively; a snake reared its head from the grass; the fireflies wove their mocking lights about them. From afar a tiger called. Nabby Adams raged with thirst.

'Fourteen fifty,' he panted. 'And not a bloody penny more. And lucky to get that. The bastard,' he added. 'The drunken bastard. Not a penny more.'

5

'He he he,' said Inche Kamaruddin, showing his small teeth in a gay smile. 'If you make dose stupid mistakes den you cannot hope to pass de examination. If you do dat den you must fail.' He smiled brilliantly, encouragingly.

'Yes,' said Victor Crabbe. 'But there don't seem to be any rules.' On the table lay his exercise, a piece of transliteration into Arabic script. The words sprawled, from right to left, in clumsy uncoordinated curves, sprinkled with dots. It was a warm night, despite the rain that had fallen, and busy with insect life. All around them flying ants were landing, ready to copulate, shed their wings, and die. Flying beetles sang fretfully in the rafters of the veranda, and little bugs and pallid moths had been drinking the sweat from his neck. The hand that held the pen dripped sweat on to the paper. His face, he knew, must look wet and greasy and callow to his Malay teacher. Inche Kamaruddin smiled and smiled, deploring his stupidity in a look of ineffable happiness.

'Dere are no rules,' smiled Inche Kamaruddin. 'Dat is de first ting dat you must learn. Every word is different from every oder word. De words must be learnt separately. De English look for rules all de time. But in de East dere are no rules. He he he.' He chortled, rubbing his hands in joy.

'All right,' said Crabbe. 'Now let's have a look at these special words for Malay royalty. Though why the hell they should have words different from other people ...'

'He he he. Dey have always had dat. Dat is de custom. When de ordinary people go to sleep you must say dat dey *tidor*. But de sultans always *beradu*. De root of dat word means dat dere was a singing contest among de concubines. And de one dat won slept wid de sultan. He he he.' He rubbed his groin in a transport of vicarious concupiscence.

'And does the Sultan of Lanchap have these talent competitions?'

'De present Sultan? Now it is different.' Eagerly Inche Kamaruddin picked up a copy of a Malay newspaper from a pile of books and other teaching aids. 'Dere is today's news, you see.' Crabbe squinted at the Arabic letters, deciphering slowly. 'If you read Jawi fluently den you keep up to date wid de latest scandal. He he he.'

'He's going to marry again? A Chinese?'

'De Sultan lost a lot of money at de Singapore races and de Penang races and de races at Kuala Lumpur. De Sultan owes a lot of money.'

'My amah says he owes some to her father.'

'Dat is quite possible. He he he. Dis Chinese girl is de daughter of a tin miner, de richest tin miner in de State. Dis will be de Sultan's tent wife. He he he.' This was a rich joke. Inche Kamaruddin rocked with glee.

'How you love a bit of scandal.' Crabbe smiled at his teacher tolerantly. Inche Kamaruddin was ecstatic. Soon he became a little more serious and said:

'Dere is more trouble at de Mansor School, I see. De Headmaster had his motor-car scratched and his tyres slashed de oder day.'

'I didn't know that,' said Crabbe. 'He didn't mention it to anybody.'

'Of course he did not mention it,' smiled Inche Kamaruddin. 'Dat would be to lose face. But he beat tree prefects wid a stick, and now dis is revenge. Dere is worse to come. Dere is going to be a rebellion.'

'They can't do that, you know. That only happens in school stories.'

'Dey will try. Dey are becoming politically-minded. Dey

are talking about de white oppressors.' Inche Kamaruddin grinned widely and shook with joy.

'How do you manage to hear these things?'

'He he he. Dere are ways and means. Dere will be big trouble at de Mansor School, noting is more certain dan dat.'

'So. And what do your spies in Kuala Lumpur say about the official attitude to the present régime?'

'In de Mansor School? Dey know noting about it. De autorities are very pleased wid de way dat Mr Boodby is running de School. But dey are not very pleased wid you.' Inche Kamaruddin grinned and shook and sang 'He he he' down the scale.

'Oh?' said Crabbe in disquiet. 'And why not?'

'Dey are getting reports about you not doing de tings Mr Boodby asks you to do. And dere is a story about you being friendly wid de Malay women. But you must not worry about dese tings. U.M.N.O. is quite pleased wid you and when U.M.N.O. is running de country dere will be no difficulty about you getting one of de good jobs. But first,' Inche Kamaruddin tried for a moment to look very grave, 'first,' his face gradually lightened, 'you must get your examination. Dey will want Englishmen who can speak de language.' Inche Kamaruddin banged the rattan table with his neat brown fist. '*Misti lulus. Misti lulus.* You must pass de examination. But you will not pass de examination if you make dese stupid mistakes.' He grinned widely and engagingly and then collapsed into quiet mirth.

'All right,' said Crabbe. 'Let's read some more of the *Hikayat Abdullah*.' Inwardly he was disturbed, but it was a cardinal rule in the East not to show one's true feelings. The truth about anything had to be wrapped up and could only be seen and handled after the patient untying of much string and paper. The truth about one's feelings must be masked in a show of indifference or even the lineaments of a very different emotion. Calmly now he translated the sophisticated Malay of the *munshi* who had been the protégé and friend of Stamford Raffles.

' "One day Tuan Raffles said to me, '*Tuan*, I intend to go home by ship in three days' time, so get together all my books in Malay.' When I heard this my heart beat strongly and my soul had lost its courage. When he told me that he was sailing back to Europe, I could not stand it any longer. I felt that I had lost my father and my mother, and my eyes swam with tears." '

'Yes, yes.' Inche Kamaruddin danced up and down on his chair. 'You have got de meaning of dat.'

'They felt differently about us then,' said Crabbe. 'They felt that we had something to give.'

'You still have something to give,' insisted Inche Kamaruddin, 'but in a free Malaya dat shall be ruled by de Malays.'

'And the Chinese? And the Indians, the Eurasians?'

'Dey do not count,' grinned Inche Kamaruddin. 'Dey are not de friends of de Malays. Malaya is a country for de Malays.'

The work of translation stopped, and the old political wrangle began again. Crabbe was reasonable, pointing out that the Chinese had made the country economically rich, that the British had brought rule and justice, that the majority of the Malays were Indonesian immigrants. Inche Kamaruddin grew heated, waving excited arms, grinning passionately, finally shouting, '*Merdeka! Merdeka!* Freedom, independence, self-determination for de Malays!'

'*Merdeka* itself is a Sanskrit word,' said Crabbe, 'a foreign importation.'

From the nearest dormitory a young boy, wakened by the noise, could be heard crying. 'We'd better stop now,' said Crabbe. 'I've got to do my little prowl round the dormitories.'

Inche Kamaruddin went downstairs to his bicycle, waving his hand in farewell, showing all his teeth in the last big grin of the evening. 'On Tursday, den,' he called quietly.

'Thursday,' said Crabbe. '*Terima kaseh, inche. Selamat jalan.*'

Crabbe began to wander round the still, dark dormitories, thinking of what his teacher had told him. There were few secrets to be kept in Malaya. What he had thought to be a discreet liaison was obviously already stale knowledge round the town, stale knowledge to Boothby. The side had been let down. He had broken the unwritten laws of the white man. He had rejected the world of the Club, the week-end golf, the dinner invitations, the tennis parties. He did not drive a car. He walked round the town, sweating, waving his hand to his Asian friends. He had had an affair with a Malay divorcee. And of course Fenella was no better. She had rejected the white woman's world – *mah jong* and bridge and coffee parties – for different reasons.

He felt suddenly a stab of anxiety about Fenella. Tonight was the night of the first meeting of the Film Society in Timah. He had refused to go, saying that he could not cancel his Malay lesson. She had said it was pointless taking Malay lessons, pointless taking Government examinations when they did not intend to stay in the country. He had said that he did not see why they should not stay in the country. He liked the country and, if she wished to be a dutiful wife, she should try to like it too. It was up to her to go wherever her husband went. If he had determined on a career in this country, well, her duty was plain. If she did not wish to be a dutiful wife, then she had better not be a wife at all, she had better leave him. He would not have said so much if his nerves had not been on edge with a trying morning in the School. She had cried, said he did not love her, and all the rest of it. He had tried to retract, but she had burst out with the inevitable reference to his first wife. Then he had become hard, cold and stupid. At seven o'clock Alladad Khan had brought round the car and she had gone off to Timah alone; alone, that is, save for Alladad Khan's respectful and discreet presence. He did not expect her back for another hour. Now he worried a little about the possibility of an ambush, the car breaking down miles from anywhere, Fenella afraid in the black night. This, he supposed, was a sort of love. He shrugged it away, refused to think about it further, walking soft-footed between the rows of boys' beds.

From the prefects' room came the light hissing of talk. A blue glow, as of a shaded lamp, showed under the door. Crabbe walked stealthily towards it, stood outside, hardly breathing, listening. He could not understand what was being said; he knew hardly any Chinese. It was evident, however, that this was no ordinary conversation, apt for a dorm-feast; there was too much of one voice. Then came the hint of catechism: the question, the quiet chorused answer. Crabbe opened the door and entered.

Shiu Hung opened a surprised mouth, raising his eye-brows above spectacles which had slipped down his nose. The other boys, all Chinese, looked up from the floors and beds where they sat. All were wearing pyjamas.

'What's going on?' said Crabbe.

'We are having a meeting, sir.' said Shiu Hung. 'We have formed a Chinese society.'

'Where are the other prefects, Narayanasamy and the rest of them?'

'They lent us the room, sir. They are down below reading in the lavatories.'

'You know about the lights-out rule?'

No answer. Crabbe looked at the boys. Two or three were prefects, the rest merely seniors.

'What kind of society is this?' asked Crabbe.

'It is a Chinese society, sir.'

'You said that. What does the society propose to do?'

'To discuss things, sir, things of world interest.'

'What's that book?' asked Crabbe.

'This, sir?' Shiu Hung handed the thick pamphlet to him. 'It's a book on economic theory, sir.'

Crabbe looked at the fantastic columns of ideograms. He only knew one or two: the symbols for 'man', 'field', 'light', 'tree', 'house' – pictograms really, straightforward drawings of straightforward things. He suddenly shot a question at one of the crouching boys:

'You. State the doctrine of Surplus Value.'

The boy, bewildered, shook his head. Shiu Hung remained suave, impassive.

'Shiu Hung,' said Crabbe, 'how shall the revolution be accomplished in Malaya?'

'What revolution, sir?'

'Look here,' said Crabbe. 'I suspect the worst. I suspect that this is an indoctrination class.'

'I do not know the word, sir,' said Shiu Hung.

'Watch your step,' said Crabbe. 'I'm taking this book away. I'll find out what's in it.'

'It is a good book, sir, on economic theory. We are interested in these things and we have a right, sir, to discuss them in our own language. We are given no other opportunity to meet for this purpose. It is either prep. or games or debates in English.'

'You're here to get an English education,' said Crabbe. 'Whether that's a good or bad thing is not for me to say. If you want to form a discussion-group ask me about it. And you're breaking the rules by not being in bed by lights-out. I'll have to report this. Now get to bed, all of you.'

Crabbe went back to his flat, much disturbed. He poured himself a large whisky and sat for a time, smoking, looking at the pamphlet. The big garish ideograms on the cover meant nothing to him. He would ask Lee, the mathematics master, what the contents were. But he was certain that Boothby would do nothing. He was also certain that other indoctrination sessions were being held in the other houses. Indoctrination meant victimization. Also there was the big public school tradition of not sneaking.

He strolled restlessly about the big living-room, stopping at last to examine the titles of books behind the smeared glass of the standard-pattern bookcase. Some of the books dated from his university days – poets like Auden and Spender, novels by Upward, Dos Passos, André Malraux. In those days he had himself for a time been a Communist; it was the thing to be, especially at the time of the Spanish War. He remembered the loose-mouthed student of engineering who had the complete works of Lenin and was glib in his application of Dialectical Materialism to all human functions – drinking, love-making, films, literature. He remembered the girls who swore and chain-smoked and cultivated a deliberate lack of allure, the parties where he met them, the songs they sang at the parties:

> 'Three, three, the Comintern.
> Two, two, the opposites,
> Interpenetrating though.
> One is Workers' Unity
> And evermore shall be so.'

Those memories now had the smell of old apples, they were a dried pressed flower. Were these boys the same as he had been, fired with an adolescent desire really to reform the world, as little to be taken seriously? Shiu Hung was a good student of History. Crabbe wanted him to go to England, to read for a degree there. He had a future before him. Did he really see the ambushes, the eviscerations, the beheadings of the innocent as a wholesome and necessary step to the fulfilment of a freer and happier East? Or did he, young as he was, know what power was and desire it?

Crabbe heard a car singing in a rising scale round the bend of the long drive. His watch said nearly twelve. The car stopped in the porch, he heard brief words and a slammed door, then the car was off again, singing down the riverside road that led to the town. He heard Fenella mounting the stairs. He went to the door to meet her.

'Hello, darling,' he said. She seemed flushed and happy, the afternoon's quarrel forgotten. 'Here I am,' she said. They kissed.

'Was it a good film?'

'Well.' She went ahead of him into the living-room. 'Let

me have a drink first. Wake up Ibrahim and ask him to fetch some ice.'

'Ibrahim's not back yet. He too went to the cinema.'

'Never mind. This water seems cold enough.' She sat down with a flop of languor and drank some diluted gin.

'Well,' she said. 'It's rather a long story. We never got to Timah.'

'Never got there?'

'Do you know anything about this driver, What's-his-name Khan?'

'Nothing. Why?'

'Well, we broke down on the road. At least, he said we'd broken down. He managed to drive the car into one of the estates – conveniently near, I thought, a bit too convenient. Admittedly the car was coughing a bit, but I think we could have got to Timah. He said he knew some of the Special Constables there and also the estate driver. He said he could get the car repaired.'

'He spoke in English?'

'No, Malay. But I could follow him. I really must get down to learning the language, Vic. It's silly not to know Malay when you're living in Malaya.'

'Really, my dear. This is quite a new note.'

'Well, actually, there was a lot I wanted to find out to-night, but nobody spoke English. Everybody knew some Malay.'

'What did you want to find out?'

'Oh, it's a long story. We went to this estate and there was a sort of party going on. It was mostly Tamils. There seemed to be some sort of religious ceremony, but it wasn't really religious either. The most incredible thing. You've no idea.'

'Such as?'

'Well, some of them walked in their bare feet on broken glass and others stuck knives into their cheeks, and one man swallowed a sword. And they sang songs. And we had a foul-smelling drink called toddy.'

'Ah.'

'Have you ever drunk it?'

'Yes, a little.'

'Well, it's all right if you hold your nose. It's quite intoxicating in a gentle sort of way.'

'That's true.'

'I had quite a lot of that. They kept handing it round. Really, the whole evening was most interesting. Like something out of *The Golden Bough*.'

'But you missed the film.'

'Yes, I missed the film. Still, I never much fancied *The Battleship Potemkin*, really. But I mustn't miss the next one.'

Just before she went to sleep Fenella said, 'You know, that Khan man, the driver, is rather nice really. Very attentive. I only wish I could understand what he's saying to me. It all sounds quite complimentary. This is like something in a novel, isn't it?' she added. 'Like one of those cheap novels about Cairo and what-not.' She giggled a little, and then swam off into sleep, snoring very faintly.

While she slept happily two men were happily awake. One was Alladad Khan. He swelled with pride as he took off his shirt before the mirror. He flexed his muscles and examined his teeth. He tried various facial poses, ending with a lascivious leer which, he realized, did not really suit him. He recomposed his face to a quiet dignity much more becoming a Khan. Then to the mirror he spoke some words of English. 'Beautiful,' he said. He sought for an adverb to go with it. 'Bloody beautiful,' he said. Tomorrow he must borrow that little book from Hari Singh. Then he turned to his wife's photograph and sneered dramatically at the strong long nose and the confident arm leaning on his own new-married image. 'Silly bastard,' he said. 'Bloody liar.' Then, satisfied, he got into bed.

He lay smoking a last cigarette. Smoking in bed was forbidden by his wife, because once he had burnt the sheet. His wife was not here to enforce the law, but, Allah, she would soon be back, complete with a squalling baby. When she returned he would assert his manhood a bit more. Any further mention of her brother and he would use rude language. He might even strike her gently, though hitting a woman was not conduct befitting a Khan.

Tida' apa.

Mrs Crabbe had, he thought, been given a very good evening, and it had cost nothing. At first she had been frightened, but a pint or so of fresh toddy had soon made that pass. His friends, he thought, had behaved very well. They had never belched nor spat excessively. They had smiled frequently and encouragingly. She had obviously been interested in the things she had seen. It was a good thing she had not been able to understand the songs she had heard.

Next time he would make the car break down near a *kedai*, one of the more refined *kedais* where ice was obtainable. There they could have a good long talk. By then he should know a little English.

'Bloody good,' he said. Then, content, he turned towards the wall and addressed himself to sleep.

The other happy man was Nabby Adams. Old Robin Hood had brought him to Penang. There was to be a conference of Contingent Transport Officers at Butterworth the next day, and Hood needed Nabby Adams's technical advice. Nabby Adams was now sitting in a rather high-class *kedai*, doing very nicely indeed.

Nabby Adams had arrived in Penang with two dollars. Hood had given him the money for a hotel room but nothing for expenses. The two dollars had to be husbanded carefully. First, a bottle for breakfast had to be bought. This bottle had been bought and then stored carefully in the same cupboard as the chamber-pot. This left one dollar for the evening, one dollar to taste the varied pleasures of a civilized city that has been called the Pearl of the Orient.

Nabby Adams had entered a *kedai* and ordered himself a small bottle of Anchor. Now, it normally happens that when one has much money in one's pockets that is the time when other drinkers, even strangers, are at their most generous. When one has nothing nothing will come of nothing. On this occasion things went differently. A Chinese jeweller had said, 'A drink for the police-lieutenant. It is they who are clearing this country of Communist scum.' Nabby Adams had been bought a large bottle of Tiger. He protested that he had no money to return this generosity. He had been told that that was no matter, that nothing was too good for police-lieutenants. Soon friends of the Chinese jeweller came in and were greeted warmly by the Chinese jeweller. They too were appreciative of expatriate police-lieutenants and they too bought him large bottles of Tiger. It was not long before Nabby Adams had eight unopened large bottles of Tiger on the table before him. Then somebody had said, 'The police-lieutenant is drinking very slowly.'

Somebody had said, 'Too slowly.'

Somebody had suggested, 'Perhaps if the police-lieutenant had a brandy before each bottle of beer it would help him to get them down.'

This was thought to be a good idea. Soon eight glasses of brandy appeared on the table. They helped the beer down considerably. And now Nabby Adams was speaking rapid Urdu to a couple of Bengali business-men who frequently nodded gravely in agreement. Occasionally the Chinese jeweller would sway over to the table and shout:

'More drink for the police-lieutenant. It is only fitting that they should be repaid for their bravery.'

It was, joking on one side, the best bloody evening that Nabby Adams had had for a long time.

Meanwhile Victor Crabbe was dreaming. He was in Boothby's office. This office expanded and contracted like a huge yawning mouth. Boothby was sitting in his chair with Rahimah on his knee. Rahimah was evidently very fond of Boothby for she kissed him frequently, even when he was yawning. Boothby was glancing through a Chinese pamphlet, saying, 'If you'd been in this Federation as long as me you'd be able to read this language. All it says is that terrorist activities must be intensified, especially in this

School. That's your trouble, Crabbe, you're inexperienced. You can't take orders, you can't exercise discipline, the boys laugh at you behind your back.'

On a ledge, high up near the ceiling, Fenella lay languidly, saying, 'Oh, darling, I'm so happy, so happy.' Boothby said, 'All right, boys, give him a joy-ride.' The Chief Clerk and the two peons came in, wearing caps marked with the *bintang tiga,* the three stars. They bundled him into a smart Abelard, into the driving seat, and said, 'You're on your own.' But he was not on his own. The muffled figure in the passenger-seat said, 'Oh, darling, I'm so happy, so happy.' Over the bridge-fence they went. 'Who ever heard of ice in Malaya?' yawned Boothby. Nabby Adams said, 'I can't abide it cold.' Over they went, into the dark January waters.

6

'So I thought you might like to go there,' said Nabby Adams.

'Yes,' said Crabbe. 'Let's go and have a few beers.' He was smarting from the day's failures. 'Do sit down, Alladad Khan. I mean, *sila dudok*.'

'*Shukria, sahib.*' Alladad Khan sat gingerly on one of the four chairs ranged about the table, under the spinning fan, and stroked his moustache, glancing shyly round. So this was where she lived. Fine P.W.D. furniture, and many books in an unknown language, and on the walls coloured pictures. And there on a small table ice in a jug and gin. But where was she?

'I think my wife might quite like it,' said Crabbe. 'Have some gin, Nabby.'

'No, thanks,' said Nabby Adams. 'No water. I like to taste it as it is.' He drank with no grimace a bulging mouthful of the raw spirit. Alladad Khan accepted shyly the same and burst into a shock of coughing.

'That's his bloody trouble,' said Nabby Adams evenly. 'Thinks he can drink and he can't. Go on,' he added, 'get it up even if it's only a bucketful.'

It was unfortunate that she should enter just then. He, Alladad Khan, red with coughing under his brown, eyes full of tears, fire in his gullet. He had meant to be calm, gentlemanly, saying in careful English, 'Good evening, memsahib. Thank you, memsahib.' She entered, graceful in thin flowery stuff, gracious and solicitous.

'Don't mind about him, Mrs Crabbe,' said Nabby Adams, remaining calmly seated. 'He's only coughing his art up.'

Fenella heard this with appreciation. Coughing his art up. That could apply to any of the tubercular poets. She must use it sometime.

'There's a big fair up at the Istana,' said Crabbe. 'Side-shows, dancing.'

'And two beer-tents,' said Nabby Adams. 'It's the Sultan's birthday, you see. Tomorrow, that is. And I thought you might like to go to it. You'll be safe with two men. And him,' he added.

'Yes,' said Fenella. 'I should like that.'

'There's no hurry,' said Nabby Adams. 'Doesn't start till nine.' He looked appreciatively at the bottles on the sideboard. That had been a bloody good idea of Alladad Khan's, to come up here like that with the suggestion. He must come here again. Crabbe probably had beer in the kitchen as well.

Alladad Khan had stopped coughing. Now he said, with careful articulation, 'Good evening, memsahib.'

'Oh,' said Fenella. 'Good evening.'

'Bit late in the day, aren't you?' said Nabby Adams with contempt. He then launched into long Urdu. Alladad Khan replied in long Urdu, his eyes flashing and melting. Nabby Adams grunted and said, 'I'll take one of your cigarettes, if you don't mind, Mr Crabbe.'

'What was all that about?' asked Fenella.

'He says his heart is heavy that he made a bloody fool of himself like that,' said Nabby Adams. Then he gaped in horror. 'I beg your pardon, Mrs Crabbe. It just slipped out, that did, I didn't mean to say that, not before a lady, I do beg your pardon, really I do.'

Nabby Adams, forgiven, drank more neat gin. Alladad Khan was soothed with some sherry. Allah, that was a good drink. He smacked his lips. Rich, aromatic, sustaining. Allah, he must buy some of that.

'You don't mind me coming in these clothes, do you?' announced Nabby Adams. 'I didn't go back to the mess, you see. Me and him had to go out on a job.' He looked down at the stained shirt and long, long crumpled trousers. 'I didn't get a bath, neither. But I think you can bath too much. No, joking on one side, I think you can. Now, I know some people who bath as much as twice a day. Honest. Keir does. You wouldn't know him, Mrs Crabbe. Not that you'd want to. Mean? Mean as bl ... Mean as dirt. It doesn't cost him any money to have a bath. That's how he passes the time.' Nabby Adams now risked one of his little jokes. 'I had a damn good wash on the boat coming over,' he said.

'Really?' said Fenella.

'That'll do me until the end of the tour.'

Crabbe brooded on the day's humiliations. The Chinese pamphlet had been a catechism on the teaching of Karl Marx. He had taken it in to Boothby, and Boothby had yawned. He then said:

'I know all about it. This lad – what's his name? – came in to tell me that he was trying to show these younger kids where Communism goes wrong. He said that you weren't very sympathetic about it and that he understood it was the job of the staff to try and teach the youth of Malaya the truth about Communism. Well, now, I don't see what you're bellyaching about. It's down in your syllabus here. Just a minute.' He leafed through a file. 'Here. "Nineteenth century political ideas. Utilitarianism. Bentham and Mill. The Co-operative Movement and Robert Owen." Here it is. "Socialism. Karl Marx and the Economic Interpretation of History." Well, he was only trying to do what you don't seem to have done.'

'We haven't got as far as that yet.'

'All right. But don't blame this lad for trying to do your work for you. He's a good lad anyway. You say so yourself in that report I asked for. You said his scholarship should most certainly be renewed.'

'I tell you I don't like it. There was too much of the air of a secret society about it. Late at night. Breaking the lights-out rule as well.'

'Internal discipline is your own affair. Don't bring it to me.'

'Unless it happens to relate to offences of an erotic nature?'

'I don't quite get you.'

'Young men talking to girls in a house-boy's room.'

'Yes,' said Boothby with vigour. 'Yes. That reminds me. Mahmud bin What's-his-name in your House. He was seen with a girl in the grounds, arm in arm, love's young dream. You didn't do anything about that, did you?'

'I didn't know anything about it.'

'There you are,' said Boothby in heavy triumph. 'But I did. If these lads want to work late for exams and out of general interest and what-not, then you start interfering. Fornication goes on under your nose and you don't see that, oh no. Perhaps because you don't want to see it.'

'And what exactly do you mean by that?'

'What I say.'

'Look here, Boothby,' said Victor Crabbe. 'How would you like a nice sharp jab on the nose?'

Boothby looked in astonishment, open-mouthed. Then he grinned, and, as his mouth was already half-way there, thought he might as well yawn. He yawned. 'Go on,' he said. 'I'll say no more about it. You're new, that's your trouble. You can get away with a lot in this country if you keep it quiet. You'll learn.'

Back in Light House, in the yawning afternoon, Crabbe had had a quiet talk with Shiu Hung. On the veranda the boy had listened politely, responded politely, sipping orange-crush.

'I want you to be honest with me.'

'About what, sir?'

'I want to know what was really going on last night. I promise you that whatever you tell me won't go any further.'

'I told you what was going on, sir.'

'Yes, yes, but you didn't tell me the whole story. I want to know what's really going on in the minds of these boys.'

'Yes, sir.'

'Would it surprise you,' Crabbe had leaned forward con-

spiratorially, 'surprise you to know that I myself am some
thing of a radical in politics?'

'No, sir. You have talked in class of a free Malaya.'

Ah. Crabbe said, 'How are we to get a free Malaya?'

'Through representation, sir. Through free elections
and a party system.'

'What parties?'

'Parties that represent the people, sir.'

'Does the Malayan Communist Party represent the
people?'

'Certainly not, sir. It represents Red China.'

'Have you any feelings about Red China?'

'I am a Malayan, sir. I was born here.'

'Shall I tell you, in confidence, what I think? I think
that in a free country there should be room for all shades
of political opinion, for all political creeds. To make it an
offence to belong to a particular party does not seem to
me to be consistent with the much-vaunted principle of
freedom.'

'You think that the Emergency Regulations should be
repealed, sir?'

'I . . .' Crabbe looked into the impassive eyes, set tight
and slant, as in a perpetual mask of mockery. 'I will ask
you what you think.'

'They cannot be repealed, sir. The Communists are torturing and killing the innocent. They are holding back
all our schemes for social and economic progress. They are
evil, sir. They must be destroyed.'

'Would you yourself be willing to destroy them, given
the chance?'

'Yes, sir.'

'You are Chinese. Think. If your father or brother or
sister were hiding in this jungle torturing and killing, as
you say, the innocent, would you be willing to help destroy
your own kith and kin?'

'My own . . .?'

'Kith and kin. Your own flesh and blood.'

'Oh, yes, sir.'

'You would kill, for instance, your sister?'

'Oh, yes, sir.'

'Thank you. That's all I want to know.'

Shiu Hung got up, puzzled. 'I can go now, sir?'

'Yes, you can go now.'

Had he really got anything out of the boy? Adolescents will reel off shibboleths they have heard or read, they will be brutal and callous enough in speech. In any case, even if Shiu Hung were running a Communist study-group, did it matter very much? Doctrinaire blather, a pubescent rash. Could they do anything that mattered? Crabbe suddenly saw himself as a witch-hunting little senator, looking for burglars under the bed, listening at keyholes, tapping wires. Was it perhaps not better that boys should stay up late reading Marx, rather than ingesting the film-myths or breathing heavily over the comic-strips? Crabbe felt vaguely ashamed of himself but still disturbed.

He came to. Ibrahim had entered the room, flaunting red curls, simpering, with faintly swaying hips, at Alladad Khan. Alladad Khan looked embarrassed.

'*Makan malam ini, mem?*'

'No dinner,' said Fenella. 'We're going out.'

Nabby Adams made another little joke. '*Ada baik?*' he said to Ibrahim.

'*Ada buik, tuan.*'

'Motor-bike or pedal-bike?' said Nabby Adams. The bottles on the sideboard had put him in a good humour. Ibrahim went out on oiled haunches, simpering finally from the doorway at Alladad Khan. Nabby Adams said, 'You get a lot of them like that. When I was in India there was what I thought was a woman in the next washhouse. I was stripped off, see, Mrs Crabbe, having a swill-down. Needed it, because I was smelling a bit. Well, it seemed to me she had her hair all down her back, so I thought, well, if she's come in here she knows what to expect. Well, I went in there, Mrs Crabbe, and she turned round and I got the shock of my life, because she had a beard. It was a man really, a Sikh, you see, Mrs Crabbe, and they're not allowed to have the scissors of the razor touch their body. Well, I said I was sorry and begged his pardon, but he was all for it, if you see what I mean, Mrs Crabbe. Oh,' he added, 'perhaps I shouldn't have started to tell that story.'

When Nabby Adams had finished half a bottle of gin, neat, and Alladad Khan had, absorbed in the wonder of it all, taken three glasses of sherry, it was time for them to go. Alladad Khan drove carefully along streets festive with banners saying 'LONG LIVE THE SULTAN'. Inche Sidek, the local Health Inspector, had been round the shops all day selling these banners at exorbitant prices, threatening every *towkay* with closure on the grounds of inadequate sanitation if he did not buy. Crowds of walkers and cyclists infested the road to the Istana. As the car entered the Istana grounds policemen saluted Nabby Adams. He waved a languid paw at them, lolling in deep cushions.

'You see,' he said. 'They let us through without a murmur.' Other motorists were nosing and inching and sidling into the crammed parking-place outside the gates. 'It's useful to have a police officer with you sometimes,' he said, remembering the gin he had drunk and the beer he would drink, all at Crabbe's expense.

The grounds were gay with tree-slung fairy-lights, with fire and smoke of food-sellers, noise of show-booths, of *ronggeng* music, Chinese opera, Indian drums, brown and yellow faces above best clothes, glistening eyes wide in the shine of the Sultan's treat. The car parked under the stars, the four walked down the main drive, Nabby Adams huge, a minaret to the upturned eyes of the open-mouthed children. They stopped by the *wayang kulit*.

'This is a kind of a shadow-play,' explained Nabby Adams unnecessarily. Into the lighted screen swam little heroic figures, fluttering like moths, moustached Indian warriors with swords stiffly upheld, playing-card kings, toy gods, striking a kitten's impotent tiger-terror. The unmoving lips of great cardboard princesses were fed with the showman's rapid epic Malay. All the time the little drums beat and the tiny bells tinkled in water-drops. The crowd gaped, absorbed, all save those at the back; they, sea to Nabby Adams's pharos, gazed in awe at the queer quartet: the golden-haired woman, the white schoolmaster, the brown swaying Indian, the yellowstone rock of Nabby Adams. Perhaps this, too, had been provided by the Sultan?

Like the high, lighted Chinese shows, flanked by huge monolithic picture-writing slogans, where the jugglers juggled with flaming torches and the thin women caterwauled to a single saxophone and thudding drum. Like the Malay play with its stock characters: the comic money-lenders and the father ruined by his prodigal son; the stock descent from decent middle-class house to *attap* hut, the squeezed-out drop of philosophy: *Tida' apa*. Like the songs in Hindustani with endless, breathless phrases; like the *ronggeng* platform where the girls danced without a pause, the grinning young Malay men awaiting their turns to advance and retreat with swaying hips and arms held out as for a tentative embrace.

'I can do that,' said Nabby Adams. Stern eyes, powered by gin, were on the delicate girls in their best *bajus* and sarongs, going backwards to the platform's edge, forward again towards the band, moving arms held out to the partners whom they must not touch, who must not touch them. Nabby Adams looked at the waiting queue of slim-waisted, liquid-brown, smiling youth. 'When that queue's gone down a bit,' he said, 'I'll have a go at that.'

They sought an open-air table by the nearest beer-tent. Around them were the flares and fires of the *sateh*-sellers, the stalls piled with peanuts and coconut slices, rambutans, coloured sweets, bananas, warmish yellowish soft drinks. Crabbe bought *sateh* for all: tiny knobs and wedges of fire-hot meat on wooden skewers, to be dipped in a luke-warm sauce of fire and eaten with slivers of sweet potato and cucumber. The beer came, and with it a saucer of ice, quick to change back to warm water under the sweating night.

'It won't do him any good to drink beer after all that sherry,' said Nabby Adams. 'Still, if he thinks he can do it he can try. He'll spew his art up, Mrs Crabbe,' he said seriously, clinically. 'You wait and see.' He entered a long tunnel of rumbling Urdu. Emetic art, thought Fenella. James Joyce? Henry Miller? She was learning a lot from this huge crumpled man. Alladad Khan, not at all crumpled, ironed and starched in white shirt and black trousers, sat close to her. How pink the nails seemed on his brown hand.

To their table came Inche Sidek, fat and wheezy, bubbling rapid approximate English in ever-rising intonation. 'My God,' he piped high. 'My God, it has been a lot of work, seeing that there is enough lavatories to go round, and that there is properly trenches digged for the dirty water to run away down. My God, I tell you. Lady,' he said, 'lady, you will drink a little with me. I will send round a bottle of brandy from my table.'

Nabby Adams said, 'They only sell beer.'

'My God,' said Inche Sidek. 'Getting into my car I find that there is three bottles of brandy in the back seat. I do not ask questions. There is three bottles. Three star. It is a present, so I do not ask questions.'

'*Haram*,' said Crabbe.

'My God,' said Inche Sidek. 'Who is to know if drinking brandy is *haram*? I tell you, the Prophet forbid what would intoxicate. Even water will intoxicate. Me nothing will intoxicate, so for me it is not *haram*.'

From the Malay *wayang* came '*Rukun Islam*', sung chirpily by a hoarse female voice. Crabbe thought with a pang of Rahimah, his betrayal over the scratchy record in the Paradise Cabaret. How was she getting on?

To their table came, grinning through a nodding full beard, a big Sikh. He sat down without invitation, pulling up a chair between Crabbe and Fenella.

'Hari Singh,' said Alladad Khan. Hari Singh shook hands with the lady, the gentleman. Nabby Adams said, 'Bloody fool, he is,' quietly to himself. Hari Singh began to speak grumbling bad monotonous English. Alladad Khan listened jealously.

'Yes,' said Crabbe, uncomprehending.

'I beg your pardon?' said Fenella. Hari Singh pulled his chair closer to her, speaking to her eyes.

'He says it would do his heart good to buy us some beer,' said Nabby Adams. 'I wouldn't want to spoil his pleasure.'

Hari Singh rumbled that he would show them a trick. He took off his heavy signet-ring and span it on the table. He asked the lady to try it. The lady tried it and failed. Hari Singh laughed schoolboyishly through the nest of beard. He showed the lady again. The lady tried again and failed. Hari Singh came closer, span the ring to a blurred whizzing. Nabby Adams yawned. Alladad Khan glinted jealously.

Suddenly Fenella was aware of a big bare foot stroking her shod one. She was surprised, and tucked her feet under her chair. Alladad Khan saw and was mad with inner rage. Bloody Sikh, he thought. He would get him, Allah, he would get him. The bloody Sikh slid his foot back into his leather sandal.

'We ought to go in there, really,' said Nabby Adams, looking towards the great Hollywood vision of Baghdad, the vast vulgar floodlit Istana. 'Gambling going on. Thousands of dollars changing hands. Them Chinese, mainly. Money no object.'

'It's a mug's game.' said Crabbe.

'That's right,' said Nabby Adams. 'When you come to think of it. Like horses. And all the horse-racing's crooked in this country. The jockeys and the trainers is a load of old shit. I said that to them in the Club there, and they said, "Do you know who that is there, that's Bert Rugby, biggest trainer in the country." And I said, "Well then, he must be part of the load of old shit.'" He sat back, unsmiling, seeing no shame in pure logic.

Alladad Khan made a long passionate speech in Urdu. Nabby Adams listened attentively.

'What does he say?' asked Crabbe.

'He says we ought to get away from here,' said Nabby Adams, 'and go somewhere else.'

'My God,' said Crabbe, 'he's right.' He saw what he had half-expected to see all evening. Rahimah, holding on to the hand of a small brown boy, was approaching the table, ready to greet and be greeted. She was dressed in Malay costume, walking gravely on high-heeled shoes. Crabbe knew she would greet him lovingly with wide smile and soft words. Fenella's face was hidden by the turban of Hari Singh, who was now reading her palm, bending low over it, squeezing it often. Now, before it was too late . . .

'I see what you mean,' said Nabby Adams. Crabbe, feigning not to see Rahimah, rushed over to the beer-tent with money for the beer they had drunk. Alladad Khan escorted Fenella quickly away, his hands and lips voluble with apologies. That he should let this happen to her. How could he blame himself enough? A fellow-Punjabi, but to-morrow hell would open for this rascal. His beard should be pulled out, that soapy smile sponged from his mouth by an avenging fist. Allah, brave punishments would be devised for this false Sikh.

'What's all this about?' asked Fenella. 'What's going on?'

'He says his heart is heavy that that bloke should have behaved like that,' translated Nabby Adams. 'He says he's going to give him what for.'

This time they entered a beer-tent, secure under canvas from importunate Sikhs, from ghosts of old romances. More beer. Alladad Khan began to feel that he looked green. Allah, he had changed like a traffic-signal this evening. But even here there was no peace for, soon, a slim Bengali from the bazaar appeared, offering whisky from a pocket-flask, eager to tell the lady of new fabrics from exotic America, just now in stock, cheap, so cheap, if the lady would come round and see tomorrow . . . They were joined by one of the letter-writers, relaxing from the labours of recording others' sorrows, whines, entreaties on a clanking second-hand Oliver. He would talk of the meaning of life with the lady.

'Sister,' he said, 'sister. There is much pain and grief in the world, but God sees it all, and God will see that the wicked will be punished. Like, for instance, my father-in-law, who has cheated me but recently of twenty-five dollars. The story is a long one, sister, but you have a sympathetic face and will advise me best of course of action to be taken to put this scheming rogue behind inhospitable bars.'

'Oh God,' moaned Nabby Adams, 'look who's here.'

Grinning with mad teeth, a thin brown man in a *dhoti* had arrived at the table. Without ceremony he made straight for the Bengali from the bazaar, abusing him in careful English.

'And so I find you, cheat that you are, puffing yourself up in the company of the upper classes. And of the money that is rightfully mine you are without doubt not telling these ladies and gentlemen. Yet you would not be the rich man you now are had I not scraped the bottoms of my empty coffers to give help to one who seemed to be a friend. Friend!' He laughed drunkenly, scornfully, theatrically.

'It is best to ignore such,' said the Bengali to Crabbe. 'He will soon go away if he is ignored.'

'I will not be ignored. The whole world shall know of moral turpitude of a false friend.'

'I am no friend of drunkards,' said the Bengali with sneering scorn.

'It is you who are drunken bastard too,' danced the other. 'And false bastard. And liar. As your father were before you.'

'You will not speak so of my father.'

'And your mother also.'

The Bengali rose. 'Oh Christ,' said Nabby Adams. 'Out of here quick.'

'*Banchoad!*'

The final insult. 'The Bengali's launched punch sent

the glasses and bottles flying. Nabby Adams led his party out hurriedly.

'My dress!' screeched Fenella.

'Never mind. Quick, over there, near them dancers. The police will be on the job in a minute.'

They merged with the *ronggeng*-watchers.

'Better get up on that platform,' said Nabby Adams, 'and do a dance. Make out we've been dancing a long time.'

'All of us?' said Crabbe.

'You and me. He's not up to it. Three parts pissed.'

'But I can't.'

An electric-lighted dream-world. The Malays, who awaited their turns to dance, courteously let the two white men go before them. Crabbe saw the sweating faces of the band, rakish *songkok* over saxophone, a young *haji* playing the drums. In a delirium he saw huge Nabby Adams, tall as a crumpled tower, stiffly backing and advancing, drawing and drawn by his pigmy partner, an invisible cat's-cradle wound on wiggling dancing fingers.

The crowd clapped and cheered.

'Victor!' cried Fenella. 'Victor! Come down!'

But Crabbe was paralysed, staring with open mouth at Nabby Adams's hip-wagging partner. A red bang of hair, a stylish sarong, a cheerful greeting to Crabbe – '*Tabek, tuan*' – skilled high-heeled shoes, an undulant bottom. It was Ibrahim.

'Victor! Come down at once!'

Soon, subdued, they sought their car and drove home. Nabby Adams drove. He was excessively careful, old-womanishly apprehensive – 'What's this man going to do now? Is he going to turn here or go straight on? I wish that bugger would make up his mind. Is this woman going to cross or isn't she?' – but soon he steered the Abelard into the lighted porch of Light House. There was a pause. Then Nabby Adams said:

'Do you mind if I come up and have a drink of water? I'm parched.'

They went up. Nabby Adams was given a warm bottle of Tiger beer. Alladad Khan sat meditating, his head in his hands. Nabby Adams spoke long rumbling Urdu to him. Alladad Khan groaned occasional answers. Fenella suddenly burst into tears and ran into the bedroom. Crabbe followed.

'What's the matter, dear?'

'Oh, it's no good, no good,' she wailed. 'You try to mix with them and they take, they take . . .'

'Yes, dear?'

'. . . Advantage. Just because I'm the only white woman there. They think . . . They think . . .'

'Yes, dear?'

'. . . I'm a whore or something. And they start fights.' She wailed to the cobwebbed ceiling.

'Never mind, dear.' Crabbe held her sweating, shaking body in his arms.

'They wouldn't do it . . . to the others.' She sniffed up tears. 'It would be all *mem, mem*, no *mem* . . .'

'It doesn't mean anything, dear.'

'I'm going home,' said Fenella. 'I can't stand it. They're all bad . . . all bad.'

'We'll discuss this afterwards, dear,' said Crabbe. 'Now just wipe your eyes and come and say good night to these two.'

When Crabbe went back to his guests, his guests were no longer there. Or so it seemed. But then he heard pulsing contented snores from the veranda. On the planter's chair Nabby Adams was stretched, overlapping greatly, asleep in crumpled shirt and slacks. He stirred, grunting, aware in his sleep of a presence, opened leathery eyelids and said a little in Urdu. Then he opened his eyes wider and said, 'Just five minutes.' He closed them again, settled more comfortably to snore. It was the first of many five-minute naps, stretched by the principle of the relativity of time to dawn or near-dawn, he was to take in that house. From the lavatory loud retchings could be heard, prayers, moans, repentance. 'Him,' said Nabby Adams in his sleep. 'His art up.'

Fenella came in to say good-night to her guests. She saw and heard.

'Oh, it's too bad,' she wailed.

Nabby Adams groaned and requested silence in dream-Urdu.

'Too bad,' she cried. 'They take advantage all the time. I'm going back on the next boat.'

'Never mind, dear,' said Crabbe.

In the lavatory Alladad Khan heard; his heart was torn by the tears of beauty in distress. But he could do nothing now, nothing. He rested his sweating head on the cold wall-tiles. That he, a Khan, should have behaved so, should have betrayed his name, his race. And he had meant that tonight should be so different. Laughter and politeness and attentiveness and a few drinks. A few drinks. In agony he retched, bringing his heart up.

7

Undulating through the market, who so gay as Ibrahim? He, in crepitating silk, hair-clips holding curls in place, basket swinging, fist clutched tightly round two crumpled dollar notes, went to do the morning's shopping.

The market was covered, dark and sweltering. Ibrahim had to mince delicately along foul aisles between rows of ramshackle stalls. Old women crouched over bags of Siamese rice, skeps of red and green peppers, purple egg-plants, bristly rambutans, pineapples, durians. Flies buzzed over fish and among the meat bones, ravaged, that lay for the cats to gnaw. Here and there an old man slept on his stall with, for bedfellows, skinny dressed chickens or dried fish-strips. One vendor had pillowed his head on a wash-bowl full of bruised apples. Thin, pot-bellied Chinese blew cigarette-ash on to sheep carcases or tight white cabbages. The air was all smell – curry-stuff, durian, fish and flesh – and the noise was of hoicking and chaffering. Ibrahim loved the market.

Ibrahim greeted his friends gaily, provocatively, argued shrilly about the price of golden bananas and horn bananas, bought chillis and half a coconut for curry. He wondered whether he should buy, as a little surprise for *Tuan*, a couple of turtle's eggs, or perhaps a small blue bird in a cage or maybe a toy xylophone. Ibrahim liked giving little presents. Moreover he felt it only right that *Tuan* should get back a bit of the money that he, Ibrahim, regularly stole from *Tuan*'s trousers or from the drawer in the desk. His father had once told him that no good Muslim servant would ever steal from his master. Well, this was not really stealing; it was buying for the house little things that were needed – plastic horses, wax fruit, paper flowers, portraits of film-stars, a brood of ducklings, a tame civet-cat, yellow perfume made in Hong Kong. He, Ibrahim, was entitled to a little commission when he could buy these things more cheaply than his master or mistress. Moreover, Ibrahim often stole things from the School kitchen below. Rice, curry powder and tinned grapes had not cost *Tuan* a penny in the last month. But, in any case, taking money from *Tuan*'s desk or pocket was really a kind of mild sexual outrage, an act of revenge on *Tuan* for being married, having a mistress, and remaining unresponsive to the epicene charms of him, Ibrahim bin Mohamed Salleh.

Ibrahim bin Mohamed Salleh thought he would now have a small bottle of Fraser and Neave's Orange Crush at the open-air drinking-shop that adjoined the market. He watched with pleasure the food-sellers swirling the frying *mee* round in their *kualis* over primitive charcoal fires. He, Ibrahim, had an electric cooker, a nest of bright aluminium saucepans, a day-long-humming refrigerator. He also had a hundred dollars a month, as well as what he made on the side. He was doing very nicely.

Suddenly a black cloud covered the sun and the orange-crush no longer glistened golden. Ibrahim, watching the swirling *mee* in the *kuali*, had suddenly remembered his wife. He blushed, remembering, thinking of how his mother had meant it all for the best, believing that it would make him settle down – settle down! And he then only seventeen years old! – that it would bring his feet to the true one path of Muslim manhood. The marriage had not been a success, naturally. Ibrahim had cried, resisting the rites of the wedding-night. Fatimah, big and heavy-browed, had used the word '*nusus*' against him, one of the strongest of the Islamic terms of opprobrium, normally applicable only to a woman who refuses cohabitation. Ibrahim had run away from his mother's house and found a post in the Malay Regiment Officers' Mess. Fatimah had tracked him down and tried to hit him with a *kuali* in the mess kitchen. Ibrahim had screamed. And escaping later to the post of cook in Tuan Crabbe's household he had once again been discovered. He had pleaded, he had prayed, he had begged her to go back to her people in Johore, he would give her her train-fare, he would make her an allowance. Often, at the evening *waktu*, when he turned towards Mecca, he had voiced a petition to the Deity:

> 'Allah, merciful Allah,
> Please make my wife go back to Johore.'

But Allah had not budged. He had allowed Fatimah to chase him with a carving knife, to scream her wrongs to a cinema queue, when he, Ibrahim, was arm-in-arm with a soldier friend. Only when Ibrahim was at the point of final despair, ready to run amok – that would have been a pity, because he genuinely did not want to kill anybody, especially Tuan Crabbe – only then had she agreed to go to Johore for a short time, to see her parents and tell them of her wrongs. But she had said she would be back. She would be back.

Ibrahim closed his eyes for a minute and prayed, 'Allah, make her go down with a dread disease, make the train crash, make her be killed by the Communists. But please, please do not let her return.'

When he opened his eyes he started violently and spilled some of his orange-crush, for standing before him was a woman. Allah, he had thought for a moment it was she, Fatimah. But it was not; it was the mistress of Tuan Crabbe with, clinging to her hand, a small thin finger-sucking boy.

'Peace be with you.'

'With you be peace.'

'There is a little help you can give me,' she said, sitting down, the child on her knee.

'How? What help?'

'Your master has deserted me.'

'Oh.' Ibrahim crossed his legs, shrugged his shoulders, bunched up his face in a gesture of no sympathy.

117

'I have lost his love.'

'But in that matter I cannot help you, even if I wished to.'

'I have here,' said Rahimah, opening her handbag, 'a thing that will restore that love.' She showed Ibrahim a small phial. 'I obtained this of 'Che Mat the *pawang* in Kelapa. It is a powerful medicine for drawing a man back to one's heart.'

'I have heard of these things,' said Ibrahim indifferently.

'It can be put in drink and has no taste. I ask you to put this in your master's drink. I can pay you a little for this help.'

'But how am I to know that it will not kill him?'

'You have my word and the assurance of the *pawang*. He is a very skilful *pawang* and I am told this medicine has never yet failed.'

'And how much will you give me?'

'Five dollars.'

'It is not enough.'

'Allah, you can have a man axed or knifed for two dollars fifty. Five dollars is enough, nay it is generous, for so small a piece of help.'

Ibrahim fingered the tiny phial. 'And if I am discovered and lose my position?'

'You cannot be discovered.'

Ibrahim thought for a while, sipping his orange crush. There was some very good sarong material in the bazaar, two dollars a *hela*. 'Make it ten dollars,' he said.

'Six.'

'Eight.'

'*Baik-lah*.' She gave him a five-dollar note, two single dollars and a handful of small change. 'You will swear to do this?'

'One does not swear.'

'You will promise?'

'I promise.'

She shook his hand and departed. Ibrahim watched the

118

weaving of her small buttocks, watched the finger-sucking child who clung to her. Women, he thought. They will cling to a man like a liana, like a jungle leech. How he hated women. He looked again at the small phial, uncorked it and smelt the viscous potion. There was no smell. Well, he had promised, but the fulfilment of the promise could be postponed. There was no hurry. He did not like meddling with these things. He thought for a moment of the things that magic had accomplished in this very town. The jealous mistress of the Crown Prince who had made his second wife's hair fall out; the Tamil in the Town Board Offices who had died of a fever induced by image-sucking because he had had a Malay clerk dismissed unfairly; the innumerable wives who had refocillated a dying passion in their husbands; husbands who had regained the love of their wives ...

Allah! Ibrahim cringed and began to sweat. Supposing she ... But Fatimah would not ... Yet she could ... *Allah, Taala*, she might. No, no, no. Allah Most High! It was possible. Even now, in Johore, where, it was well known, there were powerful *pawangs*, she might be brewing something up, something to draw his heart back to hers, to make him *want* to do that horrible obscene thing. ... And again. He swallowed dryly, trembled. She too might seek revenge, regard him as one who had wounded her womanhood by rejecting her advances. She might now be sticking pins in a little wax image of him, Ibrahim bin Mohamed Salleh. *La ilaha illa'lah!*

Ibrahim dropped the deadly phial into the shopping-basket to nest among the red peppers and coconut. To-night he would go to the small shrine by the servants' quarters and place upon it bananas and lighted candles. Good spirits haunted that spot, a loving couple who, long ago, taking a walk there, had been whisked up to Heaven like the Prophet himself. They assuredly would help one of a sinless heart. Whimpering to himself Ibrahim went back to Light House, there to start cooking lunch for *Mem* and *Tuan*.

Already cooking lunch was Fatimah, but not Fatimah binte Razak, wife of Ibrahim bin Mohamed Salleh. This was Fatimah Bibi, wife of Alladad Khan, Police Transport corporal. She had been back a week now, and had found, as she had expected, their quarters in the Police Barracks filthy – floors strewn with cigarette ends, spiders busy in all corners, sheets that had not been to the *dhobi* for weeks. She had reviled her husband while, busy with broom, she had restored order and cleanliness to the tiny quarters. What had he been doing, she would like to know, while she had been close to death's door bearing his child. *His* child, yes, the fruit of his importunity. He had, without doubt, been around the town drinking with his atheistical friends, he had perhaps even been taking sly mouthfuls of pork and godless bacon. She knew him, let him not think she did not. And he had replied, maddeningly, with that shiftless Malay expression. '*Tida' apa.*'

Fatimah Bibi let the curry simmer on the charcoal stove. The chapattis need not be started just yet. She went to the cradle in their bedroom and smiled at the fruit of his, Alladad Khan's, importunity. Little Hadijah Bibi lay in milk-fed baby bliss. Fatimah Bibi frowned when she remembered that her husband had said, when she had first fed the child in his presence, that she reminded him of the second *Surah* of the Koran. She had smiled at first, thinking that perhaps he perceived in her something of the holiness of Muslim motherhood. Then she had recalled the sub-title of the second *Surah* – *Al Baqarah*: The Cow. Her strong face, ruddered with a nose that bespoke will in long line and flared nostril, took on an expression that boded no good for him, Alladad Khan. Thank Allah that the women of the Punjab had been reared in no submissive tradition, unlike their sisters of Malaya and the Arab lands. Alladad Khan must be brought to heel. His spending-money must be strictly rationed; so must the pleasure he sought from her in bed. The withholding of that, the granting of that: therein lay woman's power. And again she could always invoke that paragon, her brother. He had done well, he spoke English, he had a commanding presence, he had the will to succeed. She did not believe Alladad Khan when he told her that Abdul Khan had once been taken home drunk from a party in Sungai Kajar. Nor did she believe the stories of a love affair with an English girl when he had been at the Police College. Abdul Khan would do the right thing always, keeping himself pure till a girl came along who had those qualities he revered in his sister. A girl of the clan, naturally, a good Muslim, demurely beautiful, a good manager, frugal, controlled, intelligent.

Hadijah Bibi began to cry, beating tiny fists, kicking little brown legs ringleted with fat. Fatimah Bibi picked up the child, soothing in Punjabi, crooning in Punjabi, holding to her strong body, her big breasts, the brown mite she had borne for him, Alladad Khan.

Who now entered, calling:

'It would seem that this child is like her mother, always complaining.'

Fatimah Bibi turned on him, but, suddenly guilty, remembered that she had not yet cooked the chapattis.

'Here, nurse the child. You should have warned me you would come in early for tiffin. It is not nearly ready.'

'I am no earlier,' said Alladad Khan, 'and no later than usual. Heaven forbid that I should so far forget myself as to come home early.'

'Take the child and do not drop her. That,' said Fatimah Bibi, as she handed over the precious brown burden, 'is no way to hold a child. You show no love for her. You handle her as you would handle a carburettor.'

'A carburettor is a useful thing. Without it a car will not go.'

'May God punish you for such sayings,' said Fatimah Bibi, as she went to the kitchen.

Alladad Khan, left alone, dandled unhandily his child in unfatherly arms. He wanted to finger his moustache, but could not. Allah, two women in the house now, both, as is the way of women, ready to rule one's last drop of blood. The child cried loudly, and Alladad Khan said to it quietly, 'Bloody liar. Bastard.' But no, that last word could not be used in this context. He had discovered its meaning, had found it in Hari Singh's little dictionary. Hari Singh. Alladad Khan's face darkened. Still unpunished, still unrepentant. A fortnight had passed since Hari Singh had committed this unforgivable, filthily libidinous act. Yet how could he, Alladad Khan, approach the matter directly? For he must give no inkling to his subordinates of his deep self-interest in the ethical issue. He had said to Hari Singh, 'It is unseemly for you to behave in that way with a white woman.' And he had replied, 'Let us have no hypocrisy, Corporal. You would do the same had you the courage. Are they not women like other women, with this difference however: that as the cinema shows us, they are much more accessible and, for that matter, much more wanton than our own women are? She did not protest, that is quite certain.'

'That is because she is a lady and would not, as is the way of the English, exhibit her feelings in public. But to me she expressed shame and abhorrence. Indeed, she wept.'

'She wept? In your presence? That argues some degree of intimacy.'

'She was overcome, she could hold back tears no longer. And that added to her shame.'

'It is time that the white man and the white woman wept. God knows that they have many wrongs to repent of, wrongs committed in our country in the name of the British Raj. And even now India is not free, at least the Sikhs are not. If there is Pakistan, why have not we our Sikhistan?' And so on

Alladad Khan had been harsh in his official dealings with Hari Singh, and Hari Singh had reported Alladad Khan, complaining of injustice and tyranny. Alladad Khan had been gently reprimanded. It was all very difficult. But, Allah, the time would come.

'What are you doing to that poor child to make her cry so?' complained his wife from the kitchen. Indeed, the weeping and howling had not ceased, had increased rather. Alladad Khan realized why; he had been tightening his grip on the child's small body, as on the neck of Hari Singh.

'Be quiet,' said Alladad Khan indifferently. He rocked the child to and fro like a cocktail-shaker. Soon the child, in the middle of a frog-mouthed yell, decided to stop breathing. Alladad Khan became frightened, ran with the baby to the kitchen. His wife took the precious, precious mite as it drank in a pint of air and began screaming again.

'My baby, my jewel, my precious little one. Oh, what a cruel father you have, my sweet one.' The child howled agreement.

'*Tida' apa*,' said Alladad Khan, and began smoothing his moustache.

The baby quietened and laid again in its cradle, the two sat down to tiffin. Alladad Khan had little appetite. He dutifully broke off a piece of chapatti and bathed it in the rather watery curry. Since that meal at the Crabbes he had begun to fancy more exotic food. Langsheer hodpod, or something like that, had been the name of that dish. Exciting, full of meat, rich in gravy. No rice, no chapattis. He said to his wife:

'Why must we have always, every day, the same food? Bread at midday and rice at night. Always the same. No variety, no surprise.'

Acidly she said, her mouth stained with curry sauce, 'I suppose you have developed a taste for pig's flesh while I have been away. I suppose you will not be satisfied till you have for your tiffin a pork chop and a glass of beer, and for your evening meal a piece of fried bacon and a bottle of whisky. God forgive you. I dread to think of the influence you will be having on the child.'

He said evenly, 'The menu you suggest lacks variety, but it would perhaps be a little more interesting than the eternal curry and rice, curry and chapattis I seem to be condemned to eat.'

As she was eating with her fingers there was nothing to slam down on the table. But she rose, terrible in her wrath, and reviled him bitterly.

'You were bad enough when I went away, but Allah knows that you are now more like an unclean spirit than a man. You are making my life a hell. You have no love in you, no fatherly feeling, none of the qualities of a husband except an unwholesome lust which has given me more pain than I can describe, the pain of bearing you a child which you will not love, which, it seems, you are even trying to kill. I was a fool to marry you.'

'You had no choice. Nor had I. Your brother was determined to get you off his hands and marry you to the first Khan who came along. You did not think yourself a fool then.' Alladad Khan pointed with a trembling arm to the wedding portrait – the strong nose, the smiling teeth, the arm laid on the knee of the shy bridegroom. 'You did not think me then a devil out of hell. Allah knows I did not wish to give up my freedom. I was bludgeoned into marriage, I was told I was betraying the clan if I remained single while you were panting for a husband. And if I had not married you, if I had waited . . .'

The baby had started crying again. Alladad Khan looked gloomily down at the cold curry, the broken bits of chapatti while his wife ran in to the bedroom, crying soothing words.

Tida' apa. No, that would not do any more. He longed for the evening, longed to be with Victor Crabbe and Fenella Crabbe. Strangely, not just with her, but with both of them. He was beginning to understand certain things now, things that he hoped would clarify themselves in time and, for some reason, with their help.

Alladad Khan composed himself, shrugged, twisted his moustache. He picked up his beret from the chair and buckled on his belt. He then went over to the Police Canteen and sat for half an hour over a cup of coffee and

Hari Singh's little book. He mouthed quietly to himself:

'This is a man. He is a big man. Is he a man? Yes, he is a man. Is he a big man? . . .'

Among the billiards-players and dicers, oblivious of the talk and the rattle of cups, he, Alladad Khan, the student of English, sat alone, proud, indifferent, misunderstood longing for the evening.

8

Nabby Adams was by no means of a mean nature; he just
lacked the means to be generous. As time passed and he
enjoyed more and more of the hospitality of the Crabbes
Nabby Adams began to be tortured by guilt. The gin he
had drunk, the bottles of beer, the odd reviving nip of
brandy, the meals he had eaten, the cinemas visited, the
petrol consumed, all at the expense of Victor Crabbe, began to clamour – though long vapourized, forgotten or
digested – for more substantial return than mere gratitude.

'Thanks very much. You've looked after me and him
real good.'

'You've saved my life, really you have. I've stopped
shaking now. I think I can go back to the office.'

'You know, that's the only thing I've been craving for
in the eating line: a bit of gorgonzola and an onion and a
couple of beers.'

'I had a real good sleep there, Mrs Crabbe. It's funny,
I can always sleep in your house, any time of the day or
night. I toss and turn all the time when I'm in the Mess.'

'I've been parched for that all morning, Victor.
Couldn't do no work for thinking about it.'

No, such expressions of gratitude were not enough. It
was time he did something for the Crabbes. Once or twice
he had brought a bottle of *samsu*, or Alladad Khan had
purchased a small bottle of gin, and these offerings had
been carried through hordes of small schoolboys, wide-
eyed with interest, to the flat at the top of the stairs. But
debts were growing, and Alladad Khan was finding it
more and more difficult to extract money from the savings-

box, even though his wife believed that the key had been lost. In the still watches she would stir and wake and ask of the stealthy naked figure that groped under the bed:

'What are you doing, disturbing me and the child with your noise?'

'I had a dream that someone was trying to steal the money-box. Thank Allah, it is still there.'

No, money must be obtained from somewhere, and legitimately at that. One of Nabby Adams's tasks was to inspect vehicles – whether military, police or civilian – that had been involved in accidents, with a view to establishing material evidence of structural flaw or integrity that could be used in court. The Chinese owners would delicately hint that, if the police-lieutenant could bring himself to state that the brakes were quite in order, he should find that he had a new friend, a true friend, a friend indeed. And it frequently happened that the brakes were in order, and Nabby Adams would say so. Then he would be offered – 'Do you smoke, Lieutenant?' – a cigarette-tin crammed with ten-dollar notes, and, groaning, Nabby Adams would have to refuse. Or, more delicate, more diabolic, 'I should be glad to maintain an account for you, Lieutenant, in any drinking-shop you care to name.' Oh, the temptation, the temptation. But it was too bloody risky. And now sundry creditors were saying that they would be quite willing to accept payment in police petrol. Nabby Adams had nearly fallen, but six feet eight inches of integrity had reared itself heavenwards just in time. Oh, the suffering, the crucifixion.

How to get some money, legitimately. Nabby Adams had insisted once that they all go to Timah races together. He had had a few hot tips from a grateful Chinese owner-driver. And so, borrowing cards of membership of the Lanchap Turf Club, they had gone, the four of them, to sit in a dilatation of hope, a contraction of despair, a perisystole of speculation. And all the bloody horses had gone down the drain, all except those backed by their Chinese neighbours on the crammed stand. They, quacking and chirping with winners' joy, had been reviled by Nabby Adams in deep grumbling Urdu, until Alladad Khan had had to say:

'*Ap khuch karah bolta.*'

'And I'll say some bloody worse things if those buggers don't keep quiet.'

To make matters worse, it was only Crabbe who had really lost, for neither Alladad Khan nor Nabby Adams had five dollars – the minimum stake – between them. After the gloomy day, money thrown down the drain, they had had to go and have a drink somewhere, and then Mrs Crabbe had started on Victor Crabbe:

'We haven't got all that much money, you know. Wasting it all on horses and then beer, and then ... Oh, it's too bad, too bad.' And then the three men had sat in gloomy silence over their beer while she snivelled into a tiny handkerchief. 'It's too bad. I'm going home on the next boat.'

'Well, go home then.'

'I will, I will.'

Nabby Adams had felt very guilty; it had all been his fault.

Nabby Adams bought monthly a lottery ticket, but he had no real hope of winning anything. That first prize – $350,000 – was a mere fable, something you pretended to believe in, like them stories in the Bible about the age of Methuselah and what-not, but which you knew deep down didn't really, couldn't really, be true.

In desperation, Nabby Adams had nearly thought of marriage. There was an old Malay woman in the town who wanted desperately to marry, because she believed that spinsters were not accepted in Heaven. She had a nice little sum tucked way. It meant that Nabby Adams would have to embrace the Muslim faith, but that wouldn't have mattered. He could still drink, like Alladad Khan, who was a bloody poor advertisement for the faith, did. But Nabby Adams could see himself as a turbaned *haji*, turning up shocked eyes at bottles of Tiger and *samsu*, far more easily than he could see himself as a married man. It was all very difficult.

And yet Nabby Adams continued to accept the hospitality of the Crabbes. A fantastic pattern of sodality began to emerge. When somebody had some money there was drinking in one of them little *kedais*. There they would sit, over their Tiger or Anchor or Carlsberg, while the flying ants beat against the naked electric bulb and the mosquitoes took tiny sips of the blood of Mrs Crabbe. Around them the gawping locals sat, amazed with an amazement that never grew less, drinking in with their syrupy coffee or tepid mineral-water the strange spectacle of the huge rumbling man with the jaundiced complexion, the neat Punjabi fingering his ample moustache, the pale schoolmaster, the film-star woman with the honeyed skin and the golden hair. Three languages rapped, fumbled or rumblingly oozed all the while. At these sessions Nabby Adams spoke only Urdu and English, Alladad Khan only Urdu and Malay, the Crabbes only English and a little Malay. And so it was always, 'What did you say then?' 'What did he say?' 'What did all that mean?'

A question would be put to Alladad Khan through Nabby Adams. Alladad Khan would hurl, expressively, eyes flashing and melting, shoulders emphasizing, out of a sincere mouth the long answer. Then Nabby Adams would translate:

'He says he don't know.'

Sometimes they would go to the cinema and, tortured by bugs, watch a long Hindustani film about Baghdad, magic horses that talked and flew, genies in bottles, swordplay, sundered love. Alladad Khan would translate the Hindustani into Malay and Nabby Adams, before he slept, would forget himself and translate the Hindustani into Urdu. Or perhaps they would go to see an American film and Fenella Crabbe would translate the American into Malay and Nabby Adams would, before he slept, translate what he understood of it into Urdu.

Many an evening they would return to the flat and then

Nabby Adams would say, 'Just five minutes,' and sleep till dawn on the planter's chair. Crabbe himself, aware of early work next day, would go to bed, leaving Alladad Khan and Fenella alone. The curious thing was that, now, Alladad Khan had no further desire to win the lady's heart. The two would sit on the veranda, talking interminably in broken Malay and broken English, and Alladad Khan began to see at last what was the relationship he desired.

It was rather complicated. He, alone, was seeking others who were alone. He was the only Khan for many states around who had come here, an exile, to live among alien races. His wife was a Malayan, born in Penang; Abdul Khan had seen England and France, but not the Punjab. Alladad Khan saw in Fenella Crabbe also an exile, cut off from her own country, cut off from the white community — alone, she had walked in the sweating heat, while the insolent cars of Government officers bore languid wives to the Club and the shops in Timah. Something was crystallizing in Alladad Khan's mind, and the time had come to unlade the burden, haltingly, though the cranes and hoists of language creaked and broke. And she, Fenella Crabbe, took gently the burden from him, questioning, drawing out.

'Why did you join the Army at thirteen?'

'I ran away from home.'

'Why did you do that?'

'It was my mother's fault. She insisted that I marry this girl, and I did not wish to marry her.'

'But surely thirteen is young to marry?'

'From my earliest days it had been arranged, perhaps even before I was born. The two families were to be united through a marriage. And when I was a small boy I was made to play with this girl, though I hated her. It was always intended that we should marry, but I would have died sooner than marry her. Even now I can say that.'

'Did you not want to marry at all?'

130

'How can one say at that age? But there was one other girl whom I believed I loved, and now, when it is too late, I am sure I loved her. We were at school together and, even when we were only twelve, we would meet and I would give her small presents. And one day I went and poured my heart out to an aunt, an aunt I thought I could trust. But she told everything to my mother. One day I came home from school and threw my books, as was my custom, into the four corners of the living-room. And, unsuspecting as I was, my mother turned on me, reproaching me, and forbidding me ever to see this other girl again. Then, just as I was, I walked out of the house and went to the recruiting-office, stating my age wrong. Thus I became a soldier.'

'And the girl you loved?'.

'She said she would wait, for ever if need be. I wrote letters and she answered. We were to marry. Then one letter came from my mother saying that she had married someone else, and that she did not want to hear from me again. And, indeed, no further letters came from her. That was because, I later discovered, they had told a similar story to her. And so I married here in Malaya. A month after my marriage I got a letter from my brother, telling me the whole story, and also a letter from this one I loved. But then it was all too late. We Punjabis do not divorce like other Muslims. When we have married a wife we cling to her only, remembering our duty.' Alladad Khan, at this point, began to cry. Fenella, shocked and overcome with pity, put her arms round him, comforting. Meanwhile Nabby Adams, prone on the planter's chair, snored on. Only those sounds in the still Malayan night: the sobbing, the inadequate words of comfort, the gentle snore of the big broken man.

Fenella Crabbe talked less now about going back to England on the next boat. She had responsibilities. Alladad Khan had opened his heart to her, the great motherless wreck of Nabby Adams had to be helped and, as Fenella was a woman, reformed.

But Nabby Adams appealed to another side of her, the bookish side. He fascinated her, he seemed a walking myth: Prometheus with the eagles of debt and drink pecking at his liver; Adam himself bewildered and Eveless outside the Garden; a Minotaur howling piteously in a labyrinth of money worries. She treasured each cliché of his, each serious anecdote of his early life, she even thought of compiling his sayings in a book of aphorisms.

'I don't bath very much here, but I had a bloody good wash on the boat coming over.'

'I mean, when you've been out with one of them tarts you look at yourself careful for a few days after, don't you, Mrs Crabbe?'

'Like yourself, Mrs Crabbe, I'm no angel. But I don't ask much. Like yourself. A couple of dozen bottles of Tiger every day and I'm quite happy. As it might be yourself, Mrs Crabbe.'

'He's nothing but a load of old shit. I mean, what else can you call him, Mrs Crabbe? There's no other way of putting it, is there?'

'I bet you was dying for that, Mrs Crabbe.' (The first queasy drink of the morning after.)

And the stories about the time when he was an undertaker's assistant. 'Well, this one had a wig, see. But I couldn't get it to stick on his head when I was laying him out in his shroud. So I called downstairs, "Mr Protheroe, have you got a bit of glue?" And then I said, "It's all right, I've found a couple of drawing-pins."' And other stories about Nabby Adams in the Northampton shoe-factory, and Nabby Adams the bookmaker's clerk, and Nabby Adams of India.

But what was Nabby Adams? She could not believe that his first name was really Abel. And the genesis of Nabby Adams. Did he really have an Indian mother, or a Eurasian father? These characters emerged in his stories as salty Northamptonshire rurals. His father had been a sexton, his mother a good hand with pastry and curing a ham. At the core of Nabby Adams lay a mystery never to be solved.

'I'm not one for church, Mrs Crabbe, but I do like a good im.'

'A good . . .?'

'Im.'

Fenella Crabbe submitted Nabby Adams to all kinds of curious experiments. She played Bach to him on the gramophone, and he said:

'That's very clever, Mrs Crabbe. You can hear five different tunes going on at the same time.'

She read to him and Alladad Khan the whole of Mr Eliot's *The Waste Land*, and Nabby Adams said:

'He's got that wrong about the pack of cards, Mrs Crabbe. There isn't no card called The Man With Three Staves. That card what he means is just an ordinary three, like as it may be the three of clubs.'

And when they came to the dark thunder-speaking finale of the poem, Alladad Khan had nodded gravely.

'Datta. Dayadhvam. Damyata.
Shantih. Shantih. Shantih.'

'He says he understands that bit, Mrs Crabbe. He says that's what the thunder says.'

Inexhaustible. Often Fenella cursed, cried, sent him away in disgrace. As, for instance, when he got up early, stole unbeknown to the drink-cupboard, and finished a whole bottle of gin before breakfast. Or when he fell up the stairs with the shocked boys of Light House looking on, saying:

'I've had it, Mrs Crabbe. I must have a sleep and a drop of something. I can't go back to the office like this.'

But there was nobody like him. Fenella Crabbe forgot about the Film Society in Timah, and she never saw *The Cabinet of Dr Caligari, Metropolis, Les Visiteurs du Soir* or *Sang d'un Poète. Tida' apa.*

9

'She would insist on coming,' said Nabby Adams. 'There wasn't doing nothing with her, yelling the house down. And by the time me and him had put her out of the car three or four times, we thought she might as well come. Although,' said Nabby Adams, 'I've got to agree she smells a bit. I hope you don't mind, Mrs Crabbe. She hasn't had a bath for a month or two. I haven't had a chance to give her one.'

'Did she have a bloody good wash on the boat coming out here?' asked Crabbe.

'Oh, she didn't come out with me,' said Nabby Adams seriously. 'She's not my dog at all. She belonged to the bloke before me. I took her over when I took his room over, see.'

'She's a nice-looking dog,' said Fenella, patting the heavy matted black hair. 'What do you call her?'

'Her name's Cough,' said Nabby Adams apologetically. 'That's all she'll answer to. I suppose the other bloke was always telling her to get from under his feet, or something like that.'

'I don't quite see that,' said Fenella.

Crabbe explained in a quick whisper. Blushing, she saw.

'We'll have to be pushing off now,' said Nabby Adams, 'if we're going to get back tonight.' He spoke Urdu to Alladad Khan who sat, bereted and uniformed, in the driver's seat. Alladad Khan produced a revolver from the cubby hole. '*Achcha,*' said Nabby Adams. 'He's got his, anyway.'

'Is it a bad road?' asked Fenella.

'There's a bad stretch,' said Nabby Adams. 'About nine miles. I shouldn't let it worry you, Mrs Crabbe, though.' Nabby Adams sat down with Crabbe on the back seat. The dog crawled all over him, licking, nuzzling, finally subsiding, grunting with content, on his knees. 'I reckon what will be will be. It stands to reason. If you don't get a bullet in your guts today you'll get run over tomorrow.' Fenella sat next to Alladad Khan.

It was Friday, the Muslim Sabbath and a free day at the School. They were going to Gila, a little town on the State border, where Nabby Adams had to inspect vehicles. Nabby Adams, unable to repay hospitality in any other way, had thought up this treat for the Crabbes. Bandits on the road and a small town whose Malay name meant 'mad'. But there were a few *kedais* on the way where Nabby Adams owed comparatively small sums. He would buy them a couple of beers. The least he could do.

'Are you sure we can get back tonight?' asked Crabbe. 'It's a long way.'

'You'll be back in time to have a good night's rest before your Sports Day,' said Nabby Adams. 'Don't you worry about that.'

Lolling back in his commandeered car, Crabbe thought about Sports Day. There was going to be trouble. He sensed that Boothby would not be yawning very much when that day was over. He had been hearing whispers, catching out boys in conspiratorial nods and glances. The time had, perhaps, come, the full-dress occasion for revenge, for striking back at the tyrannical British. He knew that something was going to happen, but precisely what he could not say. A genuine revolt? The long knives? The cremation of the School buildings?

The morning was dark, heavy-clouded and humid. Alladad Khan spoke to the windscreen a long Urdu speech. Nabby Adams listened contemptuously. 'He says he thinks it's going to rain,' he translated. 'But what does he know about it, I'd like to know. I know what he really means. He wants to push on, so he can get back to his wife and child tonight. He doesn't want me to start boozing any-where. Anyway,' said Nabby Adams, 'we'll christen the journey, so to speak. That *kedai* there, just up that road.'

In the *kedai*, a squalid hut where chickens ran and a goat waved its placid beard, there were some Sikhs, hap-pily drinking from a bottle of high-grade *samsu*. They begged the newcomers to join their party, smiling fatly behind their beards. But Alladad Khan was stern. One bottle only. Nabby Adams spoke eloquently, protesting, reviling, but Alladad Khan was adamant. They had to push on. He looked out through the dirty window at the dirty sky, clouds moving sluggishly in heavy coils.

'Who does he think he is?' said Nabby Adams. 'Order-ing his superiors about. Just because he's taken a bit of money out of his wife's saving-box he thinks he can bloody well rule me. Well, he can't.' But, meekly enough, he drank his warm beer, and, as the sky darkened yet further, consented to continue the long journey.

'Are the people really different up there?' asked Fenella. Cool libraries with anthropology sections were in her head. She automatically saw form in her mind the exor-dium of a stock monograph: 'The aborigines of the Upper Lanchap present, ethnologically and culturally, a very dif-ferent picture from the inhabitants of the coastal areas . . .'

'You'll see some of them,' said Nabby Adams. 'With blowpipes and stark ballock-naked.' Off his guard, trying to stem his dog's elaborate affection, he had let that out. Shocked, he began to apologize, but soon desisted. It was no good. He had no drawing-room talents. He had better shut up. Gloomily he closed his eyes and watched the figures dance and leer at him:

Bung Cheong	$157
Heng Seng	$39

He dozed liverishly. In his dream he was drinking in Bombay, paying for rounds with ample rupees. So grateful were his drinking companions that they came closer to him, speaking in happy pants their thirsty gratitude, and

136

one black-bearded drinker licked him wetly, juicily, on the nose. With deep grumbles, he pushed the dog away. As they rolled on, under the heavy sky, past the rubber trees and squalid villages, Crabbe slept a little too. He had not been sleeping well lately. When, at two or three in the morning, he sank into deep exhausted oblivion he always had to fight his way out from a cold coffin of water, and, waking, seek a cigarette and a book, scared of yielding again to those deceptive arms.

Alladad Khan and Fenella spoke softly together, in slow Malay garnished with a few English words. She was learning fast to understand him, to make herself understood.

'She is wearing me down,' said Alladad Khan. 'When I am out late she wants to know where I have been. She will not believe me when I say I have been on duty. Now she is saying that I have been seen with a European woman, and she cries and calls me bad names, and now she is asking her brother to try and arrange for me to be transferred into his district so that he can see what I am doing all the time. It is becoming hell.'

'Be master,' said Fenella. 'Tell her you will do what you like. You owe nothing to her. You do not even . . .'

'But there is the question of responsibility, of duty. I married her, I have to consider her.'

'If she starts whining or complaining again you must try hitting her.'

'A man should not hit a woman.'

'A woman sometimes welcomes a blow. She always knows when it is deserved.'

'You open my eyes,' said Alladad Khan.

The rain, like a football crowd, was waiting to charge and rush at the opening of the gates. The jungle that stood back sullenly and threateningly to let the road go through looked defiled and clotted in the thickening light. Mist rested half-way up the mountains. Soon the rain started in an orchestral roar.

'This will make us late,' said Alladad Khan. 'It becomes hard to see and the roads quickly become flooded.' The windscreen wipers swished softly and monotonously, like, thought Alladad Khan, like himself rocking that baby. Left to right to left to right to left. The car soon seemed islanded in water. The two at the back awoke to heavy wetness on their faces, and all the windows were shut tight. Still the water soaked in and the car floor was thinly flooded. Nabby Adams was monotonous in grumbling Urdu, swinging the deep words from left to right to left to right to left.

'We'll have to stop soon,' he said. 'We're not far off Tomcat or whatever it's called.'

'Tongkat?'

'Yes, Tomcat. There's a couple of *kedais* there. We can wait till the rain stops.' Thirst began to oppress Nabby Adams heavily. The dry mouth after the unrefreshing nap, the heat in the car, airless, the steamed windows fast battened.

Gloom sat at the next table when, the car parked in a rain-pool among jubilant ducks, they rested their elbows on the clammy marbled top and waited for beer. The rain lashed and swished and emptied down, drinking the drab land with a dropsical passion.

'I think,' said Nabby Adams, 'we'd all better go into silent prayer.' Suddenly, unbidden, a memory congealed in his mind of himself as sexton's assistant pumping the organ on Good Friday, long ago. The trees had wept, the gravestones sluiced in the spring flood. And all the time himself pumping away and then, in the last chorus of Stainer's *Crucifixion*, he had decided to leave off, to hell with it, and he left the organist stranded in mid-chord, the air groaning out to nothingness, like the air coming out of a corpse in a moan when you lift it to wash its back.

'Father, forgive them,' said Nabby Adams, 'for they know not what they do.' The dog came to lick his hand and then, smelling of old tinned peaches, tried to climb on his lap. They drank their flat washy bottled beer, and Nabby Adams felt a twinge of heartburn.

'The bloody price of it,' he said with sudden passion. He

thought of India, and forgot that it ever rained in India.

Crabbe looked at the 'No Spitting' notice on the wall and his head swam with the absurdity of four languages telling people not to spit, all on the same notice. A thin Chinese bathing girl beckoned from a calendar. From behind her, in the swimming open kitchen, came the noise of painful expectoration.

'Get it up,' said Nabby Adams, 'even if it's only a bloody bucketful.'

The gleeful savage rain knifed the road again and again and big-drummed on the tin roof and gargled and choked gaily in the gutters.

'Sometimes,' said Fenella, 'one could wish one were dead.'

Alladad Khan made a speech. They must push on. Nabby Adams felt a twinge of tooth-ache.

'Do you want something to eat first?' asked Crabbe. They looked at the plates ranged temptingly on the table before them, covered with cloudy plastic bells. There were some cakes of a sick pink colour, little red jellies made in tumbler-moulds, pallid round blobs of dough containing a cold core of minced goat's liver. They each peeled in silence a tiny banana, ingesting it like a medicine. Nabby Adams felt further twinges in tooth and duodenum.

The rain pounced on them like a pack of big wet dogs as they sought their islanded car. Push on. The rain became their world; they gaped out from their windowed tank, swishing through floods, at the drowned jungle and huts and swimming rice-fields. The road was theirs alone. No other vehicle was to be seen as they squelched on to Gila. Perhaps they had missed the announcement? Perhaps the living and the newly-risen dead had all been instructed to report at some great town of stilled factories and parked cars, no more to be used, for there, at the zenith, in the rain of the Last Day, He stood in His glory, flanked by seraphic trumpeters? And they and that witless hoicking *towkay* had missed it all, swilling beer without relish, the four of them, miles from life and the end of life.

They carried guilt, like an extra spare-wheel, in the boot.

Miraculously, in mid-afternoon, they found themselves running out of the rain-belt. They were still twenty miles from Gila. The sky was clearer, the roads dryer, there were people still alive, walking through villages, cycling, even driving an occasional car. Thankfully they wound down the windows. But they must push on, climbing steeply now.

'We're coming to it, now,' said Nabby Adams. 'Just our bloody luck, in a way. The terrorists don't come out much when it's raining. We could have done with rain here, not back there.' Behind them they could almost hear still the fierce sky-flood.

Fenella was feeling sick. Not frightened, just sick. Sick with the car-journey, sick with a little fever. But she couldn't ask them to stop, not now, not just yet. Though, in response to a long piece of Urdu from Nabby Adams, Alladad Khan was stopping . . .

'Let him handle the gun,' said Nabby Adams. 'I'll drive through this stretch.'

Should she ask them to wait a little while, just to allow her to go over there by the side of the road, so that she could . . .? But they would think she was frightened.

'Doesn't do to stop here really,' said Nabby Adams. 'Ambush here the other week. We should have changed over farther back down the road. He should have reminded me. It's his gun. Let him use it, if he has to.'

Fenella felt sicker. They now entered sheer pack jungle, the road winding through in wide curves, almost seeming to double back on itself. Speed was impossible. As Nabby Adams cautiously turned the wheel his dog woke up to the realization that her place was there, at the front, with him. She fought and squirmed from the holds of Alladad Khan and Crabbe and vaulted clumsily over to lie down at her master's feet, with the brakes and gear-lever. Nabby Adams started violently and, in a flood of violent speech, nearly drove the car into vast jungle clumps of torrid vegetation. She tried to climb on his knee. There was a struggle to remove her. Fenella held her shaking, panting body to her own, her sick nostrils full of dog-smell. Nabby Adams drove on slowly.

'It's a bad patch, this,' he said. 'You never know where they'll be. Sometimes they lay a bloody big tree-trunk across the road. Then you know you've had it. Stop it,' he said, as the dog stretched painfully to lick his nose.

Another mile. And another. The jungle was terribly silent. The road ran sluggishly between the deep beds of lianas, hacked out of sweating, breathless, obscene, sunless greenery. The tree-tops could not be seen. The sky was choked by the tangled limbs and fingers of parasite growths which choked and sucked their sky-high hosts. There was no noises. Only a snake wormed across in front of them, then swam like a fish through the green sea of jungle floor. Another mile. And another. Alladad Khan, his gun ready to aim, suddenly saw himself, Alladad Khan, in a film, his gun ready to aim. Ha! How far away she seemed, she and her squalling milky brat. Adventure. He heard the atmospheric music of the soundtrack.

Another mile. 'What's that?' Crabbe rapped. A movement behind a tree, a shaking of parasite leaves.

'A bloody monkey,' said Nabby Adams.

Another mile. Fenella would have to, here and now, never mind what they thought, if only she could get hold of her handkerchief . . . The dog gave her a gamy kiss.

Another mile. Not a sound, only the engine and the slow tyres and the breathing. Now it was like going into the horrible essence of green life, shut in by it, annihilating all that's made . . .

They turned and came into clearer road. They could see the sky. The jungle was retreating. 'We're through now,' said Nabby Adams. 'We're all right now. Thank Christ for that. God,' he added, 'I'd give my left bloody leg for a nice bottle of Tiger.'

Fenella said, shaken, 'Would you mind stopping, just for a minute? I've got to . . .'

By the side of the road the three men ministered to her, encouraged her.

'Get it up,' said Nabby Adams. 'Go on, all up. Think of one of them pink cakes in that shop.'

Behind them the jungle crouched, impotent now, locked in its cage again.

10

Ibrahim was nearly ready to depart. He had the flat to himself today and ample leisure to gather together his *barang* and choose a few keepsakes from the possessions of his master and mistress. Aminah, the *amah*, had been given two days off to visit a sick aunt in Taiping. So, with only the pounding rain for company, Ibrahim ruled for a few hours the decaying Residency and sensually had his will of it.

It was better that he should go. Worry had been wearing him down to the bone these last few weeks. It was better that he should go and hide himself in a place where his wife could not find him, whose location the Johore *pawangs* could not fix. He had been lucky to meet the fat planter from down the Timah road. He had met him in the cinema. Ibrahim knew the fat planter well, had often seen him in the company of a fair young man from the Drainage and Irrigation Department. But lately the fair young man had been seen much in the company of a new man, a white faced Customs officer with innocent glasses on his tiny nose, and Ibrahim surmised that the fat planter was hurt and lonely. He had told Ibrahim so and offered him the post of cook and friend in his big empty bungalow on the huge estate. No one surely, thought Ibrahim, would ever find him there. There was an estate shop and, three miles away, a small *kampong*, and, if Ibrahim should wish to taste the pleasures of civilization, it was easier to get to Tahi Panas than to Kuala Hantu. And the pay was good: one hundred and twenty dollars a month and all found. It was, undoubtedly, a change for the better.

For worry had been making him a bad servant lately. Twofold worry. He had taken Rahimah's eight dollars and bought himself a lovely new sarong and a few trinkets besides, but that deadly potion lay still in the *barang*-box under Ibrahim's bed. Ibrahim was convinced that it was a lethal concoction. He had been hearing that Rahimah now hated Tuan Crabbe and hated Mem Crabbe also, and that she wished them both dead. Or, if not dead, maimed, deformed, *Mem* certainly bereft of her shining hair, *Tuan* deprived of his potency. He had heard these stories round the bazaar and in the market. And then he had received a nasty letter from Rahimah, written curtly in tiny Jawi script. '*Belum lagi pegang janji . . .*' He had not fulfilled the agreement, he agreed, but now he knew what she, with woman's deceit and treachery and down-right wickedness, wished him to do. He could not do it. And Rahimah had threatened him with dire punishments. She would get the *pawang* to stick pins in his image, to raise ghosts which would drive him mad and make him, in screaming desperation, hurl himself from the high bal-cony.

Two women after him. Ibrahim groaned. But it was well known that they had no power over you if they did not know where you were. The last week or so had been hell. Serving the soup one night he had suddenly screamed and dropped the plates. For a mat by the door of the dining-room had suddenly raised itself, danced a couple of steps nearer to the table, and then stopped. Ibrahim had heard of the demon that disguises itself as a mat, but never before had he seen one. Leaving the mess of steam-ing broth and broken china on the floor, he had rushed out to his kitchen, there to utter terrified prayer on his knees. And then, one quiet night, washing up the dinner dishes, he had become convinced that there was a *hantu dapur* lurking behind the refrigerator, ready to do mis-chief and smash everything up unless appeased with offer-ings of bananas and rice or an invitation to a party. And, most frightening of all, Ibrahim had been sure that there was a *penanggalan* floating outside his bedroom window. He almost saw the waving head and neck and long string of tangled hanging intestines. He almost heard the squeal of 'Siuh, siuh, siuh'. Thank Allah, these usually only sought houses where there were new babies, thirsting for infant blood. Perhaps the Tamil cleaner in the next quarters, where there was a new baby every year and the annual duty of adding to God's Kingdom had just been fulfilled. And then somebody had told him that a grave-yard ghost had been seen tumbling and rolling in its gravesheet over the lawn at the front of the house. No wonder he was getting thin, no wonder he could not do his work properly.

Tuan had been displeased with him lately and called him harsh names. And *Mem* had kept saying, as she tasted the curry or felt the plates he had forgotten to heat, something that sounded like '*Tu bed, tu bed*'. Yes, it was as well that he should be going. Ibrahim needed a friend rather than a master, someone who would be kind and loving, even when the curry had too much chilli in it or the mashed potatoes were watery and cold.

Ibrahim now packed his belongings in his box and his imitation-leather attaché-case. He packed also his mist-ress's tortoise-shell combs, two cards of hair-clips, a bras-siere and a silk slip. Also a feathery fan he had always liked. He took a packet of *Tuan's* razor-blades (a gift for his new master) and a couple of tins of cigarettes. He could also do with some bed-sheets. He knew the drawer where these were kept. Also, of course, he must have money.

To his annoyance there was no money in the desk-drawers. There was no money anywhere, except a few worthless coins in a little lacquer jug. *Tuan* had let him down. Still, he could sell something. There were two un-opened bottles of gin which would bring him twenty dollars. The sherry bottle was only half-full; he could not do anything with that.

Ibrahim eventually sat down in one of the arm-chairs in the lounge, drinking a glass of orange-squash, looking again at the deadly phial which Rahimah had entrusted to him. The rain lashed and thundered down still, the river was rising. The trishaw he had ordered would be coming for him soon. This would take him as far as the town's end. Then he could get a bus to Kelapa. Then he could walk to the estate, leaving his box in a *kedai* to be called back for. He turned and turned the phial over, feeling guilty. He had taken the money and spent it. If it was a deadly poison he could not be blamed. He had acted in all innocence. Perhaps, again, it was not a deadly poison; surely Rahimah would not be so foolish? But love, he thought shuddering, does strange things to a woman. And, in any case, *Tuan* and *Mem* had wronged him, Ibrahim bin Mohamed Salleh. Ibrahim tried to feel hard and bitter, but found it difficult. He pondered for a long time, trying to generate resentment. He had done his best to please them, but they had not been grateful. This was too cold and that was too hot, and this had not enough salt in it and that had too much. And they had not even noticed that he had been losing weight and had things on his mind.

When the bell of the trishaw-man could be heard from below, ringing forlornly through the passionate rain, Ibrahim made his decision. He went over to the drink-cupboard and emptied the contents of the phial into the sherry. The colour of the sherry was unchanged, the smell – he sniffed the heady, vinous vapour – the same. Perhaps it was really quite harmless, after all. Besides, thought Ibrahim, the Prophet had forbidden strong drink, and if anything happened to a person who drank strong drink that was perhaps a just punishment. Anyway, he had ful-filled his part of the bargain. Perhaps Allah would reward him for his fidelity to promises, perhaps Allah would en-sure that his wife died of fever or of Communists.

Ibrahim felt clean and virtuous. There was only one thing he had to do now. He took a piece of paper from the desk-drawer and a pencil from the desk-top. He began to write, in laborious Romanized Malay, his farewell mes-sage.

Tuan. And now what? *Saya sudah lepas kerja* ... True. He had left the job. *Sebab saya di-janji kerja yang lebeh baik*. He had been offered a better job. *Saya tidak mahu gaji sa-bagai kerja di-buat oleh saya bulan ini*. He did not want any wages for this month. He had taken his wages in kind. He felt again virtuous and great-hearted because he had given his services and not received any money for them; also he felt deliciously ill-used. He poised the pencil over his scrawl. The trishaw bell rang impatiently through the dismal rain. There seemed nothing further to say. He added *Yang benar, Ibrahim bin Mohamed Salleh* – yours truly, and, as an afterthought, *yang ma'afkan* – who forgives you.

Then, in purity of heart, he took his goods to the door of the flat. It was still raining hard. He wrapped round his shoulders the plastic raincoat of his late mistress and, in a mist of quiet virtue, went out to the trishaw and the beginning of his new life.

'It's no good,' said Nabby Adams. 'It's no good even starting to look at them vehicles today. I'd never get finished,
so there's not much point in getting started. It was the rain
and what-not. We'd have managed to get here early if it
hadn't been for that rain and Mrs Crabbe not feeling so
good and that puncture. We'll have to stay the night. They
can put us up in the police station. There's a nice little
lock-up there.'

'I must get back,' said Crabbe. 'I'm working tomorrow.'

They were sitting in a *kedai* on the single street of Gila,
acting, it seemed, a sort of play for the entire population
of the town and the nearest *kampong*. Their audience was
uncritical and appreciative. Tiny smiling people squatted
in rows before their wall-side table, and behind the squat-
ters were others on chairs, and behind those the latecomers
who had to stand. The play, after its opening scene, in
which Nabby Adams had cracked his head smartly on a
hanging oil-lamp, must seem to lack action, thought
Crabbe. But the townsfolk and their neighbour villagers
had little entertainment in their lives and, presumably,
they had to be thankful for a brown man with a gun and
a huge liverish rumbling man and a pale wet schoolmaster
in sweaty whites and a rather tatty golden-haired goddess.
Also there was no lack of sound off-stage. Cough, the dog,
was shut up in the car yelling and whining, answered
loudly by her own canine audience.

Primitive drama being primarily relIgous, small brown
smiling matrons kept bringing their infants to Fenella to
be touched and blessed. Half-naked *orang darat*, their

148

blowpipes sleeping at their sides, smoked strong local shag wrapped in dried leaves and watched and listened.

'I don't see how you can,' said Nabby Adams. 'You won't drive and I need him here to translate for me.'

'It's not a question of "won't drive",' said Crabbe bitterly and with heat. 'There's just something in me that won't let me.'

'I don't fancy sleeping in a prison,' said Fenella. 'We ought to get back. Oh, why can't you drive, Victor?'

'Why do you need him here to translate for you?' said Crabbe nastily. 'Why don't you speak the bloody language yourself? You've been here long enough.'

'Why don't you drive a bloody car yourself?' asked Nabby Adams.

'That's a different thing.'

'Why is it?'

'Hush, hush,' said Fenella. 'Please don't quarrel.'

The audience, pleased with the rough and rapid passage of irritable language, smiled to each other. At the back some newcomers were being given a résumé of the plot.

Alladad Khan, seated upstage, gave a lengthy speech. Nabby Adams gave one back. Finally he said, in English, 'He says he'll take you back and then get here himself again tomorrow morning. Although that's going to be a bloody nuisance.'

'Why is it?' asked Crabbe.

'What am I going to do, stuck out here on my own?'

'You've got the dog.'

'She's got no money. He has.'

'Here's ten dollars,' said Crabbe.

But Nabby Adams was not to be lonely after all. A new character entered, accompanied by little men wearing clothes and wrist-watches. He was brown and nearly bald and he greeted Nabby Adams in the English of a Cockney Jew.

'Hallo, chum. Still hitting it hard, eh?'

'It's Ranjit Singh,' said Nabby Adams. 'He looks after these here *Sakais*. Get a chair,' he invited.

'You mustn't call them *Sakais,* chum. They don't like it.' Ranjit Singh, now that his name had been announced, looked strangely beardless to the Crabbes. The clean shave and the naked bald head had a Black Mass quality. Ranjit Singh exhibited his apostasy to the whole world. His wife was a Eurasian Catholic, his children were at a convent school, he himself, abandoning the faith of the Sikhs, had become a devout agnostic. He held the post of Assistant Protector of Aborigines, and his task was to win the little men over to the true cause and to enlist their specialist jungle-skills in the fight against the terrorist. In fact they were incapable of being corrupted ideologically by the Communists, but they responded strongly to the more intelligible and sensible corruptions with which they were bribed and rewarded out of Government funds. They liked wrist-watches and Player's cigarettes; their wives took quickly to lipstick and brassières. The ineluctable process which Crabbe was implementing in the class-room was spreading even to the core of the snaky, leechy jungle. The three little men found chairs, accepted beer and joined the play. The introduction of local talent did not, however, please the audience. They wanted the exotic and mythical. Murmurings and spittings of betel juice began to spread through the assembly. Still, they waited. Perhaps the play would end as it had begun – with the big man's cracking his head again and the awful rumble of unintelligible words.

Ranjit Singh now took the desecrated host in the form of a cigarette. As the beer went round and the light thickened and the oil-lamp was lit, Crabbe saw the beginnings of a session burgeoning. He said:

'We must think about going, you know. It's a long way back.'

'Going?' said Ranjit Singe. 'You've got to stay and see the dancing, chum.'

'Dancing?' said Fenella.

'Oh, just a bit of a hop,' said Ranjit Singh. 'A bit of a party, really, because I've just got back here from Timah. Any excuse for a party. We'll have to get through a bit of jungle, though. On foot. A car's no good.'

Fenella's first flush of *Golden Bough* enthusiasm was mitigated somewhat by this. But, still, aboriginal dancing. ... The monograph droned on: 'The culture-pattern of the *orang darat* is necessarily limited. The jungle houses them and feeds them and provides them with an anthropomorphic pantheon of the kind which is familiar to us from our observations of primitive life in the Congo, the Amazon and other centres where a rudimentary civilization seems to have been arrested at what may be termed the "Bamboo Level". Morality is simple, government patriarchal, and the practice of the arts confined to primitive and unhandy ornamentation of weapons and cooking utensils. ... In the dance, however, the *orang darat* has achieved a considerable standard of rhythmic complexity and a high order of agility ...'

One of the *orang darat* asked Fenella in courteous Malay if she would like some more beer. She came to, startled, and refused with equal courtesy.

'We must get back,' said Crabbe.

'But, darling,' said Fenella, 'we must see the dances, we must. We can travel all night, after all.'

'And Alladad Khan?'

'He can get back here by mid-morning. He won't mind.'

The play came to an end. The characters took their bows. Nabby Adams cracked his head again on the hanging lamp. The audience was pleased and, gently, began to go home, chattering with animation, discussing, comparin ...

'We ought to have taken the bloody hat round,' said Nabby Adams.

The way through the jungle was lighted by fire-flies and a couple of electric torches. The *orang darat* went first, sure-footed. A tiger called, far away, and things scuttled under Fenella's feet. Leeches dropped on her and, surfeited, fell off again. It was not long, however, before they saw flares and crude huts in a clearing. There were tiny muscular men in trousers and small women, gaping at the apparition of Fenella, wearing brassières and almost nothing else. The women chattered eagerly together, discussing her, clicking and sliding in a tongue with many words but no inflections.

It was, to Fenella, a disappointing evening. A toddy jug went round and with it little glutinous rice-cakes. The natives were hospitable. But their dances were nothing more than a happy romp and their songs artless and simple as five-finger exercises. Two drums beat easy rhythms and an old man blew a flute, first with his mouth, then with his nose. It was, except for the toddy, a mere jolly Boy Scout evening . . .

At midnight they saw Nabby Adams and his dog safely bedded down in the lock-up, a beer-bottle filled with already stale toddy safely bedded down beside them. 'This will do nicely for my breakfast,' said Nabby Adams. 'I'll try and get her a bit of fish or something.'

And so the journey back. Fenella went to sleep, stretched on the rear cushions. Alladad Khan and Crabbe, exhilarated by toddy, talked metaphysics in Malay.

'The question is whether a thing is really there if we are not there to see it.'

'You could hear it, or smell it.'

'No, no. I mean . . . (I wish I could think of the right Malay word.) I mean if we could not be aware of it with our . . .'

'Senses?'

'Yes, our senses. We could not be sure it existed.'

'So this jungle perhaps exists only in our heads?'

'Perhaps. And this car. And you only exist in my head, too.'

'And my wife only exists in my head? And the child?'

'It is possible.'

'It would be a big relief,' said Alladad Khan, sighing. Slowly, with skill, he steered through the nine-mile stretch of bad land. The toddy put out its tongue and made long noses at the hidden enemies.

It was when they were well past danger, but also well away from even the smallest *attap* homestead, that the car broke down. Alladad Khan poked and pulled and swore in the dark. Fenella awoke.

'What's the trouble?'

'Something's gone wrong with the engine. Christ knows what. We'll never get back tonight, not unless we can stop somebody and get help.'

'But what are we going to do?'

'We'll have to sleep here.'

'Sleep here?' Fenella wailed. Alladad Khan tugged and fiddled at the car's guts. How he hated engines, how they hated him.

It was no good. They settled for sleep, after half an hour of waiting for a saviour vehicle to appear on that deserted road. They awoke shortly after the first comfortless doze to find that the rain had started again. They wound up the windows and, in suffocating heat, with the rain pouring with a myriad metallic fists on the car-roof, lay, wooing sleep, Crabbe and Fenella now both on the back seat, slouching in the corners, and Alladad Khan in the front.

They pretended to each other to be asleep, each wrapped in his few cubic feet of dark, each with his own pounding private rain. They were all obsessed with the world of dark and the world of spinning thundering water. Everything seemed a long way away, bed and home and anything that could be thought about comfortably. But, each separately, the rain and the blackness had absorbed them, and each seemed strange to the other. Once a lorry swished and hurtled past, lighting each one to the other as a hunched mound of silver and black.

Alladad Khan woke to a strangeness, a lack of noise, after an hour of dreaming. Rain was no longer falling, but the car-floor was flooded. The sky had cleared and the moon shone. Alladad Khan saw that it was near the end of the true, lunar month. Silently he wound down the windows, letting in the strong rank smell of wet grass and trees and earth. Crabbe watched him let the windows down, without speaking or stirring. Fenella was asleep, snoring very faintly. When Alladad Khan seemed asleep again, Crabbe put his arm gently round Fenella's shoulders and let her sleeping weight fall against him. He was filled with a terrible compassion for her and longed for it to be love. Alladad Khan, quietly awake, watched him. The moon moved imperceptibly towards setting.

Alladad Khan woke to the far crying of *kampong* cocks in the dark. That noise had been the farmyard aubade in the Punjab in his dream. He had been a boy again, sleeping in the same bed as his brother. He would wake soon to breakfast and school. He woke to Malaya and a strange bed, strangers breathing rhythmically behind him. He felt completely alone but curiously confident, as though he understood that aloneness was the answer the philosophers had been looking for.

The last awakening was in the grey spreading light. An inquiring Chinese face was peering in at the driver's window, talking, asking. Alladad Khan geared his fumbling brain to the right language. He saw, dimly, a saloon car parked across the road.

'Need help?'

'How far from Tongkat?'

'Nearly ten miles. I am going there.'

'Could you ask the garage to send . . .?'

'Yes, yes.'

Crabbe and his wife groaned and yawned, hair tangled, eyelids gummed, dirty and exhausted. What a day this was going to be, thought Crabbe. He would never be there in time, and this was the day of the Governors' meeting, the lunch with the Sultan, the School Sports. They would telephone the flat and Ibrahim would say that *Tuan* had not yet returned. He had no excuse. It had been foolish to suppose that they ever could get back in time. At best, he would arrive when the Sports were nearly finished. A six-hour journey from Tongkat to Kuala Hantu. The work of putting the car right. At very best, he would arrive in the middle of the Sports.

He got out of the car and stretched in the morning that already gathered its heat together. It did not matter. He was too old to worry about things like that. But he was also too old to be nagged by Boothby, too old to permit himself the luxury of smashing Boothby's face in. It was best to conform, best not to cause trouble. And today he was sure that there was something that only he could do. He was sure that there was going to be trouble and that only he could handle that trouble.

Alladad Khan was looking sadly into the car-engine, saying something about an oil leak, about engines seizing up. Fenella combed her hair dismally, tried to put her face to rights. It was full day already.

They stamped around, smoking, waiting for the break-down service of the garage. It was an hour before the cheerful Chinese mechanics arrived to tow them into Tongkat. In Tongkat they were told that the leak could be remedied in about an hour and a half.

'We'll have to get a taxi,' said Crabbe.

'A taxi? All the way?' Fenella was indignant. 'If you're not back, you're not back, that's all. Ring them up now, tell them you've had a breakdown. Tell them they can expect you when they see you.'

There was a public telephone in the small post office. After much delay Crabbe got through to the School office. He heard the voice of a peon. The Chief Clerk had not yet arrived.

'Yes?'

'Tell them I'm stranded in Tongkat.'

'Yes.'

'The car's broken down.'

'Yes.'

'I'm trying to get back as quickly as I can. Tell them that.'

'Yes.'

'Is that quite clear?'

'Yes.'

Crabbe went back to the *kedai* where Fenella was drinking black coffee and staring at the billious pink cakes. 'Well, I've done all I can do,' he said. Alladad Khan twisted his moustache, aware of his wet, creased uniform and filthy boots. He said nothing, basking in a curious and unreasonable content.

It was ten o'clock before they were able to leave Tongkat. The car, holding its oil now, sped on in sunlight. Fenella lay at the back, trying to doze away her headache. Alladad Khan and Crabbe spoke metaphysics at the front.

'It is hard to say these things in a language like Malay. But this man Plato believed that all things on earth were a mere copy of a *chontoh dalam shurga*, a heavenly pattern.'

'So there is one motor-engine in the mind of God, and all others on earth try to imitate it.'

'Yes, something like that.'

'And this motor-engine of God's never breaks down?'

'Oh, no, it cannot. It is perfect.'

'I see.' Alladad Khan drove on past another rubber estate. 'But of what use is a motor-engine to God?'

'God knows.'

'That is true. God knoweth best.'

Secure and relaxed, they rolled on. 'YOU ARE NOW ENTERING A WHITE AREA.' 'YOU ARE NOW LEAVING A WHITE AREA.' 'Obviously,' said Alladad Khan, 'the Communists must be able to read English. They are gentlemen and will keep on the right side of the notice.'

At two o'clock they ate *sateh* and drank beer in a cheerless *kampong* where the people were hostile and spat. Crabbe thought, 'Now the Sports are starting; now perhaps the trouble is starting too. And I, being away from the trouble, will undoubtedly be associated with the trouble.'

'Another ninety minutes,' said Alladad Khan, 'and we should be back. Oh.' He remembered something. 'I have not telephoned to Gila.' He rushed out to the police station.

'How do you feel, dear?' asked Crabbe.

'Oh, fed up, depressed.'

'It has not been much fun, has it?'

'I can't help it,' said Fenella. 'I feel terribly homesick. It comes and it goes. I was just thinking of a nice little lunch in that Italian place in Dean Street, and then perhaps a French film at the Curzon or at Studio One. I don't think I'm really cut out for Malaya. When it's not dull it's uncomfortable. What did we get at the end of our endless journey? Only a few stupid little men doing a silly little dance. And bottles of warm Singapore beer.'

'You're a romantic,' said Crabbe. 'You expect too much. Reality's always dull, you know, but when we see that it's all there is, well – it miraculously ceases to be dull.'

'I don't think you know what you're talking about.'

'I think you're right. I'm so tired.'

'So am I.'

It was on the home stretch, on the Timah road, that reality ceased to be dull. Somnolent, off their guard, drugged by the sound of the engine and the endless unrolling of rubber estates and jungle and scrub and rare huts, they hardly took in the significance of the burnt-out car that stood, a deformity of twisted metal, barring the way. Alladad Khan exclaimed at it and swerved to the right. There was room enough to pass if the car could take that grass slope . . .

Crabbe could see distinctly the yellow men with rifles, could see the serious concentration as they aimed. He then heard the whole world crack and crack again and again. And then Alladad Khan's hands were off the wheel. In an agony of surprise he was clutching his right arm. The car went mad and Fenella screamed. Crabbe reached over and seized the wheel, brought the car into control again.

A breathless half-mile, and Alladad Khan's two feet had jammed down hard. The car stopped. Alladad Khan was panting hard, soaked in sweat, and his rolled-up sleeve was all blood, blood rilling down his arm.

'Take this handkerchief,' said Crabbe, as Alladad Khan tottered into the back. 'Make a tourniquet out of it. Stop the blood.' Fenella found a pencil in her bag, wound the handkerchief, thrust the pencil in the knot, began to twist.

Crabbe was at the wheel. 'Thank God we're not far from Sungkit Hospital,' he said. 'About ten miles.'

'It's gone in,' said Fenella, 'really deep. His arm's smashed. The bloody swine,' she added. Alladad Khan groaned. 'There, there, my dear,' she said. 'You'll be all right soon. It won't be long now.'

Crabbe accelerated, gave the car all speed. It was quite a time before he realized that he was driving again. Driving well, moreover. And really exhilarated. He almost felt like singing.

12

'No,' said Boothby, '*don't* take a pew. Remain standing.'

'I take it I can stand at ease?' asked Crabbe.

'The time for bloody stupid little jokes is over,' said Boothby. 'You've had it now. I don't mind your ruining your own career, but when you try to ruin mine as well . . .'

'I still don't know what's happened,' said Crabbe. 'I admit that I wasn't there for the lunch and the Sports, but I did what I could. I rang up the office. It wasn't my fault if you didn't get the message.'

'The whole point is,' said Boothby, 'that you'd made up your mind to be away. You knew what was going to happen.'

'Did you know?'

'Don't be a bloody fool. Only you knew about it, and you knew about it because it was your idea. You instigated it.'

'I still don't know what happened.'

'I'll bloody well tell you what happened. There they all were, the Sultan and the Mentri Besar, the British Adviser, the crowd from K.L., God knows how much royalty from all over the Federation. And they'd played the State anthem and everything was going all right and they announced the first track event.'

'Yes? And what happened?'

'You know damn well what happened. Nothing happened.'

'Nothing?'

'The little bastards just sat there. They damn well refused to take part in any single event. Except the juniors. So all we had was the egg-and-spoon race and the sack race and the bloody hop, step and jump. That was the Sports.'

'And did anybody do anything about it.'

'I screamed myself blue in the face. And then the Mentri Besar appealed to the Malay boys and quoted the Koran to them. And some of them looked a bit bloody sheepish.'

'I see. And who were the ringleaders?'

'How the hell do I know? All I know is that it was your idea.'

'In all seriousness, and keeping my temper, what makes you think so?'

'What makes me think so? I like that. Ever since you've been here you've been encouraging these boys to go against discipline. There was the business of that expulsion. And I was right about that and you damn well know I was right. But you told them I was wrong. I know all about it, don't think I don't. You told them I was a bloody tyrant. And you were behind that protest meeting when I caned those prefects. And when I docked that holiday because of the bad exam. results. It's all come out. One or two of the prefects here had the bloody sense to realize which side their bread was buttered. I've heard all about you. I've heard it all. That lad you were down on, that Chinese lad you said was a bloody Communist, he's told me a few things.'

'Such as?'

'Such as that you're a bloody Communist sympathizer yourself. You had him in your flat and you as good as told him that Communism was right and that the British were wrong in not recognizing the Communist Party. Can you deny that?'

'I was trying to draw him out. I still maintain that he *is* a Communist, and if you look carefully you'll probably find that he's at the root of your trouble. I told you before, but you wouldn't do a thing about it.'

'This Chinese lad proved himself the best bloody prefect I've got. Yesterday it was him who was pleading with them, threatening them even. He was in tears. He said the

160

School had been let down and I'd been let down and the cause of democracy had been let down. There. What have you got to say about that?'

'Only this. That you're too damned innocent to live.'

'Look here,' said Boothby, red and threatening, 'I'll tell you what's going to happen to you, Crabbe. You're being transferred, and with a bloody bad report, too. And at the end of this tour I think you'll find yourself out on your ear.'

'You know, Boothby, perhaps I'm really the innocent one. I just don't understand. I've done my best for these boys, I even thought some of these boys liked me. I thought that I was really getting somewhere with them.'

'Oh, you got somewhere with them all right. You staged a nice efficient revolt. You made me and everybody look a pack of bloody fools.'

'Boothby, I want you to believe me when I say that I had nothing to do with that business. Frankly, I've never liked you. I've always thought you were inefficient, autocratic, unsympathetic, the worst possible headmaster for a School like this. But never would I dream of doing anything disloyal, so . . .'

'Yes, I know exactly what you've thought about me. And I know exactly what you've been doing, day after day, in the class-room, on the sports field, in the dining-hall, at prefects' meetings. You've been turning them against me, and that means turning them against everything this School stands for. You've been a traitor. You are a traitor. And you'll get the reward of a bloody traitor, you just wait and see.'

'I'm sorry you feel like that, Boothby. Really sorry. You're doing me a very grave injustice.'

'You'd better look at this,' said Boothby. He handed over a typewritten sheet. 'This is a record of what you've been doing. This is a protest from one of the best boys this School's ever had.'

Crabbe read:

Dear Sir,

I hope you will forgive my writing to you like this, but I find that I am becoming increasingly disturbed by some of the things that Mr Crabbe, the History Master, is saying in class, especially about the running of the School. I know I speak for all the boys when I say that he should not say these things. He is speaking as though he should be running the School himself and is always criticizing the things that you, sir, do to make the School an efficient and happy School.

First he said the expulsion of Hamidin was wrong. Then he said it was wrong to cane prefects when they have done wrong. Then he said it was not right to deprive the School of a holiday when, as is well known, it was the only way to make the School realize that they must do better work in the examinations. Then he said that you, sir, did not listen fairly to the things the boys say when they come to see you. Also, I believe that Mr Crabbe has many wrong political ideas and talks about freedom and independence when he really means Communism.

One day he called me into his flat and asked me many questions. He seemed annoyed that I was trying to help the younger boys to see how wrong Communism is. He said to me as follows ...'

'All right,' said Crabbe. 'There's the evidence, a load of lies and half-truths. How long will it be, do you think, before my transfer comes through?'

'It's going to be bloody soon,' said Boothby. 'The sooner the better as far as I'm concerned.' At that moment the peon came in with the Sunday newspapers. Boothby scanned the front pages of the *Sunday Gazette* and the *Sunday Bugle* with grim concentration. 'There you are,' he said. 'All over the front page. If I had my way you'd be bloody well shot.'

Crabbe went out, feeling not in the least depressed. The thing was so thoroughly absurd; the truth would out, sooner or later. He felt clean with innocence, as though he had just showered. He got into his car and drove slowly back to Light House. Tomorrow he must do something about applying for a driving-licence. With keen pleasure he drove through the town, avoiding children and chickens, back to lunch, a lunch that Fenella would be preparing herself. How good people were at letting one down. Well if he were going on transfer, he would not want to take Ibrahim with him anyway. It was just as well. Still, when one thought of the thefts condoned, the bad meals cheerfully eaten, the complaints unvoiced at fantastic hair-styles and epicene hip-wagging, one felt rather hurt. He thought of Rivers, violent face contorted above the moustache which grew out of the lean British nose. Rivers now, back home, would be saying, 'Lash them, beat them, flay them alive. . . .' Was Rivers right?

No, Rivers was not right. It was best not to wear oneself out with violence. The East would always present that calm face of faint astonishment, unmoved at the anger, not understanding the bitterness. That was why it was pointless to attempt to take any action at all against this young Chinese betrayer, to protest any further to Boothby. A pattern would work itself out.

'I'm being transferred,' he said to Fenella.

'Where to?'

'I've no idea. They think I was behind the strike that was organized at the School Sports yesterday.'

'A strike?'

Crabbe told her everything. Then she said:

'So Othello's occupation will be gone.'

'Meaning?'

'Two people will be sorry to hear we're going.'

'Yes. But still, wherever we go, there's a hell of a lot of helping to be done.'

'I suppose so.'

'How about a drink before lunch?'

'Don't call it lunch. It's just a snack. That wicked boy has denuded the larder of practically everything. He's left us canned soup and a couple of tins of sardines. I always said he was no good.'

'Yes. Look here, I'm sure we had some gin. We can't have drunk all that, surely?'

'You forget the capacity of Nabby Adams.'

'Still . . . Have some sherry.'

Crabbe poured it out and then switched on the gramophone. A record was ready to play for them, one of the pile skewered on the automatic-change spindle. It started: strings rising from A to a long held F, through E to E flat, when the woodwind came in with their bitter-sweet chords. Wagner's prolonged orgasm.

Languor came late for them that Sunday afternoon. They lay in bed, smoking and sweating and wondering. How strange life was. When life seemed at its worst, then came the astonishing revelation. The annunciation and the epiphany. They slept till long after dark came, not hearing the noise downstairs.

Yawning before dinner, surrounded by his Book Club library, Boothby put down his *stengah* and went out to the shy peon who waited, still astride his bicycle, outside the open door.

'You're working late,' he said. 'What's the matter?'

'*Surat, tuan.*'

'A letter? Who from?' Boothby looked at the childish handwriting on the cheap envelope. No stamp. 'All right, you can go.'

Boothby tore the envelope open and read:

Dear Sir,

We hope you will forgive presumption and untimeliness of what follow here. We have heard that Mr Crabbe is to be expelled from the School where he has done much good and valuable work, not easily forgotten by boys he has taught. We will say that what happened at Sports yesterday was no fault of Mr Crabbe's, although Mr Crichton say it is so to some senior boys, and we would humbly say, sir, that Mr Crichton should not say like that to pupils but should keep his own council. Well, sir, to bring inordinately long missive to a timely end, what happened yesterday was the work of some boys who said it would be a good idea to do what was done, although some of us said no, it should not be. One of these boys has already been punished, to wit he has been punched on the nose and one eye has been blacked. This is termed summary justice. We beg, in conclusion, that Mr Crabbe be not expelled but allowed to continue to teach the boys who would otherwise be sorry of his departure. You will understand that it is not fitting to sign this by name but will merely subscribe, with all good wishes,

                                                    Fair Play.

Boothby read it again and yawned. His wife, a scraggy and lank blonde in a faded blue frock, said, 'Anything important, dear?'

'Nothing,' said Boothby. 'Only another of these anonymous letters. That's the only thing to do with them.' He accompanied his words with a violent tear across, and another, and another, and then threw the scraps into the waste-paper basket. Then he returned to his *stengah*.

13

Alladad Khan awoke from very refreshing sleep and remembered where he was. He had never before been in a hospital, except to visit Adams Sahib when, falling down in the Veterans' Race at the Police Sports, he had been admitted to Kuala Hantu Hospital with obscure internal injuries. It had been then that Adams Sahib had decided, for a week or more, to go steady and retire to bed immediately after the day's work. Adams Sahib had been given milk to drink three times a day and had been glad to leave the hospital.

Now he, Alladad Khan, was in hospital with an honourable wound. They had dug out the bullet from torn flesh and ligament and bound the arm up. He was to lie here for some days and rest and recover. Alladad Khan surveyed the neat white ward with its open windows, the greenery without and the sun streaming in. In other beds were men sleeping or reading gloomily or looking at the ceiling or into space. An ancient petulant Chinese was being rebuked by a Malay nurse for spitting on the floor. Allah, some men had no manners. The Malay nurse was tiny but she had a good flow of vigorous language. Alladad Khan admired her.

Alladad Khan looked to his left and saw a man dozing in a turban. The man's face was turned away from Alladad Khan. Alladad Khan wondered if he would have visitors today. Perhaps now his wife would be penitent and be the better prepared to believe his stories about having to be out late on duty. Though, thought Alladad Khan, there was little connection between being out late on duty and being hit by bandits in the early afternoon. But women were illogical and could be persuaded of a connection.

The man in the turban groaned, turned and began to sit up in bed. Alladad Khan saw that it was Hari Singh. He wondered for a second if this was a trick of Hari Singh's, to annoy Alladad Khan and retard his recovery. He said, with surprise:

'What, are *you* here?'

'As you perceive, it is I.'

'I understood you were on local leave. Are you accustomed to spend your leaves in hospital?'

'I was playing football and was injured gravely.'

'Ah. I was shot at by the Communists and a great bullet had to be extracted from my arm.'

'That, nowadays, would seem to be a common occurrence. I can assure you that this injury I sustained at football was extremely serious. Now, with God's help, it is expected that I shall recover.'

'What happened? Did you stub your big toe against the ball?'

'No. I fell and my ankle was damaged and the whole foot also has turned black.'

'Ah. Which foot, may I ask?'

'The left one.'

'It is as I thought. God is just, of that there can be no doubt.'

'I see no justice in this.'

'Who are you to speak against the ways of God? You will remember how I rebuked you, and how you laughed me to scorn, how you went crying in your great black heart to the o.c.p.d. to complain of my alleged tyranny. You will remember the crime in question for which you were justly rebuked.'

'I do not apprehend the drift of your somewhat verbose statement.'

'The time when you placed, unasked, your great importunate foot on the foot of the memsahib.'

'Oh, that? That was nothing.'

'You call it nothing, but God remembers and God punishes. Providence has long ears and great eyes and a long avenging arm. Your foot has been mauled by the foot of divine justice.'

'I would entreat you to say nothing of this to my wife Preetam and the children. They will be visiting me this morning.'

'I will say nothing directly to your wife. I will merely hint at the singular appropriateness of your punishment.'

'I beg you to be quiet about it. See, I have food here in my locker. There are bananas and chocolate and a small jar of chicken essence. You are welcome to share these things with me.'

'I shall have many gifts coming to me from my friends. I do not need your bribes. I am satisfied, however, that justice has been done, and I will say no more about this very distasteful matter.'

Preetam and two small children came, two children of indeterminate sex, one wearing a top-knot, the other dribbling in baby Punjabi. Preetam was a little fierce woman in silk trousers and a sari. There were loud and passionate greetings. Hari Singh was given fruit and cakes and a roll of magazines and newspapers. Some of the magazines were Chinese, a language which Hari Singh could not read, but they were full of photographs of cabaret girls and football stars. For Alladad Khan there were no visitors. He lay indifferently smoking, listening to the voluble family life of Hari Singh. The dribbling child came over to inspect Alladad Khan, leaving a deposit of melted chocolate on the bed-cover. Alladad Khan spoke very quiet English to it and the child went back to its father.

'Here,' said Hari Singh in loud generosity, 'is a newspaper for you to read. It is in English but, doubtless, that will present no difficulties to one who has many English friends and has studied assiduously a certain book which he has not yet returned to me.'

'It shall be returned. Though why one so eloquent with his feet should consider a book of English words important I cannot understand.'

Hari Singh laughed loud and false. 'He refers to my skill at football,' he explained to his wife.

Alladad Khan tried to read the *Timah Gazette*, but he could make out the meanings of very few words. Still, he pretended, for the benefit of Hari Singh, to be absorbed in a long article which was illustrated with the photograph of a large fish. His lips silently spelt imaginary words, and his frowning eyes read swiftly across and down. But, turning the page, he quickly became genuinely absorbed in a brief news item. There was a photograph of two happy people, one of whom he recognized immediately. Who could mistake the identity of that owner of large teeth, long nose and severe moustache? It was Abdul Khan. Yes, the news item confirmed it: Abdul Khan . . . Abdul Khan . . . Officer Commanding Police District . . . Miss Margaret Tan . . . Singapore. Alladad Khan could read little else with understanding, but the photograph made all clear. The happy slit-eyes of the middle-aged-looking Chinese woman, her loving proximity to the person of Alladad Khan's brother-in-law. So. He had married at last, so much was evident, and out of his clan. He, Alladad Khan, must do the right thing, must declare the solidarity of that proud house, but Abdul Khan was above such matters of honour, except vicariously, except when it was a question of getting his sister off his hands. Alladad Khan waited patiently till Preetam should make signs of departure. The hospital was a long way from Kuala Hantu, buses were infrequent, perhaps she would stay shrilling around with her chocolate-defiled brats till the rattle of the tiffin-trays. Thankfully, however, he heard her say soon that she had to go. The trade-van of Mohamed Zain, vendor of women's medicines in Kuala Hantu, had come that morning early to Timah, and the driver had promised to stop for her on his way back. Now he, Alladad Khan, could expend a little forgiveness on

Hari Singh and permit him to show off his English in a translation of this news item into Punjabi.

The valedictions were as voluble – all the bed-heat and lip-smacking of a marriage dug deep as a den – and nauseatingly exhibitionist as the salutations had been. Preetam was insistent that her husband take his chicken essense and keep up his strength, that he instruct the doctors and nurses to watch out for gangrene, that he demand to be weighed at frequent intervals. The children were kissed and crushed in podgy arms; then the wavings of hands and the heartfelt wishes that she should keep her courage up without him and he without her. Then the ward became quiet again.

Alladad Khan said, 'Would you care to translate this for me? There are certain words I cannot clearly make out. My eyes are watering because of the immense pain in my arm.'

Hari Singh said, 'Courage, brother. Pain comes to all of us at some time or other. No man can escape. Some flying into danger in full awareness as, for instance, myself; others adventitiously. Let me see what it is you want me to explain to you.' Hari Singh put on large reading glasses and then translated slowly. Alladad Khan lay back, listening. So. A hole-in-the-corner marriage in a registry office in Singapore. No guests. A Chinese Christian, daughter of a man rich in rubber. Allah, he had done well, the swine. Whereas he, Alladad Khan . . .

'But I knew of this,' said Hari Singh. 'I learn these things because I have many influential and well-informed friends. I could have told you before had you cared to ask me of news of your brother-in-law, but you so rarely betray interest in his doings. There is a man who has got on, who has a great future before him. He was good enough to ask me to join some friends of his at a bachelor party he held a week or so before the wedding. I was unable to attend, having family commitments and not being a drinking man. But I understand from one of those present, a Chinese Inspector, that the whisky flowed and that your brother-in-law outdid any there in his ability to imbibe and contain. He is surely a man who will get on.'

Alladad Khan was silent. His resentment began slowly to modulate first into relief, then into elation. At last he had a powerful weapon to wield against his wife. There would be no more talk of the virtues of Abdul Khan, no more threats about transfers to Abdul Khan's district, no more deprecations of God's wrath at his, Alladad Khan's, harmless transgressions and impieties. He, Alladad Khan, could now pose as the injured, the man who had sacrificed wealth for the good of the clan, the man who had been true to the traditions of his fathers. He, Alladad Khan, had not gone whoring after women who worshipped a filthy and uncircumcized God, because of a lust for the things of Mammon. And what if he, Alladad Khan, did drink a little and seek to broaden his mind through intercourse with the cultivated? He deserved something occasionally to soothe the wounds inflicted by the behaviour of one whom he had, previously, been taught to regard as the ideal Khan, the Khan in the mind of God. He, Alladad Khan, had been let down. His saint had been revealed as one of the shameful shoddy ikons that the Prophet himself had denounced and cursed at Mecca itself. He, Alladad Khan, had been very ill done to. Shot at by Communists in the pursuit of his duty, the duty that was the means of providing curry and chapattis to sleek her coy body, to convert to milk for her milky brat. Allah, there was no question of it now. He, Alladad Khan, would be master in his own barrack quarters.

He lay back smiling, dreaming of the new life, the life which was to start almost at once, as soon, in fact, as she came to visit him. He tasted, in imagination, her tears of shame and chagrin. He heard the cracked voice of penitence. He heard his own voice, the voice of her master, saying with lordly disdain or kindly condescension:

'I shall be out all night. I may be out all tomorrow night. If I should return drunk you will prepare for me that potent Western medicine called a Prairie Oyster. You will have it waiting for me.'

Or:

'If you cannot learn to behave properly you will be packed off to stay with your relatives in Kuala Lumpur until you have considered sufficiently of the demeanour appropriate to wifely status.'

Or:

'Yes, you have little entertainment, God knows. I propose to invite your brother and sister-in-law to a party in these our quarters. You will please to buy a bottle of whisky for this occasion, for your brother is inordinately fond of that beverage.'

Or:

'Divorce may be uncommon in the Punjab, but we are living at present in Malaya, whose streets are infested with the mendicant wraiths of wives who did not please their husbands. I assure you, I shall not think twice about it when I grow tired of you. Then perhaps I may follow the high example of your brother and instal a rich Chinese woman in my bed.'

Or:

But that would do for the present. A happy time stretched ahead for Alladad Khan. He would now sleep for a while and let Hari Singh rumble on to himself about the rights of Sikhs and the short-sightedness of Promotion Boards.

14

'And if you did say you knew anything about it at all you'd be a bloody liar,' said Flaherty with a kind of epileptic vigour. 'See the world, man. Get out into the highways and byways. The East,' he waved and twisted his arms ceilingwards in snake-dance gestures, 'the bloody East. And this is no more the East than that bloody boot lying over there.' He pointed with a stiff shaking arm in a soap-box orator's denunciatory gesture. 'Now I know the East. I was in it. Palestine Police from the end of the war till we packed up.'

Nabby Adams groaned from his narrow bed. If only he hadn't annoyed the Crabbes by drinking a whole bottle of gin before breakfast the previous weekend he might now be lying on that hospitable planter's chair on their veranda. As it was, he had to hear Flaherty burn away the hours of sleep in long drunken monologues. It was now nearly four in the morning, and there was nothing to drink.

'Why can't you get to flaming bed?' said Nabby Adams.

'Bed? Bed? Listen who's talking about bed. Never in his bed from one week's end to the other, and just because he decides to honour the bloody establishment with his noble presence for once in a way he thinks he can rule the bloody roost and tell his superiors how to run their own lives. I'm telling you, I'm telling you,' said Flaherty, pointing with the blunt finger of the hell-fire preacher, 'I'm telling you that the end isn't far off, not far off at all. I've watched you go down the bloody drain, inch by inch of dirty water. I've looked after you like it might be your own mother, I've rescued the perishing on more occasions than one, I've nursed you and taught you the right road, but what thanks do I ever get? I've tried to educate you, you ignorant sod, telling you about the places I've been and them bints I've been with, and giving you a bit of intelligent conversation where another man would say, "Let him stew in his own juice, for ignorance is bliss," but I've never got as much as a word of gratitude out of your big toothless mouth. I've spent good money on you. I've covered up for you, I've warned you, but you remain what you always were, a big drunken sod who leads good men astray and hasn't an ounce of decency of feeling or of gratitude for the acts of a friend in his whole blasted big body.' Flaherty glared from frowning eyes, panting.

'Did you bring any beer back, Paddy?' asked Nabby Adams.

'Beer? Beer?' Flaherty screamed and danced. 'I'll take my dying bible that if it was the Day of Judgement itself and the dead coming out of their graves and we all of us lined up for the bloody sentence and He in His awe and majesty as of a flame of fire standing in the clouds of doomsday, all you'd be thinking about would be where you could get a bottle of blasted Tiger. There'll be beer where you're going to at the last,' promised Flaherty, dripping with prophetic sweat. 'There'll be cases and cases and barrels and barrels of it and it'll all be tasting of the ashes of hell in your mouth, like lava and brimstone, scalding your guts and your stomach, so that you'll be screaming for a drop of cold water from the hands of Lazarus himself, and he in Abraham's bosom on the throne of the righteous.'

Nabby Adams was transfixed with a pang of thirst like a Teresan sword. The sharp image of that eschatological drouth made him raise himself groaning from his bed of fire. The dog clanked under the bed, ready for any adventure, stretching herself with a dog's groan as she appeared from behind the tattered slack of the mosquito-net. They plodded downstairs together, pursued by the oracular voice of Flaherty.

'Look at yourself, man. Pains in your back, and your teeth dropping out and your bloody big feet hardly able to touch the floor. And that scabby old mongrel clanking after you like a bloody ball and chain. It's coming, I tell you. The end of the world's coming for you.'

The raw light of the naked bulb showed dust and boot-mud in the empty living-room, the glacial off-white of the refrigerator's door, dirtied by ten years of lurching drunken shoulders and succour-seeking hands that groped for the lavatory. Nabby Adams drank water from one of the bottles that stood in a chilled huddle. (Neither food nor beer waited in the grid-ironed body of the big icy cupboard.) Nabby Adams gulped, wincing as odd teeth lit up with momentary pain.

Lim Kean Swee	$470
Chee Sin Hye	$276
Wun Fatt Tit	$128

Nabby Adams drank his fill, feeling his stomach churn and bubble, feeling the real thirst thirstily return. He plodded upstairs again, his dog after him, and found Flaherty out on the floor, burbling prayers to the Virgin, cluttering up Nabby Adams's bedroom. Nabby Adams looked with contemptuous distaste and decided that Flaherty had better stay there. The dog thought differently. She growled and tried to bite, but Nabby Adams soothed her with:

'All right, Cough. Let the lucky bugger alone.'

Nabby Adams then considered it a good idea to have a look in Flaherty's room. After all, if Flaherty made free with his, Nabby Adams's room, it was only fair that he should return the compliment. Nabby Adams did not believe that Flaherty had brought nothing back with him from the Malay Regiment Sergeants' Mess.

Flaherty's room was tidier than that of Nabby Adams.

Hair-brushes were arranged carefully on either side of a clean comb, and a pair of recently pressed trousers lay over a chair-back. On the wall was a picture of Flaherty, made by an Arab artist on a cartographical principle. Grid-lines had been ruled over a passport photograph, and then, square by enlarged square, the face had been transferred in horrid magnification on to a large sheet of cartridge paper. The artist had given Flaherty a preternaturally high colour, somehow suggesting a painted corpse, and added, from imagination, sloping shoulders and a big red tie. This portrait smiled without pleasure at Nabby Adams as he began his search. There was no beer in the wardrobe, nor under the bed, nor in four of the drawers of the dressing-table. But the fifth drawer revealed treasure. Nabby Adams looked, like hungry Gulliver eyeing Lilliputian sirloins, at a neat collection of tiny bottles containing single glassfuls of various liqueurs. There were about a dozen of these bottles, all different, some round, some square, some doubly bulbous, some fluting up from a globular bottom. Nabby Adams surveyed them all with pity. Poor devil, he thought. His little collection, saved up as a boy saves up fireworks against Guy Fawkes Night, to be gloated over in solitude, fingered and smoothed lovingly before bedtime. Poor bugger.

Nabby Adams ingested successively Cherry Brandy Drambuie, Crème de Menthe, Cointreau, John Haig, Benedictine, Three Star, Sloe Gin, Kümmel, Kirsch. The terrible thirst abated somewhat, and Nabby Adams soon had leisure to feel shame. So he had come to this: stealing a child's toys, as good as robbing a gollywog money-box, in order to slake his selfish and inordinate hunger. Leaving the bottles stacked neatly in the drawer – they still looked pretty – he returned to his own room, his dog after him. There lay Flaherty, flat out, his face contorted to a mask of deep thought. Nabby Adams found a paper packet of Capstan in Flaherty's shirt-pocket, and, lighting himself a crushed and creased tube, lay again under the mosquito-net, taking stock of himself.

It had, perhaps, not been a very edifying life. On the booze in England, in India, in Malaya. Always owing, often drunk, sometimes incapable. Three times in hospital, three times warned solemnly to cut it out. What had he achieved? He knew nothing of anything really. A bit about motor-engines, army discipline, grave-digging, undertaking, sleeper-laying, boot-and-shoe manufacture, turf clerking, bus-conducting, Urdu grammar, organ-pumping, women, neck massage, but little else. There was this Crabbe, with a lot of books and talking about music and this ology and that ology. And there was he, Nabby Adams, whose only reading was the daily paper, who had only possessed three books in his life. One had been called The Something-or-other of the Unconscious which a bloke called Ennis had left in the guard-room and everybody had said was hot stuff, though it wasn't really; one had been a Hindustani glossary of motor-engine parts; the other had been a funny book called *Three Men in a Boat*. There was nothing to show, nothing. Only moral debts and debts of money, only imagined miles of empties and cigarette-ends.

Nabby Adams heard the *bilal* calling over the dark, saying that there was no God but Allah. Another day was starting for the faithful. But for the faithless it was better that the night should prolong itself, even into the sunlight of Sunday morning. If he had been at the Crabbes' place he would be stirring gently now in delicious sleep, fully dressed, on the planter's chair. And then that boy of the Crabbes, or, as it was now, that *amah* of theirs, would bring him a cup of tea in gentle morning light. Unless, of course, Cough happened to be guarding the chair, in which case jealous growls would send the tea back. And then a couple of gins for breakfast and then the first beers of the day in a *kedai*. Nabby Adams looked back to a week ago as to an innocent childhood. He had been driven out of that Eden as his father had been driven out of his, because of his sinful desire to taste what was forbidden. In his, Nabby Adams's, case, not an apple but the bottom of the solitary bottle of gin. In shame and anger he fell asleep, to lie abounden in a bond of dreams of a happy, coloured India, safe in the far past.

He awoke at first light to hear moans from the floor and growls from under the bed. Flaherty had come to, parched and sick and stiff as a board.

'Oh God, my bloody back. I'm paralysed, man, my face has gone all dead. Oh, why did you leave me here? Why didn't you show the act of a Christian and put me to bed, as you knew was your duty? Oh, I'm going to die.' Flaherty tottered out. Nabby Adams heard a heavy weight collapsing on bed-springs, a groan or two, then silence.

He awoke again when the sun had made the air all lemon-yellow and begun to taint the damp coolness. A figure stood by the bed, stealthily drinking tea. Through glued eyelids Nabby Adams saw Jock Keir, mean as bloody dirt, stealing the cup of tea which the cook-boy had brought for Nabby Adams. Stealing it because he knew that Nabby Adams rarely touched tea, because, saving heavily, Keir refused to pay anything for messing and preferred to send out for a single day's meal of fifty cents' worth of curry. Nabby Adams closed his eyes again.

At nine o'clock Nabby Adams was fully awake and very thirsty. He lay for a while wondering how to raise the dollar he needed. Vorpal wouldn't lend him one, Keir wouldn't, Flaherty couldn't, not just now. The *kuki*? No, not again. Nabby Adams put on his trousers and slippers and went downstairs. A week ago he had paid off ten dollars of his debt to the old *towkay* across the road. Crabbe had lent him the ten dollars. Surely one small bottle was not too much to ask?

In the living-room the cloth had been laid and two bottles of sauce stood near three egg-cups. Nobody had had breakfast yet. The cook-boy stood anxiously by.

'*Saya t'ada wang, tuan.*'

'I know you've got no bloody money. I wouldn't ask you even if you had.' Proudly man and dog went out and crossed the road.

In the *kampang* street Sunday was just another day. The *kedais* had been long open and the Malay children had long since departed for school. Nabby Adams grimly sought the shop of Guan Moh Chan, Cough clanking after him, his upper body's crumpled pyjama stripes proclaiming to all the world the urgency of his quest. The dark shop was full of family. The old man scolded a young shapeless woman who carried one baby and led another by the hand into the black depths of the living quarters. Three sons quacked to each other, sprawled about the single table, one probing his golden mouth with a toothpick. Nabby Adams spoke:

'*Satu botol.*'

The old wrinkled man chortled regretfully, sorting out the account books.

'I know all about that,' said Nabby Adams. 'I'll bring some money next time.'

'*Dua latus linggit,*' began the old man.

'*Dua ratus ringgit.* Two hundred bloody dollars. Look here,' said Nabby Adams, 'if you give me one bottle now it's not going to make all that difference, is it?' The family listened, uncomprehending, inscrutable. 'I mean, if I owe all that bloody much already, one dollar's not going to break anybody's heart.'

The old man said, '*Satu botol, satu linggit.*'

'But I haven't got a bloody dollar. Look.' Nabby Adams pulled from his trouser-pocket an old wallet, made in India long ago, torn at the seams, holding only an identity-card, a folded letter and a lottery ticket. He looked at the lottery ticket. Not a bloody chance. 'Here,' he said, 'take this. It cost a dollar. It might be worth three hundred thousand. I'll risk it. A bloody good chance like that for one bottle of Anchor.'

The old man looked carefully at the number of the ticket. His sons came over to look also. One son foolishly registered mild excitement but was quelled with a quack from his father. 'Something about the bloody number,' thought Nabby Adams. The Chinese went in a lot for lucky numbers.

Nabby Adams was given a small dusty bottle of Anchor beer to hide in his hand. He went off with it, hearing quacking from the whole bloody family. Bloody fools. As though there was anything in the lucky number idea. A lucky number for him, Nabby Adams, anyway. He had got a small bottle of beer out of it. That was the most he had ever got out of a lottery ticket.

The Chinese shopkeeper and his family watched the stiff retreating form of Nabby Adams and the wagging rump of his dog. Then they looked again at the number, quacking with great excitement. Ostensibly Christian, they were all profound Taoists in fact, and what excited them now was an arrangement of nine numbers which could easily be resolved into the Magic Square:

$$4\ 9\ 2\ 3\ 5\ 7\ 8\ 1\ 6$$

The Noah of China, Emperor Yu, walked along the banks of a tributary of the Yellow River one day after the Great Flood. He saw a tortoise rising from the river with a strange pattern on its back. Miraculously, this pattern resolved itself in his eyes into the Magic Square, the ideal arrangement of the *yin-yang* digits. Out of this came a plan for reconstructing the world and devising the perfect system of government.

Slowly the third son wrote out the number on Nabby Adams's lottery ticket in the form of a square:

$$
\begin{array}{ccc}
4 & 9 & 2 \\
3 & 5 & 7 \\
8 & 1 & 6
\end{array}
$$

Yes, yes, it was! Whichever way you added up, across or down or diagonally, you got the number 15, symbol of Man Perfected. Their dancing excitement was succeeded by a feeling of awe. Perhaps this huge yellow man was really a sort of god, perhaps it was their duty to feed him with all the beer he wanted. See how that dog follows him everywhere; he has power over animals. He is bigger than the common run of men; he speaks a strange tongue. And now he gives a piece of paper with the Magic Square telescoped on it.

'We must wait till the result is put in the newspaper. Then when we win we can give him perhaps a chicken or perhaps even a small pig.'

'He does not eat.'

'Then perhaps six bottles of beer.'

'And his bill?'

'He does not know it, but his bill has been paid already. There is a man he has helped with his car which was in a bad accident and he would not take a bribe so this man came to me and said I must send the bills to him. This I have done, but he, the big man, does not know that yet. Nor shall he ever be told by me.'

The sons chortled at their old father's cunning. Then one son said:

'Surely today is the day of the lottery draw?'

'Find out moonshine.' They went to their Chinese calendar. 'Yes, it is today that the winning numbers are published. The English papers are out now, but the Chinese paper will arrive at noon.'

'It is but a short time to wait. How providential that we should be given the winning ticket but three hours before the result is announced. This big man shall most certainly be rewarded with a gift of beer.'

The big man had entered the shabby living-room of the mess. Keir was sneering over his Sunday paper, while Vorpal cracked a boiled egg.

'Can't beat a bit of the old egg-fruit-*lah*. Though this one's a bit on the high side. Seen better days-*lah*.'

Keir said, 'Somebody in Lanchap's got the winning number. Not me, anyway. It's a mug's game. Million-to-one chance. If you don't spend a dollar you know you've got a dollar. That's two-and-fourpence back home, and you can do a lot with two-and-fourpence.'

'Somebody in Lanchap?' said Nabby Adams.

'Yes,' sneered Keir. 'Are you the lucky man?'

But Nabby Adams was off, the bottle still hidden in his vast paw. Breathless, the dog followed after.

In the *kedai* Nabby Adams said, 'Here's your bottle back. Let's have a look at that bloody ticket.'

The *towkay* indicated deep regret. A transaction had been completed, could not be revoked. Nabby Adams was now bloody sure that that was one of the winning tickets, that they had seen the blasted results already, that was why that young bastard had got so bloody excited and the old man had tried to shut his bloody trap for him.

'Look here,' said Nabby Adams. 'I want that ticket. Here's your beer. You get your beer back; I get my ticket back. You savvy?'

The old man offered Nabby Adams a dollar note. Nabby Adams went wild and his dog barked. 'If I don't get that bloody ticket back I'll break the bloody shop up.' He threatened, huge, angry. The Chinese family realized that the anger of even a minor god was a thing to be reckoned with. The *towkay* took down from a shelf a small bundle of lottery tickets and offered a ticket to Nabby Adams. Nabby Adams looked at it suspiciously.

'Can take beer too,' said the old man.

'This isn't the right ticket,' said Nabby Adams. 'You're trying it on. Why are you so bloody eager to give me the bottle of beer as well?'

'Is ticket,' said the *towkay*.

'Is bloody not,' said Nabby Adams. 'Give me the right one or I'll smash it all up, all the bloody lot, beginning with that bloody shelf of condensed milk there.' A huge flailing arm was ready. The dog barked. The *towkay* tut-tutted and clucked and, searching carefully through the sheaf of tickets, chose another one which he gave to Nabby Adams.

'Come to your bloody senses,' said Nabby Adams. 'That's more like it.' He scanned the number – 112673225 – and wished to God he could remember whether it was the right one.

'And I'll keep the beer,' said Nabby Adams.

Ten minutes later Nabby Adams sat dumbfounded, the bottle still unopened, over the front page of the Sunday paper. It couldn't be true. It was all a bloody practical joke.

112673225.

Vorpal drank a fourth cup of tea and said, 'Something wrong with old Nabby-*lah*. First time I ever seen him not want any breakfast-*lah*. Crying out for beer and when he's got it he won't touch it-*lah*.' Keir sneered and went to suck his empty teeth on the veranda. Nabby Adams closed one eye, opened it, closed the other, and quizzed the number again. There were so many bloody numbers and he couldn't keep the paper steady. Clamped to the paper with his thumb was the ticket.

112673225.

Such a bloody long number. He tried again slowly. 1126. 1126. That was all right. He trembled and blood sang in his ears so that he couldn't hear what Vorpal was saying. Steady now. He breathed in deeply and tried the number from the end. 5223. 5223. Christ, this was all right too. He began to feel very sick. Now the bloody figure in the middle, if he could get that far. But which way to go? From the beginning or the end? He almost closed his eyes and tried to focus on the heart of the trembling number, almost praying that it wouldn't be 7, that there would be no need for palpitations and perhaps fainting and all the new life that this would mean. He wanted to be left alone, in debt, always thirsty. He took a shot at the core of the long number and nearly reeled over.

7.

Oh Christ, it was true.

'You don't look so good, Nabby,' said Vorpal with anxiety. Then he moved forward, staring at the prodigy, and Keir came in from the veranda too, as Nabby Adams crumpled and crashed off his chair. The house rumbled seismically at the heavy fall. The dog barked. The two men tried to lift the huge dead weight.

'Leave him there-*lah*,' ordered Vorpal. 'Get some bloody brandy, quick.'

'There isn't any,' said Keir. 'It wouldn't last two minutes if there was, not with him about.'

'Well, get that bloody beer-bottle open,' urged Vorpal. 'Pour it down his throat-*lah*. Come on, man.'

'It's caught up with him at last,' sneered Keir.

Vorpal tipped beer down Nabby Adams's gullet, and the frothy brew spilled over stubbly chin and faded pyjama-jacket. All the time the dog danced and barked.

'He's coming round-*lah*,' said Vorpal. 'Speak to me, Nabby. How do you feel now-*lah*? Christ, you gave us a turn-*lah*.'

'I've won,' groaned Nabby Adams. 'I've won. I've bloody won. I've won, I tell you. I've won the bloody first prize. The first bloody prize. I've won. Oh.' And he passed out again.

The two men, awed as in the presence of imminent death, could only look down on the huge wreck which the dog, whimpering, ranged over, looking for places to lick. The lavish cold tongue, laving his frothy lips, brought Nabby Adams back to life. He groaned.

'I've bloody well won. I've won. The first bloody prize.'

'And by Christ, he has too.' Vorpal held paper and ticket, scanning, checking, re-checking, confirming.

'There must be a mistake,' said Keir, pale, forgetting to sneer.

'There's no mistake. It's there in black and white. Look, man.'

'I've won. I've won. Oh Christ, I've won.'

'There, there, Nabby,' soothed Vorpal. 'You're with friends-*lah*. You'll feel a bit better in a minute. I'll send the *kuki* out for some beer.'

'I've won, I've won, I tell you. Oh God.'

'Three-hundred and fifty thousand bucks,' said Vorpal. 'Settling day one week from now-*lah*.'

'Three hundred and fifty thou ...' Keir sat down, limp as a leaf.

'I've won.' Nabby Adams was calmer now, resigned, pale as death, reconciled to the dread sentence. He sat, wretched, on a chair, and absently patted the dog.

'You've won, boy,' said Vorpal. '*Kuki*!' he called. 'We're going to celebrate-*lah*. A case of Tiger.'

'Carlsberg,' said Nabby Adams, 'It's a bit dearer, but it's a better beer.'

'Carlsberg,' said Vorpal. 'Brandy. Champagne-*lah*. Any bloody thing you like.'

Nabby Adams gloomily scanned the winning ticket, his hands still hardly able to hold it.

'For God's sake don't lose that,' said Vorpal. I'll look after it for you.'

'No,' said Nabby Adams. 'He'll look after it. It's safer with him.'

'Who?'

'Crabbe. Crabbe'll look after it. I'll give it to Crabbe. It'll be all right with him.'

The *kuki*, staggering back with a clinking case of beer, said that this was a present for the big *tuan*. On top of the bottles was a skinny chicken, glistening with refrigerator-ice.

'It's always the bloody same,' said Nabby Adams gloomily. 'When you've got it you go on getting it. I wish I was bloody dead.'

'You will be,' sneered Keir, 'You soon will be.'

Then a strange thing happened. The dog Cough bared her teeth at Keir and with a profound belly-growl advanced on him.

'Take her away! Call her off!' Keir backed on to the porch, Cough's naked teeth ready to lunge. 'Bloody dog!' Then Keir ran into the street, Cough, out for blood, after him. Man and dog disappeared, gaining speed. Nabby Adams could seen astonished faces of Malays looking off-stage. He decapitated a bottle of Carlsberg.

'I've won,' he said, before drinking.

15

The river was rising steadily when term ended. It was still possible to drive through the streets of Kuala Hantu, but dwellers near the river's edge had taken to the roofs and the bazaar had had to close down. Up-stream the rain thundered and soon, in time for Christmas – the birthday of the Prophet Isa – Kuala Hantu would resound to the whip-lashings of the frenzied sky. Then there would be cosy isolation for those who lived up the hill, the boats would ply between the stone and wood islands, and the prices of foodstuffs would mount drunkenly. Meantime there was Crabbe's farewell party at Kong Huat's – five dollars a head for all members of the staff, drink extra, no pork in deference to the Muslims.

It was a tradition in the Mansor School that a departing master should be given a Chinese dinner. Though wives were barred, there was no roystering, no doubtful jokes, little inebriation. It was just another staff-meeting, with Boothby yawning at the head of the table, the agenda consisting of equivocal dishes which were served in no special order, just dumped on the table as they were ready. Thus one could never be sure when the meal had ended. On one occasion chicken legs had appeared during the speeches, on another the ice-cream had come first. *Tida' apa*.

The staff was very pleased at some news that had just come through, on the very day of the dinner in fact. Boothby was also leaving. He was being transferred to an obscure school somewhere in Pahang. It was providential that the news should have come through when it did, for now one farewell dinner could serve for two people, and everybody had thus saved five dollars.

In the dingy upper room of Kong Huat's Crabbe looked round for the last time at his colleagues: Mr Raj's sad jowl; the golden sullen Adonis Mr Roper, looking bitterly at Boothby as though Boothby had fathered him; Gervase Michael, the black Catholic Tamil; Lee, the Chinese mathematician, fingering peanut-shells as though they were the balls of an abacus; Inche Jamaluddin, quizzing over shy spectacles; Tuan Haji Mohamed Noor, who spoke no English and smiled benevolently now, like one who knows he is saved; Crichton, with Australian apple cheeks like a Pommie; MacNee the Ulsterman; the squirming four Malay probationers; Hung the geographer; Wallis the art man; Inche Abu Zakaria, skilled in woodwork; Solomons the scientist; Gora Singh, huge-bellied, grey-bearded, his turban almost meeting steel spectacles.

'Awwwwwwwww!' And, of course, Boothby.

'You do not like shark's fin soup, Mr Boothby?' said Gora Singh. 'It is very rich and glutinous. It is good for the stomach.'

'Can't stand fish of any kind,' said Boothby. 'It brings me out in spots.'

'I have a sister,' said Inche Jamaluddin, 'who similarly cannot eat mushrooms. She swells like one who is pregnant almost at the very smell of them. That is one of the reasons why she was married at the age of twelve. The other reason was because of the Japanese. They had some little decency. They would not put married girls into the common soldier's brothels.'

'Shark's fin soup is aphrodisiacal in its effect,' said Mr Raj. 'The Taoists believe that the duality of *yin* and *yang* functions even in diet. Steamed fish and chicken and vegetable soup and even mushrooms are considered to be cooling foods, edible materializations of the *yang*, the pure primal air. The *yin*, or earth element, inheres in fried dishes and especially in shark's fin soup. Am I right, Mr Lee?'

'You may well be. As an empiricist I am concerned only

with the external accidents of the things I eat. And I know nothing of metaphysics.'

'Plenty of jaw-brykers flying around,' said Crichton. 'Aphro whatsits and whatnots.'

'You will perceive that Mr Boothby has no need of aphrodisiacs,' said Gora Singh with heavy humour. 'He will not eat his soup. He is a better man than any of us, ha ha.' Gora Singh spooned more of the almost solid soup into his own bowl, poured in soya sauce and added sliced chillis, and then ate with much relish and sucking. His great paunch intervened between him and the table, and fishy gouts kept bespattering beard and shirt on the spoon's long journeys.

After the soup came sweet-and-sour prawns. ' A *yin* dish,' said Mr Raj. 'A heat food.'

'This is most unfortunate for Mr Boothby,' said Gora Singh with a large smile. 'Here is more fish, and fish brings him out in spots. He is, so far, not having a very good dinner.'

'I'm all right,' sulked Boothby. He leaned his elbows on the table and yawned. 'Awwwwwwww!'

'I have long wished to know, Mr Boothby,' said Inche Abu Zakaria, 'whether that is perhaps an ailment. I have often felt pity for you because of it. It is perhaps a disease of which I have read called the gapes.'

'That is a disease of poultry,' said Mr Gervase Michael. 'We had chickens which had it badly. I forget now how it was cured. One chicken certainly we lost.'

'Mr Boothby is no chicken,' said Gora Singh, the life and soul of the party. 'Ha ha.' He tore into his sweet-and-sour prawns, taking Boothby's share as well as his own.

'I don't understand what you're talking about,' said Boothby. 'Unless perhaps someone's trying to be funny.'

Gora Singh suddenly roared with grey-bearded laughter. He put down his fork and said, 'Ha ha ha, a crab is a fish, Mr Crabbe. I have just thought of it. Ha ha ha. That is very funny. Mr Boothby will come out in spots, Mr

Crabbe, if he tries to devour you. Ha ha ha, that is very funny.' He explained the joke in Malay to Haji Mohamed Noor. It took a long time, and, when it was evident that the Haji would never grasp the point, the next course had arrived.

'Look here,' said Boothby, 'is this a put-up job, or something? Don't I get anything to eat at all?'

'I can assure you, Mr Boothby,' said Mr Roper, 'that we knew nothing of your being allergic to fish. When I was deputed to arrange this dinner I merely told the management here to give us a varied Chinese meal. That they have, so far, done. I am sorry you cannot eat fish.' He then gracefully scooped himself a portion of the *ikan merah* which lay, covered with cucumber, in a shallow pool of sauce.

'*Yin,*' said Mr Raj.

The next dish was an innocuous mess of fried vegetables. Boothby ate greedily and then began to hiccough.

'One should hold the breath and take many sips of water,' suggested Inche Jamaluddin.

'A sudden shock is best,' said Hung. 'A blow between the shoulders.'

'Or between the eyes,' said Crabbe, 'like this.' He took from his jacket-pocket the winning lottery-ticket. 'Examine the number, gentlemen.'

'So it was your ticket! Well!'

'I had heard it was a policeman in the town.'

'A man in Kelapa, I was told.'

'Well, this is most surprising.'

'To think it was Mr Crabbe.'

'Secretive about it, weren't you?' said Solomons.

'Too right you were.'

'Well.'

'Mr Crabbe.'

'A very, very rich man.'

It cured Boothby's hiccoughs.

'Now,' said Crabbe, 'I can go back to England whenever I like. I can expose many things in the Press. I can perhaps even ruin a few careers. This represents a lot of money. Money is power.'

'You could start a school.'

'On the most scientific pedagogical principles,' said Mr Raj.

'You could travel the world.'

'You need never work again.'

'Well.'

'To think it was Mr Crabbe all the time.'

Everybody was too excited to be much interested in the next course. Everybody except Boothby. Boothby banged his fist on the table and said:

'The lot of you! The whole bloody lot of you! You've all worked against me! You've all tried to ruin me! But just wait, that's all, just wait. I'll get the whole bloody lot of you if it's the last thing I do. Stop talking!' he yelled to Gora Singh. 'When I'm bloody well talking you'll kindly shut up. I'm still Headmaster!'

'I was translating for the Haji's benefit,' said Gora Singh. 'And you will not speak to me in that manner.'

'I'll speak as I bloody well like!'

'Boothby,' said Crabbe, 'you've had it. Sit down and eat your nice fish.'

Boothby screamed, picked up a large dish of fried rice garnished with shrimps, and then hurled it at Crabbe. He missed and struck a fly-blown picture of Sun Yet Sen.

Then they heard steady chanting from below.

'It's the seniors,' said Mr Roper, turning round in his chair to look down from the window.

'I'll get them too,' raved Boothby. 'They're all in it. Who gave them permission to be out, eh? Who gave them permission?'

'It's end of term,' said Crichton.

The words of the chant were discernible.

'We want Crabbe! We want Crabbe! We want Crabbe!'

Boothby, red hair all anyhow, turned in triumph. 'You

see, you bastard. You didn't get away with it. They want you. God help you if they get you.'

'We want Crabbe!'

'You see!' Boothby grinned horribly. Then a single voice was raised from below, cutting clearly through the chant:

'Crabbe for Headmaster!'

Raggedly the cry was taken up. There were cheers, and then:

'Crabbe for Head! Crabbe for Head!'

Boothby shook his fists, standing at the stair-head. 'Rotten to the core! Treachery and corruption! Just you wait, that's all, just you wait!' Then, gasping for breath, he began to stamp down the stairs. They heard him stumble and swear half-way down. Then he could be heard stamping out the back way, seeking his car.

'Now we can finish our dinner,' said Gora Singh. 'It was as well he did not stay. The other two courses are also fish. Though, of course, there is ice-cream.'

'Crabbe for Head!'

The noise of angry gears and a fretful engine. Boothby was going home. The car sang into the distance.

'Before you start thinking me mean for not ordering champagne and cigars,' said Crabbe, 'I'd better say now that I didn't really win the lottery. It was just a cure for hiccoughs.'

'I thought that was not the winning number.'

'Yes, I know the number well.'

'I knew all the time it was a joke. Ha ha ha.'

'It was very clever.'

'It was obvious,' said Mr Raj. 'You are not the type of person who would ever win a great fortune. You are not a lucky person. It is evident from your face.'

'Crabbe for Head!' A little desultory now, a little liturgical.

'Well, that's a relief,' said Crichton. 'If you don't mind my saying so.'

'It made him very angry.'

'That was the intention.'

'Ha ha. A very good joke.'

'So Mr Crabbe is a poor man again.'

'He will deign to finish this simple fare and wash it down with nothing more Lucullan than beer.'

'Well,' said somebody, 'Poor Boothby. Nobody could say he went out like a lamb.'

'He was only an imitation lion,' said Mr Raj. 'His teeth were false and his claws were made of cardboard. I feel very sorry for him.'

'He was not a bad Headmaster,' said Inche Jamaluddin, 'as Headmasters go. In twenty years at the Mansor School I have known many far worse.'

'He lost his temper too much.'

'He yawned all the time.'

'The British,' said Mr Raj, 'have done heroic work in the tropics. When one considers how temperate and gentle is their northern island . . .'

'Islands,' corrected MacNeice.

'. . . one marvels at their fundamental strength of will. The time is coming for them to leave the East. At least, the time is coming for those who will not be absorbed. One cannot fight against the jungle or the sun. To resist is to invite madness. Mr Boothby is mad. It is a great pity. If he had stayed at home . . .'

'Crabbe for Head!'

'Close the window,' said Crabbe. 'We can switch on the other fan.'

'They are going now,' said Mr Roper. 'Their exuberance does not last very long.'

'If he stayed at home he would have been a decent little schoolmaster. He has had too much power. In a few years he will retire and then he will drag on his empty life, freed by an adequate pension from the need to work. But he will be recognizably mad. People will laugh at him and not wish to play golf or tennis with him. And he will bore people with his unintelligible talk about a country he could never learn to understand. It is a pity. His life has been ruined.'

'And will my life be ruined too?' asked Crabbe.

'Oh yes,' said Mr Raj calmly. 'But with you it will not be a pity. The country will absorb you and you will cease to be Victor Crabbe. You will less and less find it possible to do the work for which you were sent here. You will lose function and identity. You will be swallowed up and become another kind of eccentric. You may become a Muslim. You may forget your English, or at least lose your English accent. You may end in a *kampong*, no longer a foreigner, an old brownish man with many wives and children, one of the elders whom the young will be encouraged to consult on matters of the heart. You will be ruined.'

'Crabbe for Head!' A few straggling voices, already losing interest.

'That cry is your death-warrant,' said Mr Raj. 'The proletariat is always wrong.'

The rain began to come down heavily. The ants flew into the electric lamp. Sweat gleamed on brown and white and yellow foreheads. Mosquitoes began to nip thin-socked or bare ankles. There were no more voices calling from below.

'Tomorrow,' said Mr Raj, 'we shall awaken to a flooded world.'

16

Sergeant Alladad Khan, the three new brass chevrons not glittering at all in the dull rainy light, came back by river from the workshops at Kelapa. He was erect in the stern of the police launch and Kassim was at the wheel, unhandy as ever. Allah, the world was all river now. The river had thirstily engulfed much of the main street, all the dirty lanes by the bazaar, had even climbed up the stone steps of the old Residency, virtually marooning the Crabbes. Tree-tops rose bushily from the grey sheets of water, and snakes were lodging in the branches. An old Chinese man had stood by his housedoor to pray the flood away from his family; he had been carried off by a crocodile. Old boats had been capsized or been sucked down – the seams uncaulked – loaded with household chattels. These were bad but thrilling days. For here was he, Alladad Khan, chugging back to the swilling yard of the Transport Office, riding the flood like the Prophet Noah, lord of the river, granted the freedom of the waters. Allah, there was something more dignified, more befitting a man, about this stately progress than the rasping of brakes and jerking of gears on the dusty jolting road.

Lord of the river but of little more. For she had soon learned, as women will, to adjust herself to her brother's defection and treacherously-acquired prosperity. Was it not evident that his career would be advanced by this cunning marriage? For he was meeting all the best people now, and – as for his wife – obviously so good a Muslim would bring her in time to the true faith. His drinking was a sort of self-elected martyrdom, a mere means to gaining greater strength through the right social contacts. Abdul Khan had told her so himself.

As for her attitude to him, Alladad Khan – well, it was much the same as before. Except that she was quite pleased with his promotion, proud of his wound in the arm, and soothed with the presents he had been able to buy her with money given freely and generously by Adams Sahib. And he, Alladad Khan, had decided that the child was not unlike himself – an unaggressive nose, an intelligent forehead, eyes both lively and melting. This child he dandled now in his arms, singing old songs of the Punjab, and she approved of the fond fatherliness he evinced. She let him go out occasionally and did not complain overmuch if he returned with bright eyes and rolling gait. One thing she still would not allow was that horrible erotic act which was a commonplace of American and European films, but she took complaisantly enough now to his other husbandly advances.

It was as well, thought Alladad Khan, that he construct something on which to rejoice, for soon he would be losing his friends. The first week after Christmas the Crabbes would be flying to another State; a month later Adams Sahib would be leaving the Federation for ever. He, Alladad Khan, would be alone. Perhaps, however, he could ensure against being completely alone by cultivating the few roods of garden wished upon him. He would try to love his wife, he would protect and cherish his daughter, he would continue to learn English, he would have a shelf of books and a few pictures on the walls. Perhaps some day he would have a son, and, when he retired to the Punjab, there would be a few acres and cows and horses and a vista of progeny carrying in its head, retailing round the winter fire, the legends of him, Alladad Khan – soldier, dreamer, policeman, cosmopolitan, cultivated, free-thinking. It was not much, but it was something.

She would wish the son to be called Abdul Khan, but there he would most definitely put his foot down.

Alladad Khan was interested to note that, in the sparse

speedy river traffic, a boat careered gaily along containing a raja and the raja's new mistress. The raja was a young dissipated man in a European suit; Alladad Khan knew him well by sight. The girl he knew even better. She had formerly been the mistress of Victor Crabbe. Now she seemed happy enough with her smart *baju* and slinky sarong, her gold-studded handbag, her ear-rings of Kelantan silver, her dissipated but probably virile young raja. Allah, women had no faith.

None except one.

And at Kelapa he had seen that faithless boy, tittering around, the minion of a paunched planter. In the store by the workshops he had seen him, buying food for the bungalow, but also spending wild money on gaudy trinkets and childish toys – a doll's house lavatory, a jack-in-the-box, paper flowers and wax fruit. He had moved provocative girlish shoulders at Alladad Khan and tossed his tinted hair. The world was speedboat-speeding to its final collapse. Friends go and women and boys are faithless and God may not exist. There remains the flat in the Police Barracks, however, and in it a long-nosed wife with cannibal teeth, a baby, a bed, chapattis hissing and jumping on the stove.

And things one likes to remember.

'Kassim!' he shouted. 'Bloody fool! Silly bastard!' For Kassim was gloomily steering straight for the yard wall by the Transport Office, speed unslackened, the boat's nose ready for a bullet impact with red brick. Alladad Khan took control.

'*Minta ma'af,* Corporal,' said Kassim.

'Sergeant,' corrected Alladad Khan, 'sergeant. Allah will you never learn? Three stripes is sergeant.'

'I have much on my mind,' said Kassim. 'There is my new wife and the money is difficult. I should be glad to be merely a corporal.'

'Promotion comes when one has proved one's ability.'

'But that is not fair. You have but one wife and you do

not need all the money you have as a sergeant. I have three wives now and it is very hard.'

'Hari Singh has been promised the rank of corporal. Admittedly, he has as little ability in matters of transport as yourself, but he at least knows some English and plays football for the Police Circle.'

'I never have time for these things, Corporal.'

'There is no God but Allah,' swore Alladad Khan. 'Will you never learn?'

'But I have no opportunity to go to the evening classes. There seems always so much to do in the house.'

'We will say no more,' said Alladad Khan, alighting to tread some inches of flood-water. 'Wait here. The *tuan* and myself must go out together soon to the big school-house on the hill. You must be ready to take much *barang* on board. Today is a big day with the Christians. It is called Christmas Eve. They celebrate the birth of the Prophet Isa.'

'That is why there is a free day tomorrow.'

'Yes. And the day after. I beseech you to do as little as possible in the house. We shall require you to be fit and eager for the resumption of work. Take your wives for a trip on the river. You are reaching an age when energy must be conserved.'

'Yes, Corporal,' said Kassim.

17

The evening of the eve of Christmas promised to bloom
and fade lovely over the waters. Warm light shot through
the rainy western cloud, catching the hair of the jungle
and irradiating the misty wreaths on the mountain-tops.
Crabbe and his wife stood high above the town, having
climbed to the roof of the crumbling watch-tower to look
at the streets of water, the huge swollen river, the craft
gliding or chuffing upon it. Even below, beyond the highest flight of stone stairs, little boats bobbed and rode. In
one of them was a recognizable figure, being rowed home.
Crabbe waved and the figure waved back in high laughter
that rang faintly over the wet waste.

'*Misti lulus!* He he he he!'

Then, still waving and tittering, he was borne away to
wife and seven children and the roof of his tiny flooded
home.

'Christmas Eve,' said Fenella. 'Cold streets and warm
pubs and all the children excited. Camaraderie for a brief
unreal space, toasts and back-slappings. For something
they don't even understand, let alone believe in. And the
carols.' She began to sing, unmusically, in a badly pitched
key:

> 'The holly and the ivy,
> When they are both full-grown,
> Of all the trees . . .'

Then she put her face in her hands and sobbed. Crabbe
comforted her.

'It means nothing here,' he said. 'This is the land of
a later prophet. But, whoever he was, he could have been
born here more fittingly than amid fancied winter snow.
The *towkays* hoicking at the *kampong* couple, the chil-

198

dren staring up from the monsoon drains – though that's not possible now, of course – and the search for a room in a Chinese hotel. And then the *timbu* in the Sikh stable and the birth in the smell of dung.'

'I can't help it,' said Fenella, wiping her eyes. 'It's always the same. Something to do with lost innocence, I suppose.'

The swift twilight began to run like a fishing-line off a reel. From below came an approaching chugging and then a hail:

'Ahoy!'

Crabbe and Fenella looked down to see a launch mooring by the steps, a huge man talking petulantly in Urdu, several crates, the craft overweighted.

'Ahoy!'

'The bloody thing nearly capsized,' came a distant grumbling voice. 'We had to throw one bloody crate of Anchor overboard.'

'I'll come down and help!' shouted Crabbe.

It was slow and sweating work lugging crates of beer for Nabby Adams, sherry for Alladad Khan, champagne for the Crabbes up the stairs to the near-denuded flat. Houseboys were called from their vacation to help. Nabby Adams dispensed lordly gratuities.

'*Terima kaseh, tuan.*'

'*Terima kaseh.*'

'*Terima kaseh banyak, tuan.*'

'*Sama sama,*' said Alladad Khan.

'*Samsu samsu,*' said Nabby Adams. 'Who the bloody hell does he think he is, anyway? It's my bloody money, not his.'

Nabby Adams, indulgent of the weaknesses of others, had brought cold chickens and pork pies, tins of ham, wedges of cheese, loaves, melting slabs of butter, fruit, marmalade, jars of pickled onions, crackers, Christmas puddings, slabs of dried fish, pink cakes, bottled mushrooms, figs, chocolates, cough-sweets, canned soups, Dutch cigars, potted shrimps, smoked salmon, caviare, tinned pâté, hard-boiled eggs, and a hunk of meat for a dripping dog that sprayed the stairs with its happy tail.

'Would insist on coming,' said Nabby Adams. 'She jumped out of the bloody window and swam after us. So we had to pull her on board.'

They sat on coverless armchairs in the pictureless, bookless flat. Only a group photograph, delivered that morning by post-boat, had been too late for the crates and boxes.

'It's the Upper School,' said Crabbe, 'and there's me in the middle of the front row.'

'And who's this Chinese kid with the black eye?' asked Nabby Adams.

'He's the *musah dalam selimut*,' said Crabbe. 'The enemy in the blanket. But not here any more. He's going to Singapore. There's more scope there in the Chinese schools.'

There was distant gunfire.

'Still at it,' said Nabby Adams. 'Not even on Christmas Eve can they let up.'

Bottle-tops were levered off, drawn, popped. They all drank from beer-glasses.

'So you've made up your mind, Nabby?' said Crabbe.

'Yes. Back to Bombay. I'll settle down there. There's no place like it.'

'But what will you *do*?' asked Fenella.

'Well, nothing really, Mrs Crabbe. I'll just live there. There's no place like Bombay.'

'You can't drink there any more,' said Crabbe. 'Prohibition's in force.'

'Well, I can really,' said Nabby Adams. 'You see, I've got this.' He took from a note-crammed wallet a crumpled letter. Crabbe unfolded it and read:

'This is to certify that the bearer is a confirmed alcoholic and may be served with intoxicating liquors in any hotel where he requests them.

'P. Vivekananda. M.B., Ch.B., Madras.'

'If you want a drink when you're in India, Mrs Crabbe,' said Nabby Adams seriously, 'you just get one of them. Then you'll have no trouble.'

They drank and ate. Nabby Adams consented to take a little cheese and a small piece of bread. Alladad Khan tore a chicken with his teeth.

'It makes me real sick to see him,' said Nabby Adams, 'gorging like that. No moderation somehow when he starts anything. And I got him them three bloody stripes before this came through, because I needed the extra money he'd get. And not a bit bloody grateful.' He spoke long Urdu. 'And he won't come with me to Bombay. Says he'll stay here. Oh,' said Nabby Adams, 'that reminds me. You two have been real good to me and him. And you held that ticket for me when I would have lost the bloody thing. Well, you're getting ten per cent. That's only fair. Thirty-five thousand. I've put it in the bank for you already.'

'We couldn't, really . . .'

'It's terribly kind, but . . .'

'You're always saying as how you want to get back home and start a school or a pub or something. Well, here's your chance. What's thirty-five thousand to me?'

'It's awfully kind,' said Fenella, 'but really . . .'

'I don't think she wants to go home now,' said Crabbe. 'She wants to stay here.'

'Yes,' said Fenella. 'I want to stay here.'

'Well, you keep the money just the same,' said Nabby Adams. 'You can have a bloody good piss-up with that.' Then he stared in horror. 'I didn't mean that, honest I didn't, it just slipped out like, Mrs Crabbe, honest, I'm sorry, really I am.'

'*Ap khuch karab bolta,*' said Alladad Khan.

'And I'll say something a bloody sight worse if you start pulling me up,' said Nabby Adams. 'Full of himself since he got his third stripe.' He gave a lengthy speech in Urdu. Alladad Khan worked away at a chicken-leg, indifferent.

They drank and ate.

'Christmas Eve,' said Nabby Adams. 'I used to pump the bloody organ for the carols, proper pissed usually . . .' He began a glazed look of horror.

'Well, what else can you call it?' said Crabbe quickly.

'That's right,' said Nabby Adams with serious warmth. 'What else can you call it? Anyway, there was one that I used to like, more of a im really than a Christmas carol.' Nabby Adams coughed and cleared his throat and began to sing in a graveyard bass:

> 'O come, all ye faithful,
> Joyful and triumphant,
> O come ye, O come ye
> To Beth Lee Em.'

Fenella began to cry, and Alladad Khan made a serious, concerned statement in chiding Urdu. Nabby Adams, disturbed, said:

'I'm sorry, Mrs Crabbe, I know I've not got much of a voice and you being musical and all, but I didn't think it was that bad it'd make you cry, honest.'

They drank, and the evening poured itself out in a long bubbling or frothing or aromatic stream, and Alladad Khan sang a Punjabi hunting song and addressed the Crabbes seriously in Urdu, and the Crabbes addressed Nabby Adams in Malay, and it became Whitsun more than Christmas, for the Tower of Babel lay with the empty bottles.

At length Nabby Adams looked towards the planter's chair on the veranda, and said:

'Just five minutes.'

Alladad Khan sang quietly to himself, eyes glazed, sherry bottle in hand; Crabbe began to sing a counterpoint, seriously, sonorously:

> 'The holly and the ivy,
> When they are both full-grown,
> Of all the trees that are in the wood,
> The holly bears the crown.'

Alladad Khan left him to sing on his own, pale beneath the warm brown, off to the lavatory. Fenella cried and cried.

'His art up,' said Nabby Adams sleepily. Then he snored gently, the dog clankingly searching for fleas beside the planter's chair, unaware as yet of her booked passage to India.

Fenella sobbed. Crabbe took her in his arms and comforted her. Then midnight sounded from the half-drowned town clock. Above the broken meats, the drained bottles, the insect noises, the gunfire, the snores and the retchings he wished her a merry Christmas.

The Enemy in the Blanket

'Their coming and going is sure in the night : in the plains of Asia (saith he), the storks meet on such a set day, he that comes last is torn to pieces, and so they get them gone.'

ROBERT BURTON:
'A Digression on the Air'

The Malay State of Dahaga and its towns and inhabitants do not really exist.

I

The Chinese captain and the Malay second pilot worked stolidly through the check-list.

'Lap-straps, no smoking?'

'*Sudah*.'[1]

'Hydraulic hand-pump?'

'*Tutup*.'[2]

'Carburettor heat?'

'*Sejuk*.'[3]

It was Chinese New Year, the first day of the Year of the Monkey. The passengers had driven through the hot morning town to the airport, slowed or stopped by the Lion-dance swaying through the streets. Young slim-waisted Chinese had crashed gongs, looking somehow Mexican in wide-brimmed straw hats and the brisk sweating dancer had leapt and run and bowed and advanced and retreated. He had been encased from the shoulders up in the round ugly lion head, while, yards of fluttering cloth away, a small boy had pranced as the tail. Into the open mouth of the Lion people had stuffed, for good luck, little red parcels of *ang pows*. But here, on the brown-grassed airfield, it was just another flying day, nearly time for take-off to the northern fringe of the peninsula.

In Victor Crabbe's mouth a tongue was stuffed like a parcel, a *pow* by no means *ang*. In his head a Lion-dance circled and thumped to loud gong-crashes. Last night he had been smothered with Chinese New Year hospitality. Bird's nest, shark's fin, sucking pig, boiled duck, bamboo shoots, bean sprouts, huge staring fish, sweet-and-sour prawns, stuffed gourds, crisp fried rice and chicken-wings.

1. Done.   2. Shut.   3. Cold.

And whisky. Glass after glass of it, neat. *Kung Hee Fatt Choy*. That meant roughly, a Happy New Year. One mustn't lose face; one couldn't say, 'No more whisky'. He lolled back, eyes closed, ears closed too to his wife's quiet weeping.

Fenella Crabbe sniffed into her handkerchief, and the Sikh traveller in the seat across the aisle smiled with sympathy. It was hard to leave old friends, a loved house, a known town. But duty was duty. Where the British were sent, there they had to go. That was how they had built their Empire, an Empire now crashing about their ears. The Sikh smiled at the vanity of human aspirations. He had been, in his earlier, less prosperous, days, a fortune-teller. He was not that now, he was . . .

Fenella Crabbe read yet again the anonymous letter. It had been delivered into her hands by a small Tamil boy as they stepped into the taxi that morning. It was typed — heavy old office-Oliver type – on greyish paper. The letter ran:

Dear Sister,
My heart has swelled often and again with humble appreciation that you and your husband not like rest of white men in this country. For they suck from bounteous earth like greedy pigs from udder of mother-sow the great riches of rubber which Indians planted in pre-historic ages. Laughing haughtily, they drink at white men's club and spurn their brothers of skin of different hue. But your husband and you, Sister, in no manner like that. For you have freely mingled and show love to your poorer brothers and sisters.

But, O Sister, perhaps you are misguided. Perhaps, in poetic words of base Indian, you love not wisely but too well. And here I refer to your husband the teacher whose brain, though it contain knowledge to bestow in overflowing measure and bounty on eager learning youth, it can yet stoop to base act of sexuality. For it is known that he has for many months sated uncontrolled lust on simple Malay girl who is widow and orphan, both. And she herself believing that the child that is natural consequence shall have white skin and she become object of revilement among her people.

Sister, I tell you in all truth, which is precious jewel, though worn on toad's head. And I say that you warn him to show care in new place whither you go. For there men are men of strong passions and much subject to the green-eyed monster that mocks the meat it feeds on. And they will hit him on the head with little axes and English blood will stain Malayan soil.

Closing now with good wishes and hopes and blessing of our one father God of your new state and much happiness in work and social amenities.

The Voice of the East.

Postscript. You ask others here and they telling you the self-same story.

'For God's sake, stop crying,' said Crabbe.

The number two engine back-fired. Soon there was an all-enclosing vibration, perhaps like the rumble of blood that surrounds the torpid foetus. The Chinese pilot released the brakes, advanced the throttles.

'And to think this was going on all the time,' shouted Fenella, barely audible above the engines. 'I thought we had no secrets from each other.'

The gongs throbbed through the engines and the Lion jumped and came down with a crash in his brain. 'But it finished long ago. There was no point in telling you.'

'And she's going to have a baby.'

'WHAT?'

'A BABY.'

'Well, it won't be mine. I can prove it.'

'You're disgusting. I'm going to leave you.'

'WHAT?'

'LEAVE YOU.'

The Sikh traveller smiled in his beard. They quarrelled among themselves. The beginnings of dissolution. But the future was bright for him, Mohinder Singh. Let them not say that the Sikhs were fit only for the police or the bullock-cart or the hard bed of the night watchman. Let them not say that the Sikhs had no aptitude for business.

Crabbe took a glucose sweet from the air hostess and crunched irritably. Fool. She needn't have known. But, unthinking, he had said, wearily, that she wasn't a widow but a divorcée and wasn't an orphan but had a very vigorous set of parents and grandparents away in a remote village. And that, of course, had done it. If only he hadn't been feeling crapulous, if only he didn't still feel crapulous. Crabbe looked with favour at the air hostess. Her name, according to the little board by the cockpit door, was Molly de Cruz. Eurasian. Crabbe had a swift cinematic vision of the glory of Malacca and the coming of the urgent Portuguese. She was long-legged, ample under the uniform jacket, a sweep of rich hair under her cap. Now she danced up the aisle with newspapers, handing out *The Timah Gazette* and *The Singapore Bugle*, a Malay journal in proud sweeping Arabic headlines, a cramped sheaf of drilled Chinese ideograms. Crabbe shook his head at her, smiling refusal with what he hoped was debauched charm. Fenella bent angry brows over a front page, taking in nothing of the Singapore riots, the 'Clear Out British' banners above toothy smiles and brown feet, the smirk of a new strip-tease artiste from Hong Kong.

Deep below them was deep jungle and, to the west, the Malacca Straits. They moved with speed towards the air of a strange land, Negeri Dahaga, Malay country washed by the China Sea, a State of poor honest fishermen and rice-planters. It was a land which had been tardy in yielding to the kindly pressure of the British, and Chinese and Indian traders had been slow to follow the promise of peace and cold justice: Malay land, where the Chinese kept to their shops and ate pork in secret. A mere fifty years before, the Siamese had waived, as also with the neighbour States of Kelantan and Trengganu, the *bunga mas*, the rich golden flower of tribute. A British Adviser had come at a time when a gardened Residency and Sikh guards and a coach-and-four had long been a commonplace on the West Coast. And there the Adviser had found, and his successors found still, that the State was only nominally in the hands of a Sultan. Dahaga was ruled feudally by an hereditary officer called the Abang, a man with such titles as Scourge of the Wicked, Friend of the Oppressed, Loved of God, Father of a Thousand, who claimed descent from the faeces of the White Bull of Siva.

Traditionally, even the installation of the Abang was far more magnificent than the Sultan's coronation. Silver trumpets clamoured and drums thumped and Javanese xylophones clattered with an ominous noise of dry bones. An age-old Hindu prayer was intoned while the Islamic leaders looked placidly on. The names of some of the Abang's ancestors were chanted, great heroes who had tried to subdue the world to the True Faith: Al Iskander the Great, Aristotle, Mansor Shah, Averroes, D'Albuquerque, Abu Bakar and others. The Abang's feet were washed in goat's milk and his testes blessed and anointed behind a gold-thread curtain. Veiled girls danced to the skirl of Indian pipes, rich curries were eaten and mounds of cold rice distributed to the poor. And the Sultan smiled and fidgeted and was sent away to supervise his four quarrelling wives and play chess with his attendants, seeing himself, crowned but impotent, static or retreating on the chequered board. Meanwhile the Abang ruled, collecting many dues, lounging in limousines, impatient of the gentle restraints of Western law. From the West he desired only cars and fair-haired women.

The chief town, Kenching, was bulbous with mosques and loud with the cries of many muezzins. Islam was powerful. During the fasting months police squads dragged out sinful daytime eaters from house or coffeeshop. Non-attendance at the mosque on Friday – if discovered – was heavily fined. Polygamy was practised and divorcée prostitutes were thick on the evening streets. But ancient Hinduism and primitive magic prevailed in villages and suburbs. The *bomoh*, or magician, cured pox and fever, presided at weddings and grew rich on the fees of fishermen who begged prayers for a good catch. Gods of the sea and gods of the rice-grain were invoked, threatened, rewarded. And from the north came Siamese Buddhism to complicate further the religious patterns of Dahaga.

History? The State had no history. It had not changed in many centuries, not since the Chinese had stepped ashore and soon retreated, carrying its name back in three ideograms: DA HA GA. The British had hardly disturbed the timeless pattern. The rivers were still the main roads, though the railway train puffed in from the south once a week and an aeroplane came daily. There were cinemas and a few hotels, some British commercial firms in poky offices. But Dahaga regarded all these as a rash that might go, leaving the smooth timeless body unchanged. Or the British might be absorbed, as the Siamese had been in the days of the Occupation, when the Japanese had moved west and south, leaving Dahaga to their jackal friends from Thailand. The future would be like the past – shadow-plays about mythical heroes, bull-fights and cock-fights, top-spinning and kite-flying, sympathetic magic, axeing, love-potions, coconuts, rice, the eternal rule of the Abang.

All that Victor Crabbe knew was that he was appointed headmaster to a school where the medium of instruction was English. That such a school should exist at all in Dahaga was probably due to an oversight on the part of some Abang of the past, one who had tasted whisky and become momentarily Anglophile or had grunted in his sleep what sounded like assent to the gentle recommendations of a British Adviser. Victor Crabbe had never been a headmaster before, and it was as much apprehension as crapula that had distracted him into admitting that the anonymous letter-writer had spoken some truth. Otherwise he would have said, 'The only thing to do with such letters is to burn them and forget about them.' But he had always been convinced that Fenella would find out sooner or later about his liaison with Rahimah. It had never seemed necessary to volunteer the information. He had just felt that, if she found out, she would laugh in her gay sophisticated way and cry, 'But, darling, how amusing. What was it like?' And in a way, he didn't want her to take it so light-heartedly, because Rahimah had meant something to him. So he let things slide. Now here she was, sobbing like any suburban housewife, all jealous woman, eyes red and cheeks swollen, threatening to leave him. However, this too might be part of a New Year hangover. She had washed down the boiled duck with much gin. Best to say nothing and wait.

Crabbe looked at what he could see of the other passengers. A squat Chinese, deep in his newspaper of ideograms. A turbaned *haji* asleep. Two Malay wives, meek behind their husband. Meek perhaps with air-sickness, for Malay women were normally all earth and spirit. A red-haired Englishman with briefcase and dark glasses. A bald Tamil, blue-black above the white shirt. And a smiling Sikh.

The Sikh was smiling with full-bearded compassion at Fenella, who was retching quietly into a paper bag. The intrepid British of the past, who had ruled the waves. Ah, they were becoming an effete race. The least thing upset them now. And the man next to her, her husband, he too had turned green. The white man had turned green. Ah, very good. He, Mohinder Singh, had never felt better.

'I feel so ill,' said Fenella, and she flopped back in her seat. Crabbe took her hand and she suffered the pressure of his fingers.

'Never mind, darling.'

'How could you?' she whispered, from a lifeless mouth, eyes closed.

'It won't happen again.'

Though it probably would, despite the passionate men with axes.

Soon the tawny land of Dahaga began to ogle them and then, brazenly, to raise its arms towards them from its sleepy sandy beds. Its coconut-palms swayed mannequin-like, voluptuous in the sea-wind. They saw the white-washed name on a long attap roof, the whispered introduction rising to a shout: KENCHING.

Molly de Cruz brought round her charger of glucose sweets. LAP-STRAPS. NO SMOKING, said the electric sign.

They dropped to earth and the aircraft changed from a flying ship to a great awkward lolloping bus.

Mohinder Singh slowly lost his full-bearded smile of confidence. He became agitated. There was something he had to communicate to the memsahib. She had been sick, she still looked green (ha!), but she walked now with grace towards the aircraft's open mouth, towards the huge sunlight and marine sky outside. Mohinder Singh followed the man her husband, struggling with something in the back pocket of his white trousers. At leisure, below, he would, if only he could find the accursed thing.

'They said he'd never meet us,' said Crabbe. 'I can't see a single European waiting anywhere.' They walked towards the terminal of two long huts, their luggage trundled after them. Two Malay women in sarongs, white powder, high heels greeted their fellow-wives. Their husband, who carried only a paper carrier, marched off his hens to a waiting car, his belly proud before him. The Chinese passenger was greeted in loud Hokkien by a loose-shirted yellow cadaver, all big teeth and spectacles. The red-haired Englishman shambled off with his briefcase. The Crabbes had much luggage, it had to be passed by the Customs official, they had to wait. But there was definitely no one waiting for them.

'You ought to check on these things,' said Fenella.

'It was in the letter, in black and white,' said Crabbe. 'Official.'

Mohinder Singh pulled out his wallet and began to search desperately. Identity card. Lottery ticket. A broken comb. A picture of his fat small niece. A soiled paper with Chinese magic numbers. A folded pamphlet about Guru Gobind Singh. Some ten-dollar notes. But not what he was looking for.

On the counter of the stifling Customs shed the Crabbes' luggage was ranged. A Siamese girl in a short-skirted uniform asked them if they had anything to declare. No, they had nothing.

Standing splay-footed at the back of the terminal were

Malays of a kind that Crabbe had never seen before. Their legs were bare and muscular, bidding their feet hold down the earth as though, in this place of flying ships, the very sandy soil might take off. On their heads were dish-towels wrapped in loose turban-style, with apices waving in the wind. They wore torn sports-shirts and old sarongs. Their faces were lined and their eyes keen. They were silent. In their hands . . .

Crabbe felt fear tremble through his hangover. No, this was impossible. Damn it all, he'd only just arrived. Had the word been passed already? Had they been told off by her relatives on the West Coast, the message drumming through the thick jungle? In their hands were long cloth bundles, but their fingers clutched a recognizable heft, and Crabbe felt in anticipation the sharp axe-edge pierce his skull or, at best, the thud of the dull heavy blunt back.

'Lady,' said Mohinder Singh. 'It is misfortune that I mislay my business card. My name is Mohinder Singh. You are coming to Kenching. You will want many things for your fine house. My shop is very new shop on Jalan Laksomana. Fine silks and curtainings and cloths of all kinds. Bedspreads. Camphor-wood chests. You come and you will be satisfied. For babies all things too.'

'Don't mention babies,' said Crabbe.

'Look,' said Fenella. 'They're coming here. For us. They've got weapons.'

'Yes,' said Crabbe. 'They've got weapons.'

'This is all your fault,' said Fenella, unreasonably. 'Messing about with native women.'

'Don't retreat,' said Crabbe. 'Look them in the eye.'

The men advanced steadily, five of them, a small boy in the rear, he too with a bundle, learning the trade. The Customs girl paid no attention, chatting to one of the air-port underlings. Soon the eldest axe-man, a vigorous patriarch, snarled briefly at the others, who then just stood and stared without rancour at the intended victim. With a relief so immense that it brought the hangover hurtling back, Crabbe saw that their quarry was the shopkeeper Sikh.

'What's he saying?' asked Fenella. The patriarch was using a terse barking language that seemed all vowels and glottal checks. But Crabbe could understand something of this strange dialect, for his Malay tutor in Kuala Hantu had given him an account of its phonology. The senior axe-man approached the cowering Sikh and told him that there was no animosity on the part either of himself or of his colleagues. He was just doing this for a friend. The Sikh well knew that the friend was soon to appear in court on a charge of stealing one tea-towel from the Sikh's shop. It would be a good thing for the Sikh to drop the charge. Indeed, he was now about to be formally warned to drop the charge, for friends must be helped, without friendship the world is nothing. If he would heed this warning he would not thereafter be molested further. All this was told in rapid root-words with little structural linking. Then the warning came.

The axe thudded but dully on the Sikh's mass of turban and unshorn hair. The Sikh sat on the ground and moaned a while. The patriarch took from the waist of his sarong two cigarettes. He told the Sikh that this was the only payment he had taken as the work was done for a friend. He put one cigarette in his own mouth and handed the other to the Sikh. To show there was no real animosity. A job, as you might say.

'Foolish old man,' said one of the axe-gripping juniors. 'He is a *Benggali tonchit*. It is against their religion to smoke.'

'True,' said the patriarch. 'The world is full of pork-stuffing infidels. Let us go.' And off they went, the small boy waiting respectfully to bring up the rear.

'What a shame,' said Fenella to Mohinder Singh. 'Are you dreadfully hurt?'

'See,' said Mohinder Singh, 'my business cards were in my turban. They dislodged with the strike of the weapon. In Dahaga such things happen. Law and order not possible. Please take one card, lady.' And he tottered off to the rear of the terminal. Soon he could be seen on a bicycle, twisting drunkenly down the road.

'Now what do we do?' asked Fenella. 'We can't stay here all day. I feel terrible. I don't think I'm going to like it here. For God's sake ask somebody something.'

Crabbe asked the Customs girl. Did she know where Mr Talbot lived? She did not. Mr Talbot was the State Education Officer. She knew of no such appointment. Did she know of a school called the Haji Ali College? She had never heard of it. How far was it from the airport to the town? That she knew: eight milestones. Was it possible to get a taxi? Not from here. Was there a telephone available? There was not.

'Helpful, aren't they?' said Crabbe. The sun had started its afternoon stint, and the sweat welled in his shirt.

'We'll have to go somewhere,' said Fenella. 'I feel like death. Is there no way we can get into the town?'

'Hitch-hike, that seems to be the only way,' said Crabbe. 'That looks like the main road. Let's get on to it.'

'Oh, what an awful bloody mess,' moaned Fenella. 'You never could organize anything. Time and time again you let me down.'

Crabbe asked the Customs girls and the interested ground-staff of three if they could leave their luggage here at the airport and call for it later. The girl replied that it was not advisable, as there were many thieves. Perhaps, suggested Crabbe, it could be stored in some office that had a lock and key? That was not possible, for there was no such office.

Now at that moment two of the turbaned Malay axe-men reappeared, this time without their axes. They both pedalled decrepit trishaws and one of them called out: '*Taksi, tuan?*'

'Where?' said Fenella with hope. 'I can't see any taxi.'

'They call these things taxis,' said Crabbe. 'Come on, better than nothing.'

And so the luggage was piled on to one trishaw, and

Fenella and Victor Crabbe wedged themselves into the cane seat of the other. They had to sit close, like lovers, and Crabbe even had to put his arm round her back.

'Don't sit so near,' she said. 'I hate you to touch me.'

'Oh, hell,' he snapped. 'I'll walk if you want me to.' He was hating everything and everybody. But he did not move. Soon the sullen journey commenced, hard muscular legs circling, on the sandy road to the town. On their right was the conventional tropical paradise of sea and palms, slim girls bathing in soaked sarongs, attap huts and waving children. On their left were paddy-fields and massive buffaloes. Above them merciless blue and the sun at its zenith.

A few cars passed them, small Austins with huge families crammed inside, the children waving derisively. Once a Cadillac passed, empty but for a proud smoking uniformed chauffeur, bearing as number-plate the legend 'ABANG'.

'Ominous that,' said Crabbe. 'Tyres, I mean. I wonder how our car will fare on this road. When it gets here.'

'If it gets here. I suppose you've messed that arrangement up, too.'

'Oh, shut up.'

'You shut up. How dare you speak to me like that.'

'Oh, shut up.'

But then they stopped their wrangling, for ahead of them a car had halted. A dusty car, and from it peered a face, a European face, and then a greeting arm.

'A sort of Livingstone and Stanley,' said Crabbe. 'Nice of him.'

The face was pale, the eyes pale, the hair almost white, the eyebrows invisible, the eyelashes seemingly singed away. It was a young face, however, pointed, pixyish.

'Better if I gave you a lift,' said the stranger. 'You shouldn't really go around on those things, you know. I mean, white men don't do it, and all the rest of it, not here they don't, and besides there's an Emergency on. Communists leap from the sea, like Proteus. You must be new here. No car?'

'It's coming by train. Look here, I know you. In England somewhere. Or Army?'

'I was Air Force. You a University man? I was at . . .'

'You read Law. I read History. Something-man something-man . . .'

'Hardman.'

'Hardman, by God. Robert Hardman. Well, of all the . . .'

'Rupert Hardman.'

'I'm Crabbe.'

'Well, good God, who would have thought . . .'

Handshakes, pommellings, cries of incredulity. Patiently Fenella waited. At length she said, 'Manners, Victor.'

'Victor, of course. And this is Mrs Crabbe?'

'Sorry. Rupert Hardman. Fenella. And what are you doing here?'

'Law. Still law. You posted here?'

'Education: I should have been met. By Talbot. Do you know the man? We were trying to get into town. I suppose somebody there would . . .'

'Not in town. He lives somewhere near here, I know. Have you much luggage?'

'A few cases. The rest is coming by train. With the car.'

'Well, well, incredible. Get in. I'll take you to Talbot's place. Queer sort of chap. Queer sort of set-up. The whole place, I mean. You must come round to the hotel sometime. The Grand, a bit of a misnomer. Talbot's a bit off the beaten track.'

They paid off the trishaw men and loaded the luggage into the boot and on to the back seat. Fenella looked curiously at the pale-headed lawyer, the shabby upholstery, the stuffed ashtray which spoke of failure.

'Mortimer's out here, too. You remember him?'

'He was the chap who . . .'

'That's right. He's doing well. Married a Chinese widow. Money in tin.'

'And you? Married? Doing well? This is incredible, you know. I mean, meeting like this.'

Hardman shrugged his thin shoulders. 'I shall be. Both, I think. Fairly soon. That is, if everything goes right. Things don't always go right, you know. Not here.'

'I know.'

Hardman turned left, entering a lane bumpy with sand-drifts and ruts. The car jolted and bounced and creaked. 'Springs not very good, I'm afraid. This gear keeps slipping, too. I shall be getting a new car. At least, I think so. A Plymouth or a Jaguar or something. Let Austin have his swink to him reserved.'

'I've got an Abelard. Second-hand.'

'You'd better sell it. Quickly. There aren't many of those on the East Coast. There aren't any in Dahaga.'

'What do you mean, sell it?'

'It's just down here,' said Hardman. They passed attap shacks and many hens and naked cheerful children who cried, '*Tabek!*' in greeting. A goat bleated her flock off the road. 'Hiya, kids,' said Hardman. Soon they came to a lone bungalow with a back-cloth of swamp and coconut palms. The palms carried no fruit.

'Very bad soil,' said Hardman. 'Nothing grows here. A lot of malaria, too. It's those damned swamps. And then sand-fly fever. And snakes. And iguanas. Big ones.'

'You make it sound most attractive,' said Fenella. 'And what does one do in the evenings?'

'Oh, there's a club. In town. But nobody ever speaks to anybody there. It seems to be one of the rules. And you can go to the pictures. Indonesian epics and Indian visions of Baghdad, a very ill-lit Baghdad. It's best to stay at home and drink. Drink a lot. If you can afford it. Oh, you can bathe. But it's a bit treacherous. Look, this is where Talbot lives. Do you mind if I leave you here? He'll look after you. Actually, I don't particularly want to see his wife. Nor him, for that matter. Do look me up. At the Grand. And then we can talk. Soon, I think, I shall be able to buy you a beer. Perhaps two. At least, I hope so.' He smiled at them wanly, reversed into a patch of coarse high grass, then bumped off back to the main road, his exhaust belching irritably.

'What a very extraordinary man,' said Fenella. They stood on the bottom step of the bungalow, their luggage all about them.

'Oh, he's all right,' said Crabbe. 'You'll like him, once you get to know him. I wonder why he came out here.'

'I wonder why anybody ever comes out here. I wonder why the hell we did.'

'Never mind, darling.' Crabbe took her arm, smiling ingratiatingly. The sun had started up again the gongs in his head, and the Lion-dance returned twisting and jumping and bowing. But he felt hope, because he felt hungry. 'Let's go and see if anybody's at home. Perhaps they'll give us something to eat.'

So he knocked on the wooden wall beside the open door and braced himself to enter the life of the State of Dahaga.

2

'You see,' he said, in sudden irritation, 'they're still here. Spite of their bloody promises. Every day it's the same. You and me working our guts out in the sun, and them there in their motor-cars, going off to drink their whisky under a big fan.' The brown, lined, lean workman leant on his heavy road-tool, whatever it was, and gawped indignantly at the passing car. His companion spat on to the scorched road and said, 'They've let us down. They said when they got in there wouldn't be a white man left in the country. They said they'd all be buried alive.' He spoke a thick strangulated Malay dialect, the tongue of Dahaga.

'Burnt alive.'

'And now they've been in power since last August, and the white men are still here.'

'Like what I said at first. They're still here.'

'You can't trust the political men. Ties round their necks and kissing the babies. Promise you this and promise you that. And the white men are still here.'

'Still here. Like what I said.'

'I reckon we've done enough work for one day. We're only working for them.' The car had long passed, but he spat in its direction, and the spit was swallowed by the large afternoon heat.

'I reckon we ought to lay off now.'

A fat Tamil overseer came over to them, speaking toothy Malay, the Malay of the Tamils of another State, Greek to these workmen. Behind him the heavy steamroller gleamed in gold of a Victorian coat-of-arms and seethed in boiling impotence. The two workmen listened stolidly, understanding one word in ten, understanding clearly the drift of the whole speech. When he had gone one said to the other:

'In the other States it's the Tamils does the dirty work.'

'So they ought, black sods. Adam's shit, my father used to call them.'

'Drunk on toddy every night.'

'I reckon we ought to do a bit more and then lay off.'

'All right. Till that monkey's finished throwing those nuts down from that tree over there. And then lay off.'

They watched for a moment a *berok*, or coconut monkey, hurling down nuts to its master. The master gave it sharp orders, telling it only to pick the young soft-fleshed nuts. With an ill grace it obeyed. Languidly the two workmen pounded the road with their heavy tools, whatever they were called, the loose ends of their head-cloths agitated by the faint breeze.

The white man in the car sped on towards the town. Rupert Hardman was very much a white man, and all too aware of it. His skin was deficient in pigment, but only in moments of extreme depression, when pale eyes stared back bitterly from the mirror, did he call himself an albino. He was not quite that, there was just a rather unusual deficiency in pigmentation. A day on the beach and his thin body grew angry and peeled in its rage. His face grew tatters of curling white-tipped scarf-skin. His body, in spite of himself, sheered away from the sun as a cat, stiff with distended claws, sheers away from bath-water.

Perhaps it was only right that, nature having done one thing, war should finish things off. Rupert Hardman fingered with his left hand the skin around his nose and mouth. It was an old habit, ten years old. He had crashed towards the end of the war and his face had been ravaged by fire. The white man had been burnt alive. He still remembered the smell of the Sunday roast, he the joint, the cockpit the oven. Walking down the English suburban street, after eleven o'clock mass, with doors open to the warm family dinner smell, had always brought it back, and he had regularly escaped to the pub, just open at twelve, to drink cold beer. They said the doctors had done a marvellous job. The nurses cooed, perhaps a bit too much. When he plunged into the mirror he had not been displeased. Could you call it Rupert Hardman? That didn't seem to matter. It was an acceptable face, especially under the peaked officer's cap which hid the pale hair. And then leave.

In the village pub, the silly girl had greeted him and said:

'Ow, what's happened to you? You look like you've torn your fice and sewn it up yourself. Ever so funny.'

But Crabbe hadn't looked as if he'd noticed. Crabbe had never noticed very much, though, the world of sensory phenomena meaning less to Crabbe than the world of idea and speculation. So it had been at the University, when Hardman, in his first year, had gone to hear Crabbe talk to the Communist Group, Crabbe the well-known and brilliant, for whom everyone prophesied a First. Crabbe had had no interest in the coming revolution, no love for the proletariat, only an abstract passion for the dialectical process, which he applied skilfully to everything. But Crabbe, as Hardman remembered, had been interested in a girl: a dark girl, small, usually dressed in a jumper and a tweed skirt, animated, talented, a student of music. Surely Crabbe had intended to marry this girl? Surely, now he came to think of it, Crabbe did marry this girl, during the war? Yet this woman whom he had met today, introduced as Mrs Crabbe, was tall and fair and vaguely patrician. Not, thought Hardman, really Crabbe's type at all. This chance meeting stirred up the whole past in Hardman's mind as he drove expertly on to the town. The palm trees and the brown bodies and the China Sea became, despite the years of familiarity, suddenly strange, genuinely exotic, and he saw himself from the outside, driving a car in a Malay State to a Malay town, having spent the night in another Malay town where he had conducted the defence in a Malayan Court, his home Malay, his income – such as it was – derived from Malayan clients, wondering how the hell all this had happened, what he was doing here anyway, and thinking, with a sudden start of sweat that had nothing to do with the heat, that he was really imprisoned here, couldn't raise a passage to England, and if he returned there what was he to do anyway?

Yet Crabbe had brought back a whiff of nostalgia. Old oak in cool musty chambers, periodicals that were press-wet, not five weeks late, the queue for the ballet, a live orchestra, draught beer, ice on the roads and not just in the ice-box. Europe. 'Better fifty years of Europe than a cycle of Cathay.' That was Tennyson. It would have done that bearded gin-guzzling shag-smoking laureate of the antimacassars a lot of good to come out here and ...

Cycles along Jalan Laksamana, main street of Kenching, and there the Cathay Cinema advertising an Indonesian film called *Hati Ibu* – 'A Mother's Heart'. A huge brown weeping face and, in the background of the poster, the rising generation in jeans and Hawaiian shirts, off for a spree, forgetting the old ways, unmoved by a mother's tears. In the next-door kiosk a sulky ripe Malay girl offered lottery tickets for sale. Sweat shone on the lean shoulders of a turbaned fisherman, his silver-gleaming catch hanging from a pole. There was loud leisurely chaffering in the market over rambutans, aubergines, red and green peppers, Chinese oranges, white cabbages, dried fish-strips and red-raw buffalo-meat. The smells rose into the high blue coastal air. Hardman turned left and made for the Grand Hotel, and the reek of the river greeted him.

He wondered what it would feel like to be a Muslim, even in name only, and what sort of a life he could have with her. He seemed to be letting Europe down. Was it for this that the Crusades had been fought and Aquinas had tamed the Aristotelian beast into a *Summa*? But money was more important than faith. At least, now it was. Faith could come later.

In the hotel Auntie's husky whisky-bloom bass boomed down the telephone. She stood, as though speaking down the telephone in a play, on a kind of dais before an audience of Asian tea-drinkers. She had a vast flattened bosom and red hanging jowls and, as she spoke, her fat shook.

'I have my way to pay too. I have my creditors to meet. If you cannot afford to drink then you should not drink. Besides, it is forbidden by your religion to drink. That makes it all the more worse that you should run up debts. I know, I know. At the end of last month you promised me too. And now it is the end of another month. I have it here.' She intoned to the tea-drinkers: 'Che Abdul Kadir bin Mohamed Salleh. Haji Ali College. One hundred and fifty-five dollars.' The tea-drinkers listened, the slightest pain of sympathy in their eyes. One or two men took down the name on cigarette packets. Blackmailers? Agents of the Supreme Council of Islam?

'Tomorrow,' said Auntie. 'Tomorrow at the latest. There are men up the road with little axes. They are only too glad to earn two, three dollars. To them to strike a man with an axe, it is nothing. It is to them an honest living.' Calmly she put down the receiver. Her turtle-lidded eyes caught Rupert Hardman escaping up the stairs.

'Mr Hardman.'

'Oh, hello, Auntie.' Rupert Hardman turned at the stair-head, a great nervous boyish smile on his thin face.

Auntie's heart melted, as it always did. Her huge body seemed to sag at the joints, as with incipient fever. 'I will come up,' she said, 'just for a moment.'

She mounted the stairs, pausing at each step, pausing at each phrase. 'All the time money trouble. That is the big disease of Malaya. Not T.B. Not malaria. And you are as bad.' The banister groaned. 'As the rest.'

'Everything's going to be all right, Auntie. Just wait, that's all.'

'I wait. I go on waiting. I think I wait too long.'

Rupert Hardman entered his little room and switched on the bedside fan. The blades whirred comfortingly and coolly and the upper structure of the fan moved sedately from side to side, shedding coolness with royal bounty, now here, now there, crassly impartial. Hardman lay on the bed and looked up at the new blue distemper of the ceiling.

'You do not take off your shoes,' said Auntie, entering. 'You put dirt on the bed. That make a lot of laundry.'

'You always tickle my feet.'

'There were perhaps men who were glad to have their feet tickled by me.' Auntie lowered her bulk on to the single chair.

'When was that, Auntie, and where was that? When you danced the czardas with Admiral Horthy? When Petrograd was a snowy furry fairyland?'

'And what is to become of me here, sixty already, and nothing saved up, and the bills coming in and nobody paying their bills?'

'Blistered in Brussels, patched and peeled in London? Or nothing so exotic. Say, after *schnapps* and *rijstafel* in some Djakarta joint. I want to sleep. I've had a tiring two days. And I've eaten nothing.'

'How can you eat when you pay no bills? Credit does not last forever.'

'Auntie,' said Hardman. 'I shall pay my bill.' He suddenly felt hopeless and excited. 'In full. And then it is quite certain that I shall go somewhere where they are not always asking for money. Somewhere where they will give me money.'

'There.' She came over and sat at the foot of the bed. 'You get worried. I do not forget what Redshaw and Tubb did for me in Singapore. They are a very good firm. It is such a pity you got out of them. You would now be sitting pretty.'

'They were a lot of blasted rogues. Sharp practice. I don't want to talk about them.'

'And so. Because they get me off they are a lot of blasted rogues. So.' Auntie rang the bell on the wall by the bed.

'It's not that. I'm not concerned with morals. Not as a

lawyer. If you wanted to run what you did run it's your own affair. I suppose it's as honest as anything else.'

'What did I run?' Auntie let out a pint of indignant air. 'It was legitimate business. I only say you were a fool to get out of a firm like that. To be a lawyer on your own, that needs money. You have to have an office. How can you afford an office when you cannot pay my bills even?'

'I shall pay my bills. I shall get an office. And very soon. God help me.'

'These two days then, you have been getting money?'

'Yesterday,' said Rupert Hardman, incisively, forensically. 'I had a case down south in the State of Kelantan, in the chief town of Kota Bharu. There, Auntie, I met nice people and stayed in a nice hotel kept by a very nice Russian lady, a lady who said I need not hurry about paying my bill, because she knew of my great ability and said that my credit was good. The case I had was a case of rape. It was a small Chinese shopkeeper who had taken advantage of one of his Malay assistants. I tell you this to prove to you that I have briefs. That means fees. But I cannot force my clients to pay any quicker than they wish to pay. One must be leisurely in these matters. One must give the impression that one can wait for ever for the fees.'

'Yes, yes,' said Auntie, soothingly. There was a knock at the door. 'Come in,' she called. 'I mean, *masok*.'

Rupert Hardman laughed, his good humour somewhat restored. The Chinese Number One boy came in. 'Whisky,' said Auntie.

'And a raw beef sandwich,' added Hardman. '*Masok*,' he laughed. At the door the boy hesitated. 'No, no, no.' said Hardman, 'I didn't mean you.' The boy went out. 'I meant this case of rape. The prosecution went on about had he done this and had he done that, and had there been any attempt to, shall we say, force his attentions on her, and had he perhaps been importunate in demanding her favours, and had there finally, let me see, this is most embarrassing, had he, shall we say, succeeded, if one may use the term, in effecting, let us say, any degree of penetration.

The interpreter listened very patiently and then he just asked the girl, "*Sudah masok?*" and she replied, quick as a flash, "*Sudah*".'

'*Masok!*' shrieked Auntie, all trembling jelly. The boy was standing patiently with the drinks. '*Sudah masok*,' he said patiently.

'Yes, yes, yes.' Auntie coughed gargantuanly. 'Now you can go out.'

'Raw beef sandwiches,' said Rupert Hardman, 'with a raw onion.'

Auntie turned to Hardman, came closer, put a huge mottled paw on his thin ankle. 'It is not that I mind about the money. Your money, to me it means nothing. I am always grateful to Redshaw and Tubb.'

'But I'm no longer with Redshaw and Tubb.'

'Yes,' said Auntie vaguely. 'I see that. But there are so many ways in which you can help me. You are a young man of education. You are friendly with many Europeans.'

'That's not going to count much from now on. Expatriates are going to have their throats cut.'

'Ach.' Auntie frowned hugely. 'That is all nonsense. The Europeans will never go.'

'They said that in Indonesia. Look at it now.' Rupert Hardman poured water from the thermos jug into his whisky. 'Where the hell are my sandwiches?' He petulantly drank the sharp cool potion.

'For example, you know women. Nice women. Women who are well-dressed and of education.'

'Yes, Auntie?' Hardman looked up at her, smiling sweetly, gently.

'And gentlemen, of course. We want nice people to come here. There are nice business men who come from Bangkok, they want to meet nice people. Nice English people.'

'Yes, Auntie.'

'This could be a nice place. People drinking cocktails and laughing and talking very gay. Refined dinner-parties. And dancing to the radiogram.'

'And nice refined seduction afterwards?'

Auntie boiled with large sudden anger. 'Ach. You have only dirty thoughts in your mind. About me you have always had such thoughts.'

'No, Auntie,' said Hardman, sweetly, seriously. 'I really and truly haven't.'

Auntie smiled roguishly, hideously, and tweaked Hardman's ankle. 'You are a bad boy,' she said.

The boy came in with the sandwiches. Hardman devoured them wholemeal, munching with the swollen cheeks of a child. Auntie said, 'You eat only sandwiches. Tonight you must eat a hot meal, with a spoon. There is chicken curry. With *gula Melaka* to follow.'

'I shall eat out.'

'You will not get much to eat with what you have in your pockets.'

'There are many places where they're only too pleased for me to run up bills.'

The Number Two boy came in to say that the Crown Prince was on the telephone. Something about a *mah jong* game. Auntie said, 'Ach,' and made her fat stately way to the door. 'At least,' she said, turning, 'you are not in debt to me for *mah jong*. That is more than the Crown Prince can say.'

When she had gone Hardman took off his clothes and slept restlessly for an hour or two. He could hear clearly through his dreams the quarrelling of the Chinese couple in the next room, the crying of a child opposite, the oscillations, and intermittent bursts of Hindi song from the radio down the corridor. His dreams were vague and historical. He was the Saracen spy in the entourage of Richard Coeur de Lion. He was a Spanish propagandist of the subtle doctrines of Averroes. As he was waking in the rose of the brief evening he was the muezzin announcing that there was no God but Allah. But the muezzin was outside, calling the sunset prayer from the loudspeaker opposite the Bank. He remembered he had an appointment, so he arose, showered his meagre body, and changed his trousers and shirt. He also put on a tie, remembering that he was an Englishman in the tropics. He was not in the Colonial Service, but he was still a white man. A very white man.

Early dusk was on the town. Hardman crossed the road, dodging trishaws and homeward cycles. He sought a drinking *kedai*, climbing steps to reach the high covered pavement that was snug above the flood-level. The monsoon was far off, months and months of sun stretched before him, heat in which the fine logic of the law-books would blur. But he would soon, he hoped, be settled in, with a name-plate outside and the law-books gathering mould on their shelves, litigation creaking on under the heavy indifferent rains or the big brassy law-abiding sun.

The *kedai* was gloomy, empty save for the man that Hardman had arranged to meet. The creased moon-faced Chinese grinned above his glass of beer at the marble table. The table bore a saucer of small bananas and a smoky glass case of pastries. The big beer-bottle was half-full and the Chinese called for another glass.

'Have you decided about the rent?' asked Hardman.

'Thirty-five dollars a week.'

'That's a bit heavy. After all, the position isn't all that good.'

'Lawyers make much money.'

'This one doesn't.'

'And also two-thousand key-money.'

'That's a bit thick.'

'I should ask three thousand.'

'It's not strictly legal, you know, to ask anything. You should be satisfied with a month's rent in advance.'

'That is what is usually done. It is the custom. Custom is a kind of law.'

'But two thousand dollars!'

'I have many inquiries about the shop. There were two men around today. One said he was very interested and would talk about it with his wife and see me tomorrow.'

Rupert Hardman sipped his beer. It tasted very bitter.

He owed three months' rent for Club chambers in Kuala Lumpur. He owed for his car. He owed various hotel bills. He had spent too much money on a girl called Enid.

'You wish not to take the premises?'

'No. Yes. Wait.' Hardman looked at the small quizzical eyes, Chinese eyes, eyes of an alien code of ethics, eyes he could look at but never look into. Better fifty years of Europe. 'I'll come and see you tomorrow. Early. I think I'll be taking the premises. It's a question of getting the money together.'

'Cash.'

'Hung,' said a voice like a gong. 'Hardman, you bastard.' A small brown man with huge teeth and a wide-gaited moustache was upon him, embracing him with loving arms and a rough cheek. It was Haji Zainal Abidin. 'Hardman, the bastard,' he announced, 'who threw the Koran on the floor and put his heel on it. The man with no respect for another man's religion.'

'That's not true,' said Hardman. 'You threw it on the floor yourself. You said the Koran was too sacred to be translated. You said an English Koran was blasphemy. You stamped on it.'

'No respect for another man's religion,' said Haji Zainal Abidin. 'He has seen the light. I have shown him the light. But still he has a prepuce.' He laughed raucously, showing a red throat and uncountable teeth. 'That is a good word,' he said. 'I said that today to my boss. "Mr Cheesy," I said, "the time is coming when there will be no prepuces left in our country. The prepuces," I said, "will be sent home with their owners." "And what is a prepuce?" he said.' Haji Zainal Abidin laughed loud and harsh. 'To think that I speak the white man's tongue better than the white man.'

'On a point of anatomical fact,' said Hardman, 'I have no prepuce. It was removed when I was a child.'

Haji Zainal Abidin sulked for an instant. Then he recovered and, in great good humour, introduced a dim Indian who had entered with him. The Indian was smiling and very drunk.

234

'This is my colleague,' said Haji Zainal Abidin. 'It is his day off today and he tries to spend it in his usual manner. He becomes drunk and he goes and buys things. Fortunately today is Chinese New Year and many shops are closed. But he has already bought two refrigerators, a radiogram and a Sunbeam Talbot. He has signed cheques for all these things and he has not two cents to rub together. But the men in the shops mostly know him now. Today it was mostly the assistants he saw, because the *towkays* were away drinking. But I have been round and got back the cheques. One day he will find it very difficult. Two years ago they deliver a bulldozer to him and he says he knows nothing about it. That will happen again, only perhaps that time it will be a cinema.'

Haji Zainal Abidin did not proclaim, either in dress or demeanour, the pentecostal grace that traditionally descends on one who has made the pilgrimage to Mecca. He wore no turban, a natty cravat with a horse-head pin was tucked inside his open nylon shirt, his flannel trousers were well-creased and his shoes highly polished. He exhaled a heartening smell of hops, hardly concealed by the breath of garlic. He was in his late forties and depressingly vigorous. He called for beer. Mr Hung said he had to be going.

'Tomorrow,' said Hardman.

'You owe him money,' shouted Haji Zainal Abidin. 'Everybody owes Hung money.'

'I want to open up an office,' said Hardman. 'That's all.'

Haji Zainal Abidin became serious, confidential. 'Money,' he said. 'You need money. I know.' He leaned over, pushing a great nose, great eyes and the cleft in his moustache into the face of Hardman. 'I have told you, there is only one way.'

'I know. I've thought about it. I've been thinking about little else.'

'What is holding you back?'

'You know what's holding me back. Or rather, what's been holding me back.'

'There you go again,' raged Haji Zainal Abidin. 'Because she is a Malay. Race prejudice. Race hatred. I tell you again, you English bastard, there will be no peace on the earth until race hatred ceases. Because you are a white man you despise us. You despise me because I am a Malay. You call me a Malay bastard. Well, I am not a Malay. I am an Afghan.' He sat back in triumph. The dim Indian began to sing quietly to himself.

'It's not that. You know it's not that, you silly Afghan bastard.'

Haji Zainal Abidin roared with great laughter. Then he said, 'She is a young woman. She is only forty-two. And as for her other two husbands, you need not believe the stories. They were both estate-managers. It is highly probable that the Communists killed them. If you are a good husband to her, there is nothing she will not do for you. Nothing.' He winked hugely, seriously. 'She has money.'

'It surprises me that nobody has snapped her up already,' said Hardman. 'You, for instance. You've only got one wife at the moment.'

Haji Zainal Abidin leaned forward, froth on his lips, his face a devil's mask of cunning, his teeth set as though he carried a knife between them. 'I have had four wives,' he said. 'I have fourteen, fifteen children. I am not sure of the number. Of these wives only my first wife is left. She is the only woman for me. Late, I realized that she was always that. She has had staying-power. She is the only woman in the world for whom I have any appetite. Any *appetite*.' He bit off the word itself with something like appetite. Hardman felt his own saliva stir. 'There are no women like the Arab women,' said Haji Zainal Abidin dreamily, lyrically. 'No women for beauty or fidelity. She was twelve when I first met her in her father's house, with her dark eyes flashing like fire above the veil. That was in Mecca itself. She is not only a child of Mecca but a lady of the line of the Prophet. A lady, yes. More of a lady than these Malay women, who are not true Muslims. They walk about in their powder and high heels, drinking beer publicly. They have no shame.'

'There's no way out, is there?' said Hardman. 'If I marry her I'll have to enter Islam?'

'And why should you not?' stormed Haji Zainal Abidin. 'It is the true religion, you Christian bastard. It is the only one. The rest are mere imitations.'

'Oh, you just don't understand.' Hardman felt hopeless again. Soon he said, 'You'll have to help me find a name. A Muslim name.'

'It is a pleasure,' said Haji Zainal Abidin. 'It is my duty, too, for you are my friend. You shall become also my son in God. You shall be Abdullah bin Haji Zainal Abidin. No, no. There are better names than Abdullah. I must think of a really good one.' He thought.

'Tonight, then,' said Hardman, 'I shall propose.'

'There are many good names. I was just going through the names of my sons. I cannot remember them all. Latif? Redzwan? Redzwan is a good name. It means grace.'

'I can't be called Grace. That's a girl's name.'

'You shall be called what I say,' Haji Zainal Abidin nudged the Indian, his sleeping partner. 'Wake up! This is a solemn moment.'

'I shall go round to her house after dinner,' said Hardman with gloom.

'We shall all go,' cried Haji Zainal Abidin. 'We shall have a party. We shall go round and collect the others. We shall buy beer. We shall call for Kadir first. He has a motor-cycle and sidecar. Kadir is a good name. Abdul Kadir. You shall be called Abdul Kadir. Abdul Kadir bin Haji Zainal Abidin. That shall be your name.'

'LL.B. Barister-at-law. A bit of a mouthful.'

'Let us go,' said Hardman's father in God. He stood up and seized his Indian friend by the scruff. The Indian woke smiling. 'This is a great occasion. An infidel has been called home to the true way. Allah be praised.' He drained his beer standing, sighed with satisfaction, banged down

the tall glass. He led the way out, singing in a thin muezzin's wail.

Rupert Hardman followed him into the dim-lit dark,
Abdul Kadir bin Haji Zainal Abidin, heir to two cultures.
Allah be praised.

3

'There must be somebody at home,' said Fenella. 'There's a car.'

'A Land Rover.'

'Try again.'

Crabbe rapped once more, but the faint wooden noise seemed swallowed by vast Malayan distances, and they became oppressed by a great loneliness. The lizards darted into familiar sand-holes; the sun howled down; a distant goat wavered a plaintive call. Things went indifferently on, and nobody wanted the Crabbes. Perhaps they, like their side-walking namesakes, should dig holes and then bed down in sight of the vast empty sea, rejected of the warm-blooded inland world. But Victor Crabbe decided on action. He walked into the house and looked shyly round a large sitting-room, all buff-painted wood, pictures, mats, gin-tables, books, Trengganu fans, Kelantan silver, empty chairs. Uncertainly he called: 'Is anyone at home?'

The silence chewed this over. Then, sluggishly, the emptiness stirred itself into movement. A door opened, one of the three doors that presumably led to bedrooms. A man, appeared, wearing the uniform of the Home Guard, three stars on his shoulders. He was dark-haired, moustached, big, his face a cliché of handsomeness – straight nose, cleft chin, deep brown humorous eyes, small ears, a healthy tan: a face no intelligent woman would look at twice. Crabbe could see that the uniform had only recently been reassumed: there was a certain carelessness about buttons, the shorts were somewhat baggy, the hair had been hurriedly welshcombed. He listened with sympathy to the soft Scottish voice.

'Would you be looking for Talbot? He's not normally back till about three. Mrs Talbot will be coming out in a wee while. She and I have been rehearsing a scene from a play that we're going to do. We were shouting a wee bit, so we couldn't have heard you knock. Just arrived, I suppose? I'm Bannon-Fraser.'

Hand-shakes. Bannon-Fraser smiled with interest at Fenella. 'We don't see many fair-haired ladies out here,' he said, 'not nowadays. You've probably heard all about that.'

'No,' said Fenella, 'I haven't.'

'Oh,' said Bannon-Fraser, 'it's the Abang. You've heard about the Abang?'

'I've read about him,' said Crabbe. 'At least, I've read about the office, the Abang-paradigm, you might say. What has the Abang got to do with fair-haired women?'

'What's he got to do?' Bannon-Fraser laughed, showing, inevitably, strong white teeth. 'What's he got to do with fair-haired women? He loves 'em, laddie, can't have too many of them.' The schoolboy salacity disappeared from his look. Seriously he said to Fenella, 'I'm sorry. I shouldn't have said that. You're in Education, aren't you? Well, you'll be all right, I suppose. It's only at the Drainage and Irrigation level that he starts any funny business. Or Agricultural Department. Of the earth earthy. I should think Education's a bit outside his scope. I've got to go now. Mrs T. will be up, out, any minute now. Do come round to the mess sometime. Or see you at the club. We'll have a drink,' he added, as though this thought were a sudden inspiration. Then he left with the hurry of a man who has fulfilled a duty that, with the long passage of time, has become more and more perfunctory, a function that has developed economy of action, a routine as gratifying as the fiftieth cigarette of the day. Crabbe and Fenella decided to sit down, hearing the Land Rover roar away up the road.

There was a picture on the wall that caught Crabbe's

attention, an obviously amateur picture. Female breasts, greatly elongated, grew up, tufted like brushes at the points, into a forest. The dendromorphs were painted in nursery colours, like children's beakers. Crabbe's appetite receded. Fascinated, he looked at others: a snake entering a woman's mouth; a stylized satyr leaping out of a cuplike navel; a parade of pink haunches. Each picture carried the bold vermilion initials: A.T. Soon they were both wandering about the room, colliding at intervals and saying, 'Sorry.'

'Trying to shock,' said Fenella, as the two of them craned at a sort of erotic Laocoon, poster-paint flesh and ill-proportioned limbs. 'He wants everybody to think he's interestingly depraved. It's all very childish.'

'You don't have to look at them,' said a voice. They turned guiltily. 'I do these for my own amusement.' The speaker lounged at the bedroom door, her mouth wagging a cigarette. She was slim and seemed to be wearing a sort of ballet practice dress. Her face was that of a boy gangleader, smooth with the innocence of one who, by the same quirk as blinds a man to the mystery of whistling or riding a bicycle, has never mastered the art of affection or compassion or properly learned the moral dichotomy. Her eyes were small and her lips thin, her black hair parted demurely in Madonna-style. Her voice was faint, as if her vocal cords had been eroded by some acid. Crabbe suddenly heard the voice of a Malay girl who, a year ago, had enticed him from a lonely roadside: '*Tuan maha mainmain?*' But *Tuan* had not wanted to play: in the strained whisper spoke the aristocratic disease of love.

'I'm Anne Talbot,' she said. 'I suppose you must be expected or something. My husband never tells me anything. Please sit down, both of you.' Fenella flushed: she had not stood up, she had merely been standing. She remembered vaguely a film about a Restoration trollop promoted to duchess: 'No ceremony here, ladies.' She did not sit down until she had finished counting fifty. The counting also kept her mouth shut.

Crabbe announced his name and, for some reason, suddenly felt ashamed of it. It carried the wrong connotations – crustaceans, pubic parasites, instead of innocent wild apples.

'Crabbe,' said Mrs Talbot. 'Crabbe. That's a nice name. It reminds me of wild apples.' (I was wrong, he thought, in thinking them innocent.) 'I used to be very fond of crab-apple jelly, back in England, of course, when I was a young girl. I never get it now. Never. There are a lot of things I don't get.' She leaned back in her armchair and blew smoke feebly. 'One becomes so very tired of it all.'

Fenella was now seated. She looked at Crabbe and Crabbe looked at the floor and both felt a slight chill of premonition adding its draught to that of the ceiling-fan. Crabbe felt also shame. All this had been set out years ago in the stories of a man still well remembered in the East. Willie Maugham, damn fine bridge-player, real asset to the club, remembered me, put me in a book. Things were all too simple. That Elizabethan play of adultery and jealousy, Fenella remembered, that play with the unironic title of *A Woman Killed with Kindness*, had reflected a civilization a thousand times more complex. Fenella and Crabbe looked at each other briefly, and the business of the anonymous letter was already torn up.

'A drink,' said Mrs Talbot. 'Our servants have taken the day off. I can't understand how two Malays could possibly have Chinese cousins, but that was their story, so off they've gone to celebrate the New Year. Perhaps you, Mr Crabbe, would like to give us some gin and vermouth. It's all in that cupboard. And there's ice in the refrigerator.'

'I don't particularly want a drink,' said Fenella.

'Nor I,' said Crabbe, 'particularly.'

'Well,' said Mrs Talbot, 'I do.' She gave Crabbe a five-second glance of her small eyes and a grimace of her thin red lips, then she shrugged her very thin shoulders, got up, and lounged to the drink-cupboard. Crabbe made a frog's mouth and slightly raised his hands at Fenella. Then a car-noise approached and was ground out in front of the bungalow. They both breathed relief. Heavy feet mounted and Crabbe rose.

'Don't tell me, don't tell me,' said Talbot. 'It's Bishop. We're back together again. God, it's been a long time. Mrs Bishop, how are you? Young and beautiful as ever, despite the heavy weight of the years. And the other boys, how are they, Bishop?'

It was the moon-face of a yokel, a lock of straw-straight hair kissing one lens of the cheerful spectacles. The fleshy face and paunchy stumpy body, clad in a blue shirt and what looked like running shorts, spoke of a hopeless euphoria. Talbot seemed in his middle forties. He was evidently reaping the dank straw harvest of marrying a much younger wife. He was too cheerful. Soon, it was evident, he would talk with enthusiasm of his hobby, probably something laborious and harmless. The face was not that of a man of talent or temperament: it was too knobby and unlined, and the metal-gleaming teeth were too readily shown in an empty desperate smile.

'Crabbe,' said Crabbe. 'You may have had a letter about me.'

'Crabbe,' said Talbot. 'I thought you were Bishop. You're very like Bishop. And of course there must be a connection somewhere. Let me see. Yes. Bishop was an eighteenth-century drink. Dr Johnson was very fond of it. And you use crab-apples for making lamb's wool. That, you'll remember, was an Elizabethan drink. "When roasted crabs hiss in the bowl." ' He made 'bowl' rhyme with 'owl'. 'Or perhaps there was a Bishop Crabbe. There must be somewhere in Anthony Trollope. Are you any relation to the poet?'

'Distant. But my grandmother was a Grimes.'

'Well, well.' Talbot seemed pleased. 'I suppose you've come to take over the College. I must say they've been pretty quick. Foss only went two days ago.'

'They kept us hanging about for a month. Back in Kuala Hantu.'

'Oh, God, that horrible place. Well, well. This calls for a drink. Anne, give us all a drink.'

'They said they didn't want a drink. They were absolutely certain that they didn't want a drink.' Mrs Talbot came back with a full glass for herself.

'You see,' said Crabbe, 'it's the old business of an empty stomach.'

'My dear fellow,' said Talbot. He spoke as if Crabbe had committed a sin which was canonically mortal but because he, Talbot, was a Jesuit of the world, could be softened and attenuated till it disappeared like ectoplasm through the confessional grille. 'My dear fellow.' And then Crabbe knew what Talbot consoled himself with. The successful grew fat on plovers and cream; the unsuccessful on bread and jam and swigs from the custard-jug. 'My dear fellow, you ought to eat. That's the trouble with my wife. Thin as a rake, because she won't bother to order anything. Says she's not hungry. I'm always hungry. This climate has different effects on different people. I always have my lunch out. There's a little Chinese place where they give you a really tasty and filling soup, packed with chicken and abalone and vegetables with plenty of toast and butter, and then I always have a couple of baked crabs.'

'Yes,' said Crabbe.

'With rice and chilli sauce. And then a pancake or so, rather soggy, but I don't dislike them that way, with jam and a kind of whipped cream they serve in a tea-cup. Anne, what is there to eat?'

'There's nothing laid on, and the servants have gone. There, I'll give you that as a free gift. You can start writing an intelligible poem for a change.'

Talbot laughed indulgently, as if to say, 'Isn't she a one?' He turned adoringly to her and said, 'There must be something in the larder. Dig something out.'

'Crabs are good at digging,' said Mrs Talbot. 'Perhaps Mr Crabbe would like to help me.'

'Yes, yes, do that, Crabbe. And then I can talk to Mrs Bishop.'

Crabbe and Mrs Talbot entered the sun-hot store-room. There were many tins and jars. 'You can have cocktail sausages and gherkins,' she said, 'and tinned cheese and anchovies and pork liver paté. Or beetroot and Gentleman's Relish. We could have a little picnic. We could eat off the leaf, as the Malays say.' She was not near him, but the hot room diffused her scent. If he were to kiss her now she would taste it as casually and dispassionately as a fingerful of Gentleman's Relish or a cold lean sausage. He remembered his hunger and said, 'This, I think. And perhaps this.'

'What a greedy boy you are. Just like Herbert. Come on then, let's empty things on to plates.' She led him into the kitchen.

Sawing at bread she cut her finger. That was to be expected also. 'Oh, look, blood! Dripping over everything. Oh dear, dear, I can't stand the sight of it.' She danced prettily up and down enticing him to say: 'Poor little finger. Let me kiss the blood off.'

'Run some water over it,' said Crabbe.

'Oh, well, if it drips into the beetroot it won't show, will it? And nobody will know, will they? Except you and me.' Crabbe felt curiously uneasy, as if the harmless canned provisions were the raw materials of necromancy. He remembered Dahaga's sinister reputation for magic, but then shook the silly fancy away. After all, it was her blood, not his.

When they got back to the lounge, carrying two tray-loads of plates, they found Talbot in the middle of one of his own poems. He was intoning harshly and without nuances from a heavily corrected manuscript:

'... Cracks open the leaden corncrake sky with crass, angelic
Wails as round as cornfruit, sharp as crowfoot, clawfoot,
Rash, brash, loutish gouts of lime or vinegar strokes
Till the crinkled fish start from their lace of bone ...'

Fenella sat with her head lowered, embarrassed. So adolescent. And yet the theme was not the lustful itch of adolescence. The subject was food, sheer food. It was a picture of Talbot at breakfast or a chipped-potato supper. Or probably all meals coalesced with him in an orgy of thick bread-and-marge and an array of sauce-bottles. The poem rang with the bells that called Pavlov's dogs to salivation. Fenella was sensitive to the harmonics of words. She was a poet herself.

Talbot looked up brightly at the loaded trays. 'A bit peckish,' he said. 'I had lunch early.' Then he speared a sausage and spooned out mixed pickles.

'Now,' said Crabbe, 'tell me all about it.'

'Yes.' Talbot caught a trio of sardines and bathed them in pickle-sauce. 'Yes. You mean about Haji Ali College?'

'Well, it was named after Haji Ali.'

'One of the great men of the State?'

'Yes. I see you know all about it.'

'No.'

Talbot squirled a couple of anchovies in. 'A hero chiefly because he once cheated a Chinese shopkeeper. By God, that takes some doing. But also he was a poor boy who made good. He graduated from sneak-thief, axe-man and occasional pirate to *haji*.' The ward *haji* seemed to induce appetite in Talbot. He took in a dessertspoonful of mustard pickle and continued through saffron lips: 'He reformed and determined that his last theft should enable him to make the pilgrimage. By God, he did it. He went to Mecca and came back with a turban. Then he became town magician and I gather he was pretty good. He cured the Sultan of . . .'

'Darling, not while our guests are eating.'

'Anyway, when he died there was universal mourning. Drums going all night, black kids sacrificed to obscure Hindu gods. Then they started building this school. At first the idea was to call it after the Abang, but Haji Ali's

246

ghost appeared to the workmen and things began to go wrong. You know the sort of thing – scaffolding rotting at the roots and the bricks condemned as pure jelly.' Bewildered, Talbot looked around and finally lit on a jar of Brand's Chicken Essence. He poured some into tomato juice, added salt, and drank with a sigh. 'Got to watch vitamins. Bulk isn't enough. That's where the Malays make a mistake. Rice, rice and more rice.'

'But look at their waist-lines, dear.'

'Anyway, to continue. The whole damn structure fell down, a month off opening day. A workman said that Haji Ali had appeared to him in a dream and sworn at him in Arabic. The workman said that he had had a vision – the school appeared as a vast fish curry at a huge feast of workmen. Then Haji Ali arrived, amid cheers, and he poured a sort of thin chutney over the whole thing. But the whole thing went up in smoke, leaving a big ruin of white rice. And the voice of the Lord was heard in a kind of stereophonic sound, saying: "Woe to the children of the scripture, for their aspirations shall become as garlic on the wind." And so they thought it better to re-name the College, and everything went right, and there's been no trouble since.'

'Tell me about it,' said Crabbe.

'Well.' Talbot cut a slice of tinned cheese. 'You've got about a thousand pupils and a staff of Malays, Indians, Chinese and Eurasians. They're all going to hate your guts, especially the Senior Master. He's a Tamil called Jaganathan, and he was definitely promised the headship when Foss went home. Of course, it was only an electioneering promise, and that sort of promise doesn't mean a thing, but these poor devils had never had an election before, and they genuinely believed all that stuff about cutting the white man's throat. Poor old Jaganathan drummed up a lot of votes for the man who made the promise about the headship, so you can understand how he's going to feel about you.'

'It's hardly my fault, is it? People shouldn't make promises they can't keep. Besides, this Jaganathan doesn't sound too bright.'

'He's not, but that doesn't matter. He's been in the college for fifteen years, he's got a lot of contacts, and he's well in with the local magic boys. You've heard about those?'

'A little. Do you mean he's going to stick pins in my image?'

'He might.' Comfortably Talbot looked round the fast-emptying plates and finally settled on a huge red round of beetroot. He put this whole into his mouth. As he talked it lolled for a second or two like an extra tongue. Mrs Talbot smiled grimly at Crabbe, and Crabbe began to feel warmer towards her. 'Anyway, he's not a graduate. Of course, nobody sees that that's important. They all think that our skin is our only piece of parchment. We carry our whiteness like a diploma. I say, that's not bad. I can use that.'

'And the house?' asked Fenella.

'It's a good house. The situation may seem rather peculiar, because it looks as though it's set in the middle of a *kampong*. But that was because of Foss. He used to encourage the Malays to come and sit on his veranda and he'd tell them stories about the great world beyond the seas. Foss was a bit touched. A bachelor, you know. Never drank, never went to the Club. He had a vision of himself as a kind of saviour of the down-trodden brown man. He gave money away right and left, and it wasn't long before the local Malays began to carry their houses and dump them down near his, so that he became the centre of a whole new *kampong*. You've seen them do that, have you? The whole damn village carrying a house on their shoulders, yelling like mad. They do it a lot round here. Portable *kampongs*.'

'Perhaps now that we've come they'll carry them away again,' said Crabbe.

'Well, that's up to you, old boy. You'll see them coming round tonight, ready for a bed-time story. I shouldn't give them the brush-off if I were you. They're a touchy lot and they carry axes.'

'Look,' said Fenella, 'when's the next plane back?'

'But old Foss wasn't so Malay-struck that he didn't provide himself with one of the best Chinese cooks in the State. I've had some marvellous meals there. I tried to entice him away, but he wouldn't come. Says he's too old to start chopping and changing now. So he goes with the house.'

'Do you mean to say that we have a first-class cook laid on?' said Crabbe.

'You're lucky, old man. Ah Wing is the goods. He's a bit cracked, of course, laughing away to himself all the time, and he's a bit deaf, so that it's no good giving him any orders. Just let him carry on in his own way, and you'll be more than satisfied.'

'Well,' said Crabbe. He sat back, dazed. 'I can hardly wait.'

'I'm going home,' said Fenella. 'I'm definitely going home. As soon as you can book me a passage.'

'Don't talk like that,' said Talbot, happy and replete. 'You're going to love it here. You just wait and see.'

'Just wait and see,' said Mrs Talbot with some bitterness. 'It's a white woman's paradise.'

'Well, if you'll forgive me,' said Talbot, 'I've got to be on my way. You know the tradition. Chinese New Year they like you to drop in and have the odd bite with them and a glass of whisky. I've got several calls to make. Do come and see us again when you're settled in. I must read you some more of my verse, Mrs Bishop.'

'Crabbe,' said Fenella.

'I beg your pardon?' Talbot looked vaguely insulted.

'Can you take us to the house?' said Crabbe. 'Our car's still on its way. Besides, we just don't know our way around.' He glanced at Mrs Talbot. 'Topographically, I mean.'

'Delighted,' said Talbot. He went ahead, his plenilunar

buttocks tight in the very short shorts. 'This your luggage?'

'Thank you so much,' said Crabbe, smiling with his mouth at Mrs Talbot who lay languid in her armchair, 'for your hospitality.'

'Delighted,' she said. 'Any time. I like being hospitable.'

4

'Che Normah binte Abdul Aziz was supervising the clearing-up after the party. It was a party that had ended early; the last maudlin protestations of eternal amity, the trite philosophizings, the long visits to the back-yard *jamban* rebuked by the false-dawn call of the muezzin. The clearing-up was prolonged and squeamish: there was much mess revealed by the sunlight. Abdul Kadir had tried to make things go, as he always did. He had emptied most of the bottled beer, a quart of stout, a flask of Beehive Brandy, half a bottle of Wincarnis and the remains of the whisky into a kitchen pail. He had seasoned this foaming broth with red peppers and invited all to drink deep. This had been his sole contribution to the victualling of the party. Cheerful, quarrelsome, always in working shorts, his crew-cut bullet-head rendered scholarly by rimless glasses, he was never solvent. He regularly apologized for the fact, calling at friends' houses to express regret for his inability to return past hospitality, continuing the apologies over the hastily-laid extra dinner-place, the beer that had to be sent for, forgetting the apologies over the final nightcap, when he would ask such provocative questions as: 'What is religion?' 'Why do we allow the white man to stay?' 'Why cannot Islam develop a more progressive outlook?' It was such questions as these that slammed the cork in his host's bottle.

His friends were, in a distracted way, ashamed of him, but the shame was of such long standing that it had transmitted itself into a kind of special affection. His penury was looked upon as a sort of holy idiocy, and he was granted such privileges as swigging a whole bottle of Benedictine at a sitting, being sick in the ash-trays, using vile English obscenities he had learned in the Navy. Much could be excused him anyway, for he was no true Malay. He was a mixture of Arab, Chinese and Dutch, with a mere formal sprinkling of Malay floating, like those red peppers, on the surface. His friends, complacently pitying this eccentric product of miscegenation, would forget the foreign bodies in their own blood. Haji Zainal Abidin would cease to be mainly Afghan; 'Che Abdullah no longer spoke the Siamese he had sucked from his mother; little Hussein forgot that his father was a Bugis. When they talked about Malay self-determination, they really meant that Islam should frighten the Chinese with visions of hell; but perhaps they did not even mean that. They themselves were too fond of the bottle to be good Muslims; they even kissed women and ate doubtful meat. They did not really know what they wanted. The middle-class of Kenching who carried Muslim names and were not too dark, not too light, were united by the most tenuous of bonds. One of these bonds was 'Che Guru Abdul Kadir, the hairy-legged goat who carried their sins on his back, who defined a vague smoky image of the true Malay (who did not exist), the true Islam (not really desirable) in terms of what these things were not. Certainly a beer or two and an occasional Friday abstention from mosque did not seem so heinous when Abdul Kadir lay cursing in his vomit.

'Che Normah wrinkled her flat splay nose in disgust as the servant swabbed the doorstep. She liked a party, but she did not like a party to get out of hand. When she had been mistress of two rubber estates the parties had been more decorous: much whisky had been taken, ribald songs sung, but the white man usually knew when he had gone too far, he could usually be controlled. ('Che Normah knew a great deal about controlling white men.) Give a little alcohol, however, to men like Mat bin Hussein, Din, Ariffin, Haji Zainal Abidin, and you could always expect the worst. Here was the pretty Chinese table whose top had been greased smearily by the flat feet of Ariffin doing his little dance. There was the Persian carpet on which Din had allowed clumsily-opened beer to froth freely. Bits of broken glass lay about, ready to ambush bare feet. Even 'Che Isa the normally lady-like colleague of the accursed Abdul Kadir, had behaved sillily, making up to married men. Only Rupert had been reasonably restrained. ('Che Normah pronounced the name in the Malay manner, metathetically: Ruperet, the final dental initiated but not exploded. She had been practising the name a lot lately.) But Rupert was a white man and could be controlled. A very white man. And to think that that fool of a *haji* had proposed naming him after that drunken improvident lout Kadir. Normah had put her foot down. He was to be called Abdullah. That was to be his mosque-name and his burial-name. In the house he was still to be called Ruperet.

'Che Normah was a good Malay and a good Muslim. That is to say, her family was Achinese and came from Northern Sumatra and she herself liked to wear European dress occasionally, to drink stout and pink gin and to express ignorance about the content of the Koran. The Achinese are proverbially hot-blooded and quick on the draw, but the only knives 'Che Normah carried were in her eyes and her tongue. She gave the lie to the European superstition – chiefly a missionary superstition – that the women of the East are down-trodden. Her two husbands – the first Dutch and the second English – had wilted under her blasts of unpredictable passion and her robust sexual demands. The Communist bullets that had rendered her twice a widow had merely anticipated, in a single violent instant, what attrition would more subtly have achieved.

Haji Zainal Abidin had been too cautious in telling Hardman that both had 'probably' been killed by Communists. There was no doubt about those two identical ends: tappers had stood open-mouthed and impassively around while execution had been performed. But possibly Haji Zainal Abidin had had in mind a subtler and more forensic question: that of ultimate responsibility. Mac-beth had used no knife on Banquo, but he had none the less killed him. The Communist terrorists, whose trade was death, had frequently been known to put, at the request of tappers, an unpopular foreman out of the way. They were at times glad enough to be hired assassins and were content with a payment of rice and a few tins of corned beef. It might or might not be significant that both Willem Pijper and John Hythe had been shot a few days before they were due for repatriation. A Muslim marriage does not need a civil contract to make it legal in a Muslim state, but in a Christian country marriage is not marriage unless there be benefit of registrar. It is just possible that both Pijper and Hythe were frivolous in their attitude to marrying 'Che Normah, that they merely wanted, in the American phrase, to get 'shacked-up', and the Muslim names they assumed were an amusing fancy dress. But 'Che Normah was no Cho Cho San. Allah had spoken in the Communist rifle-shots, and 'Che Normah had become doubly a wealthy widow: bonuses lay snug in the Anglo-Chinese Bank, the rubber companies had paid handsome compensation, there had been life insurance. Now, mistress of a house that was her own, she contemplated marriage once again, perhaps for the last time. She had worked out details of the marriage contract herself and, if she was to pay heavily for Rupert Hardman, she was determined on getting her money's worth. It was promotion, this new marriage: Hardman was a professional man, not a glorified foreman. There would be invitations to the Residency on the Queen's Birthday, dances at the Club, the prestige of going about on the arm of a man whose untannable skin could not be mistaken for that of a Eurasian. John Hythe had – only once – come back drunk from the club to announce with passion that someone had called him a *Serani*. The brown face and arms of an open-air worker, the marriage to a Malay – the catty club-women had been only too ready to look for a touch of the tarbrush. He had stormed and volubly regretted his marriage and she had knifed him back with her more deadly tongue, ending by throwing a chair at him and then, excited, taking him to bed. Willem Pijper had indulged in no such cries of wounded blood: he probably had been Eurasian.

It was a good solid house, fanless but airy. As the servant cleaned up, 'Che Normah looked round its rooms with approval, not regretting the high price she had paid for it. Its view was good. From the porch she could see the Law Courts and the Bank and the Great Mosque, a piquant anthology of architectural styles: Colonial Palladian; a timid approach to Corbusier; Hollywood Alhambran. And there would be no question of her husband coming home smelling of chlorophyll tablets and pleading a long day in court. She would be able to see him going in and coming out. The office was a different matter: that was to be on Jalan Laksamana, but Jalan Laksamana was full of her spies. 'Che Normah went to the back door and looked out on her cool garden: a rain-tree and a flame-of-the-forest, gaudy Malayan flowers that officials of the Agricultural Department had, as a labour of love, classified in cold Latin, but to which liberal peasants had given grosser names, names which 'Che Normah hardly knew, for all flowers with her were subsumed in the general term *bunga*. For her only the life of the flesh was important. At her feet was a clump of the leaves called touch-me-not, leaves which pretended death and curled up at the approach of foot or hand. For some reason, seeing them do this, 'Che Normah smiled secretly.

'Che Normah was a handsome woman. (Another smug European fallacy is that Eastern women lose their beauty quickly.) 'Che Normah was forty-two, but her hair was lustrous under its perm, her coffee skin smooth, eyes large, chin firm. She was lavish in build, with great thighs but a slim waist, bathycolpous as any Homeric heroine. Her walk evoked images from such Malay poets as had felt the influence of the Persians: melons in the melon-season, twin moons that never waned (but, she ensured, never waxed either). She ate sparsely of rice but was fond of salads of cucumber, lady's fingers and red peppers, a little tender meat from Singapore Cold Storage, the choicer kinds of sea-food. She ate only when she was hungry. She could dance but played no games. She knew some Dutch and spoke a high-pitched stressless English. Her Malay was the Malay of the State of Lanchap, the State where, to use the idiom, her blood had first been poured, and she spoke it fierily, with crisp glottal checks, with much bubbling reduplication. (Optionally, Malay repeats words to express plurality and intensity. The connotations of both these terms were appropriate to 'Che Normah.)

Today her betrothed had a case in court. The court, she knew, rose for tiffin at twelve-thirty, and soon it would be time for her to watch him come out, thin and very white, elegant enough in unpaid-for palm-beach suiting. (So many bills of his had to be paid; well, she would pay them.) She was prepared, until the marriage contract had actually been signed, to forgo her proleptic right to control his movements and associations. There was plenty of time. But, almost sentimentally she wanted to rehearse the part of the doorstep-waiting wife, the hand waving at the approaching lean figure, the white boyish face perhaps breaking into a smile of greeting. Realistic like all Achinese, she knew that the greeting smile would not last for long, or, if it did last, it would become twisted. But she tried to retain this rare mood of sentimentality, even tried to intensify it by applying it to the past as well as the future, and so went for her photograph album and sat down, barefooted, on the step.

Studio photographs; herself in rich Malay dress; in a frothy evening frock; a profile with bare brown shoulders. And the innumerable snapshots: herself and a Japanese girl-friend in pre-war Singapore; a group on the estate, her doomed Dutchman next to her; herself in bathing costume, leaning back provocatively in the sun; a Chinese dinner, with her second husband fumbling chopsticks to his mouth; Willem smiling vacantly, an arm about her. The sentimental mood did not last. Her eyes hardened.

Soon she brought to the door-step a plate of cold curried

beef, fiery pepper-choked fibres, and forked it in delicately. Then, unaware of irony, she hummed 'One Fine Day' while picking her teeth. 'A man, a little man, is approaching across the *padang*.' She did not know the words.

Before twelve-thirty the court recessed. She saw her betrothed come out, talking to a white-suited Tamil, making forensic gestures, his brief under his arm. Then she saw him prepare to move off and then someone come on to the scene up left, and accost him gently.

The storms began to stir in her eyes, for, despite everything, she was still a daughter of Islam, and the man that Rupert Hardman was talking to was just the man he should not be talking to. She banged her fist on the empty curry plate and it cracked in two.

5

Having telephoned his client, still waiting at the Club, to say that his case (breach of contract, brought by a servant) would not now come up till the afternoon, Rupert Hardman left the court-house, wiping irritably his face and the back of his neck, his brief under his arm, listening to the chatter of the Tamil interpreter whose name he had forgotten. Chinese cases are brisk, the litigants want to get back to business, but with Indians there is an unhealthy love of the law, and a petty case of the theft of ten dollars had evoked high drama – wailings, rendings of shirts already rent, flashing eyes and poetry, babies exhibited theatrically at moments of crisis. The case was likely to eat away a great deal of the afternoon – because of a certain dramaturgical rhythm its length could roughly be judged – and certainly the audience would not object. The law was a poor man's circus and the public benches were crammed with *aficionados* of the short answer and the long answer, the crescendo and the climax, the thumping of breast and elevation of eyes, the tears and the hard-luck story.

'Our worthy magistrate,' said the Tamil interpreter, 'is too enamoured with the niceties of English idiom. He told the Chinese defendant that he would let him off this time but that henceforth he must paddle his own canoe. Our friend Wong translated this for him too literally, saying that the defendant must expiate his crime by taking a sampan up and down the river. Whereupon the defendant said he would take anything but a sampan, anything – a fine of a thousand dollars, a week's gaol – but how could he now, at his age, forsake his business and become a sampan-man. You see thus the stupidity of the Malays. A Malay magistrate takes everything too far, including the English language, and our worthy 'Che Yunus is no exception to the rule.'

Hardman nodded, remembering that 'Che Yunus had reviled a Tamil witness, a convert to Islam, because he gave his name as Abdulla bin Abdullah. Had he no imagination, did he think so little of the faith he had entered as to take the most obvious, the least inspiring name that came to hand? 'Che Yunus was ready to dismiss him from the witness-stand, as a man without a name, until counsel had gently intervened.

'Che Normah had decreed that Rupert Hardman's new name should be Abdullah bin Abdullah.

Hardman now became irritable and expressed impatience at the long waiting in the heat, the frivolous attitude of the East to the calm processes of Western Law. He waved his arm in a gesture of weariness. The Tamil nodded, saying: 'It is the heat, Mr Hardman. It is getting you down. How long since you have had leave?'

'Leave? How can I afford leave?'

'Soon, I hear, you will be able to afford it. But will you then be able to take it?'

Hardman did not answer. There were obviously no secrets in this town. Haji Zainal Abidin had done his rounds, announcing loudly to the world that another infidel had seen the light, the terms of the contract, the size of the marriage settlement, Allah be praised, boy! another beer.

'I hope I can take it,' grinned Hardman at length. The Tamil took his leave, his face gleaming in the sun like a polished door-knocker, strong arm raised in most cordial valediction.

Hardman started off in the direction of the car-park. Then Georges Laforgue appeared from around the corner and accosted him in French.

'Is it true what I hear?'

'What do you hear, Georges?' Hardman smiled with affection and embarrassment and shame.

'You are to be married.'

'Yes, Georges. I'm sorry.'

'You had better come to my house. I can cook you a little lunch. Your car is here?'

Father Laforgue was a missionary who had been ten years in China, four of them in prison, a year now in Dahaga and two years yet to come before leave. He was somewhat younger than Hardman but looking far younger than he should. The fair cropped head and glasses and innocent eyes suggested a Mid-Western campus; only the mouth was mobile, adult, French. His office was displayed frankly in a long white tropical soutane that spoke of the clinic more than the altar, and the sweeping aseptic dress made sense for Hardman out of the words of *Finnegans Wake*: 'He does not believe in our psychous of the Real Absence, neither miracle wheat nor soul-surgery of P. P. Quemby.' Sooner or later everything in *Finnegans Wake* made sense: it was just a question of waiting.

'You're probably right,' said Hardman. 'If we're seen together in the street you'll probably end by being thrown out of the State. Here it is.' They got into the worn dusty car, oven-like with a morning's slow soaking of metallic heat, and Hardman started it and crept, with much horning, into the stream of lunch-time bicycles and trishaws. They clattered down Jalan Hang Tuah, turned into Jalan Rumah Jahat – chickens and children and mountainous rubbish on the road – and then, on Jalan China, came to Father Laforgue's little house. Father Laforgue lived at the end of a row of shops, all of them carrying names in bold ideograms, and he himself had his name and his calling painted on a board in white Chinese characters. Thus he became one with his Chinese parishioners, announcing a trade as honest as that of the dentist, the seller of rice-wine, the brothel-keeper, the purveyor of quack rejuvenators and aphrodisiacs, or the vendor of shark's-fin strips.

The street-door was always open, for there was nothing to steal, and Hardman was led into the single large room, dark and airless. It was dirty too, for Father Laforgue kept no servant. Once he had tried, and the Parish Committee had granted eighty dollars a month as fair wages, but lubricious eyes had suspected and tongues eventually broadcast the worst: a Chinese boy had meant pederasty, an old woman gerontophily, an intelligent monkey would have meant bestiality. It was best to do for oneself and risk the charge of auto-erotic practices. Celibacy is not merely unknown to Islam, it is unintelligible.

Hardman sat on one of the two hard chairs and saw on the table an open book which he knew to be the *Analects* of Confucius, row after falling row of ideograms preserving – outside phonetic change and above dialectal differences – that eminently seductive and dangerous common sense of old China. There were other books on the single book-shelf, all Chinese – Shang Yang, Tzu Ssu, Hui Shih, Kung-sun Lung, Chuang Chou, Han Fei, Pan Ku, Wang Ch'ung. Nowhere to be seen was the work of a new slick Thomist, Maritain, von Hügel, even Augustine or Jerome or Liguori. Georges Laforgue knew the meaning of the term 'seduction'.

Shyly the priest said, 'There is nothing to drink. No, wait. I have some rice-spirit. We could drink that with altar-wine.'

'That's all right, Georges.'

Father Laforgue sat down, folded hands on lap, and waited.

'You knew I had to do this,' said Hardman, 'but it doesn't mean anything. How could it?'

'It must mean something. Why else do it?' Of the two Hardman spoke by far the better French. Diffidence smothered the knowledge of authority that rested beneath Father Laforgue's equivocal Catholicism. In China he had spoken good Mandarin, and in ten years this had become his first tongue. Here he found himself with a parish of

Hokkien and Cantonese speakers and a few English people whose language he could hardly talk. His French, severed from its sources of nourishment, grown coarse through lack of use, halted and wavered, searching for the right word which Mandarin was always ready to supply. He understood the confessions he heard only because he had compiled a sort of traveller's guide to the chief sins, practising as a colonial doctor practises, the stock questions and description of symptoms set out in polyglot lists to be learnt parrot-fashion.

'You know I had to get money. I'm being quite honest with you. No other way suggested itself. But, you see, it can't mean anything. I haven't apostatized; I'm just pretending to be a Muslim.'

'It isn't just a question of what you believe but of what you do,' said Father Laforgue. 'By the mere act of going to the mosque . . .'

'But I shan't go to the mosque.'

'But you will not be able to receive the sacraments, go to mass. You'll be under Islamic law, remember. Islam is mainly custom, mainly observance. There is very little real doctrine in it, only this belief in one God, which they think so original.'

'I'd thought of that, but . . .'

'And don't you see, you'll be living in sin. You'll be cohabiting with this woman, outside a state of matrimony.'

'And supposing I cohabit only in the strict literal sense?'

'You mean?'

'Supposing I merely live with her, in the same house, having no carnal knowledge?'

Father Laforgue smiled, looking wise and bitter. 'You know your own nature well enough. Human nature. And I think you must know the law of Islam on that point. She can claim divorce on the grounds of non-consummation. They have an Arabic term for it.'

'*Nusus.*'

'I think that is the word. And then she can demand the

whole of her money back, the marriage money. There is a Malay word for that.'

'The *mas kahwin*.'

'Yes. You know it all.'

'And you know it all.'

'There was the case of a Tamil Catholic who changed his faith to marry a Malay. It was here, it happened while you were away. I was nearly thrown out of the State for trying to talk to him. I learned a lot about Islam at that time.'

Hardman knew that they both knew that there was no compromise possible, no more façade, no stealing off to masses said in cellars, sacraments administered when the town was asleep, no avoiding the marriage-bed. 'Look here, Georges,' he said. 'I know what I'm doing, and what worries me most is your position. I don't want you to feel you have to try and win me back, putting yourself in bad with the Islamic authorities. You can write me off. For the time being, that is. I'll just have to take a chance. But you can't afford to go back for the lost sheep, at least your parish can't afford that you should do that.'

Father Laforgue sighed. 'You know my duty as far as that goes.'

'It's not as though I'm a real Catholic,' said Hardman. 'I'm a convert, and a very recent one at that. People are always dubious about war-time marriages, and war-time conversions are sometimes just as shaky. If it hadn't been for that wing-commander having visions and this other business of the crash, well, it just wouldn't have happened.'

'How do you know?'

'I'm pretty sure.'

'But the fact is that it did happen. Conversions are often a matter of sheer accident. You had better have some lunch.'

'I can help you.'

'There is not much to do. We can have some *mee*

and a little fried pork. Or are you allowed to eat that now?'

Hardman grinned. 'In public, no.'

'I like a man to be whole-hearted. If you are going to be a Muslim why not be a real one? It is better than being tepid. You remember it says: "Because thou art neither hot nor cold . . ." '

' "I shall vomit thee out of my mouth." '

'You stay there and rest. You will find some Chinese cigarettes somewhere. I will do the cooking.'

Standing over the frying-pan Father Laforgue caught, in the smell of the *mee* and the pork, the smell of the hilly province where he had lived and worked for so long. Those ten years had impaired his orthodoxy. A soldier of Rome in a far outpost, he was cut off from orders, from new policies and definitions, and had to administer the law in terms of what was expedient. The doctor, curing diseases in a savage territory, may well have to meet the medicineman half-way and submit to the intoning of spells and the sticking of talismans between the patients' teeth before plunging his scalpel into the distempered part. And so Father Laforgue had been willing to falsify the doctrine of the Trinity in a polytheistic parish, had learned not to be outraged at meeting Chinese priests who had married. More and more he had discovered a sympathy for the charismatic churches against which St Paul had fulminated. He had held fast to his main function, primarily a thaumaturgical one: he could forgive sins, he could turn the bread and wine into God, he could save a dying child, from Limbo. Little else mattered.

And he was so sick for China that he wondered whether anything mattered now except his returning there. The Chinese Government had become more moderate recently. They would permit priests to work there now, so long as they were careful not to allow their teaching to conflict with the official philosophy. A priest, of course, was essentially a crying witness against the Communist metaphysic; he was nothing if he was not that. But Georges Laforgue clung to a hope. He might yet find himself back in those cool hills with their incredible stars and that mad logical world of the Chinese villagers. France meant nothing to him. Europeans had sometimes invited him to dinner and given him stuffed aubergines and onion soup and Nuits St Georges and what they said was good coffee. They had gushed about Normandy and the Côte d'Or and little places on the Left Bank. They had played him records of French cabaret music. They had evinced, in their curious French mixed with Malay (both were foreign languages, both occupied the same compartment, they were bound to get mixed), a nostalgia for France which amused him slightly, bored him much, flattered him not at all. He rarely received invitations now to the mass-produced houses of the Public Works Department. He dined with the Chinese and spoke with the children, many of whom were learning Mandarin at school. And he had this English friend Rupert Hardman.

'I suppose,' he said, as he laid the table and put down the soya sauce, 'I suppose that I am not doing things at all in the right way. I should tell you that I am the voice of the Church, which is the voice of God, and tell you to get down on your knees and repent. And then you would feel a great deal happier.'

'That's perfectly true. I know I'm not going to be happy.'

'And yet you do it.'

'I have my function. I am a lawyer. I must fulfil that function. I cannot fulfil it with a background of debts and without an office. It's as simple as that. If you had shown me a nice rich Chinese widow it would have been easier, but . . . Well, I take what I can.'

'I do not understand. You are a well-qualified man. You should be already rich. Lawyers make much money in this country.'

'You can blame Redshaw and Tubb. They asked me to come and work in Singapore. They were crooks, as I found out too late. There were no repatriation terms. I had to leave, on a question of principle, and I had to stay in Malaya. There just wasn't enough money for a passage home.'

'That is, I suppose, amusing. You leave your firm because of a very high principle, and now you embrace very low principles yourself.'

'But that was professional honour.'

'And so you set professional honour above God.' Saying this, Georges Laforgue felt shame. The big words were beginning to sound empty in his mouth. Hardman had at least been seduced by honour; he himself only by hills and ridiculous impious peasants. St Paul had been right there. Better not to have been born. But then he had been Saul. Or had he just quoted it from someone else? He ought to look that up, but he had nowhere to look it up in. He shrugged it away.

'And I shall be rich,' said Hardman. 'Then I shall give her all her money back. And then I shall pronounce the magic formula of divorce.'

'Leaving one more divorcée abandoned to walk the streets.'

'She'll never need to walk the streets.'

'Right and wrong are so terribly mixed up,' said Georges Laforgue. 'I find it better not to think about them. I prefer to think of Confucius and human-heartedness. Now sit down and eat. I am afraid you will have to drink tepid water. I have no refrigerator.'

'We shall still go on seeing each other,' said Hardman. 'We shall still be friends.'

'Yes,' said Father Laforgue, 'we shall still be friends. How could we be otherwise?' He pincered into his mouth a fragment of fried pork. 'But friends must meet, and it seems to me that we shall never be able to meet.'

'Oh, there are places. There's the Bijou Cabaret, for example. Police officers go there to pick up their nightly whores. We can meet there and talk philosophy, under cover of girls and beer. It will be quite easy.'

'You know,' said Father Laforgue, probing with his chopsticks, 'my reactions are most unorthodox. I feel less hurt about your entering Islam than I would if you were to become a Protestant. That is wrong, for Protestantism is a disreputable younger brother but still of the family. Whereas Islam is the old enemy.'

'The fact is,' said Hardman. Waspish red peppers bit his tongue. 'The fact ith that Catholithithm and Ithlam have more to thay to each other . . .' (he drank some water) '. . . than have orthodox and heterodox Christianity. It was a quarrel between men when all is said and done, and there was a healthy mutual respect. Both claimed Aristotle as master of them that know, and Dante put Averroes in a very mild place. What I mean is that you can't take Luther or Calvin or Wesley very seriously, and hence they don't count. But you can take Islam very seriously and you can compare wounds and swop photographs, and you can say: "We're old enemies and old enemies are more than new friends." It's like bull-fighting and the moment of truth, when the toreador and the bull become one.'

'You will come back,' said Father Laforgue, nodding. 'I know that. But it is important that you do not come back too late. Anyway,' he added, with little conviction, 'prayer may help.'

'I must go back to the Law,' said Hardman. 'And before that I have to give some money to a parishioner of yours, a man called Hung.'

'Hung is a good man.'

'He's certainly wealthy enough to be able to afford to be good. And today he's going to be wealthier by two thousand dollars. More than thirty pieces of silver,' he added, grinning.

'Be very careful in traffic,' said Father Laforgue. 'Death awaits in a pinprick. And we shall see each other soon.'

'As friends.'

'As friends.'

When Hardman had gone, Father Laforgue, leaving

the plates on the table to gather grease, turned with relief to the *Analects*. He picked out, as on a guitar-string, the notes of monosyllabic wisdom: 'If a man be really bent on human-heartedness then he cannot be wicked ...' But neither the words nor the meaning brought tears to his eyes. '... A wise man is not perplexed, nor is a human-hearted man unhappy, and a courageous man is never frightened.' He felt hopeless at being neither wise, courageous nor human-hearted.

For Hardman the afternoon went well. The premises on Jalan Laksamana were secured, Hung counting the limp notes greedily, and Auntie's bill was paid. Then in court Hardman demolished the Chinese cook who demanded two-months' pay from his ex-employer, alleging that he had not been given the statutory month's notice but had been summarily dismissed with harsh words. Hardman left the plaintiff a quivering sniveller, his treacheries and villainies open to the world, defeated and rebuked, ordered by the magistrate to pay costs at the rate of five dollars a month. Hardman's client, a paunched planter, was pleased – 'Wasn't going to let that fat Chinese sod get away with it' – and he cordially invited Hardman to drink victorious whisky with him in the Club. Hardman drank quite a lot of whisky, listening to the planter's bellyaches and gripes: he was wealthy but rejected of women; even his wife, pinched, raw-boned and big-nosed, had left him for another man, a man with whom she now lived in sin in the Australian outback. Hardman was attentive and courteous, anticipating an eventual divorce suit.

When Hardman left the Club he was happy and somewhat amorous, warm images flushing his pineal gland, his marriage presented to him as an adventure, and a line from *Antony and Cleopatra* ringing clear: 'The beds i' the East are soft.' He drove jerkily to his fiancée's house and was met by a monsoon of abuse. 'Che Normah flashed the twin blades of her Achinese eyes and daggered him with metallic-clattering Malay. There was a lot of reduplication, and from the swirling pot of her anger he picked out *chakap-chakap* and *orang-orang Nasrani* as the main ingredients. He was accused of chatting-chatting with man-man Christian. His pale eyes glittering with whisky, he tried to take her hand, saying loud:

> 'When thy mistress some rich anger shows,
> Imprison her soft hand and let her rave.'

She would have none of this, reiterating: 'Christian men not good. Japanese Christian and Germans Christian and all bad men who have come to Malaya Christian. Christians believe in three Gods, contrary to Muslim teaching.' Her Japanese girl-friend, she argued, had been Christian, and look what the Japanese had done in Malaya. And now the Chinese Communists were killing and torturing, and they too were Christian...

'On a point of factual accuracy,' Hardman kept trying to say, 'on a mere point of accuracy...'

Hardman was thin but he was wiry. He put his arms round her ample body and kissed her heavily. She struggled in vain, only once freeing her mouth to forbid him any contact with the *padre*. Then the energy of her anger was converted to a passion of submission to his caresses, and soon, among the cushions on the floor, he anticipated the consummation of his marriage.

Convalescent, sweating, almost sober, he said: 'Is it true what you told me about not being able to have children?'

'Allah has denied me that blessing.'

'Are you sure it's only Allah?'

'What do you mean?'

He lay back in cigarette-smoking languor, with the silks and perfumes of the *Arabian Nights* all about him. Soon a girl would bring coffee. Minarets rose in frail spires of smoke, and the camel-bells of the robed traders thinned into the distance as the caravan passed through the gateway. It was an acceptable world.

'You must promise me that,' said 'Che Normah. 'Not to see that *padre* again.'

'But he's my friend.'

'You will have new friends.'

'All right,' lied Hardman. 'I promise.'

She embraced him with undiminished ardour and he began to feel a reluctant admiration for those Muslims who could not get along with fewer than four wives. Perhaps the West was really effete.

Next day the marriage contract was signed.

6

The thermometer in Crabbe's office read one hundred and six degrees.

It was not really the office, it was a book-store. The real office had become a class-room, housing the twelfth stream of the third standard, and soon – the *kampongs* milling out children in strict Malthusian geometrical progression – the store itself would become yet another class-room. Then Crabbe would have to take his telephone and type-writer into the lavatory. He went to the lavatory now, without typewriter or telephone, to pull off his shirt, wipe down his body with a towel already damp, and drink thirstily of the tap-water, brownish and sun-warm. For a fortnight now he had intended to buy a large thermos jug and a table-fan. His prodigious dryness was due to the heat, too much smoking, and to a great salty breakfast.

The excessive smoking was the fault of Haji Ali College; the Pantagruelian breakfast was Ah Wing's regular notion of what an expatriate officer should eat before going off to work. Crabbe had consumed grape-fruit, iced papaya, por-ridge, kippers, eggs and bacon with sausages and a mutton chop, and toast and honey. At least, these things had been set before him, and Ah Wing had watched intently from the kitchen door. Crabbe now saw that he would have to beg Ah Wing to go and work for Talbot, a man who would meet his challenge gladly, might even call for second help-ings and more bread. But perhaps Ah Wing would cun-ningly recognize Talbot's greed as pathological and des-pise him more than he despised Crabbe, deliberately burn-ing his steaks and under-boiling his potatoes. Somewhere in Ah Wing's past was a frock-coated whiskered law-bringer who had established the pattern of square meals and substantial heavers. Perhaps Ah Wing was to be seen on some historical photograph of the eighteen-seventies, grinning behind a solid row of thick-limbed pioneers, all of whom had given their names to ports, hills, and city streets. Certainly, in the gravy soups, turbot, hare, roast saddles, cabinet puddings, boiled eggs at tea-time and bread and butter and meat paste with the morning tray, one tasted one's own decadence: a tradition had been preserved in order to humiliate. Perhaps it really was time the British limped out of Malaya.

Ah Wing was a fantastic model of Chinese conservatism. He had not at first been willing to recognize that Crabbe was a married man and had set only one place at table. At length, grudgingly, he had obeyed his master's sign-language. And habits of long repatriated officers seemed fossilized in certain rituals: a large bottle of beer was brought to the bedside on the morning of the Sabbath; twice Ah Wing had entered Crabbe's unlocked bathroom and started to scrub his back; once Fenella had been rudely shaken from her dawn sleep and told, in rough gestures, to go.

But Ah Wing's private life – in so far as it showed chinks of light in Crabbe's kitchen-dealings with him – exhibited a much more formidable conservatism, dizzying Crabbe wth vistas of ancient China. He had once caught Ah Wing eating a live mouse. A day later he was proposing to send a black cat after it (black cats were said to be tastier than tabbies). Then there was Ah Wing's store of medicines – tiger's teeth in vinegar, a large lizard in brandy, compounds of lead and horrible egg-nogs. Crabbe discovered that his cook had a great reputation with the local Malays, with whom he did a roaring trade in – eventually lethal – aphrodisiacs. The village *bomoh* was jealous of Ah Wing and called him an infidel. And indeed Ah Wing's religion, though not quite animistic, was too complex and obscure for inquiry.

The local Malays were a problem. They squatted on

Crabbe's veranda every night, waiting for tales of distant lands and Western marvels. Crabbe had now established the routine of reading them love *pantuns* – mysterious four-line poems he had found in a Malay anthology – and discovered that a few verses went a long way, producing ecstatic cries, grunts of deep approval, profound nods and writhing of bodies. Here at least was a healthy literary tradition. It was Fenella who suffered most. The Malays were fascinated by her fair hair, and children were brought along to clutch it stickily, as against the King's Evil. The women asked her about her underwear, begged for discarded brassières, and went round the lounge, handling the ornaments and wanting to know how much they cost. It had taken Crabbe some time to become accustomed to Malay elders squatting on the dining-room floor and using the second bedroom for reciting their prayers. His predecessor had been decidedly too chummy. And Fenella was still scared of taking a bath, for a spirit of sincere inquiry sent serious Malay youths to the bathroom window to find out if white women differed materially from brown ones. It was not easy, and Fenella talked more and more about going back to England.

'Take it easy, darling,' he would say. 'We've got to be absorbed into these customs. We're still too tough to be ingested quickly, but we've got to try and soften ourselves to a bolus, we've got to yield.'

'What lovely metaphors you choose.'

'I mean what I say. If we're going to live in Malaya, work for Malaya, we must shed a great deal of our Westernness. We're too ready to be shocked and we're too reserved.'

'I've tried. You know I've tried. I thought I'd succeeded in fitting into Malaya, but now I know I never shall. I've got to go home.'

'But we've nothing to go back to.'

'Are you so blind? Don't you see the beginning of the end already? They don't want us here. They're talking about Malaya for the Malayans. There's no room for Europeans any more.'

'That's what they think. But who's to do the work if we don't? They're not ready to take over yet. In their hearts they know it.'

Did they know it? Crabbe was having trouble with his senior master, Jaganathan. Jaganathan was quite sure of his own competence to take over from the white man. In the oven of an office he and Crabbe had occasionally raised their voices, and the Malay clerks had looked up with interest. Jaganathan was a black tub of a man, with a jutting rice-round belly and black trunks of legs below his white shorts. But his head was angular and carven like a huge piece of coal, polished with sweat and reflecting light in all its facets, the steel-rimmed spectacles always flashing tiny crystal moons of impatience or irritation. His middle-aged voice whined and crooned and sometimes grew husky and panting when he was deeply moved – as now, this morning, with Crabbe coming out of the lavatory, adjusting his shirt, feeling sweat rill down the hollow of his back.

'I am telling you, Mr Crabbe, these peoples are very angry that you will not admit their children. They are good peoples, they want to give education to their children, and they are angry that the white man will not allow them education. Then they see that two white children, the children of white men, are allowed in the school and they are not. They will be very angry to you, they will injure your car, they will throw stones at your windows.'

'Look here, Mr Jaganathan, that decision isn't mine, and you damn well know it isn't. These two expatriate officers were promised places in this school for their kids. That promise was one of the conditions of their consenting to be posted here. It was a promise made at high level, some time ago. What do you want? Do you want to deny education to the children of expatriates?'

'They should make their own arrangements for education. They have money and they should start private schools. They should not take the bread of learning from the mouths of Asians.' Crabbe guessed that Jaganathan had been making a speech somewhere; the metaphor came out too glibly.

'And I wish you'd see sense about this money business,' said Crabbe. 'I'm sick to death of being told that I'm bloated with the blood of the down-trodden Asian. Your salary is a good deal higher than mine.'

'Look at my experience. I have been teaching for many, many more years than you, Mr Crabbe.'

'Look at my qualifications,' said Crabbe with heat. 'Those had to be worked for, you know, and paid for. You'd better start realizing that some of us are out here to work for Malaya, and that the work we do requires some sort of specialist knowledge, and that we don't regard our white skin as any qualification at all. Sometimes I wish to God I weren't white, so that I could get people to stop looking at my face as if it were either that of a leper or a jackbooted tyrant and start thinking of what I am, what I'm trying to do, not of a mere accident of pigmentation.'

Jaganathan wheezed a queer chuckle which joggled his belly. 'You sometimes become very angry man, Mr Crabbe. It is not a good thing to become angry in a hot climate. The white man is not used to this climate, he is not born to it. It is better to be calm.' Then his voice took on a peculiar sing-song quality, and he seemed to be soothing Crabbe, repeating the words, 'Be calm, be calm, be calm,' smiling and throwing the crystal lights of his glasses on to Crabbe's eyes. For a moment Crabbe had a strange conviction that Jaganathan was trying to hypnotize him. Certainly he felt spent and he tasted the fish-course of his breakfast in a wave of nausea and got a distant view, as on a radar-screen, of an approaching headache.

'All right,' said Crabbe. 'I'm sorry.' He felt a certain shame. He could not hope to help Malaya if he made enemies, lost his temper with the influential, lashed out at his henchmen. He sat down behind his desk, wiped the back of his neck with a soaked handkerchief.

'You are not looking very well, Mr Crabbe,' said Jaganathan. 'The work is very hard here. Why do you not take a little time off, lie down for a little while? There is no reason why you should not go home now.'

'I'm all right,' said Crabbe. 'Thanks for your solicitude.'

'I think perhaps you have a headache.'

Crabbe looked at him sharply. 'I've no headache,' he said. Now, if you'll excuse me, I'm going to take a walk round the school. I want to see some of the teaching.'

'They will not like that, Mr Crabbe. They will resent it. They are qualified teachers here.'

'There are quite a few probationers. It's one of my jobs to see how they are getting on.'

'I will come with you, Mr Crabbe.'

The headache was taking shape, firming. 'Thank you, Mr Jaganathan. I believe you yourself have a class now. If you'll excuse me.' He pushed past, went out.

Crabbe got his biggest shocks from two of the experienced teachers. A shrill Tamil woman in a bright sari was giving a history lesson. Crabbe stood outside the classroom and, unseen, listened to an account of British tyranny in India.

'. . . And the British hate the Indians so much they build a prison called the Black Hole of Calcutta and they put thousands of Indians in this very small dark room where there was no air and the Indians died . . .'

He gulped, wondering whether to laugh or cry, and passed on down the stone corridor to the class-room of 'Che Abdul Kadir. Kadir was evidently in the throes of a hangover and was throwing around, like stink-bombs, ripe pellets of lower-deck invective.

'. . . For fuck's sake, if you are going to speak this bloody language, take your finger out. Any work I give you you do not bloody well do. I stand here in great pain because I am a sick man, and I see you little bastards doing no bloody work at all grinning at me like fucking apes as if it did not matter. But . . .' He slapped the desk and contorted his Dutch-Chinese face anew. '. . . It does bloody matter. There is the future of the fucking country at stake. If you little bastards do not work then there is chaos.' Suddenly his expression changed and with a sort of pedantic eagerness he wrote, in large capitals, the word CHAOS on the blackboard. Then he stood back and looked at it, the corners of his mouth lifting in a vapid smile. 'Look at that word,' he said. 'It is going to be an important word soon. See how it is spelt.' He admired the word, licking his lips and at one point sticking out a bilious tongue. 'Write it down in your books.' The word seemed to cure his hangover, for he became vigorous and friendly, patting children on the back, running horny fingers through their hair, striding up and down in good humour. Meanwhile the children, looking up at each several letter with open mouths, wrote. Then Crabbe, who had been standing unseen, peering in through the glass door, entered the class-room.

'Class stand!' yelled Kadir.

Small brown faces and an occasional yellow one, wide eyes and wondering mouths. They stood and sat down again. 'Look here,' said Crabbe, 'you can't use words like that.' The children strained to hear his low voice.

'Chaos? It is not a rude word.'

'No, no. I mean the other ones. "Bastard" and "bloody" and so on. Those aren't used in polite society.' Crabbe was seasonable, affable, smiling, catching the breath of stale hops from Abdul Kadir.

'Those are common English words. All sailors in the British Navy use those words. I teach these children English as it is spoken, not from dusty books.'

'Yes, yes.' Crabbe was patient. 'But don't you see ...'

At the end of the long morning the headache raged and the tin of cigarettes was nearly empty. His task seemed hopeless. One young Tamil teacher had assimilated the sound-system of English so thoroughly to that of his mother-tongue that none of the Chinese and Malay children understood him. Others could not be heard beyond the first two rows. A lot of them were teaching nonsense – New York is the capital of America; Shakespeare lived in the Middle Ages; the Malays founded Singapore; 'without' is a pronoun; the kidneys secrete bile. And a loose fluid arithmetic flourished in the number-melting heat, so that most answers could be marked right. Before the final bell a bright Malay boy of fourteen came in. He wanted time off to attend a 'Voice of Youth' rally in Tahi Panas. The rally was to be held on a Saturday, a holiday on the West Coast but not in the strict Muslim State of Dahaga. He could travel down on the Friday, he said, and be back in time for work on the Sunday.

'But your work comes first,' said Crabbe. 'You can't afford to start taking time off at this stage in your career.'

'This is an important meeting, sir. It is to assert the solidarity of Malay youth against the intruder.'

'The intruder?'

'The non-Malays, sir. Such as the white man, sir.'

'It doesn't seem a very laudable sort of thing to do. At least, it doesn't seem important enough to justify my giving you a day off.'

'I can't go, sir?'

'I think it would be better if you didn't.'

The Malay boy's eyes melted and his mouth drooped. 'Have a heart, sir,' he said. 'For fuck's sake.'

That night Crabbe went to the Grand Hotel to meet Hardman. Hardman had seemed shy of seeing him, and Crabbe had received no invitation to the wedding celebrations. But they had encountered each other on Jalan Laksamana in an ironmonger's shop, and Crabbe had suggested a few drinks together, finally fixing a time and a place. At the bar of the Grand, under the match-dousing fan and the cheeping house-lizards, surrounded by throat-hawkings and naked Chinese calendars, they drank beer and so warmed up the engine.

'But why did you come here?' said Crabbe.

'I might ask the same of you. Neither of us is exactly a Colonial type.'

'Oh, it's a long story. My wife died.'

'I thought there must be something like that. I puzzled about it quite a bit. There was that dark girl, the one who did music, wasn't there? You were always pretty thick, and I remember someone telling me during the war that you'd got married. I'm sorry.'

'Oh, one gets over it. It was a ghastly business. A car smash. The damn thing went into a river. I got out all right. It was January, a very cold January. Then I married Fenella. I'd known her before: she was a post-graduate student when I was lecturing. I just couldn't get warm again. I used to shiver in bed. It was partly accident my coming here – you know, answering an advertisement when I was tight – and also a kind of heliotropism, turning towards the heat. I just can't stand the cold.'

'I can understand that. Look here, do you remember what I used to look like in the old days?'

'You were always pretty pale. I don't think you've changed much.'

'You don't notice anything queer about my nose and mouth?'

'Oh, that. I thought it was a sort of peeling, sunburn or something. Isn't it?'

Hardman grinned and thrust his disfigurement into a full beer-glass. Then he said, 'I had to get out because of this. Damned egotism, I suppose. It was a 'plane crash. Anyway, I'd worked up such a beautiful mumbling self-consciousness about it that I became pretty useless in court. You know, like Oscar Wilde, covering my mouth up with my hand and muffling all my rhetoric. Redshaw and Tubb in Singapore wanted somebody to join them, so I came out. My point was, I suppose, that all white men here are white to the same degree, and people – Asians, I mean – would stare anyway. So what the hell. Look, let's have some whisky.'

'Yes. Whisky. And now you're married.'

'Now I'm married. I'm sorry I didn't invite you to the reception.'

'As you said. Did you have the usual Malay business – you in uniform and kris, recalling the glories of ancient Malacca, and the medicine-man's mumbo-jumbo?'

'You don't have that when one of you's been married

before. Just a contract and then orange crush for the mosque officials and then alcohol for the rest of the boys. It strikes me I'm a better Muslim than most of them. God, what a night. Abdul Kadir ...

'Yes. For fuck's sake.'

'Oh, they're all right. They're a bit more alive than the Club boys.'

'And the wife?'

'You know, she's pretty good.' Hardman drank some whisky and water. 'I think it's going to work out all right. Mind you. Malay women are pretty demanding.'

'So I've heard.' Crabbe opened his mouth to speak of Rahimah, then shut it again. She obviously still meant something to him.

'It's not lasciviousness, not really. It's a means of checking whether you've been with another woman.'

On that cue-line Mrs Talbot entered. She swung open the bar-door and stood glaring, her eyes a little out of focus, her lipstick smeary, dishevelled. She was wearing a smart crisp cocktail dress, patterned with lozenges of local silver thread. She had evidently been drinking. She said:

'Where is he?'

'Who?' said Crabbe politely, coldly, standing.

'You know damn well. Bannon-Fraser. He's upstairs, isn't he?'

'Madam,' said Hardman. 'I've just no idea.' At a single table a couple of Chinese drinkers looked up incuriously. Then Auntie appeared, huge, with great welcoming arms. 'Ah,' she said, 'this is great pleasure. You do not honour us as often as you should.'

'Is Mr Bannon-Fraser upstairs?'

'Mr Bannon-Fraser is not here, not tonight.'

'He's upstairs, with that bitch.'

'He is with no bitch, at least here he is not. Elsewhere he may be.'

'I'm going up to look.' Mrs Talbot made towards the main room.

'That is private,' said Auntie. 'That is for residents.' Her bulk barred the way. 'You come over here to the bar and have a little drink. With me.' She steered Mrs Talbot across, her beef-red ham-hand on the fragile arm. Mrs Talbot flopped on to a bar-stool, elbows on the counter, then started to snivel. 'All alike,' she sniffed. 'You're all alike.' Then she turned on Hardman viciously. 'You with your bloody Catholic virtue,' she said. 'Not too virtuous to ...'

'All right.' Hardman snapped it out. 'Not here.'

'What's it going to be, my dear?' said Auntie ingratiatingly. 'Gin?'

'Double whisky.'

'Look here,' said Hardman to Crabbe, 'I've got to go. I promised I'd be back by ten.' He winked and jerked his head in the direction of Mrs Talbot's back, bowed over the bar. 'Drop in at the office sometime.'

'I'm going myself,' said Crabbe. Then he looked at Mrs Talbot, wife of the State Education Officer, getting drunk, not herself, alone, not fit to drive. 'In a minute or so,' he added. Hardman winked again and went out quietly. Auntie waved, winking, conspiratorial.

'It is so nice to see you here,' said Auntie to Mrs Talbot. 'It would be nice to see you more often. Sometimes we have parties, with nice people from Bangkok and Penang. They like to meet nice European people.'

'Oh God, God,' said Mrs Talbot. 'I don't want to meet anyone ever again.' She drained her whisky and called 'Boy!'

'Look here,' said Crabbe, 'have a tomato juice. Chilled. Have you eaten anything?'

She laughed without mirth. 'There's always eating in our house. Non-stop performance. For God's sake don't mention food to me.'

'Don't have any more whisky,' said Crabbe. 'Please.'

She lolled her head at him. 'You trying to protect me from the worse side of my nature or something?' She lisped slightly, little-girlish, looking at him still while drinking whisky steadily from the full glass.

'Let me take you home,' said Crabbe.

'You think I'm not fit to drive or something?' It was the same high child's voice of innocence.

'Come on, let me take you home. He'll be worried about you.'

'Who? Bannon-Fraser? He'll be worried when I see him.' The voice had modulated to full woman. 'I'll give him something to worry about. The swine. The worm.'

'We have nice people coming here,' said Auntie. 'There is a radiogram. There can be dancing.'

'You can leave your car here,' said Crabbe. 'A boy can bring it along in the morning. Come on, let me take you home.'

'You keep harping on that.' The little-girl coquette. 'You got designs on me? Oo, how exciting.'

'And there is a new cook,' said Auntie. 'Chinese. He is paid a hundred and fifty a month.'

'One for the road,' said Mrs Talbot, 'before Mr Crabbe takes me to my lonely bed. Or his lonely bed. Which?' She goggled at him, swaying, some scum at the corners of her mouth.

'Come on,' said Crabbe, taking her arm.

Outside it was drizzling. Mrs Talbot lost her balance, fell to the wall. 'Steady,' said Crabbe. He put an arm round her. 'My car's here, round the corner.'

The Abelard stood, smooth and ghostly in the faint street lighting. It was evident that nobody would get home in it, not that night. All the tyres were slashed. Mr Jaganathan's good peoples, their vicarious thirst for learning thwarted by the wicked white man, had presumably sipped a small revenge. Crabbe, holding up Mrs Talbot, swore.

'Look what the swine have done to my tyres.'

Mrs Talbot saw the joke. She laughed full-throatedly, almost soberly. 'It's not at all funny,' said Crabbe.

'Now you'll have to come home with me,' she said.

'Give me your ignition-key.'

'No. I drive my own car.'

'You can't, not tonight. Give me that key.'

'No. Get inside.'

Crabbe hesitated. She seemed somewhat more sober. Her speech was not slurred. She fitted the ignition-key into the switch deftly.

'Well. Are you coming?'

She drove too fast but her reactions were normal enough. She darted from side to side of the road but was quick with her brakes. A home-going trishaw driver missed death by many yards.

'Look,' said Crabbe, 'this isn't the way.' She had branched off the main road and was speeding towards the airport. She paid no attention. 'This isn't the way,' he repeated.

'No, dear. I know it isn't the way.'

'Then what the hell are you doing?'

'Don't you know, dear? There's a nice quiet spot up this road where you and I can be rather cosy.'

'But, damn it all . . .'

'Just what I say. Damn it all. And *them* all. You're only young once.'

Physical pleasure is in itself a good, and some mystics say that God is good precisely as the taste of an apple is good. Anyway, one should not withdraw from the proffered good, despite morality, honour, personal pride (having her revenge on Bannon-Fraser), the knowledge that sooner or later there will be a hell of a row. Crabbe took what he was offered, as one would take slices of orange or a peeled banana. Meanwhile the drizzle rattled on the car-roof and the red light of the control-tower glowed – in vain.

7

'Brother, brother! Do not be forever in your shop. Come today and drink with us.'

Mohinder Singh hesitated. It was all very well for *them*. Kartar Singh was a police constable, fat and happy in the realization that even now, two years before retirement, he would not gain promotion. Teja Singh was a deep sigh of rock-bottom insouciance, night-watchman outside a Chinese hotel. Neither had anything to lose. He, Mohinder Singh, had his way to make, a great deal to lose, the big sale of the year to miss on a random wanton day off. He hesitated.

Kartar Singh was so fat as to generate in the beholder a re-orientation of aesthetic standards. His was a fatness too great to be gross, a triumphant fatness somehow admirable, an affirmative paean, not a dirge of wasted muscle and over-indulged guts. This fatness *was* Kartar Singh: it was the flesh singing, in bulging cantilenas and plump pedal-notes, a congenital and contented stupidity, a stupidity itself as positive as the sun. A mere week before, Kartar Singh had been patrolling the streets with a younger constable – a keen Malay boy – and the clock above the bank had struck the hour. 'We are finished now,' said the boy. 'It is time for us to report off duty at the station.' 'How do you know?' said Kartar Singh. 'The clock has just struck,' said the Malay. Kartar Singh laughed heartily and said, 'Don't be silly, that is nothing. The clock is always making that noise.'

Teja Singh was all dirty grey hair and straggling piebald beard, dirty whites and a turban that always needed adjusting. He slept all night on his watchman's bed and he slept off his sleep during the day. Now he was taking a rare holiday from sleep.

'See,' said Kartar Singh. 'Here is a bottle of good *samsu* I have received as a bribe from a Chinese. It is a very light colour. That shows it is good. Take money from your till, brother, for we have none, and let us go to some *kedai* for a day's merrymaking.'

Mohinder Singh hesitated. He looked round his shop – the rolls of cloth, the soapstone elephants, the underpants, the dummy teats, the razor-blades, the single camphor-wood chest and said, 'It is difficult. A shopkeeper should keep to his shop.'

'Not always, brother. We Sikhs must have our occasional meetings. We are so few, and the other races are so many. We must show a solid face to the world, show that we are one. Come, brother, dip your hand in that over-flowing till and accompanying us to some *kedai* for a day's merrymaking.'

Mohinder Singh took from the till all that it contained – two dollar notes and a handful of small change – and locked his shop door. He glanced suspiciously at the withered Chinese who sat in underpants, picking his teeth, outside the druggist's shop next door, and also at the Malay tailor on the other side. 'I should not be doing this,' he said : 'the rent has not been paid this month.'

'What is rent, brother? It is the tyranny of landlords. Let us go.'

Arm in arm they proceeded along the covered five-foot way, greeting various acquaintances. They entered Cheng Leong's Muslim Eating Shop, took a central table, and called loudly for glasses. Then they uncorked their *samsu* and drank to each other.

'What is to become of us,' asked Teja Singh, 'when they have their independence? I see bad times ahead for Sikhs.'

'The Sikhs against the world,' said Kartar Singh. 'What are a few Malays and a few more Chinese? We are a warrior race, we can fight for our rights.'

'Where is your bangle?' asked Mohinder Singh. 'You

are not wearing the bangle on your wrist. A Sikh should not be without his bangle.'

'I found a way of using it to open beer bottles, brother. By ill luck it broke. But I shall get another one.'

'We have been pushed around,' said Teja Singh. 'We are human beings, like any other people living in the world. But where will you see your wealthy Sikhs, or your Sikhs in their offices with many telephones and riding in their big cars? I say the Sikhs have been cheated, and when this independence comes they will be cheated even more.'

Two Malay workmen entered, old dish-towels round their heads. They had been pounding the road and were tired. They wanted two glasses of iced water. One looked at the huge belly of Kartar Singh with contempt and said to his colleague:

'There they are, the fat sods. Bearded prawns, my father used to call them. They carry shit in their heads just like prawns, he used to say.'

'Fat at our expense. No work to do. Drinking the day away. Sucking the marrow from the bones of the Malays.'

'Right. But things are going to be different soon. Sikhs and Chinese and Tamils and white men . . . Did you hear of that new white man who runs the school?'

'No.'

'He has a wife with gold hair, but he spent the whole night at that fat white woman's hotel, sleeping with another woman. His car was outside all night. When the fathers and mothers of some of the school-children found out they slashed his tyres.'

'Ah.'

'And he was with another white woman in a car just by the flying-ship place. Half the night, they say. That's what things are coming to. Godlessness and sleeping with women. And such men are to teach in the schools. But things are going to be different soon.'

'There is a white man who has married a Malay woman and has entered the Faith. You have heard that? He is a very white man.'

'Entered the Faith. They pretend to enter the Faith to marry our girls. And then when they go home it is all finished. I have heard too many such stories. And this man certainly has a wife in his own country. They are a treacherous lot.'

'There will be a reckoning soon.'

'Yes. Call for two more glasses of cold water.'

The *samsu* was going down well. Mohinder Singh said, 'No one can deny that at least one Sikh has shown enterprise. There are very few in trade. But, please God, I shall yet have a car and assistants and a telephone. And then you will be proud of me.'

'We all show enterprise,' said Kartar Singh. 'It requires enterprise to be a good policeman. And perhaps,' he added, 'to be a good night-watchman. The Sikhs are everywhere engaged in the important things. Guarding the lives of those who are sleeping, guarding valuable property, tending cattle so that there shall be fresh milk, and in the post offices and on the railway stations you will find them. They are the backbone of this country.'

'We will drink to the Sikhs,' said Mohinder Singh.

One of the Malay workmen belched briefly on a gulp of cold water. The Sikhs looked across, dark fiery eyes over warriors' beards, the ghostly swords of their ancestors at the ready. 'Ignore them,' said Teja Singh.

The bottle went round and round, and turbans were cocked awry. A Chinese came in for a cup of coffee, a harmless youth who was a clerk in the Airways office. He smoked a cigarette over a newspaper.

'There he is,' said one of the Malay workmen. 'A pincered crab. Smoking his cigarette like a bloody raja and pretending to read that paper. It stands to reason you can't write down words that way. Like kids' drawings.'

'Their time is coming,' said the other. 'There won't be a Chinese alive when we get independence.'

'Another glass of water. Then we'd better get back to work.'

Customers came and went, but the Sikhs stayed. They

became happier and happier, the potent lead-poison of *samsu* heartening them, crying great music through their arteries. Soon Kartar Singh obliged with a song:

> 'A bird sat high on a banyan tree,
> Carolling night and carolling day,
> And on the heads of the passers-by . . .'

'Look,' said Teja Singh, 'we have no more *samsu*. And we have spent Mohinder Singh's money on nuts.'

'We will sell something,' said Mohinder Singh recklessly. 'We will sell something from the shop. Better, we will take camphorwood chest to the pawnbroker's. He will lend us good money on it.'

> 'And each bemerded passer-by
> Cried loud in anger on that bird
> Carolling night and carolling day,
> Wiping from his eye . . .'

'A third at least of its value,' cried Mohinder Singh. 'One cannot work all the time. Even the self-employed man is entitled to his relaxation. We will go now.'

'I must go to work at ten o'clock,' said Teja Singh. 'The watchmen of the shops are less lucky. They seek their watchman's bed at six. I have greater responsibilities and must not abuse them.'

'We shall not be late. See, the sun is but setting. There is time enough.'

> 'And still that bird upon the tree,
> Carolling night and carolling day,
> Ignored the plaints of the passers-by . . .'

But, sitting by the opening of Ismail's Muslim Eating Shop, Inder Singh was spooning in soup, tall, thin, saturnine, his beard, contrary to the laws of religion, trimmed in a Mephistophelian manner, his turban neat and starched, so that it could be doffed and donned like a skull-cap. He was midway between the old Sikh and the new — bald and smoking — and read the modern books of the

288

West. He was a teacher at the Haji Ali College. He greeted his co-religionists and offered them beer.

> 'Let us like birds upon the tree,
> Carolling night and carolling day,
> Ignore each hairless passer-by,
> And say . . .'

'And how is the white man there?' asked Teja Singh, politely.

'As the rest,' said Inder Singh. 'He has much to learn. He sweats too much. His shirt is like cellophane at all hours of the morning.'

'And his wife, the gold-haired one?' asked Mohinder Singh. 'She flew with me that time, she and I, from Timah.'

'She grows thin and never smiles.'

'Ah.'

They drank and laughed full-beardedly, rolling in their chairs. The *kedai* had a tame bird which hopped from table to table, chirping and pecking rice-grains. This they petted, calling it pet-names, accusing it of being a spy, of being able to fly back to their wives and tell tales of their spendthrift bibulosity. They had a very good time.

'Now I must go home to my wife,' said Kartar Singh. 'About now she expects me.'

There were great obscene jokes about strongly made beds and convenient positions. In high spirits, Kartar Singh told the story about the man who took the wrong bottle of urine to the Medical Officer. It was a very good evening.

Down Jalan Laksamana they staggered. Next to Mohinder Singh's shop the Chinese druggist still sat, reading a newspaper in the neon-light, a toothpick fixed in his mouth. He looked up at Mohinder Singh staggering, arms round his friends, and rebuked him in staccato Chinese Malay.

'Early this evening,' he said, 'a red-haired dog came, a woman with gold hair. She wanted to buy many things from your shop. She wanted a camphorwood chest . . .'

'No!'

'And many yards of silk. And also a comb. And glasses and tea-cups. And also mattresses . . .'

'No!'

It was not all lies. He was right about the comb.

'This may be as a warning. If you are to do trade you must do trade. It is not right for a shop-man to go roistering off . . .'

'Why did you not call me? You know where I was . . .'

'And leave my shop? It is the first rule of trade – always to be there. There is only one man on this street who is not always there, except for you, Sikh. He is the white lawyer. He too has no trade sense. But if you wish to learn the hard way . . .'

Mohinder Singh turned on his fat friend and gave him a feeble punch in the belly. The old Chinese cackled with pleasure.

'You come seducing me from the right way, spending money from the till. How shall I succeed like this? Now you give me the trouble of going up to the white woman's house with the things she wishes to buy. And there is the cost of a taxi, of two taxis. You are no true friend . . .'

'You will not hit me in the belly like that. I tell you, men have died for less. If you dare to do that again . . .'

'It is not right,' said Teja Singh, 'to hit him again off his guard. He was not expecting that . . .'

'You are a false friend. Now I am ruined. Now my honour is besmirched.'

A little crowd had collected, including two Malay workmen with towels round their heads. One said to the other:

'Hairy sods. When they're not drinking they're fighting.'

'More money than sense,' said his friend. 'Shit in their heads.'

'Like prawns.'

'Like prawns.'

The Sikhs had grown heated. Angry words flew. Soon Kartar Singh cried:

'If you continue to abuse me, I shall call the police.' The word started something off in his slow mind. 'Police.

By God, I am the police.' He sought in his pocket for a whistle.

'Ruined . . . Moreover . . .'

'And it is certainly no friendly act . . .'

'And when you come to consider it soberly . . .'

'If you dare to do that again . . .'

'Apart from that . . .'

Crabbe and Fenella drove past, on their way to the party at the Istana. 'Look,' said Fenella, 'it's beginning. Riots, fights, brawls. Tomorrow it will be murders. Oh, let's go home, Victor. Let's go home.'

'Quiet, dear,' said Crabbe. 'Do please be quiet.'

8

'Look,' said Crabbe, warm orange crush in his hand. 'I'm not starting anything.'

'Oh, you make me sick.' Anne Talbot looked demurely ravishing, as was her intention, in a very low-cut evening frock of bottle-green, choker of Kelantan silver, ear-rings in the shape of small sharp *krises*. She was painted, white-washed, rouged, scented, heady, intimidating, goddess-like, irresistible, like any other personable woman in evening dress, more especially here where the flash-point was low, under a tropic moon, among palms, orchids, hibiscus, brown polished bodies. 'Sick, sick, sick.'

'And I didn't start anything,' said Crabbe, 'as you know.' He was sweating into his white tuxedo, his shirt dark with wet, feeling heavy, lumpish, boorish, the orange crush in his hand growing warmer and more undrinkable.

'It isn't a question of who starts,' said Anne Talbot. 'It's all a question of what starts. Look,' she added, 'that Asian over there, the one in glasses, is pouring something into the glass of that other man, the one with a turban and a moustache. I'm sure it's gin. Do go and see if you can get some. Here, take my glass.'

'Yes,' said Crabbe. 'Kadir and Haji Zainal Abidin. But I'm not starting anything.'

At the flood-lighted end of the Great Hall, under high gilt beams, the Sultan sat on his throne, Yang Maha Mulia Sultan Idris ibni Al-Marhum Sultan Yassin, smiling somewhat foolishly as though drugged for the occasion, the occasion of his sixty-third birthday. Smoke rose high – cigarette and golden table-lighters brought round by un-deferential white-coated flunkeys – but there was nothing to drink except orange crush – officially. In the lavatories, behind screens, pillars, out among the bushes, flasks and bottles flashed amid giggles and guffaws, and improvident newcomers to the State grew sour in sight of the hilarity of the long-seasoned.

The Abang, God bless his name, was talking to Fenella. He wore Malay evening dress of rich tunic, trousers and apron, his well-shaped head sleek under a velvet *songkok*. He was a handsome man, his face a fine blend of Bugis and Siamese, his hair black and thick at fifty, his moustache luxuriant, shaking the confining bars of its recent neat clipping. He spoke English well, using it efficiently like any other tool of government, but unseduced by the connotations of its words. He had been taught it by a Japanese alumnus of an American university, and nothing could have better emphasized his independence of the fussy British arm of protection than those drawled sound-track vowels and brash folky idioms. He was talking to Fenella because he proposed, at leisure, to attempt her seduction. There was no question of personal attraction: it was a tradition among his ancestors that power had been granted to the family by the fair-haired Ghost Princess and that the blood of the family must be refreshed whenever possible by copulation with blonde women. He now attempted to make a preliminary appointment with her – lunch at the Istana – in the hallowed language of film.

'You're kind of pretty. Pretty as a picture. I guess they all tell you that.'

'Really . . .' Fenella looked well in black, her skin faintly flushed with sun, the rich gold in tight curls above her tiny ears.

'I reckon you and me could get together. We could meet some place and talk. We could have a real long talk and get kind of better acquainted.'

'My husband . . .'

'I guess I haven't had the pleasure of making his acquaintance. I understand he's a very lovely person, though. They tell me he's making a real fine job of the College.'

'I mean, I don't want to seem rude or anything . . .'

'I guess he'll be understanding. He won't think you're rude or anything. How's about lunch tomorrow?'

Rupert Hardman slunk about self-consciously in a *songkok*. His wife, magnificent in a tight European gown, had insisted that he wear this token of his conversion, and after a quarrel in which he had seen, perhaps for the first time, the potential heat of her temper, he had submitted with an ill grace. He felt foolish under the black oval cap and he sought strong drink from Abdul Kadir. Haji Zainal Abidin greeted Hardman with loud harsh laughter and a vista of red throat and many teeth. He cried:

'Tonight they try to make us both bloody fools, me in my *haji*'s turban and you in that stupid little cap. Still,' he said, gulping orange crush that was fat with gin, 'we must proclaim to the world that we are of the Faith. Not like this bloody fool here who looks like a bloody tramp.'

Abdul Kadir had come straight from a party in one of the town *kedais*, and had had little time to change. He had borrowed a pair of white trousers too small for him, and his shirt, lacking collar-buttons, gaped at the throat, disdaining the weak construction of a loosely knotted tie. He blinked nervously over his glasses, trying to hide in a huge hairy hand his flask of gin. Soon, Hardman foresaw, he would grow nautical, jolly Jack in port for the night, cursing and blinding, but, like a court jester, without rebuke.

'For fuck's sake,' said Kadir. 'What kind of a fucking party is this, anyway?' Hardman took his slug of gin and moved off to talk to the fat young Protector of Aborigines. The exposition of Kadir's nocturnal symphony was beginning.

'False pretences,' said the fat young Protector of Aborigines. 'Everything is granted under false pretences in this damn place.' He poured orange crush into his lively greasy face, and said: 'I understood this was a straightforward anthropological job. But, damn it all, it's political – trying to get the aborigines on the right side, bribing them with

nicotine to accept the democratic faith. And I can't learn
the language. Nobody's ever thought of giving it an alphabet, and I'm essentially a visual type. In Africa they put me
in a native hut for six months, made me live with a family,
just to learn the language. It was no damned good.'

'No?'

'After six months all I could do was point at things –
that's what my hosts did – and when I got back to Nairobi
I found I was making unequivocal gestures at the women
in the Club, and that didn't go down at all well.' He
sighed. 'I find anthropology much more attractive in a
library. Sir James Frazer did a lot of harm really, making
the whole thing so Hellenic and aseptic. I don't think I'm
really cut out for field work.'

'But it is important,' said Mr Jaganathan, polished and
round in his white dinner jacket, 'that you do your best to
combat Communism in these primitive communities. It is
insidious ideology.' Mr Jaganathan had again been making a speech somewhere.

'Oh, we talk too much about ideologies,' said Hardman.
'When people are only concerned with ideology it's harmless enough, a kind of intellectual game, one that we all
played when we were undergraduates. In the late thirties
and early forties it was very popular, but it didn't tie up
in any way with machine-guns and barricades and gas-
chambers. It was, to use our friend's term, Hellenic and
aseptic.'

'I am shocked to hear these things,' said Mr Jaganathan, a great gush of insincerity coming from his inclined left armpit. 'For here the British always prided
themselves on bringing the justice and the institutions of
their traditional parliamentary democracy. And they who
came here were always the kind of persons you mention –
good clever young men from the universities.'

'It doesn't last,' said Hardman. 'Why look at your boss
over there: Conservative, Christian, almost reactionary.'
He gestured towards Crabbe, who was delivering a long
frowning speech to Mrs Talbot. 'He was a great Com-

munist when I knew him, leader of the Communist Group and all that sort of thing. His conversation was thick with Lenin. But he changed.'

'That is very interesting what you tell me,' said Mr Jaganathan. 'I did not know Mr Crabbe was a Communist.' He drank to his discovery.

'You are very kind,' said Fenella to the Abang. 'I must see if I can persuade my husband to let me come.' She looked for her husband and found Anne Talbot simpering at him in a far corner. 'But I don't think he will mind.'

'That's swell,' said the Abang. 'I'll send a car round for you. Would you like to see my cars? I've got a swell collection, finest in the Federation, every kind you can think of.'

'We have an Abelard,' said Fenella.

'An Abelard? That's one kind I don't have. You don't see many in these parts. An Abelard. Well . . .' He began to steer Fenella to the royal garages at the back of the Istana.

'I don't think I'd better,' said Fenella. 'People are looking.'

'Of course they're looking. It isn't often they see a dame like you.'

To the sound of a bugle, covers were whisked off the buffet tables that were ranged on each side of the long hall. Plates of cold meat were disclosed, rolls, platters of rice and brown viscous curry. There was a rush, headed by Talbot.

Crabbe found himself set upon by starving rajas who stabbed forks into his hand. They stabbed indiscriminately – here a slice of dried-up beef, there a chicken-wing, here a dripping hunk of cold curried mutton, there a human hand. Talbot fought his way out, protesting loudly, holding his spoils clear of the stabbing. From the dark recesses of the hall odd dark men had appeared, the scavengers. Crabbe observed a tall intellectual-looking Indian in a creased suit; he was cramming his pockets with meat passed to him by a tiny raja. Crabbe was interested to note that the flunkeys joined in with the guests, laughingly grabbing ice-cream and dishes of pickle, and that rank was forgotten in this elemental clawing for food. Every man for himself, including the Abang. The essential Malaya is jungle.

After refreshments came dancing. The sole dance band of Dahaga sat in the musicians' gallery, discoursing approximate versions of popular tunes, in unison and without bar-lines. Cars went and came bearing more gin and whisky. The brightly coloured wrapper of orange crush passed around, the dry bread of delectable hilarious sandwiches.

'Would it interest you to know,' whispered Anne Talbot, all close mobile perfume and softness and warmth, 'that I love you.'

'Even if it were true,' said Crabbe, 'it wouldn't elate me, it would worry me. God knows I've enough trouble.' He muffed a reverse turn. 'Sorry.'

'But it's true,' said Anne Talbot. 'Why don't you hold me closer? Fenella's not looking. She's otherwise occupied.'

Fenella sat with the Abang.

'Oh, Anne,' said Crabbe, 'for God's sake don't start anything.'

'You can always fabricate a conference in Kuala Lumpur. 'And I can always visit a friend in Singapore.'

'No. Please, no.'

'No,' said the Secretary of the State War Executive Committee, a ginger man with a Lancashire accent, 'it's not finished yet, not by any means. And won't be for a long time.'

'I'm sorry to hear that,' said Hardman.

'Ruperet,' came a shrill voice from the dance-floor, 'put on your *songkok*.'

'These political boys want us to think it's over. It's one way of getting us out, see. But they're still there in the jungle, and we can't get at them. There's a screen of aborigines all round them, and they're getting food and weapons and doing fine. And then these independence boys accuse us of taking things. Do you know, we brought them a couple of packs and rifles and even a cap with a star on it – genuine stuff, captured in the jungle – and they said, bold as brass, that we'd bought it at Whiteaway's.'

'Too bad.'

'But there's food getting through. God knows how, but it's getting through. The rice ration's down to nearly damn-all in the *kampongs*, but we keep finding dumps of grub in the jungles. We're worried to death and you'd think we'd get a bit of sympathy. Damn it all, it's their country, not ours . . .'

'For fuck's sake, take your fucking hands off me.'

'Come on, Kadir, like a good boy. We'll get some nice black coffee down the road.'

'I'm not fucking drunk.'

'Nobody said you were. A bit tired, that's all. It's been a long day.'

'Don't fucking touch me.'

'Come on now. Grab his other arm, Kassim.'

'We could have such a good time in K.L. There's a nice little hotel where nobody ever goes.'

'I guess you're always being told you're beautiful. I won't say what the other guys say. I'll just say that you look like something special to me.'

'I was given a special piece of information tonight. Our Mr Crabbe is known to have been prominent Communist.'

'No.'

'Yes. But then I say always that beneath every Christian you will find Communist leanings. It is the same sort of faith. But Hindus are always good peoples. We have too many gods to become Communist.'

'Yes.'

'But this is to be thought about seriously. It is terrible that the College should be run by prominent Communist.'

'Terrible.'

At midnight the party ended. The Sultan was bowed off to his quarters, to the accompaniment of a sketchy version of the State anthem, and the guests sought their cars. At the portals of the Istana the Abang met Crabbe for the first time. He shook his hand warmly, his eyes bright with pity, for Crabbe was doubly to suffer: he was to be robbed of his car, he was to be cuckolded.

Crabbe and Fenella drove home sulkily. As they neared the *kampong*, one said to the other:

'I didn't see much of you this evening.'

'Nor I of you.'

'What was going on anyway?'

'Exactly. What was going on?'

'I was just being sociable.'

'One can take sociability too far. Everybody was looking at the pair of you.'

'Everybody was looking at the pair of you.'

'Oh, well, it doesn't matter.'

'No. I don't suppose anything matters.'

Crabbe slept fitfully that night, the moon on his face, the China Sea in his ears. At four in the morning he awoke, sweating and terrified by the old dream, dream of a ghost he had thought exorcised for good. He was with his first wife in the car on the freezing January road. The skid, the crashed fence, the dive of the whirling car to the icy water of the river, the bubbling, the still body in the passenger-seat, the frantic ascent through fathoms of lead to the cold breath of the living night, the crime which could not be expiated.

He sat up in bed and smoked a cigarette. The faint noises were attributes of night's silence – the small clicks of the hunting house-lizards, the power-house drone of the refrigerator, the distant frog-croaks, Fenella's steady breathing. He looked at her still shape on the neighbour bed, and felt pity. She had given so much to him but could never receive in return the warmth he bestowed even on a casual mistress. It could not be helped: there was just nobody to take the place of the first, the only. And yet he had thought there was a chance, especially when his fear of driving a car again had been banished by another fear – that time when Alladad Khan had been shot in the arm by the ambushing terrorists and there had been nothing for it but to seize the steering-wheel. But the dream had come back and a sinking realization that Fenella was not to him what she should be, and hearing the sea's beating now he shuddered at the thought of water closing over his head again, of his being enclosed by the element of another woman.

He got up, unable to seek sleep again, frightened of re-entering that dream again, and left the bedroom. In the lounge he poured himself some whisky and sipped it very slowly. On the table, he noticed, was a poem that Fenella had started. The manuscript was much scarred with fastidious alterations, searchings for the right word and rhythm. He read it, pitying.

> Land where the birds have no song, the flowers
>   No scent, and time no movement; here
> The rhythms of northern earth are frozen, the hours
>   Set like ice-cubes; the running of the year
>
> Is stopped and comma'd only by the moon's feasts,
>   And the sun is Allah, never an avatar;
> In sight of that constant eye life crumbles, wastes
> To the contented champing patterns of the beasts
>   Which live in day's denomination. Far
>
> The life of years and works that yet a day's
>   Flight can restore . . .

It was not a very good poem – confused, the rhythm crude. Poor Fenella. But the fact of her unhappiness was very much to be taken into account, and certainly she would never be happy here in the East. It was not her fault. She belonged to the North, the world of spring and autumn and the cultures that spring out of a weakening and strengthening sun – winter sables over bare shoulders that would glow in central heating, books by the fire and myths out of the fire. She wanted to go home, but not without him. Twice he had suggested that she go back to London, to wait till the end of the tour and long leave together. But what after that? He proposed to come back, work for Malaya till retirement, or for as long as Malaya would let him. And, unable to give her much love, he at least should give her part of what she wanted – to be with him, living somewhere where she could have her libraries and music and ballet and conversation about art, for it did not matter much to him where he lived. Except that he felt his place now was in Malaya, his duty to show Malaya those aspects of the West which were not wholly evil, to prepare Malaya for the taking over of the dangerous Western engine.

He went back to bed and dozed till the dawn came – the mass-produced invariable tropical dawn, greeted by no bird-chorus, a dawn assignable to all months in this land of no seasons. The *kampong* folk would now be eating cold rice and the fishermen would be tramping down to the beach. And in the kitchen Ah Wing would happily be putting the kettle on and gathering the materials for another gargantuan breakfast. She was right about the day's denomination, the single cubes of time – the porridge, then the kippers, then the bacon and eggs, then the routine of work: the champing pattern of the beast that occasionally looked up at the moon. Right or wrong, it was his way; since that January night he had lost the desire for more complex and civilized patterns.

9

The Abang, of course, was aware that his days were numbered. He did not repine. He and his forebears had had their fill of power, possessions, women. Money was salted away in Australia, there were rubber and tin shares, a fleet of cars, jewels, precious stones, heirlooms of all kinds. Whatever happened, the Abang and his numerous progeny would never starve. It might be necessary for him to spend a glamorous exile in Cannes or Monaco or Capri, places to which he had not yet been, but he had a rough idea of what the West was like, and he had visions of new kinds of power, perhaps being lifted – like certain other royal sons of the Prophet – to heights of Occidental myth through marriage with Hollywood film-stars. He saw himself in a smart suit and a *songkok*, bowed into the opulent suites of Ritzes and Waldorfs and baring, under dark glasses, a hairy chest to a milder sun by a snakeless sea. He saw himself entering the Casino, he heard the flush of respect for exiled royalty.

Royalty. There was the joke, of course. There was not a drop of royal blood in his well-set randy body. Meanwhile, there were true rajas picking up a few dollars a month as school-teachers, *tengkus* working in shops. Back in the misty reaches of the annals of Dahaga – part history, part legend – some vigorous peasant had obtained a hold over a sultan senile or insane with tertiary syphilis, and the myth had come into being. He himself did not believe in the story of the descent from the faeces of a sacred bull, or in the magical accolade of the Ghost Princess, but he accepted the power of a tradition which could raise earth-red blood above that watery blue which ran in some of the lowliest channels of the State. The rajas and the *tengkus* bowed with joined hands to one whose very title was a rough *kampong* shout, for 'Abang' was the name one called contemptuously at boy-servants whose real names one did not know. *Abang* means 'elder brother'.

The Abang had read George Orwell and was struck by the exquisite appropriateness of the title of the Ruler of Oceania. It had amused him for a time to consider sticking posters throughout Dahaga, posters bearing, below the image of his own powerful head, the legend: *SI-ABANG MEMANDANG AWAK*. But it was doubtful if his Malay subjects would have seen the point. All right, he was watching them. Why was he watching them? Did he admire their beauty, or something? If he was watching them, they could equally well be watching him. Where was all this watching getting anyone? What was there to watch, anyway? But, of course, all his subjects were proles.

The rule of the Abang, in an age when the techniques existed to lapidify any rule to permanency, was, because of the very rise of a party, doomed. There was this new thing, politics; there were these cries of *Merdeka!* A new class was arising – small intellectuals, failed B.A.s, frustrated lawyers, teachers with the gift of the gab. Another year, and there would be independence. Sultans would be in an anomalous position, and Abangs would be in no position at all. Centralization, directives, much paper, a spectacled bureaucracy, but this time not a haughty white face to be seen anywhere in the air-conditioned offices. The British would be pulling out soon and, with them, the last of the feudal rulers.

It was, in a sense, curious that the end of colonialism meant also the end of a grotesque seigniory in Dahaga. In another sense, it was not. The British were much given to anomalies – anomalies of character, anomalous ethics, constitutional anomalies. But there would be no anomalies in the new régime: there would be a bright white light to sweep away the romantic, Gothic shadows. And then, if the dynamo failed, another dynamo would be imported and there would be a bright red light. There was going to be a dream of order – perhaps, thought the Abang, itself a kind of romanticism, but a romanticism dangerous because self-deceptive – based on a racial mystique, most probably. But the Abang feared the red hordes whose advance parties crouched in the jungle. They had no dream: their feet were firm on the ground, they were driven by a deadly logic.

There were the people to consider, the *ra'ayat*, the proles. Their lot would not be improved. The *kampong*-life, the *padi*-planting, the fishing, the magic, the superstitious mumbling of the Koran, the poverty – these would continue. And the rulers would be far from them, forging with pain a new language, apt for governmental directives, which the peasant would not understand. Malay hegemony would mean nothing to the real Malay.

Now, in the twilight of their rule, the Abang began to feel a sort of warmth towards the British. Haughty, white, fat, ugly, by no means *sympathique*, cold, perhaps avaricious – you could call them all these things, but Malaya would be empty without them. The common enemy was also the common law-giver; coldness could mean justice. It was too large to be friendly, too late to try to learn. But one could at least dislike with sympathy and smile through one's valedictory jeers.

Today, he remembered, a white woman was coming to lunch with him. Perhaps she would be the last of the series but, in a sense, the first. Soon he might be living in her world, himself the exile. He would treat her kindly, he would revere her as a symbol, his seduction of her would be civilized, delayed. He would send his best car for her, his politest chauffeur.

The Abang left his apartments and descended the polished staircase – no hazard for bare feet – and sought, at the back of the Istana, the royal garages. There lay his stud of polished darlings, the belamped streamlined docile monsters of years of collecting. Syces were cleaning them down, whistling. Daimler, Buick, Rolls, Bentley, Jaguar, Austin Princess, Hudson – names like a roll of heroines. Every known breed except an Abelard. This was to come. He had already ascertained that the one recently arrived in the State was in excellent condition, with four brand-new tyres. Curiously enough, it was owned by the husband of the white woman coming to lunch. Well, perhaps this would be his last acquisition. It was somewhat unjust that one man had to be wronged twice, but that was probably symbolic: the Prawns or Shrimps or whatever their ridiculous fishy name was, had to be the last sacrifice, because they were the last in. No new expatriates would come to Dahaga now, except perhaps for Indonesian philologists or theologians, and the Lobsters or Crayfish were a sort of tangible twilight.

Drizzle began to mewl out of a dark marine sky. He would play chess with the Sultan. The old boy would appreciate it, poor hag-ridden stooge. The Abang walked to the Sultan's wing. Entering it, he saw in the open office of the A.D.C. the Muslim date. The fasting month was not far off now, and perhaps he had better not covet wives or goods during that time of holy abstinence. The Crabs – it must be Crabs – would have to be cracked open soon. He would send a formal request for the Abelard today, when the Buick went to collect the gold-haired wife.

The Sultan sat alone, wearing a sports-shirt and an old sarong, biting his nails. He grinned up at his visitor.

'What news, *tuanku*? News good?' said the Abang.

'News good.'

'Like play chess?'

'Can.'

They set out the pieces on the huge board – the elephant, the *hajis*, the horses, the chief minister towering above the impotent raja. While the rain beat at the windows, above the noise of typing, the song from the kitchens, they played, and the Abang played badly. He was not surprised at being beaten – it was all somehow symbolic. The Sultan grinned triumph when he ranged his second elephant next to his first, cutting off retreat from the Abang's raja.

'*Sah-mat!*'

'Yes. Raja dead.'

'Not play well today. Why?'

'Not know. Will be time to learn. Much time.'

10

'Tell me,' said Crabbe, 'would you say I was fat?'

The mosquitoes were biting badly tonight – it was an ankle-slapping evening – and there were flying-ant wings in the whisky glasses.

Hardman scrutinized jowl and waistline with careful pale eyes. 'Not exactly fat. I should imagine you've put on a bit of weight since you came here. Of course, at the university you were what I'd call an ascetic type – lean jaw and concave belly. Now, well, neither of us is getting any younger. Can you pull that in?'

'Oh, yes. Easily.'

'H'm.'

Fenella had gone to bed early, fretful, out of sorts. People were always saying this was no climate for a white woman.

'Why this sudden concern about adiposity?' asked Hardman.

'Oh, it was something Fenella said. She said all I thought about was my fat guts, and that I didn't give a damn about her, and that I was becoming hoggish and boorish and thick-skinned. You know the sort of thing – you're a married man.'

'I don't get that from Normah. At least, I don't think so. She speaks a bit too fast for me at times.'

'More whisky?'

'Thanks.'

In the *kampong* the drums were beating for a wedding or a funeral. In the kitchen Ah Wing washed up his many platters, singing an endless plainchant. The cicadas triple-tongued – tickity-tickity – and a big beetle clumsily boomed and beat the wall.

'You're sure you don't mind my asking Georges to come here?'

'Delighted. I'm afraid my French isn't what it used to be, though.'

'That hasn't got fat.'

'No.' Crabbe drank, brooded a moment, and said, 'We had a bit of trouble. Apparently she made some damned silly arrangement about having lunch at the Istana. I wouldn't let her go. I think I did the right thing.'

'Oh, yes, you did the right thing.'

'But then she started saying she never had any fun, that she was stuck out here with nothing to do, surrounded by a lot of half-washed peasants.'

'They're a very clean people.'

'That's what I said. Anyway, she accused me of carrying on with women, and that she was expected to be the good little stay-at-home, having no fun.'

'Why the plural?'

'What plural? Oh, that. It's something that happened in Kuala Hantu. I've been a model of fidelity since.'

'Yes.' Hardman grinned. 'So I've noticed.'

'Look here, I'm a bit worried about this Abang. He sent a car round for her at lunch-time, and I had a hell of a job getting rid of it. I said that *mem* couldn't go, she had fever. Strangely enough, she's developed a touch of it this evening.'

'All these sandflies. And you've certainly got a good line in mosquitoes up here.' He smacked his neck. 'That's another one less.'

'But I couldn't get that driver to go away. He'd have stayed all afternoon if I hadn't given him five dollars. And he gave me this.'

Hardman opened the large crested envelope and translated slowly to himself:

From the Abang, Scourge of the Wicked, Medicine of the Sick, Comforter of the Afflicted, Money of the Poor, Hope of the Impotent, etc., etc., Greetings.

It has graciously pleased the Abang to be desirous of adding your motor-car to his collection, the which is known to be a wonder and a prodigy in the whole of the Eastern world. A fair price will be given. Be so good as to deliver the vehicle at your earliest convenience, together with all relevant documents, so that transference of ownership may be officially effected in due pursuance of the regulations.

From the Istana, Kenching, the 12th day of the month Sha-aban, in the year of the Hijrah, 1374.

'What do they want of us?' said Crabbe. 'They work us to death, and they also want our wives and our chattels. It's a bit thick, to say the least. What's the legal position?'

'As far as your wife's having lunch with him is concerned? That, of course, is entirely up to you, or her. She knows what will happen, of course?'

'I've told her. But all women say that they can take care of themselves. She says he's got nice eyes and he wouldn't do anything he shouldn't.'

'Yes. As far as the car's concerned, that's entirely up to you again. He's merely inviting you to sell him your car.'

'He's not. He's ordering me to sell it. And there's no reference to an actual price.'

'It says "a fair price". That means presumably what any reputable garage would give you for it. Of course, you'd have to wait for your money.'

'How long?'

'Indefinitely.'

'And if I refuse to sell?'

'They find some excuse for throwing you out of the State.'

'I see.' They both drank whisky. Insect activity went merrily, indifferently, on over the crass bourdon of the drums. Ah Wing filed the last of his plates and went singing away to the mysteries of his own quarters. A Malay elder crawled on to the veranda, greeted Crabbe with an edentulous '*Tabek!*' and then crouched in a dark corner, chewing a quid of sireh with hard gums.

'It's a hard life,' said Crabbe, 'to say the least of it.'

'Oh, it is.'

'Is there nothing I can do?'

'Don't let him get your wife alone. He'll exercise his *droit de seigneur* with as much ceremony as an orang-outang.'

'That means keeping her in purdah.'

'In a sense, that's true. If she joined Islam she'd be safe, of course. The Abang is deeply religious.'

'Then *I'd* have to become a Muslim, too?'

'Quite right. You'd be in a better position all round if you did. You'd be in the family.'

'And how do you like being in the family?'

'As far as the car is concerned, I'd just temporize. Reply courteously to this letter, tell him you're only too delighted to sell him the car; but there are one or two things that have to be put right first, because you wouldn't like him to receive it in a condition unbefitting his exalted position and his known connoisseurship. That kind of thing.'

'And how long can I do that for?'

'Till your transfer comes through.'

'But I can't apply for a transfer, after being here only a couple of months.'

'Who said anything about applying?'

'Have you been hearing something?'

The squeal of the wheels of a trishaw outside, and then Father Laforgue was mounting the steps of the veranda. He apologized volubly for being late. The creaking engine of Crabbe's French was cranked up slowly while Hardman gurgled away with a wealth of easy idiom.

'Whisky, *mon père*?'

'Thank you.'

'How is the work, Georges?'

'Not bad. I have finished Wang Ch'ung. It is interesting to compare with Han Fei. There is much research to do there.'

'And the parish?'

'It goes. You, I believe, *monsieur*, have an old parishioner of mine in your school. Mahalingam is his name. I lost him when he married a Malay girl. He was an indifferent Catholic. He is perhaps now an indifferent Muslim.'

'*Je ne sais pas. Il est malade.*'

'Oh, yes?' Father Laforgue showed little interest: Mahalingam was no longer one of his patients.

Conversation did not go well. Father Laforgue tried to speak English and Crabbe tried to speak French. He brought up the topic of birth control and the need to enforce it in the pullulating East.

'*Saya ingat*, I mean, *je pense qu'il faut l'introduire* . . .'

'Church say it not O.K. God say it not O.K.' But he was not very interested. Nor did Hardman and he have much to say to each other. It was as though religion had shut a door between them. Crabbe called for more ice. When Ah Wing toddled in, bow-legged, a mummy, all wrinkles and tendons, Father Laforgue greeted him with enthusiasm in words that sounded to Crabbe like vibraphone strokes. Ah Wing replied in an old man's happy lunatic sing-song. Father Laforgue was delighted.

'It is very very close, his dialect, to that of my old province.' He pinged away and Ah Wing, shading his deaf ear with a hollowed hand, listened avidly, half-comprehending, and pinged back. 'Is it in order,' asked Father Laforgue, 'if I ask him to sit down?'

'Well . . .'

'It might give him ideas above his station,' said Hardman.

'I understand. The English are very particular on these matters. Perhaps we could go away to his kitchen for a short while and talk there?' Father Laforgue, arm round Ah Wing's shoulders, went off happily, leaving his full glass of whisky and water to the flying ants.

'What have you heard?' resumed Crabbe.

'Oh, I haven't heard anything. But I've just got a feeling you won't last long out here.'

'Why not?'

'Enemies. You have enemies.'

'Oh, that.' Crabbe sat back in relief. 'I thought you meant real enemies. I mean, Jaganathan's nothing . . .'

'All your enemies are real enough,' said Hardman. 'They're out to get you, every one of you. The white man's day is coming to an end. *Götterdämmerung*. You've had it.'

'You talk as though you're no longer a white man.' Crabbe looked at the bloodless face, pale hair, rabbit's eyes.

'I'm not. I have a stake in the country. I can never be thrown out. I shall retire some day, having made my pile out of honest practice, and perhaps go and live in the south of France. Till then, and it may not be all that far off, I shall be respected as a Malayan, a good son of Islam, a hard worker who keeps his money in the country. You know what they call you expatriates? White leeches.'

'And are you making much money?'

Hardman moved his thin shoulders. 'Not yet. I haven't had much of a chance yet. There's a bit of competition, you know. There's this new Chinese lawyer with the Balliol accent. But I shall win through. It's something to look as though you're making money. I've got a Jaguar. I've got some decent clothes. I don't have to worry too much about dunning people for fees. All that inspires confidence.' He poured himself more whisky, his mended mouth set complacently. Crabbe felt a slight stir of distaste.

'Has it been worth it?'

'Has what been worth it?'

'Your marrying a Malay widow, your giving up the European way of life, your complete deracination.'

'I'm digging in here. I shall have roots.'

'But think of European architecture, and the art galleries, and London on a wet day, river fog, the country in autumn, pubs decorated for Christmas, book-shops, a live symphony orchestra . . .'

'The exile's dream of home,' grinned Hardman. 'My dear Victor, what a sea-change. Is this our old ruthless dialectician, our hard-as-nails pillar of pure reason? You *must* be getting fat, you know.'

'God,' thought Crabbe, 'I'm talking like Fenella. What devil made me do that?'

'There speaks the old Empire-builder,' said Hardman. 'You're a bit late, old man. You've only got to the third drama of the cycle. After the grubbing for Rhinegold come the thundering hoofs. And then Rhodes and Raffles, Siegfrieds in armour and bad verse. And always this ghastly "What do they know of England?" Why did you come out here?'

'I told you before,' said Crabbe wearily.

'I know. You spouted some nonsense about heliotropism and applying for a job when you were tight. How about the metaphysical level, the level of ideas? I mean, knowing you, unless you've changed all that much . . .'

'Well,' Crabbe puffed at a cigarette that was damp with the night air, 'I suppose part of me thought that England was all television and strikes and nobody giving a damn about culture. I thought they needed me more out here.'

'They didn't need you. They needed somebody else, and only long enough to teach them how to manage a strike and erect a television transmitter. And that's not your line, Victor.'

'I can teach them how to think. I can inculcate some idea of values.'

'You'll never teach them how to think. And you know damn well they've got their own values, and they're not going to change those for any high-minded, pink-kneed colonial officer. They're ready to take over now. It's probably going to be a hell of a mess, but that's not the point. Whether the fruit's going to be good or rotten, the time is ripe.'

It was Crabbe's turn to sneer. 'And of course there's always the army of unalterable law.'

'Not such an army. That's why I'm in a good position. But you can't deny that law is part of the machine. They can do without you, but not without me.'

'What do you want me to do then? Go home?'

'Oh, they'll find something for you, for a time, anyway. But not in the history seminar with bright-eyed brown-skins eagerly lapping the milk of culture. You'll become part of the executive engine, easily replaceable when the time comes, and translate nationalist politics into directives for the new leaders of youth. And I shall find that my work is not so ignoble after all. Certainly it'll be rather more creative than yours.'

'You've changed, Rupert. Changed a hell of a lot.'

'Yes, I've changed. I had a crash at the end of the war, remember, and before that a few years of always expecting to crash. God gave me one face and the war gave me another.' He had had four large whiskies and it was beginning to show. 'That's why I'm all for Justice. For Law, anyway.' He took more whisky. Father Laforgue walked cheerfully back into the silence, a silence loud enough with the busy factory jungle-noise, the hunting cries of the house-lizards, the crack of the beetles against the wall, and still the *kampong* drum.

'He has some remarkable things,' he said. 'Some remarkable medicines.' He held up an aspirin-bottle of vomit-coloured liquid. 'He gave me this for the toothache.' He sat down and picked up his warm whisky, its surface autumn-littered with ant-wings, and looked at his host and friend contentedly. 'He is a very remarkable old man. He lives completely in the past. And he is very kind, he has many of the old Chinese virtues. The Chinese will never let their friends down, and they always help those in need. They always help poor relatives, for instance.'

'*Doucement*,' said Crabbe, '*s'il vous plaît*. He speaks too fast for me,' he said, turning to Hardman.

'Your servant here,' said Father Laforgue, at the same speed but rather more loudly, 'sends money regularly to his sister in China, and he is very good even to his son-in-law, who lives in the jungle.'

'I still don't quite get that,' said Crabbe.

'He helps his son-in-law,' said Hardman. 'In the jungle.'

'His son-in-law is a soldier,' said Father Laforgue. 'He has a gun and he spends his time shooting in the jungle. But he gets very little food, and your servant sends it to him. That is very strange, of course, because I always understood that soldiers had good rations.'

Crabbe began to feel slightly sick.

'He says the aborigines are very helpful because they take the food into the jungle and they give it to your servant's son-in-law and he shares it with his comrades. The Chinese are very generous. Even though I was in one of their prisons for a long time, I can still say that. They are the most generous people in the world. And loyal too.' He beamed, not noticing, perhaps because of the shadows, perhaps because of his absorption in the Chinese dream-world, Crabbe's increasing pallor. 'I could you tell many stories of how the Chinese have been generous to me. There was, for example, the time when the great wind blew down my small church . . .'

'Now,' said Hardman to Crabbe, 'you really do need legal advice.'

I I

Victor Crabbe went to bed very late, very weary. He, Hardman and Father Laforgue had spent a stuffy hour in Ah Wing's quarters, where the guileless old man had been harangued and cross-examined, all to little purpose. The session had been a linguistic nightmare – English to French to Chinese or just French to Chinese and then all the way back again, with reproaches and threats in Malay from Crabbe, the cries of a wounded bird. Neither priest nor servant could be convinced that one of the most ghastly offences against the Emergency Regulations had been committed. Crabbe's head reeled. As in a cotton-wool-padded world of 'flu delirium, they threw the ball of question and answer from hand to hand, watching it change shape and colour, dropping it, losing it, all against a foetid background of preserved lizards, tiger's teeth and whiskers, ancient eggs, fat cats, a picture of Sun Yat Sen. At the end of it all Ah Wing remained unshaken. He sat tailor-wise on his bed, picking the horny soles of his feet, a fixed smile on his mouth empty of teeth, now and again nodding delightedly, often misunderstanding, mishearing. The ball was lost frequently in the hazards of his deafness. His logic was simple: if his daughter's husband needed the odd handful of rice was it not his plain family duty to provide it? Solidarity. The concept of the State had never even had a chance to wither away in his mind; the holy Family stood solid. But, said Crabbe, the Communists were evil, cruel, they wanted to overthrow established order and rule with the rubber truncheon and the firing squad. He even began to tell stories about eviscerations and decapitations. It made no difference. Ah Wing seemed rather pleased than otherwise at the prospect of Red China ruling Malaya. Blood was thicker than ideology. The son-in-law, moreover, was a young man who had always worked hard and had fought bravely against the Japanese. He was a good boy. He the Enemy of Mankind? Nonsense.

It was genuine innocence, the most dangerous thing in the world. Crabbe shook when he considered his own position. He always paid the food bills himself – Fenella was no housekeeper – and he had never troubled to check the invoices. Fenella had, admittedly, once commented on the amount of waste that went on, but Crabbe had taken no notice. Now he had visions of terrorists sitting down to the kippers he sent back uneaten, large joints ravaged by only a few cuttings, cold fried eggs in newspapers, mounds of cooked rice taken back to the kitchen on curry evenings. Ah Wing had not even stolen anything: he had used only the servant's privilege of appropriating rinds, crumbs and tail-ends.

None of the orthodox measures seemed to fit the situation. Ah Wing should be handed over to the police, but then so should Crabbe himself. The Security Forces should be tipped off, and then Crabbe would have some awkward explaining to do. Ah Wing should at least be dismissed, but in his senile innocence he would sooner or later let out his story to a Chinese ear, and there were people, not necessarily Chinese, who would be pleased to see Crabbe convicted of consorting with the enemy. It was not wise to send Ah Wing away from this isolated Eden. He never went to town, he met only Malays with no strong interest in the Emergency, odd Sakais with blow-pipes and the drivers of tradesman's vans. How about the tradesmen themselves? It was unlikely that they would be suspicious, especially as more than one general dealer was patronized by the Crabbes. And even if, in some *kedai* off-duty, shop-keepers spoke of the mountains of meat consumed by the new headmaster, they might well remember the days of lavish dinner-parties and glory that the past had returned.

317

And there was Talbot's great diseased appetite to corroborate a belief that expatriate educationists ate hoggishly. The future could be made safe for Ah Wing's master – reduce the orders at once – but Ah Wing would have to paddle his own sampan. It was the past that worried Crabbe – 'EXPAT TEACHER SENT SUPPLIES TO C.T. HIDEOUT'. Presumably Hardman and Father Laforgue could be trusted. But the whole business had been most unfortunate. Only one issue was good: foodbills would be smaller, and Crabbe would lose weight and save money.

Still, he woke to the last of the giant breakfasts with the sour taste of foreboding in his mouth. The morning's work and its many cigarettes helped to confuse the source of the sourness. The term was coming to an end with the approach of the Muslim fasting month, and examination marks were being handed in. One master called (Crabbe could never get over this) Mr Gunga Din came hotly to state that he had it on unimpeached evidence that Abdul Kadir had sold examination questions to his class – two dollars a question – and that Crabbe would find this confirmed in the astronomical marks of Abdul Kadir's wealthier pupils. Also Crabbe had read some history answers which glorified a mythical Indian rule in nineteenth-century Malaya and vilified the depraved British who crushed it out:

'Sir Raffles kill many Malays for not paying cruel taxes and build big prison for Malays and Indians and Chinese to be tortured and children have heads cut off by soldiers as cruel joke to laughing English.'

Five minutes after the final bell of the morning he was at his desk with a full ash-tray and a sheaf of unintelligible estimates. Mr Jaganathan, polished and grave, walked in.

'I wish to speak with you, Mr Crabbe. I think it better we go out to talk, for these Malay clerks know much English. What I have to say is very serious.'

'You mean about Abdul Kadir?'

'I think it better we go out to talk.'

They went on to the dry grass of the playing-field. The sun rode high and the air was loud with children and home-going bicycle-bells. Mr Jaganathan, his head dewed by the sun, his armpits spilling over their damp patches, spoke.

'Mr Crabbe, I have found out all about you.'

'I beg your pardon?'

'It is too late to beg pardon, Mr Crabbe. What I have found out is very, very serious. It is so serious that I will tell nobody. But you will realize there is only one thing you can do.'

Crabbe thought: 'It hasn't taken long.' Bitterly he remembered that there can be no secrets in a colonial community. But still he presented to Jaganathan the face of bewilderment, with anger ready to show at any moment.

'Perhaps you had better make yourself clear, Mr Jaganathan.'

'I will make myself clear. Not to mince matters, I will say here and now without preliminaries of any kind whatsoever that I know about your politics.'

'A government officer has no politics, Mr Jaganathan. You have been in the service long enough to know that.'

'That makes it all the more worse, Mr Crabbe, that your politics should be of the kind they are. Not to beat about the bush, Mr Crabbe, I will say that I have found out you are prominent Communist and that you are here to help Communist terrorists in the jungle under the disguise of teaching the little ones of Malaya.'

'That, Mr Jaganathan, is a most serious accusation. I hope you realize the gravity of what you are saying.'

'I realize it all too well, Mr Crabbe. I realize also the gravity of your being in this school, in charge of innocent minds which it is your intention to corrupt with vile Communist indoctrination.'

'I refuse to get angry, Mr Jaganathan. If what you're saying were not so slanderous I should be tempted to laugh. What evidence have you got to support these wild statements?'

'It is evidence of what was told me by a man who knows you well, Mr Crabbe. It is a man you have known many years. He studied with you at the same university, and he says even there you were prominent Communist.'

'You mean Mr Hardman?'

'None other, Mr Crabbe. It is but a matter of very short time indeed that I have it from his word of mouth. Moreover, there was witness in the shape of the gentleman in charge of the aborigines. I am very grieved about all this, Mr Crabbe.' Grief sweated from him all over; his shirt wept with grief.

'I see. And naturally you believe this gentleman?'

'I do not wish to, Mr Crabbe. But I must think of these poor innocent children.'

'Right, Mr Jaganathan.' Crabbe felt more empty than angry. Betrayal has always to be expected. What in God's name had Hardman got against him? Crabbe thought he knew: the old envy of the odd little albino freshman, shy of women, for the successful and prominent third-year student who was engaged to a pretty and talented girl. Envy, too, because Hardman had suffered from the war more than Crabbe had. And then the intrusion on Hardman's new rootless world, on his penury, his eccentric marriage. Hardman had acted quickly. But was all this enough to justify such a betrayal? Perhaps so; one never ceased to learn, never ceased to be astonished.

'Mr Jaganathan,' said Crabbe slowly. 'You may do precisely what you please. I do not propose to deny or confirm this allegation to you. If you wish to believe this incredible story, you may. You may act on it as soon as you wish. But remember that you will require evidence, very conclusive evidence. This is a most grave accusation, remember. I would ask you, for your own sake, to think most carefully before you act.'

'But, Mr Crabbe, I do not wish to act. I know it is my duty to do so, but I have read my Shakespeare and I know of the quality of mercy.' Mercy rilled down his face, strained through his shirt. 'It is quite easy, the thing you have to do. You have merely to ask for a transfer. I do not wish to ruin your career. I only wish you not to be corrupting these poor children here in this school where I have worked so long.'

'But, you know, Mr Jaganathan, you should wish to ruin my career. If I had conclusive evidence that you were a Communist I should immediately start ruining your career. I should go immediately to the police about you. I should only be happy if you were under lock and key.'

Mr Jaganathan smiled in sweaty benignity. 'You are a young man, Mr Crabbe. Perhaps already you learn the error of your ways. Perhaps you do not know precisely what you do. I give you a chance.'

'What is your evidence? asked Crabbe. 'Frankly, I believe all this is bluff, Mr Jaganathan. Ever since I came to the school you've wanted me out of it. This is your first full-dress attempt to drive me away. You can't do it, you know. You know as well as I, that there's nothing in this damned silly piece of slander. Hardman's got something against me, so have you. You say I'm a Communist. All right, I could say the same about you, about the Abang, the Sultan, the High Commissioner. But I've got to have evidence, strong evidence. You know damn well that you wouldn't dare go to the police about this business. It's just sheer unscrupulous nastiness, and you're going to suffer for this ...' His temper was rising too fast. He gulped, stopped, Jaganathan calmed him with a smile and gesture.

'There, there, Mr Crabbe. It is not good that you lose your control like that. This is very bad climate for losing control. I see your heart beating through your shirt. Now just go home and lie down for a little while and rest and think of what I have said. I can be your friend, Mr Crabbe. I ask very, very little, and then you are perfectly safe with me. Now go and rest, Mr Crabbe, rest, rest, rest.' Crabbe felt listless, hearing the sing-song soothing voice, remembering another time when Jaganathan had counselled rest, in that same voice, remembering Talbot's words about the 'magic boys'. He raised his eyes to Jaganathan's, but found he was squinting into the sun, that he could not look at Jaganathan. It was all bloody nonsense, of course.

'You'll suffer for this, Jaganathan,' he said. 'By God you will.'

'You will suffer, Mr Crabbe, if you are not more sensible. You go home now and rest, and then write a short note to Kuala Lumpur asking for a transfer. It is quite simple. You have never liked it here, Mr Crabbe, you have always hated it. You will be happier somewhere else, much, much happier.'

Crabbe stumbled off, up the grass slope, to his car, trying to think. Evidence. Suppose Hardman maliciously got hold of Ah Wing and used the innocent Father Laforgue to interpret, suppose he gave Jaganathan that first-hand evidence ... Suppose, worse, he contacted the Security Forces and got them to watch for the next Sakai emissaries, to seek out the path to the hide-out. Why, why, why? Did Hardman want him out of the way so badly? Did he want to wreck his career? What was the real motive behind it? Or was it just some peculiar malice, age-old, living in this primitive State, demons older than Islam or even Hinduism, exiled to the jungle, working silently through the axemen, the magicians, the betrayers of friends, the men who were, almost despite themselves, cruel to their wives, as he was to Fenella?

He arrived home to find the table set for one, and on the table a folded note.

'The Abang called personally and asked me to go with him to the Bedebah Waterfalls. I didn't see why not. I may be late. Don't worry. F.'

Crabbe ate his way grimly through the last of the huge Edwardian luncheons – ox-tail soup, grilled sole, Scotch eggs, beef and four vegetables, caramel cream, Camembert. He eyed with something near to hate the happily chirping Ah Wing. He tried warning him again, but his Malay was not of a kind that Ah Wing understood, and he knew no Chinese. Ah Wing nodded brightly, crowing assent to he knew not what, going off singing to the kitchen. After lunch Crabbe sat around, restless, trying to read, sour-faced even at the rhythmic haunches of Fatimah, the young amah, who undulated down to the bedroom with an armful of laundered clothes. Empty time stretched before him – afternoon school was a loud chant of Koran and vernacular languages, outside the white man's province – and he needed Fenella now, perhaps, he realized, for the first time for a long time.

He was lonely, worried. He ought to contact Hardman and have it out with him, but that was no work for an afternoon fainting with heat. Perhaps he ought to drive down to the Waterfalls and confront the Abang. Finally he decided to go and see Anne Talbot. Talbot would certainly be in his office and Anne would certainly be at home. He wanted comfort, even the comfort of that apneumatic bosom and those thin thighs.

He found she was ready enough to give comfort. They wore the afternoon away, sweating in the fanless bedroom, at last drowsing while a cock crowed near by and the sea beat and the coconut palms rustled with questing *beroks*. Meanwhile, in the sun-hot town, three Sikhs drank.

'Brother,' said Kartar Singh, 'that your business does not prosper is a sign. It is a sign that trade is an ignoble occupation for men of our race. It is God himself telling you that buying and selling ill befit a warrior son of the great Guru. Brother, get out while there is time. Our life is service, not gain. We, the warriors, protect the weaker and more timid citizenry of the shops and offices, by night as well as by day.' Gracefully he had acknowledged the value of Teja Singh's supine occupation. Teja Singh, mindful of the courtesy, raised his glass of *samsu* and solemnly drank.

'It is competition,' said Mohinder Singh. 'The Chinese and Bengalis and Tamils are men of no honour. They sell too cheap. But, misguided, the fools of the town patronize them. I am losing money, brothers, I am losing it fast.'

'What is money?' said Kartar Singh. 'It is nothing.'

'It is useful for buying *samsu*,' said Teja Singh.

'Come,' said Kartar Singh, we will have a song.' He raised his tuneless voice in a doubtful ballad:

> 'Beasts and men are made the same —
>   Here a one and there a two,
> And with these three they play the game
>   Of doing what they have to do.'

Two Malay workmen, dish-towels round their heads, came in to drink iced water.

'There they go, hairy sods, drinking all day.'

'Doing no work.'

'Let them have their pleasure. They won't have it much longer.'

'The reckoning is coming.'

'Shit for brains.'

'Like prawns.'

The *samsu* flowed freely, Kartar Singh had overlooked a parking offence that day, and the grateful Chinese driver had slipped him five dollars. As the magical flower of the brief twilight lulled them, the yodel of the muezzin turning to Mecca, the lights coming on in the shops, only Mohinder Singh felt remorse.

'I have failed,' he said. 'Failed. Here am I grateful for the hospitality of a police constable, when it is I who should be crowding this table with bottles.'

'And so you will, brother, so you will. It is not too late to start again. In the police there are many opportunities. And,' he nodded his great beard at Teja Singh, 'also even in the night watchman's profession.'

'It is now we need money,' said Teji Singh. 'I have but thirty cents. The bottle is empty.'

The scanty ration of intellect that sweltered in Kartar Singh's monumental fat today had determined to expend itself. What the hell.

'The white woman, brother,' he cried. 'Have you forgotten? Have you forgotten that she wants to buy up your shop? Camphorwood chests and blankets and sheets and cutlery and plates. We will go to her house. We will take these things to her. We shall be paid. We may even be offered whisky.'

'Can we?' Mohinder Singh was sapped of confidence. 'We may be turned away. And then we shall have wasted trishaw fares and also have lost face.'

'Lost face? It is only the cowardly Chinese who talk of that. We Sikhs are men of courage, of adventure. If we fail, we fail. But we shall not fail.'

Kartar Singh was exhibiting signs of a talent for salesmanship. He was showing enterprise. Mohinder Singh did not like this.

'I think it is not a good idea,' he said.

'And so you will drink all day at my expense, and when the chance is given you to repay hospitality, you will not take it. That I call the attitude of an ingrate.'

'It was you who persuaded me to come and drink. I was unwilling.'

'Not so unwilling. You needed only three minutes' persuading.'

'You will remember that before you lost me valuable trade. It was inconsiderate, to say the least.'

'It was *this* trade, brother, trade that you seem anxious to lose without any help from me or anyone else.'

'Are you implying . . .'

'Brothers, brothers,' soothed Teja Singh, 'we must not quarrel.'

'No, we will not quarrel,' said Kartar Singh. 'I accept his apology. Come, we will go. We will have a little adventure.'

They staggered down to the shop, unlocked it with difficulty, and then called loudly for trishaws. Soon they were loading goods on to them, while the mummified Chinese druggist next door looked on sardonically.

'I knew you would never make a shopkeeper. You take too much time off.'

'These,' said Kartar Singh, 'we are selling. We will beat you *towkays* at your own game. We seek custom in the highways and by-ways. We do not sit on our bottoms, picking our teeth, waiting for people to come. We go to them.' Kartar Singh, this one night, was inspired.

'So he is not closing down?'

'We are not closing down,' said Kartar Singh. After all his talk about the ignominy of trade, Mohinder Singh did not like this new proprietorial attitude, this lordly plurality. But he said nothing. Clumsily they loaded three trishaws with miscellaneous goods. They locked the shop. They called for two further trishaws – one for Teja Singh and Mohinder Singh, one for Kartar Singh. Again Mohinder Singh did not like this, though it was evident that the policeman's great bulk could not be accommodated in less than a full seat. Still, Mohinder Singh would have much preferred it if he himself had led the procession in lone comfort, instead of being pressed against the crumpled and grubby person of one who was, after all, and all questions of racial solidarity aside, his social inferior. It was certainly not pleasant either to see Kartar Singh taking charge of the sweating and swaying cortège like some gross god of wine re-arisen, bringing fatness and loud words to the humble village folk.

At one point on the dark road the camphorwood chest crashed to the dust, but helpful *kampong* boys restored it to its seat. Later a roll of muslin fell and unwound snakily. But to Kartar Singh's simple heroic soul these mishaps were part of some picaresque adventure, a pretext for plump laughter and even song.

At length they reached the house of the Crabbes, a civilized outpost among crude Malay dwellings. 'See,' said Kartar Singh in triumph, 'the lights are lit. They will now be drinking their whisky before the evening meal. We will provide diversion. We will be welcome and offered refreshment. Was I not right, brothers, to suggest this small excursion? Will it not bring us both pleasure and profit?'

But, mounting to the veranda, they were amazed to see great activity and to hear loud Chinese words and Malay screams. 'Surely,' said Teja Singh, 'that Chinese is not lord of the house. Certainly it is not seemly for him to be chasing a young girl like that.'

'Ha,' said Kartar Singh, 'that young girl I know. She is the daughter of Abu Bakar. He was in the police with me, a corporal. I have seen her often at his house. Now what is that old man trying to do?'

'She is carrying a black cat,' said Mohinder Singh.

'That will afford her little protection.'

The pursuer and pursued disappeared down a dark corridor. The pursued reappeared from another direction, screaming and still clutching the black cat. Ah Wing, not yet winded, was soon after her.

'Here we must step in,' said Kartar Singh bravely. 'What he is doing is not right.' From his left breast pocket he produced a whistle and blew it. Then he strode into the house, followed by his friends. In a solid heavy-bearded line they confronted Ah Wing. The girl fled to her quarters.

'Are you not ashamed?' said Kartar Singh. 'An old man like you, and a girl so young and defenceless.'

He spoke in Malay. Ah Wing replied in the same tongue, or an obscure version of it, and the only intelligible word was 'Makan'.

'Makan' has too many meanings. It primarily means to eat, but it is often used of the action of the cock and the hen, the bull and the cow, supererogatory in a language rich in motor and sensory terms. Kartar Singh, his one rare day of imagination not yet set, took this secondary meaning. He forgot that the Malays revere cats and that the Chinese merely relish them. He wagged a solemn finger at Ah Wing warning him, telling him that the sins of the flesh were the last to be forgiven. Then, seeming to relent, he said, 'We have come to see your master. We will wait. Bring us refreshment.'

Ah Wing seemed not to understand, so Teja Singh used two words of the universal language, potent words on which the sun never sets.

'Police. Whisky.'

Ah Wing scuttled off. The Sikhs sat in lordly ease on the veranda. *Kampong* dwellers appeared, curious, responding tardily to the whistle. Kardar Singh addressed them.

'It is nothing. The police have everything under control. It is but this foolish old Chinese seeking to cover a virgin and thus regain lost youth. That is their superstition. Ah, my old friend Abu Bakar. It is a long time since we last met. Yes, your daughter. Ha, ha, it is nothing. This old Chinese was after her. But we got here in time. The Sikhs are always in time.'

His words had some effect. Murmuring began. Tough swarthy faces turned to each other in glottal complaint. But two days before there had been a small Sino–Malay brush-up in the town: two Malay workmen, turban dishcloths on their heads, had seen a Chinese at his evening meal and accused him of eating pork. A row had started; other Malays had appeared; the eater – who had been consuming innocent *halal* market beef – called on his sons to come from the back of the shop and support him. Hard words had been exchanged; the police came. In the minds of some who heard of the incident there grew the notion that the day of wrath was at hand; the hour when the Malays should be freed of their Chinese creditors was approaching; independence would soon be here. The guileless Ah Wing was now in an awkward position, especially as the suitor of the young amah, Fatimah, heard the words of Kartar Singh. He was a young carpenter and in his spare time, a shadow-play master. Often he had prayed to the ox-hide figure of Pa' Dogok, hero of the ancient Hindu legends which he nightly presented, to soften the heart of the haughty maiden. And now a Chinese, an old one at that, a pork-stuffing pincered crab, had dared to attempt what he himself blushed to dream of. Anger rose in the crowd. There was talk of axes.

'I beg you,' said Kartar Singh, 'not to take this further. He did nothing. I came in time. I have punished him with my tongue. That was sharper than any axe. I beg you …

Law and order ... I shall be forced to blow my whistle again ...'

'*Besok*,' called somebody. 'Tomorrow.' The cry was taken up.

'Tonight,' called another. '*Malam ini.*'

'Not tonight,' said Kartar Singh. 'I shall blow my whistle.'

The crowd dispersed murmuring. But Ah Wing, listening in his quarters, heard certain dread key-words. He had known that the Malays did not approve of eating cats, but surely axeing was going a little too far?

'He is a long time coming with that whisky,' said Teja Singh.

'And where are the white people?' asked Mohinder Singh. 'It is already late and they have not come for their meal. For my part, I could eat something.'

'What is his name?' said Teja Singh. 'Call him.'

'Did I not do well?' said Kartar Singh. 'Do you not think I quelled the mob efficiently?'

'We had better go,' said Mohinder Singh. 'They are not coming. We have waited long enough. I told you this was not a good idea.'

'There is always tomorrow,' said Kartar Singh. 'We will come again tomorrow. Still, we did not come in vain. I did my duty.'

'The trishaw drivers rang impatient bells. The three Sikhs descended.

'Gone,' cried Mohinder Singh. 'The camphorwood chest. It is gone.'

'And the roll of cloth,' said Teja Singh. 'That is gone, too.'

'Boy,' cried Mohinder Singh to one of the drivers, 'what do you know of this? Who has been thieving here?'

All the drivers looked blank.

'This is all your fault again,' raged Mohinder Singh to the fat constable. 'It is always your fault. Every time you force me to come out with you something goes wrong. Now perhaps you are content. I am ruined.'

'You will not use that language to me,' said Kartar Singh. 'You will not accuse me in that manner.'

'You have ruined me. I always knew you would. That has been your intention.'

'You will not speak like that ...'

'You fat pig. You bladder of disgusting lard ...'

'If you dare ...'

'The boys want their money,' said Teja Singh. 'They will not take us back until they have been paid.'

'Friend! Heaven preserve me from such friends ...'

'I will use violence ...'

'You would not know how to ...'

'Have a care ...'

Teja Singh quietly gave to one of the trishaw drivers the remains of a tea-set. In lieu of cash. Quietly he drove off in the dark to his work. He left the other two to their argument. His night-watchman's bed awaited him. The day had tired him out; he stretched in delicious anticipation of a night's honest toil.

12

She had absolutely no right to go off like that, especially after all the trouble he had had the previous day, telling lies and dispensing dollars. Didn't she realize that she was making an absolute fool of him, the laughing-stock of the town, didn't she know the Abang's reputation, didn't she realize that he had only one aim in mind, and by God he would fulfil that aim before very long if Crabbe did not prevent him?

Or had he fulfilled it already?

How dare he indulge in such nasty insinuations! The Abang had been charming, attentive, a model of propriety. Whatever his reputation was, it was something of a change to receive such attentions after all these months, nay years, in which she might as well have been a dirty clothes basket for all the notice her husband took of her. Plenty of time to chase other women, no time at all for his own wife. And for all his promises, it was still going on.

What was still going on?

Oh, she wasn't such a fool. She saw what was happening under her very nose. Making eyes at Anne Talbot, she recognized all the symptoms. If he was going to live his own life she was going to live hers. Did he not realize that he had not evinced the slightest desire to make love to his own wife for months now? She had been losing confidence in herself; now at last a little of it was being regained. If he didn't think she was attractive there were others who did.

And so on.

Friday and a school holiday. But Crabbe was awake and up early, long before the time of the bedside tray, aware that something had changed, that something was wrong.

In shorts, sandals and a Hawaiian shirt, unwashed and unshaven, he went to the kitchen and found it cool and deserted. He called Ah Wing but there was no reply. Perhaps he was ill, perhaps – he swiftly quelled the cruel hope – the old man had died in his sleep. He knocked at Ah Wing's door once, twice, then tried the handle. It was unlocked. The room was empty of all the old eggs and lizards and horrible medicines that furnished Ah Wing's life. Only a picture of Yat Sen remained on the wall, staring glassy-eyed at the new China, amid the smells of the old. Ah Wing had vanished.

Crabbe called Fatimah. Soon she appeared, hair down her back, plump young brown shoulders naked above the sarong she was knotting under her arms. After her sidled a black cat, mewing.

'*Tuan?*'

'Where is Ah Wing?'

'Gone, *tuan*. Taken all his belongings.'

Where had he gone? She did not know. All she knew was that two aborigines in torn shirts and nothing else had come to the back of the house late the previous night and Ah Wing had followed them. She had not wanted to disturb *Tuan* and *Mem* in the middle of their quarrel to tell them of this.

'Why did he go?'

'*Dia takut kapak kechil, tuan.*'

So he was frightened of the little axes, was he? Crabbe began to feel an enormous relief welling up in him, like warm blood after a cold shower. Ah Wing had gone, presumably to join his son-in-law in the jungle, to chirp happily over the cooking-pot among snakes and leeches and rusting rifles, gone out of Crabbe's life for ever. Why he feared the axes Crabbe did not trouble to ask: everybody found cause to fear the axes sooner or later. It was providential that Ah Wing had found cause to fear them at this particular moment of time. Crabbe, elated, would have flung his arms around the desirable plump body of Fatimah and kissed the moist bee-stung lips in gratitude for the words of release they had uttered had he not also fear of the axes. He merely smiled and went back to the kitchen to boil the kettle for tea.

As he sat drinking it and eating bread and marmalade he thought: 'Now, Mr Jaganathan, you can do your damnedest. And, Mr Hardman, you have it coming to you as well.' There was nothing anyone could do now: the jungle road was closed, the thread of the labyrinth was broken, the tangible evidence had been devoured by the huge green mouth of the forest, and the teeth had snapped shut. And Crabbe himself would celebrate his new-found security with a brief holiday in Kuala Lumpur, in the willing arms of Anne Talbot.

He went back to the bedroom and woke Fenella rudely.

'We've no cook. If you want breakfast you'll have to get it yourself. I'm going off to see Jaganathan.'

'No cook? What do you mean?'

'Ah Wing has left. Don't ask me why. He's just gone, that's all.'

'You seem very pleased about it.'

'I am.'

Jaganathan's house was a sweltering wooden structure half-way between the College and the town. When Crabbe drew up before it he heard the loud noise of a Tamil day that had long started. Outside the house black pot-bellied children shrieked and tumbled; from within came the sound of loud female scolding. A large dog – brown, shapeless, old but visibly dentate – stretched its chain to taut metal and cursed Crabbe.

'Good dog, good dog. Come on, shake paws, blast you.'

Mr Jaganathan came to the door, a black flabby sweating chest above a tartan sarong. He greeted Crabbe affably and bade him enter.

'I can't.'

'The English are said to be so fond of dogs.' Indulgently Mr Jaganathan grasped the thick studded collar of the growling hound and let Crabbe go in.

The living-room was full of children, mostly naked. One

small boy was eating a cold chapatti on the dusty floor, a baby lying on the dining table, cried piteously for the breast. Jaganathan led Crabbe to an alcove and shooed away two marriageable girls in saris who were seated quietly at their homework. With wide hospitable gestures Jaganathan showed Crabbe to a chair, and the two men looked at each other over a glass-topped table in which were embedded family snapshots, cut-outs of Indian film stars and a Chinese mineral water advertisement.

'You have been thinking, Mr Crabbe, as I advised you?'

'Oh, yes, Mr Jaganathan.'

'It is very hot day. We do not have fans in this class of government quarters. You would like a refreshing drink Mr Crabbe? I have whisky.'

'No, thank you, Mr Jaganathan.' They always began their interviews thus, with a great travesty of politeness.

'And what conclusion have you come to, Mr Crabbe?'

'That I am most certainly not going to do as you suggest, Mr Jaganathan. That if one of us is to go, it is certainly not going to be me.'

Jaganathan smiled winningly, and said, 'I think we will both have some whisky, Mr Crabbe. I have some bottles of soda outside in the well. They should be cool enough.'

'You drink by all means, Mr Jaganathan. Not for me, thank you.'

Jaganathan called loudly and a trembling boy appeared.

'This fellow is my eldest son,' said Jaganathan. 'He is a good-for-nothing. He is only fit to run errands and do work of a menial.' Jaganathan spoke loud burring Tamil, hit the boy on the head, and then watched him run off.

'The other day, Mr Crabbe, you talked of evidence. Today I will show you my evidence.'

'Show?'

'Yes, Mr Crabbe. I have a brother-in-law in Singapore. He is in the library of the University there. The University receives publications of all the big universities in England, Mr Crabbe. I asked him to do little research, Mr Crabbe, and he looked up all back numbers of the magazine of your University Union, Mr Crabbe. The result is most interesting.'

A naked female child came round to Crabbe, drooling. Mr Jaganathan took the child on his knee, watching, with pride, its slow dribble.

'You wrote many articles, Mr Crabbe, on universal necessity for Communism.'

'Did I, Mr Jaganathan? You know, I'd completely forgotten.'

'Now you will remember, Mr Crabbe.'

Crabbe began to feel a certain disappointment. Was this, then, to be the evidence? Jaganathan called loudly again, and again the boy appeared, this time carrying a whisky bottle and a brief-case. Jaganathan roared with anger and cuffed the boy.

'The fool brings neither glasses nor soda-water.'

'Unlike some of your Hindu gods, Mr Jaganathan, he would appear to have only two hands.'

'Now, Mr Crabbe, pardon me one moment.' He put the naked child down on the floor. It crawled over to Crabbe and began to dribble on to his sandals. Jaganathan opened the brief-case and extracted a brochure with a red cover. Crabbe's heart turned over as the past came hurtling back. It was a copy of *Vista*, the undergraduate magazine to which he himself had in fact often contributed, had, for one year, edited. How strange that here, eight thousand miles and a whole life away, part of one's past should be recorded waiting to spring out at one in a Tamil house full of bawling children, hens clucking outside, the fat black sweating hand holding it out. How very strange.

'Look at it, Mr Crabbe, and decide whether this is not evidence. And not this only. There are other issues in which you have written on this same topic.'

'This is a long, long time ago, Mr Jaganathan.'

'It seems not long. It was in that year that I first came to teach at Haji Ali College. Look at it well, Mr Crabbe.'

Crabbe looked at it well. His heart turned over again as he opened it at an article entitled 'Stravinsky and the Tradition'. The name of the writer of the article ... He breathed heavily, felt faint.

'You see, Mr Crabbe. You have done very, very foolish thing.'

And here a poem by Hardman, a very bad poem. Crabbe saw a blur of print only before he steadied himself to look at it.

> The one woman I long for,
>   Straight as an apple tree,
> And in her voice all summer,
>   Bird and breeze and bee.

And then an article by Victor Crabbe, arrogant, ignorant, juvenile:

The deterministic principle that Marx took over from Hegel is often lost sight of by those who work for the cause. The class struggle is inevitable, an ineluctable part of the dialetical process, and the revolution, however slow its coming, nevertheless has to come ...

'And here, Mr Crabbe, you talk of the Communist revolution in the East. You say that that is next important arena where standard of living is lowest in the world. You also say ...'

'It was a long time ago,' said Crabbe faintly. He took out his handkerchief and mopped his left eye. 'A very long time ago.'

'I see you are overcome by shame, Mr Crabbe. For that reason I do not wish to be too hard. You have only to do as I say.'

'How little you understand,' said Crabbe. 'That's a dead world. That was another me. We all believed in it then. It was our new myth, our new hope. It was all very foolish.'

'Very foolish. And now you are beginning to see consequence of your foolishness.'

And she too, dark hair, blue jumper, sitting beside him on the floor, drinking tea, occasionally adding her voice to the discussion. Once, to the group, she had played records of Mossolov and Shostakovitch.

'Oh, God, man,' cried Crabbe, 'it was wholesome, it was good. It was youth. It was right for us then. We wanted to improve the world. We honestly thought that we loved mankind. Perhaps we did. Oh, we found out that we'd been following a false god, but at the time it seemed the only religion for a man of any feeling or intelligence. These articles represent a part of me that I'm not at all ashamed of. I wouldn't retract them. They were true for that stage in my development. But they don't represent me now.'

'You say you wouldn't retract them, Mr Crabbe?'

'Jaganathan, you're a bloody fool. I'd be doing a great disservice to Malaya if I got out and let you take over.'

'You will kindly not call me bloody fool in my own house, Mr Crabbe.' Jaganathan shook. 'Who are you to say I could not run this school? I was running this school when you were still writing your wicked articles about the necessity of Communist bandits in the East. While you were only a foolish young soldier I was running this school.'

'Were your masters pleased with you, Mr Jaganathan?'

'They were pleased with me, Mr Crabbe. They knew I was efficient and they said so often.'

'The Japanese prized efficiency, didn't they? It's no good, Jaganathan, you'll never understand the feeling we had in those days. We were on fire, ready to fight anyone. I don't think we could have done what you did. I may be wrong, but I don't think so. And now if the Communists took over here you'd just be the same. Anything for a bit of personal power. You make me sick.'

'Mr Crabbe, I will not stand for such words in my house. You shall go now.'

'Oh, I'll go. But if you want a fight, Jaganathan, you can bloody well have one. I can fight dirty too.'

'I will not fight. I will do my duty. I will have those articles typed in many copies and I will give them to the staff. And they will see what you are, and you will get no more co-operation from them. And I shall call a meeting of the parents and they shall know too. You will have only trouble now, Crabbe, nothing but trouble.'

Crabbe raised his eyebrows. This was the first time Jaganathan had ever addressed him without the conventional honorific. He grinned. 'Kindly remember you are speaking to your headmaster, Mr Jaganathan.'

'You will not be that for long.'

'Long enough, Mr Jaganathan.' Crabbe picked his way delicately through a writhing pattern of children and reached the door. There the dog cursed him again. He cursed back this time. Startled, the dog retreated to the sugar-box which was its kennel. A black baby stared, sucking its thumb.

Crabbe, as he drove slowly back to his house, thought not of the declaration of war with Jaganathan, but of his own youth, disclosed so unexpectedly in those childish pages that smelt of the apple-loft. His heart jumped again with the shock of her memory leaping out at him from a pompous and ill-informed article. He saw her, smelt her, felt the dark curls above the white neck, held her. He hardly noticed the Jaguar drawing up on the other side of the palm-fringed road. It was Hardman, and with him was Father Laforgue. Both were solemn. The priest gave no greeting, staring straight ahead, holding something with care as if fearful of spilling it.

'I wanted to see you,' said Crabbe. 'I've got a bloody big bone to pick.'

'Not now.' Hardman whispered. 'This is serious.'

'This is serious, too. What the hell are you whispering for?'

'Be quiet. Can't you see what he's carrying? Where does Mahalingam live?'

'Mahalingam?'

'You know,' Hardman was impatient. 'That teacher who's ill. He's dying now. He wants to make his peace. He sent for Georges.'

'Dying? Nobody told me; nobody tells me anything.'

'Quick. Where does he live?'

'In the new married quarters. Round by the water-works.'

'Take us there. Quick. There's no time to lose.'

'Dying? Nobody ever told me.' Crabbe reversed his car on to a shallow dune at the road's side, set his direction once more away from home. 'He's a Muslim, isn't he?'

'He was. Hurry up. We may be too late.'

Crabbe had never met Mahalingam and he suddenly felt ashamed of the fact. He knew where he lived, for he addressed a monthly pay cheque to him. He did not even know what disease he was suffering from. That was bad. Bad headmastership. He sped down the main road, the Jaguar purring after him, turned right by a decayed coconut plantation, turned left by the water-works, at length came to a block of bright new buildings. Where Mahalingam lived, or was dying, was evident from a ghoulish knot of people standing outside an open door, waiting.

'I had better go in alone,' said Father Laforgue. He whispered too, aware that, despite the wide hot blue air and the noise of children, he carried with him the Eucharist, core and focus of a silence of worshippers. He went in, Malays stepping back awkwardly, half resentfully, half fearful of magic they did not know. The white *padre* was going to kill Mahalingam, but that, it seemed, was what Mahalingam wanted. The wife, sullen-eyed, followed Father Laforgue into the house.

'There's going to be a hell of a row about this,' said Hardman, seated at his wheel. 'I hope nobody's going to talk too much. The authorities will come down on poor old Georges like a ton of bricks.'

'I'd no idea he was dying.' Crabbe was almost apologizing to Hardman. Suddenly he changed his tone to the truculent, remembering other business. 'What have you been saying to Jaganathan?'

'Saying? What do you mean? Who is Jaganathan?'

'You know damn well who Jaganathan is. You've been talking to him, haven't you? About me.'

'Jaganathan? Is that your Tamil friend? Teacher at the school?'

'Oh, come off it. You know who he is. You've been telling him about my supposed Communist sympathies, haven't you? There's no point in denying it. What I want to know is, why? What in God's name have you got against me?'

'Let's get this straight, Victor. Who's been telling you all this?'

'Jaganathan himself. He said there was somebody else present when you told him. What exactly have you been saying to him?'

'But, honestly, Victor, I just can't think of a time when I ever spoke to the man. I don't think I've even met him.' Hardman's white face was screwed up in what looked like honest bewilderment.

'What have you got against me? That's all I want to know. What harm have I ever done you?'

'But I don't see when I could have met him. I'm genuinely trying to think back.'

'Not after that business with Ah Wing? You won't have to do much thinking back. I put it to you, as you lawyers say, that, for some reason best known to yourself, you got in touch with Jaganathan and informed him that I was sending food supplies to the Communists. Isn't that it?'

'Good God, man.' Hardman looked shocked. 'Do you honestly think I'd do that?'

'Well, what put the idea into his head? He's even gone to the trouble of getting old copies of the university magazine from Singapore. He's going to circulate some of the articles I wrote. He's going to raise a very unpleasant kind of hell. And it's you who started him off.'

'Oh, God,' said Hardman. 'What a stupid thing. I remember now, I did meet him. I talked to him for about five minutes at the Istana. It was the Sultan's birthday. I said there was no harm in intellectual Communism. I said that, in our day, most young men were theoretical Communists. I must have instanced you as an example. I probably said that even you had been an intellectual Communist.'

'Well, you've let me in for a hell of a lot of trouble.'

'But he can't do anything. I mean, you wrote those articles ages ago, when people thought very differently...'

'I wish to God you'd keep your big mouth shut in future. Don't you see, people here aren't going to think in terms of phases. As far as they're concerned, what I believed when I was twenty I still believe. Time stands still in the East. They've got a lovely stick to beat another white oppressor with now. I suppose that's what you want. You told me yourself you're no longer a white man.'

'Look here, Victor, have a bit of sense. Nobody can do anything. The people in Government would just laugh. So would the police, for that matter.'

'I know, I know. But that doesn't mean that I'm not going to have trouble here. God knows it's hard enough to do this job, without strikes and broken windows and slashed tyres and, probably, axes. Don't you see what you've done, you bloody idiot? You've just about ruined my career.'

'Oh, come, that's going a bit far.'

'That's what you want, isn't it? You want me out of the way. You don't want me here laughing at the bloody mess you've made of your own career. That's it, isn't it? You don't want faces out of the past...'

'Look here, you're talking sheer damned nonsense...'

Father Laforgue came to the door, stern, rebuking them with an upheld finger. They became aware also that the Malays, mild, interested, concerned, were watching, their mouths open.

'This is just a little undignified, isn't it?' said Hardman. 'Rowing when there's a death going on in there. If you want to talk to me, please come to my office. I don't like brawling in the streets.'

'Oh, go to...' Crabbe shut his mouth on the obscenity, got into his car, started it viciously, and drove off, thinking: 'Three quarrels in twelve hours. It isn't right, it isn't like me; the tropics are getting me down; but I didn't start it all. What gets into other people?' Hardman, colour in his cheeks, lit a cigarette, trembled doing it, waited, watching the Abelard corner clumsily. When Father Laforgue came out he looked pleased.

'I think it is quite possible he will recover. Extreme Unction often restores health. I often saw it in China. It is like a medicine.'

'Yes.' Hardman put the car into gear, drove away slowly.

'I think these people will be quiet about it. The wife was impressed, in spite of herself. They were quite amazed when he cheered up so visibly.'

'Really?'

'One could make many converts here. I am sure of that. But Islam is so repressive. There is no freedom of conscience. It is very like Calvinism.'

'I suppose it is.'

'Drop me outside the town. I can pick up a trishaw. We must not be seen together. We do not want any trouble.'

'No.'

'What is the matter with you, Rupert? You are not saying very much.' Father Laforgue chuckled. 'I think I understand. I think you have had an embarrassing experience.'

'Oh?'

'It is not easy to throw things over, just like that. You still believe, you see. It was like meeting a woman you think you no longer love. But your heart beats fast, just the same. And your mouth becomes very dry. I know nothing of such experiences, but I can well imagine what it is like. I am happier than you are, much happier. You can drop me here.'

Father Laforgue stood by the roadside, vainly waiting for a trishaw to cruise by. But it was the Sabbath, and most men were going to the mosque. Hardman drove home, hearing several times on his way the thin wail of the muezzin calling the faithful to prayer.

13

The thinnest of shavings of silver, the new moon was sighted. Cannons sounded, the fasting month began. In the hot daytime sleep wrapped the town, servants and workmen drooped. Everywhere the air was loud with hawking and spitting, for even to swallow saliva was an infraction of the law. Only at nightfall came animation, as the fast was broken with brittle cakes and deep draughts of water. Then came the rice and the burning sauces, drum-beats, old men gathering to read the Koran. In the middle of the night the lights came on again, the last meal swallowed against time, and then, in pitch dark, the booming of the cannon, the first spitting of the long, dry stomach-rumbling day.

Now came the end of Hardman's long honeymoon. The silk girls bringing sherbet had gone, the beds i' the East were no longer soft. The khaki police scoured the town in the name of the Prophet and found easy prey in Hardman. On the third day of the fast he absently lit a cigarette on Jalan Laksamana, was apprehended by two bony constables and carried off to the Chief Kathi.

'You can no longer claim the privilege of the white man. You are to us no longer a white man but a son of Islam. It is breaking the fast, contrary to the law, to smoke a cigarette. It is, moreover, foolishness to do so in public. Fined ten dollars.'

'But smoking isn't the same as eating. I mean, the smoke goes into the lungs, not the stomach.'

'Nothing must pass your lips during the hours of fasting.' The Kathi was a gentle old man but hard as a rock. 'Fined ten dollars.'

It was now that Hardman began to feel himself cut off completely from his own kind. He might before have deplored the fact that Islam left so little to the individual conscience, but his objections had been academic, because the teeth of Islam had not yet touched him. Now he was made to feel like a schoolboy chewing toffee in class. He saw the other Europeans eating publicly during the daytime, swallowing beer in *kedais*, come roistering out of the Club. The adolescent drinking-parties at lunch-time now seemed strangely adult. Even around the club the police hovered: he was such easy prey, desirable prey too, because he was still a white man. He was getting the worst of both worlds.

Cut off from Crabbe, he was also cut off from Georges Laforgue. That safe meeting place was denied him now. And in his home tempers grew ever more ragged with thirst and hunger. But he dreaded the breaking of the fast too, for Normah's advances became ritualistic and regular. Because all fleshly enjoyments were banished during the day, it became almost a religious duty for her to drag him to bed shortly after the evening gun was shot off. He became thinner, paler, more nervous, and was obsessed by a kind of claustrophobia, often waking at night in a frightful dream of smothering.

And there was no release. He could no longer look at himself from the outside, for there was no one to talk to now. He was genuinely drifting away from the West, and the fancy dress of Islam began to feel like his ordinary clothes. Suffocated, one day he drove twenty miles to a Government Rest House that stood by a ferry on the banks of the Sungai Dahaga. There he ordered beer from the adenoidal Chinese manager and drank the afternoon away, greedily swilling bottle after bottle, feeling gradually his adulthood return. For some reason he began to scribble *pensées* in his pocket diary:

'*The Arabian Nights* is essentially a book for boys.'

'The Koran is obviously the work of an illiterate.'

'Proclaiming the oneness of God is like proclaiming the wetness of water.'

'I shall go mad.'

He was not paying his way. His practice was not flourishing. He was a kept man. He drove back singing Parry's 'Jerusalem', entering the town as the gun was fired. He had a feeling that the police would stop him to smell his breath, that probably already the authorities had learnt of his afternoon's debauch, but to hell with the lot of them. He was civilized, adult. He was a barrister, a scholar, a cosmopolitan. He had drunk wine in Italy, eaten octopus by the Middle Sea, seen castles in Germany, talked with poets in Soho. He enclosed these people here, he was bigger than they.

As he approached the house he remembered that it was not his but his wife's. He felt fear stir through the thick beery euphoria. He dared not go home. Impulsively he drove to the Club – was he not entitled to? The fasting day was over; he was breaking no law – and soaked whisky with a sweat-shirted, hairy-kneed gang of planters in for the day.

At eleven o'clock one planter said: 'Come back to dinner.'

'Dinner? Now?'

'A few drinks first. Then dinner. Never have dinner before midnight.' He swayed happily on his bar-stool.

'Love to,' said Hardman. He steadied himself against the billiard-table.

'Stay the night if you like. Plenty of beds. Everybody come and spend the night.'

'Yes,' said Hardman. 'Spend the night. Called away on a case. Forgot to inform the wife. Yes.' He felt safe. The protecting flag fluttered above, proud in the hostile air. Sanctuary. He was with his own kind.

It is unwise ever to feel safe. Bombs have been hurled into Residencies. 'Che Normah had every right to enter the Club of which her husband was a full member.

She would not let him drive back. The car, her car,

could stay the night outside the Club. She had kept her trishaw waiting. They were pedalled slowly back, wedged together, and 'Che Normah said little, for she could afford self-control. In the house the army attacked, knives flew at him, a transfixed Saint Sebastian. A thousand voices seemed to fill the hundred-watt-lit room. It was superb, it was the glory of God in a tropical storm, it was mountains and jungles, fire and avalanches. She was Cassandra, Medea, harpies and furies. Red-hot Malay flowed like steel from a furnace. Hardman was pinned by her eyes, buoyed up by her cosmic energy, a scrap of paper in a maelstrom of hot air.

Then he spoke. He screeched an Arabic word. In his whisky-confused mind it seemed an exorciser's charm, but it was a term that had lodged, like a fragment of food in a tooth, from the grind of his legal reading. It was the Islamic formula of divorce.

'*Talak!*'

She stopped, amazed, shocked, incredulous as if hearing a child utter a dirty word.

'*Talak!*'

'That is twice,' she said. 'It has to be three times.' She looked at him, fascinated, as though he were cutting his cheek with a razor-blade.

'*Talak!*'

'That is three times,' she said. 'That is divorce.' Then, calm, as though well satisfied, she sat down and took a cigarette. She said, in English, 'You are silly boy'. Then she followed up in good clear slow Malay, 'You must not say that. It is very dangerous.'

Hardman danced up and down, sweating violently, incoherent, croaking obscenities, ending with a refrain like the end of an Upanishad.

'Bitch! Bitch! Bitch!'

'You must never, never say that again. You must not try to divorce me. One man tried it before. It is very, very dangerous for you to say that.' She looked at him, her eyes softened, almost indulgently. 'You see, it would be the end of you.' She had not even seemed to hear the flow of execration. She held the Arabic word like a weapon wrested from a naughty child, a weapon more deadly than the child knows. One is too shocked to think that a child can get such a weapon to be cross with the child; one even feels a paradoxical respect for the child, seeing that a child can be dangerous. The word was magical enough; it had quietened the devils. But Normah's cigarette-smoking calm, her softer, more thoughtful eyes, her slow words were deadlier than any devils. Hardman's foodless day, his full stomach of beer and whisky began to send queasy messages. The sweat was all over his body.

'Have you eaten?' said Normah. He shook his head. 'There is cold curry.' He shook his head again. 'You must eat. You will be ill.'

'Don't want to eat.' He was spent. He sat on the floor, his forehead against the cool wall, eyes closed, but aware that she was appraising him as though he were a choice exhibit at the slave-market.

'Come to bed, then.'

'Don't want to come to bed.'

'Ruperet,' she said, honey in her mouth, as she undressed him with cool brown fingers, 'you are not to say things like that again. It can be very bad for you if you say things like that. I will forget that you said it and you will forget that you said it. We will say no more about it. We shall be very, very happy together and love each other. Now you will come to bed.'

He was led off, white nakedness, tottering, thin with bird's bones, the cosmopolitan, the scholar, the man who enclosed these people. He passed out quickly. The beds i' the East are soft.

14

'It's just pouring out of me,' said Anne Talbot. 'They talk about love in the tropics. It's just adding heat to heat.' She lay back exhausted on the hard single bed. 'A temperate zone. Winter. Frost on the window. And when you get into bed first you shiver. That's for me.'

'It is hot tonight,' said Crabbe. He wiped himself all over with a bed-sheet. 'A pity there's no fan.'

'No fan, no bath, no civilized lavatory. Hawking and spitting on the stairs. Whatever made you choose this place?'

'Secrecy. Nobody cares here. Nobody knows.' Outside in the narrow street, British troops, repressed after their jungle stints, roared with drink, spilling long-saved dollars. Later they would fight, pass out, or pant in venery. From below, in the hotel bar, the noise of the juke-box filtered up. Crabbe looked out, rubbing sweat from his back. 'We couldn't very well stay at any of the reputable places. Malaya's only a parish.'

'Nine o'clock,' said Anne Talbot, peering at her watch on the table, flopping again on to the soaked pillow. 'You choose the absurdest times. Too early for sleep, too late to get dressed again.'

'I choose?' He sat beside her.

'You're developing a paunch. Just like Herbert, but not quite as big. But, then, you're younger. And you smell.' She turned over on to her face. Her voice came muffled. 'You smell of man.'

'That's the tropics again. We all smell in the tropics. And Herbert, you'll remember, smells of more than himself. Onions and cheese and cocoa.'

'Oh, shut up about Herbert.'

The small room looked squalid, clothes strewn about, two empty glasses, a plate on which ants crawled. From next door a portable radio oscillated, swelled up in a burst of Hindustani, modulated to a chatter of Chinese. The hundred-watt bulb, naked, beat down warm on their nakedness.

'The Muddy Estuary,' said Crabbe. 'Or, as Jean Cocteau called it, *Kouala L'impure*. Listen to that.' Howls and a smash of glass came from the street below. 'Come on, we'll go out. We'll have a drink somewhere.'

"Where? We can't go to the Club, we can't go to the Harlequin. The town's full of conferring headmasters. They all know us. Certainly, they all know me.'

'Yes.' There actually was a headmasters' conference. That palliated a little the sense of guilt. And Anne was, so Talbot believed, staying with a woman friend who was in Radio Malaya.

'Come on, we'll go somewhere.' Crabbe wanted to get out of the sweating airless room with its tortured grey sheets.

They dressed. Applying lipstick, Anne said, 'Tell me. When you talk about love, is that just the voice of tumescence?'

'Partly.'

'Because I've got to get out. I'm not going to live with him any longer. He not only eats but drinks as well. Then he becomes all hairy arms. The only room I can lock myself in is the lavatory. You can't spend the rest of your life in the lavatory.'

'When did this happen.'

'It often happens. It happened the night before I left.'

'Poor darling,' said Crabbe. He kissed her left ear. She looked at him, not too warmly, in the mirror.

'The point is,' she said, 'what are you going to do about it?'

'What am I going to do?'

'Yes, dear. You have a certain responsibility towards me, you know.' Crabbe, in tight tie and palm-beach suit, sat on the unused bed and scooped sweat off his forehead. 'What do you want me to do?' he asked.

'The time will come when he'll have to divorce me. He knows that. He can't put it off indefinitely. When he's a big enough laughing-stock he'll do something. He's got his precious career to think about.'

'And where do I come in?'

She turned from the mirror, reintegrated, demure, after her self-indulgence of the previous hour. 'You can send Fenella home,' she said. 'She's always moaning about wanting to go home.'

'She won't go home without me.'

'She'll go home soon enough. She'll go home for good.'

'You want me to get a divorce? Is that it?'

'You please yourself about that. You've certainly got ample grounds.'

'She says that the Abang hasn't done anything wrong. She says he just worships her from afar. Anyway, what do you want?'

'I want to get away from Herbert.'

'You don't have to stay with him, you know. You can always get out.'

'How? Where do I go? What do I use for money? I can't even get the fare home unless he authorizes it.'

Crabbe lit a cigarette, looked at her through the smoke. 'I still don't see where I come in. Do you want us to be married?'

'No. I'll never marry again. I want to be free. Give me one of those.' He lit her cigarette.

'I see. You just want to use me, is that it? You want me to help create so big a scandal that he'll let you go. And then what do you do?'

'I stay with you.'

Crabbe gazed in astonishment at the demure boy-gangster's face. 'And what exactly happens to my precious career?'

'You haven't got one. Not here, anyway. You've left it all too late. When you've finished this tour you won't come back. Unless you accept a contract with the Government. If you stay in the Oversea Civil Service you'll have to go somewhere else. Borneo, Hong Kong ... There aren't many places left, are there? But Herbert will probably see his time out.'

'How do you know all this?'

'Oh, information's coming through. They want the white men out quickly.'

'So it's all been in vain,' said Crabbe, gazing at the bare floor. 'It's too late.' Was it worth fighting Jaganathan? Hardman was right: the twilight was here, the twilight in which man can do some work, but unhandily. Not enough light, bats fly into your eyes, mosquitoes bite. If you loved, your love was rarely returned. Malaya didn't want him.

'Be honest, Victor,' she said. 'You don't want marriage. You're like me. You want love with the door open. I could make you happy for as long as you wanted. Or as long as I wanted.'

'There was a time when I was really married. I think it only happens once.'

'You were lucky. Listen Victor.' She sat beside him. 'I've been good. Haven't I? Really good. Nobody knows about us. Not a soul. I've been clever.'

'Fenella suspects something.'

'Not much. And I've got some decency. I don't flaunt things. And we're being careful here, aren't we? All too damn careful. But I do care for you, you see, I care for you quite a lot.'

'I care for you, too,' he said lamely, putting a hot hand on her cool one. She drew it away, concerned only with what she was saying.

'If you care for me, for God's sake don't let me suffer. We can be together till the end of your tour. You can save something. You can get me home. That's the least you can do. But I can't go on with him, I just can't. He's making me physically sick, just his being there, gorging and mouthing his filthy poetry, and then smelling of whisky and coming for me with his hairy arms.' Somehow this did not sound like Talbot, the mild, yokel-locked, moon-faced, fat-boy-buttocked.

Crabbe sighed, 'It's so difficult,' he began.

'Difficult? How about my difficulties? You just don't begin to understand. You're ready enough to take me to bed, aren't you. You make enough noise about loving me. But when it comes to a real bit of help, you're just like the rest of them ...'

'The rest of them?'

'The rest of them. All men. Selfish. Out for what they can get. Oh, come on, let's go for that drink.'

They went down the narrow stairs, seeing on the bare treads odd dirty plates and bottles of soya sauce. The manager of the hotel stood at its entrance, sucking a tooth-pick, dressed in vest and underpants. He gave them no greeting. In the hot street Malay and Indian urchins called '*Taksi, tuan?*' and begged for small coins. Troops lurched singing, and a fat Chinese prostitute spat loudly into the monsoon-drain. Anne and Crabbe walked to a drinking-shop outside which stood a posse of military police.

Smoke, shouting talk and loud metallic music hit them. Crabbe ordered beer. At the bar leaned a moustached plump-shouldered young man in an evening gown. Loud and sloppy-mouthed the troops sang, mindless of the whores who clung to them. A glass was smashed in a far corner.

'This is not quite my line,' said Anne. 'And we can't talk here.' A reinforcement of fresh troops staggered in, one man soaked and dripping, his hair sticky with the chrism of poured beer, another with his pocket crammed with sauce-bottles. Above the partition of the alcove where Anne and Crabbe were sitting a wandering hand appeared. It groped and lighted on Anne's hair. She cried out, inaudible in the solid noise, and Crabbe touched the hand with his lighted cigarette. The hand disappeared back to its own world and was not seen again.

Half-way through their beer they saw the main fight start. It came into their view, segment after segment, like a groaning thudding wave, heralded by a piling-up of chairs and tables, flopping bottles and broken glass. The fight was an anthology of all the techniques – punching, kicking, jagged bottles into faces. A young wild-haired Tamil kicked high like a ballet dancer, a fair-haired New Zealand private bit his opponent's ear. The wave broke at the juke-box which tottered in a flicker of coloured lights. The military police entered and, under their cover, Crabbe and Anne left.

They took a taxi to Campbell Road where, in the vast open-air eating-hell, they ordered beer, chicken soup and fried *mee*.

'You know,' said Anne, 'the whole thing's just turning out to be sordid. I didn't expect it to be like this at all. And we could have so good a time. You know that.'

Crabbe took her hand. 'We'll think about it,' he said. The gloom of the twilight was settling on him. Did anything matter any more? Perhaps the days of circumspection were over. Perhaps Anne really understood him. Perhaps what she wanted he wanted too.

'Oh, God,' said Anne. 'We're back in Kenching. Look who's over there.'

At a small table, bowing to them, was Father Laforgue. He was in his surgical white, smiling, happy with a crowd of animated Chinese.

'But what on earth's he doing here?' wondered Crabbe. 'He can't afford any holidays.'

'Perhaps there's an ecclesiastical conference as well,' said Anne.

Father Laforgue came over. He shook hands and spoke rapid French.

'A drink, Father?'

He shook his head. '*Merci.*'

'What are you doing in this gallery?'

'I am no longer in Dahaga,' said Father Laforgue. 'I have been ejected.'

'Slower, slower, please.'

'They have thrown me out.' He spoke without bitterness. 'You will remember when this teacher of yours was dying. He was not so ill as he thought. Moreover, the sacrament of Extreme Unction often has the power to restore health when God sees it to be expedient. This may well have happened. And, to show his gratitude, he has denounced me to the Islamic authorities. Or, rather, I think it was his wife who did this. Our good friend Rupert is in great trouble also. His wife was very annoyed to learn that Rupert had taken me to Mahalingam's house in his car. Or, rather, she says it is her car. She is having one of their holy men to come and exorcise it.' Father Laforgue smiled. 'In some ways it is very amusing, of course. But I am very sorry for Rupert. He is having great trouble with the authorities now, and his wife has been most angry with him. All this because we try to help a man who is dying.'

'When did this happen?' asked Crabbe.

'The day before yesterday I was given my notice to quit. I was given only twenty-four hours. Some of my Chinese friends raised the money for my air passage and they are arranging to send on my books. I reported here yesterday and I now await instructions. He continued to smile. 'I am not sorry for myself. Here I have met many Chinese, far more than in Dahaga. And there is a Chinese schoolmaster here who is writing a book on Chinese philosophy. But it is poor Rupert I am thinking about. Although, in a way, it is a kind of judgement on him. God is not mocked.'

'Do have a drink.'

'No. If you will excuse me, I will return to my friends. We are to have some shark's fin soup. On the east coast you cannot get good shark's fin soup. Here you can. And then we are to go to a midnight showing of a Chinese film. You see, there is plenty to do here.'

'Your parish will miss you,' said Crabbe.

'My parish. Yes, my parish.' Father Laforgue shrugged his shoulders. 'They will get somebody else.' Candidly he added, 'Somebody better. Good-night, Mr Crabbe. Good-night, Mrs Crabbe.' He had no longer much of a memory for European faces.

Sweating again that night in the stifling room, Crabbe felt a sort of love well up for Anne. It was the sort of love she seemed to want. A love with the door open, she had said. For him there had only been one time when he had wanted the door locked and bolted, enclosing a love that must never escape. That door was still locked and bolted, but now he was on the outside, only in sleep hammering vainly to be let in again.

The day before the end of the conference he returned to the hotel at midday. Anne was seated at the small bar, drinking, talking quietly but earnestly with a man in uniform. The only other occupant of the room was a dishevelled soldier, drinking steadily, spilling drink among screwed-up dollar bills which were scattered over the table. He drooled incessantly, alternately moaning and cursing in a low somniloquist's voice. Anne turned as Crabbe entered, feigning surprise. Crabbe then saw that the man in uniform was Bannon-Fraser.

'Victor,' she cried. 'What are you doing in K.L.?'

He played up. Good girl, she was protecting his reputation.

'It's a small world,' said Bannon-Fraser. 'I'm on a course here. Damn silly to send me on a course just when my contract's coming to an end. But typical, I suppose.'

'Are they renewing your contract?' asked Crabbe. Behind them, the forlorn soldier suddenly cursed loud and clear.

'Really,' said Anne.

'They got him! They got him, the bastards! Best bloody pal a man ever had.'

'No, they're not,' said Bannon-Fraser. 'In spite of the fact that the Emergency's still in full swing. Still, I'm not worrying. I've got myself fixed up with a job in Singapore. With a Chinese transport firm. I've nothing to go back home for, and I like Singapore. The pay's good, too.'

'Congratulations,' said Crabbe. He sipped the gin Bannon-Fraser had bought for him. 'What are you doing here?' he said to Anne. He enjoyed these harmless charades.

'Seeing a specialist. It's my old trouble again.' She turned innocent eyes on him. 'I can't sleep at nights with it.'

'I didn't know you frequented dives like this.'

'Well, I don't normally. But I was looking at the shops and felt thirsty and this place looked reasonably quiet. And I was just sipping a harmless orange squash when Jock walked in. As he says, it's a small world.' Crabbe did not smile back. Had this been arranged? The bar-boy tapped him on the arm and gave him some letters. Forwarded bills, by the look of them.

'Yes, I'm staying here,' said Crabbe. 'How the poor live.'

'But how frightful,' said Anne. 'It's so squalid. The sort of place people might go for a week-end.'

'Yes,' said Crabbe. 'That sort of place.' He gazed at her levelly. '*Nostalgie de la boue* on my part.'

'I've got to lunch with a chap at the Selangor Club,' said Bannon-Fraser. 'I'm sorry to shoot off like this. Can I give you a lift, Anne? You didn't tell me where you were staying, by the way.'

'With a friend.'

'Have a drink!' called the soldier. 'Best bloody pal a man ever had.'

'Well, can I take you there or anything? Or perhaps Crabbe wants to give you lunch.'

'Victor has his reputation to think of,' said Anne. 'He can't be seen lunching with the wife of his superior officer.'

'My reputation can take care of itself,' said Crabbe. 'If yours can. I should be honoured if you would lunch with me.'

'Toffy-nosed bastards!' mumbled the soldier. 'Won't have a drink.'

Bannon-Fraser gave a smooth demonstration of man-management. 'Sorry, old chap,' he said. 'We can't stay. Some other time. And do watch your language in front of a lady, there's a good chap.'

'They killed him, I tell you. Those bastards killed him.'

'I know, and they've nearly killed me. Well, I've got to be going,' said Bannon-Fraser. 'Could we all meet, do you think, tonight? Do the town and all the rest of it. Safety in numbers.' He turned on to Anne an advertisement-smile, put on his cap, looking, all clichés of handsomeness, every inch a Home Guard officer.

'That would be nice,' said Anne.

'Look here,' said Crabbe. 'We'll come too. That is, if you'd like to,' he added, to Anne. 'I believe the food's rather good at the Selangor Club. You could give us a lift,' he said to Bannon-Fraser.

'I don't particularly want any lunch,' said Anne. 'I rarely eat it.'

'If you'll excuse me,' said Bannon-Fraser. 'Let's meet at the Harlequin about eight. Will that be all right?' Smiling, young, muscular, paunchless, probably odourless, he went. The soldier called after him:

'Stuck-up bastard.'

'Well,' said Crabbe. 'Was this all arranged?'

'Was what arranged?'

'You knew he was here, didn't you? Knew he was in K.L.?'

'I'd heard vaguely that he was on a course, yes.'

'And it's starting all over again, isn't it?'

'Oh, Victor.' She fingered her wrist. 'That was all over a long time ago.'

'Now you're just friends.'

'Oh, that is possible, you know.'

'Come and sit down here, lady,' said the soldier. 'Have a drink with me.'

'Fancy you being jealous,' she said. 'Remember what you were always saying.'

'What?'

'That you didn't want to start anything.'

The soldier now lurched towards the bar, put an arm round each of them and looked blearily into their faces. He smelt of everything the bar stocked, his strawy hair was wild, and he had splashed beer over his jungle-green. 'They killed him,' he said. 'He was ambushed. That's why I'm getting pissed, see? You get pissed with me,' he invited.

'Please stop pawing me,' said Anne sharply. 'Victor, tell him to go away.'

'Go away,' said Crabbe.

'Found his body, they did, full of holes, see? That's why I'm ...'

Anne wrenched herself away and went towards the door. Crabbe followed. The white-hot light of the street hit them, noise of cars, bicycles, brown urchins.

'That was rather unfortunate,' he said.

'Oh, it's so sordid, sordid. I shan't go back there. I shall go somewhere else.'

'It won't be for much longer.'

'No, it won't.'

'Please, Anne.' Crabbe tried to take her arm. 'Don't be angry.'

She slowed her walk. 'I'm not angry. I'm just tired, that's all. I'm not having much of a life. And think what I've got to go back to.'

'That won't be for long, either.'

'I wonder.'

That night they did the town. It was all very decorous. They drank in the bars of reputable hotels, Crabbe and Bannon-Fraser neck-tied and jacketed, spilling, among other members of their race and class, their colonial bromides on the conditioned air, Bannon-Fraser, handsome, vacuous, neatly locked with Anne on the small dance-floors, telling innocent jokes at the bar, greeting friends with a warm chubby laugh. At midnight they left the air-conditioned dream-world and entered the oven of the street.

'I'll drop you first, shall I, Crabbe?' Here it was, then.

'Yes, do that.'

Outside the hotel in the rough singing drunken street, the Sikh watchman asleep on his *charpoy,* the manager standing indifferent, sucking his tooth-pick, Crabbe said good-night.

'Good-night, Victor,' said Anne, looking up from the front passenger seat.

'Good-night, old boy,' said Bannon-Fraser. 'It was a nice evening.'

15

While Crabbe was packing his bags Anne came to collect hers.

'I'll pay my own bill, Victor. That's only fair.'

'No, we came as a married couple. We'll end that way. What are you going to do?'

'We're going to Singapore.'

'But his contract hasn't finished yet.'

'There's only a month to go. He thinks they'll let him spend it here, doing some sort of office work.'

'And where are you going to stay?'

She smiled. 'Ah, that would be telling. I don't want Herbert following me, begging me to come back, revelling in a nice sweaty scene.'

'Do you honestly think I'd tell him?'

'You might, dear. I don't trust men.'

'Except Bannon-Fraser?'

'I don't even trust him. But trustworthiness isn't everything.'

'Have I to tell Herbert anything at all?'

'No. I'm going to write. Look you're not feeling bitter, are you?'

'Not particularly. You've always been pretty honest.'

'I've tried to be. What time's your plane?'

'One o'clock.'

'You'd better kiss me good-bye. You still mean a great deal to me, Victor.'

'I'll get your luggage taken downstairs.'

'No, just go. I'll see to all that.'

'Good-bye, then.' He kissed her lightly. As he opened the door she called after him:

'Victor! What are *you* going to do?'

'Oh, I shall just carry on. I suppose I'd better try being a good husband. There's a better chance of that now.'

'Can you be a good husband?'

'I once had the gift. I suppose I can find it again.'

'That's not really likely to happen, is it?'

Crabbe did not answer. 'Good-bye, Anne,' he said. 'I hope you'll be happy.'

Leaning back in his armchair high above the jungle, lulled by the engine-noises, Crabbe tried to take stock of himself. He felt very much alone. Malaya did not want him. The romantic dream he had entertained, the dream that had driven Raffles to early death, was no longer appropriate to an age in which sleep was impossible. The whole East was awake, building dams and canals, power-houses and car factories, forming committees, drawing up constitutions, having selected from the West the few tricks it could understand and use. The age of Raffles was also the age of Keats and Shelley, the East attractively misty, apt for the muffled clang of the romantic image – Cathay all golden dragons, Japan the edge of the world. Liberal-ism, itself a romantic dream, had long gone under, and there was no longer any room for the individual, there was nothing now that any one man could build. Crabbe remembered some lines from an unfinished sonnet of Hop-kins, one that Fenella had once quoted to him:

> Or what is else? There is your world within.
> There rid the dragons, root out there the sin.
> Your will is law in that small commonweal . . .

The time had come to start thinking about his private life. Perhaps there were really two kinds of marriage, both equally valid: the one that was pure inspiration, the poem come unbidden; the one that had to be built, laboriously, with pain and self-abasement, deliberate engineering, sweat and broken nails. He saw his unkindness to Fenella, the demon that urged him on to believe that it was all a mistake, that she, in some way, was the usurper. One could

not spend one's life being loyal to the dead. That was romanticism of the worst sort. In Indonesia the jungle had been cleared and rice planted. It was time he cleared the romantic jungle in which he wanted to lurk, acknowledge that life was striving not dreaming, and planted the seeds of a viable relationship between his wife and himself.

He reached Kenching in the early evening. To his surprise he found that Talbot had come to meet him. As the plane taxied, he saw the stumpy figure, greying tow hair, spectacles, plump legs in running shorts, striding up and down the length of his parked car. Alighted, Crabbe greeted him with false and guilty cheerfulness. Talbot was grim.

'Come on,' he said. 'I'm taking you home. I want to talk to you.'

'Oh, what's happened? Is it Jaganathan again?'

Talbot started the engine, clumsily put it into gear. 'You know damn well it's not that I want to talk about. It's about you and my wife.'

'Yes?' Crabbe swallowed hard.

'You've been carrying on with her in K.L., haven't you? I might have known. Bloody fool that I was. I wouldn't have thought of it if your wife hadn't put the idea into my head.'

'My wife?'

'Yes. And then this chap Hardman sees your wife in the town and says that he thought she was in K.L. with you, because that French priest sent him a post-card saying that he'd met you both, and then she put two and two together. For Christ's sake, how long has this been happening?' He drove somewhat crookedly down the main road.

'Herbert, will you wait? Wait just a couple of days.'

'She's out, she's finished. You can bloody well have her, because I won't. I didn't expect you to think about me, but you might have thought about your wife. As though she isn't having enough trouble.'

'What sort of trouble?'

'Oh, she'll tell you. Perhaps she won't. I don't think she wants to speak to you again. I don't bloody well blame her.'

'Herbert, please listen.'

'There's nothing more to say. The damage has been done. Bloody fool I must look to the people in K.L.'

'Herbert, listen. I might as well tell you, because you'll find out soon enough. She's writing to you.'

'Writing? What about?'

'Do you remember a man called Bannon-Fraser?'

Talbot stopped the car, very deliberately, by the side of the road.

'Bannon-Fraser? He's still here, isn't he?'

'He went on a course to K.L. I met him there. I met him there with Anne. They're going off together.'

Talbot thought for a moment and said, 'You needn't try and get out of it that way. You needn't try to put it all on to somebody else.'

'But it's true. She's writing to tell you. He's getting a job in Singapore. She says they're going to live together.'

'Where are they now? By Christ, if I find them both ...' Talbot looked at Crabbe sternly. 'How do I know you're telling me the truth?'

'You'll soon know. She's sending you a letter.'

'How do you know all this? Are you in on it, too? By Christ, when I find them, I'll bloody well ... Where are they? Where are they living?'

A Malay labourer paused on his way home from work. He gazed open-mouthed into the car, much struck by Talbot's agitation. Crabbe waved him away.

'I don't know. She refused to tell me.'

'I'll find them. I'll scour the whole damn town. This is the end of him. This is the end of both of them.'

'It's not worth it, Herbert. You can't do anything.'

'Do anything? I'll drag them out. I'll tell the whole damned Federation about it.' He gripped the steering-wheel hard, lowered his forehead on to the nub as if to cool it. Then he raised his eyes and said. 'What sort of a woman is she? Is she a prostitute? First she's with you, then she's with this other swine. I just don't know her. I just don't know anything.'

'We had a meal together one evening. That's all.'

Talbot started to sob, though his eyes remained dry.

'Don't you think it's better this way?' said Crabbe. 'You know it's never worked. Be honest, has it? I knew the first day I met you both that it would never work.' He patted comfortingly the fat shaking shoulder.

'She was all I had,' cried Talbot. 'I gave her everything.'

'There's plenty for you still,' said Crabbe. 'There's your work, there's your poetry. Great poetry's made out of great sorrow, you know.'

'Great sorrow,' sobbed Talbot. 'I'll never write again.'

'Look,' said Crabbe, 'go to my house. Tell Fenella all about it. She'll understand. She'll be sympathetic. You're both poets, remember. You can drop me at the school. I left my car in the school garage – safer there with a caretaker on the spot. I'll pick it up and come round in about half an hour, then we can have a meal together.'

'Yes,' said Talbot, calmer now. 'One's got to eat. One's got to carry on.' Then, almost cheerful, he said, 'You haven't got a car now.'

'What do you mean?'

'Nothing left of it. Just a mass of old iron. There's been a fire, you know. Somebody burnt the garage down. And the boys' lavatory's gone as well.'

'Jaganathan.'

'Oh, no, I don't think so. Jaganathan's been away. In Malacca, I think. But it was a hell of a fire. Hell of a job putting it out.'

'When did it happen? Why didn't somebody let me know?'

'Only a couple of days ago. It hardly seemed worth while to write to you. And Fenella's been so upset.'

'About ...?'

'Yes, about that.' In sudden Ercles vein, Talbot cried, 'When I find the pair of them, I'll kill them both. I will.

They've ruined me, made me look the biggest bloody fool ...'

Thank God he'd remembered to renew the insurance. 'And now,' thought Crabbe, with a sudden lifting of spirits, 'the Abang can have it. I've kept him waiting long enough. He shall have it, any time he likes.' 'Come on,' he said to Talbot, 'let's go home.'

Talbot needed no persuading to enter the house first. He raged in, loud and bitter about Anne's treachery, about what he would do to Bannon-Fraser. Crabbe held him in front, an umbrella against an expected squall, and soon Fenella had melted enough to accept a kiss of greeting. But she had had enough trouble. At dinner she spoke of it.

'One of the bedroom windows. A stone straight through it. And people keep shaking their fists. And then this fire at the school, and the car. It's been horrible. I stayed three nights at the Istana.'

'At the Istana?'

'Yes. They gave me one of the guest-rooms. The Abang was very kind.'

The new Malay cook brought in more potatoes for Talbot. A mass of carbohydrate induced a philosophical outlook, and Talbot, speading thick butter on his bread, began to recite, his eyes moist behind their glasses:

> 'But loss, too, is at least a thing which, in the dark,
> We can hold, feeling a sharpness, knowing that a knife
> Is a double-edged weapon, for carving as well as killing.
> The knife in the abattoir is also the knife on the table,
> The corpse becomes meat, the dead stone heart the raw
> Stuff of the sculptor's art ...'

'Do have a little more beef,' said Fenella. 'I'm afraid the gravy's rather cold now, but there's Worcestershire sauce if you'd like it.'

Talbot champed away, finally spooning in resignation with the tinned fruit salad, calm of mind reached with the last piece of cheese, all passion spent in the third drained coffee-cup. Patting his stomach, he said that he would now be getting along home. He had a poem to write.

'And I'm sorry I thought what I did, Victor. I should have known better.'

'That's all right, Herbert.'

Left alone, Fenella and Crabbe sat stiffly, embarrassed. Crabbe spoke first.

'I've had time to think. I've not been a very good husband, Fenella. Will you believe me when I say that I want to start again?'

'I can quite believe that you do. We obviously couldn't go on like that for ever.'

'And I do love you. I see that quite clearly now.'

'Do you?' She seemed cold still, withdrawn, sitting upright in the bamboo armchair. Then she got up, walked over to the glass-topped table that stood under a Paul Klee reproduction, and took a cigarette from the box there. Crabbe was aware of her grace, the gold beauty, and tried to force the name 'love' on the pity that rose in him.

'It may be too late, Victor,' she said. 'I'm not saying it is. It just may be.'

'I don't think I understand.'

'You were never very good at understanding me. You've never really tried. Curiously enough, I've been learning a lot about myself lately. I've been seeing things very clearly. For instance, I've discovered that I'm quite an attractive woman. That I'm also intelligent. That I've got quite a lot to give people.'

'All that's perfectly true.'

'But you've never told me. Never once. I'm not saying it's your fault. But there's only been one woman in your life. Be honest about it, Victor. You've always been comparing me with her. You've never been able to see me clearly.'

'It was true. But you can't be ill all your life. I've been convalescing. I know what I want now. You must give me this chance, Fenella. I can be happy with you. I want you to be happy with me.'

'Yes. I think you really mean that. It's curious that this should happen now.'

'Curious?'

'Yes. Just when somebody else is telling me the same thing.'

Crabbe started. 'You don't mean . . .?'

'Yes, Yusof's been telling me.' Crabbe frowned, puzzled. 'Yusof is the Abang. And he isn't what people think he is. He hasn't laid a hand on me. He hasn't even attempted . . .'

'Oh, Fenella,' said Crabbe, 'don't be so innocent. He'll wait, he'll lull you till it's time for him to pounce.'

'No,' said Fenella, 'he won't do that. I'm quite sure. I think I know him quite well. You see, when we meet, we just talk. Sometimes in Malay, sometimes in English. I think I've cured him of that American accent. He sounds quite reasonable now. He tells me he's never really talked to a woman before, and I can believe him. Apparently, Islam doesn't approve of women talking.'

'What do you talk about?'

'Oh, I'm really trying to teach him. He knows so little of life, really, especially *our* sort of life. And it's our sort of life he needs to learn about, because he won't be here much longer. He's been persuading me very strongly to go home. He says that when he goes to Europe – as he will, very soon – I could help him a great deal. He's not asking for anything, except my help.'

'I see.'

'So, Victor, it turns out that *I'm* really the teacher. Queer, isn't it? You come out here to bring the great gifts of the West, and you say you've failed, but *I've* not failed. I've certainly taught something.'

'And so you really want to go home?'

'I don't know. Not yet, anyway. It still depends on you.'

'I've told you, darling, I want to try. Things can be very different. And I'm going to need you more than I've ever needed anybody.'

'I wonder.'

Crabbe was about to speak, to renew his protestations,

when the noise of a motor was heard drawing up outside the house. From it came the sound of a fat voice, singing in an unknown tongue.

'I forgot to tell you,' said Fenella. 'We have police protection now. The Abang arranged it himself. A rather old Sikh constable. I don't suppose he'd be much good in a crisis, but he seems to scare away our enemies, whoever they are.'

'There's only one.'

'No. You've failed, Victor. We're not wanted any more, any of us. It's all enemies from now on. God, that sounds melodramatic. But politics, of course, is all melodrama. Unbelievably crude.'

'I'm getting resigned, you know. I heard a few things in Kuala Lumpur. We shan't be coming back, that's reasonably certain. But . . .'

'I know what you're going to say. Will I stay with you here until the time comes to pack up completely? That, as I've said, depends.'

'Because "going home" is a euphemism for . . .'

'You're not slow, Victor. I sometimes forget you can be quite bright. But you don't give me much of a chance, do you? "Going home" means what you think it means. Either it works, this being together, or it doesn't. And if it doesn't . . . Well, I'm still young. And, as Yusof says, attractive. I'm entitled to a bit of life.'

'Just what Anne says.'

'Anne? Yes, I know about that, too. Nothing's easy to hide in a country like this. But I'm not blaming you any more. I understand now. And I pity . . .'

'Pity?' Crabbe looked up at her, still standing, with an expression of small surprise, eyes narrowed in a weak show of outrage.

'We'd better go to bed. Tomorrow we'll go to the beach. It's a long time since I had a swim.'

Kartar Singh gave jovial greeting from the veranda. In return he was given beer. The Crabbes went to bed, leaving their guard to sing quietly to himself as he made his tour of the perimeter, ending up outside the bedroom itself, whence he heard no sound. The white man, as Kartar Singh knew, was cold. The white man had no red blood in his veins. This was the hour for the dancing of the springs, but from the two sundered beds came not even the sound of sleeping. Kartar Singh smiled fatly and happily resumed his round.

16

The driver of the trishaw reclined in the double wicker seat and watched them idly, picking his teeth. They had asked him to wait for an hour. One hour, two hours, three: it made no difference. He would milk the white man; he would ask him for two dollars for the double journey, and he would quite certainly, get it. The white man had more money than sense. Meanwhile it was pleasant to rest under the sun, its heat mitigated by the strong sea-wind, and bask in the knowledge that no more work need be done for at least a couple of days. Two dollars was a lot of money.

At the sea's edge north-eastern Malay shed the last tawdry clothes of civilization. The China Sea yielded fish, the trees coconuts and bananas, the drowned fields a sufficiency of rice. The women wore a single loose garment, the men showed muscular torsos flawed with benignant skin diseases. Idiocy and slow speech were the flower of much endogamy, yaws flourished unchecked by penicillin. Life was short but happy. On the wide sands lay Crabbe and his wife, half-closed eyes taking in a distant diorama of sampans.

Fenella Crabbe displayed firm golden flesh to the huge blue air and Crabbe had never before been so aware of her beauty. But the whole world here breathed easy concupiscence: the bare shoulders of the women, the naked children, the fish-smell, the sea whence life arose, the water that waited, but not passively, to be ravished, the great yellow empty bed of the beach. And so, ardently, he renewed his vows, aware too of his own warm nakedness under the monstrous aphrodisiac of a tropical sun.

'There is such a thing,' he said, 'as being blind. I acknowledge my blindness with all humility. I shall never be blind again.'

'And so you do love me?'

'I do love you. And I want to make amends in any way I can. I want to expiate everything.'

'There's a small thing you can do for me.'

'Anything.'

'I'm going into the water now. I'm going to swim. I want you to come in with me.'

Crabbe drew away from her. 'You know I can't do that.'

'But you said you'd do anything.'

'Anything reasonable, anything you need . . .'

'Surely love isn't reasonable, not always? Anyway, this is reasonable, and it's something very small. Come on, Victor, for me. Come and have a swim.'

Crabbe turned on her in passion. 'Why are you asking me to do this? What's the point of it?'

She sat up and said evenly, 'I want to see if you really love me. If you love me you'll put the past out of your mind. I want you to break with the past. I want there to be only one woman in your life, and that woman to be me. Come on.' She rose with grace, long, slim, rounded in the smart meagre bathing-dress. 'Come and have a swim.'

'I won't. I can't. You know I can't.'

'All right, you needn't swim. Just wade in. As far as your armpits. The water's perfectly safe.'

Crabbe looked up at her bitterly. She had shrunk to a calendar beauty. The mood of desire and tenderness had gone. 'I can't,' he repeated. 'You know why I can't. If I could overcome that old fear I would. But I don't know how to.'

'For years you said you'd never drive a car again. But you do drive a car now. You got over that fear. I want you to get over this.'

'I can't.'

She smiled, and Crabbe distinctly saw pity in it. 'All right. Never mind. I'm going in, anyway.'

371

She ran down the ribs of sand sending the sand-crabs scurrying to their holes. The sea sent in its flowers of surf along the long coastline, with a tiny rattle of shingle. Fenella strode in, her arms keeping balance as though she walked a tight-rope. The sand shelved gently here. Only at waist-level did the sudden dips occur, and then an upward-sloping hill would lead to a sand-bar, to a new shore islanded in the sea. Fenella strode on, rose to the bar and stood for an instant as if standing on the waves, then entered the new sea-brink, and soon was far out, swimming strongly.

Dejected, Crabbe lay on his stomach, absently tracing capital letters in the sand. Suddenly, with a shock, he saw what name he had been writing. He swiftly passed his fingers over the weak inscription, obliterating it, but not obliterating her. Fenella knew. But she must believe that he was prepared to try, that perhaps in time the past would have no more power over him. After all, no man could give everything. But she wanted him all, wanted every sullen pocket of his memory turned inside out, wanted to fill him with herself, and with herself only. But the past was not part of him; he was part of it. What more could he do? She must accept the Minotaur. The Labyrinth had many rooms, enough for a life together – walls to be covered with shelves and pictures, corridors in which the Beast echoed only once in a score of years.

Fancying he heard Fenella's voice taunting him from the sea he turned over lazily, the sun in his eyes, and saw her far out. He heard her voice again and looked more intently. He though he saw arms flailing, a churning of the sea around her. He stood up. That voice was certainly calling for help. Heart pounding, he rushed to the sea's edge, straining his eyes narrowly, hoping it was a mistake, a joke. Thinly above the sea-wind her voice called, her body churned the small patch of sea, her arms were wild. He remembered the warnings of treacherous currents, but surely that was only in the monsoon season. Or was it a sea-snake?

Sick with apprehension and hopelessness he walked into the sea. It rose thirstily, higher, lapping round his ankles, shins, knees, thighs, waist. Then, without warning, the shelf plunged a foot or so, and he found himself frantic, feeling the green foam-flowered water round his chest. He panicked, kicked, turned, sobbing, towards the shore. It was no good, it was just no good. He lay panting at the sea's lips, not daring to look back, frantically trying not to hear the thin distant voice.

'All right, darling.' Fenella was beside him, comforting him with her wet body. 'Perhaps that wasn't fair, really. But I just had to know.'

'You're all right?' Relief began to modulate to anger. All that for nothing ... 'You were only pretending?'

'Yes. It's as safe as houses. Safer. Come on, now.'

He lay gasping on dry sand, she beside him.

'I just had to know,' she repeated, swabbing her face, arms, shoulders, with a towel. 'When you thought the bandits had got us you were able to drive the car. You seem able to exorcise demons when you yourself are concerned. It's the old instinct of self-preservation. But, if my life only is involved ...'

'That's not fair. You know it's not fair. Water's elemental, it's an enemy, it's different ...'

'It's not different. You just couldn't make the effort this time, that's all. It wasn't really important enough. It doesn't matter. I'm not blaming you. But you see now that it won't work. I've known for some time now what I had to do. This was just a rather spectacular way of showing you.'

'It wasn't fair. I still say it wasn't fair.'

'That doesn't matter. I'm really sorry for you, Victor. I should have had the sense to see before. You've never really been unfaithful to me, because you never started to be faithful. All that stupid business with the Malay girl, and then this affair with Anne Talbot. It didn't mean what it seemed to mean. And now I know what I have to do.'

'What have you to do?'

'I have to go home. And perhaps, at leisure, we can arrange a divorce. There isn't any hurry. But it's all been rather a waste of time, hasn't it?'

Crabbe sulked, saying nothing.

'Thank God I'm still young. And you are too. Things will sort themselves out somehow. But not between us. Perhaps I'll find somebody to marry, somebody for whom it will be the first time. And you'll never marry again, I'm quite sure of that. You can go on being faithful to her, which means revelling in guilt. But it isn't fair for anybody to have to feel guilty about two people. You won't have to feel guilty about me again.'

He still said nothing.

'And you needn't even feel guilty about the waste of time. It's been a waste of time for both of us equally. And I think perhaps you've suffered the most.'

Crabbe said, tonelessly, 'What do you want me to do?'

'Get in touch with Federation Establishment. Get them to book me an air passage home. I'm entitled to that. I think you should be able to fix things in about a week.'

'And what will you do in England?'

'Oh, there are several things. I shall go back to Maida Vale first of all. Uncle will be glad to see me. And then there are several jobs I can get. The Abang's made me a very tempting offer. He wants me to be a sort of secretary to him. I think I should be good at that. It means travelling around. It will be good to see Europe again. But I haven't decided yet.'

'You are cold-blooded, aren't you?'

'Me? Oh, I don't think so. I've just got to make up for lost time, that's all.' She pressed his hand, smiling. 'Cheer up, darling. It's all for the best, you know.'

Crabbe recognized the feeling that passed over his limbs, the pain of life flowing back after cramp, and was surprised to find that it could be called relief.

'Now,' she said, 'we'd better get back. There's a lot to do, and I can't start too soon.'

They trudged back over the sand to the waiting trishaw and woke the snoring driver. In the narrow double seat they sat, as long before, like lovers, his arm round the back of the seat, their bodies cramped together. Paid off in the house drive, the trishaw man gaped in incredulity at the single note. Five dollars! A whole week's holiday. The white man certainly had more money than sense.

17

'But I tell you,' said Hardman wearily, 'I tell you for the tenth time that she was a client.'

'Che Normah walked the length of the sitting-room, did a brisk turn up-stage and resumed her vilifications. It had been reported to her by many, she said, not only Malays, that this Chinese woman had entered his office, dressed shamelessly and provocatively in a high-slit cheongsam, and had stayed closeted with him for an hour. Some said an hour and a half, others an hour and a quarter, yet others an hour and five minutes. But it was certainly an hour. An hour was a long time, much could happen in an hour, one did not spend a whole hour on legal business.

'But it was a complicated business,' protested Hardman. 'It was about a car accident. It took a long time to get all the details.'

She would believe all that when cats had horns. 'Ruperet,' she said, cooingly, 'Ruperet, you must be very, very careful. I expected you to be different from the other two. But you have got drunk and you have been with other women and you have cursed the name of the Prophet in the white man's club.'

'I haven't. I haven't looked at another woman.' And that was true. Normah was a full-time job. 'And I haven't said a word about the Prophet.'

'You have said that the Prophet could not read and write.'

'But he couldn't. Everybody knows that.'

'And the Kathi and the Mufti have been hearing about you and they are saying that you are not a good Moslem.

How do you think this makes me appear in the eyes of the town?' Her clear eyes caught the light and flashed silver. 'It is me you are making look a fool. But I will not be made to look a fool. The other two discovered that, but they were too late. You I give warning to. There are men up the road who have little axes.'

'Oh, I'm sick and tired of hearing about these blasted axes. Haven't the people here anything better to think about than axes, axes, axes?' His voice rose on the repetition – '*Kapak, kapak, kapak.*'

'Ruperet, I will not have you shouting at me. All the time you are shouting.'

'I am not shouting,' shouted Hardman.

'Because I am kind and forgiving, you try to take advantage all the time.'

'Look,' said Hardman, getting up from his chair, 'I'm going out.'

'Oh, no, you are not.' She stood, arms folded, by the open door, backed by harsh daylight and coarse greenery. 'Your office is closed today. I will not have you going off to see your debauched white friends and skulking behind their closed doors and desecrating the fasting month with drinking. You will stay here with me.'

'I have no white friends,' he said angrily, 'debauched or otherwise. You've seen to that. You got rid of my best friend, you had him thrown out of the State. Just because he was trying to help a dying man. And then you say that Islam is tolerant. Why, Islam is . . .'

'You will not say bad things about religion,' she said quietly, undulating a step or two towards him. 'I have warned you about that. And that white friend of yours was a very bad man. He was a Christian. He tried to kill that schoolteacher because he had entered the True Faith. He made him eat something bad and he put poison all over his body.'

'Oh, you don't know the first thing about it,' moaned Hardman. 'You just don't want to know, any of you. Look here, I'm going out. Get away from that door.'

'I will not. You are not going out.'

'I don't want to use force,' said Hardman. 'But you'd better realize once and for all, that I'm going to have my own way. I'm going to be master. And if you don't get away from that door, I shall . . .'

'What will you do?'

'I'm going out, I tell you. Don't be a fool.'

'Che Normah stayed where she was, her magnificent full body confronting his delicate weak white one. Hardman turned, and strode towards the kitchen.'

'Now where are you going, Ruperet?'

'I'm going to the *jamban*.'

'No, you are not. You think you are going to get out by the back door.'

Hardman ran for it. He clattered down the three stone steps to the big cool kitchen, into the yard. But the yard door was locked and the rusty iron key not in its accustomed hole. He heard Normah's light laughter behind him and turned angrily.

'God Almighty, am I supposed to be a prisoner?'

'I have the key and I have also the key of the car.'

Hardman leapt lightly on to the dust-bin that stood by the low yard wall. He scrambled on to the top of the wall and prepared to jump.

'Ruperet! I will not have you making a fool of me! Come back at once!'

Hardman jumped into the street, surveyed by two open-mouthed Malay workmen with dish-towels round their heads.

'Mad,' one said to the other.

'They are all mad.'

'Ruperet!'

Hardman ran to the corner and jumped into a trishaw. The driver was maddeningly slow and stupid.

'*Mana, tuan?*'

'Anywhere. No, wait. To the Haji Ali College. To the house of the *guru besar*.'

'I do not know where that is, *tuan*.'

'Get going, quick!' urged Hardman. 'Round this corner.'

Many men, women and children, clothed in bright raiment for the Sabbath, saw with a faint flicker of interest and surprise a very white man on a trishaw, and the driver pedalling with unseemly haste. Allah, his creditors were after him, or an axe-man, or perhaps his wife. The patterns of the East are few.

'So it has come to this,' thought Hardman, as they sped down the main road. 'My only refuge is a man who believes I have wronged him. But he will help, he must help.' He looked behind him once more, but there was still no sign of the pursuing Fury. He took a deep breath and drew from the breast pocket of his wet shirt a letter which he had received at the office the previous day, a letter already much crumpled, read and re-read.

My dear Hardman,

It was pleasant to hear from you after all these years. I am sorry that your Oriental venture has not been going as well as you expected. But, then, I think that the days when a man could expect to make his fortune in the East are dead and gone. Indeed, the time seems to have come for the reverse of the old process to apply, and for the East to dominate the West. We have here, in at least two Departments, very able lecturers with unpronounceable Indian names, and they are the life and soul of Faculty meetings. There seems to be a certain energy there which has long burnt itself out in Europe. However, this is as may be. I was interested in your inquiry about the possibility of your joining the Department. It so happens that there is a vacancy for a Junior Lecturer, occasioned by Gilkes being appointed (you will remember Gilkes?) to the Law Faculty of a rather disreputable minor university in, I think, Louisiana, or certainly one of the southern states of America. He wrote a book, you may remember, on the Napoleonic Code, and now he will have an opportunity to devote his life to reproducing it to young men with crew-cuts. The book was, I thought, ill-written. However, this post falls vacant in October. The salary of a Junior Lecturer is, as you know, not high, and you may find it hard to adjust yourself to a life without the luxuries which the East has, undoubtedly, accustomed you to taking for granted. However, do write and let me know if you would definitely like to be considered for this post and I will set the machinery in motion.

With all good wishes,
Yours sincerely,
E. F. Goodall.

And now he must raise the fare. He remembered that Crabbe had told him about his getting a share of a lottery prize in Kuala Hantu. Surely a loan of, say, two thousand dollars was not out of the way? After all, they were united by the tenuous cord of blood and a common Alma Mater.

Hardman saw himself, heart beating with hope and excitement, catching the plane from Singapore, watching that island drop down out of his life, and, behind it, the slim limb of the peninsula which he never wanted to see again. About leaving Normah he had no qualms. She could keep the car and his law books and the small balance in the bank. After all, she was entitled to that – restitution of the *mas kahwin* on the husband's desertion. And, once he was back in England, she could have no further claim on him, outside the tentacles of Islamic law, for the marriage had no secular legal status.

And there he would be, back in the pleasant musty smell of the Law Faculty, with Professor Goodall and his nicotined moustache, his pipe that would not draw, and there would be arguments about torts and statutes, and the soothing droning voices of the world where he really belonged, the rain and the weekly papers, the clanking trams and the sooty trees and the girl students in jumpers and silk stockings. But no, it was all nylon now. The world changed behind one's back.

Behind his back there was only the dusty road and a vista of barren coconut palms. He reached the cluster of Malay houses that enclosed Crabbe, paid off the driver, and, his throat dry, climbed the steps that led to Crabbe's veranda. The house was silent and, he thought, rather dusty. There were patches on the walls where pictures had been and no flowers in the vases. Hardman stealthily walked into the open sitting-room. There was no carpet on the floor, only the ghost of the carpet defined in an oblong of unpolished wood. The desk looked alive, however, littered as it was with papers and files and letters. Hardman could not help seeing one letter, clumsily typed:

H.H. The Abang,
The Istana,
Kenching.

This is to inform Your Highness that I have instructed Messrs Tan Cheong Po, Motor-Car Agents and Garage, Kenching, to deliver my Abelard car to the Istana, so that it may form part of Your Highness's collection. I am afraid that the car is not in first-class condition and I hope Your Highness will pardon this. However, it is perhaps appropriate that one of the last of the Western expatriates should bequeath to an Oriental potentate all that the West seems now to be able to offer to the East, namely, a burnt-out machine.

Your Highness's to Command,
Victor Crabbe.

Hardman walked quietly down the dusty corridor and peered over the half-doors of the main bedroom. There, at high noon, Crabbe lay in bed, unshaven, hair too long, smoking and reading Toynbee. Crabbe looked up blearily. On the bedside table were a bottle of gin, a jug of water, and a glass.

'Who is it? What the hell are you doing here?'

'A friendly visit. And an apology, if you'll take it.' Hardman came into the room. A toad hopped out of his way.

'Come in. Sit down on the other bed. Pour yourself a drink.'

Hardman sat on the cold unused twin bed. 'Have you heard from your wife?' he asked.

'A letter yesterday.'

'I'm sorry about that business, Victor. It was sheer carelessness on my part. I ask you to believe there was nothing malicious in it.'

'That? Oh, that doesn't matter any more. See, she sent me quite a long letter. I'd forgotten how well she can write.' Crabbe took up thin blue sheets from the floor beside his bed. 'She said it was quite a good trip. Everything was a bit of a shambles at Karachi, but Beirut, she says, is a fine place. They stop off at Beirut now, since the Cyprus trouble.'

'Trouble everywhere.'

'Yes. Do you remember a chap called Raffles?'

Was Crabbe going off his head? Was history becoming a timeless dream for him? 'You don't mean Stamford?'

'No, it's definitely Raffles. A rather nice little Jew at the Technical College.'

'Oh, *that* Raffles.'

'Yes. Fenella met him at Beirut airport. Apparently he's running a small air service of his own now. A couple of Beavers, and he's going to get another. He does a trip from Jiddah up to the Lebanon and now he's extending it as far as Marseilles.'

'Where's Jiddah?'

'Oh, that's near Mecca. You should know, being a good Muslim. That's the port that serves the cradle of your faith.'

'Victor, I want to go home.'

'But you've only just come,' said Crabbe, pouring out gin for himself, handing the bottle to Hardman. 'No, *real* home. I've been offered a job at the university. Lecturer in the Law Faculty.

'Well, congratulations. But I thought things were going all right here, from the financial point of view, I mean. I thought you were settling down.'

'I've got to get away,' said Hardman with passion. 'She's killing me.'

'Really?' Crabbe rested on his elbow, looking at Hardman with bleary interest. 'You mean, that's what she's trying to do? I must say you're not looking at all well. You've lost weight. Are they making wax-images of you and burning them over a slow fire? I'm sure that's what's happening with me. I feel lousy.'

'Is that why you stay in bed?'

'Oh, there's just nothing to get up for.'

'Look here, Victor,' plunged Hardman, 'can you lend me two thousand dollars? I can pay you back when I get home. I can send you monthly instalments.'

'Two thousand? That's a lot of money. Have you tried any of these money-lenders in the town?'

'I daren't,' said Hardman. 'Everybody would know about it. *She'd* know.'

'It's a lot of money.'

'You could do it, Victor. You're the only man I can come to. You're the only one I can trust.'

Crabbe lay on his bed, hands folded as in death, and gazed at the cobwebbed ceiling. 'You don't trust me all that much. Any more than I trust you.'

'Oh, that's all over. But, don't you see, I've got to raise the fare home. You've got the money, I know you have. You told me.'

'Did I?'

'Yes. You got part of a lottery prize. You told me. That friend of yours won the first prize and he gave you a cut.'

'Nabby Adams. Yes. And now he's in Bombay. We're all leaving. We're all deserting Malaya. It doesn't want us any more.'

'Come on, Victor, for old times' sake. Your money will be as safe as houses. You'll get it back. With interest, if you like.'

'I haven't got it. I gave it to Fenella. It was hers as much as it was mine.'

'All of it?' asked Hardman.

'All of it. I don't need much money.' Crabbe continued to lie, eyes slowly following the questing flight of a mason-wasp, flat on his back, hands folded.

'Well,' sulked Hardman, 'if you won't help . . .'

'I can't help, old boy. I wish I could. I just can't, that's all. Do have some more gin.'

'I haven't had any. I don't see how I can very well have more.'

'Yes. Like *Alice*. Alice, where art thou?' Crabbe lay on his side, his face turned away from Hardman.

'Are you tight, Victor?'

'Not tight. Just lousy. Just not very well. Do come and see me again. Call any time. Always glad to see an old friend.' His voice faded out on the last two words.

At two in the afternoon, the house silent again, the spiders busy, a toad still flopping about the room, the mason-wasp still seeking a suitable building site. Crabbe lay awake, thinking: 'Am I really such a swine? The insurance money's there, doing nothing. It would have been a friendly act.'

He raised himself up stiffly, looking for a cigarette, and thought: 'He's made his bed; he's got to lie on it. Which reminds me that this bed needs making. I'd better get up.' But he lay there still, hearing the clock march jauntily on to three o'clock, four o'clock, having nothing to get up for.

At nightfall Hardman returned, righteously indignant. He had spent part of the afternoon in the Field Force mess, hidden from the sharp eyes of Islam, drinking gloomy beer. There he had met Inche Mat bin Anjing, also hiding from the sharp eyes of Islam, drinking beer not so gloomy. Inche Mat was a local insurance agent. He informed Hardman that Crabbe had a cheque for two thousand dollars waiting for him in the office, this being the amount for which Crabbe's car had been insured, and that Crabbe had not yet troubled to come and collect it.

Hardman stumbled into the dark house, switching on lights, surprising *chichaks* scurrying over the walls. He went down to Crabbe's bedroom and assaulted his eyes with a harsh flood of light, showing up tossed bedclothes, scattered books and papers, hopping toads, Crabbe wide awake, his beard darker, his hair wilder.

'What the hell?'

'Aren't you ever going to get up? Come on, out of it.'

'I'll stay in bed if I want to.'

'You lied to me.'

'What do you mean, lied?'

'You've got two thousand dollars. I know. Insurance money on your car. I was told this afternoon.'

'What's that got to do with you?'

'Lend it me. Damn it all, you said you would if you could.'

'And so you whizz around in your big Jaguar, lord of the earth, and I'm expected to go about on foot, is that it? Damn it, man, I've got to buy a new car.'

'You could hire a car, you could use trishaws. In any case, you don't seem so very anxious to do any getting about. In bed all day.'

'That's my business.'

Hardman sat on the bed, saying, 'I daren't go home.'

'That's all right, then. You don't need two thousand dollars.'

'No, no. I daren't go back to her, to her house.'

' "Home" is an equivocal term. Fenella was always saying that. Spend the night here if you like.'

'Have you eaten anything?'

'No.'

But soon Talbot came, making sure that no man should starve. Into the bedroom he brought the meagre stocks of the store-cupboard – tinned cheese, sardines, cocktail sausages, Brand's Chicken Essence, a ragged loaf, a basin of dripping, a cold leg of lamb, H.P. sauce and the salt-cellar.

'What's happened to your cook?' asked Talbot, munching, spilling crumbs on the bed.

'I don't need a cook any more.'

'And your amah?'

'She's a lazy little bitch.'

Later that evening Police Constable Kartar Singh came, accompanied by two Sikh friends. Crabbe protested that he didn't need police protection any more, that there was nothing to protect any more. Kartar Singh said that, if he did not mind, he would continue to protect the sahib, helped now by his friend Teja Singh who had lost his job as night-watchman and might as well sleep here as anywhere else. This was, if the sahib did not mind him saying so, a cushy billet, and he would be obliged if the sahib would say nothing to the Officer Commanding Police District about no longer requiring police protection. Mohinder Singh sat gloomy, seeing in vision his life-blood dripping away as the shop's trade worsened, as the Bengalis and Tamils and Chinese counted fat takings and no man came to the shop of Mohinder Singh.

So, round the bed of Victor Crabbe, beer was drunk and cheese eaten, and more beer was sent out for. Finally Hardman lay down on the other bed, saying to Crabbe:

'Think about it, Victor. Think how much it means to me. I'll pay you back, every cent of it.'

Crabbe pretended to be asleep.

18

They were roasting him over a slow fire, a human barbecue. Jaganathan supervised the turning and the basting, saying often: 'They are good peoples. You are good peoples and I am good peoples. We are all good peoples.' Talbot dripped fat over his spitted carcase, expressing worry, finally bringing in a doctor who smelled deliciously of spirits and talked of pyrexia of unknown origin. The word 'pyrexia' began to turn and topple like a snowball going downhill, smashing itself on a black winter tree to reveal a core of stone which meant 'fire'. It also meant her putting the casserole in the oven to cook slowly while they went to hear the violinist playing the César Franck sonata. She talked animatedly about the canon in the last movement, the cyclical form, deploring the romantic treacle which glued up the neo-classicism. Talbot showed interest in the treacle and recited a passage from *Piers Plowman* about the treacle of heaven. He ate this with a spoon, waiting till the Pyrex dish be drawn from the oven. In the dish was a baked crab.

The cannon in the last movement boomed the end of the fasting month, because one spied the little crescent all were seeking. Jaganathan came to weep tears of basting fat and to say that the fight was on. There was a list of names of angry parents who had signed the petition that had not yet been written, an anthology of Oriental scripts. The amah, frightened, came in to sweep the room. Toads hopped in front of her.

When Crabbe felt cooler he heard the voice of Abdul Kadir saying, 'For fuck's sake, take your finger out. That was a bloody good article about the revolution in the East. It's the truth, and I told him it's the truth. People starving and not enough rice to go round. Unfortunately they know all about you in Kuala Lumpur, going to a hotel with another man's wife. Otherwise they'd let you bring in the revolution.'

Revolution of a cycle of Cathay. Where was Hardman? Hardman never came.

The fire returned, the eternal basting, the sheet soaked in hot fat. The man who smelled of whisky talked about hospitals. Talbot said leave it till tomorrow.

In the hot night the light was switched on. Crabbe heard the voice of an old man, happily chirping. The old man was giving him something to drink, something red-hot. Crabbe lay exhausted. The room was full of people, but this was no surprise; for a long time now the room had been full of people, some dead, some alive, some here, some eight thousand miles away. Crabbe tried to focus. One man spoke good English with a Chinese high school accent.

'I don't quite understand,' said Crabbe.

'It is the amnesty. It was in the newspaper wrapped round the rice. The Government will ask no more questions. They will pay fares to China.'

'I will pay his fare to England,' said Crabbe. 'I always meant to. But I couldn't get up. And he's not been round to see me. Look here, you're all Chinese.'

'We are all Chinese. We want to go back to China. So Ah Wing brings us to you.'

'But I can't raise all that much money. I can only find enough for the fare to England. And only for him.'

'Perhaps you are ill. I cannot quite understand what you're saying.'

'Wait,' said Crabbe. He tried to sit up. Ah Wing came round to support him. 'Just give me a minute. What's going on, anyway?'

'We have come out of the jungle. It was no good staying there. It was difficult to get food. You helped us for a long time. Then you could not help us any more. But we thank you for the help you gave us while you could.'

'No, no,' said Crabbe. He saw the young man more clearly. 'I didn't give any help. I wouldn't. You're a lot of . . . A lot of . . .'

'So now we come to give ourselves up. You have a telephone here. But they must keep their promise.'

'Who?'

'The police. The Government. They must not play tricks on us.'

Whatever Ah Wing had given him had induced clarity, even a sort of drunken cotton-wool euphoria. Crabbe looked round the room at some ten or twelve Chinese, some in ragged uniform, some in old shirts and faded grey trousers. One or two had rifles.

'That's a woman,' said Crabbe.

'Yes, that is Rose. And I am Boo Eng. Ah Wing is the father of my wife. My wife died under the Japanese.'

'What do you want me to do?' asked Crabbe.

'You can telephone the police and say that we give ourselves up if the Government will play fair.'

'Play fair?' said Crabbe. 'Where did you learn that expression?'

'I used to play basketball at school.'

'Surely,' said Crabbe, 'there's a policeman round here somewhere. I seem to remember that there was a police guard round the house or something. I've been ill, you see. It was all Jaganathan's fault. He was sticking pins in me. Or burning me. I am not sure which.'

'There is a fat Sikh outside the house. He is asleep. He has a friend who is also asleep.'

Crabbe tried to get up. He felt very weak. He was supported by Ah Wing and a grim young man with long black hair. It seemed somehow wrong for a Chinese to have long hair.

'Take your time, Mr Crabbe. There is no great hurry.'

Crabbe was assisted down the corridor to the sitting-room. Dust lay everywhere, and on a table was a pile of newspapers, delivered punctually but unread, a calendar of his illness. 'What a mess,' he said. Then, 'Who do I ask for?'

'This is a matter for the C.P.O. It is a big matter.'

Crabbe heard voices from the kitchen. 'Are there others in there?' he said.

'Oh, yes. There are perhaps thirty of us. You will not mind if some of them have a little food. Ah Wing has boiled rice for them and we found some tins of meat in your store-room.'

Shakily Crabbe made for the telephone. 'Look here,' he said. 'What time is it? I've just no idea.'

Boo Eng consulted a Rolex wrist-watch. 'It is now one o'clock in the morning. You had best contact the C.P.O. at his house. There will only be fools at the police station now.'

Obediently Crabbe asked for the C.P.O.'s house. His voice sounded drunk and the C.P.O. sleepy and annoyed, was inclined to slam the telephone down. But when Crabbe mentioned the name Boo Eng the C.P.O.'s voice became alert, as though it had put on a uniform.

'Boo Eng, you say?'

'That's the name.'

'Good God, man, hang on. Don't do a thing. Keep them there. Have you got a gun?'

'Not at the moment. But I think I can get one.'

Obligingly one of the Communist terrorists handed to Crabbe a small automatic pistol. It contained no ammunition. Obligingly another woke up Kartar Singh and his companion. It seemed only fair to let them share in the glory.

'You know,' said Crabbe, 'that stuff of Ah Wing's is pretty good. I feel a good deal better. Weak, of course, but that's inevitable. I wonder if Ah Wing would be good enough to make some tea?'

'He is still your servant. You did not give him notice, he did not give you notice. Of course he will make you tea.'

'And what was in that medicine?'

'It is very powerful. It is tiger's liver stewed in brandy. It is better than all the European medicines.'

Crabbe made the headlines. And, when the headlines were forgotten, the story still ran around the *kampongs*, of how the white man, though dying of fever, had captured single-handed thirty dangerous Communist terrorists. As, convalescing, he sat on his veranda in the cool dusk, the Malays began to gather round him once more, forgetting the time when they had their doubts about him, the stories they had languidly listened to about his being the enemy of mankind.

Crabbe told them his story, much-embroidered, for pure truth is not relished in the East. Some day, he knew, the tale would pass into timeless legend, and Crabbe's heroic feat would become one of the exploits of Hang Tuah, the brave Laksamana of Malacca, or, in lighter vein, be transmuted to a cunning trick played by the fabulous Mousedeer on a whole herd of elephants.

When Crabbe returned to his sweltering office in Haji Ali College, Jaganathan looked up from the loaded important desk with surprise and pleasure.

'Mr Crabbe, I knew all the time that you were good peoples.'

'Thank you, Mr Jaganathan.' Jaganathan did not get up. Crabbe, weak still, took a chair from one of the Malay clerks.

'You should have told me earlier that you had applied for transfer, Mr Crabbe. I cannot understand that you did not say before. It would have saved so much trouble for both of us.'

'A transfer, Mr Jaganathan?'

'Yes. You are to be moved. Perhaps you have not yet heard?'

'No, I haven't.'

'I hear these things often before other people. It is a question of knowing clerks in the right places, that is all. It is always the clerks who know.'

Jaganathan was right. Crabbe went to see Talbot almost at once, taking the long painful road to the town in a tri-shaw. He had not yet bought another second-hand car. The insurance cheque for two thousand dollars still lay snug in the office of Inche Mat bin Anjing. In the Education Office Talbot was enjoying his elevenses – a dish of smoking *mee*, a couple of curry puffs, a glass of murky iced coffee.

'Come in, Victor. You might as well get to know your new place of work. I'm sorry I've not been able to tell you the glad news before now. There's been such a hell of a lot to do. You're taking my place. You're going to be C.E.O.'

'Let's have that again, slowly. I'm still weak, remember.'

'You're taking over. I'm going to K.L. I don't suppose you'll be more than a temporary fill-in until they've found a Malay to take your place. This State's being Malayanized pretty fast, and all the top jobs are going to Malays. The Indians and Chinese aren't going to like it, but there it is. This is a Malay State. I suppose you'll be following me fairly soon, into the citadel. All the Europeans will be drawing into the centre. The end is nigh.'

'The night in which no man can work.'

'I wouldn't say that, you know. Nothing's permanent, there's always enough time if you make enough time. I'd say we've got to work now as we've never worked before. But not in the classroom and not in the office. We've just got to talk to people, that's all. Talk to them over a meal, over a couple of whiskies, try and give them a bit of a friendly warning, a bit of advice. Try and get them to think a bit. We didn't need to do that in the old days. We did the thinking for them. Now we've really got to teach them. Rapidly, earnestly, under pressure. I've writ-ten a poem about that. I've got it here somewhere.' He rummaged in a crammed in-tray. 'This is only a first draft. It needs tidying up, but I think you'll get the general idea.' In his harsh flat voice, without nuances, he in-toned his lines. The clerks took no notice, being used to him.

'In moments of crisis hunger comes, welling
 Up through the groaning tubes, and feeding-time
 Is the time of waking or perhaps the time before
 Night settles on the land, endless night.
 Light, whether of dawn or evening, turns
 The river to glow-gold syrup, the trees
 To a fairyland of fruit . . .'

His mouth watering slightly, Talbot put down the manuscript. 'You get the general idea,' he said.

'Who's going to be Head of Haji Ali College?' asked Crabbe.

'Oh, yes. One in the eye for old Jaganathan. They want a Malay, you see, and the one with most service is Abdul Kadir. I daresay Kadir will be all right. Perhaps this promotion will sober him up a bit.'

'Well,' said Crabbe. 'For fuck's sake.'

After leaving Talbot's office, Crabbe collected his two thousand dollars from Inche Mat bin Anjing. Then he sought Hardman. But Hardman's business premises were locked up, and none of the towkays in the shops on either side had any information. And the house also was empty. Nobody seemed to know anything of the whereabouts of either Hardman or 'Che Normah.

Except Haji Zainal Abidin. In the early afternoon Crabbe visited him. His house was a two-roomed wooden structure on high stilts, a rickety wooden stair leading from the yard – loud with chickens and children – to the dark warm hole of the living-room. In this living-room sat Haji Zainal Abidin's wife, busy at a Japanese sewing-machine, surrounded by further children. She was a handsome black-browed woman, her nose hooked and Arab. In Malay she told Crabbe that her husband was asleep, that she dare not wake him. She also gave Crabbe a frank come-hither glance which Crabbe ignored.

In Haji Zainal Abidin's sleeping brain the purdah curtain twitched, his wife showed her face to the intruder. Haji Zainal Abidin awoke and came into the living-room, clad in a striped sarong and a pyjama jacket, the best of both worlds.

'My dear fellow,' he said. 'I am honoured. What have we? Have we whisky? Brandy? There is only Wincarnis which my wife takes for her anaemia. Where is our Number One son? At school. Our Number Two? Only Number Five, and he cannot be trusted. It is a fat lot of use having children when they cannot be trusted to carry out even the simplest mission. Very well, we shall send little Hadijah to the corner shop. She shall bring us some beer.'

'You're very kind,' said Crabbe, 'but I didn't really intend to stay.'

'And so,' said Haji Zainal Abidin, 'because I am only a Malay you will not accept my hospitality. Because I am only a poor bloody Malay and do not live in a fine European house with a fan spinning all the time. I tell you, you English bastard, there will never be peace on earth until the Europeans have learned to treat their black brothers like brothers. Intolerance all the time.' He offered Crabbe a cigarette and noisily ordered a small pretty child to find matches.

'I'm looking for Hardman,' said Crabbe. 'Nobody seems to know where he is.'

'Hardman,' said Haji Zainal Abidin, 'my son in God. Hardman has gone away for a time. He has gone on the pilgrimage. He has seen the light.'

'Do you mean he's gone to Mecca?'

'Where else would he go on the pilgrimage? I tell you, ignorance will kill the hopes of the world.'

'Has he gone alone?'

Haji Zainal Abidin laughed loudly, showing his uncountable teeth and his red gullet. 'He wished to go alone, but his wife would not let him. She said she had as much right as he to become a *haji* and, besides, it is her money. What she says is true, but it is a pity for Hardman. The Arab women are the loveliest in the world, the only ones for which a man could have any appetite. Any *appetite*.' With appetite he stared at his wife who simpered coyly at

Crabbe. 'So you see,' said Haji Zainal Abidin, 'Hardman will come back a *haji*. Like me, a *haji*. But a very junior *haji*. I am the senior *haji* round here. I am –' he paused before delivering the *mot juste* – 'the prototypical *haji*. Do you know that word? Prototypical. I say that word to my boss this morning and he does not know the meaning. To think that I speak the white man's tongue better than the white man.' He laughed harshly and long, but still with appetite in his eyes. Crabbe judged that it was now time to leave. Haji Hardman. Well . . .

19

I have to talk to somebody or to something. I will talk to paper, a thing I have not done since I was at school. This is the diary of a Pilgrim's Progress. She, sleeping in the narrow bunk, thinks that our terminus is Mecca. She is wrong as far as I am concerned. I am going home. Raffles remembered me – but, indeed, who that has ever known me could forget this face that I see now, looking up for a moment, in the mirror of the dressing-table? The face of a very white man, one whom the sun would not accept. Though those scars are new, stigmata that Raffles has not seen. I'll say there is much kindness in the Jew. He knew of my flying career. He says that he will lend me a plane if I will take a small cargo home with me. I do not propose to inquire into the nature of the cargo. He says that the man who is on leave will bring back the plane. It seems a very sensible arrangement.

She turns over in her sleep and utters a single harsh Malay word that I do not know, that I do not wish to know. The Indian Ocean glints through the port-hole and the whole rumbling ship is asleep in the Indian Ocean afternoon. A pilgrim ship. Not like the pilgrim ships of *Lord Jim*, a mass of arms and legs and snoring mouths, page after page of them, a squalid net full of fish and broken crab-legs and tentacles, heaving in sleep towards Mecca.

Crabbe might have helped. He could have helped. Only when I am on solid English ground, under rain and northern winds, clad in my gown again, back to the world I should never have left, only then will I think of forgiving him. And what do I do about the Church? We'll see about that. Georges wasn't exactly a shining witness, ready to sell his soul to be back in China. Poor Georges. And who is saying about me: 'Poor Rupert?' Stop feeling bloody sorry for yourself.

There are people here who cook their food on the decks.

There are others who have rice thrown to them, like chickens. They gobble up the rice with a sea-air appetite. Our food is not too bad. Curries mostly. It will be good to be free of the eternal rice, away from the rice-myths, back to the corn-myths, bread and wine.

Normah isn't eating much. She's been seasick a good deal. I can always feel sorry for people who are being sick. And when I can feel pity for her that's easily turned into a sort of love. What made her like that, I wonder? She's not hungry for me or for any man. Perhaps if she'd had a child it would have been different. And now it's too late. In the East women want to identify themselves with their biological function. And that makes them all woman. Compartmentalization is our big crime in the West. Normah should have been the Great Earth Mother. Frustration in her tears at the world with ravening claws, the world being man. It will soon be time for tea.

June 16th.

The ship is a Dutch ship. I seem to be the only white pilgrim, and most of the Asiatic passengers seem to take me for a member of the crew, perpetually off duty. One Indonesian this morning addressed me in Dutch. Normah, from her languid deck-chair, answered for me. This led to a fascinating monologue about her first husband, Willem, and how she did for him after all his wickedness, drunkenness, perfidy. She has great hopes for me now and says frankly that she doubts if she will ever have to call the axemen in. It is enough that I have realized my wickedness and repented. God will forgive the repentant sinner. She sees the two of us entering heaven, hand in hand, both clad in the shining costume of pilgrims. She then suggested that we repair to our cabin for a while but I said I did not feel very well.

True enough. I played cards and drank secret gin with the chief engineer, the ship's doctor and the restaurateur in the chief's cabin last night. Normah believed that I had gone to a reading of the Koran.

June 17th.

Colombo and a few more pilgrims. Normah did not feel like leaving her bunk. I thought, with a sort of luxurious sensuality, as the launch took a number of sightseeing passengers to the misty island through moist northern-seeming sea-air, that now I could, if I wanted, make the break. But I wouldn't get very far. And undoubtedly she would suddenly turn up to drag me back by the ear, creating one of her all too special scenes, magnificent and all to much war. At Jiddah I must be very careful.

Most of the books in the ship's library are in Dutch. And so, strangely enough, and to Normah's great pleasure, I have been reading an English translation of the Koran. I wonder how, with such a repetitive farrago of platitudes, expressing so self-evident a theology and an ethic so puerile, Islam can have spread as it has. And then I remember that I am, officially, a Muslim. Nay, I am even a Muslim pilgrim.

This afternoon mail comes aboard. There is a letter for me. Raffles is really a good chap. He says it will be a midnight matter and how to get from Mecca to Jiddah late at night and where to meet him or the Arab who works for him. He knows a man who will do the sixty or so miles for me fairly cheaply. He is, strangely enough, a Malay pilgrim who decided to stay in Mecca, who makes money enough with a coughing taxi from the Holy City to the port.

June 18th.

Normah sick again this morning, despite calm sea. I write this drunk, having had bottle of Bols with the Second Officer in his naughty cabin plastered with brassière advertisements. This I say not right for pilgrim ship. I tell him that good Muslim not tolerate such pornography in holy boat. He say to hell and more Bols, Bols being the operative word. He say has girl in Hull, admire English though such bloody fools. Out like light afternoon on bottom bunk, she sleep on top bunk. Haha.

June 20.

Granted that the whole problem of life is integration, who is to tell us how to integrate and what do we mean when we say a man is thoroughly integrated? If we mean man is balanced and knows what he wants, I say he is a pipe-smoking moron with the sort of laugh that I associate only with stupidity or madness. For I would say that it is death to be properly integrated, for then there is no change and one is independent of change in the world about one. I would be as I am, a thin and white nervous wreck, having made a marriage that becomes more and more fantastic as we travel towards Aden, demi-paradise, and, having, in prospect, an Arabian Nights tale to tell to the cosy Western world reading its evening paper on the Underground. Hurray. The doctor is a very good man and he has cherry brandy in his cabin and tonight he reads to me from Robert Herrick, whose work he likes. Now why should he like Robert Herrick? I mean, what is there in that lustful lyrical Devonshire parson to appeal to a fat stolid medical man from Hilversum? And they talk about integration! Pah!

June 23rd.

Coming to Aden through dolphin-jubilant Arabian Sea. Normah has been to see doctor. He says what she will not believe. I do not believe it either. He says no possible doubt. Discuss this with doctor and second officer over Bols, followed by cherry brandy.

Ah, the shimmer of sea over the taffrail! The phosphorescent night, illuminating in marine benediction what one gives to the deep. Man is never so much alone, never so completely to grips with the fundamental problem of integration as when, under the mast and the steady star, he yields to the sea what the sea will but too readily take. And, flopping on the bench on C Deck, the lines by Blake sing out:

> Him Moira found dwelling in highest bliss,
> Creating gods (no ecstacy like this.)
> Took him, as, calmed by flowers of Beulah, Los,
> Or conscious Christ on an adventitious cross.

Moira being Fate, which the Orientals render Kismet.

June 24th.

Broiling in the Red Sea. It is the humidity. I gasp for air over a game of chess with the Chief Engineer, choking, throwing away twice-puffed cigarettes. I had forgotten it was like this. Shirts stick transparent to men's backs, women go slowly by on the deck, each exhibiting, through a dress like soaked paper, the straps of a brassière. And so we approach the Holy City.

Normah is definitely pregnant. She lies in her bunk, transformed, transfigured. I may go off to do what I like. I flirted with the Dutch stewardess who, a large blonde from Ryswyck, breathed Edam cheese after her kisses. I decide that the East has definitely spoiled me for women. Sitting with the doctor late at night, I see with shock through Herrick and cherry brandy that I have left something of myself in the East. That omphalic cord will pull like rubber over eight thousand miles. I can never be the same again.

We approach the port, Normah's fingers clasped in mine. For the first time in their lives the pilgrims bend towards the East. They have come home. I have come home, or nearly. Gods of the soaring wing and steady engine, fail me not. My big day is coming. I too bend towards the East.

20

'But we must put this on a commercial basis. That is only fair.'

All day long the cars had passed, a gleaming butter-smooth convoy, towards the port. The Abang was going. The lights were going on on Jalan Laksamana, two dark gaps in the row of shops like gold-filled teeth.

'Brother, I have done so much for you in the past. I have been your financial prop and stay. Come now, this is but a small return for many kindnesses. Moreover, it is a thing I cannot take seriously.'

'Not take seriously? But it is a science, it is based on a philosophy of the universe, it requires considerable training and skill.'

Teja Singh set up his bed outside the Grand Hotel, ready to guard the residents, the casual eaters and drinkers, the fat woman who was in charge and the thin dark woman who entertained the business men from Penang and Bangkok. Teja Singh yawned as he sat down, admiring the schoolmaster's new second-hand car.

Kartar Singh, two shining stripes on his sleeve, smiled full-beardedly at his co-religionist who bent his turban over the fat uncomplicated palm, examining the exiguous headline, the thick line of luck, the plump hump of Venus.

Victor Crabbe smiled faintly from his high stool by the bar. Next to him was perched Abdul Kadir, blinking above tie and clean shirt and creased trousers, sipping a small beer.

'I still cannot understand,' said Abdul Kadir. 'It is not as if I were a really good man. Not like our Mr Din, for instance, who has an Indian degree and does not drink and does not swear very much.'

'Grace falleth where it will,' said Crabbe. 'There is nothing that anybody can do about it.'

'It is a very strange world,' said Abdul Kadir.

Crabbe scrutinized again the photograph on the front page of the *Singapore Bugle*. It showed Chinese terrorists boarding the ship that would take them to their Mecca, to the land of hard work and drab grey uniform for all and sufficient rations and not much fun, his own undergraduate Utopia. Forget about that, forget about her blue jumper and her records of Shostakovitch, her warm white neck and the solace of her compact and willing body while the casserole simmered in the oven of their flat, the woman he could not leave alone. And that particular face, smiling wryly above the squat Chinese bodies, the large mouth and the frank eyes, the crew-cut, surely he knew that face?

'And how do you find the house?' asked Crabbe.

'It is a bloody good house. I mean,' said Abdul Kadir, 'I like the house very much. But it is too good for the likes of me.'

'You learnt that humility from the lower deck,' said Crabbe. 'Come on, enter into your inheritance, remember that this is your country.'

'But it does not seem right,' said Abdul Kadir. 'It is something new, a white man giving up his house for me, and himself living in a little hotel room. I cannot understand it.'

'The house is tied to the College,' said Crabbe. 'It is the headmaster's house. Moreover, the Englishman has but a small family or else no family at all. Or even,' he added, 'no wife. Don't worry about me. In the West we're shrivelling up. We're dried fruit. And we're used to far less luxury than you think.'

'Have a fucking beer,' said Abdul Kadir. His owlish eyes showed sudden shock. 'I mean, have a beer, Mr Crabbe.'

Two Malay workmen entered, dish-towels fastened,

turban-wise, about their heads. They ordered orange crush.

'Still here,' said one. 'The white sods are still here.'

'And those turbaned prawns with shit in their heads. But it won't be long now.'

'No, it won't be long.'

'And that Malay woman is going to have a baby. She is *bunting*.'

'*Hamil* is a politer word.'

'Why use a polite word? It is the child of that white sod who has gone.'

'He has gone for ever.'

'What does the bloody postman know? His bundles of letters from England. And the telegrams from England. He is hiding, hiding from everybody, from women in England as well as here.'

'They say he was burned.'

'That was before, in the second world *perang*.'

'His flying ship fell in a cold country. Else why should the Malay woman cry? What will happen to a man once will happen again.'

'Good riddance to the sod.'

Crabbe remembered his final story to the Malays on the veranda. The story of the man from the far country who tried to help, the man who developed miraculous powers, killing the pirates and the bandits and diseases and teaching the final marvel of the word. And as he developed wings and an unconquerable fist and the gift of invulnerability he ceased to be a man from a far country, he joined the heroes of the Malay Valhalla, he became the property of the open-mouthed tough brown men, cross-legged on the veranda, he became one of them. And Crabbe's final *pantun* as his goods were loaded on to the truck:

> *Kalau tuan mudek ka-hulu,*
> *Charikan saya bunga kemoja.*
> *Kalau tuan mati dahulu,*
> *Nantikan saya di-pintu shurga.*

'Translate it for me, Kadir. Translate it for all the world.'

'If you go up the river,' translated Kadir, the glaze of drink in his eyes, 'pluck me, pluck me . . . For fuck's sake, I've forgotten the word.'

'Frangipani.'

'Frangipani. But if you die first, wait for me . . .!'

'At the door of heaven.'

'At the door of heaven. For fuck's sake, man, what are you crying for? Have another fucking beer.'

'Your language, Kadir.'

'You have very lucky face, Mr Crabbe,' said Mohinder Singh. 'You have face of a very lucky gentleman. If you will sit down here for a moment, for two dollars only I will foretell lucky future.'

Beds in the East

To Edward Jones, Esq., M.Sc.

Allah is great, no doubt, and Juxtaposition his prophet (*Amours de Voyage*)

Good, too, Logic, of course; in itself but not in fine weather. (*The Bothie of Tober-na-Vuolich*)

— ARTHUR HUGH CLOUGH

The anonymous state
and named characters of this story
are all completely fictitious

I

Either side of the bed was the wrong side. True, it was possible to get out of it by inching slowly forward on one's fat brown rump to the foot, but that, for some reason, often woke both of them. It was better, far better, to risk waking only one. But, this lie-abed dawn of the Sabbath, which one?

Syed Omar lay for an instant debating, caught in an agony of indecision which was no grim pleasure. In common with the rest of the country, he had not absorbed all that much from the West. He could speak English, drive a car, distinguish blindfold between brands of brandy, run an office, smell out injustice a mile off, but no white official had ever spoken to him of those philosophies fashionable in post-war Europe. It was all too late now to complete the course; his elected rulers had not heard Toynbee warn of the danger of sipping, rather than draining, the West. And now the jungle, after its short doze, was ready to march coastward again.

On one side lay Maimunah, his wife; on the other lay Zainab, also his wife. He lay walled in by brown female flesh. And that was wrong, most irregular, uncleanly, contrary to the strict Islamic custom. But the house had only one bedroom and in that bedroom there was no inch of space for what was not purely functional. The Malay language was more exact than the English in calling it a sleep-room. And in his house Syed Omar did little more than sleep.

On other beds lay his children, the palpable record of his past virility, the breathing memoranda of his present responsibility. As the light came up, brown chubby limbs, careless in sleep, were defined, and innocent mouths open, as in the ecstasy of hearing music. All round the room brown blossomed in many shades – coffee of varying strengths, varying temperings of tinned milk, from the watery brew of Sin Chai's shop to the robust infusion of Ooi Boo Eng: many kinds of brown, flat and unsumptuous in the hard light, dredged from the unrecorded parts of his own and his wives' families, and eighteen or so different sizes, denoting the harvests of eighteen or more years. Syed Hassan, the eldest, his sleeping mouth pouting as into a microphone, his delinquent hair tousled; Sharifah Khairun, only four, her sarong kicked off, her perm glossy on the pillow. All the boys Syeds, all the girls Sharifahs, proud little trumpets before their individual names, proclaiming them to be of the line of the Prophet.

Syed Omar, their father, felt again the prostatic twinges which he must now accept, at dawn or false dawn, as appropriate to his forty-seven years. True, he had been drinking the night before (and now the night before began to shape itself in his mind and he began to palpitate) but that made no difference. Every morning was the same. He swung his legs over the sleeping form of Maimunah. She breathed gently to the ceiling. But, as always with one or the other, his levering hand jabbed her thigh and she woke.

It was her custom to wake, when roused accidentally thus, in shock, as though the thieves, murderers, ravishers had at last arrived. Zainab's way was to resume, almost in mid-sentence, the monologue of the evening before. He had not done this, he had not done that, what was to happen to her children (*her* children)? Syed Omar preferred, on slight reflection, the more dramatic *aubade*.

'Go back to sleep.'

'Eh? Eh? What?'

'Sleep.' Incisive, firm, so that a ripple passed over the sleepers. Syed Omar surveyed them all, splay-foot and stubby, tying his sarong at the waist, surveyed them like a general surveying the carnage. 'Sleep,' he said more soothingly, like Titania or a mass-hypnotist, but it was too late. A small child (its name did not come automatically to mind) looked up at him from clear morning eyes, and Hassan called from his unconscious, in a loud adolescent voice:

'Dig that cat.'

Syed Omar stared, wondering what this could mean, frightened, as hearing the voice of prophecy. But he padded through the wrack of stirring bodies and reached the bathroom, which was under water. It was the women of the house who were most inconvenienced, he reflected, by its being situated on an old paddy-field. He could stand, as he did now, on the top step, on the shore of the flood, and perform this first morning act with no trouble. As long as the wet season lasted, his wives would suffer from an excess of water in the wrong places, and in the dry they would suffer from no water at all. Still, the more elemental their sufferings the better: they could thus be distracted from those more sophisticated grievances which transcended season. But their grievances were nothing to his.

As he stood, long, on the step, Syed Omar reviewed the previous night. There had been a farewell dinner for Maniam. Cold curry and warm rice, toasts and speeches. Many speeches. The Chief Police Officer and the Officer Superintending Police Circle and the Officer Commanding Police District, and the Officer in Charge of the Special Branch and various other officials had stood up and spoken, some in Malay, some in English, some in both, about the good work Maniam had done. He had come for a brief time only as relief Chief Clerk, they said, but they were all sorry to see him return to Pahang, they were appreciative of the great work of reorganization he had done, they revered him as a man and loved him as a friend. With men like him sitting organizing in offices, a free Malaya had nothing to fear. Mr Godsave, the last white man of the Police Department, said that he himself would soon, with many other of his fellow-countrymen, be leaving this land he had learned to love so well (hear, hear) and, in the rigours of an English winter, often look back nostalgically at happy days spent in the East. He might say that, not only in Malaya, but also in India, he had learned to respect the ability of the Jaffna Tamils, of which race Mr Maniam was an undoubted ornament. (Here Mr Maniam had shone, ornamentally, smugly.) Mr Godsave said that the Jaffna Tamils had been brought up in a tradition of service to the State which might well be taken as a model by the other races. He concluded by saying that it was a great loss to the State Police Department that Mr Maniam should be going, but that his work would long be remembered and be an inspiration to those who had had the good fortune to work with him.

Then Syed Omar, uncalled, unexpected, had stood and said, in English:

'Much time has been spent tonight in praising Maniam. I do not stand up to praise Maniam. I stand up to say the truth about Maniam. I know his race and I know him. I know his methods and I know the methods of his race. I would say this. If Maniam wants to get on, let him get on. But let him not get on by grinding the faces of others into the dust. If he wants to climb, let him climb, but let him not climb over me. I know that he has been telling others that I am not good in my job. I know that he has been making a list of the days I have taken off. And I also know that his sister-in-law was brought specially from Kuala Lumpur so that she could meet the C.P.O. and waggle her bottom at him and show him her teeth and show how fast she could take down shorthand and how well she could type. I know I cannot take down shorthand fast, but I have never pretended to be able to take down shorthand fast. But my heart is pure and I am a man of integrity. I have always tried to do my work well. Now there comes a man to lie about me and try to have me kicked out. This is the man you have praised. I warn you, especially you Malays, that you have enemies in your midst, and this Maniam is one of them. The Jaffna Tamils will try to grind you in the dirt and snatch the rice from the mouths of your wives and children. They have no love for Malaya but only for themselves. They are a lot of bastards. Thank you.'

Syed Omar completed his morning's libation, thoughtful, surveying the rest of that lively evening. There had been no fight. There had been many restraining arms which Maniam for his part, had not needed, for he kept saying, over and over: 'I forgive him. He is still my brother. It is proper to forgive those who revile us,' somewhat like an unmuscular Christian. But Syed Omar had said: 'I swear in the name of God that there are clerks and peons who will bear witness that I have, myself, restrained them from doing physical harm to Maniam. But Maniam has not gone yet. There is still time. His plane does not leave till twelve tomorrow.' Friends had carried Syed Omar off to a coffee-shop, and there beer and adrenalin had flowed till midnight.

War, thought Syed Omar, adjusting his sarong. War, he thought, with an unholy thrill. The Malays against the world. But, entering the bare living-room he was chidden by a poster on the wall. It was a portrait of the Chief Minister, smiling benevolently and extending loving silk-clad arms. Beneath, in ornamental Arabic script, was the single legend *Keamanan*: Peace.

The children were rising, tuning up for the day. The wives had started a whining canon about the price of dried fish, arranging the while each other's hair. Hassan was already at the radio, squeezing out a remote early-rising station. At the single table, over which presided a grave portrait of the Sultan, little Hashim was doing his homework. It was Geography, and, in a labour of neatness, the child wove the words of an essay.

'What is this?' asked his father, not unkindly. Hashim was his favourite, the hope of the family, the only child who wore glasses:

'Ceylon, Father.'

'Ceylon? Ceylon? Who gave you Ceylon?'

'Mr Parameswaran, Father.'

Syed Omar breathed over the child's thin shoulders, reading: 'Jaffna is the most important part of Ceylon. The Jaffna Tamils come from there. They are hard-working people and very clever. In Malaya are many Jaffna Tamils. They are in many government things. They help to run Malaya properly.'

Syed Omar, enraged, clutched and crumpled the essay, uttering a stricken cry. Hashim, astonished, looked on and then began to wail. Syed Omar blindly clawed the child's atlas and crunched Ceylon and Jaffna with it, and all the encircling ocean. Soon the wives came and Hassan gave an adolescent guffaw.

Syed Omar cried: 'It is for you I do this, for you! But no appreciation, no thought! I am nobody in this house, nobody! I am going out!'

He began to descend the house stairs to the flooded path, but found he was unshod and half-naked. He returned sheepishly and sulked in a corner. Hassan, having forgotten to switch off his grin, grinned at the radio dial and then produced from the set a sudden brassy blast which opened Syed Omar's sweat-ducts. He panted in the corner, his eyes misty.

Maimunah said: 'Cannot afford to tear up books with the wage you bring in. A disgrace.' Zainab comforted the snivelling Hashim: 'There, there. Bad, bad Father.'

Syed Omar said, sarcastically: 'Enough of this nonsense. My breakfast, if you please. In four hours' time I must be at the airport.'

At that moment, in profound crapula, the élite of the Jaffna Tamils of the town were already drinking coffee, black and bitter. After the Police party had come the party in Vythilingam's house. Vythilingam was the State Veterinary Officer and with him Maniam had been staying. Maniam was a nephew of Vythilingam, or perhaps an uncle or a cousin: relationship was not clearly defined, but relationship existed. Indeed, relationship existed between all the Jaffna Tamils who sat in their striped sarongs this Friday morning and day of Maniam's departure, silent and aching. Jaffna is a small community. The party that had just ended had been, in some measure Hellenic, a black shining parody of the Symposium at which Socrates had spoken of the virtues of intellectual love and Alcibiades had come in tight, slobbering his admiration for the snub-nosed master. Alcibiades was Arumugam, the Air Control Officer, whose manly beauty was marred by a high squeaking voice with curious gargling undertones. Socrates was Sundralingam, the doctor. He, with flashing glasses, had spoken at length of the nugatory value of the heterosexual relationship: women were there solely to produce more Jaffna Tamils, the romantic poets had written nonsense, to place woman on a pedestal was a Western perversion. Arumugam had kept saying: 'How right you are,' his eunuch's voice somehow giving a sour-grapes quality to the agreement. But it was all really sour grapes. All close to, or in, the thirties, they had not yet found wives. Women there were in the town but not women of the right sort. They wanted women of good caste and of the right colour, worthy of professional men. Kularatnam, the State Inspector of Motor Vehicles, had not come to the party. He was in disgrace, for it was known he was carrying on with a plump and well-favoured Malay princess who kept a bookshop.

Vythilingam knew that he too would soon be in disgrace. As his guests sucked at their coffee, he said tentatively: 'Could anyone . . .' The word would not come out. He had not so much a slight stutter as a slight hesitation. He raised his mild face to the ceiling, as though the better to exhibit the glottal spasm. 'Anyone . . .' If it was food he was going to suggest, they all thought not. 'Not just yet,' said Sockalingam, the dentist. 'Anyone . . .' Their language was English, the language of professional men. '. . . eat some fried eggs with onions?'

After so much effort, 'No' would seem an ungracious answer. They grunted and Vythilingam called his Siamese servant. Vythilingam glanced mildly round at the company, their faces creasing with pain as the sharp light from the window caught their hangovers. 'We'll all feel ...' Maniam shook his head with a sad smile '. . . better . . .' But behind the mildness what tigers, what jungles. The speech hesitation was a symptom of the most complicated tensions. The hands that performed their veterinary duties with such tenderness and skill could cheerfully throttle necks. Vythilingam knew how to hate. First, he hated the British. He had smarted from what he called British injustice ever since he could remember. He had seen ill-qualified tow-haired officials promoted over his head. In Kuala Lumpur once a British soldier called him a nigger. A former white State Veterinary Officer had once said to him: 'Of course, you've only got a colonial degree ...' Another white man had once tried to take him into a white man's club, and the Chinese steward, lackey of the British, had ejected him. The white man had shrugged his shoulders, said: 'Sorry, old boy,' and then walked in on his own. But before that, before he was born even, his father, a clerk in Ceylon, had actually been struck on the face by an Englishman. Or, at least, that was a tradition in the family. Out of this hatred of the British stemmed hatred for his mother, for she had, after his father's death, married an Englishman, a tea planter settled in Ceylon. And that was why he was going to spite his mother by marrying a woman she had not even met, let alone chosen. And yet in his choice of a wife there was something masochistic. Rosemary's reputation was known; he would, by obscure logic, become retrospectively a cuckold. Her caste, as her name, the name of a Christian, proclaimed, was of the lowest, and that hurt, and yet that would hurt his mother more, and yet perhaps it would not, because what had she done but marry a Christian? But it should not hurt him really, nor should the knowledge of her looseness, for he was a Communist and race and religion and caste did not matter, morality was a bourgeois device of oppression. And yet he kept his Communism quiet, because he was a Government officer. But if he was a Communist he should be in the jungle now, stinging the effete capitalist régime with odd bullets. But he did not really like the Chinese. And he was not really fighting the oppressive British, whatever he did, for they were leaving Malaya anyhow. And again, he was only really happy when injecting penicillin into ailing cows, or putting thermometers into the anuses of sick cats, and he would literally not hurt a fly, which all reeked of Hinduism, and his mother, though she had married a Christian, was still a devout Hindu.

The Siamese boy brought in plates containing wormy shreds of over-fried egg, seasoned with blackened bits of onion. Everyone languidly picked at this breakfast. The sun rose higher, the day warmed. Dr Sundralingam spoke his first words of the day, and, as if, against his will, time had been wasting, he said urgently to Maniam:

'Do you think you can get Samy that job?' Samy was Kanikasamy, first cousin to Sundralingam. 'You know the people down there; I don't.'

'I think so,' said Maniam. 'The Malays just can't do the work. The fools won't see it, they won't accept it. But I think I can fix up a vacancy. The pay won't be much at first, but there are bound to be other vacancies, higher up the scale. Don't worry.'

'And do you think it's going to be all right for Neelam?' asked Arumugam. His high voice smote wounded nerves like a fortissimo flute. Neelam was the sister-in-law of Maniam and a cousin or niece or aunt of everybody present.

'Yes. Syed Omar will be out. That's definite. If only you could have heard him last night ...'

'You'll have to be careful. He is very hot-blooded.'

'It is all talk,' smiled Maniam. 'They talk and talk and shout but they never do anything. Besides, it is too late for him to do anything.'

'Be careful, just the same,' warned Arumugam.

Vythilingam covertly looked at his watch. Soon it would be time for him to shave, dress, and, his professional black bag on the seat beside him, drive to Rosemary's house. In that house there were several cats, eight or nine of them, all of them presents from Vythilingam. She had once complained of mice. This was the only way he could visit her, the professional way, solicitous for the cats' welfare, ready with Vitamin B injections, penicillin, tonic drops, for she was panicky about what the neighbours would say if they saw men visiting her purely socially. Supposing spiteful people wrote to her boy-friend in England, saying she was carrying on? Then her boy-friend would never marry her. But Vythilingam knew that her boy-friend would never marry her anyway. Once, at a dance, he had seen this boy-friend, proud and white in his dinner-jacket, circling in a waltz, Rosemary in his arms. This boy-friend, dancing, had caught the eye of a friend of his, a loutish ginger salesman of tobacco. He had made, taking his right hand from Rosemary's back to do it, an unmistakable ithyphallic sign and followed it with a wink. The British never kept their promises. And that Rosemary had been defiled by this Englishman gave Vythilingam a twinge of curious grim elation. His marriage to her would be a gesture of many kinds of revenge.

'I think now,' said Vythilingam, 'we ought . . .'

'There is plenty of time,' said Maniam. 'My plane doesn't go till midday.'

'Ought . . .'

Black but comely, Rosemary Michael sat in the full sunlight of her living-room, re-reading the last letter from Joe. Everywhere cats lolled, fought, played, stalked, washed: the many cats of a spinster, but Rosemary was only a spinster in the strict sense of denotation. She was eminently, eminently nubile.

The perfection of her beauty was absurd. The lack of flaw was a kind of deformity. It was not possible to say what racial type of beauty she exemplified: the eyes, black, were all East – houris, harems, beds scented with Biblical spices; nose and lips were pan-Mediterranean. Her body, clad now in a wide-skirted, crisp imported model, was that of the Shulamite and Italian film stars. The décolletage, with its promise of round, brown, infinitely smooth, vertiginous sensual treasure, was a torment to the blood. Yet only to the white man were these treasures revealed, for Rosemary could not stand the touch of brown fingers. The list of her lovers was formidable, ranging from the District Officer to the manager of the local Cold Storage. Many had promised marriage, but all had gone home, the promise unfulfilled. For Rosemary had little to offer, except her body, her fragments of training college learning, her ability to arrange flowers, and her quite considerable capacity for all kinds of sensuous pleasure. She desperately wanted marriage with a European, but she didn't want marriage without love. Love, of course, was the familiar hoarse entreaty after the evening's drinking and Rosemary would quickly enough yield to the entreaty, hearing the love grow hoarser and more urgent and thinking too, 'How can he fail to go on wanting me for ever once he knows what I'm capable of giving?' And true, the men did go on wanting her for a long time, till the end of the tour or till transfer or till Rosemary's voice – inexpertly Sloane Square after much drinking – made them cringe with embarrassment. And other things got them down – her inordinate passion for Worcester sauce, her wanting to be wanted all the time, her tears, tears which didn't humanize her face by making it pathetically ugly but just made it not a face at all, her lack of 'reality-control' (she just didn't literally know whether she was lying or telling the truth). And now, all over Malaya, the white men were leaving – the brown sauce-stain spreading over the table-cloth – and time was getting short.

But Joe was still writing, and Joe had promised to send her an engagement ring, and Joe said he was still looking for a job, a good job, so that she wouldn't have to work once she was married. Rosemary believed him, and a proof of her faith was her three-months' fidelity, despite the occasional crying-out of her warm woman's blood. Again she read:

... I keep thinking of you and I all the time in bed together. Honestly, darling, on these long winter nights when I am lying on my own I want you more than ever. Yesterday I saw old Mac and we had a couple of drinks together, just like old times, and he introduced me to his sister who is really a smasher, but I wouldn't have anything to do with her, because I keep thinking of you. I do hope you are keeping yourself for me and not seeing other men. You can see Crabbe, of course, because Crabbe is by way of being your boss and there wouldn't be any funny business with Crabbe anyway, him being past all that. Well, darling, I am looking for a good job still, but there are not many cars being sold now, and who knows I may be back in good old Malaya before long if Mac can get me in with this new export firm. But I know you would want me to definitely try and fix something up here, you knowing England and liking it so much. Well now I have come to the end of the paper, these airmail letter-forms are too small, aren't they, so close now with fondest love from your Joe.

That was really a lovely letter, much nicer than the one in which he had told her not to send any Christmas presents to his father and mother, as his family did not go in much for presents. He had been really rude about it, but he had at least added: 'Save the money, darling, to help furnish our little house.' Rosemary had a shrewd idea that Joe had not told his parents anything about her, and that perhaps was a bad sign. Perhaps they had this absurd colour prejudice.

And yet, she reflected, she had seen little enough of this absurd colour prejudice when she had been in Liverpool, doing her course of teacher training. How the men had been after her! She had been treated royally. Her story then had been that she was part Hawaiian and part Javanese, a romantic combination, and she had not denied the soft flattering suggestion that perhaps she was of princes' stock. The middle-class low-caste Christian Tamil family in Kuala Hantu had then ceased to exist. And the distinguished, grey-haired managing director who had asked for her hand (if she wished, they could have separate bedrooms) and the tall young men at Claridge's and the appearance on 'In Town Tonight' and in the *Daily Mirror* and modelling for Norman Hartnell. How graciously the Queen had bowed to her! But, no, perhaps that hadn't really happened. Surely, though, the Secretary of State for the Colonies had pleaded with her not to return to Malaya, that night they were dancing among chandeliers and decorations-will-be-worn, massed flowers and champagne. It all happened, of course it all happened.

What happened now was that the front door of the small Education Department house was pushed open and massed flowers entered. Behind the massed flowers was Jalil, the Turk, a man who worked in the Town Board offices but had shares in a couple of rubber plantations. Emir Jalil, as he liked to be called, put the flowers rudely on the table and then, without invitation, sat down in the only other arm-chair. He was squat, short-necked, beady-eyed, strong-nosed, fifty, wore a cravat in his open shirt and breathed heavily, being asthmatic. The cats, knowing he hated cats, approached him with fascination, and one tough Tom, with a face like Disraeli, tried to climb on to his knee. Emir Jalil brushed it off roughly.

'You shouldn't come here,' said Rosemary excitedly in English. 'You know you shouldn't. I gave the amah instructions not to let you in. Supposing somebody sees you, with all those flowers too? Supposing somebody writes him a letter? Ooooh!' (a pure round open Tamil O.) 'Go now, please go now, please go!'

'Come eat,' said Jalil. 'Come drink. Come make jolly time.' He coughed long and sighed after it.

'I can't,' said Rosemary, agitated. 'You know I can't. Oh, please go.'

'He not marry you,' said Jalil. 'He never marry. He tell me he not marry you.'

'No, he didn't,' said Rosemary. 'It's a lie, you're a liar. He's going to send me a ring.'

Jalil indulged in comfortable, quiet asthmatic laughter. Rosemary saw the flowers and walked briskly over to them on high heels. Her ankles were possibly, just possibly, not by any means at all certainly, a little too thin. She put the flowers in water, thinking that with Jalil it was a bit awkward making up one's mind whether one ought to shudder at the prospect of his touching one or not. She had read in a book that Turkey was really part of Europe, which meant that Jalil was a European. But how could he be? He was a Muslim and had three wives, and Europeans were Christians and had only one wife. But Jalil looked like a European. And he had money. And he could divorce his other wives. Yet he never said he loved her. If he panted at all, it was with asthma.

She brought the flowers back from the kitchen sink to the living-room. Three cats jumped up on to the table to inspect them, one – a half-Siamese – trying to lap the water. Jalil coughed and sighed again, his chest labouring, and, in a resigned sort of way, took from his shirt pocket a cigarette-case. His thick fingers, grasping the case, produced also a green card which, caught for a moment in the fresh breeze, fluttered to the floor by Rosemary's feet. Jalil wheezed up from his chair with some agility to retrieve the card, and Rosemary thought she saw guilt or anxiety, certainly a twinge of disconcertment. Rosemary herself snatched it rapidly from under a cat's hind paws and scanned it with appetite.

'I get yesterday from Postmaster,' said Jalil. 'I mean give as surprise.'

'You disgusting, disgusting, horrible ...' Rosemary stamped her foot as a substitute for the noun she could not find. 'It's mine. It says there's a parcel for me. Oh, go away, get out. I never want to see ...'

'I mean bring as surprise. Make happy.' Jalil was seated again, recomposed.

'You didn't want me to see it. You wanted to keep it from me. Because you're jealous. Oooooh!' Suddenly Rosemary was alive with excitement. 'It's the ring, it's the ring. He's sent it at last. It's in the Custom's Office.' She jerked from one emotion to the other. 'And I could have had it yesterday. And you kept it from me. Oh, you horrible, horrible pig of a man.' She kicked his right shin vigorously. Jalil gave a deep chesty chirp of laughter. 'And today the Office is closed. And I can't get it. But he's sent it, he's sent it, it's here!' Her face all alight, she was not perhaps so beautiful as in vaccine repose; the features could not stand much of the humanizing distortion which makes for a more civilized comeliness. But the teeth were all there, ridiculously white and even.

'Come drink,' said Jalil. 'Come make jolly time.'

'Not with you, not if you were the last man in the world,' she said, all pout and stormy eyes. And then she swung over. 'Oh, I must celebrate, I must, I must.'

'Be sure what in parcel first.'

'It's the ring, it must be the ring!'

'We go see. We go on way to drink and make jolly.'

'But it's closed. It's Friday. There's nobody there.'

'We go. Is watchman there. He open for me. He give parcel. Me he owe money.'

'Oh, Jalil, Jalil, can we? Oh, I could kiss you.'

Jalil did not seem to want to be kissed. He sat still, quietly asthmatically chuckling almost with no sound.

'You go get ready,' he said.

'Nothing matters now,' said Rosemary. 'They can say what they like. They can gossip all they want to. I'm engaged, engaged!' She pranced into her bedroom, singing horribly high, then pranced back again to the photograph, framed in silver, which stood on her Public Works Department escritoire. 'Oh, my Joe, my Joe,' she crooned, flattening her breasts with the hugged picture, then drawing it away, adoring it, then covering the mean mouth, the pale wavy hair and the knowing eyes with kisses. 'My Joe, Joe, Joe, Joe.' Then she pranced off again to her dressing-table. Jalil coughed, sighed and chuckled comfortably.

When she was ready, Vythilingam was standing shyly by the open door. Jalil was still in the arm-chair, breathing deeply and seeming to brood on the picture of Vythilingam hovering awkwardly, as though he were really a picture.

'Oh, Vy,' cried Rosemary, 'it's come, the ring's come, I'm engaged!' She had already begun to celebrate: too much lipstick, like too much drink, her hair pulled back stark – the style she favoured for dances – into a top-knot secured by a round silver grip.

Vythilingam exhibited his working larynx, his eyes up to the ceiling as though inspecting damp. His lips chewed. 'I know, I know,' sang Rosemary. 'It's marvellous, isn't it? It's made me almost speechless, too. I'm going off to get it now, Vy. Oooooh, I can hardly wait.'

Vythilingam began: 'I...'

'Tigger,' said Rosemary, 'has been a bit off his food.' She nodded at a great striped creature that sat like a hen, hatching malevolence. 'Do give him something to make him eat, there's a dear. Oh, I'm so happy.' She was off down the path to Jalil's car. Jalil got up, as if with effort, and made a kind of warbling noise to Vythilingam, a throaty descending half-octave of chromatics, nodding not unpleasantly the while, and he lumbered out. The cats surveyed Vythilingam expectantly, without unease, as though he and they were opposing teams lined up.

In the airport stood Crabbe, leaning on the bar, the only white in a sea of brown. Malays were everywhere – on the bar-stools, drinking iced water or nothing, round the rattan tables, promenading up and down as in an opera interval, crouching miner-like, sitting tailor-wise, standing, leaning, surrounding Crabbe with a faint smell of warmth, a hint of musk. They had come from the town and the kampongs to watch the pilgrims return. They had come early, time being no object. Crabbe caught stern fishermen's faces, the resigned droop of poor farmers, the up-looking open-mouthed wonder of the children, perhaps seeing white skin for the first time but too polite to chatter about the prodigy. The women sailed along or sat in long patience. Hard light defined their clear flat features, the extravagant sarong-patterns, flowing in from the naked airstrip, accentuating the pallor that gazed back at Crabbe from the mirror behind the bar. Crabbe looked at himself: hair now riding back from his forehead, the beginnings of a jowl. He looked down at his paunch, pulled it in, flinched at the effort, let it out again. He thought it was perhaps better to be middle-aged, less trouble. That growing old was a matter of volition was a discovery he had only recently made, and it pleased him. It was infantile, of course, like the pleasure of controlling excretion, but transitional periods of history had always appealed to him most – Silver Ages, Hamlet eras, when past and future were equally palpable and, opposing, could produce current. Not that he wanted action. But, of course, that was true of the phase, and that was why the phase didn't last long. Imagine a Silver Age *Æneid*! And so let middle age come, him grow paunchy, no longer show his profile to women, stand at the Club bar rather than dance. He felt he wanted nothing further from women, anyway, his first wife dead, his second wife having left him. His state appealed to him – an Education Officer waiting to hand over to the brown man he was training, in the twilight of British rule. Suddenly, poking with a match the swollen cigarette-ends in the water of the ash-tray, he saw all this as romantic – the last legionary, his aloneness, the lost cause really lost – and instinctively he pulled in his paunch, stroked down his hair to cover the naked part of the scalp, and wiped the sweat off his cheeks. He caught the eye of a Malay girl in the mirror and smiled wanly, hiding his teeth. She moved out of the mirror, smiling though, and in something like good humour he ordered more beer.

Moving through the crowd towards him he recognized Syed Omar, plump, bothered, in a shirt with a newspaper pattern. Syed Omar nearly tripped over a child on the floor, apologized to the mother, greeted a Malay farmer with a false smile and then stood by Crabbe, saying:

'Where is the bastard? Has the bastard arrived yet?'

'Which particular one?'

'The Tamil bastard, Maniam, the one who has tried to have me kicked out.'

'Have a drink, Omar.'

'A large brandy. I'll get him, I promise you I'll get him. Last night was no opportunity. I know they have told you, and everyone else, that I am a coward, but I was prevented last night, you see, prevented from having my revenge.' He gripped his left breast, on which rode the printed photograph of a Hollywood star, and said: 'I swear to you in the name of God I will get him.' Crabbe read, on the right sleeve of Syed Omar's shirt: 'Thanksgiving dinner is an unalterably American tradition. It must include roast turkey, cranberry sauce, creamed onions, potatoes, pumpkin and mincemeat pies. Since Pilgrim times, housewives have seized upon the stuffing of the bird as the one ingredient in this time-honoured menu upon which they can exercise their individuality.' Then Syed Omar's hairless arm began. 'Those creamed onions sound good,' said Crabbe. He looked inside Syed Omar's sleeve to see if the article continued on the hem.

'Yes, there is muscle there,' said Syed Omar, 'enough muscle for that hairless bastard.'

'Some Tamils went upstairs to the control tower,' said Crabbe. 'I don't know this Maniam, but I'm quite sure I heard Arumugam's voice. He must be on duty up there.' Syed Omar's brandy came and he sucked at it impatiently. After the sucking came tilting and pouring. He put the glass down.

'I'm going up there,' he said.

'Oh, look here, Omar,' said Crabbe. 'Don't start anything, not today. The pilgrims are coming back, you know. It's not my job to start telling you all about peace on earth and what-not, but I do think you might let it rest. You can't do any good.'

'To him it is not good I intend to do.'

'Forget it. Have another drink.'

'No. While I am hot, while I am angry I will go.' He resisted the friendly restraining hand of Crabbe, which clutched the article on Thanksgiving Day stuffings, and went. Crabbe watched the swim-suited film star on his back disappear in the crowd. He heard Syed Omar's voice, arguing with the Chinese official at the Customs barrier. He heard the voice climbing the stair to the control tower. Then he heard the approaching plane. The Malays heard it too and some went out to the airfield fence and the car park, straining their eyes to the west, where Mecca lay, whence, logically, the aircraft must appear. But its noise soon began to fill the south.

It landed in the outfield and slowly, clumsily approached, on fat, flat tyres. And now the Malays began to unleash their excitement. They wanted to get at the pilgrims, to touch them, to receive a blessing. The fence was too high to climb, so they moved – excited but orderly – towards the open sliding door which led to the control tower, the Customs barrier, the aircraft itself. They had already seen a Malay go through that doorway.

A Chinese, thin, nervous, in whites and a peaked cap, barred their way, saying: '*Tidak di-benar masok.* You cannot come in here.' They pressed on. The Chinese said: 'Please go back. It is not allowed.' He tried to slide the door shut. His voice held no authority, he was nervous of kampong Malays; some had already got through, the door could not be closed. And now Crabbe left the bar, nervous himself because the plane had brought back from Singapore what he believed to be a precious burden. Crabbe tried to cut his way through the crowd, which yielded softly, courteously enough. Taller than any member of that crowd, he could see quite clearly the Chinese official do a foolish thing; he feebly pushed at the foremost man; with pork-defiled paws he laid hands on a Muslim. The glory of Mecca already shone on these simple folk. They could see, the foremost of them, the loose Arab robes, the Bedouin head-dresses, the turbans of the pilgrims who were already coming from the aircraft, hands ready to greet and bless though clutching cooking-pans and parcels. The kampong people would have no infidel between them and the glory. The official went to the wall, in a posture of crucifixion. His fellow leaped the documentation counter to help, shouting: 'Back! Back!' He was entangled in Malays, and one fisherman thrust him aside like a curtain. The bar-boy ran out for a policeman. Now Crabbe was among them, shouting too. Him they would not harm. Englishmen being, though infidel, yet the race of past District Officers, judges, doctors, men perhaps, in their time, more helpful than otherwise, powerful but mild. Yet the more eager of the kampong people were already approaching the pilgrims with loud religious greetings, the rest of the crowd was following, and, ahead of the pilgrims, was the Chinese boy with the brief-case whom Crabbe had come to meet. They would tear him out of the way, they would knock him down and trample on him and perhaps his brief-case would be kicked away, lost, stolen. Crabbe ran, panting with middle age, and pulled the Chinese boy from the pilgrims and those who greeted them and embraced them, dragging him to a safe nook at the foot of the control tower stairs. The boy was frightened, saying: 'What is this? What is happening?' But Crabbe had no breath.

Clamour before them, fright and anger and joy, and now clamour above and behind them. Syed Omar was being kicked down the stairs by Dr Sundralingam, and Arumugam's voice was piping loud. One sees so much violence on the screen, in the papers, reads about it, accepts it as part of the pattern, but one is always shocked anew by the aspects which records can't catch: the smell of sweat, the blood moving on the face, the hoarse breathlessness, the cracked voices speaking strange words. Sundralingam was nearly shirtless, Syed Omar's hair spiky, one of his sandals missing. But the Hollywood actress still posed in smiling languor, and the Thanksgiving Day article was intact. Syed Omar lay, his hands over his head, like a camel-boy in a sandstorm. The pilgrims passed him, some smiling gravely at what they considered to be an extravagant posture of veneration. Sundralingam and Arumugam were back up the stairs, perhaps to tend Maniam's wounds, Arumugam squeaking, Sundralingam panting and rumbling.

The crowd was clearing. The police had arrived, Malay police, standing shyly, doing nothing. The Chinese officials were drinking brandy in the office, quacking clipped indignation. The incident – if it was an incident – was over. 'But this won't do,' said Crabbe, 'this won't do at all.' Syed Omar, groaning, sat up. His forehead was bruised and his lip swollen. He felt his teeth methodically, one after the other, with a vibrato movement of finger and thumb.

'It won't do, will it?' said Crabbe. Syed Omar made a throaty animal noise. 'Come and have some more brandy.'

The place was fast emptying of Malays: the pilgrims had arrived, it would soon be time for mosque. At the bar were a few passengers and also Emir Jalil, asthmatic but benign, and Rosemary Michael, pouting and unhappy. Crabbe, his arm on the Chinese boy's elbow, gave greeting. Syed Omar followed, twisting an eye-tooth like a violin-peg.

'Was fight,' said Jalil. 'We miss big fight.' Rosemary pouted. 'She not very happy. She think he send ring, but he not send ring. He not send anything.'

'Oh, shut up, Jalil. Shut up, shut up.' Rosemary began to cry quietly into her gin. Jalil chuckled silently.

'How unhappy we all are,' said Crabbe. But the Chinese boy seemed neither unhappy nor happy. He waited, courteous, his brief-case under his arm.

'The pig,' said Rosemary in gargoyle anger, 'the bloody pig. He wants to hurt me, that's all.' She cried. 'Look at it,' she cried, 'and I thought it was going to be the ring.' She cried bitterly. Syed Omar handled his back in a rheumatism pose, groaning. Crabbe examined the object, rising jauntily from bunched brown paper. It was a ghastly metal model of Blackpool Tower, its silver paint chipped. The note said "Thinking of you here, Rosemary. Having lovely time at college. The men will not leave me alone! Janet.'

'Janet da Silva,' said Crabbe. 'That's nice of her.'

'And two dollars' Customs charge,' wailed Rosemary. Suddenly she stopped wailing and looked at Crabbe in a kind of horror. 'Oh,' she said. 'I mustn't stay here. People will talk. Take me home, Victor. It's all right for you to take me home. Joe said so.' She cried again at the name. 'And I thought I was engaged. It would have been all right if I was engaged.'

'You stay here,' said Crabbe soothingly. 'You have a nice drink with Jalil and Omar. They'll look after you. Robert and I have things to talk about.'

'Take me home, Victor.'

Some of the passengers began to look at Crabbe with curiosity and envy. Crabbe said: 'No. You stay here. Jalil will take you home. Come on Robert, we'd better be going.'

Jalil watched them go out together. He said: 'He not like women any more. He like only boys.'

'Oh, shut up, Jalil.'

'He like Chinese boys. Me, women I like.'

2

The violins carried their sawing figuration up to the last chord, while the viola hinted at a sort of parody of the main theme and the 'cello plunged right down to its dark bottom string. Then the tape wound to the end, broke free and swished round and round. Crabbe switched the machine off. The silence contained an image of the quarter as a whole, clear and yet as though seen from a distance, so that the shape was more apparent than the details. The first movement had seemed to suggest a programme, each instrument presenting in turn a national style – a gurgling Indian cantilena on the 'cello, a kampong tune on the viola, a pentatonic song on the second violin and some pure Western atonality on the first. And then a scherzo working all these out stridently, ending with no resolution. A slow movement suggesting a sort of tropical afternoon atmosphere. A brief finale, ironic variations on a somewhat vapid 'brotherhood of man' motif. It was a young work, boyish in many ways, but it held together, it was coherent, and it showed remarkable technical competence. Its composer had never heard a live quartet, knew the masterpieces only from broadcasts and gramophone records, and some of the orchestral works he studied – Mahler, Berg, Schönberg – he had never heard at all. And yet the score of the symphony Crabbe held on his knee – neat spidery dots and lines and curves, showing a kinship to Chinese calligraphy – seemed confident in its handling of orchestral forces on a perhaps too large scale, its use of unorthodox combinations – xylophone, harps, piccolo and three trumpets, for example – and its precise signals of dynamics and expression.

Crabbe looked at Robert Loo – Mozart, Beethoven, Brahms, Loo – and felt irritated that he showed no sign of either pride or humility, no excitement, not even a craftsman's dissatisfaction. He merely examined closely one of the parts of his quartet, saying: 'The second violin played A natural instead of A flat. That was my fault. I made a mistake in copying it out.'

Crabbe asked yet again: 'What did they say about it?'

'As I told you, not very much. Mr Crispin said that the violin writing was awkward in places, Mr Sharpe said that one piece of treble stopping on the viola was impossible, Mr Bodmin said he enjoyed the 'cello part.'

'And what about Schwarz?'

'Oh, yes. Mr Schwarz asked to be remembered to you. He said it was a pity that Mrs Crabbe married, because she had a promising musical career. And he said he was sorry she died.'

Just like that. Musicians could be inhuman, musicians were mere functions, themselves instruments played by music. But, after all, he was only eighteen with an eighteen-year-old's callousness; after all, English was only his second language and he was deaf to its harmonics. But Crabbe saw Robert Loo now as a rather dreary boy, not very intelligent, emotionally less mature than he should be, strapped to a talent which had, quite arbitrarily, chosen him, driving him to teach himself to read music at fourteen, pore over Stainer, Prout, Higgs, Forsyth at sixteen, at eighteen produce two works which, Crabbe thought, were probably works of genius. Crabbe felt sure that he did not really like Robert Loo. He was hurt at the lack of gratitude (surely it could not be shyness, when one saw the large confidence of the symphony?) for the trouble Crabbe had taken and the money he had spent – air fares to Singapore and back, pocket money, hotel expenses, the letters to Schwarz and to the people in Radio Malaya who had arranged the recording. Robert Loo took all this calmly, as he would take everything else Crabbe gave. And the things given would have to include a scholarship to

England – wangled God knows how – and a performance of the symphony.

'What did Schwarz say about the symphony?'

'Very crude, he said. But he only seemed to be interested in the string parts. But he copied some of the themes out in a manuscript book. He said he would show them to his friends in England.'

'Did he indeed? That means we can look forward to a tasteful little piece called *Oriental Sketchbook* or *Souvenir de Singapore* or something equally corny. Schwarz always did like other people's themes.'

'It doesn't matter.'

'Well, we don't seem to have got very far. I know we've got a recording of the quartet – that's something – but I thought Schwarz might have been willing to do more. He's got all the contacts. I haven't any. But minor musicians are never very generous, I suppose. Music's a corrupting art.'

'I don't understand that.'

'You don't have to. Just carry on composing, that's your line. Keep out of the world of action. I'll try the British Council and the Information Department and – oh, there are lots of things I can do. We'll get that symphony performed. We'll get you to Europe.'

No thanks. Robert Loo said only: 'I don't think my father will let me go to Europe. There is the business, you see, and I am the eldest son. He wants me to take a course in accountancy.'

'I'll have to speak to your father again. Doesn't he realize that you're the first real composer that Malaya's produced?' Crabbe took a cigarette from the box on the gin-table. 'But I don't suppose it can mean very much to him. A lot of people think that music's just there, like bananas, and anyway it's not a thing you can write down on paper.'

'He did not want me to go to Singapore. He said it was the wrong time, because it was the end of the month and it's then that we send out the bills. Now they will be late. But I told him that you insisted because the Schwarz Quartet would only be there for two days and it was a good idea for me to see Mr Schwarz.'

'And so your father blames me?'

'Oh, yes, to some extent.' Robert Loo returned Crabbe's look calmly. 'It makes it easier for me, you see. I don't want too much trouble. I cannot work if people are shouting all the time. But you are in the Government and my father thinks you can give orders to people, and you don't mind having trouble.'

'Look here, Robert,' said Crabbe in irritation, 'what the hell do you want?'

'I want to have a quiet life and to go on writing music.'

'Don't you want to study? You're clever, but you don't know everything. How can you at your age?'

'I can find things out in my own way. I've had to do that. The headmaster at school knew I was composing but he didn't help. Nobody wanted to help. And so I can help myself.'

'I see. The white man let you down, did he?'

'I didn't say that. I meant that they thought what I was doing was mad. They left me alone and let me do it. I suppose I should be grateful for that. But they didn't want to help.'

'Haven't I helped?'

'Oh, yes.' Robert Loo sounded neither convinced nor convincing. 'Thank you,' he added, formally. 'I've heard my quartet. It has been a confirmation. I knew it would sound like that.'

'But have you no curiosity? Don't you want to hear a live orchestra? There are fine ones in Europe, you know.'

'Of course. I've heard them on records. I suppose it would be nice,' he added, again without much conviction.

'Don't you want to hear your own symphony?'

'Oh, but I've heard it.' Robert Loo smiled patiently. 'I hear it every time I look at the score.'

Crabbe got up from the arm-chair and walked the sitting-room. He entered a belt of sun from the window,

434

gazed out for an instant on palms and Government houses, wondered dizzily for a moment what he was doing here anyway, and poured himself gin and water.

'So,' said Crabbe to the boy's back – thin nape, plastered hair, white shirt soiled by travel – 'you just write for yourself, is that it? You don't think other people might want to hear it. And you've no particular love for your country.'

'My country?' The boy looked around, puzzled.

'Some day Malaya might be proud to have a major composer.'

'Oh, I see.' He giggled. 'I don't think that will happen.'

'Music can be a big thing to a country finding itself. Music presents a sort of image of unity.'

'I don't see that.'

'No, I suppose not. Your job, as I say, is just to compose. But even a composer has to have some sense of responsibility. The best composers have been patriotic.'

'Elgar is not one of the best composers,' said Robert Loo, with a boy's smug dogmatism. 'His music makes me feel sick.'

'But look what Sibelius has done for Finland,' said Crabbe. 'And de Falla for Spain. And Bartok and Kodaly ...'

'The people of Malaya only want American jazz, and ronggeng music. I am not composing for Malaya. I am composing because I want to compose. Have to compose,' he amended, and then looked embarrassed, because he had admitted to a demon, an obsession. He had very nearly been seen without his clothes.

'Well, I'm going to do my best anyway,' said Crabbe. 'For this.' He pointed with his cigarette at the manuscript of the symphony. 'And you're going to be made to study. I shan't rest till I see you on that boat.' But, of course, he reflected, one never knew whether one was doing the right thing. He might go to London and, corrupted by a new ambience, produce music in the style of Rubbra or Herbert Howells. In Paris he might be emptied of what was peculiarly his own and filled with Nadia Boul-

435

anger. He needed advice, and the only person Crabbe could have trusted to give it was dead. Crabbe knew enough about music to be satisfied that Robert Loo's voice was his own and, at the same time, Malaya's. The waltz and the ländler were never far from Schönberg's music; similarly, Robert Loo had sucked in hundreds of polyglot street songs with his mother's milk, absorbed the rhythms of many Eastern languages and reproduced them on wind and strings. It was Malayan music, but would Malaya ever hear it?

'Tell me, Robert,' said Crabbe roughly, 'have you ever been with a woman?'

'No.'

'Do you have any strong affection for anybody or anything, apart from music?'

The boy thought seriously for half a minute and then said. 'I think I like my mother. I'm not sure about my father. I used to be very fond of my youngest sister.' He paused, evidently trying honestly to add to a catalogue whose exiguity seemed to chill the warm room. 'I quite admire cats,' he said. 'There is something about them,' he added, 'which . . .' He could not find the words. 'Which is quite admirable,' he ended lamely.

'Poor Robert,' said Crabbe, coming over to him and pressing his very thin shoulder. 'Poor, poor Robert.'

Robert Loo looked up at Crabbe, genuine bewilderment in his small lashless eyes.

'But I don't understand, Mr Crabbe. I just don't understand. I have everything I want. You must not feel sorry for me.'

Manian had missed the plane. Deliberately. He could have walked on to it without help, he could have survived the journey without undue nausea – despite the kick in the belly – but he was ashamed and angry about the spreading purple under his left eye and the big blubber upper lip. Now he lay on the spare bed in Dr Sundralingam's house, saying: 'What would they say if I walked into the office like this? They might laugh. And the C.P.O. might be angry about it. He might think that I had been fighting.'

'So you have been,' said Sundralingam, 'in a way.'

'I swear to God I never touched him. But he took unfair advantage. He got me against the wall under the Greenwich Mean Time. And there were all the instruments and radios and meters there. Supposing I had been responsible for breaking one of those things. And the aircraft was coming in too. He took very unfair advantage.' The words came out half-chewed, what with the swollen lips and the stiff jaw.

'We fought for you,' squeaked Arumugam. 'The first duty is to a friend.' He still had growling in his ears the noise of the Australian pilot asking for wind velocity and saying: 'What the hell goes on there?' The fight had been broadcast, must have been heard in half the aircraft and airports of the peninsula.

'I can't remember the best treatment for a black eye,' said Sundralingam. 'I have been on this yaws campaign for so long now that I've forgotten my general medicine. Some people recommend a beef-steak, but I don't think that is quite right for a Hindu. Perhaps a pork chop?'

'Not enough blood,' squealed Arumugam. 'You've got to have blood.' He sounded like young Master Pavy playing Hieronimo.

'Cold water compresses,' prescribed Dr Sundralingam. 'And stay in bed. I'll send an official note to Pahang.'

'Will I be safe here?' chewed Maniam fearfully. 'Will I be safe alone here during the day?'

'My servant's here all the time,' soothed Sundralingam. 'He's a Malay, but he's all right.' The Malay stood by the sick-room door, hunched, heavy-jawed, simian, the end-product of God knew what mingling of Achinese pirates, aboriginal bushmen, Bugis bandits, long-hut head-hunters. He took in Maniam's broken face with relish, crooning to himself.

'If he definitely loses his job,' quavered Maniam thickly, 'if that happens, he may try to get me again. He may send axe-men. Perhaps I should have got the plane after all.'

But he saw in vision the laughing office and heard the questioning C.P.O. 'No, I couldn't. I see that. I'll have to stay here. But do spread it round that I've gone back. Say I've gone back by train.'

'Yes, yes, yes.'

'Vythilingam let us down,' shrilled Arumugam. 'He was cruiserweight champion at Calcutta University, you know. He would have made very short work of our Malay friend.'

'Where was Vythilingam?' asked Maniam.

Parameswaran, the schoolmaster, who had been sitting still and pipe-puffing at the foot of the bed, now removed his pipe. 'I can guess where he was,' he said. 'I will bet he was at the house of my colleague, Miss Rosemary Michael.'

'But he took his black bag with him.'

'That is a blind,' said Mr Parameswaran. 'He is ashamed of it being known that he goes there.' He put back his pipe and nodded several times. Middle-aged, grizzled, with a comfortable paunch, a golf-tee sticking like a nipple through his shirt-pocket, he was the photographic negative of any suburban Englishman. He was a Jaffna Tamil, but also a Rotarian. He knew lines from the *Golden Treasury*, apt for after-dinner speeches, and even a few Latin tags. He was not quite trustworthy, he trembled on the brink of a bigger world than Jaffna. Not that he had travelled very far. 'A home-keeping youth,' he was fond of saying. Also he had a wife and family (the wife disappointingly, above suspicion – pure red-blooded Jaffna) and he never came to the agapes. But he seemed to know about them and he seemed not to approve.

'Are you sure of this?' asked Sundralingam. 'It sounds quite unlike Vythilingam.'

'No. It is only a guess. But she has mentioned his name in the staff-room to other ladies as being one of the innumerable men who have been seduced by her charms.'

'Seduced?' echoed Arumugam in a squeal of horror.

'Seduced by her charms. That is what she alleges. She alleges it about many men, however.'

'I don't know the lady,' munched Maniam. 'I've never met her.'

'Oh, she is, I suppose, not unattractive,' said Parameswaran. 'She is not to my taste, however. She is also Christian and immodest.'

'She's of very low caste,' said Sundralingam. 'I knew her parents in Kuala Hantu. She knows I knew them, but still she once told me that she was a Balinese princess. On another occasion she said she was partly English and partly Spanish. It was her Spanish blood, she said, that made her get brown so easily. In England, she said, she was quite pale. She despises her own race, you see.'

'Of course,' admitted Maniam, 'she must be ashamed of her caste.'

'There is too much of all this,' said Sundralingam. 'Too much despising of one's own race and too much despising of other people's races. That is going to be the big trouble of Malaya. You take this man Syed Omar. He has a mad hatred of Tamils. He imagines big Tamil conspiracies against him. Now he will nurse an even bigger hatred than before because of the thrashing he got today. But I personally did not want to thrash him, nor, I think, did Arumugam. You will believe me, perhaps, when I say that I felt sorry for him when he lay at the foot of the stairs. It was pathetic to see him with his poor cheap shirt on, all decorated with film stars, lying there in his blood.'

Maniam protested through his sore mouth. 'Look what he did to me. He deserved all he got.'

'Yes, yes. But he should never conceive these hatreds. The trouble starts in his poor misguided brain.' There were glistening pin-points in Sundralingam's large brown eyes.

'There is no occasion to get sentimental,' said Parameswaran. 'I know the family and the family is rotten. I've taught seven of Syed Omar's children. The eldest, Hassan, is the lowest of the low. Lazy, truculent, dishonest, with his long hair and his American clothes, slouching round the town with companions equally low. There's a core of shiftlessness about the Malays. They know they're no good, but they try to bluster their way out of things. Look what they're trying to do here. They're trying to close the bars and the dance-halls and the Chinese pork-market, in the sacred name of Islam. But they've no real belief in Islam. They're hypocrites, using Islam to assert themselves and lord it over people. They pretend to be the master-race, but the real work is done by others, as we know, and if Malaya were left to the Malays it wouldn't survive for five minutes.'

'True,' said Arumugam's piccolo. 'Without the Malays it would be a good country perhaps.'

'The name Malaya is unfortunate,' said Sundralingam. 'But it may yet get back its original Indian name of Lang-kasuka. That has already been proposed. Still,' he added, 'if only people would get on with their work – the Malays in the kampongs and in the paddy-fields and the Indians in the professions and the Chinese in trade – I think all people could be quite happy together. It is the ambition of the Malays which is going to prove so tragic. For them,' he smiled, not without compassion.

'Trouble is coming, certainly,' cried Arumugam. 'But if we all stick together there will be no difficulty.'

'That,' said Sundralingam, 'is why we mustn't have Vythilingam doing anything he should not do. I do hope there is nothing in this rumour of yours,' turning to Para-meswaran.

Parameswaran, intent on puffing, raised one eyebrow and grimaced non-committally.

Maniam suddenly cried in terror, 'I have just thought,' he said. The Malay servant lounged by the door, not yet sated of the innocent entertainment Maniam's ruined face provided. 'I have just thought,' he repeated. 'This servant of yours will talk in the market about my being here. And perhaps Syed Omar will find out.' He tried to get out of bed, but Parameswaran immediately sat on his left foot, at the same time pushing him back to the pillow and say-ing: 'Don't be a coward, man.'

'I think,' said Maniam, 'I had better get back to Pahang after all. I can get the evening mail train. I can steal quietly to my house. Nobody will see.'

'Don't be a coward,' repeated Parameswaran. 'Aren't you ashamed? Fancy being frightened of a Malay.'

'I am no coward,' declared Maniam from his ventrilo-quist's mouth. 'I just don't want any more of his dirty tricks.'

'There is no need to worry,' said Sundralingam. 'If Syed Omar tries it again we will set Vythilingam on to him. If you worry you will make a slow recovery. Try to relax.'

Arumugam called over the Malay servant. '*Mari sini*,' he piped. The Malay servant shambled over, mouth open. 'Do not say this *tuan* is still here,' ordered Arumugam in bad Malay. The servant nodded, his eyes all animal won-der. 'Keep quiet about it and you will get ten dollars.'

'You see,' said Sundralingam. 'Nobody will know.'

'Your old man knocked that Tamil about so much that he can't go back to Pahang.' Thus Idris bin Sudin, friend of Syed Hassan. 'He's staying at that doctor's place.' Has-san guffawed.

The four friends sat in a hot drinking-stall, drinking warm orange crush, beguiling the tedium of the long Sab-bath afternoon. The stall was one of many in the Park of Happiness, a palisaded Venusberg set in mud. There was an open-air stage for ronggeng dancing, a foetid cabaret with a beer-bar, two houses of ill-fame disguised as coffee-shops, and a tattered cinema-screen whereon was shown the endless epic of the Javanese shadow-play. The Sabbath would not end till sunset; till then these vessels of pleasure must lie becalmed. Only the wooden and attap huts were sleepily open for the thirsty, each Chinese *towkay* dozing over his abacus, the Malay waitress sulking over an old copy of *Film*.

Of the four, only Azman wore full uniform. It was his turn to wear it. The drainpipe trousers, the serge jacket with the velvet collar, the string tie – they had bought these cheap from a hard-up private of the Special Air Service. Hamzah, Hassan and Idris were cooler, but far less smart, in jeans and shirt-sleeves rolled up to the armpits. This, however, was the authentic tropical dress. But a greater solidarity with their brothers of the West was the desire of all of them, and each was only too eager to sweat and stifle in these romantic garments, the armour of a new chivalry. But they were fair with each other: nobody ever tried to jump the roster. Soon each would have a suit of his own; in the meantime the common hair-style identified them as one tight cell of an international movement: it flowed down the neck, a congealed glossy stream, trickled over on to the cheeks in side-burns, and tousled lustrously on to the low brown forehead. Each had a pocket-knife, for whittling wood or carving cryptic signs on café tables, not yet used for any dire purpose, though the flash of the blade – shooting up from the handle at the touch of the spring – made a brave and intimidating show. They were boys who wished nobody any real harm, romantics who were distrustful of order, preferring colour to form. They liked to muddy the lake, the enemies of complacency, their music the siren of the police-car and their own hearts pounding up the dark alley.

'He got him,' said Hassan. 'He's tried to get my dad thrown out of his job, see, and that's why my dad bashed him. Beat him up, knocked his teeth out, kicked him in the guts, made him spew his liver up, smashed his nose.' He gleefully performed a pantomime of violence and his friends chortled.

They spoke a vivid back-street Malay, unlike the new cold instrument of the Government, with odd splashes of film American to raise their fantasies to a more heroic level. So now Idris interjected cries of 'Yer yeller! Yer chicken!' while two-fisting the edge of the table. Azman said: 'He roughed your dad, though. Your dad was kicked down the stairs.'

'He didn't do it,' said Hassan. 'It was the other two. That doctor and him with the girl's voice.' He fluted a parody of Arumugam and then suddenly felt depressed. His dad shouldn't have done it. It was old-fashioned, that business of punching and kicking, it was Wild West. And his dad was an old man, too. It was a bit undignified. Fish-hooks, knives, razors, bicycle-chains – that was different, that was modern. He felt ashamed of his dad and wanted to change the subject.

'Move on,' he suggested. 'Let's move on. There's nothing happening here.'

'*Ai, mek!*' called Hamzah. The sulky girl came to their table. She was pretty and her low-cut *baju* showed a delicious expanse of warm milky-brown neck. The boys teased her, guffawing rawly. Hamzah said: 'I gave you five dollars. I want some change.'

'Not paid yet.'

'Have paid. Gave five dollars.'

'Correct, correct!' cried the others. The girl went over to the dozing *towkay*.

'Eh, *towkay*, have paid five dollars. Want change!'

'She says not paid. You pay one dollar.'

'Have paid. Change!'

The cameras whirred. Azman, teeth bared, frowning in menace, moved to the counter. Very slow, perfectly timed, only the pad of his feet on the sound-track. No music until the knife slowly drawn, raised, pointed, the click and hiss of the shot-out blade down-beated furious chords. 'All right, bub. We won't argue. We don't argue, see?' Menacing, caressing tones. 'Keep your money. Chicken feed. But we don't come here again, see?' On the last hissed word the knife-point flashed at the towkay's throat. Cut. Put that in the can. Out they all went, jovial, happy laughing boys, waving a cheerful good-bye. Man, that was acting.

Hands in pockets, they kicked odd stones along Ibrahim Avenue, singing in authentic American. Trishaw-drivers coasted up and down the long glaring road, looking for custom, but the Friday siesta still held. 'Only you,' sang the boys, 'can make my darkness bright.' Hassan saw,

443

suspended before him, from the hot blue sky, retreating from him as he walked, a microphone. With kissing lip he let the words trickle into it.

'There he is,' said Azman, stopping in mid-song. 'One crab leaving the house of another.' The Malays of this State called all Chinese 'pincered crabs', an allusion to their chopsticks.

'The wonder boy,' said Hamzah. They stood, waiting for Robert Loo to approach. His father's shop was near the Park of Happiness. He walked somewhat mincingly, thin, in soiled whites, his brief-case under his arm. They had been in the same English school together, all of them, but Robert Loo had left a year ago, complete with certificate. The Malay boys plodded on, moustached in the Third Form, the gap to the Fourth just too wide for them to leap. They resented this, a slur on their adulthood. They resented the treachery of the examiners, obviously in the pay of the Chinese. They resented the Chinese, too rich and too bloody clever. They resented Robert Loo's brief-case. They resented Robert Loo.

'I know what you got in there,' said Idris. 'You been robbing a bank. That's the loot.' His Malay was too rapid and too colloquial for Robert Loo to follow. Robert Loo smiled urbanely.

'It's the documents,' said Hamzah. 'He's selling them to the enemy.'

'Open up,' said Azman in American. 'It's de F.B.I.'

'It's only music,' said Robert Loo, smiling. 'You wouldn't be interested.'

'I can't hear anything,' said Hamzah. 'I must be going deaf.' He put his hand-cupped ear to the case, dropping his jaw like a stage zany. Laughter.

'Music on paper,' said Robert Loo. 'Music has to be written, you know.' He spoke in Malay, and, having spoken, realized the absurdity of what he had been saying. The Malay word for 'music' was *bunyi-bunyian*, which just meant 'sounds'. And of course, you couldn't write sounds. 'I must be getting along,' he said.

'Let's see,' said Hassan. He whisked the brief-case from under Robert Loo's arm and the straps not being fastened, plunged in his hand and pulled out the bulky score of the symphony.

'Music,' he said. 'So this is music.' Holding the score away from mock-long-sighted eyes, pushing out his belly, he began to sing:

> 'Only yew-ew-ew-ew-ew
> Can make the darkness bright.'

'All right,' said Crabbe's voice. 'Cut it out.' Robert Loo just stood there, showing neither anxiety nor relief, not even contempt. 'Give it back,' said Crabbe. He was breathing angrily, his hands on his spreading hips. 'Go on, give it back.' Sullen and puzzled, Hassan obeyed. All the boys were sullen and puzzled. What was all the fuss about anyway? After all, it was only a joke. And this was Friday anyway, and everybody was off duty, and Crabbe had no right to play the schoolmaster. A trishaw-driver hovered, interested. Crabbe called him. 'Go on,' he said to Robert Loo. 'Get up. He'll take you home.' He gave the driver a fifty-cent piece, still seeming to suppress anger. Robert Loo climbed aboard, his restored brief-case under his arm, silent. 'Go now,' said Crabbe to the driver. '*Pergi, pergi.*' The Malays watched, puzzled, as Robert Loo, without a backward glance, was borne jerkily away. Crabbe waited till the trishaw was a hundred yards down the road. He turned to the Malays, saying:

'What sort of a country are you trying to make? You've got it in for everybody. For the Chinese and the Indians and the Eurasians and the white men. You can't see a Chinese without wanting to persecute him. You want to knock the stuffing out of the Tamils. I suppose you'd like to have a go at me, wouldn't you? For God's sake, grow up. You've all got to live together here, you've got to ... Oh, never mind.' He went back to his house.

'*Apa ada?*' said Hamzah. 'What's the matter with him?' The others shook their abundant locks in puzzlement.

Slowly enlightenment blossomed in Hassan's head. 'I think I know,' he said. He was ignorant, but he had seen something of the world. 'But perhaps I'm wrong,' he added.

'What is it, then?'

'I don't know.'

'What did you say you knew for, then?'

'Ah, never mind.'

They threw a few harmless pebbles at Crabbe's car, parked in the porch, and then went on their way, singing. Hamzah suggested going to the Chinese gramophone shop, to pretend to want to buy some records. A good idea, they all agreed. That would pass the time nicely. Then sunset would be presented formally by the muezzin, the whores and hostesses appear, and adventure tremble in the shadows.

Lim Cheng Po come to tea. He took it in the English manner, enjoyed the tomato sandwiches and the fruit cake, said in his Balliol voice: 'A pity one can't get crumpets here.' He was a solicitor from Penang. He came over for two days every two months to see how his assistant, who handled the cases this side of the peninsula, was faring, occasionally to take a case himself. He also visited his friends, of whom Crabbe was one. To Crabbe he was a breath of home, an unalloyed essence of Englishry. He was Henley and Ascot, vicarage garden parties, tepid bitter, Gothic railway stations, London fog, the melancholy of a Sunday summer evening. He was plump and not unhandsome, his Chinese blood hardly apparent. Only the eyes were lashless and small and the nose slightly squat. But the English voice and the English gestures swallowed up these details, as a pan of gravy soup might swallow up a shred of shark's fin. He talked now about the troubles in Penang that had just ended – terrorism and a curfew on that one-time peaceful island – and the troubles that, so he had heard, were soon to start in Perak. He had been warned to cancel his trip to Ipoh.

'Who starts it all?' asked Crabbe.

'My dear chap, that's rather a naïve question, isn't it? It just starts. Some blame the Malays, others the Chinese. Perhaps a Malay shakes his fist at a Chettiar money lender and, for some obscure reason, that sets off a brawl in a Chinese cabaret. Or a British tommy gets tight in K.L. and the Tamils start spitting at a Sikh policeman. The fact is that the component races of this exquisite and impossible country just don't get on. There was, it's true, a sort of illusion of getting on when the British were in full control. But self-determination's a ridiculous idea in a mixed-up place like this. There's no nation. There's no common culture, language, literature, religion. I know the Malays want to impose all these things on the others, but that obviously won't work. Damn it all, their language isn't civilized, they've got about two or three books, dull and ill-written, their version of Islam is unrealistic and hypocritical.' He drank his tea and, like any Englishman in the tropics, began to sweat after it. 'When we British finally leave there's going to be hell. And we're leaving pretty fast.'

'I didn't know you thought of leaving.'

'Yes. Back to London, I think. I have my contacts there, and my friends.'

'The Malays are to blame, in a way,' said Crabbe. 'I'm disappointed in them.'

'Blame the middle-class Malays, if you like, the political men, but don't blame the kampong blokes. For them the world hardly changes. But there should never have been a Malay middle-class, they're just not the middle-class type at all. They're supposed to be poor and picturesque, sons of the soil.'

'And yet,' said Crabbe, 'I don't like to think that it's impossible to do something about it, even at this late hour. There are lots of things we neglected in the past, but you can't really blame anybody. Perpetual Malayan summer, perpetual British rule. No seasons, no change. It was all very satisfactory, it worked. And, remember, there was no imposition of British rule. People just came because the

447

British were there. Even the Malays. They flocked in from Sumatra, Java . . .'

'Just what do you think can be done?'

'Oh, I don't know . . . A bit of adult education, I suppose. Of course, religion's a problem, a nasty problem.'

'What a thing to say,' grinned Lim Cheng Po. 'What do you want? Nineteenth-century rationalism? Voltairian deism? We're living in a religious age, you know. I suppose Anglicanism might be a solution. An Anglican Malay is an interesting conception, I admit.

'One could inculcate a little scepticism underneath the outward conformity,' said Crabbe.

'That's pure Anglicanism, isn't it? And what would you do about your food taboos? It's always those that seem to spark off your massacres. It's just a hundred years since that nasty business in India. The Hindus and Muslims don't seem to have developed a more rational attitude towards beef dripping and swine fat, despite a century of the civilizing British.'

'One could spread the light a bit. One could discuss inter-racial marriage, for instance . . .

'Discussion won't get you far.'

'It's a beginning,' said Crabbe. 'Discussion is a beginning. Even just getting all the races in one room is something.'

'They're talking in Singapore about an Inter-racial Liaison Committee. It won't do any good.'

'Oh, Cheng Po, you're such a wet blanket. You're so damned Chinese.'

'Chinese?' Lim Cheng Po looked offended. 'What do you mean by that remark?'

'You've got this sort of divine disdain. You don't really believe that all the other Eastern races are anything more than a sort of comic turn. That absolves you from the task of doing anything for them. You've no sense of responsibility, that's your trouble.'

'Oh, I don't know,' said Cheng Po slowly. 'I've got a wife and children. I've got a father living in Hounslow.

I give tithes of all I possess. I work so damned hard precisely because I've got a sense of responsibility. I worry about my family.'

'But you've no nation, no allegiance to a bigger group than the family. You're not quite so bad as Robert Loo, admittedly. He's completely heartless. His only allegiance is to the few quires of manuscript paper I bought him. And yet, strangely enough, it's he who's convinced me that something can be done in Malaya. It may be pure illusion, of course, but the image is there, in his music. It's a national image. He's made a genuine synthesis of Malayan elements in his string quartet, and I think he's made an even better job of it in his symphony. Not that I've heard that yet. I must get it performed.'

Cheng Po yawned. 'Music bores me,' he said. 'And your liberal idealism bores me quite as much. Let Malaya sort out its own problems. As for me, I've got enough to think about without getting mixed up in other people's politics. My youngest daughter has measles. My wife wants a car of her own. The curtains of the flat need replacing.'

'Pale tea under the mulberries. A single flower in an exquisite bowl. Ideograms, painted with superb calligraphy, hanging on the walls,' mocked Crabbe.

'If you like. Cricket on Sunday. A few martinis between church and luncheon. Gladioli by the open window. That's your world as much as mine.'

'You'll never understand us,' said Crabbe. 'Never, never, never. Our mandarin world's dead and gone, and that's all you're looking for in England. You think the old China will stay alive in England, but you're wrong. It died forty years ago. I'm a typical Englishman of my class – a crank idealist. What do you think I'm doing here in early middle age?'

'Deriving an exquisite masochistic pleasure out of being misunderstood. Doing as much as you can for the natives' (he minced the word like a stage memsahib), 'so that you can rub your hands over a mounting hoard of no appreciation.'

'As you please. But I've got a year left before I have to

go home, and I'm going to try something useful. Though what exactly I don't know...'

The western sky put on a Bayreuth montage of Valhalla. Towards it the Muslims would now be turning, bowing like Zoroastrians to the flames. It was genuinely the magic hour, the only one of the day. Both men, in whites and wicker chairs on the veranda, facing the bougainvillea and the papaya tree, felt themselves begin to enter a novel about the East. It would soon be time for gin and bitters. A soft-footed servant would bring the silver tray, and then blue would begin to soak everything, the frogs would croak and the coppersmith bird make a noise like a plumber. Oriental night. *As I sit here now, with the London fog swirling about my diggings, the gas fire popping and my landlady preparing the evening rissoles, those incredible nights come back to me, in all their mystery and perfume* ...

Rosemary Michael entered without knocking, bearing her ridiculous beauty on clacking high heels across the sitting-room. 'Victor!' she called and then said: 'Oh, you've got a visitor.'

'This,' said Crabbe, 'is my friend Mr Lim, the last Englishman.'

'How do you do?'

'How do you do?'

Rosemary listened to the Balliol intonation with hope and wonder. She could see, with her woman's miss-nothing eyes, that Mr Lim was not an Englishman, but she was fluttered and confused by his voice. She was also a little tight. Clumsily she gave Mr Lim her choicest, most exclusive Sloane Square vowels and, sitting down, a ravishing glimpse of her round brown knees.

'Have you come to live here, Mr Lim?'

'No, no, just a visit. My home's in Penang, actually.'

'Do you know London, Mr Lim? I love London. I positively adore it.'

'Yes, I know London.'

'Do you know Shaftesbury Avenue and Piccadilly Circus and Tottenham Court Road?'

'Oh, yes.'

'And Green Park and Hyde Park Corner and Knightsbridge and South Kensington?'

'Yes, yes, the whole Piccadilly Line.'

'Oh, that's marvellous, isn't it marvellous, Victor, just marvellous!'

Lim Cheng Po was an Anglican and a cricketer, but he allowed a small Chinese man to enter his brain and, with a tiny smile, hint that Crabbe's mistress had arrived and it was time to be going. He said:

'It's time I was going. Thank you for your hospitality, Victor. Good-bye, Miss . . .'

'Rosemary. My friends call me Rosemary.'

'An exquisite name and highly appropriate in its exquisiteness.'

'Oh, Mr Lim.' She became all girl. As Lim Cheng Po drove off she stood by the window to wave to him, and then came running back to the veranda.

'Oh, Victor, what a very nice man. And what a lovely voice. Do you think he was attracted to me?'

'Who could fail?'

'Oh, Victor,' she simpered. Then she pouted, kicking her shoes off as she lay back in the chair, saying: 'I've been getting tight with Jalil.'

'What will Joe say about that? Somebody's bound to write and tell him.'

'I don't care. To hell with Joe. He let me down very very badly. I expected a ring and all I got was that horrible Blackpool Tower. I'll never forgive him.'

'But he didn't send the Blackpool Tower.'

'No, he didn't send me anything. Oh, Victor, Victor, I'm so unhappy.'

'Have a drink.'

'But I'm hungwy.' A pathetic little-girl's rhotacismus.

'Have some dinner then. I dine at seven-thirty on Fri-

days. Have a drink first.' Crabbe shouted to his servant:
'*Dua orang!*'

Rosemary had several gins and then became reminiscent. 'Oh, Victor, it was so marvellous. They had me on television wearing my *sari* and gave me a whole ten minutes' interview, and then next day you should have seen the letters I received. Fifty, no, a hundred offers of marriage. But I said I'd wait for Mr Right even if I had to wait all my life and . . .'

'And now you've found Mr Right.'

'No, no, Victor. I hate him for treating me like that, me, who could have married a managing director and an M.P. and a bishop and, oh, yes, a duke, Lord Possett his name was.'

'This duke?'

'Yes. But I kept myself to myself. I sent back their flowers, and their mink coats, and I never slept with anyone, Victor, not with anyone, and I could have slept with anyone I wanted to. I was a virgin till Joe came along, Victor, and I gave him everything. Everything.' She screwed back the tears and looked inhuman. 'He's had everything from me.'

'And now you hate him.'

'I love him, Victor, I love him. He's the only man in the world.'

'You mean you enjoy sleeping with him?'

'Yes, Victor, I love him. It was love at first sight.'

Rosemary made a hearty dinner. There was roast chicken and bread sauce and Rosemary vigorously swamped everything first with ketchup and then with Lea and Perrin's, refreshing her plate with these condiments frequently through the meal. With her coffee she had a Cointreau and then a Drambuie. Then she lay back in her arm-chair.

'Victor,' she said, 'is it true what Jalil says?'

'About Joe?'

'No, about you. He says you don't like women any more.'

'I like some women.'

'He says you prefer little boys.'

'Does he, by God?'

'Everybody's talking about you and this Loo boy. That's what Jalil says.'

'Really?'

'Is it true, Victor?'

'No, Rosemary, it's not true. He writes music and I'm trying to help him.'

Rosemary giggled. 'I don't believe that.'

'Please yourself, my dear.'

Rosemary fell into a posture of deeper languor, limbs spread, voice sleepy.

'Victor.'

'Yes?'

'Are Chinese the same as Englishmen?'

'Yes.'

'How do you know?'

'It's just something one takes for granted.'

'Oh.' The coppersmith bird hammered slow minutes.

'Victor.'

'Yes?'

'You can if you want to.'

'Can what?'

'Oh, Victor, Victor.' She sat up and cried vigorously. 'I'm so lonely, so lonely, and nobody in the world loves me.'

'Oh, yes, a lot of people love you.'

'It's true what Jalil says about you, it's true, it's true. I've never been so insulted in all my life.'

'Perhaps I'm not as susceptible as His Grace.'

'I'm going home, going home.'

'I'll run you.' With great eagerness Crabbe went to the porch where his car was parked.

'I'll walk home, thank you. I don't want a lift in your car. I hate you. You're as bad as the rest of them, and I thought you were different.' She put on her shoes angrily and clomped out with her ridiculous beauty, leaving the room no emptier than before. Crabbe settled down to an evening's reading.

3

The job of Victor Crabbe was, appropriately, a somewhat crepuscular one. He, as acting Chief Education Officer of the State, was slowly handing his post over to a Malay. Sometimes this Malay, a youngish man with a most charming smile, would be deferential to Crabbe, showing great anxiety to learn, at other times he would enter the office as though, in sleep, an angel had visited him, teaching him all in painless hypnopaedia. Then the Malay, still with great charm, would tell Crabbe what to do – settle a strike of pupils in a local school; write a letter in courtly English to the Director, apologizing for the loss of a receipt voucher; sign the letter; send out for coffee and curry puffs; generally make himself useful. The Malay himself would sit at the desk and smoke cigarettes through a Ronson holder, telephone Chinese contractors and give them hell – first announcing his official title loudly – and occasionally brood dramatically over thick files. So Crabbe demoted himself to the rank of the Duke in *Measure for Measure*, a god whom all men might touch, and wandered round the schools of the town to give funny lessons to the children ('the white man always make us laugh, make very happy'). Sometimes he would try to do more spectacular good, and this morning he visited the State Information Officer with schemes in his mind.

Nik Hassan liked to be called 'Nicky'. It was *chic* to have an English name in his circle. His friends Izuddin and Farid were called 'Izzy' and 'Fred' and Lokman bin Daud usually signed himself 'Lockman B. Dowd'. Very big-executive, very American, and a quite legitimate transliteration of the Islamic name. Nik Hassan had tried to mould his personality round the connotations of his nickname, and he sat like the boss of a gambling-joint behind his harmless official desk, moustached and smart in the busy hum of the air-conditioner. Crabbe greeted him and smiled dutifully at the counter-greeting. Nicky and Vicky. Education and Information. The comedy-team of the new Malaya.

First Crabbe told Nik Hassan about Robert Loo and his symphony.

'You see,' said Crabbe, 'apart from its aesthetic value – and I'm not really capable of judging that – it's just come at the right time from the political point of view.'

'Music? Politics?'

'Yes. You know, of course, that they made Paderewski Prime Minister of Poland. Paderewski was a great pianist.'

'A bit before my time.'

'This symphony could be played as a big gesture of independence. "We in Malaya have thrown off the shackles of an alien culture. We have got past the nose-flute and the two-stringed fiddle. We are adult. We have a national music of our own." Imagine a full orchestra playing this symphony in the capital, imagine it on the radio – "the first real music out of Malaya", imagine the pride of the average Malayan. You *must* do something about it.'

'Look here, Vicky, the average Malayan won't care a damn. You know that as well as I do.'

'Yes, but that's not the point. It's culture, and you've got to have culture in a civilized country, whether the people want it or not. That's one of the stock clichés – "our national culture". Well, here's the first bit of national culture you've ever had: not Indian, not Chinese, not Malay – Malayan, just that.'

'What sort of a thing is it?' asked Nik Hassan suspiciously. 'Is it modern – you know, Gershwin stuff? Has it got a good tune? Do you really think it's any good?'

'I'm pretty sure it's good. I've not heard it, but I've read it. Whether it's good or not is not really the point, anyway. It's a work of art, it's extremely competent, it's probably highly original. But don't expect sound-track slush. It's not got a good tune anywhere in it, but it's terrifically organized, tremendously concentrated. That boy's a genius.'

'Chinese, isn't he? Pity about that.' Nik Hassan made a sour gangster's face. 'Pity he's not a Malay. Though, of course, he could use a what-you-call . . .'

'Pseudonym?'

'That's right, a Malay pseudonym. It might carry a bit more weight. After all, everybody knows the Chinese are clever. We're a bit sick of hearing it. We're just dying for a Malay genius to turn up.'

'Well, here's a Malayan genius for you. I'm pretty sure about that.'

'If,' said Nik Hassan, 'if it's any good, they might think about playing it as part of the Independence celebrations. There's no harm in trying. It shows that we're alive in this State, anyway. Do you think he'd object to having a Malay what-you-call? You know, something like Abdullah bin Abdullah? It would make quite a bit of difference up in Kuala Lumpur.'

'He,' said Crabbe, 'wouldn't mind in the slightest. He's quite devoid of ambition. But, frankly, I should mind very much. Why should he hide his real name, when he's got as much right to the country as you people have? Damn it all, the Chinese have done as much as anybody, if not more, to, to . . .'

'All right, all right,' said Nik Hassan. 'I know. My dear fellow, I know. But it's a question of the line, you see. It's a line we've got to try and follow. I mean, to be honest, the line of the Chinese is supposed to be trade, isn't it? Money in the bank and a fleet of Cadillacs. The Malays have got nothing. The time's come to give them something. And, now I come to think of it, a little thing like this . . .'

'Not so little.'

'It could be a boost. A boost. Is there any singing in it? You know, patriotic Malay words. That would help a good deal.'

'There's no singing. But,' said Crabbe, 'yes. Yes. It's an idea. A choral finale. Beethoven did it; why not Loo? It might sell the work to the public.'

'And if you could get the orchestra to stand up at intervals and shout "*Merdeka!*" Now that really would sell it. They really would make it political. That would get it performed.'

'But,' said Crabbe, 'it's a kind of desecration. You can't do that to a serious piece of music.'

'You're keen on getting it performed, aren't you? You said it was a political thing. Well, make it really political and it might bring the house down. But,' said Nik Hassan, 'is it good? Really good? I don't want to look a bloody fool, sending off a lot of tripe to K.L. I mean, we've only got your word for it.'

'You can take my word.'

'Well ...' Nik Hassan handed Crabbe a small Dutch cigar and lit it for him. 'We're friends, aren't we?'

'Oh, yes, Nicky, of course we're friends.'

'If I were you, Vicky, I'd stop seeing that boy.'

'So people are talking, are they?'

'What did you expect? It was a godsend to the gossips. What with your wife going back to U.K. and you not knocking about with women these days, and then your always having this lad around at your place.'

'Not so often.'

'Often enough. Anyway, they're talking. And, you see, it puts me in a funny position when I do this job for you ...'

'I'll send the damned thing off myself.'

'And then, if it's any good, they'll want to know how I came to miss it. All I want is for you to tell me, quite honestly ...'

'You can go to hell, Nicky. Why should I have to go round denying rumours? If people want to think what they presumably are thinking, I can't stop them. I'd be a fool to try and stop them. And you think it, too, don't you?'

'No, not really. I mean, it's a bit queer you're not bothering with women – that Rosemary girl's after you all the time; I've seen it – and damn it all, I'm broad-minded enough, there's a lot of it goes on, but I mean, it's your own affair isn't it? You don't want to start bringing anybody else into it. It makes it awkward for other people, you see.'

'My dear, dear Nik . . .'

'Nicky. They're talking about giving me the big Australian job. Have you heard that?'

'No. Congratulations.'

Nik Hassan did not seem really pleased. 'They're watching me, that's the trouble. Watching me all the time, seeing if I'm up to it. And you're never sure whether you're doing the right thing. If you drink, you're going against Islam, and if you don't drink you've got no social talents. If you've got more than one wife, they say that won't go down well in a Christian country. But, damn it.' He turned, face wrinkled and arms wide in perplexity. 'Look at my wife, just look at her. A woman like her was all right in the old days. You know, no drink in the house and chewing *sireh* after meals and belching in public. And not a word of English. And not a damn word of decent Malay conversation for that matter. How am I going to get on, running a big department in Canberra? How are we all going to get on?'

'You'll get on all right, Nicky. You worry too much.'

'Perhaps I do. But supposing somebody here starts telling K.L. that I'm helping – Sorry, I won't say that. And supposing somebody says that I'm not helping to cultivate local talent. Where am I? Oh, Vicky, won't you tell me the truth?'

'There's nothing in it, Nicky. Nothing at all. You can trust me.'

'I used to. Now I don't think I can trust anybody. We're starting our independence in an atmosphere of mistrust.'

'But I've no stake in the country, not any more. It's only

people like me who can really help. And it's that very mistrust I want to do something about. I want to try and cultivate better inter-racial understanding, for one thing. I had an idea last night, in bed. Why can't we have meetings, say, once a week, to try and mix up the races a bit more? We could discuss things, we could have dances, we could encourage young people of different races to go about together. We need a headquarters of some kind, of course. You know, a sort of club-house.'

'Where's the money coming from?'

'Well, how about the Residency? The British Adviser's finished here. That place isn't doing anything any more. We could have a subscription, we could make money on dances and shows. A caretaker and a couple of gardeners wouldn't cost much. Of course, there's the electric light bill . . .'

Nik Hassan shook his head. 'Nothing doing. The Sultan's taking that place over.'

'But, damn it, he's got three palaces already.'

'Now he's got four. That's out. There's one thing though. I just thought of it. You remember Wigmore, the planter?'

'Yes, poor old Wigmore.' Wigmore had been shot by Communist terrorists on his own estate. A fat harmless man, thirty years in the country.

'His will has been proved. He left twenty thousand dollars to that Tamil girl he'd been living with. He also left twenty thousand dollars to the state.'

'What for?'

'God knows he'd got enough out of the state in his lifetime. It's a vague sort of bequest. It just says: "for the improvement of the lot of the people". He was a vague sort of chap. Drank too much, of course. If only he'd left it to a dog's home or the hospital, or something. Now there's got to be a committee to decide how the money's to be used.'

'Who's on the committee?'

'Oh, we'll all be on it. We'll argue about it for a year, I

suppose. And then the Sultan will claim the money for a new car. Of course, it's not a lot.'

It wasn't a lot, but it was enough. Enough to send Robert Loo to Europe. Enough to buy a building of some sort. Enough for both?

'Vague as you say,' said Crabbe.

'Very vague. The Sultan could interpret a new car as improving the lot of the people, I suppose. The people are happy seeing their Sultan happy. I wonder if I could do the same thing about getting an honourable divorce? Buy my wife off, marry a new one – *soignée*, educated, a drinker, somebody who'd go down well in Australia.'

'There's always Rosemary.'

'Oh God, man, she's too bloody dark. Black as the ace of spades. I can't stand the touch of a black skin.'

Robert Loo was wishing he had more practical knowledge of the violin. The muse had told him peremptorily to start writing a violin concerto; that is to say, she had hurled themes at him, fully orchestrated, with a solo violin soaring and plunging in the foreground, and this solo part insisted on being rich in harmonics and intricate multiple stoppings. Behind these sharp images was a bigger, duller image which would only be fully realized when the work was complete, for it was the image of the work itself. Robert Loo sat in his father's shop, neatly sketching first and second subjects for the first movement, the music-paper next to the abacus, occasionally laying down his pen to move his fingers – with the grace of one playing an instrument – over the wire-threaded wooden balls with which the amounts of bills were calculated.

His father's shop had started by selling provisions; then it had seemed a natural transition to install tables and chairs and turn the place into an unambitious restaurant; later a first-class licence brought in a scant drinking clientèle allowed by law to sit over their spirits till midnight. It meant a long day for everybody in the family, but nobody really minded: a Chinese *towkay*'s children will, with the thriftiness of the race, find fulfilment and diversion where they can. Life does not go on in some place remote from the coffee-urn and the cash-till; life is where you live.

Robert Loo sat, quite content, behind the counter, against a cyclorama of tins of milk and corned beef. The shop was bright with sunlight, trade calendars, drink posters, the yapping of two younger brothers who made up orders for delivery. A solitary Malay blew into a saucer of black coffee. Outside were all the colours of the East and all the languages. But Robert Loo gazed on a world more real and shot with sounds and colours more intense than any the shop or the street could show. Two flutes in counterpoint, the sudden citrous tang of the oboe – the auditory images were so vivid, the thrill of creating them so deliriously pungent, that the outside world was burned up. Only when he heard a faint snatch of whistled song outside, or when a younger brother shouted in Cantonese– making a tone-pattern that was on the edge of music – did Robert Loo frown. It annoyed him that the sounds that impinged on the outer ear could get so much in the way. He was not yet perfect; only when he was like Beethoven, deaf, would he have final control. But he could feel satisfied with the conquest and the grinding into the dirt of the last four or five years. The small library of musical textbooks in his bedroom, the help from Crabbe, the original spark when that other Englishman, Ennis, had shown him music for the first time and saturated him in the sound of his records and his piano–he could look back tolerantly on all this. He was free now, or nearly free. He was on his own.

But something about this violin concerto disturbed him. It was a visual image of the soloist that kept obtruding. He could *see* the concerto being performed, and, though the orchestra was shadowy, the soloist's fingers, the soloist's arm were terrifyingly vivid, as in a dream of fever. The fingers were strong and long, the arm was bare, and a kind of technicolor blue quivered behind. The bowing arm, the fingers on the strings, and then the violin itself, polished

461

brown, and the soloist's chin pillowed on it. Startled, he saw it was a woman. Who? Was this some memory of a film, of a photograph in a book on musical celebrities? Open-mouthed, he stared at the big luminous mirror opposite. It was set too high to reflect him, it carried only a shelf of looking-glass beer and the moving blades of the ceiling-fan. But this letting-in of the three-dimensional world exorcised the vision. He returned to his manuscript paper, sketched a passage of solo treble-stopping, and then suddenly the long fingers were on his, showing him that this was impracticable, that you could not, see, stretch the little finger so far when, see, the first finger had to be down here . . .

His father, Loo Kam Fatt, walked in from the street. 'It comes now,' he said. He spoke no English, he had no Christian name. He did not object to his eldest son's speaking English – that helped trade – nor did he mind that some of his children had become Christian – that could do trade no harm. Trade and gambling and a woman occasionally – that was a man's life. He had just won forty dollars on a bet that the fever-bird in the tree opposite Ng's shop would, this time, sing a passage of four notes, not three. There were thus, in him, the rudiments of a concern with music. This morning's win was a good omen for a new enterprise of his, an enterprise he had kept secret, for, coming as a surprise, it might give his eldest son all the more pleasure, because this too was to do with music, and he knew that his eldest son liked music, or certainly had used to like it. Loo Kam Fatt beamed, rubbed his towkay's paunch, and said again: 'It comes now.'

Robert Loo's three younger brothers were at the doorway, quacking with interest. The railway van had drawn up. Four men in the back of the van – Malays in shorts and torn vests – began easing out the crate, shouting instructions, counter-instructions and warnings in glottal monosyllables.

'Is what?' asked Robert Loo. But he knew what it was and felt slightly sick. One just doesn't think, doesn't expect. He should have known this would happen. He watched the crate dumped beside the counter.

'Will see now,' smiled his father. 'Will like.'

Half the street seemed anxious to help. Hashim, the idiot boy from the barber-shop next door, was pulling out nails with a crowbar. Grindingly, laths of wood yielded to brown and yellow hands, a wrenching and screaming of twisted nails fanfared the discovery of the treasure beneath. This coyly revealed itself in a growing flank of red metal as the wood came away, the shavings and masses of packing paper. Soon it stood naked and shining in sunlight, stripped of its crude cerements, a portent and a god. 'Ah,' breathed the crowd.

'Lift to corner,' said Loo Kam Fatt. To corner was pushed with happy groans and sighs, with padding of splay feet. Scavengers appeared, shining eyes darting swiftly and slyly about, to take off the wood that strewed the floor. The workers stood back to survey with awe the glass and metal music-god, whose name indeed, sprawled on its belly in flowing chrome, was APOLLO. A hundred black plates behind heavy glass, as if draining into the mysterious hidden viscera below, stood firmly on their edges. Loo Kam Fatt uncoiled the omphalic flex, saying, in tiny frustration: 'This plug not right size. Must change.' Out of air appeared a smaller plug and a screwdriver. 'Man come from Singapore,' said Loo Kam Fatt, 'after six month. Change all records. This very good.'

'Ah!' The god had begun to breathe, to glower with a glowing blue eye. This was the moment. Loo Kam Fatt, like a priest with a host, reverently put into the creature's tiny mouth a ten-cent piece. 'Now must choose.' He turned benignly to his eldest son. 'You choose, Number one son must choose. Son who like music must choose.' With gentle smiles, with the sense of an occasion, the crowd made way for the number one son. This was ceremony. This was religion. Robert Loo, his heart like a heavy breakfast, came forward to greet the god, to command it, to be sacrificed to it. Blindly he pressed a button. Inside, a turntable

463

in a staff-car, moving slowly up the rank of records, searched, failed to find, moved down again. Silently it ordered a record to come forward. The record obeyed as silently. Then it fell flat on the turntable, transfixed, and the tone-arm came down. What had been a military formation became a harem. And now . . .

Joy lit all the Asiatic voices as noise filled shop and street. Drums and red-hot brass, a wedge of saxophones bursts from the god. The god gave greeting. 'Will bring trade here,' shouted Loo Kam Fatt in his deafened happiness. 'Park now closed down. No Muslim girls allowed dance now. No beer to be sold there. People here all the time. Come to hear music. Music very good thing.'

Ten-cent pieces shone everywhere in eager waiting fingers. What was rice, what was coffee compared to the solace of art? The solo violinist waited, her bow at the ready, smiling patiently but clearly puzzled at the delay.

This music crept by Syed Omar in Police Headquarters, sitting puzzled while others were going out to lunch. He had just typed out orders to the police, instructing them that, on high religious authority, they must arrest any Muslim found drinking intoxicants, any Muslim woman plying the trade of dance-hostess, café-waitress or lady-of-the-town, any Muslim – man or woman – found in the act of committing or being about to commit or having committed adultery. They must also report any Malayan of any race or religion whatsoever found assisting or encouraging any Muslim to commit these crimes. A good morning's work, and he felt he deserved a small beer in Loo's *kedai* round the corner. But he was puzzled by a letter, a copy of which had just been given to him by the C.P.O. This letter was addressed from Police Headquarters, Kuala Beruang, Pahang; it was a glowing eulogy of Syed Omar, and it was clearly signed by Maniam. What puzzled Syed Omar was not the eulogy but the address. Why should a letter from Maniam be addressed from Pahang when Maniam was still living, convalescent, in the house of Dr

Sundralingam? He pondered for a while and then concluded that Maniam must be afraid of further vengeance from Syed Omar and thus pretended to be many miles away. The insincerity of the eulogy, of course, was to be taken for granted. It had done Syed Omar no good, for the C.P.O. had rightly divined that it was insincere and that Syed Omar must have behaved to Maniam very badly for Maniam to have written of Syed Omar in such a way. But Maniam's attempt at convincing Syed Omar that he was already back in Pahang must signify that Maniam feared that to write such a letter would cut no ice (that was the expression) with Syed Omar, and that Syed Omar was still expected to nurse hatred for Maniam and even to express that hatred in the usual manner. Probably this woman Neelambigai was now waggling her bottom in some better job than the one Syed Omar still held. So Maniam was making no sacrifice, not even humiliating himself – for it was well known that Tamils would sell their mothers, their honour, their souls to save their skins or to advance themselves. They did not know the meaning of the word humiliation, except when it applied to others, such as humble and deserving Malays like Syed Omar. Syed Omar read the letter through again:

... and so I wish to correct any false impression that may have arisen concerning my attitude to Tuan Syed Omar's character and work, owing to a quite superficial misunderstanding that arose between us shortly before my departure. I consider that Tuan Syed Omar is efficient, honourable and loyal, anxious always to give of his best, courteous to his superiors and considerate to his inferiors. I came to have the highest regard for his excellent qualities during the few months in which I worked in your Headquarters. With the coming of Malayan Independence Tuan Syed Omar should go far, as it is men like him that the country needs. ...

Still, thought Syed Omar, still, this would come in useful. It was a good testimonial, even if it was insincere. But, then, all good testimonials were insincere. That stood to reason. But now Syed Omar felt a greater anger rising to think that he had to rely on the specially insincere praises of a cowardly Tamil. He felt murderous towards Maniam. He folded the copy of the letter with great care and put it into his thin wallet. It was a good testimonial. He would get Maniam.

Rosemary Michael heard loud music coming from Loo's shop as she tripped along Jalan Post Office. Men gaped at her, whistled after her, made unequivocal gestures at her. Teeth gleamed from Indian shops in frank concupiscence. A fat Sikh constable tried to pinch her bottom. So it was always; the whole male town did homage to her beauty. Complacently she accepted the homage. The music from Loo's shop blared for her, the very sun, which she far out-did in radiance, showered its hot gold on her alone.

Oh, but she had cause for radiance. It had come, it had come at last. Well, in a sense it had come. Joe had sent her a cheque for twenty guineas. The guineas made it seem rather like a fee, but of course perhaps Joe was really being considerate and ensuring that she had a nice even number of dollars – one hundred and eighty exactly. Joe wanted her to buy an engagement ring with the money. He couldn't send one, he said, because he wasn't quite sure what size to get. And she would know better than he what kind of stones and what kind of a setting to choose.

The money, of course, was not really enough for an even moderately good ring. But perhaps Joe was not really being mean; perhaps the poor boy didn't really know how much a really good ring should cost. Perhaps he was just saving money for their little home. Still, it meant that Rosemary would now have to dig into her small reserve in the bank (she had called there on the way home to find out exactly how much it was). She must buy something really good, something commensurate with the gifts she had showered on Joe: the record-player, the golf-clubs, the Leica and the car radio. Joe must not appear less generous than she.

Joe had said in his letter that it was very likely he would

be coming back to Malaya. With this import firm or export firm or whatever it was. Then, he said, she could transfer to a school in the town where he would be working, for it would quite definitely not be this town. Rosemary did not feel too happy about this. She had thought of herself living in a nice house in Hampstead or Chiswick, the beautiful mysterious Oriental princess who had married a commoner, who was not above preparing special dishes – exotic and spicy – for her guests, but who otherwise queened it over a household of stolid British servants. Or, if not that, at least in Malaya she would be a mem, yawning all day over books from the Club library under the two fans of the sitting-room. She had not thought of herself as *working* after her marriage. But, said Joe, marriage itself would have to wait, because this firm did not believe in its employees marrying coloured women. He would only stay with this firm for a time and then he would, perhaps, get a good government job. After the initial mess-up of Independence they would be crying out again for expatriates like Joe.

Coloured women indeed! *She* a coloured woman! She walked, head up, with an indignant hip-swing past Crabbe's house, round the corner, down the lane to her own quarters. Across the road she saw a car parked, broiling in the sun. Jalil's car. Coloured woman! She was a European, at home in Paris and London, fond of European clothes and European food with plenty of Lea and Perrin's. She loved the snow, tea and crumpets by the cosy fire, fog and primroses. She was also, of course, a Javanese princess, or Balinese, or Hawaiian. But she was not a coloured woman. Hadn't her rich tan always been admired in England? Weren't Europeans always trying to get sunburnt? What did they mean by calling her a coloured woman?

She sailed on her exquisite legs down the narrow drive to her house. Inside sat Jalil, wheezing, stopping this to hum a chesty chromatic scale when he saw her. He did not, of course, stand up. The room was full of cats, flowers –

bougainvillaea, canna, lilies, hibiscus, orchids – and the music of bees. Rosemary said:

'I've told you not to come here. Jalil, I've told you again and again. What are people going to think, you coming here all the time, what are they going to think?' But this was mere ritual, performed without conviction, Jalil said:

'Come eat, come drink, come make jolly time.' This was the now traditional liturgical response. Two cats came to greet Rosemary.

'Oh, don't be silly, you know I can't, oh, you're ridiculous. Oh,' she said, 'what lovely orchids.'

'Orchids I not bring. Orchids Crabbe send round.'

'Crabbe? Victor Crabbe?' Rosemary picked up the card and read: 'To an exquisite lady these somewhat less exquisite blooms.' 'Oh,' cooed Rosemary, 'oh, how sweet. Oh, the darling.' She read the signature: 'Lim Cheng Po.'

'Crabbe send round. Come from Penang, from Chinese man.' Jalil chuckled and wheezed.

Rosemary sat down in the other armchair. 'I'm engaged, Jalil,' she said. She had always thought her announcement of this would be rather different – leaping in the air, loud song, Jalil discomfited. Then, of course, she remembered the Blackpool Tower. It was Jalil who had spoiled everything last time.

'He not send ring. I know he not send ring. I watch every day.'

'He's sent the money for the ring.'

'How much he send?'

'Ooooh, two hundred pounds.'

'Not believe.'

'All right,' said Rosemary, 'if you don't believe me you can come with me when I go to buy it. You can take me to Penang. There.' She pouted at him, triumphant.

'We go Penang make jolly time.'

'I'm engaged, you see, Jalil, engaged. And you said he never would.'

'He never marry. He tell me he never marry.'

'Well, now I can prove you're a liar. We're engaged to

468

be married, and that means we're going to be married. So there.'

'He not marry.'

'Oh, what lovely orchids,' said Rosemary again. She frowned, hearing Lim Cheng Po's voice, so English, so refined, so very English upper-class. And often she had had to tell Joe about his aitches. Well, perhaps not often, but on one or two occasions. What was the matter with her? Absently she stroked the cat with the Disraeli face. (It was on the table, sniffing the orchids.) 'I wonder why,' said Rosemary. 'I wonder why he sent them. He's only seen me once,' she smirked.

'He want sleep. Cheaper than hotel when he come from Penang.'

'Jalil, what a filthy, filthy thing to say. I hate you. Get out, go on, get out.' But Jalil chuckled and pushed down a cat from his lap. He said:

'He not marry you. He got wife in Penang. Only me marry you.'

'I'd never marry you, never, never. I'd rather marry Vy than I'd marry you. You're horrible.' Jalil rolled with pleasure at this tribute. He said:

'You want marry European. I European. I got three wives only. Is room for one more. If you not marry me I find other wife easy. Plenty Malay women want husband. I not care.'

'Oh, Jalil, you'll never understand. Never. What would I do at Christmas? I don't want Hari Raya. I don't want Deepavali. I don't want Muslim feasts or Indian feasts. I want Christmas. I want turkey and Christmas pudding and mince pies and mistletoe and snow and carol-singers. I want a Christmas tree. I want my presents!'

On the last word she broke down and her face became inhuman. Crying, indeed, on what should be the second happiest day of her life. She wept, forgetting that it was lunch-time. Jalil chuckled gently.

Vythilingam worked quietly and efficiently through the

469

long hot afternoon. He inoculated six dogs against rabies, diagnosed feline enteritis in a cat, inspected the sheep in the experimental sheep farm, confirmed that a pet monkey was suffering from pneumonia, went out in the Veterinary Department van to a kampong to treat buffalo for a new strange skin cancer that was spreading ferociously, came back to the surgery and there wrote a letter to Rosemary Michael.

His speech impediment prevented him from making a dignified oral proposal. On paper he could be fluent, even eloquent, and the stilted phrases of his letter pleased him. '... If you consent to become my wife I promise to fulfil honourably all the duties of a husband. Though not wealthy I have an adequate income, and I pledge myself to endeavour to support you in the manner to which you have been accustomed.' The dead hand of eighteenth-century Indian administration, which in no wise could be tempered by the reading of translations of Marx and Chou En Lai, this lay on his prose style. 'I remain, your sincere admirer, A. Vythilingam.' He sealed up the letter, would take it round to her house, would stand there blinking nervously while she read it.

It was necessary that he should marry soon. That morning a letter had come from his mother in Ceylon, enclosing yet another photograph of an eligible Jaffna Tamil girl. Vythilingam sneered in hatred. How well he understood the agony of that bourgeois creation of that bourgeois dramatist, pride of that detestable country. 'Frailty, thy name is woman.' He had seen quite recently a Tamil film version of *Hamlet*, over-long by about two hours, but crisp enough in its way, despite Ophelia's eight songs and the dance of the grave-diggers. That scene in the bedchamber with its rumble and gurgle of bitter Tamil vilification, the black Queen scared on the bed, that was art, that was words. But there was the question of conditioned response. If his mother should come to Malaya for a holiday, as she had once or twice threatened to, if she brought with her some girl such as this black pudding with teeth

on the photograph, it would not be easy to sustain an attitude of intransigence. He knew all too well what would
happen. Before he knew where he was he would be sitting
for his wedding photograph in his best suit with a marriage garland round his neck, tied for life to his mother's
choice. His mother must not win; that was certain. Free
will was, of course, an illusion, but one must at least seem
to exercise it.

When it was time to go, Vythilingam packed his black
bag with medicaments for Rosemary's cats. He wondered
whether the time had yet come to make her a present
of another animal. A sheep? Too large. A monkey? Des-
tructive. A parrot? Psittacosis. A cockatoo? He went out
to his car and found two men already in it, Arumugam
and Sundralingam. They greeted him jovially.

'Hallo there! You've been a long time!'

'Hail!' squeaked Arumugam, witch-like.

'We're having a party,' said Sundralingam. 'In my
house. Maniam's a great deal better.'

'I must go . . .' began Vythilingam. 'I have to go to . . .'

'My car's in the garage,' said Sundralingam, 'being ser-
viced. You can drive us home.'

'But first I must . . .' Vythilingam shrugged a nervous
chin towards his black bag. 'I have to . . .'

'No,' said Sundralingam firmly. 'We know these little
games, ha ha. You're coming with us. We'll look after
you.'

'We'll look after you,' said Arumugam, in canon at the
double octave. And then, as if a Shakespearian mood were
on him, as, indeed, it had been on Vythilingam, he began
to sing:

> 'Where the bee sucks, there suck I . . .'

'But . . .' attempted Vythilingam.

'Get in,' said Sundralingam, firmly but not unkindly.

The music-god sang loudly to the shop and the street.
Children stared with awe into its hypnotic eye, and many

beer-drinkers, more than ever before, sat tranced and wrapped in a warm overcoat of tropical night and thumping great music. Old Loo, standing by the refrigerator, looked pleased.

'Look at him there,' said Idris, sweating gently into the suit, 'cotton-wool in his ears.'

'Who?' asked Azman, tonight in tropical dress.

'Him. The wonder-boy.'

The four guffawed. Robert Loo indeed sat as though trying to weave silence round himself, two tufts of cotton-wool ineffectual valves, for the noise dwindled from a lion to ants as it met the soft obstacles, but, marching tinily rather than leaping with spread claws, still entered. The maddening image of the violinist, her dress changed, for some reason, from blue to green, was more maddening than before: she would stand there forever, her bow ready, her cheek caressing the polished wood of the fiddle, waiting, smiling, waiting. Robert Loo opened the woollen doors and the raging golden ocean entered. It was no good trying to fight.

'Here's your dad,' said Azman to Hassan. Syed Omar had entered, gay in his newspaper shirt, black slacks, sandals. He greeted his son, saying: 'So this is how you waste your time.'

Syed Hassan grinned, embarrassed by his father's loudness of voice and dress, and mumbled: 'Not doing any harm.' Syed Omar loudly ordered a brandy and ginger ale. Loo Kam Fatt said: 'Cannot do. You Malay. Police say no.' Syed Omar said. 'I am the police. You can serve me. You must serve me. I am the police.'

Syed Omar sat with the four boys and sipped his brandy and ginger ale. 'And what kind of a get-up is that?' he said, sneering at Idris's suit. 'What are you supposed to be?'

'Nothing,' said Idris.

'That's right, nothing. That's all you do, nothing. Trying to look like gangsters. You too,' he said to his son. 'I've seen you round the town wearing that same get-up.

What's happening to the Malay youth of today?' he said. 'Where are the good old Muslim principles your elders tried to teach you?'

'We're not drinking brandy, anyway,' said Azman boldly.

'Couldn't if you tried,' said Syed Omar with contempt. 'You'd spew it up.' He made a vomiting face, showing the white blade of his tongue. 'You're not the men your fathers were, nor never will be. All this Coca-Cola and jazzing about. Where are the principles your fathers fought for?'

Nobody liked to ask where or against whom they fought. They remained silent. Syed Omar said: 'What will happen to Islam when it's left to milksops like you to defend it? Tell me that.' Nobody could tell him. Suddenly the music burst like a boil and Syed Omar jumped in his seat. 'In the name of God,' he shouted, in English, 'turn down that noise.' Nobody moved. Suddenly a quiet passage started. 'That's better,' he said, as though the god itself had hastened to obedience. 'You're soft,' he resumed to the boys. 'It's all these films from America. Soft living and soft thinking. Look at that muscle,' he said to his son. 'Rolling up your sleeves as though you've got something to show.' He felt the hard roll on Hassan's upper arm, saying: 'Soft, boy, really soft.'

The boys looked at him in good-humoured contempt, at his round belly and his general flabbiness. 'I could stand up to you in the ring,' said Hamzah. 'Five rounds, I reckon I could knock you out.'

Syed Omar laughed. 'That's right,' he said. 'Pick on me. The enemies of Islam and the enemies of the Malays are all around you, and you talk about knocking me out. Me, the same age as your father, me, a member of your own race. You sit there drinking horrible sweet drinks, and all around are enemies.' He took in, in a dramatic slant-eyed gaze, the harmless drinkers. 'And all the four of you can think of is hitting a poor old man whose day is nearly over, who's given the best years of his life to making the world safe for milksops like you.' He called for more brandy and said: 'Put it on my account.'

The first show at the near-by cinema had just ended. Crabbe came in with Rosemary. Relenting of his boorishness of the other night, his crass rejection of those freely offered sensual treasures, he had taken her to see the town's first English-speaking film for months. A poor film, it had moved Rosemary deeply, its blonde heroine stirring new fantasies in her. As they sat at a table now, Rosemary said above the music: 'Just like her, Victor, fair hair and blue eyes, both my father and my mother and my brother and sister too, all of them, and just because I happened to be born dark like this they didn't want anything to do with me. They threw me out, Victor, out on to the streets, just because my skin was the wrong colour. They did, Victor. And that's why I hate them, that's way I hate my own race, that's why I'd like to cut their throats and see them lying in pools of blood at my feet.' Crabbe gazed at her in admiration. At the moment she was being the blonde film-star. Factitious passion did not make her face crumble: it merely enlarged her black eyes, dilated the Mediterranean nostrils, suggested, with its false image of a temperament that could be controlled, that she was really desirable.

'And you'd like to do that to Joe?' asked Crabbe. 'Joe lying in pools of blood at your feet?'

Rosemary looked at him as though he were mad. 'But that's the whole point, Victor,' she said. 'Joe isn't Scottish. Joe's English. I thought you knew that.'

Crabbe gave it up. He greeted old Loo with a wave, called for gin, and gestured to Robert Loo that he come over to the table. Robert Loo hesitated, his father spoke swift urgent Chinese to him and pushed him towards Crabbe.

'What was all that about?' asked Crabbe, as the boy stood shyly by. 'Come on, sit down. I want to talk to you.'

'He's really quite handsome,' drawled Rosemary, as

474

though Robert Loo were one of the 'natives', and she but newly arrived from Sloane Square. 'A bit like that nice man from Penang.'

'I must see you,' said Robert Loo, 'I have to talk to you. It's very difficult.'

'Well, sit down. Talk to me now.'

'He speaks quite good English,' said Rosemary, 'for a Chinese.'

'I can't go on like this,' said Robert Loo. 'I can't get my work done. Day after day this noise. And I can't get out.'

'Sit down,' said Crabbe. 'Tell me all about it. Calmly.'

Robert Loo sat down on the edge of a chair, hands clasped, as in a vicarage drawing-room. 'I've written only five bars in two days. It's this noise all the time. And I try to write up in my bedroom, after midnight, but my father puts out the lights.'

'What are you writing?'

'A violin concerto.'

'Ah.'

'Can you play the violin?' asked Rosemary loftily, out of a chumbling refined mouth.

'No, I can't. I mean, I know how . . .'

'I was taught the violin,' said Rosemary. 'I played it at school, and at the university. On television, too,' she added. 'Oh, all sorts of things. Symphonies by Bach, and fugues, and, oh, all sorts of things. *Ave Maria*,' she added, like a pious ejaculation. 'And *In a Persian Market*.'

'I must speak to your father again,' said Crabbe. 'It's not altogether his fault, I can see that. He wants more trade, and so forth.'

'He won't listen to you,' said Robert Loo. 'He says . . .'

'What does he say?'

'He says that people are talking.'

'You see, Victor,' said Rosemary briskly. 'I told you people were talking, didn't I? But you wouldn't listen.'

'I don't know what he means,' said Robert Loo. 'But he said you were up to no good. Please, please,' he added in panic, 'don't say that to him. He says you're a good customer and you mustn't be told anything to make you annoyed. But I still don't know what he means.'

'I'll tell you what he means,' began Rosemary with vigour and relish. 'He means . . .'

'Do be quiet, Rosemary,' said Crabbe. 'Never mind what he means. That's not the point. The point is that you must be able to go on composing. Do you get no evening off? You can always come to my place and work there.'

'He wouldn't let me go there,' said Robert Loo. 'And he says there's too much work to do here. I don't think he'll let me have any more time off.'

'I'll speak to him,' said Crabbe, not without grimness.

'Don't, don't. He sees we're talking about him now. I must get back.' And he rose from the chair.

'Sit down,' ordered Crabbe. 'So,' he said, with a certain malice, 'the real world's impinging at last.'

'Impinging?'

'You're becoming aware of other people. The artist, you see, can't function in a vacuum. If I were you,' said Crabbe, 'I'd start acting. Doing something. I'd even leave home and get a job somewhere, a job as a clerk, say. I'd assert myself.'

'I couldn't do that.' All the shock of intense Chinese conservatism confronting the heterodox, even the blasphemous. 'I couldn't. He's my father.'

'My father threw me out on the streets,' said Rosemary, 'to fend for myself. Alone in the streets of London at the age of ten. Then I was adopted by an Indian prince,' she added. 'I wasn't afraid of leaving home.'

'There's only one way, perhaps,' said Crabbe. Your father must be made to see. There's a fair chance that your symphony will be played for the Independence celebrations. If he hears that broadcast, or, better, if he actually *sees* it being played, a large audience, the applause . . . He has to take your music seriously. He must be *shown*.'

'You can come and work at my house,' said Rosemary generously. 'Any night.'

'I can't get out,' said Robert Loo. 'I said that before.

And I asked him again about becoming an accountant, but he said that he needs me here now. They're closing down so many other places, and he says we're going to get all the trade.'

'Your symphony,' said Crabbe patiently, 'is, I think, going to be played. All you have to do is to add a short finale for chorus, a patriotic ending in Malay. Your symphony must have a more popular appeal. A political appeal. You can get that done, can't you? Somehow.'

Robert Loo sneered. 'I won't change it. It's good as it is. It's what I wanted to write. They've no right to ask me to change it. Even if I could, I wouldn't.'

'Oh, Robert, Robert.' Crabbe sighed deeply, just, thought Rosemary, like Jalil. 'You'll never learn. The real world's impinging, and you can't see it. What am I going to do with you?'

But Robert Loo was looking, fascinated, at Rosemary's right hand which held, in film-star elegance, a long cigarette-holder holding a long cigarette. 'Do give me a light, darling,' she said to Crabbe. Robert Loo saw himself looking, for the first time, at a woman's hand. It was a well-shaped hand – the beauty of any one isolated part of Rosemary's body was a divine wonder. It was only the totality, the lack of the animating soul, that failed to impress: she was a valuable lesson in aesthetics, proclaiming the kinship of the sublime and absurd. Robert Loo's eyes were led, as in an artfully composed picture, up from the long delightful fingers to the cunning of the wrist, up to the smooth round brown arm to the bare shoulder. This was the real world impinging. 'I must go back,' he mumbled. Crabbe nodded bleakly, dumbly.

When Crabbe and Rosemary left, the four Malay boys, free at last of Syed Hassan's father, made tiny whistling noises at Rosemary's haunches. Then they sat a while in gloom. In a sense, all that had been said was true. They did nothing to justify their vaunted knightly trappings: the casque of hair, the one suit of sweating armour, the brave oaths and the slick knives. They had been visited, they knew, by Hamlet's father's ghost. O, what rogues and peasant slaves were they. They must start acting. Doing something.

'If my dad lost his job,' said Hassan, 'it would be his fault. A dirty Tamil.'

'We could beat him up,' suggested Azman.

'Knife him.' Thus Hamzah.

'Hit him with a bicycle chain.'

'Smash a bottle in his face.'

'Knock his teeth out.'

'Punch him in the *bodek*.'

'Here,' called Hassan angrily to Robert Loo. 'We want to pay.'

'Eighty cents.'

'Too much. Fifty.'

'Eighty cents.'

'Fifty, or we'll smash up your juke-box.'

Robert Loo smiled, said fervently: 'If only you would.'

That was not the correct response. How all occasions did inform against them. Sullenly they paid what was asked, sullenly left. Hamzah feigning a kick at the glass show-case filled with loaves and Chinese cakes.

Action. At two-thirty-five in the morning, Robert Loo, barefooted, his sleeping-sarong knotted tightly at the sternum, crept past his father's snores, past his brothers and sisters who breathed heavily in the heavy labour of sleep, and went softly downstairs. His electric torch caught rain-stains on the wall, scurrying cockroaches big as mice, forlorn empty mineral-water cases. Entering the shop, he found moonlight sitting at the tables, the great music-god asleep in the corner. This he sought. He was not going to murder, for he had no murdering weapon; he was merely going to maim. He put out his torch and, by moonlight, made from the tray of an empty Player's packet a wedge of card, trimming it with fingers and teeth to the right size. This wedge he jammed into the coin-slit of the machine, jamming it hard in, closing the passage to noise-buying ten-cent pieces. He hoped to gain from this a day of silence, time enough to sketch out a good deal of the first movement of the concerto. He heard it now, violin soaring above the muted horns and the harps, and saw the soloist, smiling in green. Then, with a shock, he saw Rosemary, and heard no music. This would not do. His breath came faster. Seeing the long elegant brown arm again, he groaned, remembering Crabbe's curious word 'impinge'. Why couldn't they leave him alone? All he wanted to do was compose his music.

4

Rosemary returned from her week-end in Penang looking curiously over-dressed. It was the effect of the engagement-ring, whose tiny stone danced and flashed hugely in the sharp Malayan light, helio-signalling many contradictory messages: 'You'd like me, wouldn't you, but you can't now, see, because I belong to another; how beautiful I am, aren't I, someone was bound to snap me up; come and get me, brave the barrier of fire; the auction's on, this is only the first bid; I am, as you can see, essentially a respectable girl.' The ring seemed ubiquitous: the glow of its spectrum filled, like a perfume, any room she had been in: its song was as loud in the town as Loo's juke-box, now repaired. But, somehow, the ring sat on her as obscenely as a nun's coif would have done.

It put into Crabbe's head the notion of a party, a party not just for her, but also for the launching of his inter-racial sodality scheme. Of that, a ring that promised marriage was an apt symbol.

'You can help, you can be hostess.'

'Oooooh, Victor, how marvellous, what a good idea, Victor, oooooh.'

'We'll have Nicky, of course, and some of the Chinese Rotarians, and the Tamils.'

'Oh, no, Victor, no, I can't bear the touch of a dark skin.'

'It's not going to be that sort of party.'

'How about those nice English boys in Boustead's, and the manager up at Durian Estate, and Jerry Framwell from Sungai Puteh, and . . .'

'No. It's not that sort of party. In some ways, it's going to be rather a serious party.'

'How can you have a serious party?' she asked in wonder, flashing her ring.

'You'll see what I mean.'

'Oooooh, Victor, in Penang the men just wouldn't leave me alone. I hardly dared leave my bedroom, and there was one very distinguished-looking man, you know, with greying hair and pots and pots of money, and he wanted to marry me, but I told him he was too late, and then Jalil was jealous and got tight and tried to get into my room at three in the morning. Oh, Victor, it was awful, awful . . .'

'Did you see Lim Cheng Po while you were there?'

She pouted. 'Yes. He was in the bar one night. Oh, I hate him, Victor, hate him. He was very polite and stiff, and, oh, Victor, he has such a lovely voice, and he just offered me a drink and then he left.'

'Well, you don't really like Asians, do you?' said Crabbe. 'You can't bear the touch of a . . .'

'Oh, I don't know, I don't know, Victor. He's not really an Asian, is he? He has such a lovely voice. Oh, Victor, Victor, why is life so difficult?'

'It's not difficult any more, Rosemary. You're engaged.'

'Yes, I'm engaged. To Joe.'

'You're engaged to Joe.'

The name hung in the air an instant like a faint common smell. It was as if, engagement having been definitely, sacramentally, achieved, Joe, its instrument, might well be discarded. Rosemary and Crabbe discussed arrangements for the party.

'Cheng Po will be over here on Wednesday. We might as well have the party then.'

'Oh, yes, Victor, what a good idea, really, that *is* a good idea.'

'I thought you hated him.'

'Oooooh, Victor, I never said that. I never said anything of the sort. How could you imagine I'd say such a thing?'

It was carefully enough planned. Many canapés – no beef to annoy the Hindus, no pig-meat to enrage the Muslims – and various beverages, including harmless hideous coloured liquids lying, a clinking reef, in a tub of icewater. Rosemary, brown bosom, flaming dress, flashing ring, high-heeled vigorously over Crabbe's large drawingroom as the sun set, setting out nuts and pretzels, perking up nodding flowers. This was, after all, on one level, her party.

When Nik Hassan came he was accompanied, to Crabbe's surprise, by his wife, 'Che Asma. She was a bulky woman in a tartan sarong and a green cardigan, who, in Malay fashion, kicked off her sandals at the door and padded on large horny feet to a hard chair in the corner. She took a wad of *sireh* from her bag and began chewing juicily, ignoring her host, dismissing her bare-shouldered hostess as a light woman, waiting for the other Malay wives to arrive. But no Malay wives had been invited. 'Che Asma had a shrewd, ugly face, obviously happiest when mobile. She curtly refused orange crush, lime juice, lemonade, and gave Rosemary an order for coffee. So coffee had to be made.

'I'm just as surprised as you are, Vicky,' said Nik Hassan, smart in a grey palm-beach suit, his fine brown eyes gloomy. 'But she would insist on coming, said I never take her anywhere. I hope to God she behaves herself.'

'Never mind, have a drink, Nicky.'

'I think,' said Nik Hassan, 'I'd better pretend to be drinking ginger ale. She watches me like a bloody hawk, man. Here.' He summoned Crabbe's boy, a shifty Chinese who loved parties, and spoke quick Malay to him. 'That's all right,' he said. 'He knows that ginger ale is a code for brandy-ginger ale.' Loudly he said: 'Ginger ale, please.'

Mrs Pereira arrived, a somewhat unappetizing Eurasian lady of fifty, headmistress of a local girls' school. Her husband had run away from her, but he still sent her enough money to pay the rent. Gushing she examined

Rosemary's ring with catty claws, saying: 'None of us ever thought he'd do it, Rosemary dear, but he's done it, hasn't he? I wonder why, now. Men, men, you can't trust any of them, can you?'

'I trust my Joe.'

'I trusted Pereira. Never mind, dear, life is what it is. You can't change human nature.'

Lim Cheng Po arrived, urbane, elegant, the soul of courtesy, with a silver bracelet for Rosemary.

'Ooooooh, that's so sweet, isn't it swect, Victor, ooooh, it's lovely, oh, I can't wait to put it on.'

'Not half exquisite enough for so exquisite a lady,' said Cheng Po. 'May I congratulate you, Victor?'

'Congratulate?'

'And may I say how pleased I am that Victor has made so exquisite a choice, and how happy I shall be to see him settled down again, and how I hope, my dear, dear lady, that you'll make each other very, very happy.'

'Oh, Victor,' Rosemary smirked all vermilion lipstick, 'do you hear what he says?'

Crabbe's head reeled seeing a new world form, in which the act of engagement came first and the choice of a betrothed followed. 'No,' he said, 'that's not it. You see, it's not me, that is to say, Rosemary is engaged to . . .' Had he, he wondered, possibly proposed to Rosemary at some time or other, and everybody remembered except himself, and Joe was a kind of code-word like ginger ale? No, no. He came to, said to Cheng Po: 'What will you drink?'

'Ah, pink gin, please, Victor.'

Pink gin, Scotch and soda, brandy and water. The guests were arriving, the room was filling, talk and smoke rode the air. But Crabbe felt that things had got off to a bad start. 'Che Asma spat out vigorously a sliver of toast with a shive of luncheon-meat on it. '*Babi!*' she cried.

'It isn't pork,' said Crabbe. 'We were very careful about that.' She shrugged, unconvinced, not willing to talk to a man anyway, waiting for the Malay wives to come. But the only other wife present was Mrs Foo, wife of Mr Foo, the dentist, smiling, slim, delicious, in a *cheongsam* that showed thighs thinner, but not less delightful, than Rosemary's. 'Che Asma spoke to the air her detestation of such exhibitionism.

And here were the Tamil brethren. For Arumugam and Sundralingam there was much to worry about: Maniam alone in the house at night; Vythilingam inclined to be naughty; Rosemary at large. But they had not been able to think of a valid excuse for not coming, especially as Vythilingam had expressed his determination to get drunk on Crabbe's liquor. Arumugam and Sundralingam knew why: another letter from Ceylon that morning, another photograph of a shining Tamil girl, with the dowry pencilled baldly on the back: $75,000; the complex machinery of Vythilingam's soul churning and grinding; even at one point in the early evening, a show of pugnacity. And now Vythilingam was jerking out mouthfuls of air at Rosemary.

'Oh, Vy, don't be silly. It's hopeless, can't you see that? Look, my ring.' The tiny diamond winked and signalled.

'I...I...don't think...'

'We're still friends, aren't we? I mean, you'll still look after the cats.'

'I...'

'Come along,' sang Arumugam, in hearty falsetto, 'come and join the boys.'

'I...don't...'

'And,' said Nick Hassan to Crabbe, 'they think it's a good idea. That's just what they'd like, they say, to open up the celebrations. A good stirring Malay song all about our glorious mountains and jungles and tigers, and all that guff. Not too long, of course. They think they can get their orchestra from Singapore. And, of course, there's always the Federation Police Band.'

'But that would just be the end of a rather long symphonic piece,' said Crabbe. 'The whole point is really the symphony itself.'

'Couldn't all that be cut out? Couldn't he just send in

the singing bit?' said Nik Hassan. He grabbed Crabbe's boy – who already smelt of Beehive brandy – and handed back his glass, saying: 'I asked for ginger ale. This is just ginger ale.'

'No,' said Crabbe, 'no. That's just it. They've got to have the whole lot.'

'They haven't *got* to.' Perhaps it was merely the presence of his wife that made him irritable. 'I'm doing you a favour, after all, Vicky.'

'*Me* a favour?'

'Well, him a favour. That boy a favour.'

'But, damn it all, man, I thought we'd been into all that. Can't you honestly see that getting this thing performed is important to Malaya?'

Rosemary's bosom and perfume and ring were upon them. 'Victor, Victor, I think that Vy's trying to get tight. Look at him.' Vythilingam had been wedged into the corner by the drink-table, a solid wall of Arumugam and Sundralingam shielding him from temptation. Vythilingam had drunk off two neat whiskies and was pouring another. Sundralingam spoke loudly and pedantically to Mrs Foo about the local yaws campaign.

'There is a most nauseating fluid exuding from the yaws sore, and the causative organism is found abundantly in that.'

Mrs Foo smiled winningly and nibbled at a sardine on a toothpick.

'As much as twenty years between the primary sore and the tertiary stage.'

Crabbe cleared his throat and called: 'Ladies and gentlemen.' The words 'spirochaete' and 'ginger ale' lagged into the near-silence. With drink Vythilingam found the gift of speech returning. He too said, goldfish-twittering to the ceiling: 'Ladies and gentlemen.'

'I don't want to talk a great deal,' said Crabbe. 'First, let me say how glad I am to see you all here, and, more particularly, express my pleasure at the sight of representatives of all the races of South-East Asia mixing freely and in obvious harmony in the house of a wicked Englishman.' There was dutiful laughter; only Arumugam nodded gravely; Vythilingam, as on a dummy flute, tried out mouth-twisting phrases. 'We hear a great deal these days,' said Crabbe, 'about the prospect of racial discord in the new, independent Malaya. These ideas have been disseminated by unscrupulous elements who see in racial dissension an admirable instrument for the furthering of their own nauseating ends. I refer, of course, to the Communists.'

There were pious noises of agreement. Rosemary stood puzzled, wondering at so strange an exordium to a speech about her and her engagement. Suddenly, surprisingly, Vythilingam said, quite clearly: 'The Communists,' and drank off more whisky.

'But,' said Crabbe, 'apart from the Communists, I don't think we can doubt that the component races of Malaya have never made much effort to understand each other. Odd superstitions and prejudices, complacency, ultra-conservatism – these have perpetually got in the way of better understanding. Moreover, the idea of a community – a single community, as opposed to many distinct communities – never seemed very important during the period of British management. There was a cold, purely legal unification provided by the State – a British importation – and a sort of superficial culture represented by American films, jazz, chocolate-bars, and refrigerators; for the rest, each race was content to keep alive fragments of culture imported from its country of origin. There never seemed any necessity to mix. But now the time has come.' He banged his fist forensically on the top of a dinner-wagon. 'There must not merely be mixing, there must be fusion.'

'Confusion,' said Vythilingam, nodding agreement. He was shushed.

'There must be inter-marriage, there must be a more liberal conception of religion, there must be art and literature and music capable of expressing the aspiration of a single unified people.' Nik Hassan grinned cynically. 'I

suggest that we attempt, here in this town ...' Here
Crabbe stopped. His heart sank at the vision on the veranda : Syed Omar, in newspaper shirt, making a spectacular entrance, crooning throatily.

'Big words,' said Syed Omar, 'big words. But they will
not help us to get jobs.' He came into the drawing-room,
blinking with drunken photophobia, and then stood swaying under the fan, his untidy hair stirred by its breeze.
'Look at them,' he said, 'wearing their suits. Black bastards.'

'Come on, now, Omar,' soothed Nik Hassan. 'Come to
the kitchen, have some black coffee.'

'Don't want any black coffee. Don't like anything black.'

'For God's sake,' whispered Crabbe, 'pull yourself together, Omar. We don't want any trouble.'

'I never wanted any trouble,' cried Syed Omar. 'I did
my work, didn't I? I did my work better than the next
man. And now I get my reward. I am out of a job.' He
sat down in the nearest arm-chair and began to sob
quietly. Everybody looked embarrassed, everybody except
Vythilingam. Vythilingam sang very quietly the song the
Japanese had sung in celebration of the fall of Singapore.
'I think,' said Mr Foo, all fat smiles, 'my wife and I had
better be going.'

'Not so soon,' said Crabbe.

'Oh,' cried Syed Omar, 'I see. You do not want to be
in the same house as a man without a job. You think I
am only a dirty jobless Malay.'

Vythilingam picked this up very clearly. 'Dirty jobless
Malay,' he smiled to the whisky bottle.

Syed Omar was on his feet. 'And if you are a clean
Tamil I would rather be a dirty Malay,' he cried. 'It is
your fault, it is the fault of your race that I am now without a job. Your Mister bloody Maniam and the whole
damned lot of you.'

'You'd better go home,' said Crabbe. 'Come on, I'll take
you.' The party, he felt, might as well be abandoned. But

487

Syed Omar shook himself free of Crabbe's arm, saying: 'I will say what I have to say to these black bastards.'

'Such filthy language,' protested Mrs Pereira. Rosemary tried to cling, in a show of apprehension, to Lim Cheng Po. Vythilingam broke through his cordon, smiling, saying very distinctly to Syed Omar: 'I know you.'

'I know you too, you bastard.'

In the scuffle that followed, nobody actually got hurt. Some of Nik Hassan's ginger ale was spilled on to Rosemary's dress, and the dress began to reek of brandy. 'Che Asma, disgusted, swept her hand across a row of spirit bottles, and two of these rolled over the floor, and Syed Omar tripped and fell over a bottle of rum, grasping, as he fell, the nearest stable object, which was Mrs Foo's right leg. The whole business was quite deplorable.

'Well,' said Idris, panting a little, 'what do we do now?'

'Quiet,' whispered Syed Hassan. 'He'll hear you.' The house of Dr Sundralingam was in darkness. But there was no doubt that Maniam was within.

'But what are we going to *do*?' asked Hamzah.

Nobody answered, for nobody really knew. Each carried in his mind a confused image of violence, and this was further confused in the mind of Hassan by a sense of filial obligation, of guilt and also, since his father had come home and said that there would be no more wages coming in and hence no more school-fees could be paid, by relief and even a curious gratitude to Maniam. Hassan envisaged for himself a fine idle adult future, feeling, at the thought, as they stood breathing quietly and quickly in the palmy darkness, a kind of promise of ecstasy in his loins, which whetted his desire to do some harmless harm or other to Maniam.

Inspired, he said: 'Handkerchiefs round our faces.'

'Have no handkerchief,' said Azman. His whisper got out of control on the last syllable, and a sudden voice-breaking bass rasped the darkness.

488

'Sssssshhhh! Fool!'

'I've got two,' breathed Idris. Tonight he was wearing the suit, and had a handkerchief in top as well as trouser pocket.

They tied these yashmaks round their faces, and, as a car went by on the road parallel to the avenue where they stood, they saw each other's big brown eyes above them, and Azman started to giggle.

'Sssssshhh!'

'Front door locked,' said Hassan. 'Must be. We'll try kitchen door. Take off that jacket,' he said to Idris. 'Take off that tie. May see. May recognize. Leave under that tree there.' Idris obeyed. Softly on sandals they trod grass; now and again a dried twig cracked underfoot, Hamzah stubbed his toe on a coconut shell, Idris squelched into an over-ripe papaya lying under its tree. Starshine above, faint rustle of palm-leaves, black, quiet, moonless. The kitchen door was locked.

'His boy sleeps here?' asked Azman voicelessly.

'Sssssshhh! Boy always go to town. Look, window there. Open.'

'Listen! Maniam's breathing in sleep?'

'Help me up,' whispered Hassan. 'Will look. Knives ready.'

Elbows on window-ledge, legs held by comrades, he looked in, darkness, saw nothing. 'In,' he whispered urgently, 'help in. Knives ready.' Hassan kneed himself up, over, in, soundlessly, feet on floor, knife out, eyes like blunter knife trying to cut darkness. No sound. 'Azman,' he whispered. 'Azman next. Then Idris. Hamzah stay out there. Watch. In here nobody.'

Idris, Azman, now in also. Azman pulled out pocket-torch, shone through room dimly with dying battery. Nobody. Sundralingam's room, perhaps. Bed empty, mosquito-net down, wardrobe, dressing-table, Chinese nude calendar on wall. Cautiously the three soft-footed out of the room, opening door creaked a little. In new room Hassan felt for light-switch.

A blaze of glory shone on Maniam sitting up startled in bed. Like 'Che Asma who, just at that moment, was knocking bottles off Crabbe's drink-table. Maniam wore a tartan sarong. His eyes wide with surprise and fear, he clutched tightly the bolster – sweat-absorbing bedfellow of sleepers in the East – known as a Dutch wife.

'What? What? Who?'

It was always as well to leave things to impulse. Hassan found the right thing to say.

'*Jangan takut*,' he said, then remembered that the language of sophisticated crime was English. 'Don't be afraid,' he amended.

'What? What? What do you want?'

'We come to protect you,' said Hassan. 'Are enemies wanting to kill you. We will stop enemies wanting to kill you.'

'What do you mean? Who are you?' Maniam's great eyes, his black skin oiled with sweat. Maniam's hands pudgily clutching his Dutch wife.

'You pay little money only. We stop enemies from killing you,' said Hassan.

'Where do you keep your cash, bub?' asked Idris hoarsely. His American was better than Hassan's English. 'You gotta hand over, see.'

Maniam eyed the knives. 'How much do you want?'

'Twenty bucks,' said Azman.

'A hundred bucks,' bid Hassan, giving Azman a rough elbow-jab. 'Pay up and you be all right.'

'I've got no money,' said Maniam.

'I bet there's money there in your trousers,' said Hassan. A pair of crumpled green slacks lay over the bedside chair. 'Pay up.'

'Or else,' added Idris. He juggled his knife in menace, dropped it on the floor, picked it up, repeated. 'Or else.'

'My wallet's in the next room,' said Maniam. 'I don't know how much is in it. I'll get and fetch it.'

'That's right, you go and fetch it,' said Hassan. 'We'll wait here.'

'Yes,' said Maniam, out of bed with eager agility. 'You wait here.'

'Idiot,' cried Idris in Malay. 'There's a telephone in there. Stop him.' Azman, nearest to Maniam, grasped his sarong, which immediately unwound down to Maniam's ankles: black round buttocks were disclosed, short hairless legs, Maniam's shame. 'Let me go,' he said in anger. He tried to get into the living-room, his dropped folds of sarong hobbled him; eluding Azman's grasp too vigorously, he was tripped by his own wide stride and the folds at his ankles; he went over, striking his nose hard on the door-knob. He lay cursing an instant, aware of a maimed face just healed, now maimed again. 'Damn you!' he cried.

'You get the money, bub,' menaced Idris. 'And no more tricks, see?'

'A car! A car coming!' cried Hamzah from without.

'Allah!'

'Out the same way,' ordered Hassan. 'Through the window, quick.'

'We get the money first,' said Idris. 'Here in trousers.'

'Out, out, I order,' ordered Hassan. 'Out now, quick, quick.'

'I bring trousers,' said Idris. He grabbed them from the chair. The naked Maniam tried to rise, called: 'Help! Murder!' as he heard the car engine come closer. The boys dashed. Azman had already scrambled out into moonless garden, clumsily landing on Hamzah the helper. Idris, trousers under arm, followed, Hassan tumbling after. The big eyes of the car, turning into the drive, caught their yashmaks, their legs doubtful whither to run. 'Help! Help!' from Maniam at the front door. 'Get them, quick! There!'

In the back of the car, Vythilingam was loudly singing: '. . . And the rising sun shall rise yet higher, destroying with its flaming fire the evil will of the wicked West, but smiling warmly on the rest,' in demotic Japanese. Arumugam was out, ready with fists, voice girling high: 'Where, where?'

The boys ran, scattered. Idris and Hamzah met the big arms of Sundralingam, realized it was not a question of catching but of recognizing, realized too late that this sort of adventure was not for small towns, but part of the culture of cities. Hamzah knifed Sundralingam gently in the forearm. Sundralingam wailed, Hamzah and Idris got away. Arumugam was down, kicked by Azman. 'Run, run!' They ran. Running, Hassan remembered the jacket, with the string-tie in the pocket, lying under the tree. To-morrow it was his turn to wear full uniform. He ran that way, ready to scoop it up from the tree's shadow. Even in this panic and flurry he saw clearly that he was rightfully the leader, having the brains to remember to remove a clue from the vicinity of the crime. (Crime? Had there been a crime?) Thus Arumugam, athletic and virile under the feminine dress of his voice, caught him, being quickly on his feet again, off his mark. Hassan struggled in mus-cular arms, his turn now to call for help, but the six fugi-tive feet were padding down the road, abandoning him. Caught in an unarmed combat grip, raised in agony to his toes, Hassan was marched, the voice squealing in his ear, towards the house and the waiting Maniam and Sundra-lingam. Vythilingam snored.

The yashmak jerked off, in the third-degree light of the house, Hassan's scared face was scanned. 'Syed Omar's son,' said Sundralingam.

'Yes, yes,' squeaked Arumugam. 'Like father, like son. This is Syed Hassan.'

'They got away with my trousers,' said Maniam.

'What is this he has?'

'That is a jacket.'

'Was there money in the pocket?' asked Sundralingam. Then he sucked the tiny wound on his arm.

'There was my wallet. Some money, yes, not much.'

'Your face,' said Arumugam. 'They hit you on the face.'

'Yes, yes, they did that, too.'

'*Pembohong*,' gnashed Hassan, 'liar.' Arumugam tightened the screw of the hold. 'Ow!' cried Hassan.

'Well,' said Sundralingam, 'I shall ring for the police. This is very, very bad. Will Syed Omar never be out of trouble?'

So comparatively early in the evening still, and the party broken up, though the drawing-room had a morning-after look and Syed Omar groaned over his black coffee.

'But damn it,' said Crabbe, 'it sounds to me as if losing your job was nobody's fault but your own.'

'Other people,' said Syed Omar, eyes shut against the light, slumped in an arm-chair, 'other people have done what I have done and have kept their jobs. I lost one file only, though I do not think I really lost it, but somebody stole it deliberately. I never claimed to be much good at typing. I have taken a few days off. I once had a bottle of whisky in the desk drawer, but that was only because I had fever. Other people have done worse and have not been given the sack. I have been framed. Maniam is at the back of it all.'

Lim Cheng Po yawned delicately and continued to keep his distance from Rosemary, who sat temptingly by him on the couch. Rosemary pouted, feeling also a twinge of superstitious foreboding because her engagement party had fizzled, or exploded, out. She looked with distaste at Syed Omar, blaming him, blaming Crabbe too, then deciding also to blame Lim Cheng Po for the failure of the evening; and it would be their fault, too, if Joe now wrote breaking off the engagement.

'And who's going to get your job?' asked Crabbe.

'I don't know, I don't know,' groaned Syed Omar. 'Some Tamil woman, I suppose, some other relation of all those black bastards.'

'Really,' protested Rosemary, from her best refined mouth.

'I suppose I'll have to find something for you,' sighed Crabbe. 'There may be a vacancy in my office. Though,' he added, 'it's not really my office now.'

Then there was the sound of transport, too heavy a sound for a private car, and headlights showed up the withered pot-plants in Crabbe's porch. 'Whoever it is,' said Crabbe, 'they've come too late for the party.' Slammed metal doors and boots, Inspector Ismail stood on the veranda, saluted, showed many teeth, and said, 'Ah, I thought he would still be here. Forgive this intrusion, Mr Crabbe. There is trouble with Syed Omar's son. Syed Omar had better come to the station.'

'Trouble? What trouble?'

'Trouble?' Syed Omar's mouth was fixed for the dentist's chair, his eyes huge now, despite the light.

'Your son and his friends tried to kill Mr Maniam with knives. They stripped off his clothes, hit him on the face, kicked him while he was down, stole his trousers and his money, assaulted Mr Arumugam too and tried to stab Dr Sundralingam to death.'

'No!'

'Oh yes,' smiled Inspector Ismail. 'We have everybody down at the station now.' He sounded happy, as though everything were set for a party, the more pleasant because unexpected. 'I think Syed Omar must come too.'

'Oh, God God God,' said Crabbe. 'Why, oh why do they do these things?'

'Unfortunately,' smiled Inspector Ismail, 'they only caught Syed Hassan. The others got away. But the gentlemen think that Syed Hassan will be enough. For the moment, anyway.'

'Look, I can't believe all that about killing and whatnot,' said Crabbe. 'Let me have a word with Maniam and the others. It was probably only a stupid childish joke, anyway. They must drop the charge.'

'But,' smiled Inspector Ismail, 'it is really a police matter. They had weapons, you see. And housebreaking is very serious.'

'I'll drive Omar down,' said Crabbe.

'Keep out of these things, Victor,' said Lim Cheng Po. 'Keep out of these Asian matters. You will find yourself in terribly deep water.'

'I'll drive him down,' said Crabbe. 'Stay here with Rosemary. Have a drink. Have something to eat. I shan't be long.'

'My son,' said Syed Omar, 'my son, my son. They are ruining us all, the whole family.' He wept.

'Come on now, pull yourself together.'

'I am impotent, impotent.'

'Oh, come on. Stay here with Rosemary, Cheng Po. I'll be back soon.'

Lim Cheng Po and Rosemary were left together, under the wind of the fan, among the dirty glasses; the faint brandy-song of the cook-boy wafted in from the kitchen. Lim Cheng Po went over to the table to get a drink, saying: 'Victor's a fool. He shouldn't do these things.' Rosemary stood up, knowing she looked her best tall and straight, like a smooth brown tree, and sobbed: 'Oh, I'm so unhappy, so unhappy.'

Lim Cheng Po turned, startled, a glass in his hand. 'Oh, my dear, dear lady, you mustn't be unhappy. What does all this business matter to you?'

'Oh,' wailed Rosemary (men are so stupid), 'oh, it isn't that. I'm so unhappy. I want to die.' She waited for consoling arms. Lim Cheng Po said: 'There, now, come and sit down. Have a drink. Tell me all about it.'

'I don't want to sit down. Oh, life is terrible, terrible.'

'There, there, there.' And here they were, comforting arms beneath a so English, a so refined voice, a smell of hair-cream, after-shaving lotion, invisible talc, Imperial Leather soap, good cloth, man. Rosemary sobbed into Lim Cheng Po's chest, sobbed dryly because tears would ruin her mascara.

'There, there, there.'

'So unhappy, so unhappy.'

'Better now?'

'So unhappy.'

Lim Cheng Po, Anglican, Royalist, cricketer, respectable husband and father, allowed his animal reflexes out for an avenue walk on the lead. Rosemary had a pleasant smell, her flesh was agreeable to palpate, to kiss her left temple lightly was less of a bore than having to say 'There, there, there' all the time. Eyes closed, she raised half-open vermilion lips to him. He was debating whether to touch them with his own when Vythilingam walked in, swaying but slightly, not very drunk.

Vythilingam had been left, apparently sleeping, in the back of his own car, while his friends, disgusted that he had once more failed them in the moment of need, had gone to the station in a police-van. But, in fact, Vythilingam had been drunkenly aware of violence proceeding outside, and he had not greatly wished to be involved. If his friends were being assaulted, that was perhaps a good thing: he was growing tired of their brother's keeper clucking over him. If his friends were assaulting others, that, too, was a good thing: the Jaffna Tamils had suffered enough from the rest of the world. He erected an impregnable tower of drunkard's snores in the back of the car, and only when silence returned to the house and its garden did he strike the stage set. Then he drove with drunken care to Rosemary's house, smiled nervously to find her not yet in, and walked, tracing wave-patterns on the road, to the house of Crabbe. There he found her being embraced by a Chinese from Penang.

The whisky ventriloquized through him, the dummy. 'Stop that,' he called, with great strength and clarity. Lim Cheng Po was only too ready to stop it. Rosemary turned, startled and thwarted.

'Vy!'

'Stop that,' he repeated, though it had already stopped.

'My dear fellow,' said Lim Cheng Po, in civilized reproof.

'You think,' said Vythilingam, 'you can do anything with me. But (he had some slight difficulty with the labial), but I am a man.' He paused, to let them take this in, to think of what to say next. 'Like other men.'

'Go home, Vy,' said Rosemary, keeping her temper. 'Go home and sleep. You've been drinking too much.'

'I wait.' He paused and swayed. 'I wait for an answer.'

'Do go home.' She stamped her delicate foot. 'Please, please go home.'

'So that. He can. He can.'

'I can what?' snapped Lim Cheng Po. He had not enjoyed any of the evening.

'Any man who comes along,' said Vythilingam. 'Any man can do it. With her.'

'Vy, what a filthy and disgusting thing to say.' Rosemary's face disintegrated. 'Get out, get out this minute, do you hear?'

'Except me.'

'Look here, old man,' said Lim Cheng Po, 'pull yourself together.' That seemed to be the leitmotif of the whole evening. 'Go home now, have a good night's sleep, you'll feel better in the morning. You're upsetting this lady, you know.'

'I only want,' said Vythilingam. 'I only want,' he repeated. 'To marry her. To ... (he stumbled over another labial plosive) ... protect her.' He nodded and swayed. 'From herself.'

'I don't want your protection,' cried Rosemary. 'Get out, get out, or Mr Lim will throw you out.'

'My dear lady ...'

'He's always after me,' cried Rosemary. 'Always annoying me. He wants me to marry him. And I won't, ever, ever.'

'Your dear Joe,' said Vythilingam, 'won't marry you.' He smiled round the room, as at a circle of invisible friends. 'Ever.'

'What do you know?' cried Rosemary in anger. 'What do you know about it? Shut up, do you hear?'

'He won't marry you. Joe only wanted one thing. And he got it.' Vythilingam nodded several times, smiling.

Rosemary peeled off Sloane Square, Hartnell, decorations-will-be-worn, fog, primroses, crumpets by the fire, and let fly vulgarly at Vythilingam. Lim Cheng Po was distressed. 'Bitch,' said Vythilingam, with some difficulty, and, with more difficulty, 'bloody bitch.' Then he added, with courtly formality, 'I ask for your hand. In marriage.'

'Never, never, never, do you hear? Never!' Rosemary's eyes flashed danger, lights on a crumbling tower. 'Now get out!'

'I think,' said Lim Cheng Po, 'I'd better take you home.' He took her wrist.

'No,' said Rosemary, 'let him go home. How dare he say such things? Filthy, filthy things! Send him away or I'll hit him!'

'I suggest you go home,' said Lim Cheng Po to Vythilingam. 'We don't want any trouble, you know. Especially in Mr Crabbe's house.'

'I ask for her hand. I wait for an answer.'

'You've got your answer. Never, never, never! I don't want to see you again, after the filthy, filthy lying things you've said! I don't want to see you again, ever!'

'Come on, dear lady,' said Lim Cheng Po, leading her to the door. Rosemary sobbed. Vythilingam swayed slightly, smiling still. A madhouse, thought Lim Cheng Po, what a madhouse Asia was. He would be glad to be out of it. The church bells on Sunday, bitter and darts in the pub, civilization. Crabbe could keep Malaya.

5

Crabbe sat at home in the early evening, gloomily drinking gin and water, waiting for the alcohol, like some great romantic symphony, to poison his nerves to a mood of quiet and resignation. It had been a hard day. The pupils of the local Anglo-Chinese School had decided to go on strike, and had maintained a day-long picket of the school yard, bearing revolutionary ideograms on cards and banners. Crabbe had been sent to investigate, but had found out nothing. The Communist cell lay hidden, somewhere in the multi-stream fourth form. He had appealed to them in English, and a Chinese Inspector of Schools had addressed them in Kuo-Yü – a language as remote as the tongue of Caedmon to the impassive hearers. The pupils had agreed to go back next day and had been much praised for their public spirit.

And this tiny revolt, by some kind of chain reaction, was connected with Syed Hassan's foolish escapade. Undistributed middles had led to a number of incredible conclusions in shop and bazaar, over sucked coffee and lingered rolls of silk. The Malays, it was said, had started to rise: parang and kris were being sharpened. They had begun to make a breakfast of the Tamils, they licked their lips at the prospect of a great Chinese dinner. It had never been young Hassan's desire to meddle in politics – he had merely wanted disinterested violence or intimidation of the most token sort – but his single night in the lock-up had made him, to other Malay youth at least, a kind of Horst Wessel. Now he was out on bail of five hundred dollars, which Crabbe, of course, had had to find. And now there were some who were saying that Crabbe was behind the coming rising of the Malays: he had, they said, secretly married his amah and had entered Islam.

Syed Hassan had betrayed his three friends very readily, arguing that, as the four shared responsibility for the crime, so they must equally share the quantum of the punishment. The English had taught him arithmetic but no ethics. The keen sight of Maniam, Arumugam and Sundralingam had apparently pierced through yashmak and darkness without difficulty, for Idris, Hamzah and Azman were immediately identified as the other criminals. For these three no bail could be found, so they had to languish behind bars. This caused further murmuring against Crabbe: why this favouritism? Why could the white man not dip deeper into his deep coffers? After all, Hamzah's father was a dredger in a tin-mine and Azman's uncle had, for three weeks at least, tapped rubber, and it was well known that the English had made themselves rich through tin and rubber, natural riches which belonged rightly to the Malayans, meaning the Malays.

So it was with relief that Crabbe read the message that the peon brought:

'Headmaster of Durian Estate School murdered. Please investigate. I would go if I could, but someone must stay in the office. Please take train tonight.'

True enough, expatriates were now expendable: it was right and proper that the new masters should stick to their offices. Crabbe looked at his watch, saw that he had an hour before the slow train left for Mawas, packed shirts and razor, and sat down comfortably to finish the bottle of gin. If he didn't, his cook would in his absence. The great Brahmsian slow movement of the sixth glass was broken rudely by the telephone's percussion.

'Is that you, Vicky? Nicky here.'

'Vicky here, Nicky.'

'It's about the money that Wigmore left. You know, the twenty thousand bucks to the State. There's going to be a meeting next week.'

'Good. I shall be there.'

'All right, if you want to, Vicky, but it won't do any good.'

'What do you mean?'

'It's already been decided. Just as I said. The Sultan wants a Cadillac.'

'But damn it, he can't do that. The terms of the will are quite clear, aren't they? It says something about the good of the State, doesn't it?'

'It's just as I said. They're prepared to argue it out. They say the highest good is the Sultan's good.'

'Who say that?'

'The Sultan and the Raja Perempuan and the Tungku Makhota and the Mentri Besar.'

'And you?'

'Well, damn it, what can I do? I've got my job to think about, and, besides, I suppose they're right really. I should leave well alone if I were you, Vicky. You don't want to get into trouble.'

'I don't mind in the slightest getting into trouble. Who's the executor of Wigmore's will?'

'Protheroe. He's the trustee as well, if you want to know. And he's not objecting.'

'For the usual reason, eh? He doesn't want to be thrown out of the State.'

'It's just not worth it, Vicky. He says the terms of the will cover a Cadillac.'

'I'm going to get Lim on the job. I'll contest this. It's a bloody disgrace.'

'Don't do anything stupid, Vicky.'

Crabbe slammed the receiver down. Then he called his cook and told him he would be away for a couple of days. 'And,' said Crabbe, 'I know exactly how much brandy's in that cupboard. And whisky.' The Chinese smiled ineffably.

Jalil wheezed at the two cats that lay on the only other arm-chair and somewhat roughly removed them. Then he sat down, breathing heavily at Rosemary's back as she,

501

feigning to ignore him, steadily filled an air mail letter form at the table. 'Who you write?' asked Jalil.

'... I am longing for you to hold me in your arms again,' wrote Rosemary, 'and tickle my ear with your moustache. Oh, darling, it sends such funny shivers through me.'

'You write him. I know,' chuckled Jalil. 'But no good. He not marry you.'

'... And am dying for the day when you and I can be together again and say these things to each other properly,' wrote Rosemary. 'All my love, dearest one.' There was enough space after her signature to implant a kiss. Rosemary raised the thin blue letter to her richly rouged lips, pressing it to them as though covering a lady-like belch with a dinner napkin. Then vigorously she folded the letter, sealing it with a little condensed milk which she allowed to trickle from the tin on to her finger-tip. Ritually she replied to Jalil:

'Oooooh, go away, Jalil, you shouldn't be here, you know you shouldn't, I told the amah not to let you in.'

'Come eat, come drink, come make jolly time.' Jalil yawned. A cat yawned.

'No,' said Rosemary. 'I'm going to bed early.'

'I come too,' said Jalil.

'Jalil, what a filthy, what a horrible, what a downright nasty thing to say.' Rosemary began to file her nails. There was silence. The brief ceremony was over.

'How long since you hear from him?' resumed Jalil.

'That's none of your business.'

'How long?'

'If you must know, we write to each other every day. We never miss. That's because we're in love, but you wouldn't know what love is.'

'I know what love is. Love is man and woman in bed.'

Rosemary smiled, superior. 'That's what you think. That's because you're an Asian. You Asians don't know anything about real love.'

'How long since you hear from him?'

'I've told you.' Rosemary's voice grew schoolmistressly sharp. 'He writes every day.'

'You get letter from him today?'

'Of course I did.'

'Yes. You get letter today. But not yet.'

'What do you mean?'

'He not write two weeks, more. Today letter come. But not yet you get.'

'Jalil,' threatened Rosemary, 'if you're up to your nasty tricks again I'll hit you. I'll throw you out. I'll call for the police. I haven't forgotten that other business with the Blackpool Tower.'

'Every day I ask Sikh in Post Office about letter for you. Today he give me. Letters more safe with me. Here is letter.' In quiet asthmatic triumph Jalil drew a blue air mail letter from his breast pocket. 'He write at last. He send bad news. I know. I not read, but I know. Now you read.'

In rage Rosemary hurled herself at Jalil. A cat fled to the kitchen, another hid under the table. The force of her onslaught toppled Jalil's chair over, and he lay, legs in the air, as she scratched at his face. He panted for a while and then began his deep chuckle as he grappled, finally seizing her wrists. They were on the floor now, and frightened cats looked on as they rolled, Rosemary spitting, trying to bite. 'This time,' wheezed Jalil, 'you get. You really get this time.'

'Pig. Swine. Rotter.' Rosemary's off-the-shoulder dress was now off more than her shoulders. Jalil's asthma roared in her right ear. Her skirt was in disarray. Cats climbed and leapt, watched with huge eyes, tails were high with fright, fur staring like quills. 'Now,' panted Jalil as though dying. Rosemary screamed for her amah, but nobody came. And still, crumpled in her left hand, she gripped the letter she had wrested. 'Only I love,' sweated Jalil. 'Now. You see. Now.' He dredged his lungs deeply and desperately for a spoonful of air. Rosemary tore at his right ear, turned it like a radio knob. Jalil hardly noticed, concentrating on breathing and his tearing hands. Then Rosemary upped with her knee.

Over in the corner she watched him crawling towards her, her own eyes big black lakes, herself panting. Panting filled the room, fan and refrigerator were silent. As Jalil got to his feet, his black Eskimo hair over his right eye, gasping towards her, Rosemary fumbled at the kitchen door, tottered through to the door of the servants' quarters, opened the door and tripped through the untidy cell (the floor paved with cigarette tins saved up for a ceremony of lights, a bulky sewing machine, cardboard boxes filled with trinkets, the amah out without permission) to reach the outer door which, thank God, was open. Crying, clutching at the letter, she ran through the oven-like evening of the empty avenue, shoeless, whimpering towards Crabbe's house.

Crabbe's house looked empty: not because of shut doors or darkness – it was not quite lamplighting time – but because there was no car in the porch. How naked a porch then seems: caddis-cases, dried shed lizard-tails, corpses of cicadas, frogs hopping freely, cigarette-ends, dust, a great smear of oil, normally hidden by the bulky metallic body, now appear as symbols of desolation. Rosemary tried the glass-and-metal front door, but it was locked; round by the servants' quarters she called: 'Boy! Boy!' but nobody came. (In fact, Crabbe's boy was there, but so was Rosemary's amah.) Rosemary went round to the veranda: there the folding doors were in place, but she rattled at panel after panel. She weakened at the knees with relief when one panel meekly swung inwards, the key panel with the tiny handle, its bolts unfastened, almost a true door. Inside the living-room that smelt of enclosed heat, she stood undecided and then called: 'Victor! Victor!' Darkness gently began to lower itself into the chairs, to settle on the surfaces of tables and cupboards. Perhaps he was in the bedroom? Rosemary padded down the long corridor, passing the second bedroom which Crabbe used as a study, to the big chamber which held his solitary single bed. 'Victor!' In the room the mosquito net was down, ghost-grey in the falling light. Crabbe was nowhere: the lavatory door stood wide, there was no sound of bath or shower. Rosemary sobbed gently, gorgeous in her disarray, the crumpled letter still in her fist. Disturbed by the noises, a toad hopped towards the bathroom, a chichak ran up the wall. Wearily she parted the mosquitonet's folds and half lay on the bed. Then she smoothed out the letter and tried to read it. The crumpled words swam, blurred, got mixed with diamonds, great splotches of tears dissolved some. But, of course, she had known all the time, had always known.

... And if you met Sheila I am sure you would be great friends. She is not a bit like you, of course, she is very English and has blue eyes. Anyway, she says she will go on working till I find something, she has a good job, she is a confidential secretary, and it is perhaps just as well that I didn't get the job with that export or import company, whatever it is. Anyway, I want you to still wear the ring, and to think of me whenever you look at it, it will perhaps bring back happy memories of you and I together. I do not regret buying it for you at all, darling, for they were good times, weren't they, and it's nice to think we each have things to remember each other by. But, as the saying goes, East is East and West is West, and it would have been very difficult for both of us, darling, if we had got married. And if we had had kids it would have been very awkward for them, wouldn't it, so perhaps everything has worked out for the best. You're bound to find a good husband soon, for you are marvellous looking, and any man who is an Asian would be proud to have such a smasher for a wife. When Sheila and I are married, which should be next month, I know when we are in bed together I shall often think of you and the things we did. Goodbye, now, dear, and God bless you, and don't think too badly of your loving Joe.

Rosemary now pumped out floods of grief on to Crabbe's pillow. Her face cracked, split, liquefied, its horrid disintegration burrowed into the worn cotton; howls and bayings and ghastly sobs and chokings racked her body and made the bed shake and tremble. (Indifferent on the wall, a male chichak hunted a female with loud chuckles.) Only the lovely patina of Rosemary's flesh, the wonder of curve and line which was not her but the whole species, only these did not join in the personal dissolution, though her limbs writhed and her breasts laboured in that transport of misery. Occasionally she gasped out 'Joe' – a flat animal cry that her slack vocal cords made unfemininely deep, that her nasopharynx, choked with mucus, robbed of all resonance. The earth did not swallow her up, but gently the dark did.

Robert Loo, hesitant in full dark, with a moon rising, heard these strange sounds clearly from the veranda. Surely that could not be Mr Crabbe? He clutched more tightly the brief-case under his arm, wondering whether to enter. Listening carefully, he decided that the voice was the voice of a woman: Mr Crabbe evidently was in bed with a woman, and he was making her cry aloud either with pain or with pleasure. The cries were like nothing he had ever heard before, but they did not frighten him, they did not even arouse much curiosity: the only significant sounds in Robert Loo's life were musical sounds, preferably imagined ones, and these sounds were too grossly external and certainly not musical. Still, Crabbe was in and, when he was sated of whatever he was doing, there was much for him to hear and certain actions for him to take. Robert Loo now entered the dark living-room with confidence. He moved over to the table where he knew there was an electric lamp, and he fumbled for the switch of this lamp. Light sprang on to the darkness, a great rose-coloured circle of it. Robert Loo sat in an arm-chair, took scoring paper from his brief-case, and then placidly began to orchestrate the bar which had waited so long to become palpable dots and lines and curves: the first bar of his violin concerto – the opening cry of the orchestra set out fully from piccolo to basses. Meanwhile the woman's sobs continued. Flutes, oboes, clarinets, the downward-leaping theme on the bassoons, the wedge of harmony on the horns. He calmly and neatly wrote out the notes with a thin-nibbed fountain-pen.

The sobs began to slow down, like somebody dying, like the end of Honegger's *Pacific 231*. The noises of pleasure or despair became articulate sounds, a name called miserably, with a modicum of hope.

'Victor!'

Robert Loo raised his head, his pen halted in the middle of a group of quavers.

'Is that you, Victor?' Then sighs, deep sniffs, a jolting of the bed. Robert wondered, a tiny crease of frown over his eyes. Crabbe apparently was not in. He must have gone out for a moment, leaving her there. Then why those strange cries?

'Victor, come down here. Victor.'

Robert Loo sat undecided. Then he put down his wad of scoring paper, his pen, and went half-way down the dark corridor leading to the dark bedroom. 'Mr Crabbe isn't here,' he said gently.

'What's that? Who is it?' A further jolt of the bed, as of someone sitting up. A touch of fear in the voice.

'It's me. It's Robert Loo. Who are you?'

'What are you doing here?' A note of greater confidence, even of curiosity.

'I came to see . . .' But this was ridiculous, this colloquy at a distance and in the dark. Walking to the bedroom, Robert Loo found the corridor light-switch. Yellow clinical light disclosed the long bare wall of the corridor, the glass louvers all along one side, busy insect life, a young black scorpion high up near the low ceiling.

'Don't put the light on,' warned Rosemary. 'Don't. I'm a sight. You mustn't see me.'

'I only wanted to ask,' said Robert Loo, standing on the threshold of the room. 'Has he gone out? When is he coming back?'

Suddenly the whole orchestra burst out again. 'Never! Never!' A huge lost howl. 'He'll never come back! I've lost him, lost him!' Another jangling of the bed as she turned to pour more tears into the already soaked pillow. Robert Loo stood and wondered further, finding himself now somehow involved in these terrible cries of suffering woman. He could hardly retreat from them: having advanced so far, having spoken, he had to say something. He was mildly surprised that Crabbe should have been carrying on some large film-like or operatic affair with a woman whose identity was becoming clear. He had read many operatic scores, only for the music, but the libretti had occasionally made a, mainly subliminal, impact. And at school they had read *Antony and Cleopatra*. 'He ploughed her, and she cropp'd.' He entered the bedroom, meeting the force of a lung-emptying sob, then the oceanic ingurgitation of air. He switched on the light.

Like some strange beast in a gauzy cage, Rosemary lay, her black hair abundant over the bed, her brown limbs sprawled in her abandon, her dress crumpled and in disarray. Stabbed by the light, she turned her swimming face in protest, her mouth square with crying.

'Turn it off, turn it off!' Her bowing arm moved – down-stroke, up-stroke – as she cleaned tears from her eyes with her fist. Robert Loo looked at that brown bare arm in mild fascination. Then he spoke.

'I'm sorry,' he said.

'You don't know what it's like, you just don't know!'

'And where has he gone to?'

'To another woman! He's left me for ever!'

'Please,' said Robert Loo. 'I think this is important.' He sat on a chair by the bed, a chair cushioned by Crabbe's striped pyjamas. 'I need to see Mr Crabbe very badly.'

Rosemary stopped crying. She looked through films of water at Robert Loo and said: 'You wouldn't know anything about it. Nothing about real love. Like Joe and me.' The name started her off again.

'Oh, I see,' said Robert Loo.

'And I've nobody to turn to, nobody!'

'Can I do anything?'

'No! No! No!' She sank again into the salty water, indulging herself before even so inadequate an audience, into the delicious warm brine-tasting depths of her grief. Robert Loo wondered what he should do. A dance hostess with whom, he knew, his father had once been friendly, had tried, in a similar transport of despair over a man (not his father) to take caustic soda. This was, he knew, the usual Chinese way. Even in his mother's cupboard there had once stood a bottle of that standard agonizing Lethe water. The Chinese were resourceful and even kept a store of death ready bottled. He remembered the story of this dance hostess: how the caustic soda had been wrenched from her fingers and she had been brought to a reasonable philosophy by Beehive brandy. He would get this shaking mound of a wretched woman some of Crabbe's brandy. He thought he knew where it was kept.

Even then, as he poured a measure into a beer-glass, he almost forgot his mission. He examined the half-scored bar, not too sure whether the horn-harmonies were well disposed. But he returned, soft and leisurely, to the bed-room, opened the mosquito-curtains and said: 'Drink this.' Between residuary sobs she drank it like water, sitting up, Robert Loo on the bed's edge, his finger-tips on the base of the glass.

The heaving of her shoulders subsided. 'Why did you come here?' she asked.

'To see Mr Crabbe. I've left home, you see.'

'Oh, so they found out, did they?'

'Found out? What?

'About you and him.'

'I don't understand. It was trouble with my father. He hit me.'

'So he'd found out, had he?'

'No, my father saw it. He saw these Malays steal the cigarettes from the shelf and run away with them. Then he blamed me. He tore up some of my music and hit me. Before some customers.'

'Oh.'

'So now I want to go to England. To study. Mr Crabbe will arrange everything.'

'England!' Like some Hollywood Pitt she howled the word in agony. 'Joe's in England. Joe, Joe, Joe!' She collapsed again, her limbs somehow tangled round Robert Loo. Even he felt he had to make some perfunctory gesture of comfort. He began to stroke her bare arm, tentatively but, as he was a musician, rhythmically. 'Nobody to turn to,' said the pillow in a choked pillowy voice. Robert Loo went on stroking, the rhythm engendering a sort of *alla marcia* slow movement. Quiet strings, a monotonous alternation of minor, or rather modal, chords. Dorian mode. At her shoulder entered a most pathetic theme on a solo trumpet. The sudden sforzando made him grip it, involuntarily, just for an instant. There was a certain creative excitement, expressed in glandular constrictions which he knew well. Rosemary moved slightly. He found that his hand had seemed to travel other-whither. 'No,' said Rosemary, 'nobody to turn to. Nobody to comfort me.'

'I'm sorry.' That trumpet-tone was curiously breathy, almost asthmatic.

'Turn out the light. I'm ashamed to be seen like this.' There was a two-way switch dangling from its cord by the bed. With his left hand Robert Loo made near-darkness. The corridor light still shone, but Rosemary's face was all but hidden. The still stroking hand met more nakedness than it had expected: it was out of its depth now, out of the shallow end of hand or arm. Not being able to swim, one could not struggle back to shore: and, anyway, there was no breath to swim with. This asphyxiation was something new, and it seemed to make drowning an urgent necessity. Another man, someone read about, someone heard singing ridiculous passionate words in opera, began to endue Robert Loo like a limp outer garment. He had become that: the head soaring somewhere, a launched balloon, the arms dangling sockets to be filled by engines expert at stroking and then caressing. Music squeaked remotely from the ceiling; a toad bellowed from the waste-pipe. There was a crescendo which seemed to require a new form of notation. Surely no one before had ever written *fffff*? Impossible. And then he saw that it was in fact impossible. The whole structure collapsed, but the memory of the act of creation, the intention of the whole vast composition mercifully hung around.

The comforters, relaxed in sarongs after the day's work, kicked off their sandals at the top of Syed Omar's steps and made their obeisances to the wives, to the elder children, and to the gloomy head of the house. Syed Hassan, withdrawn, presented only his shamed back to the household, playing the radio, fingering the knobs like a rosary of penitence.

'There he sits,' said Syed Omar, 'the bail-bird, awaiting his day of trial, the bringer of disgrace to his father.' The radio burst out angrily like a rude unfilial word. 'Turn that off!' shouted Syed Omar.

Orange crush was brought for the three visitors. 'Well,' said 'Che Yusof, late colleague of Syed Omar, most clerkly in horn-rims and neat receding hair, 'have you found anything yet?'

'I wait,' said Syed Omar. 'Crabbe has promised me a job in the Education Office. But the white man's promises, as we know, are not always fulfilled.'

'Still,' said 'Che Ramli, fat master in the Malay School, 'he found the money for the bail, did he not, this man Crabbe?'

'Yes,' said Syed Omar, 'he found it, and now I wonder why.'

'One should not be so suspicious,' said 'Che Yusof. 'It may be sheer goodness of heart, generosity of nature, a desire to help the Malays.'

'I wonder,' said Syed Omar. He turned to his son. 'You can turn that radio on again,' he said. 'Loud.' A news bulletin in bubbling Tamil gushed forth at once. 'That will do,' shouted Syed Omar. Then he bent towards his friends, and his friends bent towards him, and, fixing 'Che Yassin,

Land Office clerk, with slitted eyes and hissing teeth, Syed Omar spoke his worst fears. 'You know this man Crabbe, you know that he does not go after women, you know of his relationship with at least one Chinese boy in the town.'

'You mean,' said 'Che Ramli, 'he is a member of the tribe of the prophet Lot.'

'That is one way of putting it,' said Syed Omar. 'Now, I am fairly sure that he has as yet made no advances to my son, though this may be a beginning, this may be a means of making us all obliged to him. But already, in the coffee-shops, some people have hinted to me that the thing I fear is already actual; otherwise, they said, why should Crabbe have helped one more than another? Two men today I have struck with my fists,' said Syed Omar. 'One I merely grazed with a coffee-glass. And early this evening one man suggested to me that I myself was involved with Crabbe and his perversions.' Syed Omar swelled his chest. 'I told him in no uncertain terms that that was not so. He apologized and stood me a drink. And he then said that there were possibly some chances of employment for me in the North-Eastern Transport if I knew how to drive heavy vehicles. I told him,' said Syed Omar, his chest not yet relaxed, 'that there was no vehicle I could not drive. Thus,' he said triumphantly, 'you see that an ill wind blows some good to somebody, if not everybody.'

His friends pondered this proverb for a time, sipping their orange crush. The bubbling radio Tamil then stopped, followed immediately by a fast screeched song of urgent amorousness – drums and twangs and a high woman's voice. 'Turn off that row!' called Syed Omar. 'We can't hear ourselves drink, let alone talk!'

'You told me to turn it on,' replied Syed Hassan, 'less than a minute ago.'

'And now I tell you to turn it off!' cried Syed Omar. 'Don't argue, boy!'

'I wish you'd make up your mind,' said his son, sullenly.

'What's that?' said Syed Omar, half rising, 'what's that you say? You hear,' he said, turning to his friends, 'you hear how he answers back. I have spoiled the brat with too much kindness. Too much kindness is the only fault I can chide myself with.' He sat down, simulating the arthritic movements of a broken man. His friends tut-tutted, saying: 'Never mind, don't take on so, no cause to blame yourself, the younger generation is everywhere the same, no gratitude.'

Syed Hassan spitefully turned the radio knob to its maximum, so that the high swollen voice, garnished soon with shrieks from the valves, filled the room and made the glasses and the few cheap ornaments tingle and rattle. There were shrill and deep shouts of protest from all present. With a sour face and a thrust-out jaw Syed Hassan obeyed his father's yell, and the painful music rushed in a diminuendo to silence and a click.

'Come here, boy!'

'I'm tired, I'm sick,' cried Syed Hassan. 'On to me all the time!'

'That's right. You have disgraced me before the whole town. You are now disgracing me before my guests and friends. How dare you. HOW DARE YOU.' Syed Omar pulled up the right sleeve of his shirt, disclosing a fat un-muscular arm. The friends showed embarrassment, say-ing: 'No, no, please, no. We're going now, anyway.'

'No,' protested Syed Omar. 'He thinks he is such a big man, defying his father, defying law and order, cringing behind the white man's help. The law will, God help me, God help his poor mothers and brothers and sisters, punish him in its own time, but I have my rights too. I will not be disgraced before my friends. Come here, boy.'

The comforters were leaving, scrambling for their san-dals at the head of the house steps, in their haste shuf-fling into the wrong ones, saying: 'Sorry, yours, you seem to have taken mine, that's right, that's the one, thank you,' and so on. Meanwhile, Syed Omar, with his right arm ready, called them to stay, to witness the act of just punition. But, bowing with sketchily joined hands, they smiled their way clumsily out, down to the darkness. Syed Omar, no whit deflated, turned to his son, saying: 'Now.'

'I wish,' said Syed Hassan, his back to the wall by the radio, 'I wish that I wasn't here. I wish I was in the lock-up with the others.'

'Say that again! Say that again!' And from the women came shocked cooings.

'I'd be better off there. You wouldn't be on to me all the time. And I know what you're thinking, and I know what you said to those friends of yours.'

'Have a care, boy.' A big flat hand came up for slapping.

'All right, hit me. I don't mind.'

'You will, boy, you will!' At this point, 'Che Maimu-nah, who was evidently Syed Omar's mother, sidled in between the contestants, preaching peace. 'There will be enough tears soon, God knows. Be quiet now, both of you.'

'Keep out of this, woman. This is my affair. I am his father.'

'Sit down,' ordered Maimunah. Zainab, the other wife, said: 'Sit down, sit down, you are both waking the younger children.' Sulkily the men obeyed, but Syed Omar, un-willing to see so many feet of good strong drama discarded on the cutting-room floor, burst out with a despairing 'Ruined, ruined, ruined,' as he slumped into his chair.

'Oh, shut up,' muttered his son.

'You hear? You hear?' cried Syed Omar in gratitude. 'You ask me, you stupid women, to sit down and be quiet, do you? You want your husband to be insulted, do you, in his own house, by his own son? By God, I will choke him with my own hands.' On his feet, he made like an ape or a bear for his delinquent boy, but Syed Hassan was ready with fists.

'Strike your father, eh?' Syed Omar launched an un-handy cuff, then another. Syed Hassan side-stepped with skill, and his father's podgy left caught the wall, not hard, but enough to call forth religious cries of pain and rage.

'Keep off,' warned Syed Hassan, 'keep off, keep off.' He was cornered between the radio and a flimsy dresser that held blue crockery. Almost above him was the poster of the Chief Minister and his loving silk-clad arms, the legend, 'Peace'.

'Come here and take your punishment,' said Syed Omar. 'Come and be hit.'

'No! No!' As the breathing bulk of his father advanced, Syed Hassan downed with his head and butted. No great harm was done: Syed Omar nearly lost balance, saved himself by clutching at the dresser; only one blue plate rolled on to the floor, and it did not break. But Syed Hassan stood now in the room's centre, crying out: 'I'm going! I'm leaving! You'll never see me again!'

He was at once peppered with hot Malay and snaked about with women's arms. His father for some reason spoke violent English at him:

'Don't be a bloody fool! If you jump bail you'll be in big trouble!'

'I'm going,' said Syed Hassan in Malay. 'I go now,' he said in English. He hacked away at the lianas of brown flesh that wreathed him about. A few strides took him to the door. Here he paused before his exit, waiting for some great exit-line to come, but nothing came. The dramatic instinct of both father and son was stronger than their dramatic talent. He said, in Malay: 'You have ruined my life, all of you! May God forgive you!' Then he leapt the house steps into the night. He hurried down the soggy path, reached the road, and began walking at a great pace towards Crabbe's house. When he was satisfied that nobody was following him he slowed down, wiping the sweat from his neck and face and chest with a large soiled handkerchief.

In the town there was harsh light, and loud soothing music sang all about him. He was cooled by a new sense of freedom, heartened by the knowledge that Crabbe would help him to get away, willingly (for he was a rich man) forfeiting the bail-money, efficiently calling up cars

515

and lorries, consulting rail time-tables, devising disguises. It was the job of the British to help the Malays. That was well known, that was in the history books. And if Crabbe was slow in helping, there was always blackmail. How would Crabbe like his pederastic activities reported to K.L., eh? He wouldn't like that, would he? But, essentially, it was as a friend that he would approach him, one glad to help, knowing it was the duty he had travelled eight thousand miles to fulfil.

Turning into the avenue where the school-teachers' houses lay, Syed Hassan was surprised to meet Robert Loo; surprised, anyway, to meet him at this hour. He should be in his dad's shop, cringing at the rich music of the juke-box and dealing with the cash sales. At the end of the avenue and round the corner was Crabbe's house. Robert Loo had undoubtedly been there. *Kaum nabi Lot*: the tribe of the prophet Lot. Syed Hassan smacked the phrase on his lips, thinking of Sodom and its destruction and the prophet's salty wife. 'Hello,' he said, 'it's you, is it?'

'Yes, it's me.'

'Where've you been?'

The Chinese boy hesitated. 'To see Mr Crabbe. But he wasn't in. So I'm going home.'

Syed Hassan smiled with contempt. 'I,' he said, 'have left home.' Robert Loo looked at him with interest. The two youths, the brown and the yellow, faced each other at the cross-roads, under a dim street-lamp. 'So Crabbe's not in,' said Syed Hassan. 'We'll see, we'll see.'

'Why did you leave home?' asked Robert Loo.

'My father tried to hit me. But nobody hits me, nobody, not even my father.'

'That's strange,' said Robert Loo. 'That happened to me too.'

'Your dad tried to hit you?'

'He did hit me. Before the customers. And I walked out. It's my music, you see, I've got to go on with my music.' Robert Loo spoke with sudden passion, and Syed Hassan smiled again, saying: 'But you haven't left home. You Chinese are frightened of leaving home, you're frightened of your fathers.'

'I did leave home,' said Robert Loo, 'but I'm going back again. Just perhaps for a night. Or two nights. I've got to think, you see, I've a lot to think about.'

'And he'll hit you again. He'll beat you till you scream blue murder.' Syed Hassan spoke the words with satisfaction. 'But nobody's going to beat me.'

'Over there,' said Robert Loo, 'there's a little stall. They sell coffee and orange crush. Perhaps we'd better go over there and talk.'

'Talk,' said Syed Hassan. 'Talk's never enough. That's all my father does – talk, talk, talk. Yes,' he said, 'we'll drink some coffee. If you'll pay.'

'I'll pay.'

Syed Hassan felt somewhat ashamed of his brusqueness, his rudeness, his boasting. 'All I meant,' he said, 'was that I've no money. That's all I meant.'

'All right. I've two dollars.'

'It's very kind of you,' said Syed Hassan with stiff courtesy. 'Thank you.'

'You're very welcome.' They almost bowed each other over to the ramshackle stall, lit by a kerosene lamp, over whose cracked cups a thin Tamil presided.

'It's difficult to say these things in Malay,' said Robert Loo. 'And in Chinese, too.' He sucked the lip of the brimming coffee-cup. 'Some things the British brought with them. Along with their language.' His brow let the kerosene lamp etch out the puzzle. '*Love*,' he said. 'Do you know that word? *Love, love. I love you.* In Mandarin we say: "*Wo ai ni*." But it's not the same.'

'I know that,' said Syed Hassan. '*I love you.* It's on the films. Then they *kiss*.' He used the English word; the Malay word *chium* meant to plough the beloved's face with one's nose. It was not the same thing, despite the dictionaries.

'I'm in love,' said Robert Loo in English. He burst out

with it; he had to tell someone. 'That's why I've got to go back home, you see. I'm in love. Everything ...' He paused, juggling in his mind with Malay and English; the English words fell into his hand. 'Everything *feels* different. If my father hits me again, even that will feel different. This coffee tastes different from any coffee I've had before.'

'It's not very good coffee,' said Syed Hassan.

'I don't mean that,' said Robert Loo. 'It's a different world. It's hard to explain ...'

'In love,' mused Syed Hassan. 'Who are you in love with?'

'I can't say.' Robert Loo blushed. 'It's a secret.'

'And you've ...'

'Yes, yes. I never knew it would be like that. Everything becomes different. I feel older ...'

He felt older. Syed Hassan felt envy. That was an experience he still had not had; he felt bitter because the whole thing seemed so typical, the Chinese cutting out the Malays even in that particular business. But, in the act of formulating the words of resentment, he remembered his father. Race, race, race – his father's dinner-table theme. The Tamils had done this to him, and the Sikhs had done that, and the Chinese were pig-guzzling infidels, and as for the British ...

'Is she Chinese?' he asked.

'No,' said Robert Loo. He said it almost fearfully, startled on the brink of confidences he must not make. 'No, she's not. She's ...' Yet he wanted Syed Hassan to know and envy. Only the beloved's name must not steal forth into air which, where she was not, was rank, polluted, slave's air, 'Do not show your body to the moon, my darling, for fear that even her silver beams may smirch it.' From where did that come, where had he heard that? Was it some old Chinese poem? He thought not; it had come, like his symphonic themes, from nowhere. 'She's not Chinese,' he said at length. 'Nor Malay. She's ...' Then he recollected that he did not really know what she was;

the external world had meant so little that its great abstractions had never quite registered. Trying to assign her to the correct column of some bureaucratic form, he only became aware of her warmth and smoothness and the various scents of her – secondary attributes which nevertheless had power, in sheer memory, at this moment of savouring the enhanced taste of coffee and trying to finish the sentence he was uttering, to attack his knee-joints like monstrous rubber hammers.

'It doesn't matter,' said Syed Hassan. 'I don't really want to know.' Then, with an eagerness that was new to him, he said: 'I'd nothing against that Tamil really. What I mean is, it wasn't because he was a Tamil. My father's a fool. He doesn't know that he lost his job because one of his friends has been trying to get it for his daughter. One of his friends that was at the house tonight. 'Che Yusof it was. At least, I'm pretty sure it was. You learn a lot going round the town. More than you learn at school.'

'But,' said Robert Loo, 'they say that if you hadn't done that ... What I mean is that those Malays wouldn't have come into our shop and tried to steal. And then my father wouldn't have hit me for not seeing them. And then ...' And then, of course, he would have spent the evening as usual, a drudge thinking about the music he wanted to write, chafing under the blows of the juke-box. Tonight he seemed incapable of finishing any sentence. Curiously, now in the silence, the remembered noises of the juke-box did not seem so terrible. The mere sensuous impact of trumpet or saxophone, whatever it happened to be playing, was an echo, even though a faint echo, of that excitement and abandon. He wanted to taste, smell, hear: his senses were terribly alive.

'We ought to go to some dance-hall,' he said. 'We ought to go and drink beer and listen to music and watch the women dancing. After all, we are men.'

'There's nowhere now,' said Syed Hassan. 'We could go to your shop, of course. But the Park's been closed down by the authorities. We can't go to the Park any more.'

'And we haven't much money.'

'I've no money.'

'I suppose I'd better go home,' said Robert Loo. 'I'm not really frightened of my father. Not any more.'

'Fathers,' said Syed Hassan. 'They don't know much really. They're stupid, like kids. Ignorant. You've just got to put up with them.'

'You're going home, too?'

Syed Hassan grimaced, shrugged. 'I suppose so. We've got to remember our *tanggongan*. *Tanggongan*. What's that word in English?'

'Responsibilities.'

'Responsibilities. A good long word. We've got to remember our responsibilities.'

6

'Was it,' wondered Crabbe, 'intended for him?' The poem was called *Lines for Early Middle Age*, and it was signed Fenella Crabbe, but it was impossible that Fenella — twenty-eight or twenty-nine — should think of herself as middle-aged, or even, being a woman and a good-looking woman although a poet, have a proleptic Eliotian image of an aged eagle with tired wings demanding to be released from the dressing-mirror. Besides, there was nothing of the nobility of the eagle here. It was himself, the hanging flesh on cheeks and chest dancing as he ran up the stairs: it was the kind of farewell he had not expected:

> The afternoon hour has struck for you to
> Enter, become your body, pay
> The forced grin of affection due to
> What is now you. That is to say:
> You are this pate and mouth of missing teeth ...

'Pouring in, old boy,' said the man opposite. 'Just pouring in. Money in oil. As one door shuts, another door closes. Ha, ha. But nowhere for anybody to live. Government servants sleeping in the monsoon drains. Wives going home after a month. Ha, ha. Still, that's where you ought to go when you've left Malaya. Borneo. Borneo. I've just come back.' He thrust his head into the aisle. 'Boy!' A Chinese in a white coat responded list-lessly. 'What will you have? Beer?'

'Not Malayan beer,' said Crabbe. 'It doesn't agree with me any more. Gin and tonic, I think.'

'You heard that,' said the man to the boy. 'And beer for me. A small Polar.'

> You are these sagging bulbs and bags beneath,
> And the leering social face in that far mirror
> Recognized with shock (but no, no error) –
> That is you, too.

'But you ought to drink beer,' said the man reproach-fully. 'That's my line. I sell beer all over the East. Thirty years on the job. Three thousand a month and a car allow-ance and welcome wherever I go. Jones. You must know me. Everybody knows Tommy Jones. They may get rid of you, but they'll never get rid of old Tommy.'

'No,' said Crabbe. But the second stanza was more encouraging:

> Youth was a knife and lakes and air,
> Metal and glass; you could bestow
> Your body as a gift of swords to spare.
> It was different then. It was not you ...

'All the way along the line,' said the man. 'Last night I was given a dinner in Anjing. The towkays always do their best for old Tommy. Almost as though I was doing them a favour selling them the stuff. And the night before in Kuala Musang. And then Tikus tonight. And Ular to-morrow night. Drunk as a lord. Where do you get off?'

> Be patient. It will learn to be concise
> Again, the hot room shrink to austere ice.
> The silver will evoke a salmon's leap,
> And bone-rungs strong enough for a single step
> Will make a one-way stair.

'Needn't answer if you don't want to,' said the man huffily. 'I was only trying to make conversation, pass the time a bit.' He was thin, long-faced, domed and grey-moustached and carried a tidy paunch.

'Sorry,' said Crabbe. 'I get off at Mawas. Then I go to Durian Estate by launch. I'm sorry. I was reading this, you see. Something written by my wife. It was a bit of a shock finding it here.'

'Your missus writes for the papers, does she? Well, well.

I never did like brainy women myself. No offence. Every-one to his own taste.'

'That's one brainy woman who didn't like me much. She went home,' said Crabbe.

The man had taken the paper from Crabbe and he handled it as though it were a rag that had wiped vomit. 'You buy this sort of thing? Never have much time for reading, myself.'

'No,' said Crabbe. 'An army major got off at Pelandok and left it on the seat. I haven't seen a copy for a long time. It's a very progressive review.'

'Eh?' the man looked at Crabbe with suspicion. Then he flicked over the pages gingerly. '*The New Presbyter*, it's called,' he said. 'And then, written very small, it says: "Formerly *The Old Priest*". That sounds a damn silly name for a paper.'

'It's a kind of pulpit,' said Crabbe. 'It tells us what we've got to believe. And it has a sort of funny column. There, just next to my wife's poem. Called "Dear, Dear Isle".'

'I don't see anything funny in that.'

Crabbe sipped his gin and tonic. The tonic, manufac-tured by a Singapore firm with a monopoly, had a curious musty taste which disturbingly evoked the smell of the old Manchester Free Trade Hall. Crabbe heard the heavy brass at the end of the *Tanhäusser* Overture. His first wife, in skirt and blue jumper, stood next to him with a score. Would they never let him alone? Even on Malayan Railways, chugging through jungle, they were there. Both of them.

'That's not funny,' said the man. 'A bloke here gets a prize for sending in a cutting about a woman who put flowers on her dog's grave. That seems a very reasonable thing to do. I'm fond of dogs myself. Are you sure this is meant to be funny?'

'I think so,' said Crabbe. 'But one gets so out of touch.'

'That's it.' With vigour and eagerness the man put down the periodical. The air-mail paper rustled like thin sheets of metal. 'Out of touch, and a bloody good job too. They're all crackers back there. It stands to reason. Paying five bob for a packet of twenty. And four bob for a gin. You'd hardly believe that, would you? But it's true. I've got a sister back there. She writes to me now and again. You'd hardly believe the things they put up with back in England. I've not been back for thirty years. And I'm buggered if I'm going back. But,' he said in triumph, 'you've got to, haven't you? They're kicking you lot out. But not old Tommy. Beer's much too important.'

'It binds the races together,' said Crabbe.

'Eh? What's that?' The man listened narrowly, half incredulous. 'Say that again. By God, that's clever. That'd make a damn good advert. I'll write that down.' He searched in vain for a note-book. 'Ah, never mind, I'll remember it.' He looked at Crabbe with more favour. 'That your line, eh? Slogans and so on? Information Department and what not?'

'Education,' said Crabbe.

'You'll never educate them,' said the man with finality. He looked at space, sneering, leaning back comfortably. 'You ought to get into oil. Money there, over the water. It's a good job your lot are going. You won't never do any good.'

'You know,' said Crabbe, 'I don't think I am going. It's a funny thing, it's just suddenly come over me. There was a man, a Ceylonese, back in Kuala Hantu, and he said I'd never go. He said I'd end my days up-river. Funny. I just can't see myself getting on the boat. Or the plane. I just can't see any future beyond being here.'

'You'll go home,' said the man, 'leaving your black bastards like the rest of them. Kids all over the place with no fathers, crying out for food.'

'You ought to write for *The New Presbyter*.'

'Women,' said the man. 'I've had my pick.' He sucked his teeth. 'But I've always provided. One of the kids is in the Free School, Kenching. You'd hardly believe that, would you?'

'No.'

'Well, it's true.' Dreamily he said: 'There's always somebody waiting for me. Last night in Anjing. And in Tikus tonight. There's always somebody waiting for old Tommy. And you too, I expect. I've known some of you school-teacher bastards before. Think butter wouldn't melt in their mouths. But she'll be there in wherever-you're-going. Eh? That's true, isn't it?' He showed black teeth and tweaked Crabbe's right knee. 'A woman waiting for the old bastard.'

'Probably.'

'A woman at the end of the line. Always a woman. Have another drink.'

The train stopped at a village called Berang-berang. A Sikh went by swinging a lantern, rare lamps lit up the inevitable back-cloth of palms, bare feet padded along the platform. A Malayan family, laden with food in cardboard boxes, a callow English private in jungle green, a cheerful young Chinese in a soiled white Christian priest's habit – these got on.

'Next stop for me,' said the beer salesman. 'They'll be waiting at the station with the brass bands. It's a long time since they seen old Tommy. They won't half lay on a spread. Eh,' he said suddenly, a poking finger making for Crabbe. 'Eh, you. Don't know your name.'

'Yes?' said Crabbe.

'You come too. Not in no hurry, are you?'

'I've got to get to Mawas.'

'You can get to Mawas by road in the morning. I know. Trust old Tommy. Know this part like the back of my hand. What you got to do in Mawas?'

'A man's been killed. By the terrorists, I should imagine.'

'Oh, well, that's nothing. Nothing you can do. Plenty of that goes on these days. You come and meet some of old Tommy's pals.'

A sudden relief washed over Crabbe like shower water. He realized that, for some reason, he wanted to put off going to Durian Estate. Why, he wondered. It wasn't the corpse, which would now be buried. It wasn't the need to dispense official comfort to the bereaved, to promise official financial help. It wasn't the prospect of meeting the manager and pretending not to be embarrassed by his whisky tremor. It wasn't the thought that he himself, crossing to the tappers' lines and the schoolhouse, might well be sniped at. It was something unseen, unknown, and far more solid. And the feeling of apprehension had, for some reason, come over him on reading Fenella's poem in *The New Presbyter*.

'Yes,' he said. 'Thanks very much. I'd like to come.'

'No trouble about getting somewhere to sleep,' said the man. 'If we do sleep, that is.' He winked. 'They'll fix you up all right. Do anything for a pal of Tommy's.'

Tikus was a small town with an attap hut for a station. But that it would not be a small town for long (money in tin?) was evident from the girth and fleshy chuckles and clean white trousers of the two Chinese shopkeepers who had come to meet good old Tommy. 'Told you,' he said triumphantly to Crabbe, 'didn't I? Brass bands and all, eh?' Indeed, a small Sikh boy with a top-knot, detailed by his station-master father to collect the tickets, sat on the platform blowing a mouth-organ. 'This,' said Tommy to the towkays, 'is Mr er – Don't know your name,' he said to Crabbe. The two Chinese slapped Crabbe on the back in welcome. Any friend of old Tommy's friend of theirs. They spoke no English. The ghastly debased Malay of the bazaars chirped out of prosperous bellies as the four got into a waiting Hillman. Tommy asking about old so-and-so and old so-and-so, not seen the bastards for years.

'Old bastard!' roared one of the towkays.

'Old bastard yourself. What you laid on for us, eh? Bring on the dancing girls!'

They drove down the main street, under sodium lighting, to a filthy shop-house crammed with shining refrigerators, tape-recorders, outboard motors ('Why?' wondered

Crabbe: 'we're nowhere near the river') and brandy. A Chinese girl in pyjamas, bearing a soup-bowl, preceded them up the stairs. Good old Tommy, mounting straight after as honoured guest, whistled one sharp blast through his teeth, making the old Roman sign with snail's horn fingers that jabbed jocularly at her right buttock. The towkays roared, the girl turned at the stair-head, yapped a protest, and baptized Tommy briefly with a hot drop from the bowl. A few strips of shark's fin thatched his bald dome. 'Thinks the world of old Tommy,' he cried. 'Ha ha. That's my girl.'

Two old men, shrunken relics of old China, greeted Tommy with shy laughter, and shook hands seriously with Crabbe. The six of them sat round a table, Crabbe's foot, as he took his chair, clanking loudly against a concealed spittoon. 'Ha ha,' cried Tommy. 'Don't kick the pee-pot over.' He took charge of everything, the life and soul, smacking his lips over the soup and calling for more chilli sauce, urging his hosts to down their own brandy with the fearsome Chinese salute: *'Yam seng!'*

'Yam seng!'

'Yam seng!'

Down went the brandy, neat half-tumblers of it, and more bottles were opened.

'You,' said Tommy to Crabbe. 'Don't know your name. Shouldn't be drinking this really, you know. All right for you, you got no responsibility to the firm, but I'm never off duty, never off duty. Should be on beer. Still,' he said, 'there always tomorrow. *Yam seng!*'

'Yam seng!'

Over the fish-dish – something sole-like, exquisitely seethed in a strange sauce, garnished with roots and fruits of the country – Tommy became sentimental. 'Bloody good firm,' he said. 'Always looked after old Tommy, know a good man when they see one. Given my life to that firm. And they know it. Never let them down. Never let me down. Here, gorgeous,' he said to the pert painted serving wench, 'come and sit on old Tommy's knee.' But the time for dalliance was not yet. They had to eat their way through sweet-and-sour pork, a duck of miraculous tenderness, prawns and stuffed pumpkin, lychees in ice-water.

'*Yam seng!*'

'*Yam seng!*'

One of the two serving girls, taking up chopsticks and used dishes from the table, sang to Crabbe. The towkays smiled, listening. Old Tommy tried to join in, but was shushed. 'Wanted to make a jewess of it,' he said. 'Never mind.' It was a pentatonic tune, austere and thin as the girl's body, evidently erotic, but its eroticism checked and chilled by the pure simple melodic line. 'They're civilized,' thought Crabbe. Despite the dirty ceiling and the cigarette butts swelling in the cuspidor, they're civilized. And he felt, through the brandy, that this was perhaps the only country in the world for any man who cared about history. What an incredible head-reeling collocation of cultures. Islamic texts sprawling on the Great Wall, a twelve-legged god looking down in exophthalmic frowning benevolence.

'Extraordinary collocation of cultures,' he said to old Tommy.

'That's what I always say myself, old man.' Tommy belched loudly. 'And the very best of luck.' The girl who had baptized him on the stairs now sat on his knee, chewing gum steadily. 'That's right,' he said. 'You come to daddy.' He stroked her thin leg. 'Like going to bed with a bicycle.'

And now Crabbe had his own feather-light chattering burden. Desire for a Chinese woman did not come easily: even at their lowest social level they were works of art, engendering a hardly kinetic emotion.

'Works of art,' he said. 'This lad's a fine musician. Marvellous, marvellous. And who'll do anything for him? You won't, will you, for all your big talk?'

'Beer, beer, glorious beer,' sang Tommy. 'Fill yourself right up to here.' He was doing his duty now, doing his job. Six great bottles of one of the Hong Kong brews had been brought to wash down the brandy and the fragments of rice and *mee* and meat-fibres that clung to the back teeth. 'Beer,' cried Tommy. 'What did you call it? International something-or-other you called it. Should have written it down.' His girl, doing her job too, wiped his frothy mouth with a paper napkin.

'Binds the nations together,' said Crabbe. 'Like music. And you won't do a damn thing about it. Or about Rosemary. Or Vythilingam. Or old Syed Omar. Who'll do anything for them when I'm gone?' His girl hugged him, smoothing his back hair with a cool hand. The towkays were out of it. They sat there quietly, bemused, smiling faintly, glad that their guests were having a good time. They, too, were doing their duty, were now gently handing it over to their delegates of the long night.

'Beer's a bit warm,' said Tommy. 'Must have it cold. Remember.' He beat time with a stained forefinger, reciting a slogan in a refined accent: 'The Climate Is Torrid. Warm Beer Is Horrid.' He drank down a full six inches and again had his mouth wiped. 'But lovely stuff just the same. Knew a chap,' he said, 'big fellow, nearly seven feet tall, couldn't abide it cold. Held it in his big 'ot 'and. Made it 'ot as 'ell. He liked it that way. Nabby Adams, his name was. Police. You wouldn't know him.'

All the towkays rose as one man, ready to go, knowing that their guests were in good hands.

'In the morning,' said Tommy. 'Talk business in the morning.'

'*Terima kaseh*,' said Crabbe putting out disengaged fingers. '*Hsieh hsieh, towkay. Wan an.*'

'Knows a bit of the lingo, eh?' said Tommy. 'Me, I'm not clever that way.'

'Beer,' said Crabbe with finicking articulation, 'is itself a language.'

'By God, that's a good one. Must write that down.' But his head drooped on to the thin shoulders of the patient girl on his lap. 'Ready for bed. Take me home, love.' The towkays waved benignly from the door.

Crabbe's girl's name was Chin Chin, a name frivolous in sound but meaning 'Truth'. Led by the hand of Truth, he followed Tommy – in full song under the moon – down the empty street. Tommy's girl giggled, her arm in his, looking back to chirp Chinese words to her friend and colleague.

'Where?' asked Crabbe. 'Where we go?'

'*Sini, sini.*' It was a squalid-looking lodging-house, a vista of many stairs, a smell of turmeric and aniseed. In the distance, farther along the line, Tommy was singing, still doing his duty, advertising bottled euphoria to the sleeping town.

Chin Chin's room was small, fanless, with a bed, a cupboard, photographs of Chinese film stars with Caucasian features, the odour of hidden hung dresses. She had no underwear and was naked before Crabbe had taken off his tie. Crabbe stood, looked, wondered, tossed a coin in his head. It came down 'No.'

'No,' said Crabbe. 'Thank you, but no.'

'Not like?'

'Oh yes, like. But not now. Other time. Sleep now.'

She grimaced, wrapped a sheet round her body, lay face downwards on the bed with her limbs spread, starfish-like. In two minutes she was asleep. Crabbe found a cushion and settled with the dust on the wooden floor. Before he fell asleep he had a dim notion that he ought to be keeping his body pure for this event hidden in the near future, and he felt a tired satisfaction that he had succeeded in postponing it, even if only for a few hours.

When Robert Loo left, Rosemary lay still for a time in the dark, no particular thought in her head, feeling no particular emotion, her body quite numb. The headlights of cars occasionally shot the room with moving brief silver, and then for an instant she was in a tower, high up, above everything, with searchlights playing upon her.

The cars were going to Mr Godsave's house, where there seemed to be a party, perhaps a farewell party for Mr Godsave, the last white man in the Police Department. She heard distant drinking voices, and sometimes they seemed to be talking about her.

'Where's old Rosemary, eh?'

'Yahoooooo! Give her some stick!'

'The Trojan horse where fifty heroes slept.'

'Rosemary, my darling,' sang somebody, 'Rosemary, my dear. Rosemary da-da-da da . . .'

One of the voices was the voice of Joe. 'Then I put my hand there, and I did this, and I did that, and then I . . .' And then a great shout of drinkers' laughter. And then the grind-out of brakes and revving-up as more cars arrived.

'She was a grand girl in her way, you know.'

'Always ready, I will say that.'

'I mean, we were lucky to find her here, really.'

'Oh, God, yes, when you think of the five-dollar doses in the Park, and those bloody Chinese keeps: gimme, gimme, gimme.'

'But a bit too much for a whole tour. I mean, all right for a year or so. But not three, no, no, no.'

'Say six months.'

'Oh yes, six months would do nicely. And then, after a bit, come back for more.'

'But as a permanency . . .'

'Oh, my God, a permanency . . .'

She got out of bed, and the voices merged into the wordless noise of happy drinking. She padded to Crabbe's bathroom, switched on the light, and saw herself in the wide mirror: Medusa hair, eyes, puffed with crying, lipstick smeared where she had been inexpertly kissed by a Chinese boy, the polished brown glory of her upper body. She gasped under the cold spray of the shower, washing off and out with soap so much and so much. She scoured her teeth with Crabbe's tooth-brush, brushed her hair with Crabbe's brushes, and then put on a pair of Crabbe's silk pyjamas. And still no thought passed through her head. She sniffed and sniffed as though she had a cold, and, looking in the handkerchief drawer of Crabbe's dressing-table, found not only clean handkerchiefs but a bundle of letters. Most of them smelt old, musty, like half-eaten apples, and the dates, she noticed, belonged to another age. 'Dearest Vic.' 'My own dear Victor.' 'Darling.' Love, love, love. She read through six or seven, still sniffing. The story was that Crabbe was away, working in some college away from this woman, a place where there was no accommodation for married couples, and that, even though he was away, she thought of him all the time and missed him so much at night. Rosemary saw her mouth began to twist in the mirror, and got a swift image of stone masks she had seen above the proscenium of a Liverpool theatre. A howl came from somewhere outside, a pye-dog. She refused to cry, she had done crying. The drinking voices waxed very loud. Rosemary could not decipher the signature of the letters: Mal, May, Maya, something like that. She, too, had sent such loving letters, but Joe would not keep those in his handkerchief drawer, if he had a handkerchief drawer. He would show them to his English friends, and they would laugh at them, or they would make Zulu clicks of envious concupiscence.

'Smashing bit of stuff.'

'Get up them stairs, eh?'

'Howwwwwwwww!'

But that was the dog outside. Rosemary thought of her cats, how she had left them without food, how they relied on her, but tonight she was too weary for responsibility. Tomorrow she would not go to school, she would be ill. Tonight she would stay in Crabbe's house; her cats would not starve: they had shared three tins of pilchards at lunch-time. For a moment she hungered sentimentally for her cats: they had promised nothing, given nothing, taken all, did not pretend affection. They were a symbol of home: the cat by the fire, the fog swirling outside, the television programme just starting.

'Oh, Joe, Joe, Joe,' howled the pye-dog.

Rosemary swished silkenly down the corridor in bare feet. The sitting-room was but dimly illumined with a solitary wall-night. She switched everything on, including the dining-recess lamps, and then stood by the kitchen entrance and called: 'Boy!' There was no reply: only a heave and rustle as of somebody turning on a bed. 'Boy! Boy! Boy!' Nobody answered, nobody came. Rosemary turned back to the big bright room and poured herself brandy. She went to the refrigerator for water, and the click and swing of the heavy white door did what her call could not do. The cook-boy appeared in vest and under-pants, anxious for the safety of the pre-cooked meal he had placed in the humming cold: Crabbe's dinner or lunch, tomorrow or whenever he should return. 'There you are,' said Rosemary. 'I want food.'

'A?' A noise which God gave only to the Chinese lower classes – throaty, short, loud, interrogative, disapproving, incredulous, insolent.

'*Makan, makan. Saya mahu makan*,' shouted Rosemary. 'What's this?' She pulled from the refrigerator a dish containing a chill curry. The cook-boy tried to grab it too. They tussled for an instant, and, for some reason, Rosemary did not feel that this was undignified. 'Heat that up,' she said, letting it go, 'and make some chapattis.'

'A?'

'Chapattis, chapattis. Don't you know what chapattis are? You-all Chinese cooks call yourself cooks . . . Here, where's the flour?'

But the cook-boy had seen on the table by the refrigerator a glass of brandy waiting for water. He became loud and agitated. He slip-slopped off to the sitting-room and came back with a near-empty bottle. He wailed, he beseeched, he was near tears.

'All right,' said Rosemary. 'I'll tell tuan that I drank it. But you better start making those chapattis.'

'A?'

'If you don't start heating up that curry,' said Rosemary loudly, 'I'll say that you drank that brandy. I'll finish off the bottle and say that you drank it all.'

The cook-boy got busy. Rosemary sat in an arm-chair and switched on the radio. A play was one, some silly London play on the B.B.C. Overseas Service:

'. . . Listen to that nightingale, like some very competent imitation of a nightingale.'

'Like a gramophone record of a nightingale.'

'It's all been used before, there's nothing new. That moon over there, ridiculously bright . . .'

'Vulgarly full.'

'The night-scented stocks, proud of a perfume that any Piccadilly tart could buy.' (At the mention of Piccadilly, Rosemary's mouth began to square for tears.) 'But you know . . .'

'Yes? What do I know?'

'There are no new words either. Oh, God, I'm not afraid of being vulgar. I'm not ashamed of using the old, old clichés. You know, don't you, don't you, Rosemary? You know that I . . .'

'I think I know, Arnold, I think I've always known . . .'

'Darling . . .'

At the mention of her own name, Rosemary rose in shock and anger, ready to do injury to the mocking instrument. She blubbered instead, switching it off, hearing in the fading voice of 'Arnold' the refined stage-voice of Lim Cheng Po of Penang. 'Oh, Victor, Victor,' she sobbed. 'Where are you? I could be a good wife to you, Victor.' The loud sound of frying came from the kitchen: her tears dripped like hot fat. She sat down, sobbing – somewhat stagily now – through a litany of names of those who might comfort her, take her in their arms to say: 'Don't cry any more, darling. The bad, bad days are over now.' From the list certain names were absent. Joe, Robert Loo, Jalil. One name, surprisingly, was present:

'Vy, Vy, oh, Vy. Oh, why did I hurt you like that?'

Why should Robert Loo's name be present? His interest was purely historical: he was not to be read in any anthology. His poem had been jejune, over-brief, uncontrolled, inarticulate really, a poem not to take seriously, not even to read, merely a link in a long process of evolution: Bale divided the interlude into acts; Surrey first used blank verse; Wyatt introduced the sonnet – forgotten scullions to the great world, table-scrubbers, potato-peelers, onion-cleaners, meat-choppers for the master cook who will soon arrive from Stratford. But that cold, polite, refined Oxonian from Penang had made possible the entrance of Asia, and time and grief had handed the key to a dull and harmless Chinese boy, a boy who had at least stammered an overwhelmed gratitude, not merely yawned and said: 'Let's have a cigarette.'

The cook-boy came now and said obsequiously: '*Makan sudah siap.*' Rosemary sat at the table, mistress of an empty house, and spooned out curry on to her plate. The chapattis were pale (at home they had always been golden) and heavy (at home they had always been so light). But she tore off great pieces and dipped them in the fiery sauce and munched with appetite, letting the viscous driblets stain Crabbe's pyjama jacket. She made parcels of mutton-pieces and potatoes and posted them express. She broke large chunks of fish with her chapatti glove. She called for water, no, not water, beer.

'Beer!' she cried. The cook-boy hesitated. 'Brandy,' warned Rosemary.

Rosemary ate four chapattis, half the fish, all the mutton, most of the sauce, most of the *sambals* of shredded coconut, hard-boiled egg, chutney, banana-slices and red cabbage. And as she drained her beer she remembered something she had long convinced herself had never happened. She sixteen, in her beauty's first heady phase, the meal with that man in Kuala Hantu. A curry with chapattis on Satu Road, and afterwards, with chillis in their blood, they had not gone after all to the cinema but to his flat near Bukit Chandan. And he?

'Black as the ace of spades,' said Rosemary aloud in wonder. 'No, I couldn't. It never happened.'

But he had been handsome really. He had done an engineering course in Brighton. He had a white Jaguar which he drove at speed. He danced divinely. Where was he now? What was his name? Sundralingam? Mahalingam. *Sundra* meant beautiful, *maha* meant great. The names, now all too literally interpreted by her, were apt, apt enough. At the moment of climax their language had been Tamil, a rapid bubble of sincere sensuality.

'He was cold,' said Rosemary aloud, 'cold as that fish there.' She was now thinking of somebody else, someone in West Kensington on a January morning. 'Joe, too,' she added, 'really.' She tried crying again, but she was too full to cry. She picked her teeth with a match from the box on a side-table. She called for coffee. After some argument, quelled by the mention of brandy, coffee was made and brought. While the table was being cleared, Rosemary lounged on the couch, sipping Cointreau, her eyes in far space. In far space the men of her life marched like stars. When the boy had gone back to his quarters, Rosemary said to a Corot reproduction, hanging over Crabbe's desk: 'He's quite clever, really. And awfully kind. And I have been rotten to him. And he has got it bad. Poor, poor boy. I could do so much for him.'

Soon she lay in bed, comfortable, a cigarette in her mouth, hands behind her head, the bedside fan whizzing. 'I'm glad I gave up Joe,' she said. 'I told him that it would never work. But he insisted and insisted. And now he's leapt into somebody's arms, as they all do. Marrying on the rebound. And he'll think of me all the time when he's with her, knowing it's not the same, nowhere near as good. But I told him it wouldn't work. No qualifications, no ambitions, no money, no prospects. And me with all mine.' She snuggled down in the bed, silk against her clean, smooth body. 'And his speech was so bad. "You was" he used to say sometimes. And think of the children. Eurasian children. I'd be ashamed to show my face.'

As she turned on her right side, she saw, crumpled on the floor, almost out of sight under the bedside table, the blue air-letter that she had received that day. That was the letter saying that Joe had had to fly into the arms of another woman, that life was intolerable but he realized now that Rosemary would never change her mind. Farewell, O cruel. Rosemary got out of bed, picked up the letter, crumpled it still further, walked over to the lavatory with it and flushed it away. The words went crying away into the town drains, away to the river, to the sea. Poor Joe. Rosemary went back to bed and slept.

Robert Loo could not sleep. Excitement made his limbs dance under the thin sheet. He danced to the last movement of the Second Brandenburg Concerto, to the scherzo of Beethoven's Seventh Symphony, to the development of the *Meistersinger* Prelude to the finale of *L'Oiseau de Feu*, to Holst's Fugal Overture. But the rhythms were not enough, and what sang above the rhythms was not really relevant to his highly-charged, almost febrile state. It was too universal, too general, too mature, too little concerned with this mad spring of love. Had music ever really been able to convey that? He listened in his mind to Wagner, leafing through the love-themes of *Die Meistersinger*, the great duet in *Die Walküre*; in Beethoven there was nothing; perhaps one of the songs of Hugo Wolf?

Fever, fever. His eyes must have been bright when he entered the shop, his head burning. Why else had his father been so considerate, his mother fussing round, sending him off to bed with Aspro and brandy? Or perhaps, thought Robert Loo, it had not been that at all. His father was hopeless with accounts, his brothers worse. He, the musician, had the musician's aptitude for playing with numbers: perhaps this one night had been enough to abash his father with a sense of his son's indispensability. But no, he had been away before, sent by Crabbe to Singapore to have his quartet recorded. His quartet? He tried to hear it in his mind, but it seemed to be played on miniature instruments by elves, incredibly high up and thin. All the music he had written before this night must, of course, be immature, must be re-written or, better still, destroyed.

Most probably his father and mother had been shocked by the possibility of the break-up of the family, and his own impiety, his pulling out of a brick, was discounted in the terror of the prospect of the whole vast structure collapsing in thunder and dust. Perhaps his mother had screamed at his father, accusing him, with blows, of tyranny and exploitation, and his father had been cowed and scared of the high-pitched storm.

Robert Loo felt that he could now dictate terms. He would ask for liberal time off – most afternoons and at least two evenings. Sometimes after the closing of the shop at midnight, he would say:

'I'm just going out to see a friend. I'll be back in an hour or so.'

'Very good, my son. God knows, you work hard enough. You deserve a little relaxation. Do you need any spending money?'

'Thank you, Father. I think I've got as much as I need.' Then off, in the blue warm aromatic night, to see her, her waiting, arms open in perfume and desire, in some light gown that fell easily from her shoulders.

'But, look here, you need all this time to write your music.'

'My music? Oh, yes. Of course, my music. But I think I feel a new style developing, my second period, or perhaps my real first. That needs time to germinate.'

'And what's it going to be like, this new music?'

'I don't know yet, I just don't know. Warmer, gayer, speaking more to the heart, more rhythmical, tuneful, full of the spirit of the dance.'

'Something like this?'

Robert Loo's interlocuter, who was also Robert Loo, sprang through the open window, flew over the street, switched on a light in a high room opposite and set a loud radiogram playing. Robert Loo, lying on his bed, came fully awake and listened.

It was the fat Indian clerk who lived in a solitary room

above the chemist's shop opposite. He could be seen in silhouette, walking up and down, eating something, playing music, insomniac. The music was some standard American dance-tune, of the regulation thirty-two bars, with the regulation near-impressionist harmonies, its orchestral palette limited to brass and reeds and somewhat sedative percussion. No development, no variations, only a key-change from chorus to chorus, 'No,' said Robert Loo aloud. 'Nothing like that.' And then a voice sang, relaxed, without effort, against the pre-Raphaelitish chords of very early Debussy:

> 'Oh, love, love, love —
> Love on a hilltop high,
> Love against a cloudless sky,
> Love where the scene is
> Painted by a million stars,
> Love with martinis
> In the cabarets and bars.
> Oh, love, love, love . . .'

Robert Loo listened entranced, hardly breathing, indescribably moved. 'Oh, love, love, love. His heart yearned seeing himself in a white tuxedo, moving with grace round the small dance-floor, Rosemary in his arms, she ravishing in something backless and close-fitting. Words of love on a balcony, the band playing in the distance, under the moon, palms swaying. He felt the palms as something exotic, not the common dingy scenery of his town and state. Rosemary said:

'Let's go in and dance. That's a lovely tune the band is playing.'

He smiled, draining his martini: 'I'm glad you think so.'

'Why? did you . . .?'

'Yes, I wrote it. For you. I wrote it this afternoon when you were on the beach.' (Ah, the romance of those large striped umbrellas!)

'So that was it! And you said you had a headache!'

539

'Yes. I wanted it to be a surprise.'

'You darling.'

And, yes, he would, he would! He would revert from this stage of hard-won mastery of counterpoint, of orchestration, of thematic development, to breathed clichés of wind and voice for her, for her. All the ore that waiting lay for the later working he would melt before its time to make her ornaments for a day.

'And so you've no longer any objection to composing something for people to listen to, even to sing? An anthem for the workers of Malaya, perhaps? A Strength Through Joy song?'

'No, no! Anything, anything for her!'

He slept fitfully, and in the morning his father brought him breakfast in bed: two boiled eggs and a pot of tea. He was too surprised to say thank you.

'You eat both those eggs, son. Eggs give stamina. You can't work on fresh air.'

'No, Father.'

7

In the morning Crabbe and Tommy Jones met, quite by chance, in a Chinese *kedai*. The loud radio somewhere down the street announced ten o'clock Malayan time, and then came the news in the cheerful sing-song of Mandarin. They drank treacly coffee and wondered what they could possibly eat. The shop was dingy and gay and full of half-nakedness – vests and underpants, pimply shoulders and hairless brown legs – and rang with ground-rows of Hokkien vowels and the clop of wooden clogs. Tommy Jones looked in gloom at the clouded glass display-case of cakes in primary colours. 'Don't really fancy anything,' he said. 'You do anything last night?'

'Slept.'

'Yes, I know. Don't know what's coming over me lately. Couldn't do a thing. I could eat a bit of fried fish if they've got it.'

'With vinegar?'

'That's it.' But he made no move to ask or order.

'I've got to get transport,' said Crabbe, 'to Mawas. Do they have taxis round here?'

'Eh,' said Tommy Jones, plucking at the vest of a passing boy. 'Polar beer. A big one, cold.'

'A?' But beer was brought. Tommy Jones gulped it greedily, cutting the phlegm, and said: 'That's a bit better.' The morning film seemed to drop from his eyes, for he said to Crabbe: 'You've had a shave.'

'Yes. She brought some water in a flower-vase.'

'Oh, I'll have one later. Got to see this new Malay shop here, try and get them to take a regular order. Bit difficult with some of the Muslims.'

'You can tell them that they've just discovered a codicil to the Koran.'

'Eh?'

'Making it all right to drink.'

'You ought to be in this business,' said Tommy Jones gravely, 'You'd do all right. I'll put in a word for you when I get back to Hong Kong. Don't know your name, though.'

'I've got to get to Mawas,' said Crabbe. At that moment a Land-Rover pulled up outside the *kedai*: from its covered body came protesting squeals and loud comforting words. The man who jumped down from the driver's seat was known to Crabbe. Moneypenny, an Assistant Protector of Aborigines who was based at Mawas. He now entered the *kedai*, very big and boyish in khaki shorts, fair-haired, mad-eyed, almost as brown as a Malay, with a child's sulky mouth and native tatoo-marks on his fine throat.

'You've saved my life,' called Crabbe. 'I'm coming with you.'

Moneypenny gazed at Crabbe with eyes focused at something far behind him, as though trying to pierce impenetrable jungle. He did not smile in greeting but merely said: 'Oh, it's you, is it? You can help to hold down that blasted pig in the back.'

'Pig?'

'Jungle-pig. There's a couple of Temiars with it. The bloody fools took it for a walk on a bit of string and they got lost. Spent half the morning looking for them.' At this moment a large snout poked out from the back of the truck, small intelligent eyes looking bewildered at the street of trishaws and dustbins and idlers in sarongs. A small curly man in a yellow shirt and trousers much too big for him, evidently a cast-off gift from Moneypenny, jumped down, crooning at the pig encouragingly, showing all his teeth in a most affectionate smile. The great bristled body of the pig, pushed from behind, began to appear.

'Eh!' Moneypenny, still on his feet, shouted in a strange

language. The Temiar looked hurt but began to push the pig back again. Moneypenny sat down.

'How long you been on this job?' asked Tommy Jones.

'Six years.'

'Do they drink beer, this lot of yours?'

'They'll drink anything you give them. But they won't be able to for long. They've all got to be turned into Muslims, that's the new official policy. No more walks with pigs then.' Crabbe desperately tried to make the blue far-focused eyes come home to himself, to the table. He asked about the murder on Durian Estate.

'Oh, that. The foreman said he's been sleeping with his wife and got the Reds to do him in. And now the widow's sleeping with the foreman.'

'How did you find that out?'

'It came through on the bamboo wireless. Everything comes through.' Moneypenny refused a drink. 'Got to go back and see how our American friend's getting on. I only called in to get some condensed milk for the pig.'

Crabbe and Moneypenny said good-bye to Tommy Jones. As they prepared to mount the dusty Land-Rover Tommy Jones came running out calling to Crabbe:

'What was that about the what-you-call?'

'What what-you-call?'

'About the Prophet inventing beer?'

'No,' said Crabbe, 'not quite that.' He suggested various Jesuitical ways of persuading Muslims to reconcile their hard desert faith with the mild pleasures of the West. He realized he was still not quite sober. Moneypenny had borrowed a tin-opener from the shop, and already the jungle-pig was guzzling ecstatically, the Temiars encouraging it with gentle mooing noises and happy laughter.

'I'll tell them about you in Hong Kong,' said Tommy Jones gratefully. Moneypenny impatiently engaged gear. 'Eh!' shouted Tommy as they moved off. 'Don't know your name!' Crabbe waved smiling at the thin paunched figure standing along among the small Malay boys and the Chinese in their underwear, the prophet of harmless solace in a harsh world, not altogether ridiculous or ignoble. They never met again.

'Who,' asked Crabbe, 'is this American?' He sat next to Moneypenny; the pig no longer needed holding down: its snout ranged the sticky patches on the floor behind them. Moneypenny drove badly, almost bitterly lashing the vehicle to unnecessary speed, savagely jerking the gear-lever. Around his neck he wore a Temiar amulet: its charmed stones clinked as they bumped towards Mawas.

'Him? He's from some university or other. Under the auspices of some organization or other. He's trying to give the Temiars an alphabet. He's part of the vanguard.'

'Which vanguard?'

'The British are going. Nature abhors a vacuum. His name is Temple Haynes.'

The river had appeared on their left, far below, eye-achingly silver. The jungle could be seen beyond. Crabbe laughed, a brief snort only. 'You've got to hand it to them,' he said.

These words seemed to have a violent effect on Moneypenny. 'Christ,' he said. He lurched to the side of the road and stopped the Land-Rover. His hands were shaking. 'What in the name of God did you want to do that for?'

'Do what?'

'You laughed. Didn't you see that butterfly?'

'What butterfly?'

'Went sailing in front of the windscreen. And you laughed at a butterfly.

'I didn't see any butterfly. In any case, where's the harm?'

'Oh, my God. You've broken one of the taboos. You couldn't know it, I suppose. But for God's sake be careful in future.' He sat there, breathing heavily, Crabbe unable to say a word. The aerial factory of insects twittered away in the distance. 'And,' warned Moneypenny, 'if we get any thunder today, for God's own sweet sake don't choose that time to run a comb through your hair. It's very serious.' The pig was now snoring most gently, its Temiar guardians watching tenderly over its sleep. 'I'm going to drive slowly,' said Moneypenny. 'I don't want anything bad to happen.' They crawled along now.

Crabbe sat still and silent, as though for his photograph, thinking: 'Oh, would anybody believe it, would anybody believe it back home? They just don't know, they're all so, so innocent, sitting in their offices in Fleet Street and Holborn.'

Soon they came to the outskirts of Mawas. Moneypenny stopped, arbitrarily it seemed, at a tree-choked point indistinguishable from any other point in the long jungle continuum on both sides of the road. The river had long disappeared. But three little men in loin-cloths, armed with bamboo blow-pipes, came softly out of the mess of frond and liana and decaying palm-stumps, smiling and greeting. Moneypenny spoke briefly and made a cabalistic sign. The pig was aroused with considerate strokes and ear-tweaks, and pig and men climbed down amid a clank of empty cans, the men laughing and waving as they took their leave. In an instant the jungle had taken them.

'Well,' said Moneypenny. He sighed. 'What do you want to do? You've missed the estate launch. That went' – he looked narrowly at his wrist-watch – 'an hour ago. You'd better stay the night with me. Although Haynes has got the only spare bed.' He started the engine and wrenched the gear-lever with his teeth clenched, seemingly in hate. 'You can toss for it. One of you will have to sleep on the floor.'

'I slept on the floor last night.'

'Oh, well, you won't mind doing it again, then. Our Temple's a bit more used to gracious living.'

'Is he a nice chap?'

'Oh, yes. He talks a lot about phonemes and semantemes and bilabial fricatives. He has a van with recording apparatus in it. He's a good chap.'

They came now into Mawas, a decent-sized town for this *hulu* region: a wide main street and a few shops; a clean police station with pot plants outside; even a cinema. Here the estates – two up-river, one down – could victual themselves with rice, fish and buffalo-meat; here the tappers could make sedately merry on a night off. Moneypenny drove to a wooden shack labelled 'Department of Aborigines'. This had been translated – in fresher paint into official Malay: *'Pejabat Kaum Asli'* (literally, Office of Tribe of Originals) and, in paint hardly dry, into weird cuneiform symbols which were quite unfamiliar to Crabbe.

'That's his alphabet,' said Moneypenny. 'Temiar Alphabet Mark One. But Mark Three's already on its way.' He spoke with a kind of gloomy vicarious pride.

In the cool office sat Temple Haynes. Before him stood three tiny aborigines. On the wall hung a large sheet of glazed rag-paper with pictures on it: men, women, children, horses, pigs, houses, trains, aeroplanes, buffaloes, trees. Temple Haynes pointed at pictures in turn with a stick, inviting the little men to name them. He seemed pleased to see Moneypenny. 'I don't seem to be getting very far with this dialect,' he said. 'They keep saying the same thing. They seem to be giving everything the same name.' He read off a weird word from his notebook. 'That,' he said.

'Yes,' said Moneypenny. 'That means "picture".'

'Why do you have more than one picture of each thing?' asked Crabbe.

'That,' said Temple Haynes, 'is for plurals.' He stood up. 'I don't think I've had the pleasure.' Moneypenny admitted that he had forgotten Crabbe's name.

'Crabbe,' said Crabbe.

'Crabbe,' said Temple Haynes. 'I met a Crabbe in London. Fenella Crabbe, the poet. Are you any relation?'

'My very distant wife. Soon no longer to be a wife.'

'I'm genuinely sorry to hear that,' said Temple Haynes. 'I think very highly of her work.' The three aborigines looked up at Crabbe reproachfully.

Temple Haynes seemed pure Mayflower: unemphatic

features, clear hazel eyes as sane as Moneypenny's were mad. He wore no crew-cut: ample light-brown waves were combed neatly from a middle parting. But his sharkskin trousers were American-tailored, delicately moulding his rump as he turned round to put out a non-cancer cigarette. He wore a drip-dry cream shirt and a polka-dot bowtie. A moygashel jacket hung over a chair. 'I guess that's the lot for this morning,' he said to Moneypenny. 'Could I have them again at two?' Moneypenny coughed sounds of dismissal. The three little men made vague obeisances and shambled out.

'Where's my clerk?' asked Moneypenny. 'I've letters to write.'

'He went away,' said Haynes. 'About an hour ago. He very kindly yielded the office to me.'

'If you want lunch,' said Moneypenny, 'you can get it at Ang Siow Joo's. I never eat lunch.' He gave them both a mad look and then sat down at his desk.

Haynes and Crabbe walked in the heat outside. 'I'd read one of her things in a review back home,' said Haynes. 'A long poem about Malaya. Very impressive, I thought.'

'Never read it,' said Crabbe. 'Didn't even know about it.'

'Really?' Haynes gave Crabbe a swift sincere glance, mildly incredulous. 'Then we had this short course at the Anglo-American South-East Asian Society in London. A very useful background course. She gave two lectures. She came with a rather distinguished Malay whose name I've forgotten.'

'I haven't forgotten,' said Crabbe, thinking: 'What the hell does she know about Malaya, anyway?' 'That would be His Highness the Abang of Dahaga.'

Hearing the rasp in Crabbe's voice, Haynes glanced at him again in mild inquiry. 'Anyway,' he said, 'she's making a name. And she's a great help to all of us who are coming out here for the first time.'

'All of you?' said Crabbe. 'All of who?'

'Various organizations,' said Haynes vaguely. 'There's work to do in South-East Asia.' It was the rather smug voice of the records of *Four Quartets*, though much younger. 'I'm concerned, as you'll have guessed, with the linguistic angle. Then there's the angle of inter-racial relations. And there's method of teacher training, time-and-motion study in industry, behaviour-patterns, statistics, sociological surveys and, of course, demographic studies. A great deal to do. It'll cost a lot of money, of course, but it's the best possible investment. We can't afford to let the Communists get away with it.'

'Where are we going? 'asked Crabbe. 'Are we going to have a drink?'

Temple Haynes smiled indulgently and looked at his wrist-watch – waterproof, self-winding, with the date and the current lunar phase. 'What can one drink at this hour of the day?' he asked.

'Coca-Cola,' growled Crabbe.

Haynes laughed gaily, but there were no butterflies about. 'There's no need to feel bitter about anything,' he said. 'A lot of us contemn the drinking of that beverage as much as you Europeans seem to do. Although I must confess I found Europe full of Coca-Cola signs. No,' he continued, 'you mustn't identify us with the Hollywood or G.I. image. If you wish me to prove my adulthood, I'm quite willing to come and drink gin with you. Not that I really enjoy gin outside of a martini, and you can't get martinis here.'

They strolled into Ang Siow Joo's. It was midday and Crabbe had had no breakfast. He ordered pork rissoles and boiled Chinese cabbage. Haynes's leather case contained more than notebooks: from it he took thin sheets of rye bread, peanut butter and silver-wrapped Swiss cheese. He ate sparely, lighted a non-cancer cigarette, and amiably watched Crabbe finish his crude meal.

'This afternoon,' he said, 'I must do a little more dialectology. The real job, as you know, is isolating the phonemes, or, rather, discovering what is phonemic and what is allophonic. That is fascinating and very important.' He chattered on, and Crabbe felt lost and boorish and crude. The British, he decided, had been merely gifted amateurs: Singapore had been raised on amateur architecture, amateur town-planning, amateur education, amateur law. Now was the time for the professionals. Thoughts struck him. He said:

'What are they going to do about music?'

'Music? That, of course, is not my department. But Lewis and Roget, both from Columbia, are getting permission to initiate a pretty exhaustive survey of South-East Asian music. It will take years, of course, but they hope to produce some kind of definitive treatise, complete with copious recorded examples.'

'And if you find a promising South-East Asian composer?'

'I repeat,' said Haynes, 'that is not my province. My province is purely linguistic. But,' he smiled, 'if such a prodigy is found, I fancy that he'll be well taken care of with scholarships. I think there's already a foundation in existance to promote the encouragement of native artistic talent.'

'Take this boy's name,' said Crabbe, 'now. And his address. Pass them on. Please.'

'I think you're more in a position to do that than I,' said Haynes. 'After all, it's not my field. As I told you, I'm a . . .'

'I know,' said Crabbe impatiently. 'But I may never get the chance. Please take his name, please write to these people.'

'If you wish.' Haynes was most good-humoured and accommodating. He wrote in a pocket diary Robert Loo's name and address. 'There,' he smiled; 'I've got that down.'

'Thank you,' said Crabbe. He felt relieved: perhaps, in time, all his burdens would be lifted.

'I think now,' said Haynes, 'I'll take a brief siesta. I have work to do at two. Shall we stroll over to Moneypenny's house?'

The house was round the corner, a little way up the hill. It was filthy and bare, stripped down like its tenant, to sheer primary function, disdaining all secondary sensation. Thus the bathroom which Crabbe visited showed signs that Moneypenny now regarded even a lavatory as supererogatory. The floors were covered with rugs of peanut-shells. Everything was pared to the human limit: tapioca and taboos. The spare room, which Haynes had taken, was a sweet cool oasis, aseptically clean, swept and scoured by Haynes himself, smelling of insect-repellent, containing neat clusters of bottles on shelves: paludrine, quinine, penicillin ointment, vitamin tablets, toilet requisites of all kinds. But the rest of the house, including Moneypenny's own room, where Crabbe sought his siesta, was a growling grim annexe to the jungle where Moneypenny spent most of his time, that green monster hotel with water running through.

Crabbe slept long, not hearing Haynes's neat, timely departure. He awoke after four, hot, wet and dry-mouthed. There was nothing to drink in the house, not even cold water, for Moneypenny had long sold his refrigerator. But Crabbe remembered that the American, being of a race with as little sense of guilt as history, would not be so self-denying. Haynes's van was parked in the shack of a garage, and in it Crabbe found a deep-freeze – powered he knew not how – singing away, in its belly bottles of mineral water, clipped to its lid an opener. He sat and drank, thinking vaguely about Fenella. It was, he felt, not really remarkable that, travelling to the small world up-river, he should already have come into a finger-tip or finger-nail contact with her twice. She was making her name known at last, perhaps because free at last of him. But he could not get out of his head the feeling that this reading her last night, hearing about her today, was somehow ominous: it was as though the river and the jungle together were singling him out for attention, approaching him in terms of his own past. Death? Did this mean he was going to die? Absurd. He was fit, despite his small cushions of fat: his digestion was good; his heart, despite occasional palpitations attributable to the heat, to too much tobacco and midday drinking, was sound enough. The up-river journey was safe; he would keep out of the way of the snipers. Above all, he had no wish to die: there was plenty for him to do still, all over the dwindling Colonial Empire. He shrugged away last night's memory of Mr Raj's words in Kuala Hantu, words about his never going home, his complete assimilation to the country. That, of course, could not be, and it would be stupid to give that prophecy an ironic interpretation – leaving his bones up-river, the Englishman's grave quickly becoming a native shrine to be loaded with supplicatory bananas and flowers. And yet he still felt a desire to postpone his trip to Durian Estate.

Though less now, he thought, envisaging another day with the sane Haynes and the mad Moneypenny, their clean and dirty worlds. Tomorrow he would take the launch, get the job over, return quickly to the State capital and the stress of his problems there. He drank one more bottle of Haynes's mineral-water – slightly scented, effervescent, saccharine, with an extravagant claim on the label ('it excites the pancreas to fresh efforts') and wondered what he should do now. Then Haynes himself appeared with a plan for his evening.

Haynes seemed mildly pleased that Crabbe should be crouched in the van among the tape-recorders and cold storage. 'Welcome,' he said, 'to American territory.' And then: there's an event of some interest taking place tonight in one of the villages. A new stage for the native shadow-play has been erected, and there is to be an opening ceremony. I wish that Cunliffe could be here.'

'Cunliffe?'

'A friend soon to come to this territory. He majored in anthropology and has already published a treatise on Mexican folk ceremonies. Perhaps you would accompany me? My knowledge of Malay is slight, and I'd like to take a few notes. Perhaps photographs too.' He beamed modestly at a fine delicate instrument lying on the shelf of the van – a camera with many knobs and calibrations. 'I think even the observations of the amateur can be of some use. An amateur present is obviously better than a professional absent.'

In Moneypenny's house no dinner was served. Guests had to feed themselves with what few raw materials they could find in their host's store-cupboard, cooking these laboriously on an oil-burner whose wicks were charred and slow to yield to the match. Crabbe heated a can of soup for himself, Haynes prepared eggs Benedict and had slices of spam with a tinned salad, Moneypenny ate cold boiled tapioca, grumbling in snapped sentences about civilization.

'Another week,' he said, 'and Barlow should be back from K.L. I can't stand this sort of life,' he said, sneering at Haynes's neat plateful, 'it's artificial. I want to get back into the jungle. It's the only possible life for a man.'

'How is Barlow?' asked Crabbe.

'The same as ever. The nice little professional anthropologist, the sort of bloke who likes office-work.'

'But,' suggested Haynes with scholarly courtesy, 'you would surely be the first to admit that the professional anthropologist has his uses. I mean, the fact that he has a terminology, a classificatory system, the fact that he comes with a background of intensive comparative studies . . .'

'Balls,' bawled Moneypenny rudely. 'You've got to get into the jungle. You've got to come face to face with the living reality. There was Barlow at the university reading books and dishing up the books in his essays; there was I actually doing the job. There's no substitute for actual experience.'

'I'd venture to disagree,' ventured Haynes. 'Training . . .'

'You're just as bad,' snapped Moneypenny. Clearly he had had a boring afternoon in the office. 'Making alphabets without knowing a word of the languages.'

'Really,' protested Haynes with mildness. 'I never laid claim to be a linguist. I'm a linguistician, which is rather different. I mean, what I'm after chiefly at the moment is the phonemes. I've no wish to be able to speak any of these languages with fluency: a working knowledge is all I aspire to.'

'Yes,' said Crabbe. 'That's right. It's a question of what patterns you can make emerge out of your inchoate experiences. For instance ...'

'You,' said Moneypenny, 'can shut up. What do you know about it, anyway? Coming up here slumming, laughing your bloody head off at butterflies. When you're a guest in my house, you'll behave. Understand?'

'But ...'

'No buts,' said Moneypenny. 'You stick to your Chinese catamites and your black mistresses. Don't start telling me what to do.'

'I never said a word ...'

'Well, don't.' He began to get up from the table. 'Just don't that's all.'

'And I don't quite like what you said just then,' said Crabbe, with heat. 'About black mistresses.'

'We know what goes on,' said Moneypenny, standing with his plate by the kitchen door. 'We may be far from *civilization*,' he sneered, 'but we know all about you people. We don't want you, me and the Temiars. Leave us alone, that's all we ask.' He stomped into the kitchen, rinsed his plate sketchily, returned. 'I'm going to bed,' he said. 'You can please yourselves what you do.' He entered his bedroom.

'We will,' said Crabbe, and began to say more, but Haynes plucked his sleeve gently, shaking his head with a faint smile. 'Bloody mad,' said Crabbe.

Crabbe and Haynes drove gently to the village, four miles away, where the *wayang kulit* ceremony was to be held. 'I can't stay the night there,' said Crabbe. 'I just can't. He's so obviously cracked. He may get violent.'

'You can sleep in my room,' said Haynes. 'I've a li-lo. And the door has a lock.'

'Yes. Thanks. After all, it's only for one night.'

In the village they received a kind, an urbane, welcome. The headman even brought warm orange crush. And the shadow-play master invited them, with most courteous words, to sit on the stage itself, behind the drummers and pipers, the ox-hide shadow-puppets and the hanging lamp, the large taut cloth on which the silhouettes would be projected, to witness the humble processes by which the age-old heroic drama was enacted.

'Hindu in origin,' said Crabbe to Haynes. 'Hardly a trace of Islam in the whole thing. Take your shoes off,' he said, as they began to mount the steps. 'That's the custom.' In their socks they crouched in the corner of the attap hut, the enclosed heat most oppressive, listening to the oboist skirling away in improvisation, the drummers and gong-players trying out their sticks. The master sat cross-legged, immediately behind the screen, on each side of him the many figures – gods, demons, the comic inter-mediaries between the supernatural and sublunary worlds – the manipulation of which was his priest-like office.

'The heat,' gasped Haynes. And from Crabbe's own forehead sweat dripped or gathered into a kind of menis-cus to be scooped off. But the master, cool, brown, en-tranced, now uttered the word 'Om', identifying himself for the instant with God Himself, calling on many gods and devils to be kind and patient, not to take offence at the crude representation of their acts soon to come, not to be incensed at the ox-hide caricatures of their numinous essences. He offered a delicacy – scorched rice; he abased himself before their greatness. And he remembered the one true religion, invoking the protection of the four arch-angels of the Koran.

Soon he took in either hand a godly figure – a body and head and extravagant head-dress, all carved in lacy com-plexity, mounted on a hand-stick. These he waved at the screen, as though delicately fanning it, and the raised voices from the audience beyond it told that the spell of the tale – so well known to all, so hard for Crabbe to interpret to Haynes – was already working. 'The whole cycle,' said Crabbe, over the oboe's sinuous cantilena, the gong and the drums, 'takes a week. It's Hindu epic, the age-long struggle between gods and demons, the . . .'

'I don't feel well,' said Haynes. He didn't look well. He was ghost-white, and sweat oozed and shone on his face and bare arms. 'It's the heat.' Crabbe caught the eye of the oboist, an ancient man with dignified moustaches, and mimed that they were going round to the front, to watch the real thing, the shadows. The old man nodded that he understood and then puffed his cheeks to his instrument.

'Better,' said Haynes on the steps. He breathed the dank night air deeply. 'It was surely hot in there. I can't take all that much heat.'

Crabbe's own shirt was soaked, his trousers stuck to his rump. He reached down for his shoes, saying: 'Perhaps you ought to have a drink of something. Something cold. Let's go back, to the . . .' Then he yelled with pain. The drums and gongs were loud: only Haynes heard him. 'In my shoe,' said Crabbe, his face screwed up. 'Something stung me. What . . .' He tipped the shoe, and from it fell the squashed body of something.

'A scorpion,' said Haynes. 'A black one, very young. You'd better get that seen to.'

'Christ,' said Crabbe. 'My foot's on fire.' He hobbled towards the van, Haynes helping him.

'Well,' said Haynes, 'we are a couple of fools. This is what happens when we come out for a pleasant instructive evening.' He held his shoes in his hand still. They both padded in their socks over the short trampled grass, reaching at last the friendly civilized van. They drove towards the town. 'Somewhere here,' said Haynes, 'there's a doctor. An Indian. I met him a couple of nights ago. He'll give you a shot of something.'

The doctor was in – a lonely, talkative Tamil who gave

Crabbe penicillin and told him not to worry. 'Just rest it up for a couple of days,' he said. 'And I'll give you a sedative. Do you see anything of my friends?' he asked. 'My friends of the Jaffna confraternity? Vythilingam should be coming up any day now, to examine the cattle. And how is Arumugam? That voice is a terrible handicap, terrible. A pity he can't get in touch with a speech therapist. But I don't think there are any in Malaya.'

'There will be,' said Haynes. 'You can be quite sure of that.'

'Yes,' said the doctor, 'poor Arumugam.' Meanwhile Crabbe groaned.

'But I thought I was doing the right thing,' squealed Arumugam.

'The whole thing is most unfortunate,' said Sundralingam. 'He will be quite right to be angry.' They were sitting round the bed of Maniam in Sundralingam's house. Maniam's nose was a strange colour and painful: for the second time he had had to delay his return to Kuala Beruang. So now he fretted in his tartan sarong, clutching his Dutch wife, adding little to the worried talk of his two friends.

'But it was partly, no, mainly, your idea,' shrilled Arumugam softly but urgently. 'You said that he must not be lured away from the circle by this Rosemary woman.'

'Yes, I know, but to steal his letters was surely going too far.'

'I didn't steal them. I merely collected them from the Post Office. My idea was merely to see who they were from, and if one was from this Rosemary woman to steam that open and find out what was going on.' Arumugam's voice rose yet higher with self-righteousness. 'And then I was going to give him his letters, saying that I had collected them for him as a friendly gesture.'

'And then you put the letters in your back trousers pocket and forgot all about them.'

It was too true. Arumugam, the efficient, who whipped in with ringmaster's coolness the roaring delicate aircraft, the inheritor of Jaffna's immemorial tradition of reliability, Arumugam had slipped up badly. Then he said: 'But it was an easy mistake to make. We had so much trouble with Maniam.'

'That's right,' said Maniam, through his clogged nose, 'blabe be.'

'And there was the question of my trousers,' continued Arumugam. 'They got torn slightly when we were fighting that day with Syed Omar. And then when his son came to beat up Maniam they got stained with blood. Your blood,' he said to Sundralingam.

'It wasn't very much blood,' said Sundralingam.

'And after that I spilled coffee on them,' said Arumugam. 'So I put them away in a cupboard. And I forgot all about them. And then Vithilingam said that this Rosemary woman had sworn at him when he saw this Penang Chinese making love to her in Crabbe's house, and then he said that he hated her and he never wanted to see her again. So after that I never thought about getting his letters and I forgot about the letters I'd put in my trousers pocket. So you see,' he ended, 'it is all easily understandable.'

He crumpled the letters absently with twitching hands as he talked, Sundralingam took them from him. 'There is nothing very vital,' he said. 'A circular from Calcutta, two local bills. But this,' he said, 'is an air mail from Ceylon.'

'I suppose,' said Maniam from the bed, 'I'b to blabe for everythig.'

'No, no, not that,' protested Arumugam. 'It was just unfortunate, that's all.'

'No great harm done,' said Sundralingam. 'The letters are a fortnight late. But the postmark on this letter from Kandy is not very clear. We can make it less clear by rubbing some dirt on it and then blaming its condition on the Post Office.'

'Or the peon in the Veterinary Department,' suggested Arumugam.

'Yes. There's no great harm done. But never, never, never try anything like that again.'

'No,' piped Arumugam meekly. 'And who is this Mrs Smith?'

Sundralingam looked closely at the name and address on the back of the air-mail letter. 'I don't know,' he said. 'I never knew he had any English friends in Kandy.'

'His bother,' said Maniam. 'His bother barried ad Eglishbad.'

'His mother, of course,' cried Arumugam. 'How strange to think that Vythilingam's mother is called Smith.' And then with a naughty girl's giggle, he said: 'Let us open it up and see what she has to say.'

'Now, really,' reproved Sundralingam. 'That, as you know, is not right at all.'

'The letter is not stuck down. Tropical air-mail letter forms don't have any glue on them. It's just got a couple of staples from a stapling machine.'

'Mr Smith's office stapling machine,' said Sundralingam, turning the letter over and over. 'Why ever did she marry an Englishman?'

'Bodey,' said Maniam cynically. 'She re-barried for bodey.'

'Imagine,' said Sundralingam, fascinated, 'imagine those two bodies in bed together, the white and the black. Horrible.'

'Horrible,' squealed Arumugam. 'Let us open the letter.'

Sundralingam, with deft doctor's hands, eased out the staples. He smoothed the letter open and began to read. It was quite a short letter, written in convent-school English. Arumugam tried to read it over his shoulder, but Sundralingam said: 'Do have some manners. I will read it first and then you can read it.' Arumugam meekly sat down on the bed again.

'No,' said Sundralingam in shock. 'No, no.'

'Whatever is the matter?'

'The date?' asked Sundralingam urgently. 'What is to-day's date?'

'The twenty-third,' said Arumugam. 'But why?' His voice reached C in alt. 'Why? What's it all about?'

'When does the next plane come from Singapore?'

'Tomorrow. Why? What is all this mystery?'

Sundralingam looked up at him in deepest reproach. 'Now you'll see what you've done with your stupidity. Tomorrow she will be here.'

'Here?'

'Yes, yes. It says here that she intends to fly to Singapore on the twenty-first. It's a one-day flight from Colombo, isn't it?' He didn't wait for Arumugam's professional confirmation. 'And she's spending two days in Singapore while this girl buys new clothes. And then coming here on the next available plane.'

'What girl? Who is this girl?'

'A girl for Vythilingam. An orphan. Both her parents were killed in a car smash.'

'How much?' asked Arumugam automatically.

'Eighty thousand,' said Sundralingam automatically. 'And Vythilingam's stepfather is going to Penang on business. And she wants Vythilingam to call him "father".'

'No!'

'And she wants to be met at the airport. A fine mess you've made of things,' said Sundralingam. 'You and your great inquisitive nose.'

There was shocked silence from invalid and delinquent. At last Arumugam said: 'What shall we do?' The intonation-pattern finished almost at the upper auditory limit. 'We daren't give him the letter now. He'll kill me.'

'The letter was lost in the post,' decided Sundralingam. 'Perhaps she sent another letter after. Or a cable confirming everything. Or perhaps she has rung him up from Singapore already.'

'Do.' Maniam shook his head. 'He dever bedtioded

adythig about that. He cabeid to see be this bordig.'

'The letter got lost,' repeated Sundralingam. 'Letters sometimes do. It will be a nice surprise for Vythilingam. His mother will walk into the Veterinary Department while he is giving medicine to some small animal. With this girl. It will be such a surprise. There is no great harm done.'

'But perhaps he doesn't want to see his mother,' said Arumugam.

'Nonsense! What man doesn't want to see his mother? And this girl. Eighty thousand dollars,' said Sandralingam. 'Perhaps, after all, it is time we all married,' he sighed.

'Never!' cried Arumugam jealously.

'Anyway, it will be your duty to meet her at the airport. You will see the plane come in. You will be able to send a loudspeaker message to her asking her to meet you in the waiting-room. Then you can take her to her son.' There were tears in Sundralingam's eyes. 'Mother and son meet after long years. With future wife.'

'It will be a surprise.'

'Oh yes, it will be a lovely surprise.'

8

Rosemary sat at her Public Works Department escritoire, in a sea of fed cats, and tried to write a letter to Vythlingam. She had, as she had promised herself, taken a day off from school, having told Crabbe's boy to take a message to her amah to take a message to the school to say that she was ill. But never had she looked better. A large evening meal, deep sleep in a better bed than hers, a full evacuation, a hot bath (her own house had only a cold shower), a breakfast of bacon and eggs and sausages from Crabbe's boy – these had smoothed and restored her. She had come home, changed into a sunny model dress from Penang, tied her hair in a ribbon, fed her cats on corned beef and undiluted condensed milk, and now sat ready for a new life.

She sat wriggling on the standard-pattern Windsor chair, her pink tongue-point dancing about her lips, trying to write, wrestling with a profound stylistic problem. By her pad she had Vythilingam's stiff proposal, whose Augustan periods were intimidating and inhibited her normal chatty flow. The cats, digesting in broody attitudes, looked at her sleepily, taking in nothing of her delicious beauty.

As she shifted from ham to delectable ham, biting her tongue in concentration, the sun warmed her gently, muffled by the lettuce-green curtains but making brighter the mustard-coloured carpet, the pepper-and-salt cushions. She tried to continue her letter, but was half pleased to be interrupted by the opening of the door behind her. She said automatically:

'Oooooh, go away, Jalil, you're not supposed to come

here. I told the amah not to let you in.' Then she remembered Jalil's disgusting behaviour of the previous evening and turned to give him vinegary words. But it was not Jalil: it was a Chinese boy. Loo his name was. He stood there smiling very shyly, a clean shirt with a tie to show he was in love, pressed trousers. Rosemary could not remember his first name. 'Hello,' he said.

'Oh,' said Rosemary, 'it's you.' Then she said guiltily: 'Why aren't you at school?' His smile began to go slowly, and she remembered that he was no longer at school, but worked in a shop. So she said: 'I was only joking. It's me who should be at school.'

'I know. I've just been there and they said you were ill.'

'Oh,' said Rosemary. 'Oh, yes, I am. I've such a terrible headache.' She suddenly clapped her hand to her brow, screwing up her clear healthy eyes, whose whites were as white as peeled picnic eggs. The cats were aware of her feigning and did not look up at the sound of distress. But then some of them scattered like birds, for Robert Loo was awkwardly down on his knees, saying: 'Poor dear. Poor darling.' He blushed to say the words, as though he had stolen a theme from some other, inferior, composer.

'Oh, I'm all right, really,' she said. 'It comes and it goes.' Robert Loo remained on his knees, wondering what he should do now. Some cats sat on window-ledges, one on the table, looking at him. This was the first amateur performance they had ever seen. Robert Loo turned his embarrassed eyes away from them and noticed the writing-pad and pen, the opening words: 'My dear.' 'You're writing a letter,' he said, some new equivocal feeling rising in him.

'Yes, I've been trying to. Do get off your knees, you'll make your trousers all dusty.'

Robert Loo got up, as awkwardly as he'd got down. 'Are you writing to him?' he asked; 'to that man Joe?'

'Joe?' Rosemary smiled disdainfully. 'Oh, not to him. I've finished with him. He begged me to marry him, but I won't. I was writing to somebody else.'

Hope and despair and anxiety rose in Robert Loo. 'Is it me that you're writing to?' He was already reading in his mind two letters, like two simultaneous staves of a score: 'After last night I realize that, young as you are, you are the only one who could make me happy . . .' 'After last night I want us never to meet again. It was beautiful, but it was all a mistake, let's forget it ever happened . . .'

Rosemary smiled again, almost with the calm, wise indulgence of a mother, and stroked the nearest cat. 'Oh, no, George, not to you.' (She had remembered his name at last.)

'Why do you smile like that?' said Robert Loo, almost with agitation. 'What do you mean?'

'What could I write to you about, George?' Pleased at having remembered his name, she determined to insert it into every utterance now. But soon he must go: poor boy, he was a nice boy, but only a boy. She did not feel she was yet old enough to be worshipped by boys.

Robert Loo blushed. 'I don't know,' he said. 'I just thought . . .'

'You shouldn't follow me to school,' she said. 'And you shouldn't really come here. What are people going to think?' Then she added: 'George.'

'They'll think that I love you,' he mumbled. Then, louder, he said: 'I love you.'

'Oh, George,' she smiled, not above simpering.

'My name isn't George,' he said, mumbling again. 'It's Robert.'

'You're only a boy,' she said. 'I'm older than you. Some day you'll find some nice Chinese girl. Robert,' she added, 'I thought your name was George. It must have been somebody else I was thinking about.'

'There've been others,' he said jealously. 'I know. Lots of others.'

'Oh, yes. Lots of men have said they loved me. But all the time I was waiting for Mr Right.' She looked dreamily into air, still stroking the cat.

'Mr Wright? Who's Mr Wright?' Then he remembered a ginger tubby man in shorts, a P.W.D. official who had run up a large account in their shop. 'I know the man,' he said with bitterness. 'He's old and fat. A European.' He had the faint beginnings of an understanding of why people disliked Europeans: they took things away from the Asians.

'Oh, no,' said Rosemary, her eyes still smiling absently. 'You don't know who it is. But perhaps you soon will know.' It would, of course, be a Christian ceremony, perhaps in Penang. 'You could play the organ,' she said. 'I remember now. You're fond of music, Victor Crabbe told me.'

'I love you,' he said. 'Marry me.' Saying the words, he felt horror and excitement equally. Marriage meant becoming, almost overnight, like his father, an old man with responsibilities. But it also meant that delicious, that unspeakable, that dizzying crowd of sensations over and over again. His flesh responded to the image. He clumsily sought Rosemary's right hand, the one that was not absently stroking, and tried to kiss it. His lips smacked against it inexpertly: it was neither passion nor old-world courtesy that the cats saw.

'Oh, George,' she said, 'I mean, Robert. Don't be a silly boy.'

'I'm not a boy,' he said loudly. 'I'm a man. I'm a composer. Could your Joe do what I've done? Could he write a string quartet and a symphony and a violin concerto? I'm a man, I tell you. I'll be a great man. Not just somebody like this Mr Wright of yours in P.W.D. I'll be famous. You'll be proud . . .'

'Yes, yes,' she soothed. 'I know you're very clever. Victor Crabbe's always telling me that. But you're being silly just the same. And if you stay here any longer your father will be angry. You shouldn't leave your work like that, just to come and see me.'

'I'll do what I like,' he said. 'I'm a man.'

'Yes,' she said. 'But I must write this letter. Please go now.'

'I won't go! I'm going to kiss you. I'm going . . .'

At the door appeared masses of flowers and, behind them, the wheezing Jalil.

'Oh, Jalil,' she shouted. 'You shouldn't have come, you know you shouldn't.' And then, with relief: 'Oh, come in, Jalil, do come in. Oooooh, what lovely flowers.' In relief she got up from the chair, taking the bright and scentless bunches from Jalil's arms. Jalil was now fully disclosed, wheezing hard, noticing Robert Loo, nodding pleasantly, humming gently down a chromatic scale, then, as he lowered himself into an arm-chair, saying: 'Chinese boy. Crabbe's Chinese boy. Boys I not like.' He was unabashed, relaxed, only his chest working.

'Oh, lovely, lovely,' said Rosemary, briskly seeking jars for the flowers. 'Robert,' she said, 'be an angel and fill these with water. The amah's gone to the market.' Robert Loo noted bitterly the mature approach, the gift of flowers. All he had been able to think of was to wear a tie. He sullenly took the jar that Rosemary proffered and went to the kitchen. As the water drummed in he heard Jalil say: 'You have boy now. How much you pay him?' and Rosemary's reply: 'Oh, Jalil, what a filthy, what a cruel, unforgivable thing to say.' And then Robert Loo came out swiftly with the half-filled jar lest more be said. Cats milled round the table where Rosemary was arranging her flowers, and over one of these cats Robert Loo nearly stumbled. He recovered in time but splashed his shirt and tie. Rosemary said kindly: 'Oh, you silly boy. You've made yourself all wet.' He blushed. The cat he had come up against crouched by a table leg with its ears back, its fur stiff.

'I suppose,' said Robert Loo lamely, 'I'd better be going.'

'Oh, no,' said Rosemary swiftly. 'Do stay. Have a glass of lemon squash or something.'

'No, I must go.' His eyes tried to speak to her, but he was not one of those Chinese who have great liquid expressive eyes; his eyes were small, black, unable to convey much.

'Perhaps you'd better go too, Jalil. Thank you so much for bringing the flowers.' But Jalil put one leg over the other, settling his shoulders more comfortably against the chair. He was going to stay. 'Come drink,' he said. 'Come make jolly time.'

'Oh, Jalil!' Then Rosemary remembered that she was supposed to be ill. 'My head,' she cried dramatically, both hands on her brow like a neuralgia advertisement. 'Oh, its splitting.'

At the door Robert Loo hesitated, thinking: 'She's a liar. She lies about everything,' but feeling strong pangs of thwarted desire more painful than any headache. He would not go back to work: he would go and brood in a coffee-shop not his father's.

'You no headache,' said Jalil. 'I see amah on street. She say you want be lazy today.' He smiled, nodding his head and then wagging his foot in a different rhythm.

'I'm going,' said Robert Loo.

'Yes, yes, all right,' said Rosemary. Then to Jalil: 'I haven't forgotten about yesterday, you know. You're a pig.' She kicked the leg of his chair. 'A nasty, horrible pig.' Jalil laughed quietly. Shamed and frustrated Robert Loo had gone.

'We go in car,' said Jalil, 'to Lotong. Drink and make jolly in Rest House.'

Rosemary hesitated. It was not, she thought, a bad idea. Thirty miles, a chance to be away from the town. She had not expected these declarations from Robert Loo: she was somewhat embarrassed by the thought that it was perhaps all her fault. She did not want him coming back later in the day, more passionate, perhaps – in a boyish way – violent. And she did not want to be seen in the town here by people ready to report her healthy appearance to the headmaster. And what was the use of a day off if you couldn't have a couple of drinks and a blow in a car?

'I must write this letter first,' she said. 'It's important.'

Jalil laughed, coughed, laughed again. 'No use you

write,' he said. 'I tell you he not marry. He not love. Only me love.'

'That's just where you're wrong,' said Rosemary haughtily and triumphantly. 'I've got his proposal here.' She waved it. 'And I'm going to write to him accepting. Tomorrow,' she added.

'He never marry,' said Jalil. 'Only me marry.'

Robert Loo walked gloomily down the avenue, his hands in his pockets. As he approached the main street of the town he remembered that he was wearing a tie, so he removed his hands from his pockets to tear it off and open up the neck-buttons of his shirt. What did he want with wearing a tie? He came to the shop-window of Chung the dentist. In that window was a ghastly gilt picture of a cross-section of the human mouth and also a mirror. Above the mirror was written in Chinese: 'Take a good look at your teeth. They are undoubtedly rotten. Come inside and I will make all well again.' And from within came the noise of all being made well again – groans and the practitioner's encouraging laughter. Robert Loo looked at his face, not his teeth, and saw the smooth face of a boy, a thin neck, slim shoulders. Behind his image passed real boys, schoolboys on their way home from school, none of them wearing ties. Boy, boy, boy. Chinese boy. Portrait of the composer as a young boy. Then into the mirror flashed the face of another boy, brown, splay-nosed, his hair long, showing teeth in greeting. The greeting made Robert Loo turn to meet a shy hand ready for shaking. It was Syed Hassan.

'Where you go now?' asked Syed Hassan.

'I don't know. Just walking, just eating the wind,' said Robert Loo in Malay.

'Tomorrow,' said Hassan with pride, 'is the day of the trial. A big day.'

'What will happen to you?'

'Oh, prison, perhaps for many years. With hard labour, perhaps. Perhaps today is my last day of freedom.' He smiled proudly. 'I have committed a terrible crime.'

'Not so terrible.'

'Oh, yes,' insisted Hassan. 'Very terrible. Violence, attempted murder. Don't say it's not terrible.'

'Terrible,' agreed Robert Loo.

'Tonight we will celebrate,' suggested Hassan. 'Have you any money?'

'My father gave me ten dollars.' It was true. Inexplicably, when Robert Loo came down from his breakfast, washed and neck-tied, his father had put his fist in the till and brought out a note, saying: 'There, my son, take this. Buy yourself a little something. Life should not be all work.'

'I,' said Hassan, 'have five dollars. I cleaned the car of a P.W.D. man called Mr Wright.'

'Oh,' said Robert Loo. And then: 'What are we going to do?'

'I'll call for you this evening.' Syed Hassan winked. 'At about ten o'clock. Then you'll see what we're going to do. But,' he remembered, 'I forgot. There is the question of your beloved. When do you see her again?'

'Not for a long time,' said Robert Loo. 'She's busy.'

They parted. Robert Loo went back to his father's shop. His father was out, gambling somewhere, his mother greeted him with three raw eggs beaten up in brandy.

'Take this, son. You look very pale. And for lunch I am giving you fried pork. That makes blood.' This new solicitude was very puzzling.

But Robert Loo could eat little. After lunch he sat in his accustomed place behind the counter, totting up bills mechanically, before him the few scored pages of the violin concerto, beneath them the many blank lined pages still to be filled. It was very hot. Dust swirled outside, a few listless coffee-drinkers lounged at the tables, the day slept. The great music-god was silent, the hours were propitious for the welling-up of theme and development from a subconscious the more lively because of the torpor of the mind's surfaces. And nothing came. The solo violinist seemed to have vanished. Robert Loo took from the till a ten-cent piece and fed it to the sleeping god. It awoke languidly, searched with insolent slowness for the record Robert Loo's random hand had chosen, and then the afternoon exploded into a larger-than-life dance orchestra crying false emotions. His chin on his fist, Robert Loo sat and listened behind his counter, his heart aching, his eyes staring at nothing, while his brothers cheerfully clopped around, occasionally calling to the kitchen, as customers drifted somnambulistically in:

'*Kopi O!*'

'*Kopi O ping!*'

But he could not call for anything so simple as black coffee, hot or iced, to soothe this thirst which had no name. It was not a thirst for Rosemary, it was not that great thirst which, so Paul Claudel once said, is excited by woman but can only be slaked by God. And art seemed to give no solace. But when the record had ended and the machine dozed again, Robert Loo took a small piece of manuscript paper suitable for piano compositions and idly wrote a few bars of lush but near-astringent Debussy-ish chords. Hearing these with his mind's ear, he felt comforted, as though his self-pity were somehow connected with a great unseen plan organized by a god who was all soft lips and huge melting eyes, a god expertly invoked by Tchaikowski, or Rachmaninoff or the early works of the French impressionistic composers. He glanced over the first bars of his violin concerto and, taking their scores from his dispatch-case under the counter, the string quartet and the symphony (whose last pages his father had torn up). Clever, he thought, all that counterpoint. The work of a clever boy who was top in maths. But what did it say to him now? Where was the yearning, the heartbreak, to be comforted by the easy message of the single flowing tune and the big chords? That music was not him; it was the work of somebody else, somebody he did not like very much.

Vythilingam sat, sweating and breathing hard, in one of Rosemary's arm-chairs. She was out, the amah had said, she had gone out for the day with the Turkish gentleman. Round Vythilingam were ranged the cats, a soft army, knowing him, not disliking him despite his sharp needles and his strong medicine-feeding hands, half-attracted by the mysterious scents that his clothes had brought from the surgery. Vythilingam did not see them. Rosemary was out. Rosemary was out. The amah did not know when she would be back.

This at least was not dreaming. The wood of the chair-arms was solid beneath his nails. And now he could hear the whirr of the ceiling-fan which Rosemary, careless of electricity bills, had not turned off. That was real enough, and so now were the twitching muzzles, the yawns, the washings of furry legs like turkey drum-sticks, the panther-glidings all about him. What was dream, untrue, not to be thought of more, was his standing there in the surgery, delicately inserting the hypodermic nozzle into the anus of the ailing pet honey-bear, and then the inanely smiling herald-face of Arumugam, and then the fat handsome woman in the *sari*, and then the nervously grinning girl behind, plump, prettyish, dumb, and then the greetings . . .

One of his assistants had taken over the honey-bear, smiling whitely, aware of what was happening, hearing the words 'My boy' and Arumugam's stupid squeal about a lovely surprise.

'Oh, God, a beast, that wants discourse of reason . . . The beasts, the beasts,' he had to go and see about the beasts. Work would not wait. Yes, yes, Arumugam would take them to his house in the car. He would meet them later. But now, suffering another kiss from the handsome black woman, he had to go. Half an hour, no more. They would go out for lunch somewhere. But he had to see to the beasts.

The furry beasts grew tired of watching and nosing around one so still, limp and sweating in an arm-chair.

They went about their business, to licking saucers, to washing, to blinking in the sun. It would have been easy, thought Vythilingam, easy if they had been married. Even now, if she accepted him. But he could not pretend to his mother: she would see through all disguises, pull down his dusty curtains, that strong woman, that woman whose name was frailty. But still, of course, it wasn't true. After a brief breathing spell he would go back to empty bachelor quarters and, in the afternoon, to the cool aseptic quiet of the Veterinary Department, the whole vision exorcised by an hour or so of calm and deep breathing.

But the cats twitched and stirred, hearing with sharper ears than his the approach of a car. The amah came out, saying that perhaps *Missi* had returned. But Vythilingam knew it was not that. They were after him, the leisurely following feet. Hide? But the Veterinary Department Land-Rover was outside, twenty yards down the street. If he could get into that, rush off, shouting, if they saw and hailed him, that there was more urgent work to be done, that he couldn't stop. But he would stutter out the words, waste time, they would be on to him. This was the work of Sundralingam and Arumugam. 'Hale him out, keep him away from that woman, that corrupting unclean Christian woman. We told you we'd find him here, Mrs Smith. He comes here, but there is really nothing in it, ha, ha. Just friends. He looked after her cats, that's all. You will hear as much from his own lips. But now somebody else can look after the cats, for he will have much else to occupy him.'

No! Vythilingam, hearing already known voices, the slam of the car door, saw a way out through the kitchen, through the servants' quarters, a way out that Rosemary herself had, so little time ago, sought blindly. Now there was knocking at the front door. Vythilingam nodded vigorously, with shaking nerves, to the amah, miming that she should open the door, let in the visitors. The amah, a not very bright Malay girl, looked at Vythilingam with frowning brows of no comprehension.

'He *must* be here.' Arumugam's voice, outside the door. Vythilingam rushed through to the kitchen, the quarters beyond, as the amah at last caught his drift, went to open. He was out, stumbling over servants' litter, an overflow of cats from the house itself, under the sun. He saw known backs at the front door as he sought his own car. Let them take the Land-Rover, with its space at the back for animals of some bulk. Let them, beasts that want discourse of reason. The visitors – Arumugam, Sundralingam, the fat handsome woman, but not the grinning girl – turned in surprise as they saw him there, already in the driver's seat, switching on the ignition. His face twitched in a grin of agony as he called: 'Urgent!' And then he wrestled with the word 'must' but abandoned it, shrugging his shoulders at them, pantomiming swiftly 'Duty, duty. What can I do? I'll be back later.' They called, they began to come down to him, but the engine responded, he was in gear, he was off.

He did not know where he was driving. It was too late now, he thought. If he could have asked Rosemary, if he could have pleaded with her to say yes. And he felt that she would, for this Joe business was all over, he was sure of that, for the Turkish gentleman had told somebody and somebody had told Vythilingam. If only he could have confronted her, that handsome fat woman, together, both of them, Rosemary saying, 'He is mine. We're going to be married,' or better still, not lying but just stating proleptically: 'We are married. He's my husband first. He's your son second.' A woman to meet a woman, black eyes flashing opposing swords. 'Leave us alone. Let us be happy together. You have no power over him any longer, no rights of any kind.' But it was too late.

Where should he go? He could see no following Land-Rover in the driver's mirror. He had to hide. No. He slowed down, parked for an instant at the side of the road – it was the long empty road leading out of town – to think that it was no longer merely a question of hiding.

She had come for him. She would not rest till she got him. And he knew he would yield all too easily.

And now what about Chou En Lai and the Communist Manifesto? Eh? Were they over, then, the days of doctrinaire musings, the mere dreaming of action? Was it at last time to act?

But there were the animals to think of, there was his duty to the animals.

How about duty to mankind?

These things must be thought about later, at leisure, if there was ever to be leisure for thinking again. In the meantime, on, on. He was, he noticed, on the road to Anjing. Anjing to Mawas. By railway. His car could, or could not, be sent on later. It could, or could not, be left in the station yard to be picked up on his return. And, anyway, it was time he went to Mawas. In the routine of tending sick buffaloes and goats he could slowly arrive at some kind of decision. The train to Mawas went sometime in the evening. But where was his black bag? Of course, there it was, on the car floor beside him. That had made them suspicious, seeing it there when they drove to his house, wondering why he should plead urgent duty and yet forget to take his black bag. Why couldn't they leave him alone? But he wasn't really running away from them. It was time he went to Mawas, wasn't it? There was, in a sense, always urgent duty.

Duty, duty, duty. The car sped down the hot road, its horn, as it warned a careless old man, hesitant at the roadside, calling: 'Duty, duty.'

'It's down this street you see most of them,' said Syed Hassan. 'Now that they've closed down the Park.'

'Yes,' said Robert Loo. He did not care much one way or the other. It was dark, dark that enclosed in one big coat Crabbe in Mawas, groaning with his scorpion bite, Vythilingam in the gently ambling train. Rosemary home at last, with the door shut on Jalil, Syed Omar cursing his lot in a coffee-shop over cadged brandy and ginger ale.

And the dark brought out the prostitutes, Malay divorcées mostly, quietly moving from light to light, gaudy and graceful, like other of night's creatures.

Hassan could not hide either his fear or his excitement. He did not try to pose as a young man of the world: Robert Loo's experience stood between the two of them like another person, a person Hassan had deliberately sought as a dragoman. At one point, breathless, he said: 'What shall we do? Shall we speak to two of them?'

'I think,' said Robert Loo, 'the best thing is just to stand somewhere and wait.' And now he too felt excitement stirring: he was to know that complex of sensations again, that piece of music which was all crescendo. But was it right just to seek it blindly, in a void, with no reference to what they called love? Last night he had not looked for it at all; it had just happened. Let the same thing happen again now, let the moment arrive. And so they waited and Hassan took from his shirt pocket a packet of Rough Rider cigarettes and offered one to Robert Loo. Robert Loo refused: he had no vices. Hassan puffed till the end glowed bright and the tube itself grew almost too hot to hold. And they waited.

They did not have long to wait. The two girls were clean, though they reeked of 'Himalayan Bouquet' perfume. They were tiny though well-developed. Their costumes proclaimed modest submission to custom and religion while at the same time suggesting untold treasures beneath for the asking, or buying. They went off with their young customers, arms linked warmly, chattering to soft dark Malay, Malay of the night, off to the same house. Robert Loo's girl was called Asma binte Ismail, and she lived a floor above her colleague. It was not hard to make love to her.

At the blinding moment of climax Robert Loo saw quite clearly the kind of music he wanted to write: his vision confirmed those shafts, those bursting fragments of last night. The claims of the body, the claims of the emotions – some fine soaring melody above the lush piano chords of the soloist. The violinist had disappeared. When his body had quietened, Robert Loo saw an unbidden picture of rows of tins on his father's shelves. He frowned at first, wondering what this could mean, and then smiled faintly. He had conquered those giants – harmony, counterpoint, orchestration – long ago. And now he had conquered love.

She asked for five dollars and he gave her six.

9

'Are you sure you can make it?' asked Temple Haynes, not without anxiety. He helped Crabbe along to the rough landing-stage, a groaning Crabbe sorry for himself, a Crabbe with a bandaged foot, looking like a gouty uncle, a Crabbe whose luggage was heavier by a single shoe, who carried a walking-stick donated by a well-equipped and resourceful American.

'Got to,' clenched Crabbe. 'Won't stay there any longer with that insulting bastard.'

Haynes tut-tutted at the strong language but said: 'He did pile it on. I failed to see any connection between your laughing at butterflies and being stung by a scorpion, but then perhaps my particular line of study has made me too rational-minded.'

It was a mid-morning of huge heat, a vast river sky above, the reek and shimmer of the river below, the green jaws of the jungle opening on either hand, the launch waiting. Crabbe, through his pain, noticed a man he knew sitting alone and silent in the bows: Vythilingam of the State Veterinary Department. Boatmen and passengers – a Chinese assistant manager and a Tamil hospital dresser whom Crabbe had met before, two Malays of occupation undefined – helped Crabbe into the launch, but Vythilingam did not move, did not even seem to see.

Temple Haynes looked down into the hot, rocking, oil-smelling boat, the river dancing on his spotless shirt. 'Take it easy,' he warned. 'Don't try and do too much. And I hope to be seeing you in a week or so.'

'When you move to the capital.'

'That's right. There's so much to be done.'

'Yes.' Crabbe winced, closing his eyes in the full sunlight that made them water, and opening them again to the shining river, to the waving Haynes as the launch throbbed and bounced and made ready to move off.

Nobody spoke to anybody. Crabbe's greeting to Vythilingam met a stare of more than recognition, not friendly, but hostile, rather a stare of distracted interest as though seeing in Crabbe more than the man who had given the party a few days ago, more than the Education Officer who was slowly handing over his burden to one of the new masters. Meanwhile foot and engine and sky and river throbbed, and they moved towards the *hulu*. '*Hulu*,' thought Crabbe, trying to grasp at anything to take his mind off his foot. '*Hulu*, the head. Head of my stick. Head of the river. *Penghulu*, head of the village, head of a religion. *Hulu*, really the desolate cry of some bird up-river, an ululation of a mouth finally going under. '*Hulu*.'

The river was broad and silver, and the sunlight was merry on it. But to port and starboard jungle exerted an influence more powerful than the sun, its smell as strong as the smell of warmed wood in the boat or of the sun-warmed river. And it was finally to the jungle-gods that the Malays would be most faithful. The sun of Islam, disguising itself cunningly as a sickle moon, was appropriate only to the clearings, which meant the towns with their refrigerators and mosques, where the muezzin's call mingled well with the music of the bars. Now the towns were beginning to entertain their vain dream of realized independence – the bright fresh paint for the visitors, the new stadium and the luxury hotel. Some Arab theologian-philosopher had said that Islam decayed in the towns. Only when the decay of Islam brought the decay of the cities, when the desert, with its frail tented communities, reasserted itself, only then could the faith be renewed. But there was no desert here, no dominion of sun and oasis. There was nothing to believe in except the jungle. That was home, that was reality. Crabbe gazed in a kind of horror mixed with peace at the endless vista of soaring trunks, lianas, garish flowers. They were chugging to-wards the *hulu*, the head or fount of everything, where there was no pretence or deception.

Settled to the river life, the transiently permanent, a fragile community was possible. The Chinese assistant manager spoke, with a wide smile of insincere teeth, to Crabbe, asking, 'Did you have the bad luck to fall down when you were drunk, Mr Crabbe?' It was not an insolent question, it was Chinese and clinical. The Tamil hospital dresser bubbled away, showing teeth as good: 'The mon-soon drains are very treacherous. It is possible to break a leg when one is not walking straight.' They smiled and smiled, waiting for confirmation.

'I was struck by a scorpion,' said Crabbe, 'when I was perfectly sober.' There was polite laughter of sixty-four teeth. 'I am now Club-foot the Tyrant.' The teeth dis-appeared in sympathy. 'But I didn't kill my father and I didn't marry my mother.'

'Marry your mother,' laughed the Chinese. 'That is very good.'

'Marry my mother,' suddenly said Vythilingam. Those were his first words of the voyage, and they were spoken with unstuttered labials. He provoked a fresh silence. 'Kill my father,' he added, for good measure.

'The Japanese killed my father,' smiled the Chinese. 'They poured petrol on him and then threw a lighted match.' He laughed modestly. 'They made me watch. They were not very good people.'

'History,' said Crabbe, battering his pain with words at random. 'The best thing to do is to put all that in books and forget about it. A book is a kind of lavatory. We've got to throw up the past, otherwise we can't live in the present. The past has got to be killed.' But, in saying that, off his guard with the pain in his foot, he reverted to his own past, and pronounced the very word in the Northern style, the style of his childhood.

'Excuse me,' said the Tamil dresser. 'To which pest do

you refer? Surely all pests have to be killed? I do not quite understand the drift of your statement.'

'It was only talk,' said Crabbe. 'It didn't mean anything.'

And now the colour changed to brown, the soft brown of Malay, for one of the Malays of undefined occupation spoke, sitting on a bench by the gunwhale, his brown arms stretched out, gripping the boat's side. 'Allah,' he said, 'disposes all things. The tea-cup I broke as a child, and the lottery my father failed to win by only one number. That was only two years after I broke the tea-cup. I blamed the breaking of the tea-cup on my younger brother, and this, as it turned out, was not unjust, for four years later, two years after my father failed to win the lottery, he broke a tea-cup on his own account. Then we had more tea-cups than formerly, and my mother was never very clever at counting. So he escaped punishment, which in a sense was just, for he had already been wrongly punished.' He now gave an exhibition of Malay teeth, bits of gold glinting in the sun and river, teeth not so good as the others' teeth.

'But the lottery ticket,' said the Tamil in Malay. 'I am not able to see the drift.'

'Allah disposes all things,' repeated the Malay, his teeth hidden in solemnity. 'If my father had been pre-destined to win he would have won. It was of no use for him to prate about injustice.' He smiled around and then closed up his mouth for the rest of the voyage, leaving his boat-mates with much to think about. The broken tea-cup tinkled in their brains and the number by which this man's father had failed to win glowed dimly and faded. Meanwhile the river narrowed somewhat, and the green bodies and arms and legs of the twin jungles shambled nearer.

'But, despite your father's failure to become rich,' said the Chinese assistant manager, 'you still had more tea-cups than you could count.'

The Malay nodded, smiling, saying nothing. Ahead, on

the starboard side, the jungle began to thin out to scrub, and then came a regular forest of rubber trees. Crabbe remembered an English politician of a mystical frame of mind who, having spent two days in Malaya, wrote in a Sunday paper that the very jungles were symmetrical, neat as the trim garden of British rule. Crabbe thought of many other palm-beach-suited visitors who, through pink mists of hospitable whisky, had mistaken Malays for Chinese, mosques for Anglican churches, plantations for jungles, neat dishes of canapés for calm and happy order. But at the *hulu* or head of the river the two halves of the jungle joined up and became one, and there was no mistaking one thing for another. The jungle called 'OM', like the Malay showman of the shadow-play, one and indivisible, ultimate numen.

The launch moved into the landing-stage of Rambutan Estate, and here the Chinese and the Tamil disembarked, with smiles and waves. Beyond was a pleasance of lawn, a company bungalow magnificent in shining glass, beyond again the rubber and the coolie lines. The launch moved out to mid-river, Crabbe and Vythilingam silent, the Malays silent with cigarettes, the boatmen chattering. Next stop was Durian Estate.

After a mile of further narrowing river Crabbe celebrated the slight easing of his pain by saying a few polite words to Vythilingam, asking him why he was going to the upriver plantation. Vythilingam jerked out, with throbbing larynx, the one word: 'Beasts.'

'To examine the cattle?' Vythilingam did not nod; Crabbe said: 'I'm going to see the family of this Tamil schoolmaster who was murdered. Perhaps you knew him. He ran the estate school.'

Vythilingam turned to look at Crabbe, nodding that he thought he knew the man. He uttered the name 'Yogam.' He added: 'Not a good man. A drunkard.'

'He'll never drink again.'

Vythilingam said nothing more. It was not long before they arrived at the final river outpost of industry and civilization. Here were even wider lawns than at Rambutan Estate, with Tamil gardeners at work with hoses on flower-beds. The planter's house was no mere bungalow. It stood on high pillars, shading under its belly an armoured car for running round the many square miles of rubber, and soaring up in two storeys to a roof garden with striped umbrellas. Here the lonely manager had to drink desperately of whatever solace boat could bring and private power-station could drive. For few now would risk the holiday trip to huge curry tiffins, gin parties with dancing, moonlight swimming in the pool that stood, its water changed daily, surrounded by banyan and rain tree, bougainvillea and hibiscus, before the proud manor house. It was a nail biting life for the exile, soothed inadequately by the hum of his refrigerators, the roar of his many fans, the high fidelity tone of his record-player. He drank much before dinner, and the dinner with its many courses appeared in the early hours of the morning, the fish and the mutton dried up, the tired cook forgetting about the coffee. Coombes, thought Crabbe, poor Coombes, despite his many thousands in the bank, the welcome of plush chairs and cigars on his rare trips to the London office.

The Malays smilingly helped Crabbe ashore, leaving him with his stick and his bag while they strolled off, waving, to their lines. Vythilingam stood hesitant, his black bag of medicine and instruments swinging in his right hand, smiling nervously, saying at length: 'The cattle. Cancerous growths on the cattle.'

'You'd better come and see Coombes first,' said Crabbe, 'and have a drink or something.' Vythilingam shook his head. 'My duty,' he said without stuttering. Then he went off in the direction of the labourers' houses, the self-contained world of village shop, cows and chickens, school and first-aid post. Alone, Crabbe walked painfully towards the house, a long stretch from the riverside, hearing the boat throbbing finally, then the click-off of the engine as it was moored against the later afternoon's return journey.

As Crabbe approached the outer stairs of the house a man appeared in the doorway. He called: 'Hello, hello, hello' in hearty welcome and then athletically began to run down the wooden steps. He was a stranger to Crabbe, and Crabbe said: 'I was looking for Mr Coombes.'

'Just a day too late, old boy,' said the man. 'Here, you *are* in a bad way, aren't you? Let me give you a helping hand.' He was a big chubby man, in his middle thirties, the muscle of his rugger days now settling placidly to reminiscent fat. He was not unhandsome. He had dark polished hair, a moustache, a plummy patrician voice, fine fat brown dimpled knees between blue shorts and football stockings. His shirt was of checked cotton, and within it a loose stomach and fleshy breasts bounced gently. 'You're the education chap,' he said, as he steered Crabbe strongly up the steps. He laughed, the loud laugh of rugger dinners. 'There's a telegram about you inside. Coombes left it for me. Something about this chap getting murdered. But I don't see what you can do.'

'It's quite usual,' said Crabbe, as they reached the top of the steps and stood before the large open doorway among potted plants. 'Condolences for the widow, find out what really happened for the records, assure her that she'll get a widow's and orphans' pension. We don't know how many orphans there are.' He panted, standing there, waiting to be asked in.

'This telegram,' said the man. He picked it up from the hall table. The hall was wide, magnificent with inlays of imported oak, heads of African beasts on the walls, flowers, a suite of rattan furniture. 'It says: "Murder regretted. Am sending my assistant as I must stay in the office." And it's signed Something bin Somebody. Never could read these Malay names. Tamil's my language.' He laughed again, plummily. 'Sounds as though he'd committed the murder himself. Well, come inside, Mr Assistant. Damn cheek of that bloke calling you his assistant. You give him hell when you get back.'

'It's true in a way, you know,' said Crabbe. They went

slowly, Crabbe limping, into the vast drawing-room. 'I *am* an assistant. I'm assisting this chap to take over my job.' The drawing-room seemed an acre of polished floor-boards, with complete units for sitting or lounging – drink-table, settee, arm-chairs – placed at intervals along the walls, by the windows that looked down at river and jungle beyond, in the body of the echoing room. It was monstrous and pathetic, this lavishness, a child's tongue put out at the great green giant. On the walls were square patches unfaded by sun, where pictures had been and would be again. On the floor were treasures of this new man – gramophone records, books, papers, group photographs of rugger clubs – half unpacked. A radio-gramophone stood in the middle of the floor, a voice in the wilderness at present silent, though it was already plugged into a light socket high above. 'Where,' asked Crabbe, 'is Coombes?'

'He's been moved. Apparently this place has been getting on his nerves.' The man made a swigging motion and winked. 'He's gone to a place in Johore. Demotion really. And this is promotion for me.' He looked round with satisfaction at the vast anonymous room. 'I was in Negri Duabelas,' he said. 'I ran the Union Jack Society in Timbang. And a music club. I wasn't so isolated there as I'm going to be here. But I don't mind isolation. I've got my records and my books. I read a lot of poetry. My name's George Costard. I don't think I quite caught yours.'

Crabbe thought for an instant and then said: 'Victor.' If this man read poetry it was just possible he might have read some of Fenella's. After all, Crabbe was his name before it was hers; why should she usurp it and make it well known on her own behalf? 'Victor,' he said.

'So you're Mr Victor,' said Costard, 'assistant to Who-isit bin Whatshisname. Sit down, Victor, and take a load off that foot. You been playing soccer in your bare feet or something? I never did care for soccer. I'll get some beer from the fridge.' He went off, briskly walking the half-mile or so to the kitchen, and then called a Tamil name and Tamil orders. He walked the half-mile back again, saying: 'I've asked Tambi to bring a large bottle every twenty minutes. Is that all right with you? It saves the trouble of going to the kitchen and shouting. This is a hell of a big place.' He sat down, one big bare knee over the other, and looked at Crabbe complacently. 'Music,' he said. 'Do you care for music?' Crabbe said he did. The Tamil boy came with beer. 'Watch this,' said Costard with pride. 'This lad can do anything.' He gave Tamil orders and the Tamil boy, lean, black, sly-looking, took a random pile of thick smeared records (old style: seventy-eight revolutions per minute) and carried them over to the radio-gramophone. With practised skill he set the machine working: the first of the skewered pile submitted to the needle and, through loud scratch noises, the opening theme of Beethoven's Ninth Symphony began to emerge. 'I like it that way,' said Costard. 'I never know what I'm going to get. After this you'll probably get a bit of Schubert or Brahms or a Hebridean folk-song. I just leave it to him. I've got catholic tastes. Catholic with a small "c", of course. The family's always been Church of England. There was an Archbishop George Costard in the eighteenth century. You may have heard of him.'

Crabbe settled as comfortably as he could with his beer. 'Here we go again,' he thought. 'Drink and reminiscence. Another day of wasted time. They're right when they say we drink too much out here. And we slobber too much over ourselves. "Did you ever hear how I came out here? It's rather an interesting story, really. Have another drink and I'll tell you about it." We're all sorry for ourselves because we're not big executives or artists or happily married men in a civilized temperate climate.' Crabbe noted that the pain in his foot was going, to be followed by a numbness as though the foot were not really there.

'Some people make fun of the name,' said Costard. 'Ignorant people. Although at school I didn't suffer too much because most of the kids had heard of Custard's last stand. I don't think he'd anything to do with our family, though. I think the two names are different in origin. Costard means an apple, you know.'

Over in a flash, Beethoven's first theme having been just about stated, the record was replaced mechanically by part of the music for King George VI's Coronation, Parry's 'I was glad when they said unto me'. Costard said happily: 'You just never know what you're going to get.' Crabbe was glad Costard said that to him, changing the subject, for, off his guard, he had very nearly begun to say that his own name meant a kind of apple. 'Have a cigarette, Victor,' said Costard. The table was full of half-empty Capstan tins, and Crabbe helped himself. Again off his guard, warmed by the sound of his Christian name, he said automatically: 'Thank you, George.' Then he blushed.

'Funny,' said Costard. 'You're a Christian name man. I shouldn't have thought that. I've never found it easy to call a man by his Christian name, except my brothers, of course. It's public school training, I suppose.' He looked at Crabbe suspiciously. 'What was your school, if I may ask?'

'You wouldn't know it,' said Crabbe. 'It was a rather obscure grammar school in the north of England.'

'You a 'Varsity man?'

'Oh yes.' And he named his red-brick university.

'Oxford, me,' said Costard. 'The House. I took a first in Greats. You wouldn't think that to look at me, would you? Perhaps you wonder why I came out here at all. It's rather an interesting story, really. Look,' he said urgently, 'twenty minutes is nearly up, and you haven't finished your beer. That boy of mine's a walking clock.' He examined his watch narrowly. 'One minute to go. Time.' Sure enough, the Tamil boy smugly reappeared, bearing another large bottle. And then Parry's anthem finished triumphantly. There was the muffled fall of a new record, a click, and the sound of Schubert's 'Trout' Quintet, half-buried under the surface noise, swam sweetly forth. 'We ought to have bets on it, suggested Costard. 'I bet you five dollars the next record will be more Beethoven.'

'I can't bet,' said Crabbe. 'I just don't know what records you've got.'

'No more do I,' said Costard cheerfully. 'That's the fun of it. Some of these records down there on the floor – why, I haven't seen them for years. When we were packing up to leave Negri Duabelas my boy discovered stacks of them in the place under the stairs where I kept the Christmas decorations. What time would you like lunch?'

'Any time that suits you,' said Crabbe.

'I thought you'd say that. I normally have lunch about four. Dinner at any time after midnight. Except when I have lady guests. You must stay for dinner.'

'I really ought to go and see this woman,' said Crabbe. 'And then get back.'

'Nonsense,' said Costard warmly. 'It's a real stroke of luck, you dropping in like this. You can tell me the set-up in this state, and who the important people are, and what the local Cold Storage is like. And I can tell you my story, which is pretty interesting, really.'

'But I really came down to see this woman,' said Crabbe.

'You can't speak Tamil, can you? No. Well, I can. I'll get the dope from her and send it on in an official letter. And I don't suppose you can walk very far with that foot of yours.'

'It's not painful now. It's just a bit numb.'

'Ah. Well, when I left Oxford, I wondered for a long time what to do. The family has money, of course, so there was no immediate urgency. Yes, I know what you're thinking. You want to know why I didn't go straight into the army. But, you see, I joined up in my first year at Oxford, and finished my degree after the war. Were you in the Forces, by any chance?'

'Army too.'

'What rank?' Crabbe told him. 'I,' said Costard, 'didn't do too badly, all things considered. Captain at twenty-one isn't too bad, is it? No. I wasn't all that heroic, though they were good enough to mention me in dispatches. Anyway, after the war, I went back to Oxford and did pretty well, on the whole. A first in Greats and a Rugger Blue. Soccer's your game, I take it?'

'No.'

'Ah,' beamed Costard, as the record changed. 'What did I tell you? Beethoven. That's the Hammerklavier. I knew a girl who played that marvellously. A fragile little thing, to look at, but the strength in those wrists.' His face grew dark. 'Poor, poor girl. Poor, poor, poor little thing. But I'll come to her in due course. She's part of the story.'

'Not if it makes you sad,' said Crabbe.

'Oh, it's life. We all get over these things. We've got to, else life just couldn't go on. But she meant a lot, a hell of a lot. Perhaps, really, I'd better not speak about her. I mean, to a stranger. And I'm used to keeping it bottled up. There was never really anybody I could tell. I just couldn't. My mother was always strait-laced. Don't get me wrong; I adore her, but there were some things she could never understand.' He sighed. 'Adultery.' He sighed again. 'That's a hard word. And yet it never seemed as though we were doing wrong. I don't know why I'm telling you these things. It seemed rather as though her marriage was all wrong. He was to blame, not us.'

'On the whole,' said Crabbe in swift embarrassment, 'this isn't too bad a state to be in. The Sultan's go-ahead, modern in some of his views. There aren't so many British left now, of course, and the British Adviser's gone. But if you're a club man you'll find plenty of Asians to drink with, and there's even a sort of Rugger Club.'

'What do you mean – "sort of"?'

'They don't find it easy to get anybody to play with. They just meet and drink beer and sing songs. But they talk about rugger: most of them were educated in England.'

'Asians, you say?' Costard looked darkly. 'No,' he said. 'That's not really my line. The Asians are all right in their place, I suppose, but I don't think they ought to do that sort of thing. After all, it is an English game. And you mean to say that they sing, "If I were a marrying maid which thank the Lord I'm not, sir"? That's a kind of desecration. Oh, I know you'll probably think me stupidly conservative, and all that sort of rot, but that's the way I was brought up. I can't help it.' The record changed. They were now treated to Clara Butt singing 'Land of Hope and Glory'. She sang through a thick mist of scratches. Costard began to swing his beer-mug gently in time. Then he looked at his watch. 'I say,' he said, 'you *are* slow. Tambi will be here in . . .' He computed carefully, '. . . in exactly twenty seconds.' And, lo, Tambi appeared at that very moment. 'He's a bit too early,' said Costard. 'Still, it's a fault on the right side. I'm always punctual to a fault, personally. It's a family tradition. The old man used to knock hell out of me if I was ever late for anything. He was right, I see that now. I've always insisted on punctuality in my own underlings. It's no good their saying they haven't got watches or their watches stopped or something. Where there's a will there's a way.' Beer was poured for Costard and his guest. His feet flapping gently on the parquet, Tambi returned to his kitchen. There was a silent space, during which Dame Clara Butt, with brass behind her, was able to boom her climax to two conventionally grave, lonely, moved, head-drooping exiles. The Edwardian expansionist prayer came to an end. 'I suppose I am a bit old-fashioned, really,' admitted Costard. 'But I'm enough of a realist to know that those days are over. The Empire's cracking up, they say. Well, some of us must keep the traditions alive. That's the meaning of Conservatism, as I see it. Some of us have got to conserve.'

'But you're not an Empire-builder,' said Crabbe. 'You're a rubber-planter. You're a commercial man.' A new record started – a dance of clean dainty shepherdesses by Edward German. Costard looked at Crabbe with beetled brows and a pout of distaste.

'That's where you're wrong,' he said. 'Do you think the money matters to me? I'm in this game to keep something alive that's very, very beautiful. The feudal tradition, the enlightened patriarchal principle. You people have been throwing it all away, educating them to revolt against us. They won't be happy, any of them. It's only on the estates now that the old ideas can be preserved. I'm the father of these people. They can look up to me, bring me their troubles and let me participate in their joys. Don't you think that's good and beautiful? They're my children, all of them. I correct them, I cherish them, I show them the way that they should go. Of course, you could say that it's more than just an ideological matter with me. I suppose I'm really the paternal type.' He looked it, big and dark and comely, his large knees comfortable stools for climbing brats lisping 'Daddy'.

'And yet you've never married,' said Crabbe. 'You've no children of your own.'

'How about you?'

'Oh yes, married. No children, though. But I've been a schoolmaster for a long time. That's satisfied and finally cured any paternal instinct in me.' The Tamil boy had entered again, without a tray. Crabbe said: 'Something's gone wrong with your human clock.'

Costard smiled with infinite complacency. 'That boy's marvellous. He's counted the number of records. Now he's going to change them.' And indeed the boy lifted the pile of worn discs tenderly from the turntable and, at random, picked up a new pile – dusty ten-inchers. And now for some reason Crabbe felt a strange uneasiness in his stomach.

'Good,' said Costard, settling himself anew, listening to a boy soprano of the nineteen thirties singing 'Oh, for the wings of a dove'. Crabbe's uneasiness passed: it was pure breakfastlessness, he decided, hearing a comforting rumble from the pit. Costard insisted on silence for the creamy Mendelssohn. And then, as the march from *Aida* struck up – Sunday school outing trumpets and a smell of orange-peel – he big-drummed the air with his fist, lalling the square tune vigorously. 'Come on,' he paused to invite, 'join in. Grand stuff, this.' Crabbe smiled with the corners of his lips, and then sought an alibi in his tankard. 'Good man,' said Costard. 'You couldn't have timed that better.' For there again was Tambi with beer. And then the record changed, a piano pinking high a Poulenc-like theme. Crabbe heard absently, then listened incredulously. And Costard also was listening in a kind of stupid horrified wonder. 'No,' he said. 'No. That was lost. That was lost in Negri.' The piano slid in grotesque arpeggio to the bass register: a comic fugato, the left hand occasionally leaping up to pink a discord in the high treble. Crabbe saw the hand doing it, the sweep of the bare arm. He was on his feet. The stung foot, now quite nerveless, gave way under him, and he clung to the table. 'Where did you get that?' he asked breathlessly. 'Who gave you that? You bloody thief, you stole it.'

The Tamil boy stood looking, bewildered, a dog prepared for a whipping for no crime he knew of. '*Utundu povay!*' cried Costard, also on his feet. 'Where was it? Why didn't you tell me?' The boy cringed, '*Ni ennai vansiththup-podday!*' yelled Costard.

'What's going on?' cried Crabbe. 'Where did you get it? Who gave you that?'

Costard made a hitting gesture. The boy, understanding nothing of this wrath, this agitation, shambled off like an ape. The two Englishmen faced each other, breathing heavily.

'There was only one of those,' said Crabbe. 'She only made one. She said she'd lost it.' The music tinkled on, a gay brief satire on Scarlatti or Galuppi. 'You stole it, you stole it from her!'

Costard gazed at Crabbe, his plump English face a mask of loathing. 'So it was you, was it?' he said. 'You were the man. You bloody murderer.'

'What do you know about it? What's it to do with you?'

'You saved your own bloody skin, didn't you? You let

her drown. I know it all, I know the whole filthy story. You wanted to be rid of her, didn't you? Why couldn't you tell her like a man? I wanted her. I wanted her, do you hear?'

'No,' said Crabbe. 'No, no, no. It's not true. It can't be true. She would have told me. There weren't any secrets.'

'Oh yes, there was one. That she loathed your guts. That she was going to be with me. With me. For ever, do you hear? Only a week after that happened. I know it all, you bloody murderer. You came home once a fortnight. You'd no particular wish to be with her, but you wouldn't let her go.'

'There was no room there. It was after the war. The housing shortage. I had to be where my job was. It was the only thing I could do. I didn't mean it. God knows I didn't mean it. I tried to save her.'

'Driving like a bloody lunatic on an icy road.'

'I know, I know, I know. It was an accident. An accident. I lost control, the car went over, into the river. I tried to save her. I've suffered enough. Christ, I've suffered enough.'

'Only a week after that we were going to go away. We were going to be together.' The merry piano tinklings were gone. Scratchings, a soft click, then the 'Hebrides' Overture started. Costard sat down lumpily. 'Oh, I know it's all over,' he said. 'Nearly ten years.'

'I never knew. She never told me.'

'We kept our secret well. I never even came for her in the car. We always met in town.' He sat, his pudgy hands clasped, tears in his eyes, the corners of his mouth drooping, the large brown schoolboy knees grotesquely irrelevant, almost indecent in this context of mature anguish. 'I loved her.' Then Costard murmured her name.

'How dare you!' cried Crabbe. Feebly, tottering on his numb foot, he made for Costard, a hand up for slapping. Costard gripped Crabbe's wrist powerfully. 'No, you don't,' said Costard. 'You're a liar and a coward and a murderer. You wouldn't even tell me your real name.'

His grip loosened and his hand dropped. 'Yes, that was his name. She always said Victor. And she said she wouldn't have to change her monogram. Poor girl. Poor, poor little girl.'

'You,' said Crabbe, standing with limp arms at his sides. 'It's all lies. She loved me. There was never anybody else. You're making it all up. You've dreamed it all. None of it's true.'

Costard looked up gravely. 'It's true,' he said. 'And to think that it had to be here, eight thousand miles away. Eight thousand miles and the first man I meet in this bloody place. You've poisoned it for me. Poisoned it for me on my first day. My second day,' he amended, then put his heavy head into cupped hands. 'Oh, God, God.'

Crabbe stood limp, his numb foot somehow bearing him. The blood of realization of what all this meant had not yet flowed into his arteries. 'I'd better go,' he said.

'Yes, go, go!'

'But I still can't understand.'

'Get out, go on, get out!'

'I mean, I was bound to have suspected. She just didn't do that sort of thing. And with a man like you.'

Costard looked up. 'A man like me,' he said slowly. 'What do you mean?'

'She couldn't. It's just impossible.'

Costard rose. 'A man who could give her a bit of love. A man who was straight and honest. Not a dithering bloody would-be intellectual. You're cheap. Cheap education, cheap ideas, a half-baked bloody nobody. You didn't deserve her. Go on, get out before I throw you out. Get back to bloody town.' Crabbe picked up his stick from the side of the chair. His bag was in the hall. 'A man with a body. A man with blood. A man with something to give. Get out.' Slowly Crabbe traversed the half-acre of parquet floor. 'A man with an education. A man with a bloody family background,' Costard was shouting. 'Go on. Get to that bloody launch. They'll take you back. Tambi! Tambi!' he called. 'I'll get those bloody boatmen.' Crabbe moved on, still many yards from the door. 'You don't know what love means!' called Costard, in a voice like a loud-hailer. 'Your type never do!' Crabbe reached the hall. With some difficulty he inched down the steps, hearing Costard calling still and, feeble behind the manly voice, the voice of the pack-leader, a hundred wind and strings playing the *Tannhäuser* Overture.

In the open air, under the afternoon blast furnace in the empty blue, Crabbe stood, saying quietly: 'She just couldn't do that. It's all a trick. He's mad, that's it. That wasn't her piece on the gramophone. It was something like it. We're talking of two different people. I'll go back and we'll talk quietly and everything will come right.' He turned, thought of the weary stairs, the miles of parquet. It was too far. Too far for this foot. He moved on over lawn, past swimming-pool, orderly trees and flower-beds. Tamil gardeners showed him friendly teeth. The path turned, past wilder trees, towards the landing-stage.

Vythilingam saw a white man coming and hid himself. There were plenty of bushes. He had not been to see the cattle and the goats and the chickens. He had been sitting, his black bag at his side, trying to think, looking at the river, wondering if that jungle beyond could really take him, wondering if that jungle really held his duty. With only the mildest interest he saw Crabbe approach the waiting launch. There was nobody else about. Crabbe looked left and right, leaning on his stick. Jungle, river and sky.

Vythilingam saw Crabbe try to board the launch. He put his foot clumsily on the gunwhale. The foot seemed to crumple underneath him. Still carrying his stick and his bag, he faltered in the air for an instant and fell. Vythilingam saw water, green and white, shoot up long fingers of protest as a weight crashed the surface. He heard faint human noises, and then animal noises, and, hearing the animal noises, he rose to his feet in compassion. He stood undecided. And then, as noise subsided and the river settled and the launch moved in again, he sat down on the grass once more. Human lives were not his professional concern. Humanity? Yes, humanity, but humanity was altogether a different matter. He sat for a time thinking about humanity, seeing the great abstractions move and wave in the fronds of the jungle over the river.

10

Mr Liversedge always chewed gum quietly and imperceptibly on the bench. If anyone in court did perceive that gentle rolling of the jaws, they might well take it for an easing-in of new dentures or a symptom of mild tropical neurasthenia. In any case, it didn't matter. This was the East, where much was allowed that would be inadmissible in the Antipodes. Mr Liversedge, born in Toowoomba, educated in Brisbane, was a tough common-sensical Queenslander who saw the whole ridiculous Oriental *susah* in true proportion. Here men would murder for five dollars, here men would seek divorce because their wives sighed at the handsomeness of the film star P. Ramlee, here the very night-roaming dogs screamed blue murder if another dog bit their little toe. Mr Liversedge chewed, nodding at the lucid exposition of Mr Linn from Penang, though contemning inwardly the Pommie accent, chewing more roundly with a twitch of the nose at the rhetoric of the Tamils, especially that Tamil with a voice like a bloody sheila, and the clipped incoherencies of the police. He gave swift judgment.

'A lot of fuss about nothing. Here you have a few boys who want a bit of adventure. Where are they going to get it? At least, they're not mooning in the cinema every night, hanging round the coffee-shops. They showed initiative. They meant no real harm. Look at these knives, which the police call deadly weapons.' Mr Liversedge took one of the rusting exhibits. 'This wouldn't cut butter when it's hot. Look at the point. You couldn't harm a fly with it.' The four defendants hated Mr Liversedge for these words. This, then, was British justice. 'They stole nothing. The pair of trousers was recovered. If boys want to steal, they'll steal more than a dirty baggy pair of trousers.' Maniam blushed. He had not been able to obtain a change of clothes from Pahang. 'In this state there's real villainy going on, in the jungle, in the villages, and a lot of people who should know better are aiding and abetting it. But don't pick on a handful of harmless boys who are looking for an innocent bit of amusement. Don't waste our time. We've bigger things to do.' The four boys pumped up their hate to hissing steam. Harmless, quotha. Innocent, forsooth. 'The case is dismissed. But I'd like to warn these boys.' Warning, warn. They were being warned; that was better. 'Like to warn them to find a better outlet for their spare energy and love of adventure. Join some bigger organization. The Boy Scouts, for instance.' The four young Malays froze in horror. 'And I'd like to add that it's really the responsibility of this State to provide some kind of spare-time activity for young men of energy and initiative who otherwise might be tempted into adventure which, however harmless, might be construed by people old enough to know better as ...' He read from the sheet ironically '... attempted murder, theft, assault with battery and heavens knows what. All right, hurry up with the next case.'

The Malay interpreter worked swiftly, condensing Mr Liversedge's already condensed judgement into a few packed, flavoursome idioms. Mr Liversedge chewed gum amiably, looking round at the gay spectators, the protagonists making ready to go, Maniam and Lim both watching the time anxiously, both having planes to catch.

Outside the court Syed Omar, in collar, tie and jacket, clapped his son hard on the back. 'You heard what he said,' he said. 'He said that the Tamils only got what was coming to them. He said, in effect, that it is time the Malays chewed up the Tamils, and, by implication of course, the Chinese. For many years I have inveighed against British justice. Now I feel that there is something in it after all. Though, of course, this *hakim* is an Australian, which makes some difference. They have suffered under the yoke of the English. Perhaps that division ought to be made clear.'

'He never said that about the Tamils,' protested Syed Hassan. 'I can understand some English.'

'You have to read between the lines,' said his father. 'They are not so direct as us. They say a lot by implication. You saw the look he flashed on the Tamils, rolling his jaws in dislike. However, thank God, it is over. Now we can concentrate on our normal worries. Getting jobs, for instance. Borrowing money, for instance. Wait, the bail. That money will now go back to Crabbe. There is definitely one man I can borrow off.'

'There he goes now,' said Hamzah. 'The Tamil, off to the airport. His nose is still swollen, but he has been a long time away from Pahang. He has to go back some time.'

Syed Omar grinned viciously at the sight of the discomfited Arumugam, Sundralingam and Maniam getting into Sundralingam's car. Then he opened his mouth in the shock of remembering that he had forgotten something. 'My God,' he said. 'Yusof. There he is. There is Yusof.' He saw 'Che Yusof, his former colleague, most clerkly in horn-rims and neat receding hair, getting into a small Austin car with his daughter, the daughter that, so Syed Omar had definitely at last learned, though only indirectly, having many times been ejected from the office where he had formerly worked, where he had given to the Department his blood and sweat for many years, was now occupying his desk, showing smiling teeth and a brown bosom to the C.P.O. in the intervals of typing reports, letters and memoranda. 'My God,' said Syed Omar. He saw Mr Lim from Penang, Anglicanly elegant, climbing into the Hillman that the firm used on this side of the peninsula, a Malay driver closing the door smartly after him. 'Stop!' called Syed Omar. 'Stop! I am coming with you!'

'Don't be a fool, Father.'

'He has already made me a fool, that bastard. Wait!'

called Syed Omar. He was at the car window, saying to the astonished Mr Lim: 'Follow that car, that Austin. Quick, it is a matter of urgency.'

'Really,' said Lim Cheng Po. 'Really. I have to get to the airport. I have a plane to catch.'

'That's where he is going,' said Syed Omar. 'I know. He is going to drink beer at the bar. It will be bitter beer for him.'

'No,' said Mr Lim. 'If you're going to start any more of your nonsense, you can't expect me to help you. Find your own way.'

'It is all one can expect from a Chinese,' called Syed Omar after the departing car. 'The Chinese are our enemies. Curse you, you yellow-skinned bastard.' Then he called: 'Taxi!' Ashamed, Syed Hassan shepherded his friends away. 'To Loo's place,' he said. 'He invited us all to go there for a drink if we got off.'

'He? A Chinese?'

'He's all right.'

Syed Omar, though unable to pay the fare, gave the driver of the taxi lordly instructions. 'Che Yusof's car, like Sundralingam's and Lim Cheng Po's, was already long away, churning up dust in the rainless weather. The taxi coughed and shook at the tail of the procession. But, realized Syed Omar, as he sat back against a naked cushion spring and took off his tie and opened his shirt for action, there was no hurry. Nobody could get away. He hoped there would be a fair-sized crowd at the airport, enough people to justify the expense of all his dramatic talents, the energy of his blows. Cool air blew in from the open window. They cruised gently along, the road to themselves. Then the driver said, as they approached an attap coffee-stand on the outskirts of the village midway between town and airport:

'I need cigarettes. Pay me half my fare now and I can buy them.' He was a sly, hard, thin man of Syed Omar's age, a man who had suffered much in his time from wives and no money. He had been already five years paying for his taxi.

'When we arrive,' said Syed Omar. 'Not before. Come on, we have little time to lose.'

'Half the fare. A dollar.'

'You will have the whole fare when we arrive.'

'Show me your money. I suspect that you haven't any.' A hard life had taught him much.

'Insolence,' said Syed Omar. 'It's your job to drive me to wherever I say. Who are you to start inquiring insolently into the financial position of your betters?'

The taxi was now parked by the attap coffee-stand. The driver looked forward to a leisurely altercation. 'What do you mean, betters? I have a job and you haven't. I don't believe you have two cents to rub together.' He leaned an arm comfortably over the driver's seat. The heat beat in, the breeze of motion gone.

'Allah most high,' swore Syed Omar. 'I will argue with you another time. Your job now is not to argue but to get me to the airport. That's what I am paying you for.'

'I doubt it if I'll see many signs of paying.'

'I am of the line of the Prophet. That's what my name Syed means, though probably you're too ignorant to know that. I have my honour, and you are impugning my honour. When I take a thing I always pay for it. Now, come on, quickly. The airport.'

'Let's see the colour of your money.'

'You'll see the colour of my fist if you don't do what I say.'

'Fighting words, eh? Well, now, I'm really frightened.' The driver grinned, showing few teeth, but those golden. 'You must have a lot of muscle hidden underneath that flab.'

'I refuse to argue further with you. Do your job and you will be paid at the end of it. But you've been so insolent that you certainly won't get a tip.'

'Ha, that's a good one. No tip, he says. No fare either.'

'Look,' said Syed Omar, 'I'll go over there and get you cigarettes with my own hands. Will that satisfy you?'

'You won't get any credit here. They know your kind.'

'My kind. By God!' Syed Omar began to beat the hard shoulder of the driver. 'Go on. Do what I say. If you don't, I'll report you. I'll report you to the police, to the Town Board, to the Mentri Besar. Do your job, damn you.'

At the sound of the hard word *chelaka*, the driver said: 'Out. Go on, out. You can walk the rest of the way. You can be thankful that I've taken you half of the way for nothing.'

'Take me back to town, then.'

'Not likely. Go on, out.' The man got out of his own seat and opened the door for Syed Omar. 'The airport's in that direction,' he said, 'if you don't already know.'

'By God,' said Syed Omar, 'you'll suffer for this.' He got out, and squared up to the driver, but the driver laughed gaily and skipped back to his seat. He switched on, put the groaning vehicle into gear, turned it round skilfully and sped dustily townwards. Syed Omar shook his fist repeatedly. Meanwhile, the old woman who kept the coffee-stand sucked her gums and shook her head at the follies of the modern world.

Syed Omar began to walk to the airport. Sweat pearled his tough brown skin, his fat bounced in rhythm. No car passed for him to flag. Nay, but a car did, coming from the airport, an Austin with a known and hated number – PP 197 – and in the car 'Che Yusof and his daughter. The daughter waved and smiled. Syed Omar danced on the hot road. He had now passed the point of no return: the airport was a mile away, the town nearly three miles. He walked on, reaching an airport silver with sun on the waiting plane's body, silver glancing from the glass of the control tower, cars parked. The plane, whose tortuous route accommodated both Pahang and Penang passengers, was late taking off. Perhaps the Sultan's name was on the manifest and His Highness, aware that he was above schedules and the law, was still dawdling over early curry in the Istana. But no, there were instructions to passengers now crackling through the loudspeakers and, as Syed

Omar came near to the airfield, he could see the thin string of people turning often to smile and wave, already filing towards the air-hostess in the hole in the huge silver body. And here, as Syed Omar limped into the waiting hall, were two Tamils saying good-bye to one other, embracing, slapping, hand-pumping, one with a girl's voice piping high in most cordial valedictory emotion. Then Maniam, his nose not too red or swollen, almost, in fact, presentable to his masters in Pahang, joined the waving file, smiling back sadly. Syed Omar broke through the gentle cordon of white-clad Chinese officials. 'A last-minute message,' he improvised. 'From the police. Very urgent.' Maniam was the last of the embarking line. Syed Omar dived at him, bowled him over on the asphalt in view of the smiling wavers, the shining plane, the hot indifferent sun, and said:

'It was all your fault.' He knelt on Maniam and hit various parts of his face. Maniam wailed. 'You started it all.' One on the chest. 'We were happy till you came.' But now the officials were timidly interfering, and others were coming languidly to the scene, and even the police discussed this violence as possibly coming within the scope of their terms of reference. Syed Omar gave Maniam one good knuckling in the eye and was led off, not unsatisfied, saying: 'He started it all. He put the idea of treachery into everbody's head.' Meanwhile Maniam, disfigured, wailed forlornly.

'This time,' sighed Sundralingam, 'he had better stay in your house. I've done my share. You'd better get a bed made up for him.'

'No room,' squealed Arumugam. 'You know there's no room.'

'Vythilingam, then. It's time Vythilingam did something. Dear, dear, what a mess.'

But days passed, and Vythilingam did not return. In any case, Sundralingam had forgotten that Mrs Smith and the wealthy orphan called Chelvanajaky were already installed in Vythilingam's quarters (his predecessor had been a married man: there were rooms enough, though not now room for Maniam), Mrs Smith herself sweeping out the corners, ordering the Siamese servant to scrub (whereupon he gave in his notice), planning tasty meals for her son's return. And then mysterious news about Crabbe began to leak through many crevices and, in the manner of the East, news about Vythilingam was inferred from the external accidents of Vythilingam and Crabbe's being in the same boat, going to the same place, both disappearing at the same time. More, there were signatures left in river and on river-bank, or near it – a black bag nearly empty of medicaments, a floating stick and overnight satchel containing, among other things, a shoe. The lizards, before fleeting off, had left their tails in the clutching hand of the upper air. Bodies, it was well-known, were near-irrecoverable in that river of deep-set weeds. Nobody felt inclined to give orders to drag: let the river keep them.

'It is clear what happened,' said Sundralingam, while Mrs Smith sat dumbly but not over-sadly, for this was the East. 'Your son was heroic. He dived in after this Mr Crabbe, and Mr Crabbe himself dragged him to his death, or else both were caught in the weeds. It is sad, but life has to go on. And, for us Hindus, death is not an end but a fresh beginning. I do not need to remind you of that, Mrs Smith. Your son is already reincarnated. We do not know, of course, in what form. It would be pleasant to think that he was now one of the little animals being treated at this moment in his own dispensary, though, of course, his assistant will not be treating it very well. Or perhaps he is born again as some great future politician, some saviour of his people. But he always said there was more virtue in dumb animals than in some human beings. And he was, you will remember, himself very nearly dumb.'

'All my plans disarranged,' said Mrs Smith. Her voice was curiously deep and compelling, unlike the pretty bird-song of so many of the women of her race. Her voice was the voice of some competent chairman of a ladies' social guild, as her handsome and bulky person, with its rich *sari*, was apt for the heart of a group photograph in a local Ceylon newspaper. 'I had hoped so much,' she said. 'Perhaps I am very deeply to blame for being out of touch with him for so long. But I wrote letters, I tried to arrange marriages. I had my own commitments, you see. One cannot do everything. But,' she sighed, 'perhaps I can make amends in another life. He needed his mother, perhaps, more than we shall ever know. I do not think he was too happy. Men only do brave and desperate things when they are not too happy, and this thing was brave and desperate. What was this Englishman to him, anyway?'

'He was just an Englishman,' shrugged Sundralingam. 'But your son would save the life of a rat or of a toad if he could. I think it quite likely that he would try to save an Englishman.'

To those who doubted that Crabbe and Vythilingam – one or other or both – were dead, Sundralingam said: 'Look at the facts. Both have disappeared. People have to disappear somewhere. The river is the obvious place.'

'There is the jungle. They could both have taken to the jungle.'

'Well, yes,' Sundralingam would say. 'I think Crabbe possibly might go and join the Communists. A Tamil gentleman named Jaganathan – a gentleman who worked with Crabbe in Dahaga, whom I met in Kuala Lumpur – said that he had strong Communist leanings. Again, he may have embezzled cash or taken many bribes and now be over the border in Thailand with his ill-gotten gains. One cannot be sure. But Vythilingam is certainly dead. You can be quite sure of that.' And then Sundralingam would spend a cosy evening with Mrs Smith and Chelvanajaky, while Arumugam fretted jealously, aware of what Sundralingam was after, aware, as Sundralingam was aware, that, owing to the economic recession, fathers were cutting dowries by as much as fifty per cent and that here was a pleasingly shy and not unpersonable girl whose dowry could never be cut.

But there were men, white, whose word could naturally be relied on, who were prepared to ease the work of the police so far as Crabbe's disappearance was concerned. The Independence celebrations were coming, contingents of police had to be drilled and blancoed and starched before proceeding to Kuala Lumpur to represent the state. Crabbe's disappearance, if pursued to the point of river-dredging or keeping a file open till the body bobbed up down-stream, would mean overmuch trouble at this busy time. And so the Malay C.P.O. listened, with a Tertullian willingness to believe, to the white men's stories.

George Costard said that the boatmen, reporting to their launch for the afternoon down-stream voyage, found a stick and a bag floating, and one said he saw bubbles, and the other could not swear to it but thought he saw a hand come up and grasp at air for the last time. Costard had no doubt that Crabbe had accidentally or, for all he knew, not so accidentally drowned. He added that he had been forced to tell his coolies that this white man had deliberately taken his own life to compensate, by obscure logic, for the death of Yogam the Tamil schoolmaster – a white for a black, a restoration of the balance of life. Otherwise there would be a tendency for them to think that a sudden and unexpected death was a bad augury for the prosperity of the estate under its new manager. Small shrines were already in existence in the coolie lines, dedicated to the spirit of the man with the strange name, and offerings of crayfish (in default of saltier crustaceans) were already being made. This would not last long, however. The tiny cult would be swallowed up in the bigger ones, probably on the next Hindu feast-day. The point was that Costard's first duty, as the C.P.O. would realize, had to be to the estate and the company that owned it. Thank you, Mr Costard.

'A nice chap,' said Tommy Jones, promoting thirst in the State capital, 'but a bit queer. Didn't know his name

604

at the time, of course, but met him on the train going to Tikus, and we had a sort of night out together, though neither of us did anything really. He said he'd been told that it was up-river that he'd conk out sometime or other, and I got the idea that he wasn't all that keen on carrying on, he wouldn't mind snuffing it all that much. But I didn't pay too much attention because you don't really when a bloke talks that way. Met too many of them in my line of business. Still, he was a bit low because his wife was a bit too brainy for him or something. Anyway, she'd been writing poetry about him in some paper or other, a paper that didn't much go for putting flowers on dogs' graves. I do at least remember that bit. That made him a bit down in the mouth. He didn't seem himself the next morning either, kept talking about the Prophet Mohammed inventing beer or some such story. A bit crackers, I thought. He travelled with a pig in a Land-Rover.'

The C.P.O., sophisticated by an education at a British Police College, pretended to be scandalized. He tut-tutted at the crimes: self-murder, blasphemy, perversion.

Moneypenny's simple testimony was much appreciated at Police Headquarters. I knew something like that would happen to him. He laughed at a butterfly.'

Anyway, there was little trouble about writing Crabbe off. Crabbe was dead. His death, though little mourned, was resented by a few. Rosemary felt that he might have, sooner or later, introduced her to somebody eligible, or, perhaps in an ultimate weariness matching hers, have been tossed legitimately to her breast. Robert Loo felt, in a way, let down, for Crabbe had promised much and fulfilled little. And Syed Omar remembered something about the possibility of a situation in the Education Department, now not likely to be realized. The white man lies, or dies, or goes away, or forgets. Moreover, money cannot be borrowed from a dead man. Crabbe's cook-boy had some weeks of unemployment, which was rather a nuisance. Lim Cheng Po said an Anglican prayer or two, not too perfunctorily. The Malay whom Crabbe had been training to take over his job now took over his job with trumpets and cocktails, finding it convenient to blame missing letters and mislaid files on a defunct infidel. And the great golden day of Independence approached.

Flowers and Jalil in Rosemary's house. And on Rosemary's desk a letter hardly begun, the two words 'My dear' becoming blurred in the damp heat.

'Now,' wheezed Jalil in asthmatic triumph, 'who you marry? I tell you nobody left. Only me marry.'

'Oooooh, go away, Jalil, you're filthy, you're horrible, I wouldn't marry you if you were the last man on earth. And I told the amah not to let you in. Oh, what lovely flowers.' Cats stalked, sniffed, inspected.

'I last man on earth. You marry me.'

Rosemary looked at him. 'I've too much respect for myself. You with three wives already and me sleeping in the spare room.'

'I sleep there too.'

'Horrible, horrible pig of a man.'

'You want marry European? I European, I sick man of Europe. You want marry Asian? I Asian too. I anything you want.'

'I don't want a man with three wives.'

'I divorce other wives. Divorce one every day. In three days I bachelor.'

'And then it'll start all over again. I know. Me thrown out on the streets, a divorced woman. You're horrible.'

'We go Istanbul. My brother part shares in hotel in Beyoglu. Make jolly time.'

'Where's Istanbul?'

'Old name Constantinople.' Jalil managed the many syllables with surprising smoothness. He was really no fool. 'Big town, very big. Bazaars, many shops, hotels big too. Can eat, drink, make jolly time.'

'Oh, I don't know,' said Rosemary. 'I don't know what I want. It can't be like London, can it? I mean, it's neither one thing nor the other, is it? I mean, London's everything, isn't it?' Jalil did not understand, but he smiled with faint encouragement and a heaving chest. And now Rosemary saw films unwind swiftly in her head, a montage of the mysterious Orient which she had never visited, an Orient purged of hoicking Chinese in underpants, an Orient without a Public Works Department, an Orient visited by Europeans wearing white tuxedos not bought on an initial outfit allowance. Glamour, romance, cocktails by a shining evening river. Could Jalil sustain the part?

'You're not a Christian,' she said.

'I be anything,' said Jalil. 'In Turkey can be anything. Kemal Ataturk he make that happen.'

'Oh, I don't know, I don't know.'

'We go K.L. for *Merdeka*,' said Jalil. 'I book room in hotel.'

'Oh yes, yes,' enthused Rosemary. 'Oh, yes, that *is* a good idea. Rooms,' she amended primly.

'Room. Rooms. It same thing.' Jalil was above accidence.

But room it had to be. Kuala Hantu, clean and freshly made-up, the dirtier natives, like skin blemishes, hidden from the eyes of visitors. Kuala Hantu, self-consciously prancing and crowing in its new-found metropolitan glory, Kuala Hantu could only find them one room in a hotel on Batu Road. That, anyway, was Jalil's story. 'It no good go anywhere else,' he said, as the taxi-driver pulled their luggage from the boot. 'No good to look. I know. We stay here.' A ragged Malay child greeted them as they made for the hotel entrance, begging for the odd ten cents. His eyes were intelligent, and he had the immemorial Malay curiosity about prices and relationships. 'He your father,' he announced. Jalil chuckled ironically.

But it was worth it – the double-bed, Jalil's deep wheezy sleep – for the sake of those few glamour-brimming days. In a shower of rain the tape to a shining-new free land was cut, the keys of authority handed over. And the full-throated cries of '*Merdeka!*' Even Rosemary joined in, though her woman's eyes were really on the so-sweet clothes of the Duchess of Gloucester. Nobody said what Crabbe had once ironically said: that Karl Marx's real name was Mordeca and might well carry the same Arabic transliteration as the slogan that had brought the Alliance to power (without, which so many thought a good sign opposition). One cynic, a Malay tumpet-player who had once played in a Singapore orchestra under a French leader, would only shout the first syllable. Rosemary heard him quite distinctly and wondered why.

And the men, oh, the men. So many strong and handsome Europeans, impeccably dressed. To Rosemary's surprise, Jalil turned out to be a member of the Selangor Club, and he took her there twice to dine and drink. He merely chuckled to himself when the men flocked round, much taken with her dark beauty, standing her drinks and showing fine teeth in social laughter, for it was Jalil who took her back to the double bed.

'Oooooh, wasn't he wonderful, Jalil, that man with the little moustache, Alan, and the other man, the fair one, called Geoffrey, and that very nice elderly man, Peter or Paul or something? He said he'd take me away with him any time for a week-end and he's got pots and pots of money. And that man standing just by you, the fat one, that was Sir Ronald Somebody-or-other. Oooooh, Jalil, it was just like London.'

'You go sleep. I tired now.'

Independence achieved and celebrated, everybody went back to work. 'Many people,' said the Chinese leader-writer in the *Singapore Bugle*, 'many people seem to consider independence as licensed irresponsibility. Nothing could be further from the truth. We must all, the Malays especially, put our shoulders to the wheel and prove ourselves worthy of the great gift of freedom and self-determination. The clerks in the offices, the coolies on the rubber estates, tin-miners, fisher-folk and paddy-planters, have had their brief hour of rejoicing and now must buckle down to the hard tasks ahead. There have been too many false promises made by politicians to ignorant members of the *ra'ayat*, promises about their being no further need to work once the British disgorged the wealth they had stolen from the sons of the soil. Now perhaps those promises are being seen for what they are – mere straws and bubbles in the wind of self-advancement.' And so on. But few people read the leaders. Nobody worked any harder, though few workers (which a cynic might allege to be impossible) less hard.

But the Communists in the jungle buckled to and put their shoulders to the wheel. Independence meant little: the capitalists had been at their tricks again. In at least one state the Communists redoubled their attacks on villages, their ambushings of motorists, their decapitations and guttings of the jackals of the rubber-sucking white parasites, and sometimes of the parasites themselves. It was grossly unfair to suggest, however, as Syed Omar once suggested, that this was because Vythilingam had gone over to the rebels. But the independent Government of the Federation of Malaya acted promptly. '*Il faut en finir*,' said a Malay minister. So into at least one state troops poured, a battalion of decent National Service lads, to continue to carry, posthumously as it must be supposed, the White Man's Burden. The more subtle warfare of ideas was carried on by the Information Department and by certain American organizations which did heroic – and voluntary – work. There was more to it than just ideas, of course. The library of the United States Information Service contained plenty of good, clean non-ideological books, in Chinese, English and Malay, and – better still – provided an air-conditioned refuge from the day's heat, much appreciated by workless illiterates. Temple Haynes knew a good deal about the organic processes of speech and gave to Arumugam virtually a new voice. It happened this way: Arumugam inveighed against British injustice (retrospectively, it should be presumed) at a drunken farewell dinner for somebody or other. Temple Haynes, enjoying a cool lager at a table away from the party, heard him and was clinically interested. Arumugam sped homewards from the party, drunk, on his new motor-cycle and crashed rather badly. It was by fortunate chance that Temple Haynes was cruising in his van shortly after the crash and found Arumugam moaning in his blood. Temple Haynes got Malay assistance from a near-by attap house and took Arumugam to hospital. All the time that Arumugam lay under harsh lights on the table in the casualty ward he moaned: 'I am dying. I did not mean what I said about the British. You are an Englishman. I am sorry,' in a high voice that seemed to Haynes proleptically cherubic.

'I'm not an Englishman,' said Haynes. 'Take it easy now. You'll be all right soon.' A fierce-looking Malay hospital assistant was stitching away at Arumugam's scalp; another Malay, gentler but less efficient, was swabbing Arumugam's body-wounds with dirty water.

'Forgive me just the same,' said Arumugam. 'Forgive me before I die.'

'You're not going to die.'

'Oh yes, I must, I must.' Arumugam rolled large eyes under the lights. 'I have spoken against the British. A British motor-cycle has had its revenge.' He was still very drunk.

'Take it easy now. I've spoken against the British myself.'

While Arumugam was convalescing in a Division Two Officers' ward, Haynes came often with gifts of candy and copies of *Life* and *Time*. Arumugam was enchanted to learn that the Americans had once actually fought the British and defeated them. He told Haynes about the sufferings of the Jaffna Tamils under the British yoke and Haynes told him about the Boston Tea Party. And then Haynes quietly insinuated certain therapeutic measures into their chatty intercourse, asking Arumugam to read aloud and suggesting certain approaches to the use of the voice. Soon, surprisingly soon, the articles in *Life* and the waspish biographies of *Time* were rolled out in a manly music which Arumugam at first refused to believe his own.

'I see now,' boomed Arumugam. 'It was psychological. The British forced me to be a slave, and that voice was the voice of a slave. A slave,' he added, 'whose birthright had been cut off. We have both suffered,' he said, 'you and I, our two nations. Now we are men, not slaves. You have made a man of me.' His devotion to Haynes became considerable, and Haynes's work in certain quarters was made easy. And at Sundralingam's wedding Arumugam, as best man, could hardly be persuaded to stop making speeches. He even sang a song called "In Cellar Cool" from the *Indian Students' Song-book*.

One evening Syed Hassan and Idris and Azman and Hamzah were sitting in Loo's shop. All wore a costume suggestive of a more tranquil and prosperous age than this – Dame Clara Butt singing, in a voice not quite so deep as Arumugam's, 'Land of Hope and Glory', the gold squeezed from tropical helots enhancing the upper-class comforts of a cold climate. Their costumes were not suitable for Malayan heat, but they were stoics prepared to suffer for smartness and conformity. To their interest and joy three soldiers of the Royal Barsets came in, and they were wearing this identical uniform of drainpipe trousers and serge waisted jacket and boot-lace tie.

They strutted to the bar, bringing their plentiful backhair behind them. 'Here, John,' said one of the newcomers to Robert Loo. 'Give us three beers.' Robert Loo looked up distractedly from his music. 'And stand to attention when a corporal's talkin' to yer,' added the man jocularly. This disguised corporal then turned lordly to survey the other customers and caught sight of Syed Hassan and his friends. 'Cor,' he said. 'Teds 'ere too. O'd 'ave thought we'd meet nigger Teds?' He greeted the four Malay boys cordially, and, without invitation brought his fresh-faced party of two to their table. 'More chairs, John,' he called to one of Robert Loo's brothers. 'We're goin' ter sit 'ere,'

'What is a Ted?' asked Hamzah shyly.

'Speak English, do yer? A Ted's what you are. Teds is what we are. Teddy boys. Edwardian strutters was what they used to call 'em in the old days. Cor, flamin' 'ot in 'ere. Turn up that fan, John, will yer?'

'Why do they call you that?' asked Hassan. He found difficulty in following much of the corporal's English, but, not doubting that this was *echt* English, began to feel resentment towards those English masters of his who had taught him English. It was colonial English they had taught him, that was it. But he would soon learn this new, free, democratic English.

'Why? Because we go back to the good old days, see, when there was none of this bleedin' nonsense. No wars and what not. Beer a penny a gallon and that. Bleedin' sight more than that 'ere. 'Ere, gizza bit er music, John. What you lads goin' to 'ave?'

The Malay boys now drank beer for the first time in their lives. It was itself, as Crabbe had once said, a language. Robert Loo, at his father's behest, gave the new customers a free gift of juke-box music. He himself listened to the brave harmonics of saxophones and brass, the sedative drum-beat, not without a minimal physical tingling. Syed Hassan winked at him; he winked back – stiffly, however, not being used to such social gestures.

But there now started a sodality that was to prove more fruitful in promoting inter-racial harmony than any of Crabbe's vague dreams. Wandering down the street one night, the seven of them, they came across a Tamil youth in Edwardian costume. 'Wotcher, Sambo,' said the corporal. 'You doin' anythin'?' And later there were two Chinese boys who joined the gang, and one of these, whose name was Philip Aloysius Tan, swiftly became the gang-leader. The corporal was good-humoured about it, glad to see it; after all, the days of British rule were over.

For Rosemary the days of glorious expectation had returned. There was a lieutenant-colonel in the town, majors, captains, raw conscript lieutenants. Jalil? 'The unspeakable Turk should be immediately struck out of the question.' (Letter from Carlyle to Howard, 24th November, 1876, as Crabbe might have verified from his books had Crabbe still been alive and his books not on their way home to his widow.) Jalil was not a gentleman. Colonel Richman was, so was Major Anstruther, so were Captains Tickell and Forsyth. Lieutenants Creek, Looker, Jones, Dwyer? Callow, guffawish, no longer her meat. Major Anstruther was unmarried, a good dancer, skilled in the arts of love. He had a neat square face hair greying neatly, a neat broad body, a voice and accent like Lim Cheng Po's. To Rosemary he was England – fog, primroses, Shaftesbury Avenue, South Kensington Tube Station, the Antelope and the Captain's Cabin, the downstairs bar of the Café Royal, Kew in lilac-time; only occasionally Crewe at 3 a.m., Stoke-on-Trent on a Sunday, the smells of Warrington. She was, you might say, in love again.

There was something for everybody in the new dispensation. Syed Omar was given a van with a left-hand drive and a salary of two hundred dollars a month. (Malayan dollars, not American dollars, though at the end of his first month he had sworn to his employers that he had thought it would be American dollars, else he would not have taken the job on. He was promised an increase in the near future.) On this van was painted a picture of an eagle shaking claws with a tiger, symbolic of new friendship between the free peoples. In this van were stacked, weekly, copies of a newspaper printed in the most beautiful Arabic script, called *Suara Amerika* (The Voice of America). This newspaper had to be delivered to humble kampong folk who else would know nothing of events in the great world outside. Few of them could read, however. Still, they welcomed Syed Omar's appearances and treated him to fresh toddy and simple curries, and they never tired of laughing at the picture of the eagle shaking claws with the tiger. Syed Omar did quite a profitable side-line selling *Suara*

Amerika to various shops in the towns as wrapping-paper. But, to do justice to his loyalty, he always took a copy of the paper home with him and read extracts to his wives about the private affairs of film stars. They liked this. In the evenings too, when he was in, Syed Hassan gave his father English lessons. The two got on quite well together now, especially as Syed Hassan had a job with prospects: he was fifth driver to the Sultan and occasionally had the thrill of running the new Cadillac round town.

Robert Loo was one day summoned to the United States Information Service building. This had formerly been the British Residency: the Americans paid a generous rent to the Sultan for its use. Robert Loo was cordially greeted by two youngish American gentlemen who expressed interest in his music. He was taken to a music-room whose air-conditioning made him shiver, and he was asked to sit down at the tropicalized Bechstein and play some of his works. Robert Loo smiled.

'I'm not a pianist,' he said. 'I'm a composer.'

'You can't play the piano at all?'

'No.'

'Well, how do you know what your music sounds like?'

'I hear it in my head.'

'Well, then, perhaps you'd be good enough to leave some of your manuscripts with us.'

'I've not very much,' said Robert Loo. 'I destroyed a lot of my early work. There was a symphony and a string quartet. They were immature, so I destroyed them.'

'What have you, then?'

'This.' Robert Loo took from his case the score of a brief work. 'This,' he said, 'is a Legend for Piano and Orchestra.'

'Legend, eh?'

'I call it that. I don't know why.' Robert Loo smiled nervously.

'Well, leave it with us, and we'll call you back in a couple of days.'

Robert Loo was duly called back and treated kindly. 'You know all the tricks,' they said. 'It's very competent. You've obviously heard a lot of the better class of film music.'

'I never go to the films,' said Robert Loo.

'Well, it's a very neat pastiche of the sort of Rachmaninoff film-piano-concerto stuff you used to hear a lot of just after the war.'

'Pastiche?' Robert Loo did not know the word.

'Yes. It's funny that you haven't absorbed much of the local musical idioms. Very rich possibilities there. Look what Bartok did, for instance.'

'I want to write music from the heart,' said Robert Loo.

'Yes? Well, very commendable. I suppose in its way. Thank you, Mr Loo. It was very kind of you to give us the opportunity to look at your music.' And Robert Loo was kindly dismissed.

Mr Roget, one of these two gentlemen, wrote a friendly note to Temple Haynes, who was at the time running a course in the Phonetics of Anglo-American in Kuala Hantu.

Dear Temple,

Joe and I had a look at the music of this Chinese boy that the Englishman told you about before he died. Frankly, I don't think there's much we can do. He's got past the stage of elementary harmony and counterpoint and so on: in fact, he's technically very competent. But it's not technique we're after. We can soon give them the technique. What we want is the indigenous stuff – folk-song and dance, six-tone scales and the rest of it. Our assignment is to study indigenous music and find out some of the real native artists. This Chinese boy has sort of rejected the native stuff (for instance, there's not a trace of the Chinese pentatonic in his work) and turns out very competent imitations of imitations – second-rate cinematic romantic stuff, complete with big Rachmaninoff tunes on the violins and chords banging out on the solo piano. We've heard it all before. We can do it far better ourselves. In fact, we didn't come out these thousands of miles to see a distorted image of ourselves in a mirror. So there it is. Hope the course is going well.

615

Joe and I hope soon to do a bit of travelling round the re-
moter villages, complete with recording apparatus, of course.
A Malay here is proving helpful – Syed Omar, who says he's
descended from Mohammed – and he's going to take us around.
For a consideration, of course, but what the hell!

Be seeing you,

Harry.

There was a dance in the Officers' Mess. Rosemary sat
in her underwear under the fan of the living-room, her
bright red dress ready waiting over a chair, wondering
whether she ought to go. Tom would be coming round to
fetch her in an hour's time (she needed a full hour for her
make-up), but, perhaps for the first time in her life, she
was in the position of wondering whether she would be
doing the right thing in accepting a pleasure. On the floor
lay four of her cats ill, definitely ill, and of the other cats
some were restless, some listless. She had tried to give the
sick cats milk, but they could not keep it down. She had
been wiping the floor all day. The amah was frightened
and would not come near them. The cats' noses were hot.
Tigger, the great malevolent striped creature that normally spent so much time brooding evil and acting evil,
lay on his side, his coat matted, his breathing shallow.
Rosemary had phoned the Veterinary Department, asking
for someone to come, but nobody had come. 'Transport,'
they had said. 'No transport. Land-Rover broken down.'

'Well, get a taxi, borrow a car, anything. It's urgent.'

'Better you bring cats here.'

'I can't, I can't. There are too many of them. They're
too ill. Please, please come.'

'I try.'

'But nobody had come. Rosemary wondered what to do.
Tigger feebly tried to crawl to a corner, there to retch on
an empty stomach. Rosemary knew how precarious was
the life of any domestic animal in this country, any human
animal, for that matter: death came so easily, hardly announced, without apparent cause, often greeted with
smiles. It was a fall of rain or of coconuts, part of the pat-

tern. Here there were no myths of struggle between life and death, perhaps because there were no spring and winter myths. But Rosemary, having absorbed so much of the North, wrung her hands and cried and blamed herself. She became superstitious, she half remembered old prayers; she said:

'I know I've done wrong, I know I've sinned, but I've never done any harm to anyone. Please, God, let them get well. I won't drink again, I won't go to dances. I'll be good, honestly I will. I'll never sleep with anyone again, I promise. Please, please, let them get well.'

Rosemary said a 'Hail Mary' in English and a few words of the 'Confiteor' in Latin. She prayed to St Anthony – knocking, in her ignorance, at the wrong door – and to the Little Flower. But there was no stir of life from the torpid bodies, and the restless cats mewed and sniffed at the listless cats.

And now a car was heard approaching and now the grinding of brakes. 'Oh no,' said Rosemary, crossing her arms over her nakedness, 'oh no. He's early, he's much too early.' And then: 'I'll have to fly. I'd better go, I'll have to go, I promised. And that Brigadier's coming to the dance. A gala night. Oh, I'll have to hurry. Perhaps they'll be better when I come back. Oh, God, please make them better, and I won't have more than two drinks. Three,' she amended. She rushed into her bedroom to make up. In the bedroom she heard a perfunctory knock and then the front door open. 'You're early, Tom,' she called. 'Get yourself a drink. I shan't be long.' And then: 'Look at all my poor pussies. I'm worried to death about them.' There was no hearty English reply from the living-room, no clink of glass and bottle. 'Is that you, Jalil?' she called suspiciously. 'I told the amah not to let you in. There's no point in your staying, because I'm going out. So there.' But there was no asthmatic wheeze, no invitation to a jolly time. More suspicious still, she put on a wrap and peered round the door. Someone was busy on the floor, leaning tenderly over the sick beasts.

'Oh, Vy,' called Rosemary, coming out – un-made up, hair anyhow – in relief. 'Oh, Vy, thank God you've come. They heard my prayer. God heard it, St Anthony heard it. Oh, thank God they heard it. I'll never drink again. I'll say fifteen decades of the Rosary. I'll be good, I promise.'

Vythilingam said nothing. Expert with phial and plunger, he worked busily. But once he broke silence to say: 'Feline. Feline. Felin enteritis. Kampong cats had it. Disease spreads.'

'Oh, bless you, bless you, Vy. While you're using that, I'll get ready. I'll be late. Tom will be here soon.' And she dashed back to her cream-pots and mascara and lipstick. 'I knew,' she said between lipstick strokes, 'that you wouldn't – let me – down.' There was no reply. And soon there was a rat-tat-tat and the front door burst heartily open and there was a hearty greeting. 'Hello, girl. Where are you, Rosie?' And then: 'Oh, I beg your pardon. Didn't see you. Oh, I suppose you're the vet.'

'Shan't be a minute, Tom dear,' sang Rosemary. 'Just doing my hair. Bring my dress in, there's a dear.'

'Not sure I can trust myself, ha-ha. You and me alone in a bedroom, eh?'

'You are *naughty*, Tom.'

But Major Anstruther, a gentleman, was soon back in the living-room, watching politely the deft hands of the shy brown man on the floor. Major Anstruther did not care much for cats: he was a dog-man himself. 'Will they be all right now?' he asked politely.

Vythilingam said: 'Injection every day. Perhaps all right then.'

Anstruther had not been long in Malaya. He attributed this wog's clipped telegraphese to the shyness of one who meets socially a racial superior. He tried to put the poor man at his ease.

'Hot for the time of the year,' he said.

Vythilingam nodded, got up, put away his instruments. 'Hot,' he agreed.

'I have a Golden Labrador,' said Anstruther. 'Back in England. You fond of dogs?'

'Some.'

'It amuses some of us that the Chinese call us "running dogs",' said Anstruther. 'They don't seem to realize that it's really a kind of compliment.' He laughed. 'A dog's a noble beast.'

'Yes.'

'We'll be glad when it's over,' said Anstruther. 'This war's been going on too long. It's not a clean war, somehow. You can't get at the devils. That jungle's a nightmare.'

'Nightmare.'

'Here were are, Tom. You finished, Vy? I'm so, so grateful. I'm so glad you're back. We all wondered what had happened to you. Your mother was worried, I believe. She's gone back now. She'll be so pleased you're alive. There's *so* much news, Vy. Will you be in tomorrow? Bless you. Now we've got to fly. We mustn't keep the Brigadier waiting.'

'Oh, the Brig's always late,' said Anstruther. 'Still, we'd better go. Get ginned up a bit before the fun starts. Goodbye, Mr er – I hope we meet again.'

'Good-bye, Vy,' said the magnificent Rosemary, a vision of warm brown skin and rustling red silk. 'You're a dear.'

They were gone. The door slammed, Anstruther's cigarette smoke and Rosemary's perfume still faintly riding the air. Their laughter could be heard as they got in the car, fading as the car started and they moved off to the Mess. Vythilingam tenderly stroked Tigger, wiping with a bit of paper tissue the defiled mouth of the beast. He would get well. They would all get well. There was a medicine for everything. If one failed, you could try another. Vythilingam sighed, packed his State Veterinary Department bag, and left the cats lying there, confident that the healing juices would soon start their work. In the meantime there was bound to be a big back-log of correspondence in the office.

His car started quite well. That station-master had looked after it. And, moving gently down the avenue, Vythilingam thought that he had better pay a brief visit to his friends, the staid bachelor Sundralingam, and Arumugam of the high voice, before he returned to the office. They, at least, unchanged and yearning for better things, might welcome him back. He smiled slightly as he drove on the wrong side of the road.

It was a lovely night for Rosemary. The lights, the music, the attention. White-coated National Servicemen brought her pink gins (many, many: she forgot her promise to God and St Anthony and the Little Flower and the rest of the baroque pantheon) and occasionally winked at her appreciatively. At so many levels did she appeal. So many officers with cummerbunds round slim waists, smelling of sweet young dewy manhood, asked her to dance. And she danced so well. She told a group, graduated from one star to three and a crown, about her London experiences and decorations-will-be-worn and television appearances and Oooooh, the proposals. Everybody was very gay.

The refreshments were excellent. Canapés of many kinds, galantines to be scooped or carved, cheese and onions, no Worcestershire sauce. But you could not have everything. The mousse of crab was most tasty. At the fifth mouthful something smote Rosemary hard. It was a memory of a poetry lesson in her training college in Liverpool: an earnest Empsonian young man, not really attractive. Tears began to smudge her mascara. 'Poor Victor,' she said to an empty space by the white-clothed table, 'poor, poor Victor.'

'He came, he saw, he conquered,' said a quite handsome subaltern. 'Victor ludorum.'

'Poor Victor.' And then somebody asked her to dance.

Glossary

achcha (Urdu) – Right! Very well! Good!

ada baik (Malay) – everything's all right; I'm quite well, thank you.

amah (Malay) – a nurse; a female servant.

apa (Malay) – what.

ap khuch karab bolta (Urdu) – You've said something bad.

attap (Malay) – thatch of palm-leaves.

banchoad (Hindustani) – sister-fucker.

baju (Malay) – a coat, tunic or shirt.

barang (Malay) – belongings, luggage, things in general.

belum lagi pegang janji (Malay) – you have not fulfilled your promise.

bilal (Arabic) – a muezzin; the mosque official who is responsible for the calls to prayer.

bint (Arabic) – a woman.

bintang tiga (Malay) – lit. three stars. A nickname for Communists derived from the old three-star cap-badge.

charpoy (Urdu) – a bed.

dalam (Malay) – in, into.

dhobi (Urdu) – washing; a laundryman.

dhoti (Urdu) – a dress worn by some Indians, consisting of a cloth wound round the body.

diam (Malay) – be quiet! Shut up!

dua (Malay) – two.

haji (Arabic) – one who has made the pilgrimage to Mecca.

hantu dapur (Malay) – a kitchen ghost.

haram (Arabic) – forbidden by religion.

hela (Malay) – a yard (of material).

ikan merah (Malay) – a Malayan fish (lit. red fish).
itu chantek (Malay) – that's pretty.

jamban (Malay) – a lavatory.

kampong (Malay) – a village.
kedai (Tamil) – a shop.
khabar (Arabic) – news. *Apa khabar?* – lit. What news?
  Usual Malay greeting.
kita (Malay) – we.
kira (Malay) – a bill.
kuali (Malay) – a cooking pan.
kuki (Malay, from English) – a cook.

lauk (Malay) – the food (fish, meat, etc.) that accompanies
  rice.
lima (Malay) – five.
limbu (Malay) – an ox.
lobang (Malay) – a hole.

maalum-lah (Malay, from Arabic) – you know; you see; it's
  like this.
main (Malay) – to play; a game.
malam (Malay) – evening, night.
makan (Malay) – to eat; food.
makan sudah siap (Malay) – the meal is ready.
makan malam ini (Malay) – this evening's meal.
mee (Chinese) – a kind of spaghetti.
merdeka (Malay, from Sanskrit) – freedom, liberty. (The
  battle-cry of the United Malay Nationalist Organization.)
minta belanja (Malay) – please give me an advance on my
  wages.
minta ma'af (Malay, from Arabic) – please forgive me; I
  beg your pardon.
misti lulus (Malay) – you must pass (your examination).
munshi (Hindi) – a teacher of languages.

naraka (Arabic) – hell.
nonya (Malay) – a designation given to Chinese married
  women.

orang darat (Malay) – lit. people of the interior, the aborigines.

orang puteh (Malay) – white man, European.

padang (Malay) – an open space, a tract of land, village green.

pawang (Malay) – a magician, soothsayer.

penanggalan (Malay) – a vampire-ghost possessing only a head and floating entrails.

ringgit (Malay) – a dollar.

ronggeng (Malay) – a Javanese dance, popular in Malaya.

robai (Malay) – a term used to describe the aborigines (impolite, as it literally means 'slave').

sama sama (Malay) – formula used in response to *terima kaseh* (thank you). The same to you.

samsu (Chinese) – a cheap Chinese rice-spirit.

satu botol (Malay) – one bottle.

saya (Malay) – I, me.

saya t'ada wang (Malay)) – I have no money.

saya ta' erti (Malay) – I don't understand.

selamat (Malay, from Arabic) – safe, used in various salutatory and valedictory formulae.

selamat jalan (Malay) – good-bye (lit. safe journey).

shukria (Urdu) – thank you.

siap meja (Malay) – prepare the (billiard) table.

sila dudok (Malay) – please sit down.

songkok (Malay) – an oval velvet cap worn by Malay men.

stengah (Malay) – half; used by Europeans in ordering a small whisky and water.

surat (Malay) – a letter or testimonial.

tabek (Malay) – a Malay greeting.

terima kaseh (Malay) – lit. received with love; used for 'thank you'.

tida' apa (Malay) – it doesn't matter.

towkay – a Chinese boss or shopkeeper.

tuan (Malay) – sir, mister. *Tuan* is used as a title for

Europeans and Malay *hajis* and descendants of the Prophet.

tuan besar (Malay) – big man, boss.

tuan beli sayur? (Malay) – Is *tuan* going to buy vegetables?

tuan kasi lima linggit (Chinese version of Malay) – *Tuan* gave me five dollars.

waktu (Arabic) – one of the five prayer-times of the day.

wang (Malay) – money.

wayang kulit (Malay) – the Javanese shadow-play.